A History of Western Education

Volume Two

CIVILIZATION OF EUROPE
SIXTH TO SIXTEENTH CENTURY

James Bowen

A History of

SCHOLÆ PVBLICÆ.

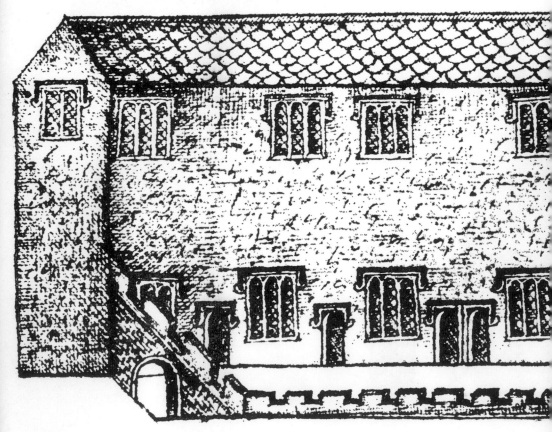

Western Education

Volume Two

CIVILIZATION OF EUROPE
SIXTH TO SIXTEENTH CENTURY

ST. MARTIN'S PRESS
NEW YORK

Margaritae

Contents

List of Illustrations

Title page: Bereblock's view of the Scholae Publicae, Oxford (ancient lecture rooms which stood where the present Bodleian quadrangle is now), 1566.

MAPS

The author and publishers wish to thank the following for permission to reproduce the illustrations that appear in this book:

Bibliothèque Nationale, Paris, for nos. 3 and 4
British Museum for nos. 12, 13 and 14
Cambridge University Library for no. 20
Institut National de Recherche et de Documentation Pédagogiques, Collections Historiques, for nos. 16 and 21
Lutherhalle, Reformations-geschichtliches Museum, Lutherstadt Wittenberg, for no. 17
Mansell Collection for nos. 1, 5, 6, 7, 8 and title page
Musée du Louvre for nos. 9 and 15
Niedersächsische Landesgalerie, Hannover, for no. 18
Öffentliche Kunstsammlung, Basle, for nos. 11 and 19
Österreichische Nationalbibliothek, Vienna, for no. 2
Staatliche Museen Preussischer Kulturbesitz, Berlin, for no. 10

Preface

The study of education has always been important in Western thought, attracting the interest of the greatest intellects in every age. Yet after several thousand years of close attention a precise definition, particularly of the more normative and ideational aspects of education, still eludes us. We do have the very strong implicit feeling that education is concerned with the maintenance of a social and cultural consciousness, with the transmission of an informed tradition that sustains civilization. Today, however, more than ever before, the study of education is of crucial significance since we expect not only the sustaining of our cultural traditions but also their critical revision and development. We demand of education that it provide a means to ever greater cultural vitality. And this, moreover, is often made without any clear realization that the demand itself is the result of historical processes.

One characteristic of education is outstanding: perhaps more than any other cultural process it carries almost all of its past with it into the present, even if this past rests in rather covert assumptions, practices, attitudes and beliefs. If we are to understand education in the fullest sense, as distinct from the more behaviouristic and prescriptive demands of particular learning and teaching situations, then we must study its history for the clarification and explanation which can be so secured. Not, of course, that this is the relatively passive reading of a chronologically organized, already existent narrative of past educational thought and practice. On the contrary, genuine history, in the tradition derived from its Greek beginnings as ἱστορία, is properly an activity of inquiry, investigation and scientific scrutiny. The historian is involved in making decisions on just what needs clarification and explanation, and in doing this his task, in part, is one of making the present intelligible. There are, of course, other tasks which historians perform; their inquiries and resulting narratives themselves help to build the collective social mind and so sustain the very traditions on which civilization rests and by which such studies are made possible.

At the present time there are many issues in education which confuse our thought and hinder our action and of these the most prominent remains the conflict between the two conceptions of education as a conservative and as a creative activity. There is no real theoretical conflict here at all since both aspects are part of the same process of the transmission and critical reconstruction of culture, yet in practice this conflict has engendered the fiercest debates and led to some of the most fundamental breaches within societies. For instance there is the rivalry between liberal and technical education with their respective antagonists considering the former a meaningless and decadent social ideal, the latter an illiberal and mindless kind of vocational training. The interesting fact remains, however, that the former conception, the *studia humanitatis*, for more than two millennia was dominant in the West and it was within such a conceptual framework that all educational issues arose and solutions or compromises were reached. In the course of that time the Christian church came to claim title over education and attempted to maintain this for more than a thousand years. In the process it had to come to terms with pagan education which already was possessed of a millennium of tradition. Paradoxically, the church not only came to terms with this tradition, it assimilated it even to the point in the thirteenth century of making the materialistic and non-theistic philosophy of Aristotle the basis of its own philsophy and educational thought and practice. This accommodation was forced upon the church by circumstances which also stimulated the growth of new forms of political and social theory, and the development of the modern political state. In recent times, particularly in the past two hundred years, the state has become increasingly concerned with the provision of education to the stage where it has not only surpassed the church – or churches as these have been considered since the Reformation

– but has made church influence subordinate or, in cases, even legislated it completely out of any educational role. The two influences of church and state remain as subjects for continued examination.

It is of the highest significance that since the entry of the state into education the controversies and conflicts on the nature, purpose and practices of education have become much greater. This is not to be taken to imply causation; rather the conditions which allowed the emergence of the organized political state have also promoted those changes which make it very difficult to make both theoretical and practical decisions in respect to education. The only really acceptable generalization we can make about the modern period is that there is a widely held implicit and nowadays explicit belief that education can and must be extended as widely as possible, even though there is no great clarity in the public mind as to why and how this extension should and can be made. There has been, however, a substantial effort on the part of numerous individuals and organizations to work at solutions to this general problem and we are now able to discern the main characteristics of educational thought in the modern period. Of these there are three which are pre-eminent: the search for an adequate rationale – or what is loosely termed a philosophy; the search for an adequate support system of institutions and processes; and the search for an adequate pedagogy, that is, for a workable method of teaching and learning.

These, then, have been the issues which have guided the selection of problems and their treatment in these volumes. In the presentation of the historical narrative it is not imagined in any way that our educational problems will be solved. On the contrary, the recognition of difficulties, their study and analysis, exhaust the historian's tasks and competencies. It remains true, however, that the identification and explication of problems – the process, that is, whereby they are raised from a position of tacit awareness to explicit formulation – is the first, necessary step towards any kind of intelligent action. History provides us with a context within which decisions can be made and further activities pursued.

In making this present investigation, certain practical considerations had to be taken into account, one of the most important being the scale within which the narrative should be constructed. Individual authorship has both its advantages and its limitations; the former include the development of a single synoptic viewpoint and the greater consistency with which problems can be investigated. Yet it is important for this to remain within the competency of a single mind. Accordingly the narrative must reflect this unity and the multitude of data and variety of interpretations must be kept subordinate. After a great deal of deliberation the present three-volume format has emerged as the most practicable, particularly since it is possible to conceive of the history of Western education occupying three phases: the ancient period of Greco-Roman civilization, the medieval millennium from the fall of Rome to the Enlightenment, and the ensuing modern period which includes not only the West in Europe but its extension to most of the world outside. Periodization, of course, is a notoriously difficult activity for any historian and it is not claimed that the present ones have any completeness. They do, however, have the advantage of allowing a reasonable space for the development of the narrative and each of the three periods has certain internal organizing concepts. Throughout the task has been conceived to be one of critical revision of standard opinion in the history of education and to do this effectively I have been guided by the one cardinal ideal of working wherever possible from the sources. In general it has been necessary to use translations although these have been checked against the original texts in what have seemed crucial instances. Modifications of translations, and those by myself, have been recorded, usually in the footnotes. This movement *ad fontes*, which if it has a Renaissance flavour is still relevant and even more pressing today, has been supported by extensive field work. I have made it a particular feature of this writing to visit as many of the original locations as possible during several years spent in the Mediterranean, northern Europe, England and America. Field investigations have been supported by the study of remains and archives in many museums and libraries and in this way I have attempted to exercise some control on the printed sources which otherwise inevitably have a sense of remoteness. Most of the locations, remains and documents mentioned in the text have been verified in the original.

Here I would like to make a few observations on the scope of the present volume and the considerations underlying its organization. Volume I deals with education in the ancient world of the Orient and Mediterranean, the essential character of which came from the dominance of Greek thought and practice. I have taken that narrative, with respect to the Greek East, up to the mutual excommunication of patriarch and pope in A.D. 1054, when Byzantine education reached a stage of exhaustion and decline. With regard to the Latin West, however, the narrative concludes earlier, with the collapse of the Roman Empire in the fifth century, for by then Greek influence had become minimal, the Roman education based upon it was moribund, and the congruence of a number of political, economic and social factors brought that period to an end. The present volume considers the emergence of the civilization of Europe with its own distinctive process of education, which gained impetus during the Carolingian revival of the eighth century and continued to develop through the Middle Ages, the Renaissance and the Reformation. While it has been a relatively simple task to begin with Charlemagne's great *renovatio*, it has been much more difficult to determine the point at which to end this volume, for, indeed, the civilization of Europe is a continuing process. For a number of cogent reasons, the sixteenth century has been chosen as the most appropriate, although there has not been a sharp break. Europe from the sixth to the sixteenth century had a large number of unifying features: it was a self-consciously Christian civilization, dominated by a strong church and with still undeveloped national states. Education, moreover, was a single process: it had an unquestioned Christian ideology; an agreed curriculum in Latin based upon the study of classical literature, both pagan and Christian; a single pedagogy, that of the master instructing *ex cathedra*; and one pervasive support system, involving progression from elementary through grammar school, to university, all under the aegis of Holy Church. This present volume is concerned with the development of that civilization and the way in which education, always considered to be the handmaiden of the church, came to assume a measure of independence and autonomy of its own. Until the late sixteenth century all of accepted educational practice, and much of Western thought, was related to advancing the cause of a Christian civilization, and for this reason the ideas of Erasmus and Luther, along with various minor figures, since they were all devoted to promoting education as *pietas litterata*, belong to the present narrative. So too does the account of the early Jesuit schools, and the work of textbook writers and educational grammarians. At the same time, however, ideas were being circulated in the sixteenth century that make distinct breaks with traditional thought and in effect mark the beginning of the modern period. Examples of this more radical literature appear in the writings in Italy of Ortensio Lando and Giambattista Gelli, and in France of François Rabelais, Michel de Montaigne and Pierre de la Ramée. Their arguments for the acceptance of the vernacular as the medium of instruction, the deposing of classical literary studies in favour of a curriculum drawn from a wider range of everyday activities and vocational needs, and their demands for the reform of the school generally, became widely discussed and in the seventeenth century were made the basis of a number of efforts at serious educational reform. Late in the sixteenth century the modern period, then, has its beginning. These writers, the voices of dissent, and the more general historical circumstances prompting their criticisms, are thus considered as the starting-point for the third and final volume on education in the modern West, both Europe and the new world.

In the preparation of this present volume I have continued to be in debt to many colleagues and institutions, and the acknowledgements given in the Preface to Volume I are equally relevant here. I would like, however, to express particular gratitude to my own University of New England for its continued support of my research activities; to my publishers for providing invaluable assistance from their scholarly readers, for the high level of editorial guidance and for the meticulous care with which the volumes have been produced. As always, I have relied very heavily upon the assistance and guidance of my wife and have increasingly made use of her own scholarly researches in the history and philosophy of science, much of which has been influential in the development of the narrative that follows. To her this work remains dedicated.

JAMES BOWEN

University of New England
Australia
May 1974

CHAPTER I

Foundations of European Education

When the great Roman Empire finally collapsed in the West, its secular, intellectual and cultural achievement had virtually disappeared. By the year A.D. 600 literacy and learning had reached their lowest levels ever, and despite the heroic efforts of a few zealous early sixth-century scholars from the surviving Roman intelligentsia – notably Boethius, Cassiodorus and Benedict – nearly all the regions of the once great Latin civilization of the West, including much of Italy itself, had become intellectually and culturally barren. The learning that did survive was, in general, conservative, encyclopedic and degenerate and, apart from a few exceptions in Italy, was maintained almost exclusively in monasteries and cathedrals. The stagnation of scholarship and lack of educational purpose comes through very clearly in the chronicles of the times, particularly in Gregory of Tours' *Historia Francorum* and Bede's *Historia ecclesiastica gentis Anglorum*. Those two writers, in common with most educated persons of the period, were acutely conscious of the plight of civilization. Gregory himself, in fact, had written his history of the Franks specifically, he states in the preface, to provide some record at a time (in the late sixth century) when 'the practice of letters perished in the cities of Gaul'. This educational perigee was, moreover, no slight, temporary setback. It persisted throughout the seventh century into the eighth and by the middle of the latter century showed no signs of improvement until the advent of the Carolingian rulers. Then came a remarkable set of events. This new dynasty initiated some reforms, and when the Frankish prince Charlemagne succeeded to the throne in 771 he brought with him a burning enthusiasm to make his kingdom the vehicle for a rebirth of Latin Christian civilization. His official policy was to effect a *renovatio* of the Frankish people, which, he recognized, would require the deliberate reconstruction of education. To achieve these purposes he found it necessary to give a corporate identity to this new civilization and in doing this he was instrumental in promoting a distinctly European consciousness and the subsequent development of a civilization of Europe with its own particular process of education.

Emergence of Europe

The term Europe is of ancient origin and was in use among the early Greeks to refer to the great peninsula to the north-west of the Mediterranean. By the fourth century A.D., with the removal of the capital of the Roman Empire to Constantinople, the western region consequently began to take on an independent character; by the seventh century this process became markedly accelerated when the two newly emerged powers of Byzantium and Islam stimulated the West to develop its own corporate identity. That need, moreover, was felt particularly by the Catholic church which was often in a precarious position with respect to temporal power. Throughout the seventh and eighth centuries the See of Rome became vigorous in seeking its identity as Western Christendom; in the year 800 it achieved this in a sense through an alliance with Charlemagne and the foundation thereby of the Holy Roman Empire. By that time Europe had become more than a geographical term; it signified a complete civilization of which its members were thoroughly conscious.[1]

For several centuries preceding that alliance the church in Rome had insisted on its primacy throughout all Christendom. The Petrine Doctrine, by which the bishops of Rome claimed direct descent from Peter, had been voiced as early as the second century and was widely current by the third. In the first decades of the fourth century Rome had kept aloof from the Arian controversy and had secured from the Council of Nicaea recognition of its authority in the West. Rome continued to maintain an organizational unity throughout the fifth and sixth centuries while the eastern sees became engaged in further destructive theological and doctrinal quarrels. By the fifth century the emperors had come to recognize the primacy of the bishop of Rome over all other Western bishops, according to him all jurisdictional authority in that region. In the absence of an emperor in the West after 476, the church in Rome assumed many of the imperial functions and even organized itself on the civil diocesan pattern. Along with the assumption of that authority grew the custom of the Roman bishops of arrogating to themselves alone the title of *papa* (in English, 'pope') which in its original Greek form of *papas* ('father') was first used by the bishops of Alexandria and had been subsequently taken over as a title by all bishops in the West.[2] The securing of papal authority in Catholic Christendom was the work of Leo the Great (r. 440–61); the organization of the papacy into a vigorous institution was the achievement of Gregory I (r. 590–604). Under Gregory the papacy intervened in a wide range of church affairs, coming to exercise a degree of authority over the monasteries which previously had been independent institutions.

Yet the Catholic church, led by a vigorous papal hierarchy, was not secure in the sixth and seventh centuries. Not all the Germanic kings were amenable to Roman hegemony, nor were they all converted to Trinitarian orthodoxy. Throughout those two centuries in which it came to power – sixth and seventh – the papacy was engaged in the considerable task of converting the pagan and Arian kings to Latin Catholicism. So began the period of widespread evangelistic activity that was marked by missions into Gothic Spain, Frankish Gaul and Celtic and Anglo-Saxon Britain. Notable successes were achieved, and by the early eighth century most of the rulers of Europe were in communion with Rome and accorded respect, if not submission, to papal authority, at least in spiritual affairs.

Much of that great missionary activity was the work of monks. The stabilization of the hitherto barbarian Europe was largely a consequence of their efforts and was accompanied by the foundation of numbers of independent monasteries, all following the Rule of Benedict, on which the Germanic rulers depended heavily since, as important centres of learning, the monasteries were extremely helpful for the conduct of the affairs of government. Charters, diplomatic dispatches, rules, regulations and fiscal accounts – all those came from the pen of the monk. So the growing church came to interpenetrate the political life of the newly emerged Europe.

Security was still not achieved by the beginning of the eighth century. The later disorders of the Roman Empire had caused the Germanic kings

EUROPE IN THE EARLY MIDDLE AGES

to be continually at enmity with each other and with the powerful hereditary nobles, both Roman and Frank, who held tenure to the land. In the
Frankish kingdom in particular, rivalry between kings and nobles was
most pronounced. This stemmed from a partition of 511, in which immediately before he died the Merovingian king Clovis divided his kingdom
among his four sons, thereby initiating more than a century of intermit-

tent conflict. Compounding the problems were the claims of the nobles to a greater share of responsibility. By 613 the noble faction had won the important concession of electing from their numbers the chief steward of the royal Frankish palace and its domains. The first such official, or mayor (Latin *major*, 'great'), was the most powerful single member of the aristocracy, Pepin of Landen, who made the mayoralty hereditary. Despite opposition, the house of Pepin maintained its claim; a century later the hereditary Merovingian kings were virtually powerless figureheads and the mayors had become *de facto* rulers.

The house of Pepin ruled vigorously. Under Charles Martel (r. 714–41) the Moslem advance from the Maghreb of north-west Africa through Spain into the Frankish domains was checked at Poitiers and the continuity of Frankish rule preserved. His son Pepin the Short (r. 741–68), dissatisfied with his mayoral rank, moved to secure recognition as legitimate sovereign. The opportunity came with the resurgence of Lombard ambition when their energetic king Luitprand (r. 719–44) began an attempt to unify all Italy under Lombard suzerainty. Luitprand's death, however, delayed the realization of that plan until the accession of Aistulf who in 751 dislodged the Byzantines in the north of Italy and thereby threatened to occupy Rome. As a result of some involved negotiations, Pepin sided with the See of Rome in return for papal approval of his deposition of the Merovingian king, Childeric III. Consequently, the Lombards were defeated by the Frankish army and in 752 Pepin was formally recognized as king of the Franks by Pope Stephen II. By the late eighth century the papacy had forged a firm alliance with the Frankish mayors who, with the accession of Pepin the Short, became the Carolingian dynasty. Under Pepin's son Charlemagne, the Carolingian rule reached its greatest development and authority and an era of stability ensued.

The Carolingian era A.D. 768–840

Rule of Charlemagne: concept of renovatio

Charlemagne, to use the now customary medieval French name (literally 'Charles the Great'), was born the elder son of Pepin in 742 and named Karl (or Charles). He acceded to the kingship in 768, ruling jointly with his brother, Karlmann (or Carlomann), until the latter's death in 771.

Charlemagne thereafter became sole king, reigning for forty-six years altogether, until 814. Almost from the beginning of his reign, Charlemagne was an unusual monarch. He was possessed of a thoroughgoing commitment to Christianity and held an unshakeable belief in the necessity of baptismal regeneration, not only of each individual person but also of the state. Just as Christian doctrine teaches that each person must be reborn in Christ, so too did the patristic *corpus*, influenced greatly by Augustine, teach that the state itself must be regenerated. Charlemagne saw himself as the divinely appointed agent of this process, and within the first years of his rule he set to the task of implementing this great *renovatio*, a renewal of the state through symbolic rebirth.[3]

To effect this he acted in various ways. The first need was to secure the external stability of his kingdom, and this required Charlemagne to wage frequent campaigns – fifty-three in all – for the first thirty-six years of his reign. By the end of the eighth century that stability was well-nigh achieved. Campaigns, alliances, marriages: by all available means he pursued his goal. The territory he came to command was considerable, in many ways as extensive in Europe as the former Roman Empire although it lacked the administrative efficiency of the earlier Empire and had little of the learning or literary achievement for which Rome remained famous. Simultaneously he began the reform of the civil government. His contemporary biographer and official secretary, Einhard, tells us that 'upon becoming ruler Charlemagne concerned himself with conflicts in the laws – chiefly due to the existence of two separate codes – and gave considerable thought to reconciling the variations and discrepancies and to the correction of errors'.[4] In addition, estates were reorganized, taxation reformed, courts of appeal and inquiry under the authority of royal messengers (*missi dominici*) established, a system of publishing royal laws and edicts, known as *capitularies*, inaugurated, and a new palace and capital built at Aachen. The demands of constant campaigning and regional supervision precluded any really fixed seat of government; Aachen was a compromise location.

Although possessing tremendous personal energy and vitality, Charlemagne could not act alone; he surrounded himself with the ablest intellects of the day, reaching to the corners of his kingdom, and beyond if necessary, to find suitable advisers. One such story appears in the life of Charlemagne, *De Carolo magno*, written by the monk Notker Balbulus (*c.* 840–912) about the year 884, some seventy years after the king's death. Upon hearing of two Irish clerics who came across to Gaul, 'at a time when the pursuit of learning was almost forgotten throughout the length and breadth of the kingdom', Charlemagne summoned them to his court and gave one the direction of a new school which contained 'a great number of boys chosen not only from the noblest families but also from middle-class and poor homes'; the other priest was given a similar charge in a monastic school near Padua.[5] The provenance of the account is unknown and it is generally believed to be false; none the less this action was considered typical of Charlemagne. His biographer Einhard records that

> Of all kings, Charlemagne was the most eager in his search for wise men and in his determination to provide them with living conditions in which they could pursue knowledge in all reasonable comfort. In this way Charlemagne was able to offer to the cultureless, and, I might say, almost completely unenlightened territory of the realm which God had entrusted to him, a new enthusiasm for all human knowledge.[6]

We have firm records that in this manner Charlemagne commanded the services of a number of distinguished intellects: Theodulf of Orléans (an exiled Spanish Visigoth), Paul the Deacon, Peter the deacon of Pisa, and Alcuin of York, who was himself accompanied by three ancillary clerics, Witzo, Fridugis and Sigulf. Along with them there was a large number of supporting scholars.

Charlemagne's motives in bringing this collection of advisers to his court seem primarily to have been those of providing himself with the necessary instruments for effecting the *renovatio* of his Frankish realm, of transforming his people from a *populus Dei* into a reborn *populus christianus*.[7] In a society as fully committed to Christian belief as the Carolingian, in which there was no conception of separate secular and religious spheres – even if pope and emperor administered the *imperium christianum* in concert – it was inevitable that his advisers should have been senior ecclesiastics. It was they who had command of god's word – as it was recorded in the Bible and the patristic writings – and who had the capability of forming this into an ideology and communicating it to society at large. These ecclesiastics, moreover, were the only educated persons in the kingdom. Probably the best illustration of the support given by these royal advisers is found in Charlemagne's involvement in the Iconoclastic Controversy. That dispute had begun in Constantinople in 726 when the Emperor Leo III had attempted to remove religious icons (Gk. *eikon*, 'likeness, image, portrait') from the churches because they were becoming objects of worship in themselves. The dispute dragged on in Byzantium, and in 787, largely owing to the stimulus of Irene, acting as regent for her son, the juvenile Emperor Constantine, a Council of Nicaea restored icons to the churches. Irene had not invited Charlemagne to the Council directly: in her view his realm was but a constituent of the Latin division of the Empire. Charlemagne construed this as a serious slight and in response he summoned a commission, most likely under Theodulf of Orléans, to refute the Council of Nicaea's decision. This refutation was issued in a four-part treatise, under the nominal authorship of Charlemagne, known as the *Libri Carolini* (*The Caroline Books*), which condemned the use of icons – painted or graven – in the Frankish realm.[8] Charlemagne not only avenged the insult, he thereby repudiated Byzantine authority over his realm.

Educational policy of Charlemagne: *the* schola palatina

It was inevitable, then, that Charlemagne's *renovatio* should assume the character of a religious educational movement. The king himself, we read in Einhard, had a tremendous enthusiasm for learning and equally high expectations of its efficacy in achieving his great aspirations for the kingdom. He was determined, Einhard wrote, 'to give his children – his daughters as much as his sons – a proper training in the liberal arts which had formed the subject of his own studies'.[9] The chronicle continues to record that Charlemagne spoke Latin as fluently as his mother tongue and that he had a considerable understanding of Greek, although he was unable to speak it fluently.[10] He learnt grammar from Peter, the deacon of Pisa, and the other liberal arts (presumably rhetoric and dialectic) from 'Alcuin, known as Albinus, who was a Saxon from Britain',[11] and in addition attempted to learn to write, for which purpose he kept tablets and note-books ('tabulasque et codicillos') beneath his pillows so that he could practise in privacy at his leisure. Regretfully, we read, owing to a late start in life, he made little progress.[12] None the less, Charlemagne recognized the value of these achievements in others and had the greatest respect for those who professed the liberal arts, rewarding them accordingly with great honours.[13]

In order to sustain the desired high calibre of thought and ideas, Charlemagne strengthened and expanded the palace school (*schola palatina*). This had been in existence for perhaps half a century, having functioned as a training centre in courtly procedure for the children of the palace. As an early move towards the upgrading of the *schola palatina* its direction was offered to the English scholar, Alcuin of York, whom Charlemagne had first met in 781 at Parma where the Englishman was engaged in a mission for his king, Eanbald.

Alcuin (c. 730/735–804) was born near York.[14] His childhood is obscure; his first documented activity was as a pupil of Egbert, himself the pupil of Bede. Alcuin then was heir to the traditions of English scholarship, and at the York cathedral school he had been given the best education of the times: Latin grammar, church doctrine and history, apologetics, and some rudimentary instruction from the quadrivium. Alcuin's general intellectual development had been guided by the prevailing Neoplatonism and his writings reveal the influence of Plato, chiefly through the medium of Boethius. It seems, in fact, that Alcuin was profoundly influenced by Boethius's De consolatione philosophiae, accepting the primacy of the role of philosophy, although Alcuin was concerned, in his mature years, to give a 'Christian' interpretation to what is fundamentally a secular theory.[15] In time Alcuin became a teacher at York, assuming increasing responsibilities until 778 when he was given full charge of the school and cathedral library. As a result of Charlemagne's persuasion at Parma, Alcuin accepted in the following year (782) an appointment to supervise the work of the palace school which, although nominally at Aachen, moved with the court. For the following fifteen years that was Alcuin's responsibility, although, so far as we can tell, the school did not really function as a teaching institution until after Alcuin had been at the court for the best part of a decade. For the first few years of his appointment Alcuin, in common with the other scholars, was fully occupied in assisting Charlemagne with the political and ideological aspects of the renovatio.

A considerable part of this aspect of the court's activities took place in the schola palatina in the form of dialogues and disputations conducted among the scholars at an advanced level. Usually the participants were identified by soubriquets, names assumed from the classical past: the king was David, Alcuin was Flaccus. Basically the new intellectual regeneratio was a linguistic movement which was forced to work with the available instruments, in this instance the classical Latin language and its methodologies of rhetoric and dialectic. It is significant, in this respect, to observe that Einhard's Vita Karoli was based upon the Latin model of Suetonius' Lives of the Caesars. In a society of such limited and degenerate educational institutions the emperor's purposes could best be effected by the skilful use of speech, properly argued and delivered. To reach the masses – and the religious sermon was the only available teaching method – a premium had to be placed upon rhetoric and dialectic.[16] We find a possibly very good example of this aspect of the court circle's activities at the *schola palatina* in Alcuin's own contribution to rhetorical theory. This is the *Disputatio de rhetorica et de virtutibus sapientissimi regis Karli et Albini magister*, known more simply as *On Rhetoric*.[17] Written in the form of a dialogue between Charlemagne and Albinus – a pseudonym of Alcuin – it appears as a relatively straightforward treatment, in Ciceronian concepts and relying heavily on Cicero's *De inventione*, of the various aspects of the subject. It illustrates Alcuin's view that rhetoric is the skill that allows the basis of an argument to be determined and analysed, and from which we can progress to a solution of the specific problem. Although *On Rhetoric* certainly took the form of a school-text it is unlikely to have been used as such. A far more plausible interpretation, and one that accords more closely with the contents, is that *On Rhetoric* is a treatise on kingship from one of Charlemagne's advisers – a *littera exhortatoria*.[18] The traditional handbook style is well exemplified in the opening passages where the following dialogue occurs:

CHARLEMAGNE. From what did rhetoric get its name?
ALCUIN. Ἀπὸ τοῦ ῥητορεύειν, that is, a fluency of discourse.
CHARLEMAGNE. To what end does it look?
ALCUIN. To the art of speaking well.
CHARLEMAGNE. In what affairs is it concerned?
ALCUIN. In public questions, that is, in questions adaptable to the ends of art, as can be inferred from the natural dispositions of the mind . . .[19]

Further on, however, the simple catechetical responses are fewer, Charlemagne's role consists in asking short leading questions. 'What official duty does each [party in a lawsuit] discharge?' (para 17); or 'How many aspects does [virtue] have?' (para 44), and Alcuin takes over the task of providing lengthy explanations, many of them running to several hundred words, and all bearing directly on the specific information and general background knowledge that a monarch concerned with just government should have.

Alcuin and the palace school

Some time in the late 780s Alcuin became more closely involved in the daily conduct of the palace school, although details are few and our knowledge depends chiefly upon inferences from his letters and miscellaneous writings. At the time of his appointment the palace school was neither scholarly nor cultivated and Alcuin recorded in a letter to Charlemagne his disapproval of the roughness of the young Frankish nobles who attended it.[20] It seems certain that his work at the school, in which he was assisted by tutors, began with instruction in simple writing and reading. From that foundation the student was enabled to proceed to the study of grammar and rhetoric. The difficulty of obtaining suitable teaching manuscripts prompted Alcuin to compose a number of his own, including the *Problems for Sharpening the Wits of Youth, Discussion between Pepin and his Schoolmaster, On Orthography* and *On Grammar*. All of those works are simple in structure, written either in catechetical form or as a dialogue between two or more persons, and are derivative in style and content, being influenced chiefly by Cicero and Bede. This kind of textbook is well illustrated in the following passage from the *Discussion between Pepin and his Schoolmaster* (*Pippini regalis et nobilissimi iuvenis disputatio cum Albino scholastico*):

PIPPINUS. What is a letter?
ALBINUS. The guardian of history.
P.   What is a word?
A.   The mind's betrayer.
P.   What creates the word?
A.   The tongue.
P.   What is the tongue?
A.   Something which whips the air.
P.   What is the air?
A.   The protection of life.
P.   What is life?
A.   The joy of the blessed, the sorrow of sinners, the expectation of death.
P.   What is death?
A.   An unavoidable occurrence, an uncertain journey, the tears of the living, the confirmation of the testament, the thief of man.[21]

This kind of presentation by controlled associations is a useful method for students who have little access to the written word and whose educational environment is mostly oral and auditory. Although this dialogue seems stilted it was in accord with the conventions of the times, and as it develops there is an increasing interpolation of didactic themes. Moreover, it must constantly be borne in mind that these dialogues were intended to teach Latin, and as correct a Latin as possible, to foreign speakers. A great deal of the pedagogical value of all of these rhetorical and grammatical textbooks simply does not come across in translation.

Following his own background in Anglo-Saxon learning, Alcuin saw the values of education focused in the contemporary ideal of *ars grammatici*, the ability to write and speak well,[22] a skill which he believed developed out of the study of rhetoric. Alcuin's own knowledge of rhetoric came from the study of Cicero and in particular from the influential *De inventione*. The classical theorists, however, of whom Aristotle and Cicero were the major figures, had never successfully separated dialectic from rhetoric, although Cicero had attempted a reconciliation by arguing that dialectic deals with universal problems, rhetoric with particular ones – those bounded by time, place and persons.[23] The considerable loss of Greek studies in the West,[24] and of Aristotle's writings in particular, had forced scholars to rely heavily on Cicero, in whose writings rhetoric was extolled as a means of discovering the truth. Alcuin accepted that viewpoint, seeing in rhetoric two major educational values: its ability to foster oratorical power and its use in analysing argument,[25] and as such it remained the highest study in his programme of learning at the court.

Encouragement of learning in the Frankish Empire

The direction of the palace school, however, although Alcuin's major, overt responsibility, was never the exclusive centre of his educational interests. From the time of his arrival, Alcuin was concerned with the improvement of education throughout the whole of the kingdom. The deterioration of learning had reached the point where large numbers, perhaps the majority of the monks and the clergy, were ignorant of Latin if not completely illiterate, and no regular programme of training them was in existence. Since the monasteries usually conducted schools only for their oblates and the Rule of the Benedictines was not concerned vitally with scholarship in any case, there were few institutional means whereby the cycle of decline could be halted. As a consequence, Alcuin was instrumental in having Charlemagne publish several decrees intended to remedy this. In the early years of his reign Charlemagne issued a capitulary requiring illiterate priests to be removed from their positions.[26] As the *renovatio* gathered momentum the number of decrees increased and one of the first significant ones that survives, in a single copy, is that sent to Baugulf, abbot of the great monastery at Fulda in Thuringia, some time around the year 787.

The text is the usual length for this kind of document – several hundred words – and deals with one specific theme: that, in addition to the pursuit of the religious monastic life, monks should be concerned with the pursuit of knowledge and with helping their brothers to learn. The reason given appears simple, which is that monks can serve god not only by living well but by speaking correctly ('ei etiam placere non negligant recte loquendo'), and each monk should be so tutored to the limits of his ability. None the less, Charlemagne reveals a greater concern in the same text: letters that he had been receiving from monasteries were poorly composed and expressed, and if monks were so lacking in their command of Latin that their letters were barbarous, how could they be secure in their understanding of the scriptural texts? It would be of decided help to monks in their religious studies if they had first mastered the art of letters. 'It is my desire', wrote the king, 'that all monks in my realm should be, to all who meet them, living examples of piety, learning, purity and eloquence.' The capitulary ends with a royal command for enthusiastic and competent monks to be chosen to give instruction in monasteries, and for the abbot to send further copies of the capitulary to his assistants and to the surrounding monasteries.[27]

Around the same time, in the year 789, Charlemagne – again with Alcuin's assistance – issued his most famous capitulary, known as the *Admonitio generalis*, which was aimed at the intellectual reform of the church. Along with stern injunctions to the clergy to strive to maintain pure lives, according to the same principles set out in the decree of *c.* 787, Charlemagne commanded the establishment of schools:

> And let schools be established in which boys may learn to read. Correct carefully the Psalms, the signs in writing, the songs, the calendar, the grammar [*psalms, notas, cantus, compotum, grammaticam*], in each monastery or bishopric, and the Catholic books; because often men desire to pray to God properly, but they pray badly because of incorrect books. And do not permit mere boys to corrupt them in reading or writing. If the Gospel, Psalter and Missal have to be copied let men of mature age do the copying, with the greatest care.[28]

From this document we probably get the most accurate account of the school studies which actually were provided for the majority of boys, as distinct from the more normative prescriptions which occur throughout the texts. Of the five studies listed, four are concerned with reading, and of these psalms, songs and grammar are easily understood. The study of 'signs in writing' – *notae* – is somewhat ambiguous, as the translation, probably the best that can be made, indicates. The Latin word embraces a wide range of meanings, all concerned with the making of marks, ciphers or brands, generally with letters of the alphabet. Neither it nor its corresponding verb *notare*, however, mean the practice of writing in the sense of producing a running script; that is *ars scribendi*. Just what the 'signs in writing' were is obscure although considering the context in which it occurs and the general direction of learning it seems reasonable to infer that *notae* designated, among other things, the *scholia* and other notations used to gloss the antiphonaries in which the psalms and songs (chants) were written.

Of greater interest here, however, is the study of the calendar, *computus*.[29] This was of central importance in the regulation of daily life in all ecclesiastical institutions, for both mundane and theological purposes, though more especially for the latter. Since the central unifying feature of Christianity is the Crucifixion, around which the church calendar revolves, the calculation of the dates of Easter and all other festivals was of the first order of importance. In the Carolingian era the computist was an important person and the practice of computing was necessarily highly skilled. A literature on this had grown up from the time of Dionysius Exiguus (*c.* A.D. 500–50) in the sixth century who attempted to set calendar studies on a precise basis and introduced the system in use to the present day. In England the Synod of Whitby, meeting in 664, accepted Dionysius' new ecclesiastical chronology; this was interpreted for the English clergy by Bede who wrote, first, *De temporibus* and then, in 725, *De ratione temporum*. These two works, along with Isidore of Seville's *De natura rerum* and parts of Book Three of his *Etymologies*, were the standard authorities in the period,[30] and all were brought across to the Frankish kingdom, although, from the evidence of surviving manuscripts – more than 125 in all – *De ratione temporum* (*On the Computing of Time*) was the most popular.[31]

There is no doubt that *De ratione temporum* was the fundamental text used in the teaching of *computus*, and to supplement this we have what appears to be an examination of computing competence based upon it. This survives in a single copy, of the eleventh century, which was first written in 809 and is now part of the Sirmondian Manuscript kept in the Bodleian Library at Oxford. It is a very compact document of a single folio containing twenty-three short, one-sentence questions and their correspondingly brief answers – in the majority of cases, four to ten words. Its *incipit* states that it is concerned with 'Topics on which assembled computists were questioned, together with a representation of the kind of answers they gave and the order in which they were rendered', while the first item sets the date:

> 1. How many years did they wish to count from the Incarnation of God to the present year? *Response*: 809.

The following questions then ask, in turn, the date of the Crucifixion, the length of Jesus' earthly life, the number of years from the beginning of the world through to the Incarnation. The document then deals in sequence with the setting of the equinox, the phases of the moon, the irregularities of calendrical dates and the procedures of intercalation. While it is impossible to be sure that it was in fact a licensing examination for computists, the document has considerable value in illustrating the approach to the study of *computus*. Very clearly, owing to the abstract conceptual skills required to grasp the principles of computation, in contrast to the brevity and simplicity of the answers, this study – and it was virtually all that existed to represent the quadrivium of the ancient mathematical studies – was probably pursued by relatively few students. As it was presented, it would have been inordinately difficult for most.

Manuscript preservation and the Caroline bookhand

Along with their concern to make some regular provision for the literacy of the clergy these decrees manifest an equal concern with the need to improve standards of book production. Misspellings and solecisms were frequently found in manuscripts along with the increasing use of various scribal shorthand devices and contractions, and these simply inhibited communication. The *Admonitio generalis* of 789 called specifically for the revision of the growing number of faulty church texts which had become corrupt through the ignorance of the copyists.[32] Meanwhile, among the scholars of the court there had been new developments in the art of writing. Throughout Europe a number of different bookhands were in use and in the various monasteries these were all used and often intermingled. In this way the various forms of late Latin script – the uncials and the subsequent half-uncials – chiefly developed in Italy, Ireland and Britain, found varying degrees of acceptance throughout the Carolingian realm. One of the most beautiful was the rounded style, derived from Roman half-uncials (or 'small' letters) which had been developed by the Irish and Northumbrian monks and then later adopted in several European monasteries, particularly Corbie, Bobbio and St Gall. Its use in the Frankish kingdom increased and around 781 the scribe Godescalc produced, most probably at Charlemagne's command, a collection of scriptural readings intended for feast days and known as a gospel lectionary. This is almost certainly the oldest surviving manuscript of the court and its script marks the introduction of a style of writing that quickly became accepted and repeated in several other service books, notably a Psalter produced for presentation to Pope Hadrian.[33] The hand used in those books, now known as Carolingian minuscule, rapidly set a standard for the scribes and became virtually the official style for the Frankish court and kingdom. Although Alcuin has often been asserted to have had a direct responsibility in the development and adoption of this minuscule there is no evidence to support the belief; certainly, however, we know that he was fundamentally interested in writing and both during and after his time at the palace school he made the proper copying and preservation of manuscripts a personal responsibility. The Carolingian minuscule script, illustrated in Plate 1, now provided the means whereby some of the deficiencies in communication could be remedied.

Meanwhile, in 796, in his sixtieth year, Alcuin had left the palace school to become abbot of the famous monastery of St Martin at Tours. This transfer was largely the result of Alcuin's advancing years and his desire for a more scholarly and contemplative environment. One of the conditions of the new appointment, however, was that he should continue to be available to counsel Charlemagne. Outside the Frankish kingdom several disturbing developments had occurred: Britain was being attacked by Vikings from Scandia who were pillaging and destroying ruthlessly; heresy and religious dissent had broken out again, this time in Spain. As a response to the Norse destruction of the English monasteries – which meant a loss of precious manuscripts – Alcuin became concerned to encourage manuscript preservation.

In the remaining few years of his life, consequently, Alcuin made the scriptorium at Tours famous throughout Western Christendom. The major task of that period was the production of an authentic version of the Latin Vulgate Bible. Under Alcuin's supervision the project was completed and on Christmas Day, A.D. 801, a copy was presented to Charlemagne. Although none of the several copies has survived, the other manuscripts of the period testify to the maturity of the Carolingian minuscule which was to remain the major script in northern Europe for the following two centuries. Those manuscripts reveal another important reform in the art of book-production. Alcuin standardized the use of the various forms of the alphabet: Roman capitals for headings, half-uncials for the preface, minuscule for the text. Alcuin was thereby responsible for introducing a convention that was transferred centuries later to the printed book and that remains in use to this day.

Alcuin's final years at Tours: vision of imperium christianum

Alciun was not to rest at Tours in any easy retirement. He found the place extremely retrograde, complaining in a letter to Charlemagne, in the year 799, that every day at Tours he had to fight against rusticity: *cum Turonica cotidie pugno rusticitate*.[34] Yet he was, in fact, kept in touch with the intellectual and theological developments of his times and Charlemagne continued to make use of his services. It has been conjectured that the treatise *On Rhetoric*, in fact, was composed while in retirement at Tours although the issue is by no means settled.[35] Certainly we know that Alcuin was summoned to deal with one major outbreak of heresy known as Adoptionism which erupted in Spain in the last decade of the eighth century.

Speculation about the nature of Christ had been growing ever since the second century. Various theories had appeared – Arianism, Monophysitism, Monothelitism – all attempting to explain Christ's nature in terms subtly different from the orthodox Trinitarian doctrine. In the eighth century two Spanish bishops, Elipand of Toledo and Felix of Urgel, embraced the Adoptionist position which held that Christ has a dual nature: the divine Christ, they maintained, is god's son by nature, the man Christ is son by god's act of adoption. The doctrine was prosecuted by Alcuin acting for Charlemagne and condemned at three Carolingian Synods, in 792, 794 and 799. Alcuin carried his case; Bishop Felix was committed to Alcuin's care in 800.

In the same year, A.D. 800, one of the most momentous events of the times took place. Charlemagne was formally crowned emperor of the Holy Roman Empire by Pope Leo III. Stephen II had only anointed Pepin the Short; with the emperor in Constantinople still regarded as supreme sovereign, it was unthinkable that the ceremony of coronation could be claimed by another ruler. The coronation of Charlemagne on Christmas Day, therefore, was an astounding occurrence, and it is still the subject of considerable scholarly dispute. The pattern of events, moreover, and the numerous motives and activities leading up to the ceremony are still quite obscure.[36] Charlemagne's own ambitions and those of the papacy, and even the personal problems of Leo III, are elements of the situation. The young emperor Constantine V (r. 780–97), ruling in Constantinople, had been blinded and had his throne usurped by his mother Irene so that, in a sense, the emperorship of the Roman Empire was vacant. That interpretation could have given cause for the attempt by either Charlemagne or the papacy to restore imperial authority to its traditional seat in the city of

Rome. In the same period, the Moslem menace continued to be felt strongly and the papal desire for a military alliance to strengthen the Roman church must have been considerable. The ancient pagan Romans had regarded their empire as a Holy Roman Empire and their emperor as Pontifex Maximus. In 800 that former conception was revived.

Alcuin played some considerable, if discreet, part in that revival. He saw in Charlemagne an heir to the *imperium christianum*. Ardent supporter of Rome that Alcuin was, and indefatigable deviser of royal policy, the notion of a new Holy Roman Empire must have appealed to him considerably. Through such an institution, civilization and culture – attacked in Britain by the Norsemen, racked with heresy in Spain, destroyed in the Orient by the Moslem advances and decaying in Byzantium under the degenerate Irene – could flourish again and so make the church secure in its claims to provide the primary inspiration. Alcuin's aim was to assist Charlemagne's plans for securing such a revival, evidence being suggested to some scholars by *On Rhetoric*.

The fulfilment of that vision did not occur. On 19 May 804 Alcuin died at Tours, probably of a stroke. Charlemagne ruled for another decade, the Empire withered after his death and Aachen slipped into rural obscurity.

Two late Carolingian scholars: Hrabanus Maurus and John the Scot

The Carolingian floruit of learning faded rapidly after Alcuin. Both Aachen and Tours lost their prominence and the scholarly succession passed to the monastery of Fulda in the north-eastern corner of the kingdom. That Benedictine abbey had been founded by the West Saxon (that is, Wessex) scholar, Wynfrith, who was elected bishop of Mainz in 722, under the name of Boniface. At his direction the great abbey was founded about 732 and its rise to prominence came with the work of Hrabanus Maurus (*c.* 776–836).

Hrabanus had been sent by Abbot Ratgar of Fulda to Tours about 802. There he had a short period of contact with Alcuin, in that time distinguishing himself as the master's greatest student. In time Hrabanus came to surpass the traditions of Tours in attempting to preserve the spirit of the Carolingian revival at Fulda, thereby providing the basis for the subsequent development of education in the region. As abbot of Fulda between 822 and 836, he continued to emphasize the liberal arts tradition, stating his views in the widely adopted tract, *Education of the Clergy (De clericorum institutione*).[37] Throughout that manifesto the spirit of Alcuin is evident in the insistence on scripture as the foundation, content and perfection of all wisdom.[38] The scriptures themselves, however, Raban points out, had been translated into numerous languages, thereby accumulating variant meanings. Their metaphorical allusions, moreover, were the subject of dispute and demanded careful examination. As a consequence, the clergy, according to Hrabanus, stood in need of a thorough training in the liberal arts to provide a proper background for study of the scriptures. Book Three opens with such an injunction:

> An ecclesiastical education should qualify the sacred office of the ministry for divine service. It is fitting that those who from an exalted station undertake the direction of life of the Church, should acquire fullness of knowledge, and that they should strive after rectitude of life and perfection of development.[39]

The means of giving this fullness of knowledge to the clergy is through an education in the liberal arts. Following the encyclopedic and etymological traditions of previous European scholarship, that of Bede, Isidore and Cassiodorus in particular, *Education of the Clergy* deals with each liberal art in turn. Priority is accorded to grammar as the foundation of the liberal arts and the basis by which correct writing and speaking can proceed. Through it alone can access be made to the literary heritage, identified in that period with poetry and history.[40] Grammar is conceived by Hrabanus as it was by Alcuin and by Bede before him – as the study of syntax, tropes, figures of speech, allusions, inferences, allegory, riddles, parables. Rhetoric and dialectic are allied skills, the former the art of using speech effectively, the latter the science of understanding – the 'science of sciences'.[41] In his discussion of dialectic, a study which had fallen into considerable disuse, Hrabanus touched upon the question of pedagogical procedure. Relatively little had been written in the immediately preceding centuries on the theory of teaching and learning and his brief treatment – a single paragraph – demonstrates the prevailing conceptions:

> Dialectic . . . teaches how to teach others; it teaches teaching itself; in it the reason marks and manifests itself according to its nature, efforts and activities; it alone is capable of knowing; it not only will, but can lead others to knowledge; its conclusions lead us to an apprehension of our being and of our origin; through it we apprehend the origin and activity of the good, of Creator and creature; it teaches us to discover the truth and unmask falsehood; it teaches us to draw conclusions; it shows us what is valid in argument

and what is not; it teaches us to recognize what is contrary to the nature of things; it teaches us to distinguish in controversy the true, the probable, and the wholly false; by means of this science we are able to investigate everything with penetration, to determine its nature with certainty, and to discuss it with circumspection.[42]

In that statement, Hrabanus kept alive an issue that was never wholly absent from Western thought: the role of reason in the discovery of truth. The line of succession from Plato and Aristotle can be traced through Porphyry and Boethius to Hrabanus Maurus. Yet in the ninth century learning was confined to the meagre sources available and reason was allowed little scope. None the less, by keeping the idea of the spirit of inquiry before men, even if in a temporarily inanimate state, Hrabanus helped lay the basis for the resurgence of interest in dialectic in the twelfth century.

Hrabanus' treatment of the quadrivium followed the usual style. Freely acknowledging his indebtedness to Plato, and even Pythagoras, he discussed all four studies – arithmetic, geometry, astronomy, harmonics – in terms of their value in facilitating the appreciation of knowledge in abstract form. And abstract form itself provided an earthly paradigm of the structure of heavenly form.

It was such a tradition that developed in the nascent Germany where Hrabanus' approach was continued by his two pupils Candidus at Fulda, and Walafrid who became abbot of Reichenau. Candidus probably accepted lay scholars at Fulda; if he did then his school was the first secular school in Germany. In time Hrabanus' standards and methods returned to the Frankish kingdom proper where, in the monastery at Ferrières in particular, the spirit of scriptural exegesis was maintained by his pupil Servatus Lupus. Even so the work of Hrabanus Maurus was still strongly conservative; he and his master Alcuin showed little inclination towards speculation or inquiry. The eighth and in turn the ninth centuries in the West were quite unmarked by any adventure of the intellect, with the noteworthy exception of the thought of John the Scot. And even John's ideas were totally outside the intellectual traditions of his times.

John Scotus Erigena (c. 810–c. 875) was born in Ireland, known also as Scotland in that period – hence his name – but virtually nothing is known of his early life. He first enters the historical record around 845 at the time of his succession to the headship of the palace school which had continued under Charlemagne's son Louis the Pious (r. 814–40) and grandson Charles the Bald (r. 843–77). John was noted for his scholarship more than for his pedagogical skill, and his famous book *Periphyseon* or *De divisione naturae* (*On the Division of Nature*) was the most remarkable work of religious and philosophical thought in the West from the sixth to the tenth century. Of considerable importance is the fact that John knew Greek quite well – his book has a Greek title although its text is Latin – and, since Greek was virtually unknown at the time in Europe, much less were there teachers of the language or schools where it could have been taught, there remains the unanswered question of how John came to know Greek. The most plausible explanation is that he learned it in some Greek land, perhaps Sicily or southern Italy, even Byzantium, and this could have been easily achieved in the first, unrecorded half of his life.[43] John's early obscurity is matched by the later events of his career – he disappeared without trace around 875. And centuries later, in 1225, his book was banned by Pope Honorius III, chiefly because of its pantheistic tone.

On the Division of Nature is none the less a work of significance to the development of European thought, and provides some illustrations of the current attitudes to learning, if for no other reason than the contrast it affords to its times. John attempted to mediate the respective claims of faith and reason, thereby giving an indication to man concerning his earthly vocation. John's own background of learning in the Greek as well as the Latin fathers is the starting-point of his thought. In addition to Origen his chief Greek influences were the writings of the fifth-century (?) Denys the Areopagite and the inseparable commentaries of St Maximus the Confessor (580–662). As well, John was acquainted closely with the Latin thinkers, mainly Augustine. Neoplatonism, then, is the basic orientation from which his thought developed.

In one sense John dealt with natural history for the first time in Europe since the encyclopedic productions of Pliny in the first century A.D., although John was not concerned primarily with nature *per se* but as evidence of the ways in which god manifests himself. This he did by a vast deductive scheme of classification. In the opening sentences of *On the Division of Nature*, which is constructed in dialogue form between Nutritor and Alumnus, literally the nurse and nursling but by metaphoric extension designating teacher and student, he asserts that we arrive at knowledge in the degree that we can understand the structure of the world or the 'division of nature'. The basic premiss is that 'the first and fundamental division of all things [*primam summaque divisionem*] which can either be grasped by the mind or lie beyond its grasp [can be designated by] a general term for them all, what in Greek is called φύσις [*physis*: nature] and in Latin *natura*.'[44] In making this analysis by classification he puts forward a fourfold taxonomy, starting with 'the causes of things' – images (*imagines*) or divine manifestations (*apparitiones divinas*) – '[which] are eternally in God and which are God, first in God, then in themselves, then the proper species and [specific] differences of the creatures themselves.'[45] This, of course, is straightforward Neoplatonic thinking and is well illustrated in his discussion on geometrical bodies. These, he explains, which

> . . . we contemplate only by the mind's eye, and which we manage to construct from the images in our memory, do not subsist in any οὐσία [*ousia*: essence] and are therefore rightly called imaginary while natural bodies are natural for the very reason that they subsist in their natural οὐσία, that is, their essences, and cannot exist without them . . . [Therefore, we] are given to understand that body is one thing and οὐσία another, since a body is sometimes without οὐσία and sometimes, so as to be a real body, is associated with οὐσία.[46]

From this approach John moves on to explain the world itself, and this he believes to be a created ordered pattern consisting in a hierarchy of forms; and one, moreover, that is not fixed but in process of continuous creation. In this way he attempts to explain change, although this explanation does not allow for the appearance of new species. The universe remains constant in its constituent elements. God is the author of such continuous creation by means of pure forms which are brought into being by the Word. God's Word – the earlier Logos doctrine – provides the archetype from whence genus, species and individuals develop. Man himself is an aspect of that cycle of endless creation, enjoying a position intermediate between the completely incorporeal angels and corporeal, inanimate objects. Yet for man, the cyclic rhythm of life was broken by the Fall; man, therefore, has the task of regaining for himself the state of divine grace from which he has fallen. At this point John incorporates the Christian revelation in his theology. Christ came to show the way to achieve grace by affirming the existence of god and providing an absolute basis for faith. Once faith is secured, the truths contained within it can be ordered by reason. Man, as a rational being, can again restore his proper relationship with god. The critical factor in John's theory is the absolute unity of faith and reason, the latter serving as man's instrument to achieve grace.

Although, as the title implies, John's treatise is concerned with nature – the Greek title too, *Periphyseon*, means 'concerning nature' – he discusses principles of taxonomy and in seeking to illustrate 'definition by place', which, he says, is regarded as being 'necessarily nowhere else but in the mind [*non alibi nisi in animo erit*]',[47] he uses the existing liberal arts to make his point, and, in doing so, he provides us with the clearest mid-ninth-century indication we have of how these studies were interpreted. 'Among the liberal arts [*disciplinis liberalibus*],' he wrote, 'also very many definitions are found, for there is no art without its definitions . . .'

> Grammar is the art which protects and controls articulate speech.
>
> Rhetoric is the art which carries out a full and elaborate examination of a set topic under the [seven] headings of person, matter, occasion, quality, place, time and opportunity, and can be briefly defined: rhetoric is the art which deals acutely and fully with a topic defined by its seven circumstances.
>
> Dialectic is the art which diligently investigates the rational common concepts of the mind.
>
> Arithmetic is the reasoned and pure art of the numbers which come under the contemplations of the mind.
>
> Geometry is the art which considers by the mind's acute observation the intervals and surfaces of plane and solid figures.
>
> Music is the art which by the light of reason studies the harmony of all things that are in motion that is knowable by natural proportions.
>
> Astronomy is the art which investigates the dimensions of the heavenly bodies and their motions and their returnings at fixed times.[48]

In these descriptions John shows an understanding of the customary classical definitions although, in respect of the available evidence of his times, these arts were not practised as such and John's knowledge may not have extended far past the definitions themselves – certainly with regard to the four mathematical studies.

John the Scot's thinking put heavy demands on men: it required the exercise of contemplation and speculation that bordered on mysticism. Such demands were difficult to achieve, particularly in the social and political climate of ninth-century Europe. His great, but abstruse and difficult doctrine remained beyond the grasp of many and exercised little direct influence on European thought. Like Alcuin and Raban, John was one of a minority of distinguished but lonely figures whose learning was restricted to a small circle of followers, generally the superior monks in the monasteries and the clergy of the cathedrals. By the ninth century the monasteries counted the majority of their members as marginally literate in the regional vernaculars, scarcely at all in Latin. The smaller churches were no better. Learning, even though it was chiefly a clerical monopoly, was restricted almost entirely to biblical commentaries and liberal arts compendia which constituted the mainstay of school instruction in the Carolingian era.

Early feudal Europe A.D. 840–1050

Feudal society after Charlemagne

The stabilization of European society achieved by Charlemagne did not survive under his successors. His son Louis the Pious (r. 814–40) created such a complex division of the Empire among his four sons, Lothar, Pepin, Ludwig and Charles, that his death in 840 was followed by a period of violent fights for succession. The Treaty of Verdun, which attempted to settle the problems in 843, was unable to prevent the continued disintegration of the Holy Roman Empire. That treaty had provided for three basic kingdoms which, since they were not integral in themselves in any real sense, broke up quickly into smaller states. By 855 there were six, and even in these sovereignty became delegated from the king through the great lords – dukes and counts – to rest ultimately in the knight holding a 'simple fief', the minimum unit of sovereignty. The king's power came to depend entirely on the willingness of his vassals (*vassi dominici*) to support him, and his ability to coerce or otherwise enforce his authority over them. The development of that enormously decentralized organization of society, known as feudalism, is not fully recorded. None the less by the end of the ninth century feudalism was the prevailing form of social and political organization throughout the former Frankish Empire, lasting until the fourteenth century.

The disintegration of the Carolingian Empire and the correlative growth of feudalism resulted from conditions internal to the continent although exacerbated by the external hostility of various non-Christian peoples: Vikings in the north, Magyars in the north-east, Moslems on the southern shores of the Mediterranean. Those antagonists, especially the Vikings, decreased communications, and the consequent diminution of trade and commerce encouraged the process of contraction to the land and the fortified castles. In the absence of strong central government and with the pressure from external invaders maintained throughout the ninth and tenth centuries, political power came to be exercised by a number of different authorities, who were, in addition, struggling constantly among themselves for ascendancy. Society was not completely fragmented and anarchic, however; some degree of stability was effected by that multiplicity of contending powers which in practice was focused in three main social orders: feudal, seigniorial, municipal.

The feudal system proper, involving the decentralization of power throughout all of the nobility, from duke and count down to knight, was the dominant social order, and its operation affected the rest of life. But it was exclusively rural and agricultural: the aristocracy survived the disintegrative pressures of the ninth and tenth centuries only by withdrawing to fortified enclosures – which in time evolved into castles – and ruling their surrounding domains from such centres of military security. The towns, since they ceased to be productive, were abandoned by the nobility; the smaller ones along with the villages were nothing more than corporations of peasants, dependent for their security on the nearest lord, and consequently under his dominion. The larger towns and the cities, even when they declined, were not abandoned by the church, however, and in them were maintained the episcopal seats. So in effect urban life, such as it was, came to be dominated in general by the church. The pattern of control over the villages, towns and cities, whether exercised by the nearby rural nobility or the urban resident clergy, was the seigniorial system. And a third main power, found chiefly in Italy, was the municipal corporation, a survival of the ancient Roman civic institution. Of those latter authorities the fifth-century foundation of Venice was the most powerful in the tenth century, although it was rivalled by others in the eleventh – Pisa and Genoa in particular. Dominant as the feudal order was, it held no universal jurisdiction. On the contrary the struggles for ascendancy between all three orders that lasted throughout the tenth to the fourteenth centuries gave the medieval period its specific character.

The pattern of learning: chivalric ideal of the nobility

During the early feudal centuries, the ninth and tenth, the decline of learning that began in the fifth century, and continued through the sixth and seventh, with a temporary halt in the eighth century under Alcuin, continued to manifest itself throughout Europe. The loss of communication and social vigour had an effect on learning, which, similarly cut off, survived only in isolated places – abbeys, cathedrals, churches, some courts and castles. Education in any deeply significant sense was no longer an active concern, while scribal activities came to be identified exclusively with the church.

The nobility had little concern with academic learning in any form. In the late Roman Empire scholarship among the ruling classes at least was considered desirable; by the tenth century that ideal had vanished. Throughout Germany, France and England the laity were largely illiterate and those secular leaders who had received some formal schooling usually had begun their careers with notions of an ecclesiastical vocation. The changed conditions of life had produced new social models, the warrior-knight became the aristocratic ideal and his training in military accomplishments had little concern with literacy.

The first stage in the inculcation of the warrior ideal began when the young noble boy was entrusted to the care of a relative for his training. Feudal military engagements were led exclusively by cavalry forces made up by the nobility. Consequently the boy's object was the acquisition of three basic skills: horsemanship, and proficiency with lance and sword. So we read in Einhard that 'As soon as they were old enough, [Charlemagne] had his sons taught to ride in the Frankish fashion, to use arms and to hunt.'[49] With those three went minor achievements, all related to the use of arms and conduct in battle. As the pattern of feudal life developed, a comprehensive code of knightly behaviour became elaborated in the concept of chivalry, the training of the young noble becoming formalized in that code. The attainment of the requisite skills was symbolized by the ceremony of knighthood around the youth's twentieth year in which he was formally admitted, by the ceremony of dubbing with the sword on the shoulders, to the ranks of the knights.

The chivalric code itself became increasingly complex and mannered as feudalism continued and the church attempted to infuse religious ideals into the code. John of Salisbury, for example, writing in the twelfth century, argued that the office of the knight is 'to defend the Church, to assail infidelity, to venerate the priesthood, to protect the poor from injuries, to pacify the province, to pour out their blood for their brothers (as the formula of their oath instructs them), and if need be, to lay down their lives',[50] the aim of such actions being to serve god by securing equity and public utility.

Chivalry acquired yet a further dimension, that of courtly love, embodied in the ideal of veneration for, and protection of noble womanhood. In places, and in later centuries, that aspect of the code received an exaggerated expression. Girls, for their part, never had any provisions made for their education as specifically as those for boys. Some literacy was provided in the few rudimentary convents that existed – although our information is very meagre indeed on this point – and some households may have given their daughters instruction in letters, as we know Charlemagne did, but he also 'made his daughters learn to spin and weave wool, use the distaff and spindle and acquire every womanly accomplishment rather than fritter away their time in idleness',[51] and it was this training which was the general standard. With such a restricted and dependent life style, medieval society compensated with this elaborate code of respect. Generally the chivalric ideal remained in operation, along with the practices, even into the thirteenth and fourteenth centuries, although by that time knightly training and life had increasingly lost their relevance to existent society. As a consequence, knights cultivated the chivalric code to the point of absurdity; courtly love was over-romanticized, thereby expressing the sharp tension between the cult of womanhood and the fact of women's subjection in real life. In the absence of real wars, knights maintained their skills through the ever-increasing tournaments, and their calling became glorified in the glamorous legends of valour and high deeds known as romances (*romans d'aventure*), epic poems designed to be recited in knightly leisure hours and to maintain the fiction of the code. Many of those – *Chanson de Roland*, *Perceval*, *Galahad*, Arthurian tales, *Lancelot*, *Tristram and Iseult* – became permanent additions to the vernacular literature.

The pattern of learning: clerics and clerks

If the nobility had little direct acquaintance with formal learning nevertheless they stood in need of it to some degree. That need was met by the clergy. Castles either maintained a resident cleric who could discharge the functions of scribe as well as priest, or else used the services of a parish priest from the rural church. The parish church itself, often including several priests, was part of the feudal system and the priest was a link in the social hierarchy, holding his church property in fief, usually from a bishop, occasionally from a lord, and rendering homage in return. Although administration of the sacraments and the care of souls formed his primary responsibility, the cleric, as the literate member of the community, performed the additional task of local scribe, and in that secondary function the designation of 'clerk' has its origins. As time progressed, increasing numbers of clerics in minor orders turned their training in formal literacy to the purely secular role of clerk.

Resurgence of monasticism: Cluniac Reform

The training of the priest itself, however, was completely unorganized. In general, there was no regular or uniform method of educating the priesthood, and by the ninth and tenth centuries illiteracy among them was increasing, a situation compounded by the ninth-century decline of the monasteries and their disinterest in any case in providing instruction for *externi*. The sixth-century foundation of Monte Cassino with its Benedictine Rule had provided the model for European monasteries and, although not an order, Benedictinism spread rapidly in the seventh and eighth centuries, becoming supported strongly by Charlemagne. In 788 that emperor established the *Regula Benedicti* as the primary rule in his domains; in 817 Louis the Pious made it obligatory throughout all of the Frankish kingdom, and in the same year issued a capitulary restricting attendance at Benedictine schools to their own oblates, which he confirmed again in 823. Despite their ascendancy the Benedictines, in fact, had no interest in providing schooling for any persons other than their own *interni* or oblates; and, regardless of the individual excellence of some monasteries in the field of scholarship, their Rule put no great emphasis on learning. Monasticism suffered from the same ills that afflicted ninth-century Europe in the period of emerging feudalism; as those foundations lost their discipline and corporate identity, even the learning that they preserved was minimal.

Impetus to reform came in 910 when Duke William of Aquitaine founded a new monastery at Cluny in French Burgundy. That action initiated the so-called Cluniac Reform of monasticism, the basic feature of which was the return to strong religious discipline. Adopting the Rule of Benedict, Cluny prospered under two of its earliest abbots, Odo (r. 926–42) and Odilo (r. 994–1049). Cluny's example was followed by a large number of new monasteries – probably more than a hundred by the end of the tenth century. In the early years of the movement, monasteries reformed from Cluny remained independent but towards the end of Odilo's time, and especially under his successor Hugh (1024–1109), dependent foundations became common. In effect, the Cluniac Reform produced a Benedictine monastic order: Cluny was the mother house, ruled by the abbot of the order, and all other monasteries were priories, controlled by priors (sub-abbots) who remained subordinate to the abbot's authority. The new order, however, did little to provide for educational reform; it was largely a rural movement, usually preferring to build in remote country locations and drawing its leaders from the aristocracy. As in the days of its original inspiration, Benedictinism emphasized the act of corporate worship, so that the performance of the liturgy became its most renowned feature. The Cluniac movement reformed monasticism, but not learning, and with their disinclination to provide schooling for the *externi* – intending secular priests – the monasteries, beginning in the tenth century, and reaching into the eleventh, ceased to operate as agencies of public education. The lacuna thus created was filled by a relatively new institution, the cathedral school.

Education of the secular clergy: emergence of cathedral schools

The dominance of the monasteries in learning was never intentional. On the contrary, attempts had been made as early as Merovingian times to fill the place of the disappearing Roman municipal schools. The two church councils of Orléans in 511 and Vaison in 529 had required every parish priest to maintain a school in his church to teach the scriptures, reading, writing and reckoning. The Vaison conclave – the second held in that town on the coastal plain of the river Rhône – was concerned chiefly with regularizing the liturgy, and to effect this it specifically required that 'all priests in charge of parishes are to receive young boys of sufficient intellect and to raise them in the Christian faith, to teach them the psalms and the lessons of scripture and God's laws'.[52] The council recommended the establishment of rural and town parish schools in order to train future parish priests. Unfortunately, we have no knowledge of the implementation of this resolution, although it seems to have been beyond the interest or capacity of most bishops. In individual places, however, if the willpower of the bishop or abbot were strong enough, and the necessary resources available, some reforms were effected, as happened in Metz under its energetic bishop Chrodegang (d. 766). Related to Pepin of Landen, and chief minister to his son Charles Martel, Chrodegang was translated to the bishopric of Metz in 742 and founded a monastery at nearby Gorze some six years later. Chrodegang attempted some reform of the cathedral schools and formulated a rule for the monastery at Gorze, *Regula Chrodegangi*, which he imposed on his secular priests as well as upon the monastics.

Similarly, Theodulph, bishop of Orléans, issued an encyclical in 786 to his parish priests enjoining them to establish schools where young boys might get some instruction and a strengthening of their faith, but we remain ignorant of the results. The temper of the times, it seems, prevented any widespread implementation of such provisions; it was partly to secure their observance that Charlemagne was moved to formulate the capitulary *Admonitio generalis* of 799. That document produced some effect, but not enough. Complaints reached Rome, including some from England, that grammar schools were still not readily available. As a result Pope

Eugenius issued a decretal in 826 instructing all bishops that it was their canonical duty to maintain schools:

> Complaints have been made that in some places no masters nor endowment for a grammar school [*studio literarum*] is found. Therefore all bishops shall bestow all care and diligence, both for their subjects and for other places in which it shall be found necessary, to establish masters and teachers [*magistri et doctores*] who shall assiduously teach grammatical studies and the principles of the liberal arts, because in these chiefly the commandments of God are manifested and declared.[53]

Indeed, throughout the ninth century there is a sufficiency of information on councils and other gatherings which considered the problem of the lack of schools. In particular, the Councils of Valence of 855 and of Savonnières of 859 both urged the establishment of at least elementary schools by bishops within their sees, but, unfortunately, there is no documentation of the responses to these decrees and information on the establishment of parish schools throughout the ninth and tenth centuries scarcely exists. At best we can infer, however, that there was a general continuation of the educational impulse provided by Charlemagne's *renovatio* and there is every ground for believing that the ninth and tenth centuries can be considered as late Carolingian, even if learning became attenuated and lost much of the zeal that it had in Alcuin's day.[54] Certainly some schools continued to function and the best direct evidence comes from the tenth century in Ottonian Germany. The biography of Bruno, brother to Otto I (r. 936–73), records that he was sent at the age of four to the bishop of Utrecht to be educated, and there, under the supervision of Bishop Baldric, 'when the boy had acquired the first rudiments of grammar he began to read, under his teacher's guidance, the poet Prudentius. . . . As time went on, his eager mind grasped all sorts of liberal studies within the range of Greek and Latin eloquence.'[55] We read further that Otto I, when he was king, relieved Bruno of the position of master of the palace school and gave him a higher rank. Bruno, however, continued to act as a director of educational activities in the kingdom and brought the liberal arts back to light: 'whatever historians, orators, poets, philosophers had to tell that was novel or great he closely investigated, aided by teachers of the language in which the books were written'.[56] Moreover, 'his Latin style was well-nigh perfect, and his influence made the style of others polished and clear'. The chronicle even goes on to relate that Bruno was always so enthusiastic for learning that he took his books on the royal journeys: 'When he followed the king he had, wherever the royal tents were pitched, the source and the materials for his studies – the source in the sacred books, the materials in the secular ones.'

While it is impossible to verify this record, it is certain that the Ottonian court was cultured, and that there was some cultivation of Greek, particularly in the time of Otto II whose wife was from the court of Constantinople. Indeed, in the time of Otto II (r. 973–83) there is an account of the work at the abbey of St Gall where the cleric Ekkehard taught. The contemporary chronicle relates that 'he was a strict and prosperous teacher; for, when he ruled both the schools [inner and outer] at St Gall, none except the smallest children dared to speak save in Latin; and, if he found any too slow for literary studies, he busied them with writing and illuminating'.[57] Here we find one of the few explicit references to two schools, one for *interni*, the other for *externi*. Beyond these references, however, there is little firm documentation and we rely chiefly on implicit evidence, which gives the impression that towards the end of the tenth century schools began to appear in increasing numbers. A book of ecclesiastical laws, for example, implies the existence of schools in churches. This same document also makes the point that it is the duty of priests to keep village schools, to teach small boys freely, and even to maintain schools in their own houses.[58]

The burden of maintaining schools, however, remained with the bishops. Since the early church paralleled the organizational structure of the Roman Empire, the episcopal seats were established in the same cities as the imperial administration, and throughout Merovingian and Carolingian times the bishops retained their residences on the sites of former Roman cities. Even though the city itself degenerated into the most primitive of towns, the bishop remained, and in the majority of places his establishment declined correspondingly. In many cases, the bishop's church – known as a cathedral, since his throne (L. *cathedra*, a chair) was kept there – was no more distinguished than any other parish church. The bulk of Roman architectural and engineering knowledge had been lost and in the remote centres no great cause existed for elaborate architecture. In terms of simple facilities, then, the bishops of many sees were unable to give more than a token effect to the school decree. Some places, those of strategic value, benefited from the relative stability and peace of the late tenth century when trade and commerce revived.

In the prototypal European cities of the late tenth century, the cathedrals grew to become significant institutions, functionally and architecturally.

Some cathedrals became particularly prominent – Liège, Reims, Laôn, Paris, Orléans, Chartres – and their schools acquired reputations for scholarship. At Chartres, established as an episcopal see perhaps in the third century, a school was founded in the cathedral in 990 by Fulbert, himself later bishop of that city (1006–28), although the exact status of Chartres's cathedral school has recently become the subject of some controversy and serious doubt.[59]

The cathedral schools grew slowly and those that prospered most were, like the six mentioned, on the main trade routes. If they were not directly stimulated by the needs of trade, they at least benefited indirectly. Learning flourishes under conditions of leisure and stability and the growth of trade in the late tenth and early eleventh centuries provided such support. The cathedral schools at first simply maintained the traditions of Western learning based on the vestigial remains of the liberal arts. The foundations of all instruction were the elements of literacy leading up to the study of grammar, which was the least emaciated survivor of the original seven disciplines. Grammar itself was studied at first from the short and catechetically arranged *Ars Minor* of the fourth-century Donatus, and this was followed by the more detailed *Systematic Grammar* (*Institutiones grammaticae*) – in eighteen books – by the sixth-century-A.D. Latin professor at Constantinople, Priscian. As the schools took more settled form, they introduced the traditional encyclopedic learning based on Martianus Capella, Boethius, Cassiodorus, Isidore and Hrabanus Maurus. In general, however, learning in the cathedral schools remained catechetical and conservative throughout the tenth and early eleventh centuries. During the mideleventh century that learning changed dramatically, in some places. Conservation was challenged by creativity, acceptance by critical questioning. For more than a century – from the year 1050 – the cathedral schools were to be the institutions of a new spirit of learning and scholarship in Europe.

Revival of the city: example of Venice

Central to the eleventh- and twelfth-century enthusiasm for learning in Europe was the revival of the city. Throughout Merovingian and Carolingian times the Roman *municipium* survived in minimal form and at times merely in name, entirely by virtue of the fact that it was the seat of the bishop and the centre of diocesan administration and consequently merited fortification. During the ninth century, a second type of fortified centre had appeared, constructed by the feudal nobility as defences before the development of the castle, and known as a *burg*. In time the burgs developed as centres of feudal administration, in many ways paralleling the episcopal *municipia*, and by the eleventh century both burgs and *municipia* provided secure bases from which the increasing numbers of merchants and traders could operate. It was the eleventh-century revival of commerce that created the medieval city.

The increased commercial activity of the eleventh century was stimulated from two directions: the vigorous activities of the Venetians and the emergence of a stable community around the North Sea after the incursions of the Vikings in the ninth and tenth centuries. Of those two stimuli, Venice was the earlier and the more sophisticated. That city-state had its origins in the fifth and sixth centuries when a defensive settlement was built in the swampy lagoons by local inhabitants fleeing from the advancing barbarians. The Lombard advance late in the sixth century precipitated further flights to the developing city. In the absence of agricultural land the Venetians turned to trade, beginning with processing and selling salt from the lagoons, and from that activity the small state expanded rapidly. At the same time Venice was not wholly independent. In conflict with its neighbours – chiefly Lombards – the city maintained its links with Byzantium, for it was the great cosmopolitan and commercial city of Constantinople that provided an outlet for trade in the first centuries of Venice's growth. Indeed, the first patron saint of Venice was Theodore, a Greek, until he was replaced in the ninth century by St Mark, and generally it seems that a Greek colony settled in the city in these formative years.[60] While Europe disintegrated into feudalism in the ninth and tenth centuries Venice built a great trading empire throughout the Adriatic, conquering small regions and constructing fortified bases from which it was able to defend its shipping routes to Constantinople. From Constantinople the Venetians retained contact with the most developed aspects of civilization, learning from the Byzantines not only the maritime crafts – from shipbuilding to navigation – but also the heritage of classical culture. In Venice the occupation of merchant, so low in prestige in the rest of Western Christendom, was honoured since it was the basis of the city's prosperity. Consequently secular learning – although restricted largely to the instrumental skills of commerce – continued in operation, and there *magistri grammatici* sustained the traditions of their occupation.

Traditions of secular learning in the West, then, were maintained chiefly in Italy, although even there in attenuated form. That region was least affected by feudalism and, furthermore, retained its links with Constantinople, parts of the peninsula in effect having remained under Byzantine suzerainty throughout feudal times apart from a period of Moslem occupation of Sicily and southern Italy in the ninth and tenth centuries. There is evidence of a book trade in Rome in the eighth century, and in the same period the first definite record exists of a papal library, that of Pope Zacharius (r. 741–52). Trade with the Byzantine and non-Western world continued according to the ancient customs of the region, and in any case Italy's topography prevented a retreat to rural isolation. Rome was still the centre of a considerable ecclesiastical administration and so stimulated some learning, at least on the part of persons who aspired to careers in the church. Those traditions survived the decline of the Carolingian Empire, and in Italy schools continued to operate independently of the church; in that region most of the educated laymen of ninth-and tenth-century Europe were to be found. Those persons were of two broad groups, the professional *literati* and the non-professional. To the former group belonged those whose living depended on some formal learning: teachers, lawyers and physicians, for example. The non-professionals were composed chiefly of those members of the upper class and nobility who sought a liberal education, or, more likely, some ecclesiastical rank. Schools existed to meet those needs, conducted by lay teachers, *magistri grammatici*, whose traditions reached back to the days of republican Rome. There is, in fact, a growing opinion among present-day scholars that, from as early as the eighth century, schools conducted by the *magister scholarum* and the *magister grammaticus* were in operation in all of the important towns of Italy, conducted by laymen for laymen.

Italy, however, was always closer to the Byzantine world than to Frankish Europe. The See of Rome remained in contact with Constantinople, even if often in respect of religious controversies and conflicts over jurisdiction. Thus the decline of learning that accompanied feudalism was not so marked in Italy, and in the twelfth century that region, along with Byzantium and the Islamic civilization – although, paradoxically, it was not an Italian movement in character – was to be instrumental in restoring learning and culture to the newly emerging civilization of Western Europe where it was first received in the cathedral schools.

Revival of trade and the stimulation of learning

Early in the eleventh century, Venice's example was followed by other Lombard cities, first Pavia, then Genoa and Pisa on the western seaboard. Those cities drew considerable strength from the fact that, in contrast to feudal France and Germany, the nobility maintained residences in them. They became populated increasingly by a new social class of traders, an urban bourgeoisie who formed themselves, so far as we can tell, into local feudatories. Although the growth of these cities was slow it was none the less steady and the cities developed from a stable basis. From them, trading activity went not only east to Constantinople and the Orient but also west. From Genoa and Pisa ships sailed to western Europe, and overland merchants again moved north through the valley of the Rhône along the routes of the old Roman highways, seeking markets within the security of the fortified burgs and *municipia*.

The Italian traders found a natural meeting place in the plain of Champagne, a large area able to be reached by traffic up the rivers Meuse, Seine and Loire, and little more than one hundred miles from the sea. This plain was in effect the geographic focus of the developing kingdom of France; on it, or in close proximity, were located more than a dozen episcopal sees, including Orléans, Reims, Laôn and Paris. The region developed not only from southern stimulation but also from the north. The Vikings settled into Europe in the ninth and tenth centuries, by the eleventh the regions surrounding the North Sea – the kingdoms of England, Scotland, Wales, Ireland, Norway, Denmark, Germany and France – were trading quite freely. That activity was entirely seaborne, and the chief commercial centre developed along the northern coast of France, focusing particularly on the county of Flanders, itself rapidly gaining prominence for the quality of its woollen goods. Flanders, where the Scheldt, Meuse and Rhine flowed into the sea, offered not only secure anchorages but ready access to the immediate hinterland of the plain of Champagne. In that natural trading region the burgs and *municipia* grew under the stimulus of commerce. Merchants settled within the protective walls, trade fairs became a common feature and attracted travellers and merchants from all over the world. The medieval city came into being.

The most prominent of all of those early cities, and destined to remain so, was Paris. Its origins reached back to the Roman conquest of Gaul, where on three islands in the junction of two of the Seine's tributaries the Romans built the important garrison of Lutetia. Its location recognized the strategic value to be gained from a command of the rivers and the surrounding plain. By holding that centre, the Romans held northern Gaul. After sinking into obscurity after the decline of Rome, the area again became militarily important when it was garrisoned by its local nobility against the Viking onslaught of the ninth century. Between 885 and 887 the counts of Paris turned back the Northmen and retained their territory. The region was held by a succession of undistinguished counts until, late in the tenth century, it was augmented by a number of neighbouring counties, becoming the dukedom of Hugh Capet (r. 956–96). Hugh had inherited all of his counties; in 987 he chose his own county of Paris as the seat of his royal administration, and in that dukedom he created the nucleus of the national state of France and the first French dynasty, the Capetian, which enjoyed a continuity of more than three centuries.

Paris of the Capetians was to become one of the great cities of medieval Europe and the greatest intellectual centre of all Western Christendom. From its modest feudal beginnings, as a result of the revival of trade that became especially prominent in Champagne, Paris developed rapidly and in time surpassed all others. The cathedral school of Paris – established in the precincts of Notre Dame – grew to strength in the period between 1050 and 1200 and by the end of the twelfth century it stood pre-eminent in Europe as a school of higher learning.

CHAPTER 2

Era of the Cathedral Schools

Eleventh-century revival in Europe

Throughout the first four millennia of man's historical existence, intellectual and educational creativity had been centred almost exclusively in the Ancient Orient and Mediterranean. Towards the end of that period Eastern vigour began to fail, Byzantium became exhausted and the Islamic Empire broke up. Initiative, then, in inquiry and learning passed to the West, where the cathedral schools of northern Europe became the institutions of a revivified scholarship. The events of that movement, gaining momentum towards the end of the eleventh century, were spectacular: not for more than a millennium had there been a comparable expenditure of intellectual energy. Even the excitement of early Christian times had not been nearly so originally creative. The patristic scholars had all worked with existing instruments – Greek philosophy and Hebrew theology – and had seen their task as one of synthesis and harmonization. Clement, Origen, Jerome, Augustine – the greatest of the Christian thinkers – wrote within this framework; further development of their thought was interrupted by the barbarian invasion of the Roman Empire and the subsequent restoration of learning was attenuated by the ensuing feudal organization of society.

Europe had always been a dependent civilization. In Roman times the West relied heavily on oriental capital, both intellectual and economic. The subsequent separation of West from East not only lessened the flow of ideas from the Orient, it also diminished the supply of goods for trade, particularly foodstuffs, on which the West had come to depend. If early feudal Europe was a retrograde civilization the cause was as much economic as intellectual; the historical record of the ninth and tenth centuries is one of an attempt to secure a proper economic and political basis to society. By the eleventh century the achievement was recognizable: economically, Europe was more than self-sufficient. Trade had revived to a remarkable extent owing to the existence of surpluses in both agricultural and manu-factured goods. At the same time a degree of centralized authority was in operation, located in the secular governments of the kings of Germany, France and England, and in the ecclesiastical institution of the papacy. The development of the authorities of church and state proceeded in conjunc-tion with the growth of commerce. Merchants and traders brought wealth to cathedral and castle; bishops and lords provided security, and both sides benefited from the interaction.

Despite the reciprocal relationships of the institutions involved in the eleventh-century revival, the church was clearly dominant; its laws governed society, its doctrines provided a morality, its schools offered what learning was available, while its clerics constituted almost the entire body of the *literati*; and, in contrast to secular power, the church was a univers-ally visible authority. That dominance did not come easily; on the contrary the church fought hard to secure its position. The struggle between church and state was already centuries old, stemming from the times of Pope Gelasius (r. 492–6), and renewed during the reign of Charlemagne. Yet, along with the rest of society, ecclesiastical power suffered an enormous decline after Charlemagne. Late in the tenth century, as a consequence of the new vigour of Europe, the papacy sought to restore that religious hegemony of society it considered its historical mission, although its rights were already becoming endangered by the rapid growth of secular authority. At a series of three synods held in southern France in 989, 990 and 994 the 'Peace of God' was proclaimed in which warfare was outlawed on the last three days of the week. Then in 1027 it proclaimed a 'Truce of God' for the purpose of outlawing warfare in certain seasons whereby the economic motive of allowing unmolested activity to the farmers during spring and fall was fused into the religious symbolisms of observing peace during the Lenten and pre-Christmas occasions respectively. The accession of Pope Leo IX (r. 1049–54) resulted in greater assertions of church power, the most consequential being the mutual excommunication of the Catholic and Orthodox churches. In 1059 Pope Nicholas II converted the cardinal clergy of Rome – the old Roman deacons – into the Papal Chapter, thereby surrounding himself with a stronger body of supporters (and, perhaps involuntarily, taking the first steps towards the creation of the College of Cardinals which, by a decree of the Third Lateran Council of 1179, gained the right, alone and independently of any secular authority, to elect the pontiff himself). During the earlier period of papal growth in the eleventh century, the climax to papal efforts at securing a stronger authority came during the incumbency of Pope Gregory VII (r. 1073–85), who sought to achieve church supremacy by a fresh assertion of the political theories generated from Augustine's writings, particularly the *City of God*.

In doing so, Gregory came into direct conflict with the emperor of Germany, Henry IV (r. 1056–1106), whose house had long resisted papal encroachment. The collapse of Carolingian authority in Germany early in the tenth century had been followed by the establishment of a Saxon dynasty by Henry I (r. 919–36). Resistance to the papacy remained an aspect of Saxon policy, and his successors, although accepting the rite of coronation, moved to secure dominance by secularizing and feudalizing the higher clergy: bishops were given temporal fiefs and required to swear fealty to the emperor. Otto I (r. 936–73) was crowned king of Italy in 962 and with its incorporation in his Empire he was able to be crowned Holy Roman Emperor. That renewed Empire was vast in extent, reaching from Rome in the south to the border of Denmark in the north; its western boundary separated it from France, its eastern from the kingdoms of Poland and Hungary – the last two but recently converted to Christianity. In the eleventh century, then, the German emperor clearly challenged the authority of the pope. The issue, in effect, was one of deciding who was to exercise ultimate authority over the Holy Roman Empire; it came to a head in the dramatic conflict between Gregory VII and Henry IV in 1076.

In that year the pope excommunicated the emperor. The immediate cause was a conflict over the imperial appointment of bishops, chiefly of Milan, since that archbishopric was the key to political and religious authority in northern Italy. Behind it lay Gregory's determination to assert papal authority. Neither side secured any real victory. Henry crossed the Alps as a penitent, and received the pope's forgiveness at Canossa, thereby securing a political checkmate. However, the incident divided the German princes, leading in turn to civil war. As a result, Germany, long disrupted by conflict with the barbarians on its eastern borders, was further divided. Meanwhile peaceful development occurred where there was greater stability, in the rapidly strengthening domain of the Capetians centred on Paris.

The preoccupation of Rome with Germany left the emerging kingdom of France relatively untroubled with political disputes. The Capetian house, ruling from 987 through to 1314, developed its power quietly and purposefully, and the renewal of trade, with its focus in the markets of Champagne, brought increasing wealth to France. The economic production of the expanding cities, erected around the episcopal sees, led to the appearance of the most spectacular symbol of medieval abundance, the great cathedrals.

The cathedral

In its simple designation the cathedral (Latin, *cathedra*, a chair) is the church in which the bishop's throne is kept. Many cathedrals in the first millennium were modest structures, all of them depending on wood for part of their construction; even those with stone walls at least had wooden roofs. Consequently, the size of the building was limited, and the timber itself gave a quality of impermanency. In the late tenth century that position started to change, particularly in Ottonian Germany. Newly developed architectural techniques offered the possibility of much greater structures, built entirely of stone.

The great stone cathedrals of Europe, mostly built between 1050 and 1350, were spectacular edifices – it has been calculated that they used more stone than all the monuments, including pyramids and temples, of Egyptian antiquity. Built on massive foundations, some set as deeply as thirty feet into the ground, cathedrals rose to enormous heights: Chartres, by no means the tallest, was raised, including the towers, some 345 feet. Christendom in its millennial existence had seen nothing to equal them. At last a structure was achieved to challenge the monuments of ancient times. And, even more importantly, the immense volume of space enclosed in the naves of the great cathedrals allowed, for the first time, entire congregations to assemble. The pagan temples were all cult edifices, entered only by an elect minority; the cathedrals provided room for thousands of worshippers; Amiens, it is said, can accommodate nearly ten thousand simultaneously.

Organization of learning in the eleventh century

The cathedral was a magnificent symbol of the changing conditions of European life, indicating the growth of a new corporate consciousness in society. The wealth that created the cathedrals changed other aspects of eleventh-century society, and for the first time in a thousand years, provision was made for a new leisured class. This was the collegiate chapter, or society of canons who formed the clergy attached to the cathedrals – and to other large churches – for their vastly increased administrative functions. Although the chapter at first was a purely technical office, it soon changed its character. The general acceptance of educational responsibility by the cathedrals in the tenth century was continued into the eleventh, and they became the obvious focus for the growing number of persons who sought the scholarly life. Eleventh-century learning, as given in the cathedrals, seemed to bear little perceptible relationship to the times; it appeared to be scarcely more than an intensification of earlier forms of learning, based upon encyclopedic conservation of the surviving liberal arts and, moreover, identified exclusively with the traditional life of clerical scholars. There was little indication that the studies sponsored by the collegiate chapter would lead increasingly throughout the twelfth and thirteenth centuries to a profound and influential examination of church, state and man and their mutual relationships. The political struggles of Gregory VII and Henry IV, for example, with their repetition in the twelfth-century encounter between Henry II of England and his archbishop, Becket, were to become subjects for study, providing some of the material for the further examination of political theory which had remained basically Augustinian, usually crude versions of the subtle and complex thought of Augustine himself. Not only political theory, but also the entire structure of man's thought was to come under exacting scrutiny in the cathedral and collegiate schools.

The cathedral schools, or collegiate schools as they were called in those churches which had a chapter but no episcopal seat, were completely ecclesiastical in character. All of their students and scholars were clerics or intending clerics and therefore in some form of holy orders, and the studies they pursued were completely verbal. Mathematics, which had numerous possibilities for practical application, was never so taught, with the single notable exception of calculating the dates of movable feasts. Instead, the vestigial mathematics that existed was based on the original

Pythagorean–Platonic model, intended as a means of searching for the underlying design of the universe. As a consequence of the extremely restricted nature of the cathedral school studies, the numerous skills and knowledges required for the pursuit of the practical matters of daily life developed through other means.

The craft guilds

In the eleventh and twelfth centuries crafts and technical accomplishments, necessary to maintaining Europe's prosperity, and exhibited in the construction of the great cathedrals, began to come within the province of societies known in English as *guilds*. The ancient Romans had formed such groupings, known as *collegia*; the term guild itself is an Old English equivalent of the German *hansa* and the French *métier*, all contemporary vernacular words being translations of the medieval latinism *universitas* which designated any group with a particular identity.

The guilds had survived from Roman times primarily as religious and fraternal organizations; when they assumed their closer connections with trade, commerce and the crafts in the eleventh and twelfth centuries they retained their religious character. The masons who were responsible for the construction of the cathedrals used their craft lodges, built alongside the cathedrals, as meeting places where they conducted the religious and fraternal rites of their society. In time the skills of their trade became part of those rites, and since many of the techniques used were guarded jealously the activities of the masonic guilds became surrounded increasingly with elements of secrecy, and membership in the guild became more difficult of access. That process became common to all of the guilds, and by the twelfth century – although our knowledge of the details is limited[1] – the custom had begun of forming closed brotherhoods, which were concerned chiefly with preserving the secrets and skills of their occupations. So developed a system of qualifications for admission that was, in effect, the technical counterpart to that developing simultaneously in the cathedral schools.

As a general rule, the guilds were preoccupied with maintaining standards of craftsmanship which they achieved in part by setting precise requirements for preliminary training and demonstrated competence before admission to the guild, or society of masters, was granted. Since the guild members came to exercise virtual monopoly over performance of the craft, membership of the society became mandatory for any person desiring to practice freely the particular calling. The achievement of master's rank in the guild, therefore, was the ultimate goal set for attainment. Progress towards that end was commenced by the young boy when he was entered around his thirteenth year as an apprentice. The period of such indentured service lasted about seven years until the second stage of primary competence was reached, the youth subsequently being designated as a journeyman. Following that stage, admission to the society of masters itself depended upon the completion of a task, or piece, appropriate to the specific guild. That example of demonstrated competence, or 'masterpiece', if accepted, represented the final examination. Interpenetrating the entire process, of course, were other less overt qualifications, and the progress of the aspirant was marked by a variety of secret and quasi-religious rites. Such requirements served to restrict membership of the guild, and since in any case the demands of the callings were beyond the skills or aspirations of many, the majority of workers remained as journeymen throughout their lives.

The craft guilds became the means by which medieval Europe maintained its technical learning, and in many instances it was the guilds that were receptive to new ideas and experiment. Not only did they revive, by diligent study, many of the practices of antiquity that had been temporarily lost, but they also became the source from which much subsequent scientific development sprang. In numerous instances the guilds were attracted to practices pursued abroad, including the technical innovations of the Moslems and the Mongols. Perhaps the most dramatic acquisition was that of gunpowder; less conspicuous but even more significant were those inventions concerned directly with literacy, paper-making and block-printing. By the twelfth century the paper-makers were an established guild; likewise the scribal guilds were employing the Chinese invention of block-printing for rubrics, those large and often highly embellished capital letters with which manuscript pages commenced. Despite the inherent conservatism of the scribes and book-binders the use of woodcut rubrics developed; in later centuries they came to encompass whole pages.

In time the guilds developed an entire literature of their own, usually written in the vernacular, and in many ways being a revival of the ancient Greek and Roman handbook tradition. The guild learnings, however, remained part of their closed systems, and in an effort to preserve that feature the guilds even set up their own elementary schools designed specifically for their members' children. So developed a dualism in learning that was to persist for centuries. Side by side were two traditions, one technical and practical, followed by the craftsmen, the other verbal and theoretical, pursued by clerics. In the twelfth and the thirteenth centuries, however, the craft tradition was overshadowed by that developing in the cathedral schools where the most dramatic aspects of human inquiry were being pursued.

The cathedral schools

The earliest schools, those of the ninth and tenth centuries, did little more than follow the encyclopedic tradition of Martianus Capella, Cassiodorus and Isidore. Although the exact developments are still imperfectly understood, it seems that the first attempt at broadening the programme of studies was made in the cathedral school at Reims when the Cluniac scholar Gerbert of Aurillac (d. 1003) acceded to its headship in 972. He acted in that capacity at various times until 999 when he was elected pope under the title Sylvester II. Much of the dissemination of learning in the period depended on the pattern of communications and the links that individual monasteries and cathedrals had with each other. Gerbert himself had been schooled at the Benedictine monastery at Aurillac, in the Haute-Auvergne, a region traditionally in touch with Spain; then, in 967, he went to the cathedral school of Vich in Catalonia where he received his advanced education and became acquainted with Arab learning. We know also that he spent some years (980–3) in Italy and from there went to Reims to take charge of the school, which was probably not very large and had perhaps two or three assistant masters. There he instituted the full programme of all seven liberal arts, according to the contemporary chronicle made by his biographer and disciple Richer. So we read that Gerbert introduced the study of dialectic through a sequence of works, beginning with the *Isagoge* – an introduction to Aristotle's *Categories* composed in Alexandria by Porphyry in the late third century A.D. – in the Latin translation of a certain Victorinus, and this was followed by the study of Aristotle's *Categories* itself, although this must have been in the translation and commentary made by Boethius. These were followed in turn by a study of Aristotle's *Peri Hermenias* (again almost certainly in the Boethian version) and Cicero's *Topics* which themselves had been derived from Aristotle.[2]

Now these are all works on dialectic and logic, and it is important to clarify the meanings of these two terms, particularly since they were to become so important in the intellectual life of the cathedral schools. Dialectic – the word comes from the Greek *dialektiké* meaning the art of discussion – had its origins with Plato who developed it as a method of verbal inquiry aimed at the discovery of truth. Plato's student Aristotle then investigated the processes of verbal argument and, having determined the patterns of correct reasoning, set these out as canons of procedure in his several books, *Categories*, *On Interpretation*, *Prior Analytics* and *Posterior Analytics*, which deal respectively with the nature of ideas, judgements and terminology, syllogistic reasoning, and definition and demonstration. These four books became known collectively in the medieval period as the *Organon* or 'instrument', although only the two former works were in common use since they alone had been translated into Latin by Boethius. The procedures set out in the *Organon* are those of logic, this term coming from the Greek *logos*, which in one of its many senses means reason. The terms dialectic and logic came to be used interchangeably as their meanings overlap greatly – *dialektiké* itself is derived from *dia* (through) and the verb *legein* (to speak), the latter being related to *logos* – although, strictly used, dialectic means the method of seeking truth by discussion, logic the procedures of correct reasoning.

Whether Gerbert himself was aware of these distinctions is not certain; none the less the *Organon* was the basis from which he selected readings and which he explained in commentary form, these serving as a preparation for his pupils for the further study of rhetoric. So Richer explains that the manner in which he provided for this was to read from and to teach ('legit itaque ac docuit') the poets Virgil and Terence, the satirists Juvenal and Persius and the historian Lucan. Then, when these learnings had been achieved he turned his students over to a sophist ('qua instructis sophistam adhibuit'), who was presumably a teacher at the school, to develop the skills of debating, hoping thereby that their theoretical learning could be put into practical effect through oratory.[3] We see here how Gerbert followed Boethius in treating logic, or dialectic, as an essentially persuasive procedure.[4]

Gerbert's main interest, however – and this stood in considerable contrast to the times – was in the quadrivium. Richer states that Gerbert commenced with arithmetic and then went on to music for which purpose he used a monochord to illustrate the mathematical basis of harmonics. In astronomy he went to considerable trouble to construct wooden models – specifically mentioned is one of the earth – which apparently included the fixed stars, and by using an artificial horizon (we are not told exactly how this was done) he was able to teach his students to recognize the constellations.[5] Clearly this mathematical interest must have been stimulated while in Arab-dominated Spain, which itself was in contact during the period with the great flourishing of scholarship throughout the Moslem domains, and we know that in 984 Gerbert dispatched at least two missions to Spain to procure works on mathematics and astrology.[6] Rather curiously, however, Gerbert's writings reveal no particular influence of Moslem mathematical thought.[7]

There is no question about Gerbert's standing as a great scholar in his day nor about the status of the school at Reims during his tenure there. Where a question does arise, however, is with respect to the standards at Reims after Gerbert departed for Rome to become pope. Certainly he left some well-educated followers, Richer and Fulbert being the most outstanding. But Richer was entirely of literary inclinations and in any case was a monk and apparently never a teacher at Reims; Fulbert had gone to Chartres. There is a suggestion that Reims had begun to decline earlier as Gerbert became increasingly preoccupied with wider political and religious matters, and that after his departure the cathedral school settled down to a quieter tempo of educational activity.[8] The school never lapsed into obscurity, however, and some fifty years later it seems to have enjoyed a revival under a master named Herimann although, unfortunately, all too little is known about him.[9] He certainly taught grammar and rhetoric and perhaps theology. But it is abundantly clear that this school, like every other one, was too dependent on the personality and academic strength of its *magister scholarum*.

As the fortunes of Reims fell somewhat, those at Chartres grew. It was there that Gerbert's most eminent student Fulbert (d. 1029) founded the cathedral school about 990 and remained in charge until his elevation to the episcopacy of the same cathedral in 1006. There is a clear record of Fulbert's scholarship; a contemporary chronicle refers to 'Bishop Fulbert of Chartres whom the whole of France praised because of his proficiency in liberal arts.'[10] At Chartres he taught grammar, arithmetic and astronomy, and some medicine – which was then an entirely verbal procedure, being based on several texts of Aristotle and of the second-century-A.D. physician Galen of Pergamum, along with a few Arabic treatises which had come in through Spain. Fulbert, however, was chiefly an ecclesiastical scholar and this was the main concern of his studies. Consequently, he developed a great interest in the study of dialectic which he considered a pre-eminent means of scrutinizing faith, although his understanding of dialectic was drawn, like Gerbert's, from Boethius. In Fulbert's day the use of dialectic as a persuasive technique was generally acceptable; there was no question of disputing a faith which rested secure in uncontested and undoubted revelation. The challenges to faith by reason, already encountered by Moslem scholars, in respect to the religion of Islam, had not yet arisen in Europe. Problems that did exist came from differing interpretations of faith, and this led scholars increasingly to turn to dialectic as a means of helping them to define the basis of belief. That method was developed by Fulbert's pupil, Berengarius (d. 1088), who became head of the monastic school at Tours. Although the exact position is uncertain, it seems that Berengar sought to use dialectic as a means of settling all questionable issues.

Controversy and conflict: the province of dialectic

The monastics: Damian, Lanfranc and Anselm

Berengar's position at Tours indicates that scholarship in the mid-eleventh century was by no means the exclusive concern of the cathedral schools. The application of dialectic to religious issues, which was the most obvious feature of the new interest in learning, was also pursued in the monastic schools, although in contrast with the cathedrals, the monastic concern was far more conservative. Berengar most likely wanted to settle issues by dialectic, not to raise them. Yet some scholars recognized the potential danger of dialectic. The bishop of Ostia, a former Benedictine ascetic and abbot, Peter Damian (c. 1007–72), went so far as to deny the validity or usefulness of dialectic at all. Mediation of the two extremes was attempted at the monastic school of Bec in Normandy by a number of significant scholars, of whom the best were all Italians who certainly brought an infusion of new thought with them from northern Italy. One important consequence was that Bec became famous as a centre of scholarship in the late eleventh century.

The first steps were taken by Lanfranc of Pavia (c. 1010–89) who was prior of Bec, and subsequently archbishop of Canterbury (1070–89). Lanfranc, we read in the contemporary chronicle of Orderic Vitalis, was born 'of noble parents who were citizens of Pavia in Italy; he had studied in the schools of the liberal arts from his childhood and had become deeply learned in civil law, intending after the custom of his countrymen to pursue a lay career'.[11] He became a highly skilled advocate, renowned for his eloquence and fluency, and this most probably was stimulated by the study of classical Latin rhetoric which had never been wholly lost in some of the Italian towns. Forced into political exile – a frequent hazard of the times – Lanfranc came to Bec, as a man 'remarkably well versed in the liberal arts'.[12] Orderic records further that he enriched Bec 'by his wisdom and painstaking administration, raising it to a condition of perfect order'.[13] His most significant contribution at Bec, however, was the conduct of the school in which

> he emerged as a master in whose teaching the fundamental texts of philosophy and the Bible were displayed. In both subjects he could unravel the most knotty problems with supreme skill. It was from this master that the Normans first learned the liberal arts, so that scholars well versed in both sacred and secular learning emerged from the school of Bec.[14]

So successful was Lanfranc that 'the fame of his learning spread all over Europe, until many flocked from France, Gascony, Brittany and Flanders to sit at his feet'.[15] The record includes the observations that he taught grammar, Aristotle's dialectic, Cicero's rhetoric and the patristic writings on both testaments, chiefly Jerome and Augustine.[16] Lanfranc continued to display his verbal skills and distinguished himself in many debates although his view was relatively simple: he held that dialectic, when used properly, explained the mysteries of God.

After Lanfranc was appointed to the archbishopric of Canterbury, his work at Bec was continued by his celebrated pupil Anselm of Aosta (1033–1109) who followed him, first as prior of Bec (1063–78), then as abbot (1078–93), and finally also as archbishop of Canterbury (England at this time being a Norman territory). Like Lanfranc, Anselm taught only in the monastery, although his scholarship attracted a wide student following. Anselm's thought is contained chiefly in his major works, *Monologion*, the subsequent *Proslogion*, and *Cur deus homo*. In the *Monologion* Anselm attempted to use dialectic as a means of verifying faith; in the *Proslogion* he advanced his thought to a different position, accepting the existence of god as a basic postulate and using dialectic as a means of verifying that prior existence. This short passage illustrates well the way in which dialectic and the procedures of logical argument came to be used in these inquiries:

> This proposition is indeed so true that its negation is inconceivable. For it is quite conceivable that there is something whose non-existence is incon-

ceivable, and this must be greater than that whose non-existence is conceivable. Wherefore, if that thing than which no greater thing is conceivable can be conceived as non-existent; then, that very thing than which a greater is inconceivable is not that than which a greater is inconceivable; which is a contradiction.

So true is it that there exists something than which a greater is inconceivable, that its non-existence is inconceivable; and this thing art Thou, O Lord our God![17]

The change in Anselm's thought is significant: Anselm found it impossible by means of reason alone to arrive at the idea of the existence of god; reason, he asserted, is useful only as a subsidiary instrument. Man's task, indeed, he concluded, is not to seek faith through the intellect, but to believe in order to understand – *credo ut intelligam*.[18] Reason, through the operation of dialectic, gives an intellectual conviction to man's primary intuitions of faith. Anselm followed in the Augustinian tradition, although his thought was restricted by his inability to gain access to the complete Platonic theory from which Christian Neoplatonism stemmed. Accepting the priority of god over all realizations in material existence, Anselm was none the less concerned with finding a rational proof for god's existence.

With the thought of Anselm, certainly one of the most creative thinkers of the period, a decisive phase in eleventh-century learning was reached. The revived interest in dialectic was now being applied to articles of belief that had long been regarded as axiomatic. Anselm's conclusions were by no means universal – his outlook supported the conservative faction, represented chiefly by those scholars outside the cathedral schools. The cathedral scholars, however, in general were not so constrained, and beginning at the same time as Anselm and continuing throughout the twelfth century, the cathedral schools became significant for the greater vitality of their thought. The first phase of that more adventurous approach occurred in the latter half of the eleventh century with an examination of some of the issues raised by Anselm hinging on the question of the form of god.

Peter Abelard and the Nominalist Controversy

It was not possible to question openly the nature of god; both the climate of church opinion and the available critical methods precluded such a direct approach. The procedure was one of indirection, of seeking answers to apparently simpler questions. One result of that paucity of concepts and restrictive social climate was that the literature gives the impression of dealing with the picayune and the trite expressed often in a tortured and convoluted style. Even in its own day this caused a revulsion among some scholars (and a much more profound reaction from the fifteenth century until the nineteenth). None the less, judgements based on these criteria are superficial and misleading; scholastic language in fact was a very sophisticated instrument (however repulsive from the literary point of view) for one of the world's most powerful and subtle types of intellectual adventure. Such an apparently minor issue, for example, is that dealing with the relationships between an individual object and the class to which it belongs. The question occurs in the writings of Boethius who, in the sixth century, had reported that Porphyry had been unable to determine whether genus and species had a real existence or were merely mental creations. Late in the eleventh century that problem erupted into a violent dispute known as the Nominalist Controversy. Two sides formed of which the majority followed orthodox Augustinian thought, insisting that genus and species indeed have an independent reality. Opposing them was a critical, even reckless, minority who initiated the controversy by asserting that such concepts are merely mental abstractions, identified by names. The former group, in the terminology of the times, were known as *realists* (in direct opposition to later uses of the term); the innovating minority were known as *nominalists*.

The origins of the issue are now obscure, although it seems to have received its first major elaboration in the teaching of Roscellinus of Compiègne (*c.* 1050–1125) at Loches. Roscelin's nominalism, however, is known only through references found in the contemporary writing of Anselm and of Peter Abelard who was Roscelin's pupil, *c.* 1095. Apart from a brief letter to Abelard nothing of Roscelin survives. The indirect evidence, however, suggests that Roscelin denied the existence of any reality outside the individual objects of physical creation, regarding universals as merely verbal labels. Clearly such a position deviated from the accepted Christian Neoplatonist position as elaborated so recently by Anselm; Roscelin was challenged, and condemned for heresy by a council at Soissons in 1092.

Roscelin's extreme nominalism was not met by judicial action alone – scholars attempted a critical refutation, represented in the work of a master in the cathedral school at Paris, William of Champeaux (1070–1121). Like Roscelin, William of Champeaux is rather obscure and also is known chiefly through the references of Peter Abelard.[19] Champeaux's defence of 'realism' had some novelty – the universal is conceived as existing not in some separate realm but actually in the individual object itself. That defence was breached by his pupil Abelard who pointed out that William of Champeaux had merely identified genus with species; and since genus is prior, species have no significance. William countered, according to Abelard's record, with the doctrine of 'indifference'. Simultaneously in each individual person, for example, coexist both similarities and differences. The sum total of the differences constitutes indivuation or species, the sum of the similarities (*indifferentia*) gives genus.

At that point the controversy was joined actively by Peter Abelard (*c.* 1079–1142) who rapidly became the centre of even greater dispute; throughout the first decades of the twelfth century Abelard was the most conspicuous scholar in all Europe. The chief biographical source for Abelard is his own account, *Historia calamitatum* (*Story of my Misfortunes*), composed some time around the years 1133–6. That document records the birthplace of Petrus Abaielardus at Palets, eight miles east of Nantes in Brittany, his early acquaintance with Roscelin and subsequent studies with Anselm of Laôn and then with William of Champeaux around the year 1100. From that time on Abelard became prominent in the controversy, using the dispute over universals as illustrative materials in his lectures on dialectic, and as the theme for his treatise *Dialectica*.[20] Abelard's approach to the question of universals is indicative of his attitude to learning and his method of teaching; it can best be understood then as a product of his whole career.

Abelard was extremely precocious; he began his studies with Roscelin some time around his sixteenth birthday. In the following fifteen years he travelled to various teachers, including William of Champeaux and Anselm of Laôn, and engaged himself in teaching rhetoric and dialectic, those two studies then being known together as the Old Logic. He appeared in Paris, teaching in its emerging cathedral school of Notre Dame around 1113–14, attracting a wide and enthusiastic following in the process. The ensuing seven years were some of his stormiest. In that period he became involved in a tempestuous love affair – later the subject of innumerable romanticized accounts – with the young Heloise, as a consequence of which the girl was taken away by her guardian to a convent at Argenteuil; Abelard went to a monastery at St Denis near Paris. There he continued his disputation and dialectical inquiries, teaching theology and secular letters as well. His personality, coupled with his critical inquiries, aroused a strong opposition.

In 1121 he was accused of violating the monastic rules by teaching secular letters and brought to trial for heresy in respect of a now unknown book on the Trinity. A council at Soissons condemned Abelard, *in absentia* and unheard, and burned his book. Yet his interest in the dialectical scrutiny of theological topics was undiminished and he began immediately the draft of another in which he attempted to gather, for a large number of disputed religious questions, the arguments of authorities both for and against. That technique of marshalling arguments in support of and opposition to disputed points was already in use, chiefly by legal scholars and theologians, particularly by the celebrated Ivo of Chartres (1040–1116) who was the greatest canonist of the day. It was known as the method of *pro et contra*.[21] Abelard gave it a greater precision and more skilful application to the dialectical treatment of disputed theological topics in his influential *Sic et non* (*Yes and No*) which was first drafted around 1122–6 and issued eventually, in its final form, towards the end of his life.

After his condemnation at Soissons, Abelard was perhaps even more sought after as a teacher and founded a school at Quincey on the Seine. Yet the years brought him no peace; he disappears occasionally from the historical record, having spent periods as a teacher at a school he founded on the river Ardugon at Troyes and as abbot of St Gildas. The attacks on Abelard were maintained by conservatives led by the powerful Cistercian abbot, Bernard of Clairvaux. After several years of complete obscurity, Abelard reappeared in 1136 at the cathedral school of Paris where he again became the centre of controversy for his counter-attacks on his chief antagonist, Bernard of Clairvaux. In that period, the last six years of his life, Abelard composed his mature works, chiefly his *Ethica*, *Theologia Christiana* (which probably contained the materials condemned at Soissons in 1121), *Dialectica* and *Sic et non*. Bernard was a powerful conservative and not easily defeated; Abelard's numerous publications provided much possible material for attack. 'Read if you please', wrote Bernard in a letter addressed to all of the bishops and cardinals of the Curia, the papal court in Rome,

> that book of Peter Abailard which he calls a book of Theology. . . . See what sort of things he says about the Holy Trinity, about the generation of the son, about the procession of the Holy Spirit, and much else that is very strange to Catholic ears and minds. Read that other book which they call the *Book of Sentences* and also the one entitled *Know Thyself*, and see how they too run riot with a whole crop of sacrileges and errors.[22]

The letter continues to exhort the Curia to consider other alleged errors, carefully insinuated, and then urges them to 'bestir yourselves' to action against the heretic.

In 1140 Bernard was successful in securing a prosecution for heresy at the council of Sens, and Abelard was summoned for trial in Rome. On the way to plead this cause, he collapsed at Cluny and after a period of illness died at the abbey of St Marcel at Chalon-sur-Saône in 1142.

The essential feature of Abelard's life work was his attempt to apply logic to received doctrines, particularly those of the greatest import. *Sic et non*, for example, referred to by Bernard as the 'Book of Sentences', deals with 157 vexed questions on faith and morals. For each point Abelard gathered opinions for and against, usually about five or six for each side, from the patristic writers and the Bible, setting them down in groups. In many cases the issues were potentially troublesome – Is god singular or not? (Q5); Is god tripartite, or not? (Q6); Does god have a free will or not? (Q34) – and whoever dared assemble the varying range of opinions, thereby exposing the numerous discontinuities of the theology of the day, was certain to arouse interest and hostility. Abelard accepted that task. Throughout all of his writing is the concern to analyse issues logically; and to separate issues from words. In a sense Abelard attempted a semantic purification of the theology of his time; his dialectical studies in particular reveal his preoccupation with the linguistic aspects of knowledge, the best illustration being afforded by his approach to the question of universals. He asks, for example, in his *Glossulae* (*Glosses on Porphyry*),

> . . . whether genera and species, so long as they are genera and species, must have some thing subject to them by nomination, or whether, if the things named were destroyed, the universal could still consist of the meaning only of the conception, as this noun *rose* when there is not a single rose to which it is common.[23]

In Abelard's view the realists had made a fundamental error in confusing the object with its name. His approach to the question of universals was to inquire into their nature – 'since it is known that genera and species are universals . . . let us inquire into the common nature of universals by studying genus and species and whether they apply to *words* or to *things* as well'[24] – to ask whether they existed and, if they did, whether that existence was material. Material existence, of course, would have led to Champeaux's position which held that genus and species coexist in the same object. Abelard had already disposed of that argument. The other extreme led to Roscelin's viewpoint: that universals are mere labels. If that were so, then existence would have no unifying quality, which to Abelard's mind was equally untenable. The solution marked an enormous step forward. Abelard distinguished logical classification from metaphysical speculation, and he regarded universals as essential to the process by which man could attach meaning to experience. In his own words, in the *Glossulae*:

> The first question was, then, to this effect, whether genera and species subsist, that is, signify something truly existent, or are placed in the understanding alone, that is, are located in empty opinion without the thing, like the following words, *chimera* and *goat-stag* which do not give rise to rational understanding.
>
> To this it must be replied that in truth they signify by nomination things truly existent, to wit, the same things as singular nouns, and in no wise are they located in empty opinion; nevertheless, they consist in a certain sense in the understanding alone and naked and pure, as has been determined, [since] when I hear *man* or *whiteness* or *white* I do not recall from the meaning of the noun all the natures or properties which are in the subject things, but from *man* I have only the conception, though confused, not discrete, of animal and rational mortal, but not of the later accidents as well. For the conceptions of individuals, too, are formed by abstraction, when, namely, it is said: this substance, this body, this animal, this man, this whiteness, this white. For by *this man* I consider only the nature of man but related to a certain subject, whereas by *man* I consider that same nature simply in itself not related to any one. Wherefore the understanding of universals is spoken of as alone and naked and pure . . .[25]

The immediate elements of experience Abelard termed *sensibles* and *singulars* which the mind organizes into meaningful patterns for which the corresponding linguistic categories are the universals which function verbally as the basis for predication and consequent meaningful discourse. In making a distinction between experience and language Abelard clarified a problem in the thought of his time. Yet his explanation was in fact no real solution at all, for if universals are merely verbal predicates, they still remain as potential referents of something. Abelard disposed of the notion that this 'something' has a material existence and made no attempt to examine the possibilities of any other metaphysical basis to universals. Such distinctions as he made, however, produced an awareness of the need to distinguish logical from metaphysical discourse. In subsequent centuries that distinction was of considerable use; in particular it influenced the development of twelfth-century grammatical theory, especially at the school of Paris.

Abelard's significance goes far beyond his attempt to apply the principles of logic to human experience, valuable and necessary as that may have been. In a period when men were attempting, for the first time in centuries, to construct a more meaningful view of the world, Abelard provided a conspicuous example of human courage. Tradition and habit, necessary mainstays of any society and particularly that of barbarian and later feudal Europe, can so frequently lead to stasis and degeneration. They must be examined constantly. That Abelard did, despite the opposition he encountered. In the history of education in particular, Abelard is one of the conspicuous examples of that intransigence of the human spirit which is encountered so rarely, that tests the limits of belief and so opposes tradition with criticism, conservation with creativity. His entire life was eloquent testimony to a refusal to compromise with the need for inquiry, wherever it may lead.

Abelard's contemporaries and the 'school' of Chartres

Abelard's dramatic experiences, however, were not unique; other thinkers continued to advance the claim of dialectic and the efficacy of the human intellect in searching for understanding, and some found themselves in similar difficulties. Perhaps the most eminent of his contemporaries in this respect was the chancellor of the cathedral school at Chartres between 1124 and 1141, Gilbert de la Porrée (1076–1154). From its late tenth-century beginnings under Fulbert, Chartres had maintained the quality of its school which was sustained by a succession of scholars committed to the ideas of Plato as these had been transmitted and received over the centuries, although the Neoplatonism which they studied was severely limited since the *Timaeus* was the sole original work available to them. We must, moreover, be careful of ascribing too much significance to the school of Chartres *qua* school; there are, in fact, some strong indications that the number of first-rate scholars there was very small.[26] One of whom we can be certain was Bernard of Chartres (*fl. c.* 1114–*c.* 1130), who was *magister scholae* there.

Evidence concerning Bernard of Chartres comes from the record made by one of his students, John of Salisbury, who studied at Chartres in his adolescent years. Bernard was guided, it is reported in John of Salisbury's contemporary *Metalogicon*, by the need to maintain a balance between the student's capacity and the teacher's diligence. Accordingly, Bernard 'urged some by admonitions, others by flogging and punishments'.[27] Studies centred on grammar and the reading of classical authors –

'grammatical figures, rhetorical colours, the subtleties of sophistry' – and 'each student was required on the following day to elaborate on some of the matter heard the day before'.[28] There is a full account of Bernard's concern to ensure that each student had learned to write and had mastered grammar with all of its formal rules. The advanced ones, we read, were able to perform exercises of *imitatio*, writing in the style of selected classical authors. Along with this was a great deal of practice and 'the boys composed daily written exercises in prose and poetry and checked each other by comparing their work'.[29]

It is possible that Bernard of Chartres may have taught Gilbert de la Porrée but there is no final convincing evidence. None the less Gilbert, both as chancellor of Chartres and bishop of Poitiers (1142–54), was a formidable and innovating intellect. He followed in the tradition of subjecting the dictates of faith to the principles of dialectical inquiry, although in contrast to Abelard his interest was metaphysical. Gilbert sought to understand the ultimate nature of existence and its relation to pure form. In similar vein to Abelard, he began with the human experience and attempted to arrive at an understanding of god; in doing so, he followed the path chosen earlier by Anselm of Aosta in *Monologion*. Gilbert, however, was not so readily frustrated; the material world in his argument represents the evidence and manifestations – *subsistences* – of being. Only through subsistences can being be known. Yet, since being, as the actualizing principle, must precede subsistence, ultimate being must itself be pure form, devoid of any material existence. Such form must be god. Gilbert's reasoning was exclusively dialectical; from the evidence of experience he was able to deduce logically the existence of god, although he depended in the final analysis on a prior notion of god, as Anselm also realized.

Yet, like Abelard, his thinking did not go unchallenged and Gilbert too attracted the attention of the conservatives. In 1147 he was accused of heresy, specifically tritheism, a doctrine which had first appeared in the fifth century in the form of monophysitism and which denies the substantial unity of the trinity. Among his contemporaries Gilbert was highly regarded, as we learn from the *Historia pontificalis*, John of Salisbury's contemporary *Memoirs of the Papal Court*. Gilbert was, John wrote, 'a man of the very keenest intelligence, who had read most things and who, I may say from intimate knowledge, after spending sixty years in reading and close study, was so learned in the liberal arts that no one could surpass him in all subjects; nay rather he was held to surpass all in every subject'.[30]

The specific charge laid against Gilbert was related to 'certain statements found in the bishop's [Gilbert's] commentary on the *De trinitate* of Boethius'.[31] Gilbert was attacked bitterly in court by a number of prominent churchmen, particularly by Suger, abbot of St Denis, and Peter Lombard, later bishop of Paris. Despite his defence, Gilbert was censured – although not condemned – by the Council of Reims the following year, 1148. The *Historia pontificalis*, however, implies that the condemnation was most likely due to Bernard of Clairvaux's own aggression rather than to any real theological error. Certainly John suggests that Bernard stimulated the issue so that it assumed more significance than it really warranted. And, in fact, the condemnation had no long-term effect in blocking the course of such speculation.

These kinds of cosmological inquiries, in fact, were rapidly becoming a major feature of the new learning of the cathedral schools, and gifted scholars like Abelard and Gilbert proved strong attractions to the increasing number of students in the emerging cities. The dialecticians of the cathedral schools, of course, were not seeking to destroy faith or to overthrow the established order of life based on ecclesiastical supremacy. On the contrary, they were convinced that their efforts would strengthen the basis by which the absolute values to life were secured. Abelard's famous dictum – 'Through doubt we are led to inquiry, through inquiry we reach to truth' – was an attempt to secure faith and the established order on a much more acceptable, and indeed unshakeable, basis. Preoccupation with dialectic merely reflected the limitations of the procedures of investigation of the times.

The newly emergent Europe, still ignorant in large part of the Moslem and even the Byzantine world, had slender intellectual resources available. In spite of Europe's increasing prosperity and the new-found leisure afforded by the cathedrals, the pioneering scholars of the late eleventh and early twelfth centuries were constrained to work with minimal instruments. Those books of Aristotle that had provided the means whereby classical and Hellenistic scholars, and subsequently Byzantine and Moslem ones as well, could further investigation were still not available in the West. The remaining four books of Aristotle on logic – *Prior Analytics* and *Posterior Analytics*, *Topics* and *Sophistical Refutations* (*Elenchi*) – along with his writings on physical, natural and social science were not known until the middle of the twelfth century.[32] Even so it was clear that a quickening of the intellect was in progress, as evidenced by the growth of student numbers in the cathedral schools – which apparently proved attractive despite the rigorous methods of masters like Bernard of Chartres – and by the readiness of students to become acquainted with such teachings, following Abelard even in his periods of disfavour. The enthusiasm for learning, however, was not hailed in all quarters; there was, in fact, a profound reaction which came from the conservative element, represented strongly in the monasteries and championed by Bernard, the most eminent monastic of the twelfth century.

Conservative reaction: Bernard of Clairvaux

In the early twelfth century the church was by no means secure in its authority, following the decline of the ninth and tenth centuries. Papal corruption, including some of the worst abuses of simony, immorality, political intrigue and malfeasance, had made the church weak in that period. In large part the authority and prestige of Western Christendom in the tenth century derived not from the papacy but from the Cluniac revival of Benedictine monasticism. That great order constituted the visible church in so many places, particularly outside the urban centres. In the eleventh century the new prosperity and the revival of urban life, coupled with the determination of the reforming popes Leo IX and Gregory VII, restored papal dignity and authority, while at the same time the rural Cluniac movement became quiescent, and in places even lapsed into laxity. The intellectual activity of the cathedral schools, in their great monumental settings, secured public attention in the first decades of the twelfth century and appeared to threaten the restored authority of the church.

Conservative reaction was initiated by the ascetic Bernard of Clairvaux (c. 1090–1153) in two ways: through an attempted further reform of the Benedictine movement and by a direct effort at suppressing the new style of dialectical inquiry. Bernard himself was of noble Burgundian lineage, and followed the custom of many of the aristocracy in choosing the religious vocation. He was in about his twenty-second year when he sought admission to the monastery at Cîteaux. That foundation, some fifty miles north of Cluny, was itself of recent origin, having been founded in 1098 by Robert of Molesme, and passing the following year to the charge of a new abbot, Alberic, who held tenure for a decade. In 1109 it was directed by the Englishman Stephen Harding who was abbot when Bernard entered in the year 1112. Three years later, in 1115, Bernard was entrusted with the mission of founding a new house. He chose a valley fifty miles to

Cîteaux's north, which he called Clairvaux. In that new location Bernard brought into existence the spirit of religious reform initiated at Cîteaux. Ascendancy soon passed to Clairvaux which became the focus of the Cistercian movement.

The Cistercian reform of Benedictinism attempted to make more fundamental changes than the tenth-century Cluniac reform. Bernard took St Benedict and the life of Monte Cassino as his model: gone was the emphasis on liturgy and music so highly regarded at Cluny; the basis of Cistercian life was a return to the simple ascetic regimen of prayer and physical labour. In principle the Cistercians repudiated secular learning and indeed were not a learned order; even though Clairvaux had a library – consisting chiefly of theological works – no school was established. On the contrary, the life of the monks was regulated by a strict observance of Benedict's original Rule, and in this Bernard was himself the prime example. We have, in fact, a number of contemporary accounts of his austere outlook and manner: Alan of Auxerre states that Bernard's physique was spare and emaciated;[33] Étienne de Bourbon's *Anecdotes* record that Bernard was thoroughly ascetic in his physical and intellectual practices. For Bernard believed that through the life of agricultural and communal work the monk is enabled to devote his mind without hindrance to a continued contemplation of the condition of his soul. From the round of simple daily activity, in Bernard's view, comes the most important of man's activities, the life of contemplation, *vita contemplativa*. Man's vocation is clearly salvation, and that cannot be achieved through any amount of dialectical activity; it comes only through a prior faith in god, a commitment to all-engaging contemplation and a life of ascetic rigour. By such strenuous means, man might hope for god's grace – that moment of exquisite ecstasy in which a vision of the ultimate is granted. In that instant when the questing soul reaches out and touches god, man receives his fullest aesthetic satisfaction; it is the moment of intensest life. Such was the doctrine of Christian mysticism taught by Bernard, through which he hoped to secure the moral regeneration of his times.

Inevitably this approach came to interact with the outside society. Bernard himself was from the nobility and sought, wherever possible, to enrol the aristocracy in his movement. The laws of primogeniture were followed to a large extent in France, and in the expanded populations of the twelfth century there was no dearth of younger sons from noble houses ready to pursue the monastic life. So in effect the new Cistercian reform was itself biased in favour of the feudal conservative order. In

opposition to the growing identification of the churches with the commercial life of the cities evident in their rich furnishings, elaborate vest-
ments and pompous ceremonies, and their support of a leisured class of
chapter canons and students, Bernard set the austerity and simplicity of
the Cistercian Rule. Clairvaux, and the daughter-houses that spread
rapidly, were absolutely stark by contrast. The monks left their woollen
habits the natural colour of scoured fleece without benefit of dye, their
buildings likewise, set commonly in the most inaccessible of rural retreats,
were unadorned – simple in architecture, as empty of furnishings as
possible. With such a conscious striving for humility and abstention, the
reform movement by its very nature was destined to conflict with the
secular church. Bernard was impelled by the need to assert the values of
asceticism and to oppose actively the obvious luxury of the urban church.
It is likely that he and his followers drew strength and comfort from
practising the very reverse of the style of life to which their rank would
have entitled them, were they first-born.

Somewhat paradoxically Bernard himself was one of the great intellects
of the age and is reckoned, with every justification, a doctor of the church.
Much of his intellectual competence was directed against the growing
dialectical movement in education, so that it suffered a real check. In the
first half of the early twelfth century it even seemed that the old controversy
of the early Christian centuries on the use of pagan authors might be
revived. Bernard's criticism of the dialecticians – chiefly Abelard and
Gilbert de la Porrée – drew strength from his acceptance of a limited role
for profane learning; his position, however, stemmed from an insistence
on the priority of faith and mystical intuition. Once that were secured, man
could use pagan works as means of reinforcing faith and intensifying his
beliefs through the historical testimony of others before him, but he could
not begin with doubt and hope to end with certainty. Bernard's conception
of the Christian way of life was opposed to that of the cathedral scholars,
and in that spirit Bernard sought to have dialectic destroyed by having its
leading practitioners discredited.

A systematic theory of education: Hugh of St Victor

The concern with dialectic and logic is, of course, the most dramatic
aspect of eleventh- and early twelfth-century learning. A balanced view

of education in this period, however, must consider the more usual processes of education in addition to the activities of the leading scholars. What, then, can be said of education in the cathedral, collegiate and monastic schools which informed the majority of the *literati* of the period? In the first instance it must be emphasized that the sum total of our knowledge is very small indeed: there are no statistics on literacy and the information that does exist still has to be secured chiefly by implication and inference from sources concerned with other issues. The extent of literacy was very circumscribed – we cannot even hazard a guess for the eleventh century except to say that it was of the order of something less than one per cent – and was limited almost entirely to boys and men in holy orders. The procedures of elementary instruction remained those handed down from classical times, and reliance on the teachings of Quintilian was common. His *Institutio oratoria*, composed in the late first century A.D., was the first important systematic manual of the theory and practice of education ever written as such, and it is important to note that for the following thousand years it alone, in a badly mutilated text with large lacunae, was available to serve this purpose – at least for those schoolmasters able to have access to a copy. Quintilian, in fact, survives rather mysteriously throughout that millennium and there are only a few authenticated instances of his work's being used. Cassiodorus knew the *Institutio oratoria* as did Lupus of Ferrières (d. *c.* 860). Stephen of Rouen, a monk at Bec, made an abridgement of the mutilated text and Bernard of Chartres applied its prescriptions to his teaching in the cathedral school.[34] It was, in fact, at the same time as Bernard was using Quintilian, in the 1120s, that the next and second systematic full-length treatise on education appeared: the *Didascalicon* written by Hugh of St Victor. This well-elaborated text, along with the other writings of Hugh, is our one major source of educational theory – and to a limited extent of practice – for the period around 1100, and from it we are able to gain a reasonably detailed knowledge of education, in its most desirable aspects at least.

Hugh of St Victor: Didascalicon

Hugh of St Victor (*c.* 1096–1141) was born in Saxony – probably at Hartingham, in the diocese of Halberstadt. His family were the nobility of Blankenburg, his uncle Reinhard the bishop of Halberstadt, and Hugh, who entered minor orders at an early age, received the customary education for the religious life from the Canons Regular (*canonici regulares*) of St

Augustine, an order which had been formed in the mid-eleventh century and had become well established in the twelfth. In 1115 Hugh went to the monastery of St Victor in Paris – made famous by William of Champeaux – and in 1133 became both prior and director of its school. This was a period of a relatively rapid increase in the numbers of cathedral and monastic schools and it was abundantly clear that despite the many prevalent idealistic notions on education – and the dramatic encounters by the great scholars must have been very confusing to the majority of unsophisticated clerics – there was a pressing need for a simple, clearly stated theory of education, supported by as full a programme of studies as possible. St Victor was one of the important schools of Paris along with those of Notre Dame and Ste Geneviève – the latter named after the city's patron saint and made famous when Abelard taught there – and it was during the first years of his appointment there as *magister scholarum* that Hugh set himself the task of writing on education.

Hugh had been deeply influenced in his own student years by the teachings of Augustine – so much so that he was nicknamed *alter Augustinus* – and he took a decidedly mystic approach to Christianity, this being set out in a number of treatises, chiefly *De sacramentis christianae fidei*. Following Augustine, Hugh believed that contemplation is the supreme pursuit of man. In Hugh's scheme, this results from the study of the external world, which yields secular knowledge and consequently allows progression to meditation on this knowledge, which in turn reveals the divine order of the cosmos, thus making us able to contemplate god himself. As a consequence of these views, Hugh set out to articulate a complete educational programme for the clergy whereby they might be able to follow this mystical way, and this is contained in three treatises: the major work *Didascalicon* and the lesser works on grammar and history, respectively, *De grammatica* and *De tribus maximis circumstantiis gestorum*.

The *Didascalicon* immediately attracts attention with its unusual Greek title. By this time it had become almost a fashion among scholars to choose Greek-sounding titles for their writings – we think of John the Scot's *Periphyseon*, Anselm's *Monologion* and *Proslogion* and John of Salisbury's *Metalogicon*. Considering the fact that Greek was virtually unknown in Europe at the time, even if these few authors had varying degrees of acquaintanceship, it is a rather curious situation and is perhaps explained by the fact that there was an increasing awareness that behind the spare Latin learning of the West there was a fuller, richer tradition of Greek scholarship to whose authority Latin authors appealed implicitly by adopting at least Greek titles. 'Didascalicon', however, is a genuine Greek word, *didaskalikon*, a term used by Plato to mean 'instructive' or 'capable of giving instruction'. This was the popular short title; the full title is a mixture of Greek and Latin, *Didascalion de studio legendi (On the Study of Teaching)*[35] and again 'didascalion', an alternative spelling, is also a proper Greek word and was adapted by Hugh to designate his manual of educational theory and procedure.

The text of *Didascalicon*, set out in five chapters, is not organized as logically and sequentially as we might like. On the contrary, it is repetitive and at times exhortatory and gives the suggestion of an oral lecture programme. There is, moreover, a confusion of ideas and terms, and a taxonomy that is at marked variance with the usual styles of classification of the day. Despite this the main lines of the argument are well set out and can be followed without a great deal of difficulty. Hugh's concern with an ascent to the contemplation of the divine order as the purpose of all serious learning appears at the outset: 'Of all things to be sought, the first is that Wisdom in which the Form of the Perfect Good stands fixed'.[36] The means of gaining wisdom is through knowledge which is considered to be philosophical inquiry, the prerogative of man alone because only he is endowed with reason. Hugh separates the pursuit of wisdom into two major activities, the contemplation of truth and the practice of virtue, both of which, despite his avowed Augustinianism, indicate the influence of Aristotelian theory. Because knowledge in his day was gained almost exclusively from reading, *Didascalicon* then sets out its further aim of advising the student on what ought to be read, the order in which it should be read and the manner of reading it, and since there is another basic division between secular and sacred knowledge, this suggests a sixfold organization – although Hugh fails to keep to this intention.

Knowledge, however, is his starting-point, and is divided into four categories: theoretical, practical, mechanical and logical. The first two divisions, theoretical and practical, deal respectively with the apprehension of truth and the regulation of morals (or the practice of virtue); the mechanical helps men in their daily vocations; the logical provides a means to clear thinking and argument. Because Hugh dismisses the practical and mechanical divisions of knowledge, we will find it more convenient to consider them first. Practical knowledge is defined as that which regulates morals, and it is subdivided further into solitary, private and public areas which are concerned respectively with ethics, economics and politics. But Hugh does not give an exhaustive analysis of these forms of knowledge; rather they are dismissed because they are 'engaged with objects of concern'. Likewise the mechanical division of knowledge is analysed into its seven components: the three areas which give an external 'cover' to nature – textiles, armament, commerce – and the four areas which provide an internal nourishment for nature – agriculture, hunting, medicine and theatrical arts. The mechanical arts, however, are unsuitable for the attainment of wisdom because they are 'adulterate': their concern is with products which imitate nature. The reader is left then with only two branches of knowledge worthy of serious pursuit: 'the theoretical alone, because it studies the truth of things [and which therefore] we call wisdom',[37] and logic because it provides the knowledge necessary for correct speaking and clear argument.

In restricting his concern to theoretical and logical knowledge, Hugh is really making a fundamental distinction between content and methods of dealing with that content, although this is never quite so explicitly recognized. Indeed there appears to be quite some confusion in Hugh's thought concerning these two divisions, and this comes from his references to the seven liberal arts. Thus he writes

> Out of all the sciences . . . the ancients . . . especially selected seven to be mastered by those who were to be educated. These seven they considered so to excel all the rest in usefulness that anyone who had been thoroughly schooled in them might afterward come to a knowledge of the others by his own inquiry and effort rather than by listening to a teacher. For these, one might say, constitute the best instruments, the best rudiments, by which the way is prepared for the mind's complete knowledge of philosophic truth. Therefore they are called by the name tri*vium* and quadri*vium*, because by them, as by certain *ways* (*viae*), a quick mind enters into the secret places of wisdom.[38]

Hugh discusses the meaning of the term 'liberal' noting that this honorific designation is applied to the arts ambiguously,

> .. . either because they require minds which are liberal, that is liberated (for these sciences pursue subtle inquiries into the causes of things), or because in antiquity only free and noble men were accustomed to study them, while the populace and the sons of men not free sought operative skill in things mechanical.[39]

Despite these two statements, and the double meaning in the latter was voiced by Aristotle too, Hugh never specifically identifies these seven liberal arts. In antiquity they were clearly understood to be the three areas of method – grammar, dialectic and rhetoric – and the four areas of content

– arithmetic, geometry, astronomy and harmonics. Yet we read in *Didascalicon* that there are six branches of theoretical knowledge, namely, the traditional areas of arithmetic, geometry, astronomy and music (into which harmonics had become transformed), along with theology and physics. It could simply be that Hugh added the latter two studies because they had developed after the period of the original classical formulation, but he does not state what the liberal arts are. In fact there is a hint that Hugh does not include the classical trivium in the liberal arts, but expands the quadrivium to seven since he writes of theology, physics and mathematics, and the latter in its four subdivisions of arithmetic, geometry, astronomy and music. Even though this means counting mathematics twice, it is a possible explanation. Regardless, these areas of content are not developed at any great length and Hugh puts a great deal of emphasis in his treatise where we might reasonably expect it: in his consideration of methods of ordering knowledge; in the discussion, that is, of logic and dialectic.

Logic, the fourth branch of knowledge, consists of grammar, which he knew came from the Greek *gramma* meaning a 'letter' of the alphabet, along with the theory of argument which further subdivides into dialectic and rhetoric. So Hugh accepts the standard trivium, even if he is unsure of its relation to the liberal arts. Grammar, we read further, 'treats of words, with their origin, formation, combination, inflection, pronunciation, and all things else pertaining directly to utterance alone'.[40] The theory of argument, 'is concerned with the conceptual content of words'[41] and Hugh's dependence on Aristotle is well illustrated in his further explanation that

> ... invention and argument are integral parts running through the whole theory of argument, whereas demonstration, probable argument, and sophistic are its divisive parts, that is, mark distinct and separate subdivisions of it.[42]

In his summary of logic as a branch of knowledge Hugh writes that

> Grammar is the knowledge of how to speak without error; dialectic is clear-sighted argument which separates the true from the false; rhetoric is the discipline of persuading to every suitable thing.[43]

Having set out the various branches of secular knowledge – and it is never quite clear if Hugh recognizes grammar, dialectic and rhetoric as the constituents of the trivium – he then proceeds in Book Four to a consideration of religious knowledge which he had earlier grouped in with the theoretical division. This area is concerned, he writes, with the study of the scriptures (*sacrae paginae*), which encompasses explanations of etymology, composition, structure and contents of both Old and New Testaments, along with considerations of the canonicity of the various books and of the *apocrypha*, since the Septuagint, which the patristic scholars of the early Christian era had generally accepted as canonical, had been, and still was, the subject of doubt and revision. Along with these prescriptions he adds exhortatory advice for the student to approach the study of *sacrae paginae* with the proper motivation. There are three classes of persons who read the scriptures: those who do so to seek fame – and are to be pitied; those who delight in reading of wondrous acts – and need help in getting beyond this; and, thirdly, those who seek strengthening of faith. This latter group is the only praiseworthy one since its members study in order

> . . . that they may forthrightly demolish enemies of truth, teach those less well informed, recognize the path of truth more perfectly themselves, and, understanding the hidden things of God more deeply, love them more intently.[44]

With this discussion of 'theology', as he calls it, as a division of knowledge, Hugh's survey of learning is completed and the reader is left to make his own further synthesis of the constituents. Hugh never considers, for example, the crucial relationships between secular and sacred knowledge; his analysis is pitched at a lower level of understanding. Throughout the work the aim is kept clear and simple; it is avowedly one of guiding the student – most likely of late adolescent age – to a study of learning as it currently existed and as it was then taught, or at least as Hugh as a superior kind of schoolmaster felt that it should be. The didactic quality of the work is one of its outstanding characteristics; Hugh leaves his readers in no doubt on this point: whereas this corpus of knowledge was known by heart by many of the ancients,

> . . . the students of our day, whether from ignorance or from unwillingness, fail to hold to a fit method of study, and therefore we find many who study but few who are wise.[45]

This admonition is supported by all of the didactic devices that Hugh can introduce into his writing: an emphatic, recapitulative style; continued explanation of terms, particularly by appeals to Greek etymology; and the effort to impose order and regularity on his materials, in the instance, for example, of postulating seven mechanical arts – to parallel the seven liberal arts – and subdividing these further into a 'trivium' (the external cover for nature) and a 'quadrivium' (the internal nourishment for nature). And all of this, as he emphasizes in an Aristotelian-type argument,[46] because

> . . . there are two things which restore the divine likeness in man, namely the contemplation of truth and the practice of virtue. [Whenever] we strive after the restoration of our nature, we perform a divine action . . . [which] we may not unfittingly call 'understanding' [*intelligentia*].[47]

At the same time, as a practical-minded schoolmaster, Hugh is well aware of the varying ranges of intelligence in his students and he is concerned to make the point that successful study will depend not only upon a well-ordered sequence of reading but also upon certain features of the student. These are three: natural endowment, practice and discipline. The first itself comes from a 'certain faculty naturally rooted in the mind'[48] (clearly reminiscent of Aristotle's 'congenital discriminative capacity'),[49] and this has two aspects: 'aptitude' which enables us to 'gather wisdom', and 'memory' which stores it. Practice is self-explanatory, and discipline designates that effort of the will that sustains continued practice. Having established these parameters, Hugh shows himself to conform to the mainstream of contemporary thinking on the natural ordering of society.

Hugh and the study of history

Hugh's educational theory, particularly with regard to the mastery of religious knowledge, is supplemented in his work on the study of history, for, it is important to observe, *Didascalicon* makes no mention of history as part of theoretical – or any other kind – of knowledge. Now history itself had never been taught explicitly as an academic study. Either it had been considered a branch of literature, as was general in classical times, or else it was included in theology as Christian writers did, following the definitive example of Augustine's monumental work, *City of God (De civitate Dei)*. Hugh sets out his ideas in his text *On the Three Most Important Circumstances of the Achievements of History (De tribus maximis circumstantiis gestorum)*,[50] in which he postulates that history 'should be placed in our memory as the first foundation of learning'.[51] History (*res gestae*), in his use of the term follows closely the established traditions of religious chronicles and annals. His *De tribus* itself is set out in eleven divisions, beginning with the creation given in Genesis, and then proceeding in turn through the Chronicles of the Hebrew testament down to the Christian period, when he includes tables of popes, rulers since the time of Christ and major Christian historiographers. Basically it is a taxonomy of events with significant dates and places of their occurrence set out in lists; it is not a connected narrative of the kind written by Bede or Gregory of Tours. For, indeed, the whole work is planned as a framework within which the *sacrae paginae* can be read, providing as sound a chronology as possible and giving an assurance – by historical appeal – of authenticity to man's religious experience.

The mnemonic approach to learning

Of greater significance to education, though, are Hugh's attitudes towards learning which *De tribus* exemplifies. Although there is a didactic structure built into *Didascalicon*, it is in no way as deliberately presented as it is in this history. The title itself is part of a wide-ranging mnemonic scheme to assist the student to remember history: the 'three circumstances' are those of people, times and places. 'There are', he says, 'three things on which a knowledge of events chiefly depends; that is, the people who performed these deeds, the places where they were performed, and the ages when they were performed.'[52] If this is achieved, Hugh argues, then a basic foundation of all learning will be secured: 'If anyone will remember these things, he will discover that he has a good foundation on which he will afterwards superimpose without difficulty whatever he has learned through reading, and he will both grasp it quickly and retain it long.'[53]

In an age in which students lacked books, and when library copies were generally chained or otherwise secured to their lecterns, the ability to recall facts was very important indeed. This is a central feature of *De tribus*, and to illustrate the need for memorization Hugh uses a vivid metaphor. 'Wisdom', he writes, 'is a treasure and your mind a coffer' in which there are separate compartments for gold, silver and various kinds of precious stones. So the student is counselled:

. . . consider how you should collect and place in [the coffers of your mind] the priceless treasures of wisdom, that you may know its compartments one by one, and, when you have placed anything to be stored in those compartments, arrange the fact in such order that, when occasion demands, you can easily find it through memory, understand it through intelligence, and bring it forth through eloquence.[54]

To achieve this Hugh sets out another mnemonic scheme whereby the contents of any book may be memorized, and this scheme also has a three-

fold division. Just as we can remember history through the three categories of people, places and times, so we can remember the contents of a
book by analysing them into number, place and time. These three new
categories are rather confusing since two of the terms repeat those of the
earlier classification. Although Hugh does not say this explicitly, he seems
to have deliberately planned a parallelism in order to further his mnemonic
argument. Number he uses to designate an artificial device for the imagin-
ary ordering of information; place refers to the physical location of this
in the text; time seems to refer – although it is used ambiguously – to the
moment when the information is learned by the student and also to the
chronology of the events given in the text being studied. So we read in *De
tribus*:

> The facts you are learning are classified in the mind in three ways: according
> to number, according to place, and according to time. Thus all the ideas or
> facts which you hear you will comprehend easily and remember a long time, if
> you learn to consider them according to this three-fold classification. Learn to
> contemplate in your mind the line of a natural number from one, as though it
> were, so to speak, drawn out in a long straight line before your mind's eye.
> Then, when you hear any number at all mentioned, learn to turn your
> attention quickly to the point where its sum total is arrested, as if the number
> itself were terminated at that final point. For example, when you hear ten,
> think of the tenth point, when you hear twelve, the twelfth point, so that you
> grasp hold of the whole according to its last point, and so on. Make this
> reasoning and this method of imagining usual and customary, so that you
> may observe – as though with your eyes – the end and final conclusion of all
> the numbers, just as if these numbers were arranged in separate places. Hear,
> now, how useful this method is for learning. For example, I wish to learn the
> psalter by heart, word for word. This is what I do: first, I think of how many
> psalms it has. I find that there are 150. I learn all of them in order, so that I
> know which is first, which is second, which is third, and so on. In just this way
> I arrange them all in order in my mind, in line of natural number, and when I
> name them one by one in their own places, where they have been put in that
> line of natural number, I notice that it is the same for me whether I am
> reciting them or thinking about them, depending on how well I have visual-
> ized them internally in my mind: 'Blessed is the man', which is the first psalm;
> 'Wherefore do they rage', which is the second one; 'Lord, how they are
> multiplied', which is the third; that is, I concentrate on the first, second, and
> third place. And I so impress this arrangement by intense concentration on
> my mind, that, when questioned, I can answer without hesitation, whether
> they are to be recited in order, or with one or two omitted; whether they are
> to be named in reverse order, or backwards from their most familiar position;

and I can name what may be the first psalm, the second, what even the twenty-seventh, the forty-eighth, or whatever psalm it may be.[55]

Hugh makes great play with the fact that his method emphasizes not only the name of the psalm but also its number, allowing the student rather quick access to the text at a time when manuscript codices had neither tables of contents nor page numbers. Without knowledge of serial order, it would be a tiresome business finding information from books, particularly since each book was copied individually and the pagination therefore would not be uniform in all copies. To assist learning, Hugh stresses such details as remembering the pattern of the pages: location of rubrics, the colours in the decorations and illuminations, even the disposition of the text on the page. He makes this aspect of learning abundantly clear:

Have you not sometime stopped to think how much more difficult it is for a boy to remember what he has read when he frequently changes his book in reading? Why is this, unless it is because the individual mental picture by which memory is strengthened cannot endure inwardly when it is shattered externally through the senses into so many figures by different books? For, when the boy is forced to learn all things in an undivided fashion, with one thing superimposed on another, and with the last always obliterating the former, nothing remains as his own or is retained as familiar by usage or practice. It is, therefore, of great value for strengthening the memory, when we are reading books, to take pains to impress on our memory not only the number and order of the verses or the sentences, but also their very colour and form, and at the same time the place and position of the letters – where we saw this or that written, in what part, in what section (at the top, middle or bottom) we have seen it arranged, in what colour we have seen the forming of the letter or the decorated appearance of the parchment.[56]

When it comes to a discussion of the third approach to memorization, that through time, Hugh is on less certain ground. He gives the impression that time refers to the moment of our reading of a particular item, although this is fused into the concept of historical time:

After division by number and place comes division by time; that is, what should be done first, what later, how much before and how much later – by how many years, months, days, this should precede that – and what should follow what. To this division pertains also this fact, that we know how to recall to our minds afterwards the memory of something even from the very nature of the time when we learn any particular idea; when we remember that one event took place at night or another event during the day, one event in the winter, another in summer; one event on a cloudy day and another on a clear one.[57]

Throughout all of the prologue the stress is upon memory, 'for in memory alone the entire training of learning consists, because, just as it does not profit anyone [who is not ready to understand] to have heard something, so it is of no value to anyone to have understood something who would not or could not retain it'.[58] Throughout this text, in fact, we find an awareness of the highly developed theories on the training of memory which had been developed in ancient Greece and transmitted through the centuries. Although many of the treatises on the art of memory – the genre was known as the *Ars memorativa* – were generally unknown in early medieval times, in Hugh's day these were beginning to be recovered and put into use in the cathedral schools as an integral aspect of education.[59]

The success of Hugh's writings was very great indeed. *Didascalicon* provided as clear a fomulation of the programme of scholarly learning in its day as could be made. Its general temper, despite Hugh's proclivities, is Aristotelian, which was becoming increasingly popular, although it is possible to discern a recognizably large admixture of Neoplatonic thought – the notion, for example, that wisdom stands fixed in the 'Form of the Perfect Good', and in the many references and allusions throughout to Augustine and Boethius. One standard measure of any work's popularity is the range of its publication and adoption, and in its time *Didascalicon* was very successful indeed: it currently survives in nearly a hundred manuscripts written out from the twelfth to the fifteenth century, distributed among forty-five libraries in western and central Europe.[60] In structure and style *Didascalicon* is unique; it follows no earlier model although there is a superficial resemblance to Cassiodorus' *Introduction to Divine and Human Readings* which also separated knowledge into two realms – but the similarity ends there. In terms of the history of Western education, *Didascalicon* is one of the few systematic, comprehensive treatments of the subject ever written. Unlike the educational writings of most thinkers which deal with limited topics, even in a range of works, *Didascalicon* attempts to be, and to a measurably successful extent succeeds in being, comprehensive. It was a major influence on much subsequent educational thought and practice. Likewise, *De tribus maximus circumstantiis gestorum* was very successful throughout all of western Europe where copies were rapidly multiplied and disseminated in the cathedral, collegiate and monastic schools.[61] Just how fully implemented the whole system was it is impossible to ascertain; what we can do is secure an impression of how Hugh saw his programme being implemented in its ideal form. This he sets out in *De vanitate mundi* which gives his conception of how a school might best proceed:

> I see a gathering of students, their number is great. I see here all ages – boys, adolescents, young men, old men. Their studies, too, are different. Some are exercising their inexperienced tongue in pronouncing new letters and producing sounds foreign to their ears. Others are learning first, by listening, the inflection of words, their composition, and their derivation; then they repeat among themselves, and, in the repetition, engrave them in their memory. Some are cutting into wax tablets with a stylus; others are drawing figures on parchments with a sure hand, in various ways and with different colours. Yet others, with a zeal most ardent, seem preoccupied with more serious studies – they argue among themselves, trying to outwit one another by a thousand ruses and artifices. I see some who are reckoning; others, vibrating a taut string against the wooden bridge of a musical instrument, are producing different melodies. Still others are explaining certain drawings and mathematical figures. Some are depicting clearly with instruments the course and position of the stars and the turning of the sky. Others are discoursing on the nature of plants, the constitution of men, and the properties of things and virtues.[62]

There were two major consequences of Hugh's work. The first was to place educational practice on a systematic, well-articulated basis of theory argued in cogent style at a level capable of being understood and applied by the ordinary schoolmaster. The second, which was to have even more profound consequences for the development of Western education, was that dialectic was put into an acceptable position: it was seen as capable of providing a limited but necessary means of access to the first realm of human inquiry (*cogitatio*) which then provides the necessary foundation to ascend to meditation (*meditatio*) and finally to contemplation (*contemplatio*). In doing this, Hugh helped modify the emotionally heightened climate of thought concerning this aspect of intellectual life and to offer the growing number of teachers a *via media* between the excesses of Abelard on the one hand, and Bernard on the other.

Towards a wider learning

The efforts of the conservatives were completely unable to reverse the obvious trend of the times. Within Europe the general temper of thought was becoming increasingly receptive to Aristotelianism, even if this was not always a conscious process, as the writings of Hugh of St Victor seem to testify. Moreover, contact between Europe and its parent civilization, represented by the two eastern powers of Byzantium and Islam, was increasing. The Moslems of Spain had always extended a measure of tolerance to Christians, and European scholars in the tenth and eleventh centuries studied at Toledo and Córdoba and other schools which far surpassed any institutions in Christian Europe. Late in the eleventh century Europe even began to mount military offensives against the Moslems in the Orient. They were conceived originally as holy wars, the first being organized in response to an appeal in 1095 by Pope Urban II for an expedition to defend the eastern Empire from Islam and, perhaps, to recover the so-called Holy Land from the Arabs. The second crusade, launched in late 1145, resulted from an appeal in 1144 by Bernard of Clairvaux himself to Louis VII of France and Conrad III of Germany for another expedition following a Christian reversal at Edessa in 1144. Unwittingly, Bernard encouraged further contact between Europe and the rest of the civilized world, of which the lasting consequence, ironically enough, was a virtual inrush of secular and rational learning into the West.

CHAPTER 3

An Age of Crisis
1150–1230

Challenges to the church

The intellectual and educational excitement in twelfth-century Europe reflected the crucial nature of the period when a new focus on human problems led scholars to question traditional concepts, which in turn brought the church itself under scrutiny. Wider acquaintance with the classical Greek and Roman tradition, through increased contact with Islam, particularly in Spain, and with Byzantium, resulted in an enrichment of European thinking, although in many ways the accession of new ideas came too quickly to be assimilated easily and twelfth-century thought was marked by disputes of the most fundamental kinds. The ferment in learning was an aspect of the overall conditions of Europe in which rapid economic growth had not been accompanied by a corresponding development of appropriate institutions, and conflicts between various secular rulers and between state and church in respect of social and political issues, had to be resolved in terms of a new pattern of relationships.

Throughout the twelfth century, and in the early decades of the thirteenth, many of the important institutions and procedures that were to give a permanent character to European society received their first definite

INCIPIT LIBER EXODVS

ÆC SUNT Cap I.
NOMINA
FILIORŪ
ISRAHEL,
QUI INGRES
SI SUNT IN   IJ
ÆGYPTŪ
CUM IACOB
SINGULI
CUM DOMI
BUS SUIS
INTROIE
RUNT

Ruben. frmeon. leui. Iuda. Iſſachar. zabulon
et beniamin. dan et nepthalim. gad et aſer

1   Alcuin's Bible, beginning of Book of Exodus.

2   Hrabanus Maurus giving his work to Pope Gregory IV, manuscript of the school of Fulda, after A.D. 831.

3   French miniature of astronomers, thirteenth century.

expression. In politics, the separation of church and state and the first signs of constitutional sovereignty appeared; in economics the growth of mercantilism, that is, the deliberate use of money as a means of fostering trade and creating further wealth, accelerated, and numbers of townsmen – traders, artisans and professionals – came to exercise a greater influence. The millennium-long dominance of Neoplatonism in theology began to be challenged by the theories of Aristotle. While intellectual life became concerned with a fresh examination of the ideas of classical Greece and Rome, and the role of reason was being defined more clearly, a new educational institution was evolved: the university.

Initially those developments, since they were as yet unarticulated, interpenetrated one another greatly. In that period of emerging pluralism, the church, diffused throughout society and holding a monopoly of learning, became involved in all of the movements. In particular it sought to exert continued control over the evolution of educational processes.

The relative calm of monastic learning, or even that of the tenth- and eleventh-century cathedral schools, was a feature of the past. Education and the life of the intellect became prominent. Schools were founded in greater numbers and attracted a larger proportion of the population, scholars became significant and often controversial public figures, universities were formed and the impact of their student bodies in some cities often remained for centuries. Throughout Europe, and especially in France, England and Italy, most persons, including the peasantry, were at least conscious of the new movements in education. In the second half of the twelfth century and through all of the thirteenth, European society was dominated by intellectual struggles. The need for men to choose from a variety of competing doctrines, institutions and allegiances was ever-present. As a consequence that century, perhaps more than any that had preceded it in the history of Western society, was an age of crisis.

Centrally involved in the changes occurring was the church, which, although enjoying its phase of greatest power both spiritually and temporally, was still far from secure. The unity of Europe, which it had sought so earnestly for nearly a millennium, was about to fragment. The emergence of powerful national states, a decline in church morale and attendant pressures for reform, the appearance of heresies and the almost imperceptible growth of some cathedral schools into practically autonomous institutions, with their interest in suspect Moslem and ancient pagan doctrines, were all seen as potentially disruptive forces that had to be met and defeated. The church's perception of itself was clear. It secured its authority in large part on historical precedent, and even claimed title to the patrimony of the Roman Empire.

In ancient Rome there had been no conception of a separation of church and state. On the contrary, the emperor was *pontifex maximus*, the office of religious leader being integral with the emperorship. The conversion of Constantine made Christianity the official church and gave succeeding Roman pontiffs claim to hegemony over the whole social and political structure, a claim strengthened considerably by the absence of real temporal authority in Rome during the barbarian incursions. The church, moreover, was in possession of a document that seemed to be, in effect, a title-deed to the Roman Empire itself. Known as the *Donation of Constantine*,[1] this document had appeared in the early ninth century and, although the circumstances of its discovery and many aspects of the text itself seemed peculiar, it was accepted – rather uneasily by some – as legitimate. As a result of church intercession, the *Donation* claimed, Constantine had been cured of leprosy, and thereby had been made aware of god's existence and power. To mark his conversion, therefore, Constantine willed the Empire to the church, in perpetuity.

The Christians themselves had seen their new faith from the beginning as the basis for a secular Christian state, and had adopted political terms to designate its offices. For church they used *ecclesia* after the Greek political assemblies, Christ was their lord: the phrase *kingdom of god* was no mere metaphor.[2] Many instances testify to a determination to provide a wider and more adequate basis to civilized life than that of imperial Rome. The Christian ambition, so eloquently expressed in Augustine's *City of God*, was for nothing less than a union of the entire civilized world, the goal of an ecumenical society.[3]

Church and state: disputes with Germany and England

It was precisely that aspiration which created the difficulties of the times. In moving towards its ecumenical ambitions in the twelfth century it was essential for Rome to secure its authority first in Germany which, following the break-up of Charlemagne's empire, remained the greatest kingdom in Europe. Yet the most visible aspect of the church's problems lay in the continued poor relationships with the German emperors, which received their most dramatic expression in the Investiture Controversy. The principle involved was that of the right of temporal lords to invest abbots and bishops with the symbols of office at the time of consecration. In accepting lay investiture, the abbots and bishops thereby accepted, according to feudal customs, a relationship of fealty to the secular rulers. Throughout the eleventh century the papacy attempted to eliminate the practice and as a consequence came into continued, and at times serious, conflict with the German emperors. Although at the Concordat of Worms in 1122 a new pope, Calixtus III, effected the Investiture Compromise with Henry V (r. 1106–26), whereby the emperor relinquished the right to invest with ring and staff but received homage from the abbot or bishop elect, only a temporary peace ensued. In 1152 the emperorship went to Frederick I, 'Barbarossa' (r. 1152–90), who ruled far more energetically and independently than his immediate predecessors. Fired with the ambition to restore the Holy Roman Empire to the greatest territorial limits of the Carolingian era, which meant the political unification of all the German and Italian states, Frederick Barbarossa began to implement his intentions almost immediately on acceding to power. It was he who used the specific title, Holy Roman Empire, to designate his view that his realm was the continuation of Charlemagne's empire, and therefore of imperial Rome itself, and he was determined to ensure that such continuity was to be resumed. But Barbarossa went even further. He claimed to be, by divine appointment, successor to the whole of the ancient Roman dominions; he was *dominus mundi*, and this meant that Byzantium too, in his view, was rightfully part of his territories. So he wrote to the Byzantine emperor, Manuel I Comnenus (r. 1143–80), that he was heir not only to the Roman west of the Empire but also to the Greek east.[4]

In extending his power Frederick was compelled to consider his strategy regarding political alignments in Italy. Sicily, under Moslem domination since the mid-ninth century, had been invaded by a small force of Normans returning from a crusade in 1016. With later assistance from Normandy, they had extended their holdings in Italy as far north as Naples, establishing themselves by the end of the eleventh century as the independent House of Tancred of Hauteville. Meanwhile, the vigorous commercial towns on the plain of Lombardy had formed a league as a means of collectively asserting their independence of imperial control, the spirit of independence spreading even to Rome where it threatened papal authority. That action aroused Frederick to discipline them. In 1154 the emperor made a temporary reconciliation with Pope Hadrian IV, and crushed the Roman insurrection. However the mutual antagonism between emperor and pope remained. Although Hadrian rewarded Frederick with imperial coronation, neither would abate his claims: the emperor to complete temporal jurisdiction over the church in his territories; the pope to recognition of the paramount authority of his spiritual office. Yet, curiously, each depended on the other: the emperor secured his title by virtue of papal coronation; the pope's authority was recognized only within the *imperium Romanum*.[5] In 1156 relations between the two were aggravated further when Hadrian effected a concordat with the Norman king of Sicily, William I (r. 1154–66), thereby giving papal recognition to the independence of the territories claimed by Frederick. The German emperor received another setback in his attempts to curb the Lombard League. By 1183, after numerous campaigns, Frederick was compelled to accept those cities as independent, self-governing units within the Empire.

The twelfth century was a time of resistance to imperial ambitions, both papal and secular. By that time Europe had assumed a much more stable pattern of political organization and a number of national states had appeared that sought to maintain their independence. In Spain the Moslems were pushed back as Portugal, Castile, Navarre and Aragon contended with the Almoravids. Around the North Sea were ranged England, Ireland, Scotland, Norway and Sweden. To the east of Europe the kingdoms of Prussia and Bulgaria had formed while Byzantium, although much reduced in territory, remained a power of some consequence. Adjacent to Germany itself, which included the papal states, were a number of kingdoms: in the south was Sicily, to the west lay France, Denmark shared the northern frontier, and Poland and Hungary occupied the eastern boundary.

While France was amenable to the papacy, Rome's relations with England were at times severely strained. The English king, Henry II (r. 1154–89), was determined to restore the ascendancy of the crown and to reform the scandalous condition of the church through royal intervention. Henry found himself in conflict with Theobald, archbishop of Canterbury. Even after Theobald died in 1161 the dispute was continued by his successor, Thomas Becket, and reached a tragic climax with Becket's murder in 1170. Despite the subsequent resolution of the Council of Avranches in 1173 formally absolving Henry of any responsibility, a sense of guilt hung over the English crown. By the end of the twelfth century Europe had reached a state of political turmoil. In England during the reign of John (r. 1189–99) opposition to the church erupted again at the very time that the papacy was attempting to achieve the domination of European politics by securing control over the successor to the Holy Roman Emperor. By a complex turn of events the Hohenstaufen succession after

Barbarossa's death in 1190 passed eventually in 1208 to a papal ward, the infant Frederick II.

At that point the issues were complicated further by war between England and France. By 1214 Western Christendom was in armed conflict, with the papacy involved deeply through Innocent III's attempt to secure papal hegemony over all the temporal rulers. In the battle of Bouvines in 1214 the French forces, in moral alliance with the papacy, defeated a combined English–German force. The church's victory was a temporary one. Conflict continued with England, while in Germany Frederick II, as he grew to manhood, became increasingly independent and virtually antagonistic towards the papacy – by 1245 he had been excommunicated four times. The hopes for an easy way towards papal control of Europe which Innocent III must have held in championing the claims of the infant were in no way justified by the young emperor. Instead Frederick abandoned the vision of a single Holy Roman Empire and centred his rule on Sicily which had been conquered by his father, Henry VI. Frederick became celebrated as a patron of learning and a scholar himself. He was interested particularly in Moslem learning, especially science, and did much to promote its study at his court,[6] thereby worsening relations with Rome which was concerned to combat Moslem influence.

Educational ideals of the twelfth century

Scholarly concern with social issues: John of Salisbury

Throughout that period of dispute between church and state the issues began to be discussed by some scholars, not solely as academic exercises, but with the deliberate intention of influencing the course of political events. One of the first significant figures to do so was the Englishman, John of Salisbury (1110/15–1180), whose activities were part of a new phase of European scholarship. John sought to examine the elements of political dispute and so construct a theoretical explication as the basis of a practical solution. In doing so, he helped to revive political philosophy, long dominated by Augustine's theories, and thus stimulated the process of relating learning to man's social needs. John's thought is an early example of a new movement of Christian humanism which was manifested in a return to the works of great writers of classical Greece and Rome and a search for guidance on how man might best cultivate himself in the interests of the good life.

According to his own account in *Metalogicon*⁷ John was born and schooled in Salisbury and from 1136 pursued his advanced studies at Chartres and Paris, where he listened to the greatest European teachers of the day, including Abelard, Thierry of Chartres, William of Conches, Gilbert de la Porrée and Robert Pullen. John met Bernard of Clairvaux in 1148 at the Council of Reims at the time of Gilbert's heresy trial; Bernard apparently was impressed with John – a curious development considering the circumstances – and wrote a letter of recommendation on his behalf to Theobald, Archbishop of Canterbury. As a consequence, John became secretary to the English archbishop in 1154, an office he retained under Thomas Becket. In 1176 he was appointed bishop of Chartres, where he remained till his death four years later.

John was a scholar in rapport with his times, applying his talents to the solution of social problems. He turned his attention to the intellectual controversies concerning the proper education of man, and to the political disputes about the respective claims of church and state, so dramatically portentous in England and Germany. In that period of crisis John was involved centrally as secretary to the English archbishop, and as an indication of his own position he completed his major works *Policraticus* and *Metalogicon*, both in 1159, and presented them to the king's chancellor, Thomas Becket. The two studies were well received and became accepted as important contributions to the political and educational thought, respectively, of the period.

Medieval political theory up to that time drew almost exclusively from Augustine's *City of God* where the principles of kingship were stated clearly. Augustine had declared sovereignty to be a ministry of god, the king's office being to govern with justice, mercy and generosity for the order and security of the state, to the greater end of strengthening the true Christian religion.⁸ Such general prescriptions were not readily adaptable in the period of emerging nationalism in the twelfth century. In particular, there was no range of political concepts adequate for resolving the issues arising in the changing society of Europe. At a time when the church was struggling to retain an indispensable place in the twelfth-century political structure, the new treatise of John of Salisbury offered a theory of the state in which the church was seen as holding an integral part. In composing *Policraticus* John attempted to help remedy deficiencies in the political theory of his time.

Despite its numerous digressions, *Policraticus* develops as a central argument a corporate theory of the state. To explain his views, John uses the metaphor of the human body: like man himself the state is considered to have an organic composition, governed by natural laws, themselves deriving from divine creation. Following the metaphor, he saw the state composed of mutually interdependent parts all designed to work in accord: the state is the head, the chivalric orders the hands, the workers are the feet, and, sustaining the entire body and giving it form as its soul, is the church. John thereby sanctioned the existence of social classes, and was able to rationalize a theory of the natural division of labour. In that theory, and in accordance with the metaphor, the state as head is concerned with direction and supervision of public affairs, with maintaining corporate health. The state, however, should not exercise any functions of intellectual or social creativity; such activity is inimical to the proper training of courtiers. John's own experiences at the court of Henry II had convinced him that courtiers were devoid of moral and ethical scruples. It is clearly the function of the church to provide that element of government: only in the person of the properly educated cleric could the right combination of moral, ethical, intellectual, social and spiritual ingredients be found. So John's theory provided for the thorough interpenetration of all civil and secular authority by the church: using a concept derived from Aristotle, he conceived the church as the soul that, diffused throughout the political body, gives it form.

The ideal type of creative leader he considered to be the educated man, the man of Latin scholarship whose vision links the historical past with the present, and so is best equipped to grapple with the problems of the future. And, in putting forward this notion, John anticipated the concept of humanism that was to become more systematically cultivated in the fourteenth and fifteenth centuries, particularly in Italy. From that ideal in *Policraticus* John developed a theory of education and in the same treatise elaborated its ideals. The aim of genuine education, in his view, is to produce the cleric whose central trait is expressed in those qualities known collectively as *civilitas*. John was acquainted with a wide range of Latin authors – indeed his *Policraticus* and *Metalogicon* are crammed full of allusions and references to ancient writers – and he knew many of the Greeks in Latin translations; he was, therefore, aware of the classical use of the term *civilitas*. Quintilian had used it, in the late first century A.D., to express the idea of the science of politics, and his younger contemporary Suetonius employed it to describe the ability to move easily in social and political life, as an equivalent to 'civility'. In the sixth century Cassiodorus revived the term in his attempt to restore public order in Rome. John of Salisbury gave the term a much more precise designation: the behaviour of the educated man in social intercourse.[9] While *civilitas* is manifested in the simple occurrences of daily life, he emphasizes that it must be derived from philosophical principles which themselves stem from the Bible. The ultimate aim of behaving in accordance with the dictates of *civilitas* is to serve virtue. In propounding his ideal of the educated man, one who holds in proper balance the necessary ethical, moral, intellectual and aesthetic qualities, John criticized, if implicitly, the prevailing code of the Cistercians, whose doctrines of asceticism and *vita contemplativa* exercised some considerable social influence.

Educational ideal of eloquence

Policraticus gives a general indication of John's humanist thought on how the study of Greek and Roman literature might best guide man in his search for right living, and this received a fuller development in his educational treatise, *Metalogicon*. This work had a double significance: it sought to elaborate some of the notions of his political theory; at the same time it was intended to provide a clear statement on educational issues that were strongly disputed in the twelfth century, quite apart from any political considerations. The argument concerning the educational value of dialectic and rhetoric – known as the 'old logic' – which had broken out in the twelfth century was stimulated further in the second quarter of that century by the introduction to Europe of the previously unused four books of Aristotle's *Organon*, known, because of their novelty, as the 'new logic'. At the time of John's appointment to Canterbury (1154) the use of this 'new logic' – *Prior Analytics, Posterior Analytics, Topics, Sophistical Refutations* – was the subject of some considerable derision and acrimony on the part of numerous, and anonymous, clerics, chiefly because its logical procedures challenged the security provided by orthodoxy and tradition. An enthusiastic supporter of the revived trivium, John applied himself immediately to the controversy and within five years had written a thoroughgoing study of the issues. Following the fashion for Greek studies, then undergoing a revival with the increased contact between west and east, John titled his work *Metalogicon*, a neologism suggesting 'a defence of the trivium'.[10]

Metalogicon is testimony to John's own thorough scholarship. The ninety-seven chapters, organized into four major sections, are closely argued and composed in the classical rhetorical style John was seeking to revive. It is set in the form of a defendant before a court, beginning with a statement of the matters under consideration, and proceeding to an elaboration of the issues with evidence from authorities, both ancient and modern, in refutation of the critics. The book then sets forward in careful detail its own positive arguments in support of the trivium, founding them on a theory of knowledge derived in the first instance from immediate experience given in sensation and imagination. From such foundations, truth is gained by the processes of reason and demonstration. John is, consequently, concerned with the nature of knowledge, and of truth itself. In the course of his examination John cites evidence from such a wide range of sources – many, of course, taken from compendia – that *Metalogicon* remains, along with *Didascalicon*, one of the most important documents on the condition of learning in Western Christendom in the later twelfth century. It is a major source from which the pedagogical and educational history of the period can be reconstructed.

The opponent whom John sets out to answer is described in the prologue as a goading critic at the court and given the pseudonym Cornificius, in a pun on the latin *cornix*, a crow.[11] It is clear however that John was really referring to the general body of hostility to the new logic. In building his case, John drew together classical statements on the verbal arts made by Aristotle, Cicero and Quintilian, all of whom he expressly acknowledged. In particular he pointed towards the importance they placed on the art of verbal eloquence in the education of the citizen. The argument, in fact, hinged on the crucial concept of eloquence since John accepted the views of those who believed that only through its achievement can man pursue his proper human vocation.

Opposition to eloquence was as ancient as its acceptance – such dispute had its origins at least as early as the first recorded sophists, and the issue had never disappeared from educational discussion. Suspicion was indeed well merited; the tricks of the demagogue and the possibilities of deceit offered by skilful argument were rarely absent from the public mind despite the assurances of propriety advanced in ancient times by Isocrates, Cicero and Quintilian. Yet it was evident to John that man stands in need of speech and some degree of linguistic facility. The early Greeks, of course, were well aware that learning is facilitated by verbal skill and that human awareness is heightened, if often in obscure ways, through properly used verbal arts. In *Metalogicon* John attempted the considerable task of examining anew that contentious and intractable problem. The Christian opposition to eloquence stemmed from the belief that the pursuit of the devout life with faith in god is an adequate and mandatory way for man. John intended to show that eloquence is a proper and necessary foundation for the progressive ascent to knowledge and truth – and that truth itself is of god.

Now John too was well aware of the inherent dangers of mere verbal facility and he demonstrated this unequivocally in several places in *Policraticus* with stringent criticisms of shallow scholars, 'those who cling to words [and] prefer to seem rather than to be wise'.[12] He observes that the seductions of verbal learning can mislead students so that 'when one of them has succeeded in making himself incomprehensible, he thinks that he has won the right of being regarded as a philosopher superior to others'.[13] In the course of this extended polemic, John demonstrates his own grasp of the problems that stem from superficial teaching and correspondingly inadequate learning; at the same time, we get a clear picture of the procedures of some classrooms of the day. 'Consider', John exhorts his readers,

> the leading teachers of philosophy of our own day, those who are most loudly acclaimed, surrounded by a noisy throng of disciples. Mark them carefully; you will find them dwelling on one rule, or on two or three words, or else they have selected (as though it were an important matter) a small number of questions suitable for dispute, on which to exercise their talent and waste their life. They do not however succeed in solving them and hand down to posterity for solution by their disciples their problems with all the ambiguity with which they have invested them. In their lecture room they invite you to battle with them, become pressing, and demand the clash of wit. If you hesitate to engage, if you delay but for a moment they are upon you. If you advance and, though unwillingly, change front, they torture words; with tricks of magic they transform themselves until you marvel at the reappearance of the slippery, changing Proteus. But he can be trapped more easily if you insist on understanding his meanings and intention despite his voluble and erratic language. He will finally be vanquished by his own meaning and be caught by the words of his mouth, if you can grasp their significance and hold it firmly.[14]

The whole point of John's invective in *Policraticus* is to alert students to the dangers of becoming mere slavish disciples and falling easy victim to the attractions of asserting authority rather than scholarship in their own teaching. The danger, John argued, is that the students are led to become interested 'not in what is said but in who said it. . . . He who becomes the slave of his teacher's point of view is prepared to argue the question of goat's wool' (that is, whether it is hair or wool – a trivial debate).[15]

John based his positive arguments for the study of the verbal arts on the assumption of an ideal form for man: the true self which represents a potential to be actualized. The self needs articulation and development through two powers of speech and reason, fused into the faculty of eloquence, which 'brings to light and in a way publishes what otherwise would be hidden in the inner recesses of man's consciousness'.[16] John saw eloquence as the means by which man achieves in fact what is pre-existent in unrealized form.[17] Since each person depends on the particular language of his own society to realize his inner potential, John argued that speech itself is therefore a convention that has to be learned. And further, if it has to be learned, then it is proper for such learning to be organized according to rules of appropriate expression which are a part of the idea of eloquence. From those assumptions John elaborated the traditional Ciceronian arguments of *De inventione* on the need for helping nature by use and exercise. Speech must be taught consciously and its right use encouraged if man is to achieve his full development. Such a science of right verbal expression John designated by the term logic,[18] composed of two constituent parts: grammar, 'the elements of language',[19] and dialectic, the science of effective argument and of verbal meaning.[20] Throughout all of John's work there is a considerable dependence on both Cicero and Quintilian; there is, in fact, a certain parallelism between, on the one hand, the defence of rhetoric by Cicero and Quintilian and, on the other, the defence of logic by John of Salisbury. Both Roman writers saw the danger of allowing rhetoric to have too large a place in higher education. Its value, they believed, would be maximized if it were grouped with other appropriate subjects. John had the same view, as expressed throughout *Metalogicon*, of logic.

Eloquence was thus regarded by John as embracing the two studies of rhetoric and dialectic. In ancient usage rhetoric designated both the art of expression itself and what was called probable argument, that is, hypothetical issues; dialectic was restricted to those issues admitting of final demonstration. In Christian times the loss of Aristotelian logic and the inadmissibility of much church doctrine to demonstrative argument led to a fusion of the two studies. John sought to separate them, in large part drawing support from the two newly translated books of *Analytics* of

Aristotle which treat of syllogistic reasoning, definition and demonstration; sections of *Metalogicon* deal explicitly with the *Analytics* and the *Topics*.

Eloquence without wisdom, John recognized, is futile;[21] dialectic must be applied to real issues, furnished by other studies.[22] However, John did not pursue the question of teaching such other disciplines. Peripheral observations suggest that he recognized the objective structure of reality which is apprehended in the first instance through experience. Beyond this he said little, although we do find some allusions and references in *Policraticus*. 'Does anyone doubt', he wrote, 'the desirability of reading the historians, the orators, and the authorities on approved mathematics, since without a knowledge of them men cannot be, or at least usually are not, liberally educated. Indeed, those who are ignorant of such writers are termed illiterate even if they can read and write.'[23] John's background at Chartres shows in his ideals of education which are those of the liberal arts. In addition to the verbal arts, the truly educated man must also have a command of 'knowledge' – and here he uses the Greek term *ma'thesis*. For, he writes rather negatively, 'intelligence dealing with the abstract [properties of mathematics] is surely no useless and idle thing when thus employed, for through it the mind ascends the ladder of the liberal arts step by step to the throne of perfect wisdom.'[24] This concept of the ordered sequence of learning is a familiar one and John's debt to Neoplatonism comes through clearly in the same context:

> *Ma'thesis* as taught in the schools consists entirely of these four forms [arithmetic, geometry, astronomy, music] and attains the perfection of worldly wisdom by these four so-called paths [quadrivium] of philosophy.[25]

John believed that man constructs his understanding of the world through the two sources of sensation and imagination. From such knowledge, truth is derived by the processes of reason and demonstration. In considering the application of reason he was confronted with the problem of the relationships between science, wisdom and faith.[26] His answer is significant: faith is an intermediary between opinion and science, and allows the affirmation in the intellect of what 'is not present'; science includes the comprehension of divine things.[27] There the argument of *Metalogicon* rested. John's further views on faith are found elsewhere. In *Policraticus* he asserts that in the domain of religion, reason and science must take second place. We must accept the fact that 'certain postulates are made which, in order that faith may be more meritorious, transcend the experience of reason. These, though reason may not impel, must be a concession to piety.' [28]

Despite his clear acceptance of Aristotle, expressed chiefly through a continued defence of him throughout *Metalogicon*, John was not concerned with attempts to use dialectic for the construction of knowledge or for the pursuit of inquiry into the natural world. His humanism was directed towards making the current moral order secure, not with examining its basis. John had, in fact, premised his *Policraticus* partly in the belief that absolute reliance on reason had been the cardinal error of the thinkers of Greek and Roman antiquity; [29] doubtless he realized that rational inquiry is a certain way of unsettling the social order and that the needs of his times were otherwise. None the less, the argument of *Metalogicon* was effective; it helped prepare the way for a wider use of the powers of human reason in investigating man and his world, and in the years immediately following it proved a steady source of inspiration for other scholars.

Moslem Spain: speculation and controversy

The recovery of Greek scholarship

Meanwhile some of the most significant intellectual developments in Europe were taking place in Spain. Since the beginnings of the eighth century that region had been under Moslem domination. When the Abbasids massacred the ruling Islamic Umayyad dynasty in Damascus in 750, the prince Abd-al-Rahman escaped to Spain and preserved a limited Umayyad rule in Córdoba, which he established as an independent caliphate in 756. Moslem Spain did not remain a rural backwater; on the contrary, its major cities – Córdoba, Seville, Granada, Toledo – became centres of scholarship and were abreast of all Moslem learning. What quickly became one of the finest libraries in the world was founded in Córdoba in 970, its collection growing, reputedly, to some 600,000 holdings in the early twelfth century. Stimulated also by its proximity to Christian Europe, Spain was well situated to receive learning. Along with Moslem thought, much of the corpus of Greek, Hellenistic and Byzantine knowledge was maintained there, and scholarship flourished in the eleventh and twelfth centuries. The political changes in that period, moreover, contributed to an even greater intermingling of learning. In the ninth and tenth centuries, Umayyad control of the northern parts of Spain had weakened under pressure of expansion by the lords of some of the minor Carolingian fiefs. Spain then broke up into several separate Moslem principalities, and in the early eleventh century two opposing groups invaded the region: from the south came an African-based tribe of vigorous Moslems, the Almoravids, later supplanted by the excessively fanatical Almohads; from the north issued a number of Christian groups, of whom the most famous leader was El Cid – Rodrigo Díaz de Vivar – who, in a series of epic engagements, captured Valencia in 1094. By the mid-twelfth century Spain was composed of five regions: the four northern Christian states of Portugal, León, Castile and Aragon, and the dominions of the Almohads in the south. Europe had extended into one of the major centres of Moslem culture and a region rich in Islamic learning.

Early in the twelfth century, then, as the Christians moved into the former Moslem territories, Western knowledge of Eastern scholarship became greatly augmented. Before long there appeared groups of translators, admittedly of obscure origins, of whom the most prominent were Adelard of Bath (*fl. c.* 1110–40), Herman of Carinthia (*fl. c.* 1140), Gerard of Cremona (*c.* 1135–*c.* 1180) and Hugo Sanctallensis (no dates; *fl.* twelfth century).[30] The chief centre was in Toledo where, on the foundation of the Arab library, the Christian archbishop Raymond established a school of translation, known as the Bayt al-Hikma, modelled on one in the cosmopolitan city of Baghdad.

Direction of this school was entrusted to Dominic Gundissalinus, a converted Jew, under whom scholars of all persuasions – Moslem, Christian and Jewish – produced Latin versions of works of Arabic and Hebrew scholarship, which included, in large part, translations from the classical and Christian past. Around 1150 Dominic himself published his *De divisione philosophiae* (*On the Divisions of Philosophy*).[31] In that influential book he separated theological studies from the human sciences, the latter being subdivided into three major parts: science of eloquence (grammar, poetry, rhetoric), logic and the science of knowledge. The third of those parts was divided further into physics, mathematics, metaphysics, ethics, economics and politics; that is, the bulk of the Aristotelian corpus. In making his classification Dominic moved towards a solution of current problems by attempting to distinguish those areas of experience amenable to treatment by reason, from those dependent on an indemonstrable faith. In so doing, he reflected the thought of Moslem thinkers across the border in the caliphate of Córdoba who were expressing similar views. Dominic's treatment is important in another respect: it illustrates how the rigid traditional classification of knowledge into the categories of the seven liberal arts was being reorganized into new arrangements.

Translation, usually under episcopal patronage, was carried on as well in a number of minor places – Barcelona, Segovia, Pamplona, León and even in nearby Christian cities across the Pyrenees: Toulouse, Béziers, Narbonne and Marseille, which also received Arabic versions.[32] The translated works were studied in such proximate centres as the cathedral schools of Marseille, Toulouse and Montpellier. Then in the course of the later twelfth century they were carried throughout Western Christendom. In a period of probably less than fifty years almost every major classical work was made available to scholars in Europe, chief among them being the medical writings of Hippocrates and Galen, the entire Aristotelian corpus, and the mathematics and astronomy of Greek and Hellenistic scholars, including Euclid and Ptolemy. In addition, the acquisitions included the commentaries, developments and further discoveries of the Moslems themselves.[33] Islamic learning, moreover, came not only from Spain, but from Sicily where the Arabs were in occupation for two centuries until the mid-eleventh century, and also from the Levant where the Christian Stephen of Antioch (*fl. c.* 1127) was an active translator from Arabic into Latin.[34] Of the greatest significance to Western intellectual and educational life, however, is the fact that the works of Aristotle which hitherto had been unknown in Europe were now made available; these were the *Prior Analytics, Posterior Analytics, Topics, Sophistical Refutations, Physics, Metaphysics, Natural Science, Ethics, Politics* and *Poetics*.[35]

The exact manner in which these works became known and disseminated is still obscure and, in many respects, the subject of controversy; none the less, their distribution was the most important influence on Western scholarship in the twelfth century. As a consequence of the accession of Aristotle to the West, learning was advanced in two aspects: a vast improvement was allowed in the procedures of logical inquiry and a stimulation was given to extend the range of human thought much more widely. The two Aristotelian books on logic, *Categories* and *On Interpretation*, which had been preserved in the translations and commentaries of Boethius, and known as the old logic, were supplemented by the other four books of the *Organon* – the *Prior Analytics* and *Posterior Analytics*, the *Topics* and *Sophistical Refutations* – which came to be known as the new logic.

The augmented and now complete *corpus Aristotelicum* affected European education in two major ways: by its direct influence on scholars who read the various books as virtually new works, and furthermore by the transmission into Christian Europe of a controversy surrounding the thought of Aristotle – and the Greek philosophers generally – which after a violent career throughout all of Islam had reached a bitter climax in Córdoba in the late twelfth century, particularly with respect to the thought of Averroes. Accompanying this was a lesser controversy over the similar work of the Jew, Moses Maimonides, which first divided the world of Hebrew thought, and then became imported into the rapidly maturing cathedral schools. The teachings of Averroes and Maimonides stimulated a bitter controversy which was to lead to an intellectual schism throughout Western Christendom.

Kalam: *Moslem application of reason to faith*

The origins of that controversy, to a considerable extent, are found in the theological history of Islam. This faith had been brought to the desert Arabs by Mohammed (*c.* A.D. 570–632) who claimed to be the chosen prophet of Allah, as the Arabs called their god. The divine revelations were recorded in the Moslem scriptures, the Koran, and these were believed, on the basis of Mohammed's statements, to be a transcript of a tablet preserved in heaven. However, difficulties arose within a century of the prophet's death, due in large part to the lack of an agreed canon, and also to ambiguities in the text itself. Furthermore, the revelations of the Koran became supplemented increasingly by inspired utterances and prescriptions ascribed to Mohammed – many of which were apocryphal – known as *hadith*. At the same time, the new faith of Islam (meaning, literally, surrender to the will of god) had spread rapidly throughout the Hellenistic Orient, and in so doing it came into continued contact with Greek philosophy which attracted many Moslem scholars since it appeared to offer explanations and solutions to their theological inquiries. Yet, at the same time, there was a strong opposition to philosophical thinking of any kind – Greek or Moslem – because it appeared to challenge faith. The result was that Islam became rent with confusion and discord.

Meanwhile, as the Moslem world became more settled, following its expansion, schools of higher learning were set up, of which the most influential model was the Bayt al-Hikma or House of Wisdom. This was

founded by the caliph al-Ma'mun in Baghdad about A.D. 830. It was conceived as an institute of science, with an observatory, and its central
studies were those of scientific and philosophical literature, particularly
that coming in from other cultures. Its library and translating offices,
therefore, were central features. Al-Ma'mun dispatched book-buying
missions for the Bayt al-Hikma to the limits of the Greek world – Alexandria and Constantinople – and possibly east to India and China. The
Bayt al-Hikma became the model from which further Moslem schools
of higher learning developed, known generically as the Dar al-Hikma,[36]
and concerned chiefly with the study of sciences and advanced secular
learning. At the same time there were established theological colleges
generally close to the mosques, known as *madrasas* whose studies were
conventionally organized into Koranic exegesis (*tafsir*), religious tradition
(*hadith*), law (*fiqh*) and theology (*kalam*). It was within the *madrasas* that a
serious split developed, which widened with the centuries, between those
orthodox theologians who regarded the Koran as absolute and to be
interpreted literally – including its elements of miracle and mystery – and
the philosophically minded scholars who accepted reason and sought to
reach spiritual truth through a combination of revelation and human
knowledge.

By the beginning of the eleventh century, the conflict between theologians and philosophers was serious indeed, the case for a rational
approach to religious belief being significantly developed by the Persian
scholar and Baghdad court official Ibn Sina (980–1037). Known in the
West by the Latin form of his name, Avicenna, his industry was prodigi-
ous;[37] in particular his *Canon of Medicine* was used widely, finding its way
into the West as well. Equally influential in Europe was his philosophy
which reached there shortly after his death and was studied with interest,
chiefly because it rationalized much of the prevailing Neoplatonism of the
times. Avicenna had accepted the Platonic notion of the incorporeal
human soul as man's link with god. He advanced, however, a theory of the
human intellect and of knowledge that seemed in many ways more
plausible than the Neoplatonic notions of innate knowledge and divine
illumination.[38] Depending heavily on Aristotelian thought, Avicenna
believed that the universe is constituted of a sequence of causes and
effects. The sequence itself is not merely random, it has a design of which
god is the author. God himself, however, being complete, is both his own
cause and effect. And since god is perfect and complete, every cause and
effect in the apparently endless sequence is really an expression of that

cosmic design. The universe, then, is contingent but also necessary. Further, the universe has a hierarchical structure closely akin to that suggested by the third-century Plotinus: god expresses himself in the whole universe through a succession of intermediate forms, reaching down from heaven, of which the last, and closest to man, is the active intellect.[39] Again, following Aristotle, Avicenna accepted the validity of sense impressions as the foundation of knowledge. They become fused into concepts, which in turn give knowledge of universals. That process, however, yields only abstract knowledge – scarcely more than stored information. It is transformed into real knowledge through illumination by the active intellect. Man consequently is linked ultimately to god; through the active intellect he receives the stamp of validity on all of his sensory impressions, experiences and thoughts, thereby gaining truth and enlightenment.

Avicenna's philosophy stimulated violent reactions from the orthodox Moslem theologians (*Mutakallimun*), the most spirited and widely disseminated response coming from al-Ghazali (1058–1111). A Persian scholar, resident largely in Baghdad, al-Ghazali belonged to a group of moderate theologians known as Ash'arites who sought a middle way between a slavishly literal acceptance of the Koran and an excessive reliance on the ideas and principles of Hellenistic philosophy. They admitted that revelation as reported in the scriptures has its irrational features and that there is, consequently, some scope for the application of reason. Al-Ghazali's attacks came in his celebrated *Tahafut al-Falasifa*, a title difficult to translate, but rendered reasonably well by the *Incoherence of Philosophy*. The intentions of that work, however, suggest that a more felicitous rendering would be 'The Bankruptcy of Philosophy'.[40]

Al-Ghazali's position is based on an occasionalist metaphysics, a doctrine holding that all of the events of the supposed linear sequence of cause and effect are not really linked causationally at all. On the contrary, every single event in the universe is seen as the result of god's intervention, each so-called effect is the 'occasion' of god's direct causation.[41] In the case of a fire, for example, al-Ghazali argued:

> The agent of the burning is God, through His creating the black in the cotton and the disconnexion of its parts, and it is God who made the cotton burn and made ashes either through the intermediation of angels or without intermediation. For fire is a dead body which has no action, and what is the proof that it is the agent? Indeed the philosophers have no other proof than the observation of the occurrence of the burning, when there is contact

with fire, but observation proves only a simultaneity, not a causation, and, in reality, there is no other cause but God.[42]

In large part al-Ghazali was reacting against the excessive emphasis on cause and effect taught by the philosophers. In their theories god is reduced to a position of virtual impotence, and his very perfection and necessary being – which means that every cause and effect is an integral aspect of god's existence – gives a thoroughly deterministic emphasis to the universe. There is no scope for man's will, for the necessary interplay between good and evil; faith itself, in fact, scarcely has any relevance. To counter that passive and deterministic view, the highly mystical al-Ghazali centred his arguments on the phenomenon of miracle. The Koran itself had been received in such a way; Islamic theology is full of miracles. Those events, by definitions, are the 'occasions' of god's intervention. If the world were in fact as consistent as the philosophers held it to be, then miracle has to be explained by causation, and that, al-Ghazali insisted, they cannot do. Al-Ghazali conceded the appearance of cause and effect, but argued that it results only from verbal predication of the observed phenomena of the natural world. It is consequently merely a linguistic or logical necessity; it is not evidence of causal necessity. Experience, in his view, merely allows us to conclude that effects come with the cause and not through it (*cum se, non per se*).[43] Al-Ghazali's conception of the universe rested in a metaphysics of atoms in process of constant movement and change, of constant creation and destruction by god. That alone is the ultimate reality. His doctrine sought to emphasize the vitality and omnipresence of god, to restore him to direct control of the events of the world in contrast to the extremely remote place given him in philosophical conceptions.

Moslem scholarship in Spain: thought of Averroes

Al-Ghazali's position provoked a response from the philosophers. but not from those in Baghdad. Early in the eleventh century the Islamic empire, in fact, had begun to decline; by mid-century it was dominated by a new minority group, the Seljuk Turks, who attempted to revive the old warrior spirit of early times. Byzantium and the West both resisted Seljuk movements and as a consequence the ensuing twelfth century was a period of military conflict between Islam and Christendom, the time of the crusades. Exhausted by those inconclusive wars, Baghdad declined and fell an easy victim to the barbarian Mongols who swept out of Asia in the thirteenth century. In 1258 Baghdad was sacked and the Moslem empire centred in Mesopotamia was shattered. Throughout those centuries of decline, learning ceased to be prosecuted so vigorously, and in the Orient itself the orthodox theologians were generally in the ascendant. The controversies of *kalam*, however, continued unabated in Spain where they revolved around the thought of Averroes.

Ibn Rush'd (1126–98),[44] or Averroes as he is known in the Latinized version of his name, was born in Córdoba and came from a family of lawyers: his grandfather was a chief justice, his father a judge. His own education was for the law, although it included a study of Greek science. His early life, however, is obscure, and he first enters the historical record around 1168 when he was introduced to the Moslem monarch, Abu Ya'qub (r. 1163–84), by the chief court physician Ibn Tufail. Averroes was presented, in part, because of Tufail's desire to advance learning at the court, particularly the study of Aristotle whose writings were becoming popular. Averroes was appointed a judge in Seville and for the following ten years or so, until 1182, he held that position and worked simultaneously at editing accurate editions of Aristotle and at writing commentaries on them. That was a productive period in his life: he wrote commentaries on the *Nicomachean Ethics, Physics, On the Soul* and *Metaphysics* at least; possibly there were others that have not survived. In the same period, moreover, there is substantial evidence to suggest that he wrote a commentary on the *Republic* of Plato.[45] Then, around 1179, Averroes produced his first major philosophical treatise, *Kitab fasl al-maqal (On the Harmony of Religion and Philosophy)*. Although that work was probably addressed to fellow lawyers and was intended purely as a legal treatise,[46] it turned out to be an influential study in epistemology. It seems to have been prompted by a need to determine the extent to which Moslem law permits the study of philosophy and logic, a problem that had arisen as a result of the reviving Moslem interest in Aristotle, and the increasing growth of opposition to his doctrines.

On the Harmony of Religion and Philosophy reveals Averroes' views on the use of reason. A short work, written with economy of style and argument, the basic proposition is put in the first chapter: Moslem law (*fiqh*) commands reflection on the universe so that man can appreciate the handiwork of god;[47] there is consequently an obligation on man to be intellectual.[48] Since the Koran is addressed to all men of varying degrees of intellectual ability, it seemed obvious to Averroes that it cannot always speak literally. Instead, it must use metaphorical and other form of figurative languages, which, however, contain the elements of truth in their apparent meanings as well. Probably following Plato, Averroes saw three classes of men:

> One class is those who are not people of interpretation at all: these are the rhetorical class. They are the overwhelming mass, for no man of sound intellect is exempted from this kind of assent. Another class is the people of dialectical interpretation: these are the dialecticians, either by nature alone or by nature and habit. Another class is the people of certain interpretation: these are the demonstrative class, by nature and training, that is, in the art of philosophy.[49]

God, in his wisdom, speaks to each class of men by appropriate means. To the simple masses, he uses direct, rhetorical speech [*khitabi*]; to those in need of persuasion he argues dialectically [*jadali*]; for the most resolute of minds, god employs the method of absolute demonstration [*burhani*]. The Koran may be read at all three levels, and, since the level of absolute demonstration demands a thorough scrutiny of the Koran to penetrate behind the veils of allegory and metaphor, Moslem law must permit scholars the use of reason.

Averroes was well aware of the problems relating to this procedure. The masses must not be disturbed from the security of their simple faith. Demonstration, in his view, 'ought not to be expressed [even] to the dialectical class, let alone to the masses',[50] an idea perhaps reinforced from his study of Plato, since Averroes in his study of the *Republic* pointed out that '. . . lying tales are necessary for the education of the citizens. There is no lawgiver who does not employ fictitious tales, because this is necessary for the masses if they are to attain happiness.'[51] Mindful of the dangers to society in general, and to scholarship in particular, Averroes counselled then, in *On the Harmony*, that although there is a need to preserve the mental tranquillity of those of 'His servants who have no access to demonstration on account of their natures, habits or lack of facilities for education',[52] this is no argument for withholding the free use of reason from the highest class.[53] Highly intelligent, educated men, virtually a guardian class, are indeed capable of exercising reason, but since they alone have the facility, it is pointless attempting to explain the operation of reason to those inferior in the intellectual scale. For Averroes, then, reason is the supreme means to faith, it gives validity to the experiences of life and the doctrines of revelation. Truth is unitary.[54] Although it is doubtful that *On the Harmony* influenced Christian thinkers directly, since there are only two surviving Arabic manuscripts, *c.* 1234–5 and *c.*

1323–4, and no Latin ones,[55] it certainly formed the basis on which Averroes developed his mature thought.

Following his belief in the efficacy of reason to determine the truth of faith given in *On the Harmony*, Averroes developed the theme at considerable length in his *magnum opus*, which was, at the same time, an attack upon al-Ghazali's *Incoherence of Philosophy*. Averroes, with a fine sense of contempt, entitled his rebuttal the *Incoherence of the Incoherence* (*Tahafut al Tahafut*).[56] This celebrated work is an exhaustive examination of the Ash'arite position of al-Ghazali, closely argued through seventeen discussions, and most likely written in 1180, the year following the composition of *On the Harmony*.[57] Beginning with the eternity of the world, and dealing in turn with the nature of god and metaphysical assertions on god's relationship to the universe, it concludes with a discussion on the logical necessity between cause and effect, the nature of the soul and of the after-life. Of its vast number of far-ranging inquiries, it is the Seventeenth Discussion, *About the Natural Sciences*, that contains Averroes' doctrines on the nature of truth and the role of reason that were to figure so prominently in the disputes of the following century. Al-Ghazali's *Incoherence of Philosophy* is badly organized; the crucial argument on causality he left until last instead of disposing of it first and using its propositions as a point of departure. Averroes, consequently, had a relatively easy task. Generally he employed the arguments of Aristotle, and Averroes' ability to reproduce skilfully the teachings of Aristotle is an outstanding feature of the *Incoherence of the Incoherence*.

The basis of the refutation of al-Ghazali's occasionalism is a simple appeal to the evidence of the senses. Averroes asserted the necessity of a fixed order in the universe. He wrote:

> For it is self-evident that things have essences and attributes which determine the special functions of each thing and through which the essences and names of things are differentiated. If a thing had not its specific nature, it would not have a special name nor a definition, and all things would be one – indeed, not even one; for it might be asked whether this one has one special act or one special passivity or not, and if it had a special act, then there would indeed exist special acts proceeding from special natures, but if it had no single special act, then the one would not be one. But if the nature of oneness is denied, the nature of being is denied, and the consequence of the denial of being is nothingness.[58]

As this passage reveals, Averroes used the evidence of verbal signification and predication to support his argument. Indeed, as he stated in another context, in *On the Harmony*, he suspected that the whole Ash'arite position stemmed from verbal difficulties, that the dispute between conservative Ash'arites (*Mutakallimun*) and rationalist philosophers was 'almost resolvable into a disagreement about naming, especially in the case of certain of the ancients'.[59]

Averroes developed in the *Incoherence of the Incoherence* the Aristotelian position, set out in the *Physics*, that the universe itself is structured of individual objects in whose essences reality inheres, bound to each other in a simple cause-and-effect relationship – 'it is self-evident that all events have four causes, agent, form, matter, and end, and that they are necessary for the existence of the effects'.[60] The crucial step is the next one: the relationship of man to that order of existence. In his view the function of the intellect is to understand the nature of reality:

> Now intelligence is nothing but the perception of things with their causes, and in this it distinguishes itself from all the other faculties of apprehension, and he who denies causes must deny the intellect. Logic implies the existence of causes and effects, and knowledge of these effects can only be rendered perfect through knowledge of their causes. Denial of cause implies the denial of knowledge, and denial of knowledge implies that nothing in this world can really be known, and that what is supposed to be known is nothing but opinion, that neither proof nor definition exist, and that the essential attributes which compose definitions are void. The man who denies the necessity of any item of knowledge must admit that even this, his own affirmation, is not necessary knowledge.[61]

Two further arguments stemmed from this: the nature of the intellect and the nature of the world so conceived. These two complete the general outline of Averroes' position.

The world itself is composed of real objects, subject to demonstrable laws: that much Averroes asserted through appeal to the evidence of the senses, and the operation of the intellect upon that evidence. A further problem remained, one that troubled all medieval theologians, Christian as well as Moslem: does the world have a determinable origin? Al-Ghazali, representing the Ash'arite position, believed, albeit insecurely, that the world had a finite creation, as a consequence of the act of god, as creator. That belief, in effect, was necessary to sustain occasionalist metaphysics, which held, even further, that the universe is sustained by continuous acts of divine creation. Yet it laid him open to rationalist attack. If god by definition is perfect, and therefore self-sufficient, then why indeed did he need to create the world? The question is a hard one to answer, and Averroes sustained his attacks throughout the First Discussion of the *Incoherence of the Incoherence*. Yet Averroes himself became caught in a difficulty: if there were no creation *ex nihilo*, then the universe must have existed externally, and if that were so god would be reduced to a virtually impotent role, difficult to define. The argument came from Aristotle, who attempted to solve the problem by suggesting that there can be an eternal order of events which at the same time had a First Cause. Aristotle never solved the contradiction adequately; neither did Averroes.[62] In general, however, Averroes came down on the side of an excessive emphasis on logical, causative determinism.

Similarly, Averroes found difficulty in deciding precisely how man is related to the world. His emphasis on the cause-and-effect structure of the world and knowledge of it, contained in a logically arranged system of verbal predication, puts a premium on man's cognitive powers. Knowledge, he argued – as Aristotle did in *On the Soul* – is one with its object. For this kind of position, mind is a necessary intermediary and the problem of how mind operates needs to be explicated.

Aristotle has suggested a dual aspect of mind or intellect: that it has a receptive or passive function, and a responsive or active function.[63] The intellect for Aristotle is an individual possession, each man being his own judge of events. Yet since the external world has an independent reality, then separate subjective experiences of the same object will be similar, if not identical. In that way, common experience and agreement are made possible. That doctrine was seized upon by later commentators and fused with the Neoplatonic concepts of a transcendent intellect and the Augustinian notion of divine illumination. Plotinus, in particular, in the third century suggested a hierarchy of intelligences reaching down from the One to man, of which the closest to man were angels, or active intelligences. It was they who offered a source for the reception of knowledge. Aristotle taught that the human mind is a writing-tablet [*to grammateion*] on which experience is written.[64] Augustine believed that god's act of illumination gives meaning to human experience. In both views, man's mind in the first instance is purely receptive; the transformation of knowledge into meaning and therefore the stimulus to action, is external to him.

Moslem theologians in their early centuries of activity absorbed all of those notions and in the writings of Avicenna there appeared the concept of a single active intelligence, external to man, enlivening his consciousness.[65] That was the position taken by Averroes, in general, although he gave it a much greater deterministic emphasis. His belief in the absolutely inexorable sequence of cause and effect, and the eternity of the world, led him to see the active intellect not merely outside man, but actually existing itself as a singular force. There was only one active intellect for all men. So, in effect, did he deny free will. In many respects, the teachings of Averroes resembled those of Plotinus. Man as part of a fixed order of existence finds his way by intellection.

Averroes' book was not well received in the Moslem world; in many places it was ignored. Across the Pyrenees in the universities of Christian Europe, however, its teachings received close attention and then violent denunciation. After the appearance of the *Incoherence of the Incoherence* the fortunes of Averroes waned. In 1182 he was appointed court physician to Abu Ya'qub. However the monarch died two years later and was succeeded by his less tolerant son Abu Yusuf (r. 1184–98/9), under whom learning became subjected to greater controls. The Almohads were not favourably disposed to theological speculation of Averroes' kind. In 1194 his teachings were condemned, his books burned and Averroes himself was sent into exile for several years. Between 1196 and 1197 all philosophy was banned in the Almohad kingdom. Subsequently Averroes was recalled when the court found itself unable to dispense entirely with his skills, but he died shortly after, in 1198.

Maimonides and the defence of intellectual speculation

In the same period that Averroes was defending causation the Jewish rabbi Maimonides was attempting to introduce rational inquiry into Hebrew religious thought. The circumstances prompting their writings were remarkably similar. Neither Islam nor Judaism possessed an authoritative office comparable to the papacy in the Christian church which could regulate religious belief and teachings. Islam had no priesthood at all, Judaism had no rabbinical hierarchy except for the position of *dayan*, leader of each particular Jewish community. Moslem orthodoxy derived, as it still does, from consensus, *ijma*; Judaic belief does likewise. Consensus, in turn, comes from the persuasive power of commentary and exegesis, and it was to exert an influence on the development of Islam that Averroes directed his energies. Above all, he was a devout believer. So, too, was Maimonides, generally regarded by the Judaic world as the greatest Jew since Old Testament times.

Moshe ben Maimon (1135–1204) was born in Córdoba, nine years after the birth there of Averroes. He came from a line of *dayans*, his father was leader or 'judge' of the Jewish community in Córdoba. In 1148, when the fanatical Almohads took that city, the family was forced to flee and for the following twelve years, until 1160, Maimonides' life is obscure. Between 1160 and 1165 the family lived in the Maghreb of North Africa, at Fez, and then migrated to Egypt where Maimonides spent the rest of his life and wrote his important treatises. As early as his sixteenth year, probably in 1151, Maimonides demonstrated his intellectual precocity with the writing of his *Treatise on Logic*. Although a simple study of grammar and formal logic, the work reveals a clear understanding of, and close reliance on, the work of Aristotle. The tenth chapter, for example, suggests that rationality is man's form and intellection is his purpose:

> Rationality we call man's difference, because it divides and differentiates the human species from others, and this rationality, that is, the faculty by which ideas are formed, constitutes the essence of man.[66]

Maimonides retained that attitude all his life and his thoroughgoing acceptance of the Aristotelian philosophy received its mature expression in his great work, *The Guide of the Perplexed (Dalalat al-hairin)*.[67]

Moslem *kalam* and, to an extent, its Christian counterpart, known as scholasticism, were influencing the numerous Jewish communities scattered throughout Europe, North Africa and the Orient. The traditional faith of the Jews, preserved in the Torah and the other books of the Old Testament, had been buttressed by the addition of interpretations and rabbinical decisions dating from as early as A.D. 200 in compilations known separately as the *Mishnah* and the *Gemara* and collectively as the Talmud, itself existing in two recensions, the Palestinian, *c.* A.D. 400 and the Babylonian, *c.* A.D. 500. Yet the Talmud did not remain authoritative; although an exegetical work, it in turn required exegesis, particularly since the Judaic laws were the basic means of preserving the corporate identity of the Jewish communities. Variant interpretations of the Torah and the Talmud, along with the increase in intellectual rationalism brought on by the revival of Aristotelian studies, chiefly from Moslem sources, had led to a perplexity among various Jews. It was for them that Maimonides wrote his various exegetical works, of which eight major ones have survived.[68] His *Guide*, coming between 1185 and 1190 at the end of his active career, represents the consummation of that activity.

In *The Guide of the Perplexed* Maimonides attempted to make faith and philosophy compatible by means of a series of exegetical essays, composed originally in the form of letters to his respected pupil Rabbi Joseph with the express intention that 'truth should be established in your mind according to the proper methods and that certainty should not come by accident'.[69] The project proved a vast one: the *Guide* is a very lengthy detailed work, subdivided in various ways by subsequent editors, but consisting basically of 177 essays. From the outset Maimonides, like Averroes, was aware of the difficulties inherent in his project: it must not disturb the simple faith of the masses. Philosophical thought for them he termed the 'slippery road of religious speculation'; it was mandatory, in his view, to preserve the *status quo*. His concern to maintain simple faith led him to reject Averroes' idea of a middle group of dialectical men. He condemned as mere troublemakers those theologians of moderate attainments who questioned belief without possessing the necessary ability to offer a better solution. Hence the *Guide* was conceived as a work of limited circulation among advanced rabbinical scholars, as well as for those promising students who are seen

> . . . to be perfect in mind and to be formed for that high rank – that is to say, demonstrative speculation and true intellectual inferences. [Such students, moreover,] should be elevated step by step, either by someone who directs [their] attention, or by [themselves], until [they] achieve perfection.[70]

Maimonides' approach to presenting the truth to the elect group marks a profound departure from that being employed by the Christian theologians: his method is one of systematic instruction. The human mind, in his view, grows and develops according to inner patterns, which are evident, and even if not understood clearly should be respected. The ascent to truth is secured by a proper training of the mind. First should come the art of logic, then the mathematical sciences, then the natural sciences, then divine science. By that means the student comes progressively to realize the distinction between knowledge of a thing and the thing in itself.[71] Such realization occurs at the moment when the barrier of language is crossed. Maimonides, like other scholars of his century, was sensitive to the fact that divine matters are necessarily discussed in human language and that truth lies beyond words, although, at the same time, it must somehow be contained in words. Maimonides saw god as being simultaneously intellect, cognizing object and cognizing subject: that is, the sum of all existence. Knowledge of god, then, comes from an understanding of his operations, in part by analogy with the natural sciences which yield cause-and-effect relationships. By such means he argued that god stands as the unmoved mover of the universe.[72] Like Averroes,

Maimonides answered the occasionalist position by asserting that such a metaphysics divests everything of any constant powers and thereby prevents any kind of knowledge whatsoever. Knowledge must proceed, he argued, from predication; we have knowledge only to the extent that we can make statements and assertions that retain their fixity. Like Aristotle, he too saw knowledge as one with its object.

Causality was affirmed by Maimonides, and even divine knowledge was asserted to come by the posterior method: by reasoning from effect to cause and by accepting the validity of the evidence of the senses. Maimonides followed Aristotle closely, and at many points he was in agreement with Averroes. Despite the fact that Maimonides and Averroes were contemporaries, and were addressing their works to a similar audience, there is no conclusive evidence that either influenced the other, although the close agreement of their doctrines at points suggests some influence.[73] The importance of Maimonides' work, like Averroes', is that it affirmed the senses and the workings of human reason and that it provided for man's knowledge of god by proof *a posteriori*. The data of revelation and the momentous act of faith can be secured by man's intellect. For both Moslem and Jew, that was seen as a step towards validating religion to the highest possible degree.

Maimonides' works were not seen in that light. Again, in a remarkable parallel to the fate of Averroes' *Incoherence of the Incoherence*, the *Guide* was not well received. It was translated from the Arabic into Hebrew[74] by Samuel Ibn Tibbon, a contemporary of Maimonides, and distributed widely, particularly among the Jews of southern Europe. For many Jews the *Guide*'s doctrines were heretical, the book stimulated controversy, and in time prompted many exegetical commentaries. Maimonides himself died in 1204; the dispute over the *Guide*, particularly on the question of whether the study of philosophy endangered the faith of young students, remained active. The Jewish community at Montpellier, in the south of France, was outraged by the *Guide* to the extent that it sought the assistance of the Christian church in having it banned and burned in the public square in 1233.[75] None the less, that proscription did not stop the ideas of the *Guide* from spreading. Like Averroes' works, it was taken up in the universities by scholars who studied it eagerly, using its arguments to support the investigations many of them were pursuing. Those first decades of the thirteenth century were alive with ideas, not only from Moslem and Jewish sources. The eagerness of the Christian church to burn the *Guide* came from its concern to extirpate heresy wherever it was to be found. For heresy was rampant within Christianity as well, particularly in southern France, where challenges to the church began appearing contemporaneously with the active periods of the writing of Averroes and Maimonides.

Heresy in Europe

Waldensian and Albigensian heresies 1170–1226

Late in the twelfth century appeared two major heresies which had developed as reactions to earlier abuses within the church. Papal aspirations to temporal power, displayed so openly in the ponitificates of the great medieval popes, Gregory VII (r. 1073–85) and Innocent III (r.1198–1216), along with the growth of the church into a strongly bureaucratic and visibly luxurious oligarchy, stimulated criticism. Earlier in the twelfth century that protest had been symbolized by the acceptable Cistercian movement brought to a state of high development by Bernard of Clairvaux; later in the same century, since the abuses in the church continued, protest developed in movements that began as pious reform and ended as social revolts. Two such movements, known as the Waldensian and Albigensian heresies, were especially prominent. The former grew from the reforming efforts of the Lyon merchant Peter Valdès, or Waldo (d. 1217), who, around 1170, in his public speeches urged the church to return to its original simple purposes of which the obvious symbol should be material poverty. The Albigensian heresy, which was far more serious, grew in the same period also in southern France, chiefly in the cathedral city of Albi where its predominantly working-class members secured support from the counts of Toulouse. Its general doctrines were drawn from oriental mystery religions, chiefly gnostic and Manichee, of the early Christian era; the heresy itself took the title of Catharism (Greek *katharos*, purity). Basically, the Albigenses followed a version of the teachings of the third-century-A.D. Persian fanatic Manichaeus (or Manes) who taught that the world is divided between the eternal forces of good and evil. Every man, the Albigenses asserted, has within him both good and evil, in their counterparts of spirit and matter. Man's task is to practise as extreme an ascetic mode of life as possible – since matter is inherently evil – and to promote the life of the spirit which can hopefully return to heaven because of such a purifying regime. The austerity of the Albigenses was often in marked contrast with the lax lives of many of the clergy, and because of their reforming zeal and opposition to orthodox Catholic doctrine and papal authority, the Albigenses were seen as a threat that could not be countenanced.

Accordingly the church moved against the heresies, at first by means of persuasion, beginning in the last years of the twelfth century. When that method failed, and threats of coercion had no effect either, conflict ensued. Open hostility erupted in 1208 when the papal legate Peter de Castelnau was assassinated by a supporter of Count Raymond of Toulouse. Innocent III seized the opportunity to use force and, despite the protests of King Philip of France, ordered a crusade. In a vast and notorious expedition lasting throughout the years 1209–15, and in a lesser campaign in 1223–6, the south of France was devastated, the Waldensians and Albigensians subdued ruthlessly. Remnants escaped to several inaccessible locations, in the Pyrenees and in northern Italy, where some descendants of the Waldensians survive to this day. Catharism was eliminated as a threat to Catholicism.[76]

Yet those heresies were harbingers of further conflict to come. By the end of the twelfth century Europe was on the eve of major changes in its intellectual life and educational attitudes. The writings of Christian scholars, notably John of Salisbury, and of such non-Christians as Averroes and Maimonides, became increasingly influential. The close study of their work in the thirteenth century was to stimulate violent conflict. The controversy that arose was pursued in the new institution of the university which, in the meantime, had emerged as a society of scholars, independent to a large extent of both pope and emperor, and determined to pursue knowledge regardless of the demands of orthodoxy or the dangers of heresy.

CHAPTER 4

Emergence of the University

Transition from cathedral schools

The task of providing a wider secular education in the eleventh and twelfth centuries had been taken up by the cathedral schools, which, from their embryonic forms in the sixth and seventh centuries, had expanded rapidly to accommodate the needs of learning and scholarship in the period of intellectual and economic activity after the European revival of the tenth century. As the twelfth century progressed into its later decades, concern with the classification and content of studies, with a view to increasing their relevance to human affairs, had become a greater pre-occupation of scholars in the cathedral schools. In that period some of those schools began to assume a more corporate character and in the relatively short period of a century they developed into the new institution of the university, or *studium generale* as it was first called, which emerged to meet the overwhelming need to provide for the training of lawyers, schoolmasters and clerics to fill the ranks of the increasingly sophisticated administrations of both church and state.

The cathedral schools, for their part, had never been conceived as fulfilling this kind of role. They were not independent institutions; rather, each was ancillary to its own cathedral, and they exhibited a diversity of standards which was to be expected where interpretations of their functions differed so widely. It seems to have been generally in the face of widespread worldliness and laxity that abbots and bishops laboured to encourage learning. Fulbert at Chartres, for example, as one of a few such dedicated bishops, was conspicuous through his efforts, but even at Chartres, despite the enormous advances made by prominent scholars, the general level of educational attainments appears to have been much more modest. Orderic Vitalis records that Fulbert's school taught boys the skills of 'reading aloud, singing, writing and all other studies necessary for the servants of God who seek true knowledge'.[1] Confirmation of the paucity of schools and masters for this period is found in the autobiography of Guibert de Nogent (c. 1053–1121/4) who became, in his mature years, abbot of the monastery at Nogent-sous-Coucy. Writing of his own education in the third quarter of the eleventh century he states:

> When I was set to learning, I had indeed already touched the rudiments, yet I could scarce put together the simplest elements when my loving mother, eager for my teaching, purposed to set me to grammar. There had been a little before, and there still reigned partly in my time, so great a scarcity of grammarians, that scarce any could be found in the towns, and few indeed in the cities.[2]

At the same time, there is, for England, a tantalizingly vague reference to the existence of schools in Winchester (*super scholis Wintoniae*) in a letter written around the period 1154–9 and sent by Archbishop Theobald to the pope, most likely Adrian IV. This letter, composed by John of Salisbury as secretary, reported a dispute between two rival masters, Jordan Fantosme and John Joichel, concerning jurisdiction over the 'schools of Winchester'. There are five separate references to schools in the document, one of which refers explicitly to the schools of the city which John was alleged to have seized in breach of some earlier promise: 'ciuitate sibi scolas usurpasse'.[3] Unfortunately, the letter is all too brief and no really helpful details of the schools are given. Certainly the existence of two rival masters seems unusual although they could be explained as two members of the same cathedral competing for the post of *magister scholarum*. None the less the continued use of the plural is interesting; it is not likely to refer to an 'inner' and an 'outer' school since these were few and restricted to monasteries; a more likely inference is that the word refers to a single institution with two divisions, elementary and grammar, and both apparently taught by the same master. At least we can be certain that such a school was in existence in Winchester, obviously of some merit, and this

4　Arabian library, miniature by al-Watisi, 1237.

5   Scenes of student life in the thirteenth century, south door of Notre Dame, Paris.

could be a reasonable indication of the prevailing position in Europe: schools, perhaps with two major divisions, were in existence, and some were flourishing, in the important cathedral centres. In the more out of the way locations, however, in many cathedrals the schools remained quite rudimentary, offering instruction in the barest elements of literacy; in some sees, how many it is impossible to determine, such schools were not set up until the thirteenth century. The need to provide schools on a wider and more systematic basis, however, was explicitly recognized by Pope Alexander III. As a result of the Third Lateran Council of 1179 which met primarily to deal with the problem of papal authority and elections – and the schism introduced by the antipope Callixtus III – Canon 18 of the Council's Decree required every cathedral to provide a school for clerics:

> The Church of God, like a pious mother, is obliged to care for the welfare of the body and the soul. Therefore, lest the poor whose parents cannot contribute to their support lack the opportunity to study and to improve, each cathedral church should provide a benefice large enough to cover the needs of a master who would teach the clergy of the respective church and, without payment, poor scholars as well. . . . Nobody should take money for the grant of the *licentia docendi* [the licence to teach] nor request anything from the teachers (as was the custom before), nor should a qualified applicant be denied the licence for teaching.[4]

These provisions, apparently, were not implemented, and as late as 1215 Innocent III in General Council issued a decretal requiring every cathedral to maintain a grammar school in addition to a master of theology. Since a prior instruction in this respect (Canon 18 of Lateran III *Decretum*) had not been observed in many churches,

> [Therefore] we, confirming the statute aforesaid, add that not only in every cathedral church, but also in others whose means shall be sufficient, a fit master shall be established to be elected by the prelate and chapter or the greater and wiser part of the chapter, to instruct the clerks of the church and others freely in the faculty of grammar after his ability.[5]

University origins: Paris, Salerno, Bologna

Some cathedrals, of course, had established schools before the end of the tenth century, a few of which rapidly became famous for their scholarship. Yet those celebrated schools – Chartres, Paris, Reims, Laôn, Liège, Orléans – had no firm institutional basis for their procedures. The quality and content of their instruction depended very much on individual

CATHEDRAL SCHOOLS AND EARLY UNIVERSITIES

masters, studies themselves were not graded into any particular sequence, and there was no formal way by which students could attest their achievements. A teacher such as Abelard was able to attract students by force of his reputation; wherever he moved he could conduct a school and secure a following. Abelard's success, of course, stemmed in like fashion from his superiority in disputing with his own masters, Roscelin and William of

Champeaux. In a constricted academic society such methods apparently worked well enough. As Europe grew in both gross population[6] and social complexity, however, it became necessary for the cathedral schools to operate according to more regular procedures, and the first indications of that movement can be discerned in the twelfth century.

The pattern of organization was taken from the medieval craft guilds. By steps now entirely obscure schoolmasters in some cathedrals followed the craft practice and organized themselves into guilds – the term in medieval Latin was *universitates* (sing. *universitas*). Their intention probably was to regularize their instruction and to ensure maintenance of adequate standards on the part of students seeking admission to the society of masters. The first cathedral school to so organize itself is not now known, although one of the earliest was Notre-Dame, and among the cathedral schools in the course of the twelfth century it became pre-eminent as a teaching guild or *universitas*. Already distinguished by the work of earlier scholars, including William of Champeaux and Peter Abelard, the school of Paris emerged as a prototype of the university and during the thirteenth century it became the model for numerous other foundations.

In this respect, however, Paris has no undisputed claim to primacy; in Italy at the same time emerged two other significant institutions of higher learning, a medical school at Salerno and a law school at Bologna. Documentation for Salerno is largely lacking; it seems to have appeared some time in the tenth century as a school of medicine. Orderic Vitalis has a clear reference to its fame in the mid-eleventh century. He tells us of a certain Ralph, who, about the year 1059,

> . . . had been a passionate student of letters from an early age and had visited the schools of Gaul and Italy to pursue his investigations into the mysteries of things. He was very learned in grammar and dialectic, astronomy and music; and so skilled in medicine [*medicina*] that in the city of Salerno, which is the ancient seat of the best medical schools, no one could equal him except one very learned woman.[7]

And this woman, about whom nothing else is known, seems to have been legendary. Regardless, Salerno remained solely a medical school and did not gain official state recognition until 1231. Throughout the twelfth and thirteenth centuries its reputation for medical studies was considerable; however, by the end of the fourteenth century Salerno declined and its influence ceased.[8]

Bologna, on the other hand, prospered as a school of law. Its origins likewise are obscure; it seems to have gained its reputation during the tenth century and to have become established as an institution in the twelfth. In contrast to Paris with its single guild of masters, two guilds came into existence at Bologna, one of students and another of masters. Although details are lacking, it seems that the student guild was organized some time around 1193 and the *collegium* of masters by 1215.[9] In turn the student guilds proliferated further into sub-guilds according to nationalities in residence, and became known exclusively as *universitates*. The masters' guilds, by contrast, were known as *collegia*, although the *universitates* enjoyed a markedly superior position and even came to exercise a quasi-totalitarian control over the masters.

By the end of the twelfth century, then, an entirely new institution of learning had come into existence in two cities, Paris and Bologna, each exhibiting a different form of organization. Paris reflected its cathedral school origins and became the centre for philosophical and theological studies; Bologna, the main legal centre in Western Europe, was stimulated by the social forces in commercial Italy that led students to seek appropriate professional training. In the thirteenth century it was Paris that became the locale of the most drastic developments in education, the results of which were to influence the direction of much European intellectual life.

Paris: *studium generale* in the thirteenth century

Growth of a corporate character

In Paris the university was never officially founded; it simply grew, almost imperceptibly, out of its cathedral school. Yet its growth was greater than that of other cathedral schools, stimulated perhaps by the favourable location of the city and the fact that it was the royal capital. At Chartres, by contrast, only fifty miles from Paris, the school that had been so eminent in the eleventh century never developed into a university, and instead declined into a grammar school. Although the cathedral school of Paris enjoyed a successful reputation at the beginning of the twelfth century which was enhanced further with the teaching of Abelard, the date of the organization of its masters into a *universitas* is unknown. The first reasonably certain reference is to the period around 1170–5; it is possible that the guild was formed somewhat earlier, perhaps by 1150.[10] Students became attracted to it in greater numbers and from the year 1180 comes the first record of the foundation of a rudimentary form of college, the Collège de Dix-huit.[11] By the beginning of the thirteenth century the *studium* at Paris was established firmly although it had not yet elaborated its constitution to any wide extent.

The term *universitas* referred only to the guild, and, in the case of Paris, this was one of masters: *universitas magistrorum Parisiensis*. Some time in the twelfth century the institution itself acquired the title of *studium generale*, literally a place of study accepting students from all regions.[12] Only later, in the fifteenth century, did *universitas* become a synonym for *studium generale* with the latter term falling into disuse.[13] The terms *studium generale* and *universitas*, moreover, as they came to be used in Italy as well as northern Europe, did not imply any claim to teach all knowledge: Salerno offered medicine alone; Bologna, it would appear, originally taught only law although it may also have offered liberal arts. Paris likewise began with the liberal arts, chiefly the trivium, although three other studies became established there subsequently, theology, canon law (the latter known also as *decretals*), and medicine to which the first reference occurs in rules of the medical faculty about 1270–4.[14] The term *faculty* (Med. L. *facultas*, strength, power, ability to do) appears around this time, representing the various subject divisions of the guild, that is, arts, theology, law and medicine. Increasingly the word faculty, although referring strictly to the studies themselves, came to replace *guild*, and so to represent the groups of scholars in each subject.

As the new institution extended its responsibility it became apparent that custom alone was an inadequate basis on which to establish the corporate authority of the *studium generale*. Society was organized according to much more formal relationships which gave a defined legal status to its various institutions, and the growing university at Paris soon found itself forced to seek official recognition in the form of a grant of legal rights. Following a riot in 1200 between students and an armed group of citizens led by the provost of the city, King Philip Augustus issued the university a charter securing students' rights to well-defined processes of law in the event of further disturbances.[15] At the same time, the appearance of what amounted to an autonomous society of clerics led the church also to become concerned with the operations of the university. Already, as early as 1170–2, the pope had intervened in Paris on behalf of student rights;[16] in 1215 the cardinal legate, Robert de Courçon, presented to the university a series of papal prescriptions concerning the qualifications of masters, their authority over students, the content of instruction and the methods of lecturing.[17]

In 1231 came the first important papal recognition, amounting virtually to a charter. The occasion prompting it was another disturbance between town and gown, occurring some years earlier at the Christmas celebrations of 1228. In that event, however, the provost was ordered by the Queen of France herself to take action against the students with the result that they found themselves unable to gain the redress promised by the royal charter of the year 1200. After unsatisfactory negotiations the masters of arts dissolved the university in the 'Great Dispersion' of 1229, many of them migrating to other *studia generalia*, including Oxford in England. Masters of theology, however, who were all members of religious orders, refused to disband. They remained, and so laid the basis for continuing friction between the two faculties of arts and theology. In 1231, in a move to restore the university, Pope Gregory IX promulgated the bull *Parens scientiarum* ('Mother of Sciences') which regulated far more explicitly the operations of the university and thereby bestowed papal protection on it. By that bull, the following provisions were made:

> Every chancellor of Paris to be named henceforth shall swear in the presence of the bishop or by his mandate in the Paris chapter, to which shall be summoned and present two masters on behalf of the university of scholars. He shall swear in good faith on his conscience, at the time and place according to the state of the city and honour and respect of the faculties, that he will not bestow the licentiate to teach theology or decretals [canon law] except to the worthy nor admit the unworthy, ratifications by persons and nations being abolished . . . The masters, moreover of theology and decretals, when they begin to lecture, shall publicly take oath that they will furnish faithful testimony on the aforesaid points. The chancellor shall also swear that he will in no wise reveal the advice of the masters to their hurt. Maintaining in their integrity the Parisian rules, liberty and law which obtain in incepting [the final process of demonstrating teaching skill in seeking the master's licence].

The bull then regulated various aspects of the social life of the university – funerals, rental for lodgings, imprisonment, summer vacations and the lectures of masters. It ended with the papal injunction

> . . . that henceforth the privileges shall be shown to the masters and scholars by our dearest son in Christ, the illustrious king of France, and fines inflicted on their malefactors so that they may lawfully study at Paris without any further delay or return of infamy or irregularity of notation. To no man then

be it licit to infringe or with rash daring to contradict this page of our provision, constitution and inhibition.[18]

By this charter the university of Paris secured explicit papal approval,
and found itself bound equally in return. Throughout the thirteenth
century, and decreasingly in the centuries that followed, the papacy sought
to maintain a firm control over Paris, and, by precedent, over all other
universities as well.

As the thirteenth century progressed, the university of Paris developed
a more sophisticated corporate character, coming to regulate a large
number of the various aspects of academic life. Official regulations dealt
with such relatively procedural matters as classroom rentals, the control
of booksellers, the prices of books and the sale of parchment, in addition
to decisions relating to the content of studies, and standards of student
competency required for the licence to teach. The surviving evidence
gives the impression of a considerable preoccupation with material
concerns, and reflects the obvious need for establishing rapidly a systematic
basis by which the newly emerged institution could operate. At the same
time there was, of course, a growing enthusiasm for learning, and masters
and students became concerned with the increasingly exciting intellectual
life of the times.

Student organization: residential colleges

Although Paris never developed as powerful a student corporation as the
universitas at Bologna, a system did emerge that provided some counter-
balance to the society of masters. Student organization at Paris first
appeared in congregations that came together for lodging, or on the model
of the Collège de Dix-huit which was designed for poor clerks. Other
hospices were founded throughout the thirteenth century of which that
endowed about 1257 by Robert de Sorbon (1201–74) for graduate masters
in arts studying in theology has remained the most celebrated. The need
for residences sprang from a variety of motives. Students were attracted
from all over Europe and stood in need of some measure of social security
since, in the faculty of arts, they were quite young, often finishing grammar
school around their fourteenth year and proceeding immediately to the
university. For such young boys there was an obvious need for supervision. In part, too, the foreign students seem to have been victimized by
townspeople, the records referring particularly to excessive rental charges

by landlords. As well there was apparently a rapid growth in the actual number of students, reinforced by those known as *vagantes* or *goliardi*, who moved to the new institutions, many of them concerned more with the social excitement of town-life than with the pursuit of learning.[19] Although these aspects of early university life have been romanticized, and probably given an unduly high proportion of attention, it remains certain none the less that the movement of students to the universities, and from one *studium* to another, was a factor in creating friction with the townspeople. As a consequence the students found it necessary to organize into corporate institutions.

Student organization: the nations

Early in the thirteenth century another form of association was evolved at Paris in addition to the residential colleges: the 'nations'. The exact origins of the nations are not known although it seems that they originated in the *studium* of Bologna, which was developing at the same time, and were copied by the students of Paris.[20] Unfortunately, much of the early documentation for Bologna is now lost and the first historically certain reference to nations comes from an injunction of Pope Honorius III in the year 1222 when he forbade the nations of Paris to seek redress for wrongs done them through the offices of a higher university official.[21]

At this point, however, it is necessary to explain more fully the notion of a 'student'. At Paris – and Bologna too – the students were not a homogeneous group. On the contrary, they came from all parts of Europe and varied widely in age and attainments. The youngest students were undergraduates studying for a first degree, necessarily in arts, which was the lineal descendant of the *artes liberales* which had been transmitted from antiquity down through the cathedral schools. By this time, however, studies had become further sophisticated and complex and had separated into four distinct areas: the liberal arts, and the three 'higher' studies of theology, law and medicine, so considered because they built upon a prior foundation of knowledge in the liberal arts. At Paris, by the early thirteenth century, four corresponding guilds of masters had developed and for entry to each of these the appropriate master's degree was necessary. At the lowest level was the undergraduate in arts who, upon graduation as a master of arts, was enabled to study in one of the three advanced faculties. The 'students', then, in the higher faculties were at the same time masters in arts. These older students were the most active in university affairs; since they were at the same time both the teachers of the under-graduates, and the students of the senior masters, they were generally subject to the greatest pressures. So they organized themselves to protect their own interests, and, by extension, those of the younger under-graduates who had no formal organizations for similar purposes.

In the years immediately following Honorius' injunction of 1222, students won for themselves the right to organize in defence of their interests, and by 1249 four distinct groupings had appeared, known as the French, Norman, Picard and English nations, so called, apparently, because their membership was drawn from each of those broadly dis-tinguishable regions. The French nation was composed of students from Paris and southern Europe generally; the Norman, those from Normandy, Brittany and other places west of Paris; the Picard, those from areas north of Paris, generally the Low Countries; the English, those from Britain, Scandinavia, Germany and the Slavic east.[22] Membership of the nations, in addition to the masters in arts, may possibly have included the under-graduates in arts.

As the nations of the relatively younger masters in arts assumed dis-tinctive identities they frequently clashed, not only with the three senior guilds of masters and with the chancellor, who exercised the power of granting degrees, but also with each other. In fact, the four nations seem to have been in a state of constant mutual enmity, helping to give student life at medieval Paris a distinctly zestful, even bellicose, flavour. The nations assumed such a corporate identity that they became the objects of the students' prior loyalty. Along with that development, it is equally clear that as the nations grew in strength they accepted the responsibility such power entailed. From their early, defensive beginnings the nations at Paris became, in the fourteenth and early fifteenth centuries, the chief agencies by which the academic work of the university proceeded. They secured the right to a large measure of self-government including the election of their own officers and chief administrator, the procurator, later shortened to the familiar *proctor*. Perhaps an even more important function than self-discipline was that of maintaining the schools of instruction themselves. These had begun to leave the precincts of the cathedral of Notre-Dame on the Île de la Cité even in Abelard's time, partly on account of his influence, and to become established across the Petit Pont on the left bank of the Seine. In that Latin quarter, so called for the language of scholarship employed there, the nations established their lecture halls. The less populous faculties had their centres elsewhere in Paris: theology at the Collège de Sorbon, law in the Clos Brunel. Medicine has not been identified with a particular location. By the end of the thirteenth century nearly all of the lectures in arts were held along the Rue du Fouarre (Street of Straw).[23]

Master's degree in arts: studies and methods

The first *universitas* to be established at Paris was a guild of artists, as its members were known. Following established traditions the liberal arts remained the basis of instruction, and became the required core of studies. All undergraduates had to enter the faculty of arts first, in many cases around their fourteenth year and directly from the grammar school, which itself was frequently established in a boarding school (*paedagogium*) attached to the university.[24] Since the thirteenth century was one of development, with little guiding precedent, it is not possible to describe a programme of studies that had any continuity in that century; on the contrary, the thirteenth century, the first for which documents exist on curriculum, was marked by a gradual expansion of studies, and, predictably, by constant conflict on the desirability of doing so. The first clear evidence of a curriculum in arts is the papal prescription of 1215, presented by the cardinal legate Robert de Courçon, which required the student to hear lectures (*lectiones*) on the old and new logic of Aristotle, the grammars of Priscian and Donatus, and Aristotle's *Topics*, along with something from the quadrivium. Expressly forbidden were the highly contentious books of Aristotle on metaphysics and natural philosophy and the books of certain heretics. Some regulation of lectures was given in the bull of 1231, *Parens scientiarum*, which reads:

> We further order that masters of arts always give one ordinary reading of Priscian and one afterwards, and those books on nature which were prohibited in provincial council for certain cause they shall not use at Paris until these shall have been examined and purged from all suspicion of errors.[25]

By 1255 the studies seem to have settled down reasonably, for in a document of that year the texts required for exposition by the masters in arts were listed. Along with those set in 1215, the list includes the works of Aristotle that earlier had been the subject of tremendous controversy – *Physics, Metaphysics, On the Soul* – with precise instructions about the time to be allotted to the various parts. This attempt at strengthening the liberal arts with the addition of Aristotle – the trivium with the new logic, the quadrivium with the physical and metaphysical works – indicates the changes that were occurring in thirteenth-century learning. Not that these introductions were achieved smoothly; on the contrary, the expansion of the university curriculum to include Aristotle was resisted bitterly by some groups, and this resistance, known as the Scholastic Controversy, became the most crucial intellectual event in Western scholarship up to that time.

The usual means by which teaching proceeded in the universities was the *lectio* method (lecturing) which consisted in the reading of, and commentary on, standard authors, and was accompanied by debate of varying degrees of formality. As early as the tenth century legal scholars had used the technique of *pro et contra* whereby the range of divergent opinions on matters of dispute was organized into categories, for and against specific propositions. That method received skilful application in the writings of the great canonist Ivo, bishop of Chartres (*c.* 1040–1116), whose monumental *Collection tripartita* had a major impact on the development of canon law, and in the equally influential work of Peter Abelard, particularly in his *Sic et non* which became the model for later writers and teachers. Argumentation and dispute became standardized methods, and by the middle of the thirteenth century at Paris, as in all other universities, these were used almost exclusively. In this period, debates were given a definite form and were known as *quaestiones disputatae*. Every two weeks a disputed question was set by a master and at the end of the fortnight, after students had examined the issues through the marshalling of arguments for and against, the master attempted to resolve the issue, or to *determine* it, in the manner of a judge, by weighing the relative merits of the arguments and the convincingness of the proofs. Some of those questions for disputation were tremendously significant, involving the finest minds of the universities; the issues could be profound, as in the case of those set by the celebrated scholar, Matthew of Aquasparta (1234/40-1302). His *quaestiones disputatae* include the following:

Question 1
The question is, whether for the knowledge of a thing the existence of the thing itself is required or whether that which is not can be the object of the understanding.

Question 2
In the second place it is inquired whether whatever is known certainly in intellectual knowledge, is known in the eternal reasons or in the light of the first truth.[26]

In its most advanced form this *quaestio* method became a feature of the magisterial life of the university. Twice a year, at Christmas and Easter, the masters themselves assembled for great debates, or *quaestiones quodlibetales* (Latin *quodlibet*, whatsoever you wish), held before large student assemblies. Those questions were intended to trace issues to their ultimate conclusions, and by the later decades of the thirteenth century, and the first few of the fourteenth, they had come to encompass the most fundamental problems of religious faith, and to attract the attention of the leading scholars of Western Christendom. When debated by masters like Thomas Aquinas, the method reached its most rigorous and incisive application and all learned Europe attended closely to the argument, using it in turn for further exhaustive inquiries. The thirteenth-century masters, in their use of the *quaestio* method, had outgrown the limitations of earlier approaches to learning. The simpler procedures of Carolingian and early feudal times, based on the study of prescriptive and authoritative texts, such as those of Cassiodorus, Isidore and Hrabanus Maurus, were inadequate.

Master's degree in arts: admission to the guild

When the student had completed his programme of studies he was ready for the first ceremony of graduation. Courçon's prescription of 1215 required the student to have reached twenty-one years of age and to have completed at least six years of studies; a subsequent regulation of 1252 required a 'bachelor coming up for the licentiate in arts at Paris [to] be twenty years old or at least in his twentieth year, and of honorable life and laudable conversation'.[27] The completion of this first formal stage of higher education was given significance by a ceremony of disputation or debate which became known as *determination*. Some time in the thirteenth century that stage was marked also by the student's right to the term *bachelor*, although the etymology of the word is extremely obscure and usage varied considerably in different studia.[28] After two years of lecturing, and apparently continued study under a master, the bachelor was then advanced, subject to securing the necessary approvals, to preliminary candidature for the master's degree, the first step of which was the conferring of the licence by the chancellor. In an elaborate ceremony, of marked ecclesiastical character, the bachelor was invested as a *licentiate*, which status gave him the right to seek admission to the master's guild. After a further period of lecturing, perhaps six months,[29] in which time the licentiate was given scope to demonstrate his scholarship, he reached the final stage, known as *inception*, which was marked by an even grander ceremony than that for the licence. The incepting master, as the advancing licentiate was termed, was formally admitted to the guild in the presence of its members. After the relevant religious solemnities the newly elected master gave his inaugural lecture, was invested with the symbols of achievement – the master's cap (*biretta*) and book – after which he took his seat on a magisterial chair with his fellows.[30]

Inception carried with it the coveted teaching credential which was in essence a papal sanction, *jus ubique docendi*, literally the privilege of teaching everywhere, although Paris and Bologna did not seek specific papal recognition of their right to confer the *jus ubique docendi* until 1291. Their ancient authority, they believed, was sufficient. All later universities, however, felt the need to secure such explicit authorization and generally, whether north or south of the Alps, they looked to the pope for this privilege. At times emperors and minor princes attempted to grant charters and so legitimize the various universities' rights to confer the *jus*, but such secular charters were generally unsuccessful in the first few centuries of university foundation.[31]

The Paris system of three grades – bachelor, licentiate, master – became formalized and copied in most other universities; the ceremonies involved in moving through the grades became fixed also in the practices of graduation and the awarding of degrees. The master's degree was the highest, but in other faculties two synonyms were used interchangeably with it, professor and doctor, the latter deriving from *doctus*, past participle of *doceo*, the Latin verb to teach.

The liberal arts, then, were the required core of studies. All undergraduates entered this faculty first and only after graduating as master of arts could they proceed, if they wished and if circumstances allowed, to one of the three higher faculties of theology, law or medicine. Not all scholars graduated in arts, and only a minority progressed to the other faculties. Statistics for this period are not available; none the less, the intellectual demands on students, and the rigorous methods of lecturing, disputing and examining used by the masters, must have operated as a selective device that allowed only the most competent to succeed.[32] Certainly the bulk of undergraduates never proceeded beyond the bachelor's degree; it is indeed doubtful if even the majority reached this stage. Those that failed to graduate, or did so without distinction, often found for themselves positions as schoolmasters; there was little that could be done to prevent them.[33] Entry to the higher faculties was difficult; graduation in them was even more demanding, in terms of the surviving evidence.

Higher studies: theology, law, medicine

Theology was the leading study at Paris. Scriptural exegesis, of course, had been a major preoccupation of Christian scholars since the second century A.D., and over the years the sacred writings had accumulated a vast ancillary literature. First to appear was the patristic corpus, but this, however, was of limited value because the Bible itself was not readily available in an authentic version. This was why the famous Latin Vulgate recension prepared under the direction of Alcuin was so significant; scholars came into possession of a standard, purified text. As this Vulgate became studied in the monastic and cathedral schools it was, naturally, the subject of commentary and criticism, which ranged from the simplest observations on matters of grammar and syntax, through problems of translation and exposition, to the weightiest issues of doctrinal interpretation. This study of the Bible, known in the cathedral school era as *sacra pagina*, led to quite an extensive literature of commentary which was usually incorporated on the pages of the Bible, either as marginal comments or in the form of interlinear interpolations. By the twelfth century these comments, or glosses (Gk. *glossa*, a tongue, and hence a commentary), had grown so numerous that some scholars began the process of abstracting them into separate collections. The first important one of these was that produced by Anselm of Laôn in the eleventh century and known as the *Glossa ordinaria*.

This was part of a widespread quickening of interest in theology which was stimulated even further by the work of Peter Abelard, and the subsequent efforts of his former student, Peter Lombard, who compiled the most authoritative and comprehensive of all the glosses. Peter Lombard (c. 1100–1160/4) was born near Novara in Lombardy, and studied successively at Bologna, Reims and Paris, ending his days as bishop of Paris. During his tenure as master at Notre-Dame in Paris he composed a great gloss, known in its day as the *Magna glosatura*, this being the widely celebrated *Four Books of Sentences (Sententiarum liber quattuor)*.[34] Peter drew together materials from a large number of sources, Greek as well as Latin, including the writings of his teacher Abelard and other contemporaries. Notable among these was the obscure Bolognese monk Gratian (d. c. 1179) who had compiled a vast and systematic collection of legal texts from patristic writings, conciliar degrees and papal pronouncements, known as the *Concordantia discordantium decretum* (*Concordance of Discordant Canons*), or, more familiarly, *Decretum Gratiani*, which appeared around 1150. Peter Lombard's *Sentences*, as its name indicates, was written in four parts which deal, respectively, with the trinity, god and his attributes; creation and angelology; salvation through the incarnation; and the sacraments. Its method also shows a significant development, for, instead of being simply a compilation of existing glosses, the *Sentences* proceed by posing a problem or position (*quaestio*) – for example, *On knowledge of the Creator through creatures, in whom the trace of the Trinity appears*[35] – and then discussing it, dialectically, by citing the arguments for and against from various authoritative sources.

Peter Lombard's text became the basis of the increasing interest in theology, and as part of the same general activity of biblical studies theologians began to compile concordances which were basically alphabetical arrangements of the key words of the Bible along with their textual locations. Further glosses consequently came to be written and assembled as independent texts, known as *postills*.[36] So, by the end of the thirteenth century, biblical scholars had developed an important set of apparatus to assist their studies: a standard text of the Bible (the Vulgate), concordances, and collections of *glossae* and *postillae*.[37] Moreover, the glosses too ceased to be mere additional commentaries; following the influence of Peter Lombard they came to include further exegetical questions (*quaestiones*). This, meantime, generated further studies which sought to gather together variant readings and to determine the correct text of the Bible in places where it had become corrupted; these emendations were known, accordingly, as *correctoria*. A major consequence of this was the production in the thirteenth century by the University of Paris of yet another attempt at a definitive version – unfortunately defective – of the Vulgate, known as the Paris Bible, the *Exemplar Parisiense*. By this time the use of the term *sacra pagina* to refer to biblical studies was discarded and replaced by either *biblia* or *scriptura*.[38]

As a parallel development to these biblical studies, chiefly in order to regularize their practices, some time in the late twelfth century theologians at Paris began to organize themselves as a separate guild. Early in the thirteenth century their corporate identity was established, and in 1207, in fact, they were the subject of a papal decree limiting their total membership at Paris to eight,[39] which was, however, not observed. The following year, the same pope, Innocent III, sent a bull to Paris complaining of irregularities in faculty behaviour, the incipit of which is addressed 'To all Doctors of Theology, Canon Law and Liberal Arts of Paris'.[40] In 1215, Robert de Courçon issued a statute concerning the theologians which reads: ' . . . concerning the theologians no one shall lecture at Paris before he is thirty-five years old, and not unless he has studied at least eight years, and has heard the books faithfully and in the schools. He is to listen in theology for five years, before he reads his own lectures in public.'[41] Then, in 1219, Pope Honorius III moved to make theology the major concern of Paris. In his bull he stated that 'we desire to spread the study of theology in order . . . to surround the Catholic faith by an unconquerable wall of warriors'.[42] The expansion of theology, however, involved prohibiting the study of civil law, which, probably stimulated by the work at Bologna, was gaining a following at Paris. Canon law, Honorius argued, would handle any legal problem that would be likely to develop. The bull ends with the injunction that 'we herewith firmly prohibit the teaching of civil law in the city of Paris and its environs'. The penalty for disobedience was excommunication. This sentiment was reinforced in the famous *Parens scientiarum* of 1231 which, although aimed primarily at enforcing a ban on the study of some of Aristotle's works, also enjoined masters and scholars in theology not to become philosophers, but to become god's learned, to avoid using the vernacular, and to dispute in Latin on 'those questions only which can be settled by theological works and the treatises of the holy fathers'.[43]

Theology, by the mid-thirteenth century, became a well-ordered faculty, following its own clearly defined procedures. The focus of its interest was on the study of histories, sentences, biblical text and glosses,[44] given by lecturers known as *biblici* and *sententiarii*. The *biblicus* lectured on the Bible, the *sententiarius* on the commentaries and glosses, but chiefly on Lombard's *Four Books of Sentences*. Indeed around 1267 the English Franciscan friar, Roger Bacon, objected that commentaries had gained preference over biblical texts:

> One manual of a master [he complained] is given preference to the text [of the Bible] in the Faculty of Theology; this is the *Book of Sentences* which is the glory of the theologians and [which is so weighty] that it takes a horse to carry it. And the man who has lectured on it dreams that he is already a master of theology, though he has not heard lectures on one-thirteenth of the Bible.[45]

So popular was the study of the *Sentences*, Bacon lamented in the same document, that the *biblicus* 'goes begging for an hour to lecture, just as it pleases the lecturer of *Sentences*'. Knowledge of the *Sentences*, indeed, became the basis for the licence, and for inception towards the master's degree.[46]

The faculty of law had been restricted in its growth by Honorius III's prohibition of 1219 which limited its studies to canon law. There is a paucity of evidence for the law faculty at Paris. Generally the procedures followed those for theology, and in place of Lombard's *Sentences* the lawyers used Gratian's *Concordantia discordantium decretum*. Between 1230 and 1234 this text, the *Decretum Gratiani*, along with a supplement consisting of the decretals of Pope Gregory IX (r. 1227–41) – which this pope had charged Raymond of Penafort with collecting – became the text of the church's canon law, *Corpus juris canonici*. In the faculty of law, however, the student was trained with the procedures necessary for the solution of specific cases, in contrast to the universal issues that occupied the artists and theologians. 'Canonical science', the lawyer Augustinus wrote, 'is a sort of practical theology.'[47] Its concerns, he stated, are with positive cases allowing a legal solution, by the method of human judgement. Since canon law put a premium on such specific activities, Augustinus added:

> I think it would be a far-sighted ordinance if the master qualified to teach theology should be required after lecturing on the *Sentences* to teach the book of the Decretals, in order that he might become more familiar with and experienced in those things which are necessary for counselling the salvation of souls.[48]

Medicine, like law, is not well documented for the thirteenth century at Paris. *Parens scientiarum* of 1231 mentions 'medical men' but only in passing; it does not regulate them as it does the artists and theologians. Explicit regulations were first promulgated some time between 1270 and 1274, and followed the procedures already established for arts and theology (and presumably law); that is, attainment first of the bachelor's degree in medicine, followed by the licence to incept for final admission to the guild. The total course in medicine required at least five and a half years of attendance at lectures, based upon the following studies:

> He should have heard twice, in ordinary lectures, the art of medicine [*Ars medica* of Galen] and once cursorily, except the *Liber urinarum* of Theophilus, which is enough to have heard once ordinarily or cursorily; the *Viaticum* [of Abu Djafar Ahmad] twice in ordinary lectures, the other books of Isaac once in ordinary, twice cursorily, except the *Particular Diets* [*Liber dietarum particularium*] which is sufficient to have heard cursorily or ordinarily; the

Antidotes of Nicholas [*Antidotarium Nicholai*] once. The *Verses* of Egidius [of Paris, *c.* 1200] are not required. Also he should have read one book of theory and one of practice. And to this he should swear; if, moreover, anyone is convicted of perjury or lying, he can be refused the licenciate.[49]

The decree does not specify the exact periods to be spent in the separate stages of bachelor and licenciate, although it seems from the text that three and a half to four years were required for the baccalaureate, the remaining years as licenciate and for inception towards the master's degree. Admission to the guild also required some tests of character, and specifically the professing of Christianity – a decree of 1271 restrained Jews, surgeons and pharmacists from practising as physicians.[50]

The study of physical medicine depended entirely on the same methods as those used in the other faculties, and the exclusion of surgeons and pharmacists emphasizes this aspect. Surgery and pharmacy themselves were organized into appropriate guilds, however, and the restriction could possibly have been a much simpler matter of agreement between competing guilds. At the same time, the medical masters were in the superior position, their guild was pre-eminent and they could dictate to the lesser ones, especially since this very decree points out that surgery and pharmacy were in a less-developed state than was the craft of the physician. Indeed, surgery was not taught at all; in this period there was little anatomy performed, and that little was on animals, often pigs, never on humans. Pharmacy was often in the hands of charlatans. The superiority of the physicians was, in fact, well founded: they possessed a considerable body of well-organized, time-hallowed knowledge, derived, like so much other learning, from the ancient classical world, through Arab and Jewish intermediaries. And it was amenable to the standard methods of presentation. The medical teachings of the time, moreover, were never expected to conform to any pragmatic tests of effectiveness. Such an attitude held little place in the learning of the day. The exposition of, and commentary on, such earlier authorities as Galen and Avicenna were the proper academic procedures.

The *studium* at Bologna

Origins of the studium: *the study of law*

While Paris was developing as a *studium generale* with a major strength in theology, Bologna became equally noteworthy for its teaching of law and associated legal studies. As in the case of Paris, it is not possible to say precisely when the *studium* at Bologna came into existence. It is generally believed that the schools of northern Italy never went out of existence during the feudal period, and it is highly probable that in Bologna, and in comparable Italian cities, the municipal foundations of Roman times continued in operation[51] and that the new *studium* was simply an expansion of one of these, stimulated by the more vigorous economic and commercial circumstances of the twelfth century. Bologna has, of course, a very favourable location in the plain of Lombardy; it is at the crossroads of highways coming from Naples, Rome and Florence in the south, Venice in the east, Milan and the further territories of France and Spain in the west. Data for the twelfth century, however, are few indeed. As early as 1119 there are references to the learned scholars of Bologna in the phrase *Bononia docta*[52] and as well to the study of law by master Gratian (d. *c.* 1179). We have only the barest details of this scholar, chiefly to the effect that he was a Camaldolese or Benedictine monk attached to the monastery of St Felix in Bologna. The early thirteenth-century *Chronicle* of Burchard of Ursberg mentions that

> . . . at this time master Gratian brought together in one work the canons and decrees that had been scattered in various books; he added to them authoritative statements of the holy fathers, organizing his work according to convenient topics in a fairly reasonable manner.[53]

This was, apparently, the famous *Concordance of Discordant Canons*, or the *Decretum Gratiani*, of *c.* 1140–50. Burchard's text suggests this period to be around 1133 but it seems most likely that the true date was after 1140 since the *Decretum Gratiani* includes decisions of Lateran II made in 1139.[54] This work consists of two sections: an outline of church law drawn from patristic texts, and conciliar and papal decrees; and a second part dealing with legal cases or *causae*, subdivided into *quaestiones* and treated in the same style as *Sic et non*. The *Decretum Gratiani* came to be glossed by a number of twelfth- and thirteenth-century canonists and, in concert with the corpus of papal decretals, became the basis of the church's canon law, the *Corpus juris canonici*.

The *Chronicle* of Burchard goes on to record:

At the same time master Wernerius [or Irnerius] revived the law books which had been neglected for a long time. Nor had anyone studied them. He did so at the request of the Countess Mathilda [of Tuscany]. He arranged them in the same order in which they had been arranged by the Emperor Justinian interpolating a few words in some places. Among these books were the *Institutes* [*Instituta*] by the above mentioned emperor; they serve as a primer and an introduction into civil law; also the edicts of the praetors and curulian aediles which bestow a solid systematic order upon the whole civil law and which are included in the book of the *Pandects* or *Digest*. To this he added the *Codex* containing the statutes of the emperors. The fourth book is that of the *Authentics* [*Autenticorum*] which the above mentioned Justinian added as a supplement and a correction to imperial law.[55]

This legal scholar Guarnerius (*fl.* early twelfth century) – Wernerius and Irnerius are variant spellings of his name – seems to have been a native of Bologna and apparently established a law school which provided a basis from which the *studium* of Bologna developed. The law books of Justinian mentioned in Burchard's *Chronicle* had always been the legal code of the Roman Empire, consisting originally of statute laws (*leges*), senate decrees (*senatus consulta*) and the decisions of Roman jurists who had the task of examining and determining the legal force of the statutes and decrees. In the sixth century the Emperor Justinian had attempted to bring order back to this corpus which had become enormously disorganized during the preceding centuries. He empowered several commissions to do this task, and between 529 and 534 they issued a much-pruned and updated law code. The body of statute law was brought out in ten volumes in 529 as the *Codex constitutionem* and revised in 534 into twelve books as the *Codex repetitae praelectionis*; the decisions of the jurists were issued in fifty books as the *Digest* (*Digesta*) and known also as the *Pandects*. These were accompanied by a textbook known as the *Institutes* and a volume of additions to the *Code* called the *Novels*. Collectively, these four parts were the complete body of civil laws: the *Corpus juris civilis*. In the regions of the empire that had been overrun by the barbarians much of the *Code* had lapsed and been supplanted by local codes; in the settled, highly civilized regions of the Roman Empire, however, the *Code* remained in operation, although with the passage of time it acquired a further body of commentary and became yet further reorganized: the body of statutes itself was separated into the *Codex* (Books I–IX) and the *Tres Libri* (Books X–XII); the *Digest* had been divided into the three sections of the *Digestum vetus*, the *Infortiatum* and the *Digestum novum*, while the *Institutes* and *Novels* remained the same although the latter were now known as the *Authenticum*.[56]

Up to the eleventh century the commentaries added to the *Code* were generally anonymous and of a grammatical or syntactical nature; it was from the efforts of Guarnerius and his students that law became the subject of a serious renewed scholarly concern. Guarnerius turned first to the fifty-volume *Digest*, giving it an interlinear gloss. These *glossae* functioned in exactly the same manner as they did in biblical studies: as explanations, elucidations, corrections, commentaries, variant readings, and so on, to the text itself. Writing the glosses was, in fact, the standard method of studying law in that period, and to do this Guarnerius drew chiefly from four basic sources of authority: the Bible, Aristotle, Boethius and other glossators, but not Roman legal scholars who were considered only as sources for study, never as authorities. By this process the *Corpus juris civilis* was carefully redacted and subjected to a thoroughgoing scrutiny. The glosses, moreover, served a number of important functions in the teaching of law: they served as notes for the orally presented *lecturae*, as materials for written texts or *summae*, and as commentaries by which future scholars could continue studies of the legal text.[57]

Following the stimulus of Guarnerius, the Bolognese school of law continued to develop and under his students the technique of glossing progressed steadily. In time – by about the mid-thirteenth century – the entire *Corpus juris civilis* became glossed juristically at Bologna and the glosses themselves were drawn together into independent texts or *apparatus*. These numerous *apparatus* were in turn brought together into one great systematic compilation, the *Glossa ordinaria*, by Accursius the Glossator (d. 1263). This large text became the standard work, recognized by all of the law schools, chiefly because it was a comprehensive, virtually complete compilation. It became the basic text for the study of law and survives in numerous manuscripts; the printed editions, published between 1468 and 1627, are in five large folio-sized volumes.[58] The school of law initiated at Bologna by Guarnerius early in the twelfth century and sustained in sequence by Bulgarus (d. 1166), Placentinus (d. 1192), Johannes Bassianus and his pupil Azo (d. 1220) reached a high point in the work of Accursius; collectively they were responsible for the recovery and systematic study of the second branch of law, the civil or *Corpus juris civilis*. In the twelfth century, then, two bodies of law, civil and canon, were in circulation and in constant process of being subjected to careful academic scrutiny.

Growth of a corporate character

It was against this background of legal studies that the *studium* at Bologna began to develop its corporate character. The study of law met a real need in the period and students soon became attracted there. Like Paris, Bologna, it seems, developed into a *studium* by custom – *ex consuetudine* – rather than by an explicitly formal foundation. The earliest document that points in this latter direction is the *Privilegium scholasticum* issued by Frederick Barbarossa at the Diet of Roncaglia in 1158. Whereas in France most *literati* were in some form of holy orders, in Italy there was a large number of scholars and students whose occupations were civil in character and who, consequently, were without the customary protection or 'benefit of clergy' afforded to all clerics – which generally meant, in practice, that the latter were subject only to ecclesiastical jurisdiction. By the provisions of the *Privilegium scholasticum*, or *Authentica habita* as it is more usually called, Frederick I extended imperial protection to all persons travelling into or out of Italy for purposes of study. It has been conjectured that this *privilegium* was granted by Frederick I to reward the jurists of the emerging *studium* at Bologna for assisting him in his claims to imperial authority,[59] but this must have been only part of the total situation. Certainly the document does not restrict the various *privilegia* to Bologna ('non solum competunt scolaribus legum, et canonum, et theologiae'), but extends them to all Italian centres of study and to all subjects, even grammar ('sed etiam scolaribus cuiuscunque facultatis, etiam si grammaticae studeant').[60] This suggests that a number of incipient *studia* were in existence in Italy in the mid-twelfth century.

The *Authentica habita* is the first recorded evidence of privilege being accorded to students. As they settled in Bologna – and doubtlessly else-where – the students organized themselves in support of their own interests. Moreover, the students of law were generally of mature age and, by virtue of their studies, were highly sensitive to their legal situation. By the end of the twelfth century they had won from the city concessions in housing rights which guaranteed security of tenure against avaricious landlords, and freedom from municipal taxes, particularly those which had been levied on textbooks. Arguing against such imposts, the thirteenth-century professor of law, Odofredus, submitted that 'no customs dues should be exacted for the books of students, because such dues are levied on goods to be sold, and no decent student would ever dream of selling his textbooks'.[61] This would have been substantially true since these law texts, having been studied and further glossed in the lectures, would be the very books which the student, once graduated as master, would need for the daily exercise of his profession.

It appears that it was under such circumstances that the mature students at Bologna began the process of banding together for mutual assistance and protection, and out of this the organization of the 'nations' seems to have been born. Although the earliest extant documents relating to nations are those for Paris, there are indications that they originated at Bologna and that they were later adopted by the Paris *studium*.[62] Unfortunately all of the university statutes of Bologna for the first half of the thirteenth century, up to 1253, have been lost, and it is consequently difficult to document the development of the *studium* as fully as we would like. At first it appears that four nations were set up, representing the major regions from whence students came, and these were the Lombard, Tuscan, Roman and Ultramontane nations, the last group being collectively all non-Italians from beyond the Alps. These four, however, later became consolidated into two: the 'foreigners' remained the Ultramontane nation – which was subdivided further – while the Italians merged together as the Cismontane (literally, 'this side of the mountain'). Once organized in this way – some time, it appears, in the early thirteenth century – the students were enabled to confront both their masters and the Commune of Bologna itself, both of whom had manœuvred themselves into positions of strength *vis-à-vis* the students.

The need for confrontation had been generated out of the unusual political situation of Bologna itself. Unlike Paris, which was a royal city and the seat of the Capetian house, Bologna was an independent city-state or commune, with authority vested in a council of six hundred, the Credenza, and exercised by a lord mayor, Il Podestà. The Italian communes were all engaged in the continued precarious exercise of playing off the rival powers of emperor and pope against each other and maintaining their own independence at the same time. Consequently, with the emergence of the *studium*, the Commune of Bologna was in a quandary: on the one hand it recognized that the *studium* was a very valuable institution, one well worth cultivating and nourishing; on the other, in a relatively small city-state it would be virtually suicidal to allow the *studium* to grow in corporate strength to the point where it could usurp the functions of the Commune, particularly since the students sought to elect their own rectors of the nations, and to give their allegiance to the latter bodies rather than to the Commune. The masters of law – *universitas magistrorum*

Bononiensis – presented no problem. They were all Bolognese citizens, and indeed this was a condition for membership of their guild in the twelfth century; they were, moreover, granted *ex officio* membership of the Credenza. Early in the thirteenth century the obviously inherent difficulties of this situation erupted. The students for their part had come to study law, and clearly their overwhelming goal was membership of the masters' guild and the conferment of the *licentia docendi*, which, of course, was denied them. The Commune, however, was not prepared to grant citizenship to students, even though in 1216 it required them to swear an oath of allegiance to the city instead of to their nations. The only final recourse open to the students was to leave, and, in a year of mounting tension during which the Commune passed decrees prohibiting them from leaving, the students vacated the city, encouraged by Pope Honorius III who on 27 May 1217 supported their right to depart. The *studium* ceased to exist for the ensuing three years, 1217–20. During this phase of the 'Great Dispersion' many students continued their studies in other cities, where the communes were often only too glad to have them, and so new *studia* began to appear on the Bolognese model. Meanwhile the Podestà of Bologna tried energetically to secure the return of the students and in 1220 important concessions were offered to them. The *studium* resumed operations but not with any stability. Relations with the Commune remained tense and a further complicating element appeared: this was the desire of Frederick II to found an imperial university in his newly chosen capital of Naples. In 1225 he ordered the *studium* to move to his capital, which they refused to do, and only after resistance by the students and successful intercession by Honorius III did Frederick withdraw his edict.[63]

Throughout all of these tribulations the students gradually gained the upper hand. They were conscious of their value to the city and became increasingly adept at gaining what advantage they could from the circumstances of the time and place. Rights and privileges relating to residence, food prices, rentals and taxes were secured by decrees, and the students eventually won exemption from civil taxes and military service. With these measures they were maintaining a favoured status granted to scholars as early as the reign of the Caesars and confirmed in the early fourth century under Constantine I who expressly provided for their freedom from *munera municipalia* in the *Corpus juris civilis*.[64] This was the effect of a decree enacted in 1243 by the Commune of Bologna which exempted doctors and scholars forthwith from military service.[65] The most important concessions won, however, were those granting the students the right to organize their own *universitates*, to elect their own rectors, and to have a major controlling interest in the conduct of the *studium*. One of the terms of return from the Great Dispersion of 1217–20 was the acceptance by the masters – the *universitas magistrorum* or, as it became, the *collegium doctorum* – of the authority of the rectors of the student nations, and the recognition of the latter as independent *universitates*. In effect, the student 'universities' now became the controlling bodies, and, since the masters had to defer to their authority, the students gained the right to appoint their own teachers. One major final power, however, always remained with the *collegium doctorum*: the right to examine and admit new members to its guild. The papacy, meantime, had become deeply involved in the affairs of the *studium* and in 1219 Honorius was able to assert a measure of ecclesiastical control by requiring, as a further condition of admission to the guild of doctors of laws (canon and civil: *in utroque jure*), the approval of the archdeacon of Bologna. There is, in fact, the strong possibility that this intervention by the church in the form of granting approval for the *licentia docendi* stimulated the further foundation of schools, since its approval would have given a prestige that otherwise would have been difficult to acquire.[66]

Throughout the thirteenth century the *studium* of Bologna continued to develop its character as a result of the interplay among the several forces of Commune, papacy, *collegium doctorum* and the *universitates*, and although the city fathers were concerned to maintain a harmonious atmosphere for studies, the history of Bologna, always a richly interwoven pattern of events, was generally one of continued struggle by the students to sustain their rights and privileges. At times the *studium* came into conflict with the papacy which was very vigorous throughout the thirteenth century in gaining as much control as possible over the emerging universities. In Paris, the church was concerned to censor the curriculum in the liberal arts and to maintain its supremacy in theology; at Bologna, its desire was to retain control over the matters of law, particularly the *Corpus juris canonici*. In this it was assisted by the Commune, which decreed in 1274 that booksellers, under threat of the enormous fine of one hundred pounds, were prohibited from selling 'copies of text books and of commentaries [or alienating] them in any way to *studia* of other cities'.[67] Between 1286 and 1289, and again in 1306–9, the university closed because of discord with the papacy. The church, however, was successful in gradually increasing its control, and this reached a significant stage of development in 1291 when Pope Nicholas IV declared that the gaining of the *licentia docendi* at Bologna in either canon or civil law would also carry the right to teach anywhere, the more highly prized *jus ubique docendi*;[68] this was confirmed in 1309 by Clement IV.[69]

Programme of studies at Bologna

While this complex interplay of forces was moulding the corporate character of the *studium* at Bologna, its studies were developing as a well-organized programme which continued to attract students, generally those of mature age and from families that were sufficiently prosperous to support them. Bologna, however, was quite different from Paris in one important respect: it never taught theology, which instead remained within the province of the monastic schools of the city, and it did not admit medicine until relatively late, at the end of the thirteenth century. Its chief claim to importance was in the study and teaching of law, and with this was associated the teaching of the liberal arts, although these were interpreted and approached in a manner quite different from that prevailing at Paris. Now Bologna too required a preliminary study in arts as a prerequisite for acceptance as a law student, but it is not as clear as it is for Paris how this operated.[70] Bologna's *studium* was renowned for its teaching of the liberal arts as early as the time of Gratian and Guarnerius, and by then they had already acquired their eminently practical character. While at Paris the liberal arts were seen and treated as propaedeutic to the study of theology, at Bologna, as they were preparatory to the study of law and may possibly have been the stimulus from which law developed, the arts were regarded as utilitarian subjects.[71] Consequently, it was the trivium that received emphasis, particularly grammar and rhetoric, both of pronounced utility as legal preliminaries. In addition there developed a uniquely Italian study which was a manifestation of the practicality of rhetoric – a kind of 'applied' rhetoric – known as *ars dictaminis*: the art of written compositions, generally in epistolary form.

The stimulus to this kind of practical development came from the overwhelmingly commercial basis on which Italian civic life was built. Moreover, the traditions of ancient Roman educational theory and practice had never totally disappeared; Bologna, it would seem, was but one of a number of *studia* which survived from earlier centuries, and there are some reasonably strong indications that several cities – perhaps Pavia, Verona, Vicenza, Florence, Siena and Padua – possessed schools of the liberal arts around the year 1200 and that they were not, as has often been conjectured, offshoots of Bologna.[72] Nevertheless, Bologna was definitely the senior *studium* in northern Italy and all other schools deferred to it, apparently following its lead. Unfortunately, there is very little data on how the liberal arts were taught in the twelfth or early thirteenth century. In that period we infer that the regular procedures followed those set down by Cicero and Quintilian and that the studies were generally those of the conventional rhetoric course. The first pronounced change originated in the teaching of Boncompagno da Signa who taught at Bologna in the first decades of the thirteenth century.

This master, literally named the 'good-companion', as he states in his *Rhetorica novissima*, was born in the Castello da Signa Franca, seven miles from Florence. In 1215 he lectured on the old style of classical rhetoric, *Rhetorica antiqua*, 'in the presence of all the professors of canon and civil law, and other doctors, and a numerous multitude of scholars' at Bologna where it was forthwith 'approved and crowned with laurel'. Boncompagno read this same *Rhetoric* at Padua in 1226. Subsequently he moved to Venice and there began to compose what he called 'an entirely new rhetoric'; this, issued as the *Rhetorica novissima*, was read at Bologna in 1235 'in the presence of the venerable Father Henry, Bishop of Bologna, Master Tancred, archdeacon and chancellor [and] the chapter and clergy of Bologna [when] it was found worthy of the glorious honour of being solemnly recited in the cathedral'.[73] The motivation for this work, Boncompagno continues in the Proem to the *Rhetorica novissima*, was threefold. In the first instance was Boethius' stricture that 'the rhetoric of the ancients consists in precepts alone without common utility'; the second, 'that students in both laws could get little or no aid from the discipline of the liberal arts except from public speaking'; the third, that the traditional rhetoric of Cicero 'is condemned by the judgement of students since it is never the subject of ordinary lectures'.[74] For these reasons, and because he believed Cicero was mistaken in basing rhetoric and its application on a belief in 'honourable causes' of origin, Boncompagno wrote his rhetoric – the eighth liberal art as he called it – to meet these objections and to make rhetoric eminently practical as a sound preliminary training for the notaries, jurists, clerks, assessors and similar occupations that the communes, chanceries and commercial offices of Italy needed in large numbers.

Boncompagno's disclaimer of Cicero – or Tullius as he is more commonly referred to in this period – is itself a piece of heightened rhetoric;

he did not reject Cicero but simply put a greater stress on the practicality of rhetoric in the composition of letters or *dictamen*.[75] Behind this study of *ars dictaminis* was a firm foundation laid in the standard manuals, particularly Cicero's *De inventione* and the pseudo-Ciceronian *Rhetorica ad Herennium*; indeed, there were continued appeals to classical authority by the masters of this subject. Magister Bono da Lucca (d. 1279) asserted that the *artes dictaminis* 'drew everything from the source of Marcus Tullius Cicero',[76] and in the same period the well-known Brunetto Latini advanced as authority the fact that 'Cicero said that the most noble part of the knowledge of government is rhetoric, which is the science of speaking'.[77] It is noteworthy that Latini's statement is in *volgare*, the Italian vernacular. The study of *ars dictaminis*, from the stimulus of Boncompagno, had not only developed a practical stress, but also moved towards a vernacular application. In the late thirteenth and early fourteenth centuries manuals of the *artes dictaminis* began to appear in *volgare* translations, including the *Rhetorica ad Herennium*, and notaries were tested on their knowledge of the vernacular for admission to their guild.[78]

Just what the relationships between the 'liberal arts' and *artes dictaminis* were is not entirely clear for the early part of the thirteenth century. It seems that at first they were fused in the same general programme and only drew apart later in the century as the eminent masters – Boncompagno da Signa, Mino da Colle di Val d'Elsa, Guido da Fava, Bono da Lucca, Brunetto Latini – developed the latter into an independent study. The liberal arts appear to have remained, or perhaps became downgraded, as a school curriculum of grammar, rhetoric and dialectic similar to that given in the French cathedral schools and taught, not in the *studium* itself but in private, independent schools about the city, the standards of which were monitored by the *studium*.[79] At the examinations for the baccalaureate – the degree which recognized completion of the arts course – the ceremony of inception was held before a convocation, or *conventus*, of the *studium*, and supervised by the jurists themselves who had the ultimate power of approval. During the course of the thirteenth century, quasi-legal studies, which depended greatly on the *artes dictaminis*, were organized as a separate independent faculty known as *ars notaria*.

Faculties, operating on the same general principles as those at Paris, seem also to have developed in the thirteenth century at Bologna, and consisted of the 'undergraduate' liberal arts, and the three 'graduate' faculties of law, *ars notaria* and, later, medicine. In 1278 there is mention of a Faculty of Sciences (*Facoltà delle scienze*) at the *studium* of Siena which seems to have been modelled on Bologna.[80] Generally, however, the main emphasis in academic organization was determined by the admission requirements for the three professional guilds, and of these we remain best informed about procedures in the study of law. In the year 1250 the master Petrus Peregrossi, a former student of Odofredus, set out the procedures he would follow in the teaching of the *Corpus juris civilis*. He begins the Proem with the advice that he is following the standard method of both 'ancient and modern doctors':

> First I will give you summaries of each title before I proceed to the text; second, I shall give you as clear and explicit a statement as I can of the purport of each law (included in the title); third, I shall read the text with a view to correcting it; fourth, I shall briefly repeat the contents of the law; fifth, I shall solve apparent contradictions, adding any general principles of law . . . and any distinctions or subtle or useful problems [*quaestiones*] arising out of the law with their solutions – as far as the Divine Providence shall enable me.[81]

Moreover, Petrus adds, difficult passages would be given further evening repetitions, and twice yearly, at Christmas and Easter, he offers to dispute *quaestiones quodlibetales*. Included in his Proem is a schedule: the *Old Digest* (*Digestum vetus*) would be commenced by early October and finished by the following August; the *Code* would be lectured on in the same period.[82]

Doubtless this exactitude stems from the professor's concern to organize his teaching effectively; it may also have been a consequence of the considerable pressure that the students were able to bring to bear. Indeed, by the end of the thirteenth century they had secured firm control over the methods of teaching. In the Statutes of the *Collegium doctorum* for the early fourteenth century this ascendancy is clearly evident. Every year, for instance, the rectors of the nations were required to appoint altogether 'four suitable scholars from each of the schools of civil and canon law, two Ultramontanes and two Cismontanes, of clerical status', who were charged with the task, under oath, of denouncing to the rectors, any teacher who had not met the lecture schedule, or had been late for classes, or had not carried out his disputations efficiently. Moreover, if the rectors failed to appoint and supervise this commission they in turn would be subject to a fine of twenty *solidi*.[83] The lecturing schedule, in fact, had become very stringently regulated. Each doctor of laws was to be in the school before the bell of St Peter's finished ringing for the end of a morning mass and straightway afterwards must commence lecturing – under pain of a nine *solidi* fine. Moreover he was not to go past the finishing bell, nor to omit any particular glosses from his treatment; in fact, as one statute provides, the university decreed that

> . . . no doctor should omit from his *punctum* [section to be treated] a single chapter, decretal, law or paragraph. . . . [Moreover] no difficult part of the text is to be left to the end of the lecture [since] by such a delay the treatment of this part might possibly be cut short by the bell ringing out the end of the hour.

The same statute continues to list similar requirements; it even extends to rule that

> . . . no doctor of canon or civil law, be he lecturer in the ordinary or extra-ordinary hours, should absent himself beyond the boundaries of the City of Bologna and stay away so long that students will either lose a lecture or will have to substitute someone else for him.[84]

In these statutes it is clear that the law students attempted to prescribe the conditions of lecturing very minutely, and to make provision for a large number of possible contingencies; at the same time it is equally true that they thereby regulated themselves and imposed an equally exacting discipline upon the student body. How many students attended these lectures, and survived to graduation, is not known; certainly they must have been relatively few. Once the course was completed, however, the rewards were considerable as the formula of the conferring of degrees in laws (*in utroque jure*) indicates. The Rector of the *collegium doctorum* would receive each candidate individually and declare:

> Since you have been presented to me as a candidate for examination in the two laws . . . and since you have undergone the difficult and rigorous examination and proved yourself to be a scholar of excellence, this circle of most illustrious and most excellent 'promoters' have judged you worthy of the laurel nobody dissenting. Therefore, by the authority of the archdeacon and the high chancellor of this *studium* which I represent, I make, declare and name you [candidate is named] a doctor in the aforementioned faculties conferring upon you the licence to teach, to ascend the master's chair, to comment, to interpret, to defend and to practise all activities of a doctor here and everywhere, in all countries and places. Moreover, you will enjoy all the privileges which are enjoyed by the fortunate persons who have deserved a position in these blessed Colleges. I hope and wish that all this will contribute to your fame, to the prestige of our Colleges and the glory of God the Almighty and the blessed virgin Mary, patroness of the Colleges.[85]

By the end of the thirteenth century Bologna, like Paris, was a well-established university with a highly developed corporate structure and programme of studies. Both of these *studia generalia* had provided a strong institutional means for the further dissemination of learning, and their examples were emulated in many places in Europe. By the year 1300, in fact, there were as many as twenty-three in operation: eleven in Italy, five in France, four in Spain, two in England, one in Portugal. A century later, a further seven were founded in Italy, four in France, three in Spain and Portugal; and in the later-starting regions of Germany and the Slavic countries, eight had come into existence. The university was henceforth to be the major educational institution throughout the West; for centuries to come it was to dominate all levels of educational activity.

CHAPTER 5

Age of Scholasticism

Beginnings of controversy: dispute over Aristotle

In the latter half of the thirteenth century many of the universities of northern Europe, that is, those dominated by, or owing some degree of allegiance to, the papacy, became involved in a violent academic dispute known as the Scholastic Controversy. The centre of the conflict was Paris although it extended to other universities, including Toulouse, Montpellier and Orléans. The apparent issue was the right of universities – expressed so forthrightly in the Paris document of 1255 – to study the newly discovered and supposedly heretical works by Aristotle, chiefly the treatises on metaphysics and natural philosophy. It has been called the Scholastic Controversy because it was conducted in the schools, by schoolmen, yet it was no irrelevant debate among idle minds: it was the most important intellectual event of the thirteenth century. The issues at stake were considerable: if the Aristotelian natural philosophy were to gain acceptance then the entire metaphysical basis of the church's traditional, Augustinian teachings, and its claims to religious authority, could be challenged. Furthermore, the way would be opened for the development of a completely naturalistic, rational explication of the universe, with obvious danger for the church.

In any event, the papacy needed to secure its links with the University of Paris, and indeed with France itself. Throughout the troubled eleventh and twelfth centuries France, enjoying the stability of Capetian rule, had been a pillar of strength. By the beginning of the thirteenth century, Rome was losing both support and influence in the peninsula of Italy. Frederick II held the kingdom of Sicily, which included not only the island but also the mainland to a point just north of Naples. As a further mark of his independence, Frederick established a university at Naples, granting it the right to confer the *jus ubique docendi*, by royal charter in 1224. To the north of Rome, the Lombard League of independent cities was growing increasingly powerful and indifferent to the church.

An entente with the universities, and especially with Paris, was mandatory. Not only had universities become the major institutions of intellectual life, they were able also to exercise considerable moral authority, and their corporate strength was such that, on occasions, they could influence royal policy. Already on reasonably good terms with Paris, the papacy sought in the early thirteenth century to strengthen its links and gain, thereby, a powerful ally. Securing those bonds, however, was a delicate task. Paris was already manifesting a spirit of independence, and was beginning to appreciate the new-found strength that a guild of intellectuals could exercise. Moreover, it was not of a single voice with respect to scholarly opinions.

The church had to proceed carefully: if it were to gain the much-needed support of Paris and the northern universities generally, it must encourage the conservative elements and at the same time ensure their political dominance. An issue was already at hand: the right of universities themselves to decide to study the contentious books of Aristotle. The intrinsic validity of the intellectual issues themselves was recognized readily by all concerned. The controversy, therefore, was a great tribulation for the church; on its outcome hinged the future of that one great institution that for centuries had sustained civilization in the West.

The mendicant orders: Franciscans and Dominicans

As events happened, the church was not without influence at Paris. The university was nominally subject to the bishop of Paris, and so to the pope, but early in the thirteenth century Rome was not anxious to test that dependence in any serious way. The church's direct influence, in fact, was exercised by the masters in the faculty of theology, who quite early in the thirteenth century set themselves apart as champions of orthodoxy, developing in the process a marked antagonism towards secular clerics in other faculties. In effect, that enmity was directed entirely at the faculty of arts. Although the faculty of theology at first was composed of secular masters, by the time of the Great Dispersion of 1229–31 its membership was made up almost entirely of the members of two new religious orders which were devoted to a militant conception of orthodoxy.

Those two new orders had their origins in the troubled period of the Waldensian and Albigensian heresies in the first years of the thirteenth century. The heresies had not been without consequence and their appearance stimulated a wave of enthusiasm for church reform. Known popularly as the Franciscans and Dominicans from the names of their respective founders, Francis of Assisi and Dominic de Guzman, the two orders, through their devotion to the ideals of austerity and poverty, became heirs to the earlier monastic reforming movements of Cluny and Clairvaux, of 910 and 1098 respectively, both of which were now in eclipse.

Although these two orders were conceived as responses to limited situations and the Dominican was concerned specifically with the Catharist heresies, they expanded their activities rapidly, and came to exercise a profound influence on the direction of church affairs. They became particularly interested in educational matters and in the course of the thirteenth century came to dominate the university of Paris, along with other northern universities, incurring the constant hostility of the secular masters. Both orders took an active part in the Scholastic Controversy and the Dominicans, who made it their own special concern, were at the centre of the dispute.

Priority in foundation cannot be assigned clearly to either order. The early records are obscure, and the only formal criterion of precedence is the year in which their rules were given papal sanction; in that respect the Franciscans were recognized five years earlier. That order was not founded with any particular corporate ambition, but grew from the inspiration provided by Francis of Assisi (1182–1226).[1] Born of a wealthy family in Italy, Francis sought quite young in life to return to the simplicity of early Christianity. He attracted a small band of followers who accepted his ideals of poverty, mendicity and humility, and together they attempted the development of a communal, semi-secluded life. Guided in their daily regimen by the principle of humility, Francis and his followers, in contrast to the elaborate hierarchical structure of the secular church, attempted to live as a brotherhood without any distinction of rank. They designated themselves quite simply as Friars Minor (Latin, *frater*, brother). Soon after beginning their corporate existence the friars accepted a rule written by Francis which was presented to Innocent III in 1209, and which received approval the following year. Although that original rule (*regula prima*) is now lost, it apparently was both short and simple, and its intentions in all likelihood were preserved carefully in two further versions, a second of 1221, and a third in 1223. Of those rules the latter, known technically as the second rule, was a shortened version of the *regula prima* of 1221 and was produced by a group of brothers in consultation with Francis. That second rule of 1223 became the accepted version and formed the basis for elaboration of the order, which grew rapidly in membership.

Emphasis in the order of Friars Minor was upon ascetic practices,[2] their chief concern being the pursuit of personal salvation, for labour was not to be sought specifically; if a friar did perform duties, his reward was to be in the necessities of life, not in money.[3] Following that principle, the rule even dissociated the Minorites from conducting schools or pursuing any of the learned callings; Article 10 expressly commanded that the friars 'should not be concerned even with giving instruction to the unlettered; instead they should direct their efforts to possessing the spirit of God'. The demands of the time, however, were otherwise; clearly the affairs of scholarship and the quickening tempo of intellectual life could not be ignored. The order split, subsequently, into two factions, a fundamentalist group who sought to follow the rule to the letter, known as *spirituals* and, in opposition, a moderate group of *conventuals* who recognized the needs of scholarly accomplishment. As daughter houses were founded, those following the conventual approach conducted schools which gave a complete grounding in the liberal arts comparable to that given in universities at the same time. That feature of Franciscan conventual life remained, and later in the thirteenth century some of the most important figures in the period's scholarship came from their schools, in particular John of Fidanza (1221–74) who became general of the order under the name Bonaventura, and Roger Bacon (1210/14–*c*. 1294) who was one of the most controversial and certainly the most embarrassing member the order ever counted.

In definite contrast to the Franciscans from the beginning was the order founded by Dominic de Guzman (1170–1221).[4] Of noble but obscure Spanish birth, Dominic became an important official of the cathedral at Osma, and it was in that place in the Spanish kingdom of Castile that he first heard of the Albigensian heresies. Then in 1206, as an aide to his bishop Diego who was travelling on a mission to Rome, Dominic became acquainted with the Albigensians while passing through southern France. His contacts with them convinced him of the sincerity of their reforming zeal and of the need for the church to attempt to convert such heretics by persuasion rather than by force. Consequently he founded a new religious society known as the Order of Preachers (*Fratres praedicatores*) whose particular mission was to travel throughout the countryside preaching the tenets of orthodoxy, and by their own example adding support to their precepts.

Dominicans embraced the ideal of poverty, although humility was never a prominent trait. On the contrary, the Order of Preachers developed rapidly as an organization committed to the techniques of eloquence and persuasion, they manifested a marked predilection for theological and other scholarly debates, and in the thirteenth century they became the intellectually militant wing of the church.

The early progress of the Dominicans, like that of the Franciscans, is poorly documented. Apparently they grew slowly in the first few years of their existence; only after receiving papal sanction from Pope Honorius III in 1215 did they gain prominence. The Dominicans founded their own schools which gave instruction in the liberal arts as they were currently available and in the course of the thirteenth century some of those schools became highly respected for the academic quality of their instruction, particularly that at Cologne which attained distinction under the direction of the outstanding scholar Albertus Magnus (Albert the Great, 1206/7–1280). However, these Dominican schools were completely internal in emphasis and conservative in outlook. None of their schools advanced educational thought: intellectual development was centred in the emerging universities. It was in those institutions that the Dominicans were to achieve their intellectual influence, the most conspicuous example being manifested in the genius of their greatest member, Thomas Aquinas.

The first Dominicans reached Paris as early as 1217, and the Franciscans followed a year or two later, although neither order was prominent at first. As the century progressed, however, they came to dominate the life of the two faculties of arts and theology. Between the years 1250 and 1280 they were responsible for the eruption of the Scholastic Controversy and a full-scale confrontation of the two competing doctrines of Augustinian Neoplatonism and Christian Aristotelianism.

The great controversy

Cosmological quest: background to conflict

The Scholastic Controversy had, in fact, been developing throughout the twelfth century, and when it became active around 1250, and reached its climax in 1277, it was the inevitable outcome of several centuries of speculation on the respective merits of the Augustinian and Aristotelian metaphysics. Unlike earlier school disputes, that over Aristotle's teachings was an event unique in the history of Western education. For the first time the issues were sustained by institutional means and were not identified solely with their protagonists. The dispute, in northern Europe, occurred almost entirely within the universities where a greatly augmented methodology was available; techniques of debate and disputation, developed throughout the eleventh and twelfth centuries, were employed by thirteenth-century scholars with great skill.

The range of intellectual concepts in Western thought, moreover, had become enlarged enormously as a result both of internal development and stimulation from the Islamic and Byzantine civilizations. The great revival of learning in the twelfth century was marked by the introduction to the West of the Latin-text *corpus Aristotelicum* along with numerous Arab commentaries on Aristotle and a ready acceptance by some Western scholars of the logical procedures offered by those works. In addition, Islamic influences provided a Western acquaintance with the Moslem method of *kalam*, that is, the use of reason and profane knowledge as aids to understanding problems arising from the study of religious belief. Christian scholars too were attracted to the use of reason as an aid to clarifying issues of faith and revelation, and a Christian counterpart to *kalam* developed, known as Scholasticism.[5] It came as a response to a strongly felt need: that of securing a thoroughgoing explication of the metaphysics of the universe and of man's relationships to it. Stated in an alternative form, it was a need to know conclusively the nature of god, the vocation he had assigned to man and how man could best fulfil that obligation. Such enlightenment had been man's quest since antiquity: intimations had appeared in the Egyptian *Memphite Theology* of more than three thousand years earlier; the search received definite canons of procedure and conceptual categories in the work of the Greek philosophers and was given a specifically religious focus by the early Christians. In the thirteenth century scholars in the universities of northern Europe, and particularly at Paris, committed themselves to achieving a final, and certain, understanding. Every available means was seized, including whatever Islam and Byzantium could offer. The universities, chiefly the principal faculties of arts and theology, directed their energies towards that religious synthesis. Lines of inquiry that had begun tentatively in the cathedral schools were developed in the universities which became the established centres of intellectual speculation. Through them were brought to a focus the traditions of previous centuries that sought a reconciliation of divergent and contradictory beliefs, and the establishment of a coherent, rational organization of all human knowledge as part of a total cosmology.

Such developments concerned the church vitally. Paris in particular, as the intellectual capital of Western Christendom, was the object of especial interest. At times the church attempted to influence the course of events, although direct intervention had to be kept to a minimum. The difficulties of the church in relation to the temporal powers of Europe, royal and civic, and even to the quasi-autonomous universities, indicated the need for it to act cautiously. Further, the critical inquiries of university scholars were not the sole challenges to orthodoxy; movements for church reform and even rival teachings, amounting to heresies, were developing among the laity. Late in the twelfth century there were two potential sources of heresy: Moslem works that were being studied in the universities, and popular movements for church reform and for new religious doctrines, particularly Catharism which spread rapidly in the south of France. Both challenges had to be met: the Waldensian and Albigensian were suppressed by direct means, the university challenge demanded more subtle control. When the two new religious orders of Franciscans and Dominicans appeared they were seen as potential instruments for securing orthodoxy. In part they were effective in this although by the end of the century these mendicants, particularly the Dominicans, were responsible for an entirely new conception of orthodoxy.

The centre of the thirteenth-century Scholastic Controversy was always in Paris where, as a consequence of their training in the methods of disputation, scholars became divided in their beliefs. Basically, there were two positions, following either the Neoplatonic doctrines of Augustine and his subsequent interpreters, or the recently revived Aristotelian theories as received from the Moslems. The methods, also, stemmed from two fundamental procedures by which reason operates: either that from cause to effect, *a priori*; or that from effect to cause, *a posteriori*. The Neoplatonists, representing the conservative faction, identified Plato's Infinite with god and saw reason as the means by which, from a basic acceptance of the order of events secured by faith, truth may be deduced. The Aristotelians, for their part, generally – although not universally – favoured arguments *a posteriori*. From human experience of the world, that is, from effects, reason can trace back to a realm of ultimates, and even to a first cause, thereby arriving at truth, and so guaranteeing the existence of god, by induction. Under such circumstances the search for truth is not always tempered by prudence or orthodoxy. In their concern to produce a really convincing proof of god's existence, the innovating Aristotelians insisted that human experience must be the starting-point of inquiry, and that absolute demonstration can come only from *a posteriori* argument – from effects traced back to cause. And, moreover, in their attempts to elaborate the posterior method, the Aristotelians not only accepted Aristotle's suspect works, such as the *Metaphysics* – which throughout most of the first half of the thirteenth century were under papal interdict – but studied carefully the Moslem commentaries, which were equally anathematized. These latter works were seen as challenges to faith; consequently the attempts of the Aristotelians to use them towards a new rationalization of religion stimulated violent reaction in a dispute that lasted for more than a century and indeed has never been resolved.

Course of the controversy

Church recognition of the dangers of some of these works came slowly and not until 1210 was there any explicit statement of disapproval. Expressions of concern had been voiced earlier: some time between 1192 and 1203 Stephen, bishop of Tournai, had written such a letter of complaint to the pope, possibly Innocent III, pointing out:

> The studies of sacred letters among us are fallen into the workshop of confusion, while both disciples applaud novelties and masters watch out for glory rather than learning. They everywhere compose new and recent *summulae* and commentaries, by which they attract, detain, and deceive their hearers, as if the works of the holy fathers were still not sufficient, who, we read, expounded holy scripture in the same spirit in which we believe the apostles and prophets composed it.[6]

Then, in 1210, a group of bishops led by the bishop of Paris published a decree prohibiting some of the writings of Aristotle:

> Neither the books of Aristotle on natural philosophy nor their commentaries are to be read at Paris in public or secret, and this we forbid under penalty of excommunication.[7]

In this context, the phrase *to be read* referred to their exposition in a lecture; the decree did not expressly prohibit any private reading. The prohibition was repeated five years later, in 1215, when Robert de Courçon, cardinal legate to Paris, prescribed methods and content for lectures in arts and theology.

> [Lecturers] shall lecture on the books of Aristotle, on dialectic old and new, . . . ethics, and . . . the fourth book of the *Topics*. They shall not lecture on the books of Aristotle on metaphysics and natural philosophy or summaries of them.[8]

The intention of the decrees of 1210 and 1215 was to restrain use of those particular Aristotelian writings until they had been expurgated properly. That activity was delayed, however, and did not commence until the university had reassembled after the Great Dispersion of 1229–31. Pope Gregory ordered an examination of the works in 1231 since, he wrote, 'we have learned that the books on nature which were prohibited at Paris in provincial council are said to contain both useful and useless matter'.[9] In 1232 the Inquisition – a special court of church inquiry that had existed for centuries – was given a much more formal character, and was charged with the conduct of an examination. Through their claims to worldly-disinterestedness, the mendicant friars, as masters of theology, dominated the membership of the Inquisition, thereby becoming potential opponents of the secular masters in arts. Gregory's action in ordering the inquiry in large part was prompted by the fact that scholars were not obeying the two earlier injunctions of 1210 and 1215; nevertheless his letter offered, as well, absolution for those masters and scholars who had violated the prohibition. In 1241, the chancellor and masters of theology, virtually all of whom were mendicants, issued a list of ten condemned propositions that had arisen from the banned Aristotelian books and commentaries. The list included a set of counter-propositions asserting the orthodoxy of the Trinity, of angels, of a corporeal heaven, of the fact that sin issued from deliberate acts by the evil angel and that redemption comes only by grace. The most important metaphysical principle is the seventh article:

> . . . we firmly believe that there is only one eternal truth which is God.[10]

Despite those actions of 1231 and 1241, scholars continued to study the condemned books, although how copies were procured at Paris is uncertain. It seems likely that they were brought from Oxford, where the ban did not apply, by English scholars, in particular by Roger Bacon and

Robert Kilwardby,[11] both of whom were at Paris around 1245. Certainly after 1240 there was a marked revival of interest at Paris in Aristotle's natural philosophy and the writings of Avicenna, Averroes and Maimonides, which by 1250 dominated the intellectual life of the university. There was, by then, a widespread acceptance of Aristotle's works; a statute of Paris of 1252 which set out requirements for determination in arts specified that the candidate must have

> ... heard the books of Aristotle on the Old Logic, namely, the *Praedicamenta* and *Periarmeniae* at least twice in ordinary lectures and once cursorily [that is, in tutorials outside regular lecture hours], the *Six Principles* at least once in ordinary lectures and once cursorily, the first three books of the *Topics* and the *Divisions* once in ordinary lectures and once cursorily, the *Topics* of Aristotle and *Elenci* . . ., the *Prior Analytics* . . ., the *Posterior Analytics* . . .; also, he shall have heard *De anima* once, or be hearing it [at present].[12]

The inclusion of *De anima* (*On the Soul*) is significant: it is one of Aristotle's *libri naturales* – the controversial books on natural philosophy. Three years later, in 1255, the masters of arts at Paris decreed the required courses in arts to include the old logic and, in addition, *Physics, Metaphysics, On Animals* (both sections, *Parts* and *Generation*), *On the Soul*, the *Short Physical Treatises* (*Parva naturalia*), *Topics, Elenchi, Prior* and *Posterior Analytics* and *Ethics*:[13] virtually the entire *corpus Aristotelicum*. The only works absent are *Politics, Rhetoric, Poetics* and *History of Animals*, and none of these was contentious. The position was similar at Oxford where the faculty of arts required from determining candidates a knowledge of all the *Organon*, 'and in addition these three books: *Physics, On the Soul, On Generation and Corruption*'.[14] Although that record dates from 1267 it seems to describe a practice of longer standing, at least of ten years.

In the case of these requirements it is significant that they were set by the faculties of arts, which were composed of secular clerics. By the middle of the thirteenth century the mendicant orders had come to dominate the faculty of theology at Paris, and, since they received their undergraduate training in arts in their own schools, they were allowed admission to the faculty of theology directly. That procedure was not accepted by the seculars; on the contrary, the practice was resisted bitterly and between 1253 and 1261, the period in which the arts curriculum specified study of Aristotle's *libri naturales*, hostility between the secular artists and the mendicant theologians became quite intense. The refusal of mendicant friars to join the Great Dispersion of 1229–31 had already aroused the hostility of the secular masters. In 1253 the same thing happened again; some friars refused to join a cessation of lectures and thereupon were expelled by the university. The threat was obvious: the mendicants sought to remain and fill the vacated chairs, thereby securing even greater control of the university, as a letter from the university to prelates and scholars generally testifies.[15] The extreme bitterness of the invective in that document reveals how strongly feeling was running against the friars. The friars, for their part, sought to ingratiate themselves with the papacy and to discharge a self-appointed mission of church reform, hence their interest in filling the offices of the reformed Inquisition. The struggle between the two faculties was mollified, if not resolved, in 1261 when a virtual separation between them was effected by the masters of Paris as a body. Henceforth, Dominicans and Franciscans could belong only to the faculty of theology, the seculars only to arts. The arts curriculum, with its stress on Aristotle, was most likely an assertion of that faculty's independence.

Despite the delimitation of areas of influence of 1261, the friars were not prepared to allow the contravention of the earlier bans which had never been lifted. Accordingly, they moved against the seculars in a campaign of persuasion and exhortation, and for that purpose the orders brought their best scholars and preachers into the university. Already some mendicants had achieved a reputation for their disputational skill, notably John of Fidanza (1221–73) who had joined the Franciscans about 1243–4. He became active as a lecturer at Paris between 1250 and 1257, when he was made general of his order and, taking the name Bonaventura, left the university, and affairs of scholarship, for the following ten years. In 1267 Bonaventura concerned himself again with developments in the university where the study of Aristotle had grown considerably. His own attitude was expressed in his theological writings, particularly the *Commentary on the Sentences*;[16] he never wrote directly on philosophy. Bonaventura accepted a limited version of the Aristotelian doctrines; he was sympathetic to Aristotle in his years at Paris, and that predisposition remained in his thought. None the less he was a convinced Augustinian and believed that faith is necessary to secure the correct functioning of reason; his position, accordingly was one of Augustinian Aristotelianism.[17] In 1267, however, Bonaventura led a vigorous attack on those groups who were inclined to allow a much greater scope to reason. Of those scholars, two in particular were attracting attention: Thomas of Aquino and Siger of Brabant. At this point, an interesting development occurred: the dispute ceased to be simply one between arts and theology. Siger represented a group of radical artists, but Thomas was a Dominican. By 1267, then, the faculty of theology itself had become divided: generally, though not completely, the Franciscans defended Augustinianism, the Dominicans advanced the claims of Aristotelianism.

Thomas Aquinas: scholastic synthesis

It had become increasingly clear that Aristotle could not be eliminated by decree and that regardless of consequences scholars were determined to study his teachings. The mendicants, as champions of the papacy and orthodoxy, turned their efforts more and more towards finding a solution to the many apparent threats to faith that were posed by the Aristotelian writings and their Moslem commentaries. In 1268 the Dominicans sent Thomas Aquinas to Paris to take up a chair of theology. A scholar of high reputation and now ranking as a preacher general of the order, Thomas had already spent a period as professor at Paris (1257–9). Since it was customary for theologians to serve only a single three-year term in the faculty of theology, the decision to re-enlist his services indicates the strength of Dominican concern with the gravity of the situation. Thomas's mission was to combat the trends towards heresy arising from interest in some doctrines of Averroes: that the world is eternal and has no finite creation *ex nihilo*, that god is not directly in control of the sequence of temporal events, that ultimate truth is secured by reason acting on the data of sensation, that there is but one single intellect informing all men. These doctrines, known at the time as Latin Averroism, were being voiced increasingly, and there were veiled accusations that Siger was espousing such a position.

Thomas Aquinas (1224/5–74)[18] was born the son of Count Landulph of Aquino and Countess Theodora of Theate. His first schooling was given at the nearby monastery of Monte Cassino; in 1239 he began studies at the University of Naples, founded fifteen years earlier by the Emperor Frederick II. It is uncertain how long Thomas remained at Naples, but in 1244 he entered the Dominican order after a period of intense family objections. His first important teacher was the great scholar Albertus Magnus who taught Thomas at a Dominican school in Cologne. When Albert went to lecture at Paris between 1245 and 1248, Thomas went with him, and returned with him in 1248 to Cologne where Albert established a Dominican *studium generale* in arts. Thomas returned to Paris four years later, in 1252, as a lecturer on Peter Lombard's *Sentences* in the faculty of theology, when he began writing his own *Commentary* on Lombard. Then, after graduating

as master of arts in 1256, and having completed his *Commentary*, Thomas
was appointed to a three-year term as professor of theology. In 1259, when
he left that position, he had begun a number of important studies, particularly his *Summa against the Gentiles* (*Summa contra Gentiles*) and his *Quodlibetal
and Disputed Questions*.[19] The following eight years are somewhat obscure;
he was at one time at the court of Pope Urban IV and at others was occupied in various Dominican houses in Italy. Thomas maintained his intellectual activity, completing around 1264 the *Summa against the Gentiles*
and some shorter works. On his return to Paris in 1268 he increased his
intellectual pace and produced his greatest works, chiefly the vast *Summa
of Theology*, which almost immediately displaced Peter Lombard's *Four
Books of Sentences*; he also completed his *Quodlibetal and Disputed Questions*
and his *Exposition of Aristotle on the Soul*. When he relinquished his appointment in 1272 he had written nearly forty books, many in multiple volumes,
ranging over the whole spectrum of theological and philosophical controversy of the century. Two years later, en route to a Council at Lyon, he
died at a Cistercian monastery at Fossanova on 7 March 1274.

The writings of Thomas Aquinas are more than skilled examinations of
controversial disputes; collectively they constitute a systematic, philosophically elaborated and comprehensive theological synthesis. For the first
time in the history of Christianity a scholar attempted to harmonize fully
the experiences of sense and intellect with the demands of faith, and to do
justice to both. The basis of his synthesis rests in his acceptance of the
reality of being. The existence of an externally real and fixed world, as
argued by Averroes and Maimonides, is a basic axiom: from it the Thomist
theology is elaborated. In many places his work reveals, and occasionally
acknowledges, the influence of Avicenna, Averroes and Maimonides.
Thomas thereby departed from a thousand years of Christian Platonism.

Not only is the external world real, in his view, but it is also knowable
by the human mind; in fact, the mind is adapted specifically to receiving
knowledge of the external world,[20] and has a capacity for abstraction.[21]
The ordered objectivity of the external world is transmitted by the senses
to the intellect where it is recorded, as on a blank tablet. In such a process
there can be no error, for the senses convey simply what *is*: truth, then, is
apprehended directly by the mind. Thomas, like the Moslem commentators, accepted Aristotle's twofold division of the mind into a passive
intellect, which receives experiences, and an active intellect, the agent of
understanding and of action. It is in the active intellect, as the agent of
understanding, that error arises as a result of faulty or inadequate interpre-

tation.[22] By locating both error and truth in the active intellect, Thomas repudiated the traditional Augustinian doctrine, derived from Plato, that the external world is illusory and that the senses are sources of error. Yet Thomas was careful to avoid asserting that the external world is itself, in its diversity, identical with truth. He recognized that any individual object is contingent: no particular man, for example, is necessary to the existence of the genus *man*. Reality in its ultimate form exists, he suggested, in the essences, or quiddities (L. *quid*, what), of objects.[23] Since man's apprehension of truth, however, is totally dependent on experience of singular objects, man's intellect is also accidental.[24] External existence is independent of the individual; ultimate truth, he argued, must reside in a permanent, divine intellect which maintains it.[25] Maintenance, in that view, implies causation.

Thomas's metaphysics of being is related closely to his epistemology; the world of being must be apprehended actively by man, and the experiences recorded by the passive intellect, meaningless in themselves, are made real by the active intellect. This is effected by a verbal process, since the intellect forms words to designate passive receptions, and these words are the means by which intelligibility (*ratio*) is achieved. Through its very actions, the active intellect becomes aware of its own operations; it knows itself, and this is the terminus of intellectual activity.[26] Man's basic quality, then, his quiddity, or *form*, is his intellect.[27] Its functioning is man's essential purpose; there is no higher activity in life beyond intellection. Again, arguing from his axioms of being, and the basic assumptions of Aristotelian metaphysics, Thomas postulated that existence is determined by four causes. Since everything acts on account of an end (the final cause), man must have a purpose, and since his form is his soul, man's purpose is the fulfilment of its activity. This activity is self-contemplation which rests ultimately in contemplation of divine causes, which are the absolute motivators of man's thought. Indeed, the highest form of human activity, the greatest possible happiness, is a consideration of the first cause,[28] the principle of actual being, that is, god.

The Thomistic system is self-sufficient except in the important respect that it is close to a thoroughgoing determinism; in fact it is little different in many of its basic features from the theory of Averroes. To avoid censure by the church, and to incorporate the essentials of Christian faith, it was important for Thomas to assert the relative freedom of the individual, to allow for free will and hence a moral realm, and also to account for the existence of creation itself. Averroes denied creation and cessation; the universe for him is in the process of constant creation by emanations, and of correlative decline. All men, moreover, are informed by the one single active intellect. That was considered a Christian heresy in the thirteenth century, and Aquinas repudiated it specifically in a short treatise *On the Unity of the Intellect*.[29]

In that famous document Thomas insisted that a moral order is mandatory, as a condition of human existence, and the operation of that order gives rise to the human will. At that point, he invoked the authority of faith. Revelation itself stands as the ultimate guide; its prescriptions are inaccessible to reason, they are indemonstrable. The basic elements of Christian belief – creation, the freedom of man's will, immortality of the soul – are all axiomatic, being given absolutely in revelation and secured constantly by faith. Thomas recognized the need to assert man's free will, of his separate independent active intellect; yet, in doing so, he was compelled to answer yet another question: why did god create the world? For, by his own premises, if the doctrine of man's free will is to stand, it is necessary to secure it in a meaningful world, the origin of which must rest in a conscious act of creation, in cause. That divine motivation, Thomas argued, is love. Only because of that disposition does god act.[30] Beyond our belief in divine love man cannot go: the absolutely divine realm, by definition, must be beyond rational access. Man's own contingent intellect cannot penetrate the workings of the absolute intellect.

The scholastic synthesis is an impressive achievement: it accounts for the experience of the senses and the rational operation of the intellect; it gives an imprimatur to man's quest for intellective understanding. Yet it denies man absolute knowledge. The quest of his contingent intellect can never be satisfied completely: contemplation of the highest good, *summum bonum*, must be incomplete. Man can never rest content in an absolutely explicated world. The ultimate mystery of the divine, the possibility of error in interpretation by the active intellect, and the need for moral choice resulting from the exercise of the will means that man's way is one of constant endeavour, one of maintaining a continually alert consciousness, of substained intellectual activity.

De magistro: *Thomas's theory of education*

Thomas not only challenged the millennium-long tradition of Augustine's philosophy, he formulated a new theory of education. Augustine's theories, expounded in several writings – *De magistro, De catechizandis rudibus, De doctrina christiana* – developed the Platonic belief in innate knowledge, that the teacher acts simply as midwife, his task being to assist the student to 'recollect' knowledge which is latently within. The teacher's active role is largely that of helping the student to clarify his inchoate ideas by means of the procedures of logic. Verification, in the traditional Christian, Neo-platonic view, comes through god's active intervention, by means of his illumination of truth in the mind of the student. Throughout the centuries of medieval Christianity, no explicit theory ever appeared to counter that doctrine. Even the great revival of the twelfth century produced no close scrutiny of Augustine's teachings. It was Thomas Aquinas who led the way in formulating a new doctrine during his first term at Paris in the period 1256–9. Among his *Disputed Questions* of that period appeared *De magistro*,[31] itself repeating one of Augustine's titles.

'Can a man, or only God teach, and be called Teacher?' was the question for debate. Following standard procedure, Thomas listed the evidence for god, in eighteen propositions, drawn from the New Testament and from Augustine. In six further propositions, he gave arguments to the contrary. Then he followed with his own interpretation, or determination. Thomas used Aristotelian arguments: the position of Augustine 'lacked a reasonable basis since it excluded proximate causes and attributed solely to first causes all effects which happen in lower natures'.[32] There is an important distinction to be made between potency and actuality: god created the world in the sense of its latent possibilities, and he provides for the actualizing of these latencies by proximate agents:

> For natural forms pre-exist in matter not actually, as some have said, but through a proximate external agent, and not through the first agent alone, as one of the opinions maintains. Similarly, according to this opinion of Aristotle, before the habits of virtue are completely formed, they exist in us in certain natural inclinations, which are the beginnings of the virtues. But afterwards, through practice in their actions, they are brought to their proper completion.[33]

So, too, with knowledge:

> Certain seeds of knowledge pre-exist in us, namely, the first concepts of understanding, which by the light of the agent intellect are immediately known through the species abstracted from sensible things. These are either complex, as axioms, or simple, as the notions of being, or the one, and so on, which the understanding grasps immediately. In these general principles, however, all the consequences are included as in certain seminal principles. When, therefore, the mind is led from these general notions to actual knowledge of

the particular things, which it knew previously in general, and, as it were, potentially, then one is said to acquire knowledge.[34]

Learning, then, for Thomas has two aspects. The first, that in which the natural reason attains understanding by its own operations, he termed learning by *discovery*: the second, that in which another person as agent aids the learner's reason, he called learning by *instruction*. In dealing with the question of instruction he regarded the transmission of knowledge as crucial to the debate. Following Augustine, Thomas agreed that knowledge is mediated by words, as signs. For Augustine, however, signs are simply stimulators that summon ideas to consciousness; meaning and verification come by illumination. Thomas believed that signs promote knowledge actively since they are directly related to their objective referents. The mind, in his theory, is adapted to the reception of knowledge, which occurs symbolically. Teaching by instruction proceeds in two ways. In one,

> . . . a person is said to teach another inasmuch as, by signs, he manifests to that other the reasoning process which he himself goes through by his own natural reason.[35]

In the other,

> . . . our intellect derives intelligible likenesses from sensible signs which are received in the sensitive faculty, and it uses these intelligible forms to produce in itself scientific knowledge;[36] [and] in the pupil, the intelligible forms of which knowledge received through teaching is constituted are caused directly by the agent intellect and mediately by the one who teaches. For the teacher sets before the pupil signs of intelligible things, and from these the agent intellect derives the intelligible likenesses and causes them to exist in the possible intellect. Hence, the words of the teacher, heard or seen in writing, have the same efficacy in causing knowledge as things which are outside the soul.[37]

And knowledge, so received, is certain and demonstrably true, if it derives from the proper first principles. That is the way of logical reasoning which is universally true. And standing as the absolute basis of first principles is god. Man 'has the certainty of scientific knowledge from God alone, who has given us the light of reason, through which we know principles'.[38]

Prior to Thomas, Christian scholars had hesitated to call man a teacher in any deeply significant sense: that role was the prerogative of god as *Archdidaskalos*. He alone, through illumination, can inform men; he alone possesses truth: man can seek only its reflection. Thomas modified that view considerably. Knowledge, he argued, can be gained by man from first principles and imparted to others; the experiences of the senses and the activities of the intellect in themselves can attain certainty, although one that is limited to earthly phenomena; the divine realm remains beyond rational access. By that doctrine, however, god as first cause, and ultimate agent, recedes from the world of events. Thomas was satisfied that he had answered the occasionalist polemic decisively, although in contrast to the philosophy of Augustine the recognition of human reason was achieved at the cost of spiritual warmth. With god removed from active control, the universe appears more stern; reason seems a much drier light than god's illumination. Reaction to Thomas was profound, although not solely on account of the frigidity and desiccation of his views. Such a position as he expounded was bound to incur papal disapproval. Belief in the constant intervention of god in daily affairs was as vital to the Christian hierarchy as it was to the Moslem occasionalists.

Attack on reason: two condemnations, 1270 and 1277

In 1270 Stephen, bishop of Paris, condemned thirteen errors of belief which were current in the thinking of the day. In his document[39] no person's name nor specific doctrine was mentioned; it is clear, none the less, that it was directed at the teachings of Averroes, and possibly at those of Aquinas and Siger of Brabant. The first article condemned the belief that the intellect of all men is one and the same in number. The tenor of all of the articles was against determinism and a view of god as utterly remote – as little more than Aristotle's unmoved mover. The condemnation by Bishop Stephen was part of a general conservative opposition. Bonaventura followed his own attack of 1267 on these growing Aristotelian doctrines – Latin Averroism as it was known – with another in 1268, and a third in 1273.

Aquinas was probably not the only intellectual at Paris responsible for the spread of those ideas; at the same time Siger of Brabant was teaching equally radical doctrines in the faculty of arts at Paris. Siger (c. 1240–c. 1281/4) was born in the duchy of Brabant, where the Meuse flows into the North Sea. He studied at Paris around the time of Aquinas' first professorship (c. 1255–60), graduated master of arts some time after 1260 and began teaching at Paris in 1266. In that period his thought was regarded as approaching heresy and it was he who seems to have prompted Bonaventura's protests of 1267 and 1268. Siger's doctrines[40] were even denounced by Thomas in *On the Unity of the Intellect*; they were probably instrumental in stimulating Stephen's condemnation of 1270. Siger did not abandon his position, although the exact nature of his teachings, and the interpretation of his writings, are still matters of considerable scholarly dispute.[41] His approach, a radical Aristotelianism, consisted essentially in a much stronger emphasis on Aristotle's teachings as an intrinsically valid philosophical system which is virtually independent of religion at all. Siger conceived god as being even more remote than Thomas did.

The marked growth in philosophical speculation continued unchecked after the death of Thomas Aquinas in 1274. In 1277 the new pope, John XXI, concerned at the growth of such philosophy at Paris, requested the bishop to conduct an inquiry. Bishop Stephen Tempier apparently went further and, acting on his own authority, issued a list of 219 condemned propositions, representing, in effect, an amplification of the condemnation of 1270.[42] No names or particular writings were specified; even the precise doctrines being condemned are difficult to identify. The condemned propositions themselves run the gamut of medieval theology, and in no recognizably logical or systematic order. From the confusion of the period – which evoked tremendous excitement throughout the academic world – it is clear that the issue was one between the conservative Augustinians, chiefly Franciscans but including some Dominicans, and an innovating group of Aristotelians. Siger of Brabant was summoned in the same year to the French Inquisition but fled to the papal court which had a reputation for being more clement. He was not condemned, but put under supervision; some years later, between 1281 and 1284, he was murdered by his insane guardian.

Opposition to the theories of Thomas was led by a fellow-Dominican, Robert Kilwardby, archbishop of Canterbury (r. 1272–9), who also condemned a set of similar propositions and forbade their teaching at Oxford. This, interestingly enough, was the same Robert who may have brought some banned books of Aristotle to Paris, thirty years before. Supporters rallied to Thomas, however; even the ageing Albertus Magnus, his former master, travelled from Cologne in 1277 to defend, in the debates, his student who had died in 1274. The Dominicans, as an order, closed their ranks and the following year at Milan Thomas's teachings were accepted as their official doctrines. Criticism by Dominicans such as Kilwardby was stifled.

Decline of scholastic debates

Franciscan reaction: Duns Scotus and William of Occam

The Augustinians remained active in opposing Thomism, and criticisms from Franciscans, in particular, continued unchecked. The basic difficulty with Thomism is that it does not allow for knowledge of god in terms of direct human experience. Thomism, in many respects, is identical with Aristotelianism, apart from the consideration of god. Yet god is not included as part of the Thomist system of knowledge; his presence is guaranteed by different sources, revelation and faith. God has the character of something tacked on. The Franciscans sensed this inadequacy, and in the following years they produced efforts to counter the Thomistic synthesis with a restatement of the Augustinian position. A number of important scholars attempted the task, of whom three Franciscans in Britain were particularly outstanding: Roger Bacon, Duns Scotus and William of Occam. Bacon (1210/14–c. 1294) asserted the traditional position with great skill, arguing especially that mathematical studies remained the most certain way to truth.

It was Duns Scotus (1265/6–1308), however, who produced the most satisfying answer to Thomism. Born in Scotland, Duns studied at the two English universities, Oxford and Cambridge, and then at Paris in 1302. He went to Oxford again for the following two years and then returned to Paris. A few years later he left for Cologne, where he died. Duns is in some ways a difficult scholar to estimate; his reputation has varied considerably and is still the subject of reappraisal. Although he accepted the reality of being and the notion that knowledge has its origins in the senses, Duns emphasized his belief that the proper object of man's intellect is being *as* being: *ens in quantum ens*. Empirical argument for him is valuable, but useful only to support knowledge given by faith. Like Bacon, Scotus sought the essential quality of being in permanent relations and necessary truths that are independent of human experience and intellectual interpretation. His revived Augustinianism, demonstrated frequently through extensive quotations,[43] proved an attractive alternative doctrine to many scholastics, and in the late thirteenth century and throughout the fourteenth it maintained a following.

In the fourteenth century, the Augustinian position was elaborated by a third Franciscan, William of Occam (c. 1300–49), who also taught at Oxford. Occam departed radically from other thirteenth-century systems and developed what amounted to a Christian occasionalism. All attempts to prove the existence of god, either *a priori* or *a posteriori*, are meaningless in his view. They impose a limitation on the Infinite, which by definition cannot be so circumscribed. In order to know, man must attend directly to the objects of experience; in them only can the workings of god be found. Occam developed his position in his famous *Seven Quodlibeta*,[44] in which he put the case for direct intuition as the basis for knowledge. Central to the problem of how man knows is the role of signification. Signs can describe but not demonstrate, they can activate the mind but they have no necessary causal relations.[45] Demonstrative proof is impossible and knowledge, which comes by direct intuition of the external world, is wholly of singular objects and events. Intuition is given symbolic representation (*signum rei*) which becomes in the intellect a concept (*intentio anime*). The notion of causation itself symbolizes a sequence of successive states of awareness. All knowledge, however, is held together by faith.

Occam was working against the prevailing current of thought. His ideas, although able to provoke some response in universities, were regarded as only the latest in a long-drawn-out series of debates that had grown increasingly mannered and convoluted and had ceased to hold interest. Europe itself was changing and the pursuit of knowledge by the quodlibetal method of disputation was no longer appropriate. Knowledge began to be defined differently to meet new needs. In Italy, in particular, another approach to matters of the intellect and to learning, and new conceptions of education were becoming popular; the old issues were now *passé* and the disputes, if not resolved, were less important. Thomas Aquinas was canonized in 1323, an act with which Pope John XXII was in great sympathy. Two years later Bishop Stephen Bourret of Paris revoked the condemnation of 1277 in so far as it 'touched or seemed to touch the teaching of blessed Thomas'.[46] The condemnation came to lack meaning. Thomism and Scotism continued as alternative philosophical explications of the Christian faith; to this day neither position has gained thoroughgoing acceptance, although Thomism has enjoyed a much wider following.

End of papal ascendancy

By the end of the thirteenth century the temporal and spiritual ascendancy sought by the papacy had not been achieved. On the contrary, that century was one of increasing secularism, nationalism and centralization. Despite the overwhelmingly theological nature of the century's scholarship, there was at the same time a strong, if less conspicuous, shift of emphasis towards legal and administrative studies. In pursuing its goals the church had been obliged to build a powerful bureaucracy, and that demanded not only theologians but also lawyers and clerks. The universities of Italy, of course, were almost totally preoccupied with legal studies, with the important consequence that their approach to philosophy was more political than theological. In that century, in fact, political philosophy, so long dominated by Augustine, developed as an independent study and in the fourteenth century began to flourish. This study focused its interests on the vexed question of sovereignty that had been chronically present throughout the medieval period; in particular, scholars continued the investigations initiated in John of Salisbury's *Policraticus* on the political jurisdiction of Rome in relation to the temporal powers. The tentative essays on the subject by Thomas Aquinas and Roger Bacon received a more vigorous expression in William of Occam's *Dialogue*, Dante's *De monarchia* of 1312, and particularly in Marsilius of Padua's highly controversial *Defender of the Peace* (*Defensor pacis*), completed in 1324.[47] Fourteenth-century political philosophy, concerned with scrutinizing the claim to secular authority of the church, reflected the church's tremendous loss of power and its inability to control speculation and learning as closely as it sought to do in the preceding century.

The major political movement of the thirteenth century was the decline of the Holy Roman Empire and the growth of a powerful French monarchy under Philip IV, the Fair (r. 1285–1314). This development, a direct result of papal activity, eventually proved to be Rome's undoing. The longstanding feud between the papacy and Frederick II ended when the emperor died in 1250. In the following seventeen years three emperors succeeded each other – Conrad IV, Manfred, Conradin – and then Italy and Sicily fell to Charles, Count of Anjou and Provence, who planned the territorial *coup* with papal connivance. Sicily was captured subsequently by the Aragonese of Spain. The Hohenstaufen dynasty was ended with the death of Frederick II, and in Germany, during the following period of the Great Interregnum, there was no emperor until 1273, when Rudolf of Habsburg was elected. An outcome of these developments was the growth of smaller, more independent states: the Austrian empire of the Habsburgs, the German kingdom of the Hohenzollerns, the republic of Switzerland, and the independent city-states of northern Italy all had their moves to autonomy stimulated by the thirteenth-century dissolution of the great

Hohenstaufen domains of Frederick II. While all of these separate states were still embryonic and so lacking in political power, France, long stable under the Capetians, profited from the disintegration of its powerful neighbour. The accession of Philip IV in 1285 was the beginning of a vigorous period of French rule.

Philip sought absolute authority in his own kingdom, which brought him into conflict in the first instance with England. The dispute of 1066 had never really ended; in 1293 it flared up over trading and fishing activities in the North Sea. War ensued and lasted until 1302. To secure the necessary funds both Edward I of England and Philip himself included church estates as taxable property, an action which provoked immediate conflict with Pope Boniface VIII (r. 1293–1303). The pope countered with his bull, *Clericis laicos*, of 1296 which provided that any cleric who paid such taxes, or any layman who levied or collected them, would, *by the act itself*, automatically incur the penalty of excommunication.[48] The result was a stalemate: Edward declared the English church beyond his protection unless they paid taxes for support of the state; Philip forbade export of money from France, thereby reducing papal revenue. By 1303 relations had deteriorated further. When Philip sought to try clerics in civil courts for civil offences, Boniface again asserted papal authority in the bull *Unam sanctam*. In a long-drawn-out metaphor on the unity of the world, symbolized in the institution of the church, the pope asserted absolute papal superiority: 'if the earthly power err it shall be judged by the spiritual power; but if the lesser spiritual power err, by the greater. But if the greatest [power err, that is, the papacy] it can be judged by God alone'.[49] Philip immediately dispatched troops under his emissary William de Nogaret who met Boniface at a summer residence at Anagni. A fracas ensued and a month later the octogenarian pope died, reputedly of shock.

Boniface's successor, Benedict XI, lived only a year and in 1305 the archbishop of Bordeaux succeeded him as Clement V. In the meantime the city of Rome had become hostile to the papacy once again and so, in 1309, the new pope removed his court to the papal territory at Avignon in France, that estate having been confiscated by the church after an Albigensian crusade of 1274. Until 1378, seven popes maintained their courts and administration at Avignon. This was followed by the Great Schism (1377–1417) in which rival popes ruled from both Avignon and Rome until the breach was finally healed at the Council of Constance (1414–18) with the election of Martin V in 1417. Throughout this period the papacy began to lose authority and the aspirations of the great medieval popes failed to be realized.

Further revolt: John Wycliffe and the 'church of the elect'

In the later fourteenth century the intellectual life of Europe underwent distinct changes. The momentous debates were over and scholarship generally became less rent with discord; few great masters were in the schools although there were many distinguished teachers of law. Even Occam, in many ways, was an anticlimactic figure; the need for a comprehensive and certain cosmology was felt no longer. In the north, however, one significant intellectual emerged, the Englishman, John Wycliffe (c. 1330–84), who became the centre of acrimonious theological dispute at Oxford after 1372. The absence of other intellectuals in the period is a puzzling feature; there is the possibility that the notorious plague of 1348–1349, the Black Death, was responsible in part.[50] That greatest epidemic in history is known to have killed some scholars, including the outstanding Thomas Bradwardine (c. 1290–1349), variously professor at Oxford and archbishop of Canterbury.

The Oxford academic John Wycliffe was responsible for introducing a new and henceforth highly significant element into Western intellectual life. This was his emphasis on the primacy of the Bible and his denial of the authority of the church. Wycliffe himself was avowedly anti-nominalist in philosophy; he was, in fact, excessively realist. In medieval terminology, realism was the position based on acceptance of the reality of universals, and in Wycliffe's arguments this was extended to the point of claiming that even the church and the Bible are but imperfect earthly manifestations of pure forms which exist in god. Consequently he rejected the institutionalized church and came to argue that the divine word rests in the 'elect' by virtue of grace. This view derived from his theological position which he received directly from Bradwardine and indirectly from the great Augustine of Hippo. In one of his last works, *On Corruption and Grace* (*De correptione et gratia*), written in A.D. 426, Augustine had argued that god's mercy is reserved for a set number of souls,[51] and this had introduced the notion of predestination. Wycliffe took up this theme as a major tenet of his theology and propounded it endlessly. The concept of god's 'grace' had always been central to Christian teaching, yet elusive of final definition. Generally it was considered to be the presence in man of god's spirit; in Wycliffe's theology, however, grace is present in only a chosen few, the 'elect', who alone will be called to heaven. This uncompromising pre-destinarianism has its puzzling aspects: we cannot know who is of the elect and who is not and must remain in a position of total ignorance. In any case, it does follow certainly that the visible church and its hier-archy, from the pope down to the lowliest cleric, have no real spiritual authority; they do not, indeed, constitute a church at all. The true church consists of the elect who are bound together by god's grace until the end.[52]

In developing this theological position, Wycliffe was at the same time working towards a political theory of dominion or lordship; both, it seems, were generated out of the political turmoil of the times. The papacy itself was in confusion on account of the seventy years of residence at Avignon and this was manifestly worsened with the rivalry of two popes, one at Avignon and one at Rome, after 1377. In 1379 Wycliffe published his treatise on the power of the papacy, *De potestate pape*, in which he argued that the Great Schism was proof of the lack of need for a pope, this being buttressed by his argument that, since it could not be known whether the pope was one of the elect, there was no necessary authority inherent in his office. Civil government was equally unstable: on the continent there was continued discord as various secular powers struggled for authority; in England the reign of Edward III, the current monarch, was chaotic and under it the church developed some of its worst abuses of simony and corruption. Some time around 1371 appeared Wycliffe's first treatise, concerning spiritual lordship, *De dominio divino*, in which he broke with the traditional view which held the church to be the divinely appointed agent of god's dominion over man. Since the true church is made up of the 'elect', he claimed, no other body can usurp its authority.

More influential, however, was his treatise on civil dominion, *De civili dominio*, written around 1376–8. In this he reasserted his previous argument, although, curiously, without ever condemning civil government. On the contrary, Wycliffe argued that all power should be exercised by two auth-orities: civil by the sovereign, spiritual by the Bible. The scriptures, of course, are the authentic, literally true, words of god; they cannot there-fore be in error. Since, however, his 'realist' view puts the Bible into the position of being a particularized 'form', then man must strive to get to its ultimate truth and this, consequently, involves man in an educational activity. Of course, only the elect in whom god's grace is present will be capable of securing access to final truth; nevertheless, since no one knows who is and is not of the elect, everyone has the incumbent imperative of searching for spiritual enlightenment. In order to bring the Bible to the masses, Wycliffe himself prepared a translation of the New Testament into Middle English, although his success in this endeavour is still a matter of doubt. And this, of course, hit at one of the most fundamental of the church's doctrines, that of being *the* authoritative teaching institution of Christian truth. The church, for its part, had always resisted any kind of unauthorized translation, and refused to countenance any role for individual interpretation of the scriptures. Apart from eliminating its own *raison d'être*, there was the practical problem that, because all religious works were in manuscript, authenticity was difficult to establish and individual access such as Wycliffe advocated would simply encourage mass production and increase considerably the chances of faulty texts.

Wycliffe himself spent virtually all of his adult years at Oxford (except the final three, 1381–4, when he retired to his benefice at Lutterworth in Leicestershire) and remained to the end of his rather short life an academic. His teachings, however, stimulated a popular movement whose members became known contemptuously as Lollards (Middle Dutch, *lollaerd*, a mumbler). Although they were persecuted, their movement of protest and reform continued, having its greatest influence in far-off Bohemia – which was linked at the time to the English crown by marriage – in the teachings of Jan Hus (1369?–1416), a rector of the university at Prague. Later, in the sixteenth century, the movement received its final, and most consequential expression in the teachings of Martin Luther. Meantime, education in Europe was not influenced markedly, except in Prague, and in parts of Bohemia. Learning remained centred in the church, and the academic traditions that had evolved through the preceding centuries became orthodoxies.

Education in the later Middle Ages

A safe and middle way: Commendation of the Clerk

Education in Europe north of the Alps appears to have developed steadily in the fourteenth and fifteenth centuries. There is little evidence of any liveliness, and the elementary and grammar schools are most obscure. The information that does exist, however, is so uniform and so mutually consistent that some conjectures can be made about the pattern of learning,[53] although it must be remembered that accounts in this period generally are normative and prescriptive; they are concerned rarely, if at all, with description of failure or shortcomings. Two documents in particular give a vivid account of educational practices and ideals of the time. One of these, *De disciplina scholarium*,[54] enjoyed widespread popularity for upwards of three centuries – until around 1500. Its content gives a detailed account of the stages of education, from the beginnings of literacy through to graduation as a master and the pursuit of the academic vocation, while commenting at the same time on the values to be gained from each stage. Although the tract claims the sixth-century Boethius as its author, internal evidence indicates that it was written, in bad Latin, possibly late in the twelfth century,[55] but more probably in the thirteenth.[56] Despite its lack of sophistication, *De disciplina scholarium* clearly met an important public need, that of offering advice to parents and scholars themselves on matters of schooling and on the loftier aims of education, abstractly conceived. There was little else available; John of Salisbury's *Metalogicon* or Hugh's *Didascalicon*, with which it was approximately contemporaneous, were hardly popular introductions to the topic. *De disciplina scholarium* is an early work of the mature medieval period and gives an account of the late twelfth century. None the less, its continuing acceptance for more than two hundred years indicates that it remained relevant, that fact being confirmed by a second, similar document of the mid-fourteenth century, which survives in apparently incomplete form, entitled *De commendatione cleri*.[57] This second anonymous treatise is also a eulogy of the scholarly life, and its content and value judgements echo those of *De disciplina scholarium*. *Commendation of the Clerk* extols the virtues of the safe and middle way of clerkly learning.

Both essays record that schooling began for the young boy in his seventh year – 'sons of seven summers ready for apprenticeship to letters'.[58] Generally, the boys who entered school came from the ranks of the townspeople; in many places in Europe, serfs and some classes of the peasantry were prohibited by law from seeking an education for their children. The pursuit of learning was still identified almost exclusively with the religious life, and was conducted entirely in Latin, with the exception of the almost completely undocumented provision of limited vernacular instruction given by private teachers and by some guilds in those subjects, chiefly elementary reading, writing and reckoning, necessary for the mastery of a craft or the needs of commerce. These latter schools appeared first in the urban, commercial centres of Europe – particularly in Italy and Germany

– in the fourteenth century and did not become established in agricultural countries such as England until the fifteenth century and even later.[59] The bulk of formal schooling in Europe, however, remained under church control, the surviving evidence giving clear support. The tenor of *Commendation of the Clerk* throughout underscores the fact. In one part, for example, that document recommends that boys with any physical defects should 'not be endowed with the nobility of letters [since . . . they] neither adorn professional chairs nor become the divine priesthood'.[60] At the same time, the author is aware that the cleric of the day discharged a multitude of duties beyond lecturing and administration of the sacraments.

In both documents, the influence of Quintilian can be observed, although his specific educational work, *Institutio oratoria*, was not in general circulation and few schoolmasters, if any, were aware even of his name. Quintilian's views apparently had considerable survival value, as indicated by certain recommendations offered in *De disciplina scholarium*: that instruction should proceed from the elements of literacy to the study of writers, including Seneca, Lucan, Ovid, Virgil and Horace; that the classical Latin be paralleled by instruction in the vernacular (Quintilian had recommended that Greek, the classical language of his day, be accompanied by instruction in the vernacular of Latin); that progression should be made to logic as 'supreme arbiter between truth and falsity and as the science of sciences'.[61] Even more convincing evidence of Quintilian's covert influence is the advice to the schoolmaster in the same treatise to be concerned with the child's individual propensities, to cultivate memory as a cardinal intellectual virtue but at the same time to remember that moderation is an equally valuable personal trait and that moral character is as important an educational goal as the cultivation of the intellect. Those injunctions are expressed just as forcefully in *Commendation of the Clerk*.[62] After a grounding in grammar, Latin literature and elementary logic, both medieval texts recommend advancement to the university, setting out in detail the standard procedure: six years of undergraduate preparation before advancing to the baccalaureate, a period as licenciate and, finally, inception as a master. The person who achieves that felicitous state, being both master of arts and cleric, a dedicated servant of god, will become, in the words of a fanciful metaphor, like a dove with wings of silver and a tail of gold.[63]

Growth of vernaculars and decline of Latin

The pattern of learning that became formalized in the fourteenth century remained in operation in the northern regions of Europe and in agricultural regions generally, for centuries to come. At the same time, the recommendations of *De disciplina scholarium* and *Commendation of the Clerk* represent idealized accounts of medieval education; they must be balanced against other evidence that suggests the absence of any provision for Latin instruction in many areas. Grammar schools in many places were rudimentary, and were conducted frequently by masters not so enlightened as those imagined by the author of *Commendation of the Clerk*.

Although Latin continued to be the language of scholarship and diplomacy, and is therefore the language of the surviving records, there is no evidence that it was taught widely. From the sixth to the ninth century Latin had ceased to be spoken in its classical form and changed progressively into a number of vernaculars or Romance languages – the word is derived from the popular Latin *romanice,* 'in the Roman tongue' – chiefly the prototypes of modern Spanish, Portuguese, Italian and French. In the same period the Germanic tribes retained their own particular tongues which in the course of time became influenced to some extent by Latin. A similar process occurred in later centuries as other peoples came into contact with Latin: in varying degrees it influenced the various Slavic, Baltic and Celtic tongues. By the tenth century, however, Latin itself was no longer the speech of any particular people. It was the language of scholarship, of diplomacy and of the church, and therefore retained universality. The fact remained that after the eleventh century Latin was approached by all persons as a foreign language, which meant that it had to be learnt by conscious effort. It took on, inevitably, those qualities of any acquired cultural pursuit: it became more contrived and mannered as scholars had their awareness of it heightened. Such a new self-consciousness had some positive effects: the language was used with greater precision, it became free of particular ethnic bias, and the process of linguistic change was reduced. Yet those features had their corresponding shortcomings: precision often led to pedantry and concern with the picayune, ethnic independence meant that persons were unable to think naturally in Latin, elimination of change resulted in rigidity and an inevitable remoteness in the language. Indeed, ever since the twelfth century Latin has remained a major concern of Western thought. Its dominance of education and the learned professions, along with inherent obstacles to its efficient use, have been a source of constant difficulty, yet, much of the Western heritage has been transmitted through Latin; indeed a great deal is retained in the so-called classical languages which needs to be recommunicated continually, and this has created tensions and ambiguities in education that have never been adequately resolved.

The decline of Latin scholarship in the sixth century, which Boethius and Cassiodorus unsuccessfully attempted to arrest, resulted in profound changes in learning, the chief one being the loss of Latin scholarship by the majority of literate persons. That process can be discerned in continuous operation after the sixth century when the *Germani* overran the empire in significant numbers; by the thirteenth and fourteenth centuries the loss of Latin by the bulk of the population was manifest. The problem was of little concern to the peasantry, but for the literate classes it had profound consequences. The various town workers, particularly artisans, craftsmen and merchants, used the vernacular almost exclusively; they were cut off from much of the knowledge of the past and increasingly cultivated regional cultures. The lesser clergy, those who performed the bulk of the church's mundane tasks, were equally ignorant of Latin and its heritage. Monastic and conventual rules, for example, by the thirteenth and fourteenth centuries were written in the vernacular, indicating the loss of Latin facility by the lesser religious. There is abundant evidence of the decline or, in many cases, the non-existence of Latin among the clergy.[64]

Since the higher ranks of the church were generally filled by the nobility, or at least the sons of well-to-do persons, it is not surprising to find the occasional bishop ignorant of Latin; political considerations in these appointments, notwithstanding Wycliffe's fulminations, were a necessary fact of life. These were precisely the circumstances that pertained to the appointment of Lewis as bishop of Durham in the fourteenth century. The *Chronicle* of Robert de Graystanes, subprior of the same cathedral, informs us that 'Lewis was of noble birth, sprung from the kings of France and Sicily . . . chaste, but unlearned, for he understood not Latin and could scarce pronounce it.'[65] This, the *Chronicle* relates, led to a great embarrassment, and the most likely inference is that such ignorant bishops were more the exception than the rule. The incident itself occurred at Lewis's enthronement:

> When, therefore, at his consecration, he should have made his formal profession, he could not read it, though he had been instructed therein for many days beforehand; and having last arrived, with many promptings from others,

at the word *Metropolitan*, which after many gasps he yet could not pronounce, at length he said in the French tongue 'let that be taken as read'.[66]

Robert emphasizes that, at this, 'all the bystanders were amazed, mourning that such a man should be consecrated bishop.'[67] Lewis, moreover, remained in the See of Durham for seventeen years (1316–33), continuing to make such ignorant gaffes; at another time, for example, 'when he was conferring Holy Orders, and could not pronounce that phrase *in aenigmate* [Cor. 13 : 12], he said in French to those that stood [near], 'By St Louis, the man was a clown that wrote this word!'[68]

The lowest levels of the clergy, however, came in general from the working classes, and among them was every range of scholarship. There is no doubt that the bulk of village priests were of marginal competence in Latin; this is obviously the motivation behind the decree of the great Synod of Oxford, convened by Archbishop Stephen Langdon in 1222 which required archdeacons

... to see on their visitations that the canon of the mass is amended, and that the priests can properly pronounce at least the words of the canon and of baptism, and that they rightly understand this part [of the service books].[69]

This was no isolated decree; its substance was enacted eleven years later at the Council of Béziers which denied priestly ordination to those 'who could not read and sing'.[70] Following the Synod of Oxford, the clerks in the diocese of Salisbury were examined by the dean and chapter, in the course of which they came across a curate called Simon, of the village of Sonning. Simon had been 'ordained subdeacon at Oxford by a certain Irish bishop named Albin, then suffragan [assistant] to the Bishop of Lincoln, from whom he received deacon's orders; and those of priest from Hugh [of Wells] now Bishop of Lincoln, four years past'.[71] Upon examination, however, Simon was found abysmally ignorant. When the examiners came to the canon, the most sacred part of the Mass, they questioned him on the meaning of the words in the passage beginning 'Te igitur, clementissime Pater . . .' ('[We] therefore [humbly pray and beseech] Thee, most merciful Father'). Upon questioning, it was discovered that Simon

... knew not the case of *Te* [Thee] nor by what word it was governed; and when we bade him look closely which could most fittingly govern it, he replied,
– *Pater* [Father (in Heaven)], for he governeth all things.[72]

The examiners continued to press Simon on other words ' . . . what *clementissime* was, and what case, and how declined; [but] he knew not'. The account continues in this sorry state until at last Simon complained that 'it seemed indecent that he should be examined before the dean, since he was already in Holy Orders'. The document ends with Simon being asked 'where he was when he received his priest's Orders' and his answer that 'he had forgotten'. The final phrase is incisively telling: 'He is illiterate' ('Sufficienter illiteratus est').[73]

Simon's case is not isolated; there are many like him on record; some years later the Franciscan Bonaventura lamented that 'few [of the clergy] are experienced enough to teach as they should, or can be trusted to do so',[74] in the course of a long and bitter diatribe, in his *Quare Fratres Minores praedicent* against the many abuses committed by an indolent and corrupt clergy. In the year 1252, a clerical examination of a similar kind to that conducted at Salisbury was held in the diocese of Rouen in France. Again the surviving evidence gives much the same picture. The examination, of course, reveals the kind of information sought, and assumes the rote learning of all of the parts of speech, with the candidate's being required to parse every word fully. In many cases, the results obtained are gibberish and show no knowledge of Latin whatsoever, except perhaps a capacity to invent pseudo-endings on the spur of the moment. A certain priest, John of Bernetot, was asked to decline the fourth conjugation verb *transire* which goes *transio, transis, transit, transimus, transitis, transiunt* in the present indicative. John starts well enough, but gets progressively worse: '*transio, transis, transivi, transire, transiundi, transitrundo, ansiundum, transimus, transior, transiris*; beyond which he would say nothing more'.[75] After the first two correct responses he had slipped to a first person perfect, then to the present infinitive and then into the realms of imagination. This document, from the *Regestrum visitationum* of Odo Rigaldi, archbishop of Rouen (1248–75), gives further details on the examining of John, and in one question he is asked the meaning of *annuam*, to which he answered '*annual*'. However, 'when asked again what "annual" was, he said "many times"; asked "how many times?" he said "every day".'[76] The same *Register* has many more, equally dismal, accounts. On 30 May 1253 a certain Geoffrey was examined and was asked *inter alia*, the meaning of *aperta* in the passage 'omnia autem aperta et nuda sunt eius oculis' ('all things are naked and open unto the eyes [of Him with Whom we have to do]'). Geoffrey wasn't sure of the answer, suggesting first a noun and then, perhaps by a lucky guess, a participle. But he was quite ignorant and the examiners, 'therefore, both because of his insufficiency, and because after due inquisition he was found to be ill-famed of continence and quarrelsomeness, thought fit not to admit him to the said rectory'.[77] In the same text is the account for 16 March 1259–60 in which the clerk Nicholas Quesnel is asked to translate Genesis 1:4, 'et vidit lucem quod esset bona' ('And [God] saw the light, that it was good'), and replies 'it was a good thing to do'. Nicholas, although he was not totally ignorant of Latin, was none the less failed by the five members of the visitation committee because 'we found him in our examination to be of utterly insufficient learning, as for example he knew neither to read competently, nor to construe, nor would he chant'.[87]

The large amount of evidence of this kind gives incontrovertible support to the frequent complaints in the contemporary literature on the poor state of priestly learning at the lower levels. Yet, it is significant to note, those very priests were the ones on whom devolved the responsibility for maintaining schools and promoting literacy. Under the circumstances, the best that they could be expected to do was to memorize what was a foreign and largely meaningless tongue, perhaps using some mnemonic or *ars memorativa* aid if they could. Certainly the overwhelming evidence provided by the surviving examinations shows that this was what they were required to do. In turn, there was little more that they could do but drill their charges in the same way – if they attempted to teach at all – and this was secured by the continued use of physical coercion: whipping with canes and flogging with a bundle of birch rods.

Yet this cyclic reinforcing of an educationally impossible system was not without its critics. In June of 1336 Pope Benedict XII issued revised constitutions, *Summi magistri*, for the Benedictine order which required, *inter alia*, improved education among their members.[79] The black monks, accordingly, were required to ensure that

> . . . in all monastic cathedral churches, priories or other conventual and solemn places of sufficient means belonging to such orders or vows, there shall henceforth be kept a master to teach their monks such primitive sciences [*sciencias primitivas*], namely, grammar, logic and philosophy.[80]

Some few years later, in 1357, the influential English bishop of Exeter, John de Grandisson (1292–1369), who occupied that chair for forty-two years, complained also about the uselessness of much grammar teaching. His *Register* records his concern

> . . . that among masters or teachers of boys and illiterate folk in our diocese, who instruct them in grammar, there prevails a preposterous and unprofitable

method and order of teaching; . . . for these masters – after their scholars have learned to read or repeat, even imperfectly, the Lord's Prayer [and other official prayers] without knowing or understanding how to construe anything of the aforesaid, or decline words or parse them – then, I say, these masters make them pass on prematurely to learn other advanced [*magistrales*] books of poetry or metre.[81]

The result, of course, was no real learning at all. John records that this 'horrible and foolish abuse' was 'already too deeprooted in our diocese'; he was moved, consequently,

. . . to depute to [his Chapter] the duty of warning and enjoining all masters and instructors whatsoever that preside over grammar schools within the limits of his archdeaconry . . . that they should not, as hitherto, teach the boys whom they receive as grammar pupils only to read or learn by heart [*discere literaliter*]; but rather that, postponing all else, they should make them construe and understand the Lord's Prayer, the Ave Maria, the Creed, the Mattins and Hours of the Blessed Virgin, and decline and parse the words therein, before permitting them to pass on to other books.[82]

As a final attempt at enforcement, the bishop added the instruction that, 'moreover we proclaim that we purpose to confer clerical orders henceforth on no boys but upon such as may be found to have learnt after this method'. How successful John was we do not know but it is true that grammar schools began around this period to improve their practices steadily.

There was, of course, no real challenge yet to Latin as the language of scholarship. None of the vernaculars was secure in that period; they possessed no important literatures and, with the possible exception of Italian, had no standard forms; Chaucer's lament in *Troilus and Criseyde* (Book V) –

> And for ther is so gret diversite
> In Englissh and in writyng of oure tonge

– applied in the thirteenth and fourteenth centuries to all of Europe's vernaculars. The knightly and courtly classes had their vernacular romances which appeared in most developed form in the Norse sagas such as *Beowulf*, and in the *chansons de geste* of the troubadours. Despite the popularity of those works, they were not great literature. Improvement was still seen to depend on the better teaching of Latin and there were some efforts at reform of the grammar schools in order to correct the deficiencies.

Arresting the decline: Gerard Groote and the
Brethren of the Common Life

The most conspicuous effort to arrest the trend came from the efforts of a
Dutch cleric, Gerard Groote (1340–84), whose vigorous efforts initiated a
reform movement known as the *Devotio moderna*.[83] Gerard's origins are
somewhat obscure. He was born near Deventer in Holland of moderately
wealthy parents who saw that he received the best education available;
he matriculated at Paris in 1355 and graduated master of arts by 1360,
later attaining some distinction as a minor church scholar. There are
records also of his attending two other major schools, the *studia* of Cologne
and Prague, and this means that he was exposed to the complete range of
European religious thought. Subsequently he moved to Utrecht where he
settled as a secular clerk, living on the income of several canonries and
prebends. It may have been there, on account of the influence of John of
Arnhem, canon of St Peters, that he became increasingly involved with
the reform of church abuses.[84] Details of Gerard's early activities in this
respect are obscure, but around 1374 he seems to have become preoccupied
with asceticism and the need for salvation. His period of significant
activity, moreover, coincided with the beginnings of the Great Schism and
the growing influence of Wycliffe's teachings; he was as sensitive as
Wycliffe to the decline of the church and he saw the need for repentance
and salvation as personal acts independent of church encouragement.

To effect his purposes, Gerard concentrated his studies on *sacra pagina*
and canon law, the latter because, although not directly relevant, none the
less helped the religious to avoid, through ignorance, '[perverting] piety
into disobedience'.[85] Secular studies, however, he eschewed; the true
followers of Christ must not spend time 'in the study of geometrics,
arithmetic, rhetoric, dialectic, grammar, songs, poetry, legal matters or
astrology'.[86] In the words of his follower Thomas à Kempis – whose
Imitation of Christ is commonly conjectured to have been based on Gerard's
teachings – at the day of judgement 'we shall not be examined on what we
have read, but on what we have done'.[87] Gerard proposed, consequently, a
programme of popular education to enable people to secure individual
access to the scriptures, and these actions, among others, aroused the
enmity of the more conservative clerics. Unlike Wycliffe, however, he
remained orthodox in his religious views and so opposition to him never
passed beyond vocal criticism. Gerard commenced his ten-year 'apostolate',
which came in the last period of his all too brief life, with his gift to the

Carthusian order in 1374 of the farm that he inherited from his parents. By 1378 his asceticism reached the point where he entered, for a year, a monastery of the Carthusians whose Rule enjoined renunciation of the world, complete asceticism and a strictly contemplative, devotional life. Gerard seems to have flourished in a social climate; perhaps for this reason he found the Carthusian regime too limiting; moreover, he had a natural talent for organization. So, in 1379, he returned to secular life, again as a deacon in Utrecht. It was at that time the *Devotio moderna* became an active movement.

This was stimulated, in the first instance, by his concern with the social problem of unmarried women who could find no acceptable status in the community. This appears to have grown out of the case of a certain Elizabeth de Gherner who had been refused admission to a convent of 'Poor Clares', an order of poverty-embracing Franciscan nuns dating from 1215. In a letter to Arnold of Lochem, Gerard objected to the position that Elizabeth 'cannot be veiled because she is insufficiently taught and is ignorant of grammar'.[88] His protest supports the belief that women's convents of the period practised a high degree of selectivity. As a result, in 1379, Gerard gave over his house to such poor women and it became virtually an irregular convent – in so far as no vows were taken – of the 'Sisters of the Common Life'.

Meanwhile, an incipient male religious 'order' had also been forming around Gerard for some time and around 1380 one was established in the Deventer vicarage of Florentius Radewijns, a close friend. In company with twelve other disciples, Gerard and Florentius, whose express intentions were to become the servants of god – *Dei servitores* (or *Deo servientes laici et clerici*) – organized themselves on quasimonastic lines as the Brethren of the Common Life (*Fratres communis vitae*) although not until 1384, the year of Gerard's death, was a formal rule adopted: that of the Augustinian canons. Their basic concern was to lead a devotional life guided by the principles of moderation and temperance. It was in that house in Deventer that Gerard instituted his educational reforms. Although he had no intention of conducting a school in the formal sense, since he did not see himself as a schoolmaster, nevertheless his conviction of the need for improved public learning was responsible for the growth of a school in Deventer, and the Brethren supported this by providing a hostel for the youths attending the school.[89] Gerard was a scholar by temperament and had always been concerned to build his library out of books of high quality. He appears generally to have maintained a personal copyist and this was one of his important contributions to the success of this 'new devotional' movement.[90] At the Deventer house he instituted the practice of making copies for the book trade; soon his small community at Deventer became recognized for the high quality of their productions, and their reputation as copyists grew. This activity attracted boys to the house where they were made welcome; before long a school was in operation, and orphans were taken in, cared for, and given instruction in the elements of literacy. Gerard was anxious to find teachers and was assisted in this by his close friend John Cele (fl. 1374–1417), rector of a city school in nearby Zwolle. The school flourished and continued after Gerard's death in 1384.

The aim of the school at Deventer was to give knowledge as a means to salvation, following the rule of the Brethren of the Common Life. The order, at the same time, expanded to Windesheim where it built a monastery and became established on a regular basis in 1387. As the order grew, so did its schools. By 1400 there were schools at Deventer, Zwolle and Windesheim which gave a Latin grammar education to boys of all classes, from orphaned paupers to wealthy scions. The school at Deventer remained the most important and in the course of the fifteenth century it had five divisions: a house for the wealthy (*Domus divitum scholarium*), a house for the middle classes (*Domus pro mediocribus*), a house for the poor (*Domus pauperium scholarium*) and two of uncertain designation, known only in terms of their physical features, the little house (*Domus parva*) and the nearby house (*Domus vicina*). Even though the schools remained true to the ideals of Gerard, that is, they sought knowledge in the form of a Latin grammar education solely for devotional ends, they became respected and imitated. John Cele used Gerard's ideas to reform the schools at Zwolle, where he organized boys into eight grades, probably the first attempt at grading a school into classes.

Throughout the fifteenth century the *Devotio moderna* spread its institutions and schools throughout Germany and the Low Countries, and became the major educational model. Some of their pupils became influential intellectual figures, particularly Thomas à Kempis who was a student in Deventer around 1398–9 in its early days, and whose book, *The Imitation of Christ* (*De imitatione Christi*), was probably the most widely read devotional book of the times after the Bible itself. Another *alumnus* was probably Erasmus of Rotterdam who was sent to school in Deventer in 1476 and who became, in his mature life, the acknowledged intellectual leader of early sixteenth-century Europe.

Despite the excellence of their instruction and their fidelity to the traditions of medieval Latin scholarship, the schools of the Brethren of the Common Life were narrow in scope. Their exclusive emphasis on the traditional trivium conserved in Latin, no matter how proficiently it was taught, their insistence on the instrumentality of knowledge to the end of salvation, and their ascetic practices limited the application of their methods to those regions, chiefly Germany and the Netherlands, that were culturally backward and beyond the ambit even of the main events of scholastic learning. They had little or no effect elsewhere. Education in the late medieval period of the fourteenth and fifteenth centuries in the regions north of the Alps followed the ideals and practices set down in *De disciplina scholarium* and *Commendation of the Clerk* institutionalized by the Brethren of the Common Life. Such procedures were the vestigial traces of a vanishing era; the conceptions of learning, of life, and even the after-life that such educational ideals and methods sought to serve were already changing in the major centres of Europe.

Following the great intellectual debates of the thirteenth century in Paris, cultural and intellectual leadership passed to Italy, particularly to the newly independent towns in the plain of Lombardy, where the issues that had dominated European thought for several centuries were less influential. There, intellectual life, and education, had been developing a totally different character, marked by a vitality, liveliness and humanity that was in marked contrast to that of the scholastic epoch.

CHAPTER 6

Italy: Classical Revival of the Trecento

Intimations of change

The struggles of the papacy with the various secular powers of Europe in the thirteenth century, which gave the period its political character, were accompanied by significant and profoundly contrasting developments in intellectual life in France and Italy. France emerged triumphant from the political conflict; church power declined and throughout the fourteenth century the papacy was unable to exercise much of the considerable authority it still claimed for itself. Italy, for its part, developed rapidly as a major European centre of commerce, and this was reflected in the style of education which appeared: law, notarial studies and accounting techniques took a place alongside the traditional liberal arts and became important studies in the grammar schools and universities.

The French court, despite its superiority over the church, remained medieval in outlook, and in the fourteenth century its energies were expended in confronting the English in the long-drawn-out encounter of the Hundred Years War. Learning in France, centred in the activities of the university in Paris, was not influenced overtly by those political events; the tenor of intellectual life in northern Europe generally was detached and abstruse. Now that the universities, particularly Paris, were no longer involved in direct conflict with the church, academic disputes lost much of their excitement and in general were maintained in a formalized and derivative style. Throughout the fifteenth century the scholastic approach was still cultivated actively in France and England, and despite a gradual widening of their intellectual horizons, many scholars remained preoccupied with the issues of the thirteenth century. Even though there were a few exceptions, notably in the work of Jean Gerson (1363–1429), chancellor of Notre-Dame and the University of Paris, the situation remained relatively static and there was little internal impetus towards change or development. The universities, like the grammar schools, were conducted by clerics and based their curricula on the Latin trivium, with logic as the supreme study. Change in northern Europe, when it became evident in the sixteenth century, was greatly stimulated by developments in education and cultural pursuits that had begun to take place in Italy as early as the thirteenth century, when political events had repercussions on all aspects of Italian life.

The political situation in Italy changed dramatically with the break-up of the Hohenstaufen empire of Frederick II during the Great Interregnum of 1250–73 that followed his death. On the plain of Lombardy, the cities which had already achieved a relative independence by 1183 in Frederick Barbarossa's reign, now seized the chance to strengthen their positions. In 1273 Rudolf of Habsburg was elected Holy Roman Emperor, and thereafter Italy separated into even more independent political units. The way was led by the papacy itself when in 1279 it extracted from Rudolf not only the recognition that his imperial power was derived from the pope but also his surrender to the church of suzerainty over central Italy, where Rome was located. Thereafter, revolts against the emperor occurred in other territories, beginning with Palermo and Florence, both in 1282. By that time, political intrigues were complicated by the activity of political parties in Italy, known as Guelfs and Ghibellines. The Guelfs supported the papacy while the Ghibellines were inclined to favour the emperor, although the allegiances of the two parties were not always so clearly disposed; the Guelfs in Florence by 1295 had split into two sub-parties, the middle-class conservative Whites and the aristocratic Blacks who formed a secession group, although this was not a general Italian phenomenon. From the complex interplay of power between those numerous factions throughout the fourteenth century northern Italy gained its particular character and this helped to create a climate in which flourished the new cultural and intellectual interests of the fourteenth century, or the

Trecento.[1] The conflict between the church and state that resulted in the removal of the papal court from the Lateran Palace in Rome to its small territorial enclave of Avignon in the south of France not only promoted political activity in Italy, it also stimulated the growth of political thought. Several vigorous spokesmen appeared, of whom the first of major significance was the Florentine, Dante Alighieri. In the writings of Dante, who was the major Italian thinker of the Trecento, distinct signs of a changing intellectual climate can be discerned and this, which was to exert a major influence on the development of European thought, was facilitated to a considerable extent by the greatly improved educational provisions now operating in the Italian communes.

Humana civilitas: the vision of Dante

Dante's education and life in Duecento Florence

The poet Dante Alighieri (1265–1321) was born and educated in Florence, and although aspects of his early years are obscure, his intellect was shaped by the schools of that city and he is by far their most eminent product. Although Dante's mature work was written during the Trecento, his education took place late in the preceding thirteenth century, the Duecento; indeed, from Dante's references in his writings – and these are quite numerous – it is possible to gain a reasonably clear account of education in Florence for this period. It is true, of course, that we are less well informed for Florence than for other Italian communes, particularly Siena and Arezzo for which data are relatively abundant. None the less, it seems that Florence had a number of teachers of elementary literacy, grammar and the literal arts who taught both boys and girls. Boncompagno da Signa, for example, had studied under an unidentified 'Latin doctor of Florence' and by 1275, when Dante was ten years of age and most likely to be ready for school, the notarial records of the city contain references to *doctores puerorum* instructing children in elementary Latin;[2] another document of 1304 mentions a certain Clementia, *doctrix puerorum*, who taught writing, along with the grammar of Donatus (the *Ars minor*), psalter and notarial studies.[3] In the absence of any firm evidence, however, it is impossible to say what kind of developments were taking place in the schools for children. Certainly they must have been in the process of steady establishment and well supported by the populace, for early in the Trecento the contem-

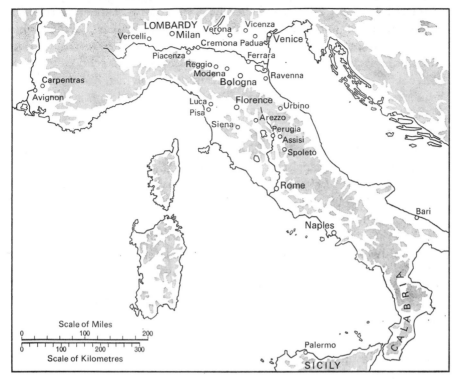

RENAISSANCE ITALY

porary chronicle of Giovanni Villani – the first to give such data – records that by 1339 Florence had a population of 90,000 of which some ten per cent, all of whom were children, were being instructed in reading. While the girls appear not to have progressed past this level, there were in existence some ten boys' schools which accepted about forty per cent of those who had thus learned to read, that is, approximately 1,800 students. There were six schools of mathematics and abacus, presumably as preparatory for accounting and commerical studies, which altogether accommodated more than 1,200 scholars, and four schools of grammar and logic for perhaps 600 boys who seem to have studied these two subjects as preparatory to law and *ars notarie*.[4] Unfortunately, the chronicle gives no further details; it does suggest, however, that during Dante's lifetime secular schools were appearing in Florence, following the practical and vocational trends already well established in Bologna, Siena, Arezzo, Padua, Venice and other communes.

Meanwhile, how did Dante receive his own education in Duecento

Florence? It is not known whether he went to any elementary school, although he does appear at some stage to have studied law. Certainly he could have been sent to one of the private masters – *doctores puerorum* – but from his own evidence he gained the significant part of his schooling in the convents of the city. Both of the mendicant orders, in fact, had established houses rather early in their career in Florence. The Franciscans had a school at the church of Santa Croce of unknown provenance which was upgraded into a *studium generale*, within the Franciscan system, in 1287. Independently of the great 'civic' universities, the mendicants had been building their own educational system. Franciscans had a three-stage sequence: the elementary *studia grammaticalia, logica et philosophica* which gave the first level of instruction for novices and were, apparently, instituted in most houses; above these were the four *studia generalia* at Toulouse, Cologne, Bologna and Florence; at the top were their three *studia principalia* which were, in effect, the schools of theology at Paris, Oxford and Cambridge. By the year 1300 the Franciscan *studium* at Florence was well established and had a library with some forty-five manuscripts. Likewise, the Dominicans had set up a system and this was organized around their simple conventual schools for beginning friars – who, apparently, like the Franciscans had already gained elementary instruction elsewhere – followed by their own *studia generalia* and capped by the three *studia theologiae* at Rome, Naples and Florence. The Dominicans, in fact, seem to have preceded the Franciscans at Florence since a Dominican school at the church of Santa Maria Novella was in existence as early as 1231; it was there that Dante received his wide-ranging religious education, and in particular his knowledge of Christian Aristotelianism along with Aquinas' interpretations. So we read in Dante's *Divine Comedy* that Thomas, and his master Albertus Magnus, are to be found in paradise,[5] along with, interestingly enough, Siger of Brabant. Dante's respect for the latter comes through in the lines from the Divine Comedy which report that Siger, 'when he lectured in the Street of Straw, syllogized unpleasant truths' ('Essa è la luce eterna di Sigieri / Che, leggendo nel vico degli strami, / Sillogizzò invidiosi veri').[6] One of Dante's most influential teachers was the literary scholar Brunetto Latini, known chiefly for his popular encyclopedia, *Il Tesoro* (*The Treasure*), and for his experiments in writing a new form of free verse (*versi sciolti*) in hendecasyllabic metre. Brunetto, Dante records in the *Inferno*, died early in life,[7] but even so exerted a strong influence on him, for he had 'on earth for hour after hour taught me of man's eternal goal'.[8] Concern with man's spiritual mission was a major element in Dante's education.

At the same time, like most Italian youths of his social class, Dante was reared in a world of politics. His early political affiliations followed those of his father whose activity for the Guelf cause had led to his temporary exile from Florence five years before Dante's birth. Dante himself grew up during a period of increasing political activism and as a young man in his seventeenth year, he was influenced profoundly by the events that led to the peaceful revolt in 1282 of the Florentine citizenry against the emperor's authority. Political participation in Florence, as in all of the Italian *municipia*, was restricted to those with definite qualifications of citizenship, generally achieved through wealth and influence in the commercial affairs of the city, or through membership of the exclusive guilds. At the age of thirty Dante was admitted to the guild of physicians and apothecaries and so was enabled to enter political life. He soon became very actively engaged and allied himself with the White Guelf (*Parte Bianca*) cause. By 1301 Dante had become increasingly antipapal in outlook and was involved in the serious intrigues between the Black and White parties. With the support of Boniface VIII the Blacks eventually gained control of the Florentine government and in 1302 accused Dante of corruption while in public office. The Whites were now totally defeated; Dante was exiled, had his property confiscated, and was then condemned to death *in absentia*. Thereupon Dante renounced his Guelfic allegiance, as he says in the *Paradiso*: 'for their brutishness will manifest itself and it is better to be a party simply of oneself'.[9] He became increasingly hostile to the papacy – though not to Christianity – and lived the rest of his life in exile in other cities of the peninsula. Those circumstances resulted in the production of two of the major intellectual documents of the century, *De monarchia* and *La Divina Commedia*. These two writings, as well as his two unfinished treatises – one on language, *De vulgari eloquentia*, and another on political theory, *Convivio* – set a new style of intellectual endeavour[10] which had a pronounced effect on the development of education in Italy. In particular they promoted the study of the vernacular and put a much greater emphasis on the role of literature and the concomitant study of the literary tradition.

Concern with the vernacular

Dante's influence on succeeding generations was exercised in large part through his attitude to the emerging vernaculars which, even in the late thirteenth century, were still not generally acceptable for literary composition. In one of his major works, *De vulgari eloquentia* (*The Eloquence of the*

Vernacular), which was begun some time between 1302 and 1305 and never completed, his attitude towards the use of the vernacular is set out clearly. Although addressed to the relatively simple question of the art of vernacular literary composition, the study deals with more profound issues and foreshadows Dante's subsequent writings.

Language and reason, in his view, are the distinctive qualities of man, placing him in an intermediate position between the divine and the animal orders of existence. At the same time, however, man is not endowed with the ability to speak any particular language; he simply has the potential, of divine origin, to use speech. Languages themselves, he recognized, are conventional in origin and usage. In stating this belief, Dante expressed his partial opposition to the school of contemporaneous grammarians, known as *Modistae*, who at the same time were advancing the theory that an ideal grammar exists outside the variety of languages and that, consequently, a major purpose of linguistic study is to find that grammar and to establish absolute rules of grammatical expression. The *Modistae* held that grammar should prescribe the rules of language, and, furthermore, that it can furnish information on the working of the human mind, since reason, in their view, operates according to the logical prescriptions of properly used grammar.[11] Analysis of grammar, in the view of the *Modistae*, elucidates the structure of logic. Dante did not depart from the *Modistae* altogether in that he sought to distinguish the accidental from the essential in language. Vocabulary, quite evidently, is arbitrary; it varies from one language to another and achieves its force entirely by conventional usage.[12] It is the syntax of arrangement (*constructio vocabulorum*) that is constant, in his view, and his observations of the many similar, but sufficiently distinguishable vernaculars in the Italy of his time, throughout which he had wandered in his years of exile, must have reinforced that belief.

In holding to the notion of a common syntax, Dante was not markedly different from the *Modistae*; in his attitude to Latin, however, he demonstrated a capacity for highly original thinking. The *Modistae* built their case around the idea of the absolute quality of Latin: in their view it was the ultimate touchstone. All other languages they believed to be debased forms. Dante himself held that view at first, since Greek was largely unknown in western Europe in this period. In the projected fifteen-book series, known as the *Convivio*, which did not proceed beyond the completion of the fourth volume in 1308, Dante argued that Latin had been derived from earlier Italian vernaculars, becoming therefore not strictly a 'true' language, but a 'meta'-language.[13] He claimed it to be superior on three counts: it is incorruptible, comprehensive and composed according to art and not usage.[14] Moreover, he continued, Latin is absolute for three further reasons which he set out in detail: for its nobility, virtue and beauty.[15] Yet the claims of the vernacular were not ignored by Dante and in the *Convivio* he showed his concern to study the vernaculars by proclaiming an intention 'to deal fully with this topic elsewhere, in a book which I intend to write – God willing – on the *Eloquence of the Vernacular*'.[16]

In this work, the *De vulgari eloquentia*, which was apparently abandoned around 1308 – the same year is conjectured both for it and the *Convivio* – Dante came to reverse his attitude completely and to adopt the position by which he is best remembered: the vernaculars are superior, and for the same reasons he had advanced to support the case for Latin. The vernaculars to which he was referring are those which preceded Latin, and are obviously not the same ones as used in his own day: they were, he said, the fertile soil from which Latin was derived. Yet Dante wrote his defence of the vernacular in Latin, presumably to reach and influence scholarly opinion, in contrast to this use of the vernacular in the *Convivio*. In his own lifetime, Dante went on to give effect to his argument through eloquent use of the vernacular in *La Divina Commedia* (*The Divine Comedy*) in which he virtually raised the Italian language to the level where it rivalled Latin, and for literary and belletristic purposes at least, displaced it increasingly thereafter.

Religious and secular sovereignty

Dante continued his political activities during his exile and by 1311 emerged strongly sympathetic to the cause of the emperor, Henry VII, who had been elected in 1308. Florence still supported the papacy: among other reasons it was politically expedient to do so. The pope in Avignon was relatively weak; support for the church meant, in effect, independence for Florence, whereas support for the emperor invited direct political control by an authority more readily disposed to enforce sovereignty. Dante, for his part, held to the most extreme of monist views and he saw all life as bound together in an ultimate unity. 'Every good thing is good in virtue of being one,'[17] and that outlook suffused all of his writing. By 1312 he articulated his political outlook in a treatise on sovereignty; this was the *De monarchia*,[18] where he argued the merits of papal and secular claims to temporal sovereignty. In that treatise, Dante asserted that effective power can only be exercised by the emperor, and that only when such authority prevails can peace and harmony ensue, giving rise to a properly civilized state: *civilitas humana*.

De monarchia deals successively with three fundamental themes: the nature of man, the vocation of man, and the best means of ensuring the attainment of that vocation. In developing his case, Dante not only explicated a political standpoint, he also implied a theory of education. Following his earlier assertions in *De vulgari eloquentia*, which in turn were derived essentially from current medieval thought, Dante conceived man as having a divine origin, with a hierarchical position between the animal and angelic realms. Man shares the quality of *being* with all existence: mineral, plant and animal. His distinctive quality, however, is more than being, it is intellection, conceived as capacity or potentiality. In this respect, Dante followed Aristotle.[19] At one point he invoked the authority of Averroes' commentary on Aristotle's *De anima* ('Et huic sententiae concordat Averrois, in *Commento* super iis quae *de Anima*'),[20] perhaps a little too explicitly, for this was partly responsible for the vigorous denunciation of *De monarchia* in 1327 by the Dominican, Guido Vernani; subsequently it was burned as heretical in Bologna in 1329, and, two centuries later in 1554, placed on the list of banned books, *Index librorum prohibitorum*. Through intellection, Dante argued, man achieves his vocation, which is happiness. As Dante's assumptions on the nature of man proceeded from the axiom of unity, so too did his conceptions of happiness and the means whereby it can be ensured. To develop his argument, Dante suggested an isomorphism between man and the state. Just as man is part of a hierarchical divine structure, and within himself is composed of a series of subordinated qualities – being, appetition, feeling, willing and thinking – of which thinking is at the summit, so too the state in essence can be conceived as a hierarchical structure, so ordered as to achieve civil equity:

> ... mankind is at its best in a state of concord; for as a man is at his best in body and soul when he is in a state of concord, the same is true of a house, a city and a kingdom, and of mankind as a whole.[21]

Concord, and equity, he argued, can be secured only in the properly regulated, unified political state. Therein lay his argument for the proper claims to temporal sovereignty by a monarch; only in such a state can man live the well-ordered life necessary to attaining his vocation of happiness. Dante's conception of the state, however, is somewhat elusive. In his day there were three versions of civil government – *civitas, regnum, imper-*

ium, terms designating respectively the city-state, such as Florence, the kingdom and the empire[22] – and in *De monarchia* he advocated the universal empire as the best form of government, although he left unanswered the question of the position of the city-state and the kingdom of Italy within it. The purpose of his thesis was to defend the principle of secular authority, in opposition to the extreme assertions of Boniface VIII in *Unam sanctam* of 1302 in which that pope claimed complete authority for his own office. The entire second part of *De monarchia* is a rationalization, conducted according to the regular procedures of medieval logic, for the legitimacy of secular government. In essence, Dante's argument sought to counter papal assertions in similar terms: god does not allow any actions contrary to nature, and since it was as a result of a natural eschatological process that the Roman people (*populus Romanus*) secured control of the world, before the appearance of Christ, therefore secular government is in accord with divine ordinance.[23] A difficulty within Dante's theory comes in large part from his frequent use of the imprecise 'Roman people', *populus Romanus*. Although the concept of the state in the period of emerging nationality that followed Dante was to become a crucial issue, its exact determination did not affect the argument of *De monarchia*.

The beatific vision

In the third part of *De monarchia*, Dante brought together the three themes in a final synthesis which offers the germs of an educational theory. In Part III of the treatise Dante sets out what appears on the surface as a traditional educational argument of the kind that had been rationalized in the cathedral schools in the immediately preceding centuries:

> Unerring Providence has therefore set man to attain two goals: the first is happiness in this life, which consists in the exercise of his own powers and is typified by the earthly paradise; the second is the happiness of eternal life, which consists in the enjoyment of the divine countenance, which man cannot attain to by his own power but only by the aid of divine illumination [*nisi lumine divino adiuta*], and is typified by the heavenly paradise. These two sorts of happiness are attained by diverse means, just as one reaches conclusions by different means. We attain to the first by means of philosophical teaching [*per philosophica documenta verimus*], being faithful to it by exercising our moral and intellectual virtues. We arrive at the second by means of spiritual teaching [*per documenta spiritualia*], which transcends human reason, in so far as we exercise the theological virtues of faith, hope and charity. These conclusions,

and the means towards them, are revealed to us, on the one hand by human reason (in the light of which the philosophers have made the human situation perfectly clear), and on the other by the Holy Spirit, who has revealed the supernatural truth necessary for our salvation by means of the prophets and sacred writers, and through the Son of God, Jesus Christ . . . and Christ's disciples.[24]

In one sense, Dante's argument can be interpreted as a reaffirmation of the medieval synthesis of Aquinas barely half a century before. There had, indeed, been a pronounced trend in that direction in European education. Yet the position is much more complex,[25] and involves a consideration of Dante's view of the church and man's need for salvation. The earthly representatives of the church, of course, receive blistering denunciations throughout the *Divine Comedy*: Brunetto Latini relates that his companions in the Inferno were 'clerics all, and famous scholars' ('. . . che tutti fur cherci / E letterati grandi, e di gran fama');[26] Pope Nicholas III, 'son of the she-bear' ('figliuol dell'orsa') was there because of his simony;[27] confined there also were the Cluniac Benedictines, described as a company of 'miserable hypocrites' ('ipocriti tristi').[28] The papacy is depicted as the office of reprobates: 'the shepherd has become a wolf, the evangelists and fathers of the church are neglected for the close study of the Decretals, the pope and his cardinals never leave this study of the laws to spare a single thought for Nazareth where Gabriel had spread his wings'.[29] What, then, did Dante feel should be the role of the church? In the first place, it should be revivified through a purging of its delinquent officials and through a redirection of its efforts. Dante's views are, in many respects, enigmatic although it is clear that he saw no role for the church as a complementary form of government; its only essential function should be that of ministering to man's need for spiritual guidance and salvation. The church should be separate from the state, acting as a guide in spiritual matters in the same way that the emperor does in secular affairs. So he argued in *De monarchia*: '. . . for, as man has a twofold end, so he needs two guiding powers; namely, the papacy to guide man to eternal life and the emperor, who leads man, through the teachings of philosophy, to earthly happiness.'[30]

Throughout the last years of his life Dante elaborated on the theme of the purification and regeneration of the church, expressing these ideas in his great vernacular poem *La Divina Commedia*. The *Comedy* – and the term in his day meant a narrative poem with a happy ending, derived from the Greek *komoidia* – is a lengthy composition in three parts – *Inferno, Purgat-*

orio, Paradiso. It is one of the greatest poems in the literature of the West, and certainly is the work by which Dante is best remembered. The details of its composition are unknown; it was written, in all likelihood, on numerous separate occasions, beginning perhaps, although by no means certainly, about 1306 and completed in 1321, barely a few months before his death. The *Comedy* exemplifies for us the philosophy underlying the life activity of Dante which, in essence, was to justify him as a poet and by means of poetry, which he considered to be the highest form of communication, to lead him – and the reader – to a divine vision. So, in a profound way, Dante differs from Thomas Aquinas who also claimed to offer a way to the highest good of beatific vision via pure intellection. In a real sense, Dante can be interpreted as a philosopher concerned primarily with the task of communication, and as such he made an immense contribution to the development of educational thought.

In many respects, it must be admitted, Dante was medieval in temperament and outlook;[31] certainly his works provide ample evidence: continued assertion of dogmatic axioms and the derivation of logical argument from them, insistence on providence and the underlying unity of all creation, and an excessive concern with jurisdictional argument. The *Comedy* has all the medieval hallmarks: it is cosmic in scope, encyclopedic in content, eschatological in outlook. It was composed in the same spirit as the vast *summae* of the philosophers, and so looked back to a disappearing age. Yet Dante was not completely medieval; indeed, much of his thought was fresh and innovatory. His use of the vernacular provided a stimulus to other writers who followed his example: Petrarch and Boccaccio in Italy, Rabelais in France, Chaucer in England. He was the first scholar to venture the opinion that the vernacular might be a worthy vehicle of human expression. Moreover, his attitude towards the church marked something of a departure: he was openly critical on many occasions and even asserted that the Donation of Constantine had led to avarice on the part of the church.[32] Hitherto no writer had expressed views quite so violently in opposition. His thought itself helped introduce a new phase in Western intellectual life. Dante may have used the conventions of the scholastics but his aims were different: he allowed free rein to his imagination, and he attempted to construct poetically a vision of civilization and to justify this historically, although he was limited severely by the lack of available historical materials and concepts. He brought out the notion of the essential unity of mankind and the need for the state to provide, by virtue of its sovereignty, appropriate conditions for *humana civilitas* which should enable men to achieve in this world the best possible mode of human existence and to make the most effective preparation for the next. Dante's thought was a harbinger of an increasing concern with man, yet his vision needed substantial support from history before it would be capable of implementation.

Petrarch and the Latin revival

Beginnings of antiquarianism

The search for the classical past, which was to become a major intellectual preoccupation of fourteenth- and fifteenth-century Italy, and which, consequently, influenced the course of education in a significantly different direction, was commencing in Dante's time, almost at the level of myth and fable, without adequate documentary sources and with little awareness of the events of the intervening centuries after imperial Rome. In *De monarchia* Dante asserted the historical supremacy of the classical Roman people; in *De vulgari eloquentia* he put the case for the recognition of Italian as the basis of a new civilization; in the *Comedy* he suggested the image of a revivified Christian Rome. Yet Dante probably had very little close acquaintance with the classical past; the bulk of his knowledge of ancient Rome came from his reading of the few extant works by the great historian Livy (59 B.C.–A.D. 17). Dante was limited, necessarily, by the circumstances of his time. Not only had the works of classical Greece disappeared almost completely from Western Europe after the barbarian migrations of the fifth century, but in large part the writings of the Romans were lost too. In some cases, classical Latin books disappeared for ever and are now known only by historical references; some were recovered, such as Cicero's *De gloria*, only to be lost again, irretrievably; yet others lay unidentified in the libraries and archives of castles, cathedrals and monasteries. The work of some authors – Virgil, Horace, Seneca and Cicero, for example – was partially extant, but the manuscripts of many others remained untouched in vaults and repositories for centuries, particularly those of the poets Catullus and Lucretius, the historian Tacitus,[33] and the great educational theorist Quintilian whose *Institutio oratoria* was only partially known.

The recovery of the classical past was stimulated by the activities of two scholars who were contemporary with Dante, a judge in Padua, Lovato

(1241–1309), and a correspondent of his in the same city, Albertino Mussato (1262–1329).[34] In his leisure hours Lovato wrote Latin verse, and in searching for classical models he discovered in the library of the abbey at Pomposa a large number of ancient manuscripts, some of which he circulated among his friends, including Mussato. So started a literary fashion for manuscript discovery and collection that spread rapidly. Throughout Italy the libraries of monasteries and cathedral chapter-houses were found to contain the newly prized documents. In Ravenna, works were discovered by the two Plinys, Gaius the Elder (A.D. 23–79) and his adopted nephew Gaius Secundus (A.D. 62–c. 114), whose surviving writings were on natural science and forensic speeches respectively. At Naples, medical tracts by Galen and Hippocrates came to light. As manuscripts were located they were copied and sold, finding a ready public. Lovato and Mussato initiated the process of recovering the classical past; the most prominent figure in that movement, however, was another scholar, younger than them by several generations.

Recovery of the Latin past: the work of Petrarch

Francesco Petracco, or Petrarca (1304–74),[35] was born in Arezzo, son of the exiled Florentine notary, Petraccolo dell'Ancisa, who was known generally by his professional title, Ser Petracco. As a result of his White Guelf allegiance and subsequent alleged intrigues, Ser Petracco fled from Florence in 1302, in the same year that Dante was expelled from that city, and he lived the rest of his life in exile. The young Francesco was born into a cultured family – his grandfather, too, was a notary – that was on personal terms with Dante. Petrarch's boyhood is obscure since the family was at times in hiding; not until 1312, when Ser Petracco sought the protection of the papal court at Avignon, and settled in nearby Carpentras, does the record become certain. In that small town Petrarch began his schooling with tuition in Latin grammar and rhetoric given by a well-known master, Convenevole da Prato, who was an exceptionally enlightened teacher. Four years later, in 1316, at the age of twelve, Petrarch was sent to the university at Montpellier where he first became acquainted with Cicero and was influenced profoundly, recalling in his later years, 'at that age I was incapable of understanding what I read, but I took so much delight in the harmonious disposition of the words that any other book I heard or read seemed to me to give off a graceless, discordant sound'.[36] The same letter, incidentally, recorded his father's opposition to Petrarch's reading

of Cicero and an attempt by his father to burn copies both of Cicero and
Virgil that Petrarch had bought and hoarded carefully. Parental opposition,
however, did not last; seeing his son's distress, Ser Petracco 'pulled out of
the fire two volumes already scorched, and . . . held out to me with one
hand Virgil and with the other Cicero's *Rhetoric*, and said: Here; take this
one as an occasional recreation for your mind and the other to comfort and
aid you in your law studies.' After four years at Montpellier, Petrarch left
in 1320 for Bologna, always the leading school of law among European
universities, to continue his legal studies. He was not deeply interested in
the subject and in 1324, in his twentieth year, he abandoned it. At Bologna,
however, he became seriously interested in the historical basis of Roman
law, and, of equal significance, he continued collecting books. His early
twenties were spent, in company with some friends, in a period of
fashionable living, concluded in 1330 by his acceptance of minor orders to
take up a clerical appointment as secretary to Cardinal Giovanni Colonna.
Petrarch found himself, for the first time, enabled to pursue freely his
interest in classical literature.

In the cardinal's employ Petrarch had access to various libraries, facilities
for travel, and the opportunity to meet with visiting dignitaries who could
guide his searches. Petrarch became conscious that he was beginning to
discharge a self-appointed mission: the discovery, copying and editing of
classical works. It is interesting to note in passing that from his activities
in that period modern book style was standardized, with wide margins
and spaced text, in contrast to the cramped and crowded pages of medieval
codices. In particular, his version of Livy is considered the first production
in the modern scholarly tradition.[37] At that time Petrarch observed how
vital his mission was to civilization's wellbeing: 'Pliny's *History of the
Roman Wars* disappeared in our own times. Our descendants will have no
knowledge of the past. I am as if on the frontiers of two peoples, looking
forward and backward.'[38] In those years Petrarch became well known in
ecclesiastical and literary circles and, being anxious to secure further
recognition of his talents, he conceived the desire to be crowned poet
laureate of Italy. That venerable custom, whereby the ancient Romans
recognized the merits of their poets by conferring a laurel crown in
festivals on the Capitoline hill, had been revived in 1315 when the university at Padua conferred the wreath on Mussato. As a result of his own
careful manipulations, Petrarch was crowned in Rome in 1341 with the
title 'magnum poetam et historicum', becoming thereby the best-known
public figure of the day. Although Petrarch had produced insufficient

literary work to justify the accolade, its wording – although not strictly grammatical – is significant: he was designated historian as well as great poet. His recognition as historian evidences the changing intellectual temper of the times; hitherto, history had not been written as such, rather it had been incorporated into other studies, generally as background material. The work of Petrarch was instrumental in creating an appreciation of history as an autonomous intellectual and cultural activity.

Petrarch had sought the title in part on the basis of his growing historical awareness and of his intention to write the greatest epic poem of all time, an account of the campaigns of Scipio Africanus the Elder against Hannibal which ended in 210 B.C. with the saving of Rome from Carthaginian domination. Although the poem, entitled *Africa*, was not completed until the end of his life, the first part was advanced for his claims to the laurels and in many respects it was a departure from the literary conventions of the day. Its hero was a classical Roman, a pagan, whose characteristic quality of virtue, in the classical sense of *virtus*, set a new ideal before the fourteenth century. Scipio had been a vigorous person who embodied Petrarch's attitude that the active life is as worthy as the contemplative, a view that was stated explicitly in a letter to Marco da Genova with an example drawn from the life of Scipio.[39] Yet Petrarch was not always consistent in this attitude, and in the *Secretum* he asserted very strongly the opposite point of view. To amplify his new-found ideals, Petrarch conceived also of a historical series of biographies of famous Romans, *De viris illustribus*. For more than thirty years he was occupied with those two vast projects, although he worked at them intermittently, giving his attention to many other works by which he is equally well remembered: his collection of the bulk of his lyrical poetry known both as the *Rime* and the *Canzoniere*; some minor poems; collected sets of letters; numerous occasional writings; and, of some philosophical importance, his polemical invective, *De sui ipsius et multorum ignorantia* (*On His Own Ignorance and That of Many Others*).[40]

Those two lifelong literary projects, *Africa* and *De viris illustribus*, symbolized Petrarch's mature commitment to cultivating a historical awareness in the intellectual community and attempting to apply its insights to the life of the times. In 1342, the year after receiving his laurels, he made his next significant attempt in this direction. Having recognized the need to understand Greek as a key to both the Christian scriptures and much of the historical past, Petrarch sought a teacher of the language, and found one in the visiting Byzantine emissary and monk, Bernard Barlaam. The effort, unfortunately, was not sustained. Barlaam was elevated to a bishop-ric and could no longer instruct him; Petrarch, for his part, sought no other teacher. There were other persons capable of teaching Greek, particularly in the vicinity of the papal court; in fact there had always been some individuals in Europe who knew Greek, even at the time of the most depressed conditions of learning: the great English scholar and bishop of Lincoln, for example, Robert Grosseteste (c. 1175–1253), had learned Greek from scholars resident in his *ménage* and himself had translated numerous works into Latin from the Greek, including Aristotle's *Ethica* and *De virtute*, as well as selections from John of Damascus, the Pseudo-Dionysius and Maximus Confessor. Sicily and Calabria, in particular, had always preserved an element of Greek culture and language, although in attenu-ated form, since the time of the original settlements of Magna Graecia, augmented at various intervals by conquest, trade and emigration from Byzantine sources. Petrarch, however, did not persevere with his Greek studies. According to some suggestions he was reluctant to continue;[41] in part, no doubt his attitude was consistent with the times. There simply was no deeply held conviction that Greek was really necessary; the literary and historical revival that Petrarch himself was leading was essentially a Latin movement[42] and it had not yet progressed to the point where it sought a more thorough self-understanding in its Greek origins.

Instead, Petrarch devoted his attentions thereafter to Latin and began collecting the letters of Cicero after making a chance discovery in 1345 of a first set, the *Letters to Atticus* (*Epistolae ad Atticum*), in the cathedral library of Verona. This was a great advance for scholarship and was to be responsible, half a century later, for a revival of the ideal of Roman repub-licanism as championed by Cicero. In addition, it stimulated Petrarch to form a collection of his own letters, on the Ciceronian model, which he commenced in 1360. In the years following his discovery of Cicero's letters, his enthusiasm increased and he has left numerous references to his quest for ancient writings. Around 1346, in a most significant letter to Giovanni Dell' Incisa, he wrote:

I am still in the thrall of one insatiable desire which hitherto I have been neither able nor willing to check. . . . I cannot get enough books. It may be that I have already more than I need, but it is with books as it is with other things: success in acquisition spurs the desire to get still more. Books, indeed, have a special charm. Gold, silver, gems, purple raiment, a house of marble, a well-tilled field, paintings, a steed with splendid trappings – things such as these give but a silent and superficial pleasure. Books delight us through and through, they talk with us, give us good counsel, they enter into a living and intimate companionship with us.

What is more, not only does a book win the reader's affection for itself, but it mentions the names of other books, so that it stirs the desire for another.[43]

This letter listed the numerous authors he had so discovered – Cicero, Varro, Ennius, Terence, Cato, Xenophon, Plato, Seneca, Augustine, Lactantius, Suetonius, Pliny, these being the major writers – and ended with an injunction to his correspondent:

Now do you, as you hold me dear, commission trustworthy and competent men to go through Tuscany for me, examining the book-chests of the religious and of other studious men, searching for things that might serve to alleviate or increase my thirst. . . . I enclose a list of the things I chiefly desire; and . . . I am sending similar requests to friends in Britain, France, and Spain.

This insatiable quest continued. The following year (1347) Petrarch accepted a commission by Giovanni Coci, the papal librarian, to reorganize Clement VI's library. In writing to Coci, Petrarch accepted the task gladly, pointing out that success, however, 'depends on the extent to which Fortune favours me in finding the emended manuscripts that you want'.[44] In that letter Petrarch again mentioned the 'shame of our times: that we should be so poor in things of real value, while riches are being heaped up with such care and toil', while at the same time asserting his own recognition that the recovery of the classical past through its literature was one of man's worthiest acquisitions. His efforts were successful. On the occasion of a journey in 1352, five years after the papal commission, he mentioned the fact that books were a large part of his luggage;[45] the following year he wrote to a friend that 'I have books of every sort, not the least of my possessions.'[46] Yet these were all Latin gains: his Plato mentioned in the letter of 1346 was a Latinized version of *Timaeus*. Not until 1354 did he make his first acquisition of a Greek text when he procured a codex of Plato's dialogues, thereby becoming the first Western European to possess a work of Plato in Greek. Petrarch was to acquire many more works of Plato, as he claimed in 1368: 'I have sixteen or more of Plato's books at home';[47] although he observed, ruefully, that he could not read them. His lack of Greek was a great handicap.

Petrarch devoted his historical attentions to more than the restoration of Latin literature. He was appalled by the neglect of the physical remains of the former empire: monuments, buildings, statuary were everywhere in process of decay and even deliberate demolition. As early as 1337, in his thirty-fourth year, Petrarch had recorded his feelings on the matter,[48] thereby anticipating and stimulating the movement of historical anti- quarianism that was to become a pronounced activity in the fifteenth century. Books and relics were the direct means by which the classical past could be restored. Yet in themselves they were but preceptors; their use was in reviving and stimulating in modern man the spirit that guided the ancients. For Petrarch, the past had many lessons, and these he set out in an intellectual and educational programme that broke decisively with the medieval tradition and became the immediate parent of the modern Western liberal arts tradition.

Moral discipline: Petrarch's attitude to education

The great value of history – and by this Petrarch chiefly meant the Roman past as exemplified in its major literary achievements – was that it taught by example. It was with this motivation, in fact, that he conceived his own *De viris illustribus* as a continuation of that tradition. Classical antiquity teaches us, he wrote, to feel rightly towards god, and to act rightly among our fellows.[49] In seeking out this concept, he emphasized the moral and ethical ideals of classical times, finding in them the best possible guide to human conduct. In Petrarch's view the good man is the morally disciplined man; from the attainment of moral discipline alone issues genuine freedom, itself the highest of human ideals. In asserting this, Petrarch echoed a sentiment of Dante's.[50] The deliberate cultivation of moral discipline, and the correlative striving towards true freedom, for Petrarch, is the vocation of man.

The way to freedom is an educational path: in his mature-age *Letter to Posterity*[51] Petrarch advances the position that morality comes through knowledge, itself contained in the three greatest categories of history, philosophy and poetry, a classification that was derived from his belief that the finest exemplars for man are Livy, Cicero, Plato, Virgil and Homer. Those three major studies are the road to knowledge, and knowledge itself is a necessary intermediary on the way to virtue. In developing this position, Petrarch followed the basic propositions of Cicero and, before him, of Plato. His own direct knowledge of Plato was minimal, even though Petrarch acknowledged his affection for the Platonic position, for example, in a number of places in *On His Own Ignorance*. It was, however, the ideas of Plato as they appeared in the general cultural tradition as Neopla-

tonism and Christian idealism, for example, that Petrarch accepted implicitly. And it was in the same spirit that Petrarch reacted to Aristotle. On
several occasions he recorded his opposition to that philosopher, although
the context makes it clear that Petrarch was quite naïve in his knowledge
and that, despite his own concern for sources, he had not and indeed could
not have consulted Aristotle in the original.[52] His objection was to current
teachings based on Aristotle, and in particular his invectives were directed
against Averroism and the excessive use of dialectic.[53] Again Petrarch
reveals no direct acquaintance with Averroes; the tenor of his objections
is more a matter of an intellectual taste that eschewed all Aristotelian and
Averroist doctrines, along with their innumerable popularized and derived
versions, than of any carefully developed philosophical position. Petrarch's
emotional outlook is summarized adequately and quite simply in his
statement, 'I will not be persuaded that any good can come from Arabia.'[54]

Cicero was the centre of his interests and the exemplar he sought
to promote: Cicero as the personification of Roman *virtus*, as master-teacher
of the Roman people, as possessor of perfect Latinity. This affection for
Cicero was part of Petrarch's vision of a revivified Rome that he mentioned
so frequently. Petrarch made no secret of his desire for the re-establishment of the *imperium Romanum*, and his acceptance of the laurels in 1341
was the first of many indications. Two years later, in 1343, the intense
visionary Niccola (or Cola) di Rienzo met Petrarch and confided in him
his dream of a new Rome. Petrarch was persuaded, and when Cola proclaimed himself tribune of Rome in 1347 after a brief, popular revolution
in the city, Petrarch supported him in letters.[55] When the course of events
over the following few years went against Cola, Petrarch quietly dissociated himself; Cola, for his part, was murdered by an avenging mob in
Rome in 1354. Although many of the details of Petrarch's relations with
the events of the revolution are unclear, it is certain that his concern was
with restoring the greatness of Rome; Petrarch may have projected into
Cola the personality of Scipio, the new saviour. The motivating spirit
throughout was Cicero, the ideal was a public *civilitas* and a personal *virtus*.
Yet when the republican cause failed, Petrarch was able to transfer his
enthusiasms equally to the papacy as a possible unifying influence. When
Urban V was elected pope in 1362, Petrarch saw his name as a portent: in
her glorious past Rome was *Urbs orbis*: the city of the world. The name of
the new pope symbolized the possibility of a return to that ancient felicitous
condition.[56]

Petrarch himself did not set out a coherent theory of education, much less a pedagogy, to accompany his ambitious ideas. He was no school-master and he had, in general, a poor opinion of that occupation, rein-forced in all likelihood by the fact that his own son Giovanni fared badly in grammar school. In 1350, Petrarch wrote to a Florentine friend and schoolmaster, Zanobi da Strada, that he considered schoolteaching to be the occupation of those who were arrested in their personality develop-ment:

> Let them teach boys who can do no better, who possess a laborious and dutiful, though sluggish mind, a murky brain, a slow wit, chill blood, a body enduring of labour, a soul scornful of glory, avid for small gains and proof against boredom . . . Leave this trade to those who enjoy reverting to childhood, who are shy of dealing with grown men and ashamed to live with their equals, who love to parade before minors, to have always someone to terrify, torture, afflict and rule, though they be hated and feared . . . Those will best teach boys who are most like them; there is a quick and easy com-munication between like creatures.[57]

Apart from the personal hostility he felt, Petrarch was simply conform-ing to generally accepted public opinion. Schoolmastering, in the absence of any fixed standards of qualification or regulation, or any systematic body of practical and theoretical literature, certainly included a disreputable element of practitioners, particularly at the elementary levels. Petrarch himself, like so many great scholars and writers before him, never attempted to set out systematically the methods and concepts by which his grand vision of the educational path to knowledge and freedom could be made available to the teacher. That was to be a concern of later centuries. None the less, throughout Petrarch's writings there are occasional indications of interest in the simpler procedures of pedagogy.

Teaching, he wrote, has for its basis a clear grasp of knowledge as an organized body of ideas, and for this he turned to the authority of Cicero and Aristotle:

> What a man understands clearly, he can clearly express and thus he can pour over into the mind of a hearer what he has in the innermost chamber of his mind. In this respect it is true what Aristotle . . . says in the first book of the *Metaphysics* [I. i. 981. b7]: 'It is a mark of one who knows that he can teach.' There is no teaching, it is true, without knowing; for, as Cicero says in the second book *On the Laws* [*De legibus*, II. xix. 47]: 'It requires a certain skill not only to know something but also to teach it.'
> However, this skill has its foundations doubtless in the clarity of intellect and knowledge. For though there is need for such skills besides knowledge,

no such skill will get clear speech out of an obscure intellect if it comes to expressing the conceptions of the mind and imprinting them on others.[58]

In seeking the basis of knowledge, Petrarch never departed from his belief that it rests in literature, expressed in the highest form in poetry, history and philosophy. As early as 1335, in a letter to Tommaso di Messina he stated an attitude that he never changed:

> Can you imagine anything . . . that is so useful or even so necessary as the first notion of letters? They are the foundation on which all our studies rest.[59]

The greatest danger, in his view, lay in a continued preoccupation with the second stage of studies, dialectic. Students must be encouraged strongly

> . . . not to throw themselves . . . into the study of dialectic, but to pass quickly through this discipline to better ones. [While] I do not condemn the liberal arts . . . there is nothing so ugly as an old man who is a dialectic debator.[60]

Petrarch thereby demonstrated his opposition to the fashion for dialectic, particularly as it was preserved north of the Alps and recommended so enthusiastically in the contemporaneous *Commendation of the Clerk*.

The three great studies of poetry, history and philosophy, however, were passive; a proper education for Petrarch had a complementary active component, identified by the Ciceronian term 'eloquence'. By that Petrarch understood the word in its full classical meaning, with connotations of honour, virtue and knowledge blended together, and he gained his understanding directly from Cicero and his twelfth-century revivalist, John of Salisbury. Not until later in life, in 1350, did Petrarch read the work of Quintilian, who stood in an intermediate relationship to Cicero and John. Petrarch certainly knew Quintilian indirectly as early as 1335, probably from reading Salisbury's *Metalogicon* where the *Institutio oratoria* is referred to on a number of occasions.[61] He made his first direct acquaintance with Quintilian's *Institutio oratoria* in 1350, in the library of Lapo da Castiglioncho (the elder) in Florence. That manuscript was incomplete, consisting only of the latter part of the work. Nevertheless it excited Petrarch who accepted a copy made by Lapo; it did not, however, moderate his views on schoolmastering. In a sense, Petrarch's attitude is made explicable by the fact that the missing books of Quintilian's great twelve-volume production included Book I which treated systematically of classroom procedures. Nothing had ever supplanted or even appeared to challenge that well-articulated statement. When the *Institutio* fell into obscurity during the first Christian millennium in the West, educational thought and practice became correspondingly impoverished, and as late as the mid-fourteenth century Petrarch's writings reflect that poverty even in the thought of the *literati*. The fact that Petrarch was unable to explain how eloquence is to be cultivated in its earliest forms, however, does not necessarily vitiate his concept of eloquence and his belief in the value of *virtus*.

Petrarch's mature years 1350–1374

During his mature years, in the quarter-century between 1350 and 1374, Petrarch was the acknowledged leader of intellectual life in Western Europe; he was the friend and confidant of popes, cardinals, princes, dukes, doges; his judgements on matters ranging from literary and educational affairs to issues of state diplomacy were sought, considered and often followed. He never held a formal teaching position, although he was offered a foundation chair in 1351, in any subject he chose, at the newly emerging university at Florence (the Studio Fiorentino). Instead, he lived a life of affluence, usually by patronage and from the prebends of his canonries – he held as many as four at a time – and travelled constantly throughout the North Italian plain. He set the style of intellectual endeavour for the following century. The Latin revival with its emphasis on classical, even pagan, models; concern with the historical past and a return to original sources (*ad fontes*); the establishment of new principles of philological inquiry; the diminishing of dialectic and the renewed interest in literature; the championing of *virtus* and the heightened self-consciousness that this entailed: these were features of subsequent scholarly life that Petrarch introduced.

In many respects, of course, his efforts had the obvious limitations that any pioneering efforts have: his attempted classical revival was severely restricted while it failed to include the Greek element; his philological and historiographical methods were still crude and imprecise. Within a century, however, his example stimulated the Greek revival and the first great movements of historical criticism since classical times. His limitations are illustrated best, perhaps, by his failure to recognize that all past events – and not merely the remote and romanticized epochs – are history. The dialectic-dabblers and the Arabs whom he scorned so much had already, through their efforts at helping recover and examine the historical past, prepared the way for him. Petrarch's freedom to write on such secular ideals as virtus, to champion the great pagan writers and to advance Cicero as the model of proper Latinity, in contrast to the prevailing medieval Latin style, and to dream of a revival of republican – or even imperial – Rome would have been difficult a century before; his ideas were stimulated by the changing political structure of Europe. The emergence of national states and their various concordats with the church led the way to the acceptance of the principle of temporal sovereignty; the church itself had become visibly luxurious, while some popes at Avignon were patently corrupt, and these were factors which limited the church's ability to maintain even a moral hegemony over affairs of the intellect.

Not that matters of sovereignty were in any way settled; on the contrary, such issues were greatly vexed, and Petrarch himself, like Dante before him, became concerned with problems of government. In the newly independent territories of every variety that existed in Italy and Germany – the principal domains of the Holy Roman Empire – concern with an effective definition of power was developing as a major interest of the intellectual classes. Even beyond Europe that concern was becoming manifest: in the period between 1375 and 1380 the Moslem scholar Ibn Khaldun of Tunis (1332–1406) composed his famous *Universal History*, the first really significant full-scale treatise on political theory in any language since Augustine's *City of God* a millennium before. Petrarch, too, dealt with this theme, although not in the form of a lengthy or systematic treatise. Rather his thoughts on political affairs are interwoven through all of his writings, particularly *Africa*. In his sixty-ninth year, however, just twelve months before his death, Petrarch did write specifically on the topic at the request of Francesco da Carrara, ruler of Padua. This took the form of a lengthy letter, virtually a treatise on princely government.[62] Petrarch discussed the need for the prince to be both morally good and just, and listed these traits specifically: the prince should preserve the civic appearance of his territory through proper repairs and maintenance, take a personal interest in public welfare and devise just and equitable taxation. In his personal demeanour, the prince should present a reserved, modest, dignified mien; he should patronize and honour exceptional men, particularly those who distinguish themselves and render public service in the administration of justice, religion, military matters and learning.

Petrarch wrote nothing on education for the people; the whole spirit of his revival was aristocratic. When he looked back to the great days of republican Rome, the first century B.C., he identified himself with the conservative elements, the *optimates*; he had no sympathy with the democratic movement, represented in ancient Rome by the *populares*. When Petrarch died, in 1374, public rumour spread that he was found still pen in hand, collapsed over his unfinished *Life of Caesar*.[63]

Extension of the classical revival: the first Greek phase

Towards Greek studies: Giovanni Boccaccio

Although the classical Latin revival of the Trecento was largely a virtuoso effort by Petrarch, it was supported and subsequently sustained by others, of whom the first and most distinguished was the Florentine scholar, Giovanni Boccaccio (1313–75), whose life spanned the same years as Petrarch – he died but a year later. Boccaccio's literary legacy has two aspects: on the one hand he achieved considerable recognition for his brilliant experiments in vernacular storytelling, known collectively as the *Decameron*, and he remains celebrated to the present day almost exclusively through that collection of ribald tales. In his own day, however, he was even more highly regarded for his serious writing, particularly the two encyclopedically structured works: *De montibus*, which is a geography based on ancient Latin sources, and *De genealogia deorum*, a history of the ancient Roman gods. The latter proved to be an extremely popular work, particularly in the late fifteenth and early sixteenth centuries. Both of these books, which were written in a formal Latin prose, in strong contrast to the vigorous style of the vernacular in the *Decameron*, displayed the influence of Petrarch in that they were concerned with the restoration of the classical past. In their concern for the encyclopedic collection of facts, they followed a well-defined Roman practice. Unlike Petrarch, however, Boccaccio was no textual critic nor was he an ardent bibliophile: his encyclopedic style was a direct expression of his concern with content rather than form, and his interest in the past was directed towards the information it could supply. None the less, Boccaccio collected an impressive number of manuscripts of quality, a selection of which he bequeathed to the monastery of Santo Spirito.

Despite the fact that Boccaccio was a contemporary of Petrarch, and was personally acquainted with him, in many respects he can be considered almost as a successor. The popularity of Boccaccio's works occurred later, at a time when Petrarch's were read decreasingly. Even more significant is

Boccaccio's anticipation of the need to search even more deeply into the past: through Latin to Greek. In this respect, his personal efforts in learning Greek were more successful than Petrarch's, although he was equally unable to stimulate a wider revival. This failure stemmed from the basic problem that the first persons then attempting to teach Greek in Italy were not themselves Greek. Barlaam is the first clearly documented teacher of Greek in this period of the classical revival. Although he made Petrarch's acquaintance while on a mission of church unity sent by the Byzantine Emperor Andronicus III, Barlaam himself was not a true Greek. He was a Calabrian with a cultural background compounded from the numerous influences of the region Greek, Roman, Lombard, Byzantine, Moslem and Norman;[64] he appears to have moved between Calabria and Constantinople according to the vagaries of adventurous opportunism. His surviving writings indicate that he was of mediocre ability, possessing only a superficial learning,[65] although neither Petrarch nor Boccaccio was aware of Barlaam's inadequacy. On the contrary, Petrarch was impressed and wrote that Barlaam 'was most excellent in Greek eloquence, and very poor in Latin; rich in ideas and quick in mind'.[66] After Barlaam left, Petrarch lamented that 'Fortune . . . deprived me of an excellent teacher.'[67] Boccaccio likewise referred to Barlaam's 'enormous knowledge' in matters of Greek scholarship.[68] In many respects their credulity is explicable, since like all beginner students they were dependent on their instructor; at the same time, however, it can reasonably be assumed that both Petrarch and Boccaccio, in view of their own considerable literary accomplishments, ought to have been more discriminating, particularly since Boccaccio recorded explicitly that he had not seen a single work by Barlaam: 'hujus ego nullam vidi opus'.[69]

In 1360, nearly twenty years after the episode with Barlaam, Boccaccio himself began to learn Greek, this time from Leontius Pilatus. Like Barlaam, Pilatus was a Calabrian and had travelled several times between Italy and Byzantium before arriving in Florence; unlike Barlaam, however, Pilatus seems to have aroused enmity wherever he went. Boccaccio was impressed, initially, and was successful in having Pilatus appointed to a newly established professorship of Greek in the Studio Fiorentino, itself the first such chair in Western Europe.[70] Pilatus remained three years, in which time Boccaccio made some progress in Greek and Pilatus made the first Latin translations of Homer's *Iliad* and *Odyssey*. Neither the translations nor Pilatus' public relations, however, were satisfactory – although his translations, in the absence of competitors, remained in circulation for the following century – and in 1363, he left. Boccaccio observed of him, in several places, that he had bestial manners, strange customs, and a disgusting appearance along with his great skill in Greek studies.[71] The truth appears more likely that Pilatus, like Barlaam, was fundamentally ignorant of the Hellenic and Byzantine traditions; that he had received a formal grammatical training which gave him, as an Italian-speaking person, a superficial acquaintance with Greek as a foreign language. Neither Barlaam nor Pilatus had any deep acquaintance with Greek literature, much less any ability to discourse at length and to expound the content of the great corpus of Greek learning. Pilatus' tenure was necessarily short-lived, and the Greek revival did not take place in Boccaccio's lifetime.

After Petrarch and Boccaccio died, however, the enthusiasm for the past that both had kindled continued unabated. Although the revival of classical learning had been developing simultaneously in other cities, of which Padua was the most important, leadership came to be exercised late in the fourteenth century by Florence, which by this time had become the dominant city-state in northern Italy. This leadership, in fact, remained centred in Florence for yet another full century, the Quattrocento.

The immediate link in the maintenance of the Petrarchan influence was his pupil, the Augustinian monk Luigi Marsili (c. 1342–94), whom Petrarch, late in life, charged with maintaining the fight against Averroism.[72] Marsili was a particularly competent and enthusiastic scholar, and in his cell at the monastery of Santo Spirito he initiated an educational innovation, that of regular meetings of a circle of like-minded friends who gathered to discuss current intellectual matters. There were classical precedents, of course: Socrates and Plato in Athens, and the Scipionic circle in Rome. Marsili's group was probably the first of the new academies that were to become increasingly popular in Europe and whose scholarly interests were pursued in marked contrast to the universities. In that secluded Augustinian monastery, set on the left bank of Florence's river Arno, daily meetings were held which ranged over a wide variety of topics, although they were generally related to the widest of cosmological inquiries: namely, the relationship of man to the universe and how man might best realize his full potential. Aspects of those discussions can be found in the writings of the most distinguished member of the group, Coluccio Salutati (1331–1406).

A vigorous personality, Salutati became prominent through his political abilities, being elected chancellor and secretary of the Florentine Republic in 1375. Within two years he had demonstrated his capacity by successfully

6   Duns Scotus, painting by Justus van Ghent.

7 School scene, tomb relief of
Cino de' Sinibaldi, *c.* 1360

negotiating a diplomatic encounter with the papal state that arose out of difficulties with food supply and resulting embargoes. For the remaining thirty years of his life he held his dominance in Florentine affairs; like Petrarch, whom he never met, although they did exchange letters, he became known in the courts, chancelleries and universities of Europe. Salutati exercised his talents equally for the improvement of learning. Although his personal scholarship never attained the first rank, he accepted fully the Petrarchan ideals of the classical revival and stimulated further efforts, in part by corresponding with every interested scholar possible. Salutati was directly responsible for taking the next great and indispensable step in the classic revival: the introduction of Greek. This time, in contrast to the abortive episode with Pilatus, the venture was successful.

Studio Fiorentino: Chrysoloras and the introduction of Greek

Until the incumbency of Salutati as Florentine chancellor, the university at Florence had not achieved any distinction; the city's intellectual reputation rested in the achievements of individuals and such literary circles as Marsili's academy. When the republic had voted to establish a *studio* back in 1321, there were, of course, already numerous other universities in existence in the Italian cities and Florence found itself competing at a disadvantage, particularly with regard to securing teachers. In the following decades, the Studio Fiorentino languished and was unable, in 1351, to attract Petrarch to a chair. Its first distinguished professor was Boccaccio who, more than fifty years after the founding of the *studio*, accepted an invitation to the faculty in 1373. Then, in 1387, under Salutati's promptings, an effort was made to regularize its procedures and to create a respectable reputation for the school. The opportunity to achieve such distinction came some years later with the arrival in Italy of a distinguished Byzantine scholar Manuel Chrysoloras (*c.* 1350?–1415). The precise time of his appearance is still uncertain, as is the nature of his mission. It seems likely that he had been sent to Italy, some time between 1393 and 1396,[73] to seek assistance for Constantinople against the encroaching Turks, although there is the distinct possibility that Chrysoloras made two visits in this period. In any event, his presence became known to Salutati, as had his reputation of being a highly regarded teacher of rhetoric and philosophy in his native city of Constantinople. Salutati thereupon commenced negotiations to bring Chrysoloras to the Studio Fiorentino as professor of Greek. In 1396 Salutati sent several letters to Chrysoloras, who had apparently returned to Constantinople,[74] and as a result of those invitations, one of which was taken personally by a leading Florentine scholar, Jacopo da Scarperia, acting as Salutati's personal emissary, Chrysoloras accepted the offer and either late in 1396 or early in 1397[75] returned to Florence as foundation professor of Greek in its university. Chrysoloras remained there for about three years, until 1400, after which his movements again become difficult to trace.

Chrysoloras' tenure at the Studio Fiorentino was a resounding success: he attracted enthusiastic, intelligent students who responded quickly to his instruction in both grammar and literature. One of those students, Palla di Nofri Strozzi, was responsible for procuring the necessary texts from Byzantium and for employing personally the finest scribes in Latin and Greek for the school. Palla even considered establishing a public library as an ancillary institution to the *studio*.[76] In those few years Chrysoloras dictated a Greek grammar which was edited by his former student Guarino Guarini, who also added a parallel Latin translation. Since it employed a catechetical method of questions and answers, in some respects resembling the thousand-year-old *Ars minor* of Donatus, it was known as *Erotemata sive quaestiones*, although its more familiar title was simply *Erotemata Chrysolorae*. This introduction to Greek was received eagerly and for more than a century was the chief text from which that language was studied in Europe. Chrysoloras' interests, however, were in Hellenic literature, and it was he who suggested the first Latin translation of Plato's *Republic*. This task he achieved, although the original codex is presumably lost, the translation surviving now only in the recension of his student Uberto Decembrio.

As a result of these activities, the Studio Fiorentino lost its lethargy and became one of the leading centres of higher learning in Italy. Bologna retained its pre-eminence as the major school of legal and notarial studies not only in Italy but in all Europe; Florence developed a comparable reputation, not for law, but for notarial studies which were becoming one of the recognized routes to public life for aspiring sons of the middle class.[77] The addition of Greek, and the corresponding enlargement of classical studies reinforced by the stature of Chrysoloras, brought Florence to the fore.

By the year 1400, when he left Florence, Chrysoloras had successfully inaugurated the revival of Greek studies. The young students who attended his lectures retained their scholarship and their enthusiasm; many of these in the following century were to become the leaders of Italian, and European, learning. Of these the most influential were Leonardo Bruni, Palla di Nofri Strozzi, Roberto de' Rossi, Niccolò Niccoli, Jacopo di Agnolo da Scarperia, Guarino Guarini and Pier Paolo Vergerio. The departure of Chrysoloras did not mean the end of his influence, and although his movements are not clearly documented, he seems to have remained in Europe, chiefly as an emissary of his emperor, Manuel Palaeologus. From the uncertain record he appears to have been in Venice around 1404, England in 1405, Paris and Venice in 1408, and Rome in 1410.[78] In all of these travels he was ostensibly engaged in an ecumenical mission, exploring the possibility of healing the breach between East and West that had existed formally since the mutual excommunication of 1054. Meanwhile, in order to heal the other great schism of the times, that within the papacy of Rome itself, a church council was convoked in 1413 to meet at Constance. Chrysoloras was instructed by Emperor Manuel to attend as a Byzantine delegate, and arrived in Constance in October 1414, the month preceding its formal opening. Before he could discharge his mission effectively, however, he died at or near Constance in April of the following year.[79]

In a sense, attendance at the Council of Constance would have represented a consummation of Chrysoloras' ecclesiastical career; yet, years before that ecumenical gathering Chrysoloras had already achieved distinction for his role in reviving Greek studies. In contrast to the inconclusive results of that Council, and of its successor, the Council of Florence (1438–45), Chrysoloras' effort at the Studio Fiorentino was of lasting significance in furthering mutual understanding. A few years after he left Florence, Chrysoloras was probably teaching at Pavia,[80] again promoting the study of Greek and thereby continuing the study of classical antiquity. The Latin movement stimulated by Petrarch and furthered by Boccaccio was finally given its necessary complement in Greek studies as a result of the work of Chrysoloras. The growing tributes to his work included the statement by his former student, Leonardo Bruni, that by 1403 the *artes liberales* were prospering vigorously in Florence.[81]

By the end of the fourteenth century the revival of classical learning in Italy was well established, both in Latin and Greek. The new awareness of the value of antiquity towards which Petrarch had laboured was now accepted, and by the year 1400 a distinct change can be discerned in affairs of the intellect. From that year onwards into the fifteenth century – the Quattrocento – scholarship in Italy and progressively throughout civilized Europe was to become based increasingly on the study of the Latin and

Greek languages and their literatures, with, however, the addition of a highly significant new element: a heightened self-consciousness of the present, and of the two classical cultures of the past. The discipline of history enters European thought.

CHAPTER 7

Italy: Humanism of the Quattrocento

Civic humanism

The issue of liberty: crisis in Florence

By the year 1400 the city-state of Florence, under the astute leadership of Coluccio Salutati, had become the main centre of the new studies in all Europe. Although other cities held individual distinction in cultural and educational activities, Florence was outstanding in terms of its total achievement; indeed that city claimed for itself the further distinction of being the exemplar of civic liberty and the model of the properly organized political state. In expounding that position, leading citizens of Florence took hold firmly of the traditions of political theory initiated by Dante, and incorporated, when it suited their argument, the work of that other great Florentine exile, Petrarch. There was a determined effort, in the period around 1400, to unite political and intellectual life; the Florentines strove to see their pre-eminence deriving from the interaction of political, civic, cultural and intellectual acitivities: the good citizen was considered to be the educated man, a proper education was the necessary basis for civic participation. The Dantean revival of *virtus* and *humana civilitas* became increasingly influential. At the same time, the concept of *libertas* was the key idea of the times: only through liberty could the best form of the state and the vocation of man be achieved. The Florentine *literati* set themselves to state their beliefs clearly, and to institute a programme of educational studies to secure them. Florentines were prominent in the intellectual and educational life of Europe throughout the fifteenth century and maintained a distinguished record, although they certainly were not alone; other communes too were enthusiastically involved in the pursuit of learning.

The heightened awareness of the issue of liberty in Europe came not only from the writings of the major political thinkers of the thirteenth century – Thomas Aquinas, Roger Bacon – and the fourteenth – William of Occam, Marsilius of Padua, Dante Alighieri – but equally from the events which stimulated their writings: the changing political structure of Europe and the resurgence of tyrannies, increasingly on a national scale. Florence's political situation in 1400 was unique in Europe, and, in fact, the cultural achievement of the Trecento was helped enormously by the relative peace and freedom existing in Italy. The rest of the continent was not so undisturbed.

European development by 1400

Throughout Europe, during the thirteenth and fourteenth centuries, the prototypes of great national states had begun to form and were engaged in frequent and often prolonged conflict. France had preserved its relative stability throughout the three centuries of Capetian rule, particularly during the years of crisis with the papacy (1303–9), which led to the removal of the papal seat to Avignon. The founder of modern France, Philip IV, died in 1314, and after a rapid succession by his three sons the Capetian house ended with the death in 1328 of Charles IV. That event precipitated a conflict over succession with England across the channel, and Navarre across the Pyrenees, that dragged on for more than a century and was known consequently as the Hundred Years War. Charles of Navarre and Edward III of England both challenged the succession of Philip VI (r. 1328–50), since Charles was the great-grandson, and Edward the grandson, of the Capetian, Philip IV. By 1337, the English were at war and their armies were in periodic conflict from the great victory of Crécy in 1346 to the equally decisive battle of Agincourt in 1415 – both bitter defeats for the French. This long period of conflict was ruinous to France and England where, as a consequence, there was social and political turmoil. This civil dislocation was exacerbated by the great plague – the

Black Death – of 1348–9, which considerably reduced the populations, particularly the peasantry, and probably many scholars as well, sufficient to retard the extension of learning, although this conjecture as yet cannot be verified. Further aggravation of the domestic problems of these countries followed. In England there were almost continuous peasant and worker strikes after 1349, and in 1374 the teachings of John Wycliffe had created a climate of religious unrest that led increasingly to civil disorder, of which the most striking example was the Peasants' Revolt of 1381, led by Wat Tyler, abetted by the Lollard priest, John Ball (d. 1381). Although there is no evidence that Wycliffe influenced Tyler directly, his doctrines were a major element in precipitating the crisis. France, for its part, was plunged into civil war, particularly in Flanders in 1382 where it was crushed ruthlessly. The net result of this century in both England and France was a condition close to anarchy.

The Holy Roman Empire continued to change. Following the Great Interregnum of 1250–73, Rudolf of Habsburg was elected emperor, and immediately thereafter set about the task of renovating his empire; one of his first territorial expansions was to march eastwards against the encroaching Bohemians. That people had developed a feudal state out of an earlier Great Moravian Empire that enters the record around 830, reaching a peak of development in the reign of Svatopluk (r. 870–94). Under their energetic king, Ottokar II, known in Czech as Premysl II (r. 1253–78), the Bohemians expanded westwards, occupying part of the Holy Roman Empire. Rudolf moved against them, defeated and slew Ottokar, and incorporated their lands in his empire. Rudolf thereupon removed his capital to the recently retrieved Vienna, which became the seat of the great, long-enduring Habsburg dynasty. From Vienna the Habsburgs attempted to extend their control westward to the Rhine but without immediate success. In the following fourteenth century, the region of Germany was in continued internal disorder; the practice of subdividing territorial inheritances (contrary to the French practice of primogeniture) created a situation whereby more than 300 separate principalities existed, with resulting conflicts over property titles and territorial expansion. Although no effective political union was forged, the efforts of the Habsburgs led to further conflicts, and this appears to have inhibited intellectual life.

Perhaps the aspect of the struggles in Germany that presented a moral to the Florentines was the example of the Hanseatic League. In the same period that the Lombard League seized its independence from Frederick the Great, the town of Lübeck on the Baltic coast of Germany was founded in 1163. This became a major trading centre for the whole of northern Europe, and a century after its foundation Lübeck was the leader of a huge confederation of free cities banded together for commercial purposes and known, appropriately, as the Hanseatic League (Ger. *hansa*, a guild). Yet their success was relatively short-lived. Another hundred years later, in the mid-fourteenth century, the league began to break up and its members became absorbed by various neighbouring principalities and by the growing kingdoms of Lithuania and Poland which, by the end of the fourteenth century, between them encompassed a vast territory from the Black Sea to the Baltic Coast.

The loss of freedom by small city-states throughout Europe in the thirteenth and fourteenth centuries occurred even among the Lombard cities. One by one they became subject to the growing tyranny of Milan, itself a city-state that had become dominated in the fourteenth century by the Visconti family. Throughout the years from 1350 to 1400 the Visconti expanded their influence, chiefly by military force, until by the end of the century many of the major cities in northern Italy – and even south of Florence – chiefly Lucca, Verona, Vicenza, Padua, Pisa, Siena, Perugia, Spoleto and Assisi, were under some form of Viscontean dominance. Bologna, Venice and Florence were still independent, although it seemed impossible for them to remain so. The Milanese leader, Giangaleazzo Visconti, in fact, planned to incorporate Florence in his domains. Despite intense diplomatic manœuvring by Florentine emissaries, in the year 1402 Giangaleazzo moved his armies into position on Florence's frontier ready for attack. Then, unexpectedly, an epidemic swept through the region; among the victims was Giangaleazzo himself. Florence secured a respite.

Humanism and the Florentine appraisal of liberty

The crisis of 1402 profoundly affected Florence, and indeed all of northern and central Italy. Had Giangaleazzo Visconti succeeded in his designs, the ideal of civic liberty, in the Florentine view, would have been submerged; the prospect was disturbing – it would have meant the loss of all the achievements of the preceding century, and the efforts of Dante and Petrarch would have been in vain. The Milanese challenge prompted Florence to strengthen its alliances; it also stimulated a vigorous intellectual reaction. The lessons of the classical revival had been well learned, and throughout the early years of the fifteenth century intellectual life in

Florence became preoccupied with a thoroughgoing appraisal of the values of liberty and the best means of securing it.[1]

The central element of the Florentine appraisal was an appeal to history – to that heightened self-consciousness that had emerged, principally in the writings of Dante and Petrarch. For his part, Petrarch was concerned particularly to see the past as relevant to the present condition, an attitude brought about in the first instance by the need to secure justification, even authority, for the republican state, and this, in effect, helped in later times to develop what were originally antiquarian concerns into the important discipline of history. The movement to see Roman history in republican rather than imperial terms was initiated by Petrarch when he found the notion in Cicero's *Letters to Atticus*; subsequently, it was also advanced by Boccaccio in his study of Tacitus' *History* (*Historiae*). Although Tacitus' work, surviving incompletely, is an account of imperial times, it expresses a continued admiration for the republican era. It was this aspect which caught the Florentine attention: not only Boccaccio, but also other leading scholars, chiefly Leonardo Bruni and Niccolò Niccoli, studied the idea. The conviction grew that the period of Rome's greatness lay in the republican past, in the *respublica romana*, and that the empire had been a retrograde development. This interpretation harmonized with the currently growing belief that Florence itself had been founded in the republican period by some of Sulla's disbanded troops. Tyranny, equated with imperialism, became synonymous in Florentine thought with unconstitutionality, a particular theme that had been developed by Salutati in *De tyranno*, itself an oblique examination of the recent Milanese confrontation.[2]

The great value of republicanism in Salutati's view is that it allows the maximum degree of personal liberty to the individual while at the same time requiring each person to put forward considerable effort on behalf of the public good. Freedom demands responsibility, and from their conjoint operation comes the best form of the state. The fourteenth-century ideal of the *vita solitaria* began to be challenged; it was seen by many as allowing but a partial development of man – his intellect – which encouraged dependency on a ruler and thereby opened the way to tyranny. The role of the scholar under the dominion of a tyrant, it was believed, was to be reduced to mere subservience, usually as a court tutor. Still fresh was the experience of the eminent Vergerio in Padua where he was in just such a menial position; his tract on education, *De ingenuis moribus*, written around 1404, providing vivid testimony of his complete dependence on the prince he served. With such examples in mind, early in the Quattro-cento the Florentines gave expression to the concept of *vita activa et civilis*: the life of social and civic activity, already historically exemplified, in romanticized accounts, in the republican periods of Greece and Rome.[3] The emphasis on *virtus* received an even greater expression.

At the same time there appeared on a wide scale the concept of civic humanism, itself the answer to the pressing question as to the best means of securing the ideal republic. The origin of the term humanism itself seems to come from the sixteenth-century word *umanista*, used colloquially by Italian university students to refer to the professor of literary studies, in distinction to the other professors whose designations as *legista, jurista, canonista* and *artista* were of longer standing,[4] although its provenance rests in Cicero's use of *humanitas* to express the idea of educational and cultural refinement, and John of Salisbury implied a similar ideal in his concept of *civilitas*. Petrarch probably helped to revive the concept through his use of the phrase *studia humaniora*, literally, the more humanly relevant studies, and, since Petrarch was concerned chiefly with the present life, he probably meant by this his own rediscovery of classical Latin literature. The use of the comparative adjective (*humaniora*) reveals Petrarch's intention to choose the better of two competing programmes: the scholastic and the humanist. After Petrarch, the term gained increasing use and relevancy; by the early Quattrocento it was in common use. Leonardo Bruni, writing in 1436, looked back to Petrarch as 'the one who restored to life the *studia humanitatis* when they were already extinct, and opened for us the path to show in what manner we could acquire learning'.[5] The term *studia humanitatis*, meaning the humanist group of studies, had acquired currency before Bruni's time, when it already was used to refer to the study of classical learning. As the Quattrocento progressed *studia humanitatis* be-came widely discussed and its educational intentions and implications acquired precise meaning.

Educational programme of humanism

Vergerio on the education of the citizen

It was Vergerio himself who provided the first systematic statement on the educational programme of humanism. Petrus Paulus Vergerius (1349–1420) – the Latin version of his name – was a native of Capo d'Istria; after a period as professor of logic and law, and possibly medicine, in Padua and Florence, he entered the service of the lord of Padua, Francesco Carrara.[6] Some time in that period, possibly in 1404, he composed in Latin a short didactic treatise addressed to the Paduan prince, Ubertinus, entitled *De ingenuis moribus* (*The Education of the Gentleman*).[7] Although humanist studies had been foreshadowed recently in Giovanni da Ravenna's autobiography (*Rationarium vitae*), where many of Petrarch's ideas were given renewed expression, Vergerio's treatise stands as the first clear exposition of the new humanist approach to education. *De ingenuis moribus* was an immediate success: manuscripts were made for nearly every learned library in Europe and by the end of the following century, the sixteenth, more than forty printed editions had appeared.[8]

The most striking feature of *De ingenuis moribus* is its incorporation of many of the ideas of the second-century-A.D. treatise *On the Education of Children* which had been incorrectly attributed to Plutarch. Around the year 1400 Vergerio had obtained a Greek manuscript of pseudo-Plutarch from Chrysoloras, and Bruni became familiar with the treatise some few years later, making the first Latin translation of this work.[9] Vergerio's title reflected pseudo-Plutarch's views that education, chiefly on account of circumstances, could be expected only by the privileged (*ingenuus*); the opening sentences continue the theme: the father has a responsibility to provide his son with a good name (that is, well-sounding), a good city (for citizenship) and an education, 'the foundation of which must be laid in the first years of life, the disposition moulded while it is susceptible and the mind trained while it is retentive'.[10] These obligations, he stresses, are particularly incumbent on the father preparing his son for service in high public offices. The chief emphasis in the early years of the child's upbringing is on the cultivation of moral discipline in the manner suggested by pseudo-Plutarch, this being secured by careful control of the child's environment so as to eliminate bad persons while at the same time providing good examples, and involving particularly a careful choice of tutors. Behaviour must be regulated to encourage moderation in all things, and, although Vergerio's treatise avoids any stringent requirements, it does lean towards a mildly ascetic attitude:

> I should prohibit the use of wine except in the smallest quantities, and even then carefully diluted, with water in the larger proportion. But in no case is it allowable to eat, drink or sleep up to the point of complete satisfaction; in all bodily pleasures we must accustom our children to retain complete and easy control of appetite.[11]

The function of moral discipline is extended to cover all aspects of the child's behaviour, including reverence to the church, to elders and to the ways of cultivated society.

Emphasis in the tract is primarily upon the content and method of higher education. Again the influence of pseudo-Plutarch is evident in Vergerio's belief that a general or liberal education is proper; he departs markedly, however, in his conception of the focus of study, replacing the Greeks' philosophy with an Italian reconstruction of the liberal arts:

> We call those studies liberal which are worthy of a free man; those studies by which we attain and practise virtue and wisdom; that education which calls forth, trains and develops those highest gifts of body and mind which ennoble men, and which are rightly judged to rank next in dignity to virtue only.[12]

In classical times the liberal studies were considered necessary because they provided the means by which the leading classes of society could cultivate civic virtue – a necessary element of government – and this attitude also underlies Vergerio's arguments for the liberal studies. Only through these, he believes, can such virtue be achieved, and in his definition of these studies, Vergerio lists the current conception, in distinct contrast to the medieval pattern of the liberal arts:

> I accord the first place to History, on grounds both of its attractiveness and of its utility, qualities which appeal equally to the scholar and to the statesman. Next in importance ranks Moral Philosophy, which indeed is, in a peculiar sense, a 'Liberal Art', in that its purpose is to teach men the secret of true freedom. History, then, gives us the concrete examples of the precepts inculcated by philosophy. . . . I would indicate as the third main branch of study, Eloquence, which indeed holds a place of distinction amongst the refined Arts. By philosophy we learn the essential truth of things, which by eloquence we so exhibit in orderly adornment as to bring conviction to differing minds. And history provides the light of experience – a cumulative wisdom fit to supplement the force of reason and the persuasion of eloquence.[13]

History, moral philosophy and eloquence – and here he is thinking of the Roman rather than the Greek contribution to these fields – are to be the basis of a liberal education. Vergerio next considers a second range of desirable studies, turning this time to the Greek experience: 'We are told that the Greeks devised for their sons a course of training in four subjects: letters, gymnastic, music and drawing.'[14] His reference here is to Aristotle (*Politics*, VIII: 3), although this is not mentioned. In a later passage Vergerio considers gymnastics to be a suitable means of cultivating military skill and he urges wider training in the art of war including 'the principles of generalship: strategy and tactics; discipline; supplies; and the ordering of camps and winter quarters'.[15] Drawing, however, is not acceptable: it 'has no place amongst our liberal studies; except insofar as it is identical with writing (which is in reality one side of the art of Drawing), [for] it belongs to the Painter's profession: the Greeks, as an art-loving people, attached to it an exceptional value.'[16] Vergerio was writing at a time when the visual arts were still controlled by the guilds, and when medieval conceptions still predominated; the great period of Italian art, now beginning to flourish, was not generally seen as directly relevant to the process of education. Apart from the obvious advantages of military skill for the leader, Vergerio really considered the two Greek studies of letters and music to be the more important, chiefly as a support to the primary studies of history, philosophy and eloquence.

Letters, Vergerio explains, consist in several sub-categories: grammar, rules of composition, logic, rhetoric and poetry. The values of these studies, he feels, should be apparent: grammar and composition are the foundations of all linguistic development; logic and rhetoric are the bases of philosophy and eloquence. 'Logic, indeed,' he writes, 'as setting forth the true method of learning, is the guide to the acquisition of knowledge in whatever subject.'[17] His tract touches on these studies only lightly; they are of such obvious instrumental value that their case, in his opinion, needs no extensive presentation. Poetry, rather surprisingly, in view of current attitudes and the vivid examples provided by Dante and Petrarch, he barely mentions; although it is seen to offer some supplement to the art of eloquence and the skill of oratory, its 'main concern [is] for the leisure side of existence'.[18] Music, likewise, is included for its recreational value; however, beyond the observation in the tract that music is also 'an aid to the inner harmony of the soul' Vergerio gives it no further consideration. The deep conceptions lying behind the idea of music as ministering to the soul are not discussed, probably because Vergerio was largely ignorant of the considerable Greek literature on the subject; moreover, for him music was largely vocal and instrumental whereas in Greece it had included history, poetry and religion. Then again, however, the bulk of the *corpus Platonicum*, where many of these concepts occur, was still not generally available; the flow of Greek manuscripts from which Latin translations were made began only around 1400 through the initial stimulus of Chrysoloras. Not until 1424, in terms of present evidence, did the first complete corpus become available when two sets of manuscripts were sent back to Florence by Johannes Aurispa, a Florentine biblio-phile.[19]

Vergerio's lack of sympathy with much of the Greek tradition of liberal learning, perhaps on account of his ignorance, is revealed in his equally brief treatment of mathematics. Arithmetic, geometry, astronomy – the three studies that with music constituted the quadrivium – are given little more than a single descriptive sentence each, concerning their instrumental value: they are 'weighty studies because they possess a peculiar element of certainty'.[20] Along with them Vergerio discusses the professional studies of medicine and law, both of which he had pursued himself. While expressing approval of these valuable fields of study, he regards them as unsuitable for the education of a gentleman because they are 'mere trades', and in this respect his outlook is reminiscent of the Aristotelian distinction between the liberal and the illiberal. In Vergerio's tract the medieval study of theology is also dismissed as treating 'of themes removed from our senses and attainable only by pure intelligence'.[21] The rational character of theology, with its ontological procedures, makes it irrelevant for his plan.

In addition to prescribing studies Vergerio deals in some detail with the method of teaching, a topic that had received very little attention since the days of Quintilian more than 1300 years previously. Indeed, throughout that period Quintilian's discussions on teaching method in the *Institutio oratoria* remained virtually the sole treatment, although the work itself was in almost complete obscurity. Vergerio's treatise reveals acquaintance with Quintilian, which is quite explicable since Petrarch's discovery and popularization of an incomplete version of the work fifty years previously. Yet Vergerio does not follow Quintilian slavishly; on the contrary he takes many points of advice but tempers them in a number of aspects, the most significant modification being in respect of memory. For Quintilian considered memory to be the cardinal trait of intellect, from which all mental development was believed to stem. Vergerio, while accepting its obvious advantages, observes that minds differ and that memory is not identical with intelligence; indeed, 'in comparison with intelligence, memory is of little worth'. As a codicil, however, he adds that 'intelligence without memory, though, so far as education is concerned, is of no value at all'.[22] He proceeds to make a twofold distinction between the quick and the slow mind of equal intelligence:

> While one boy seizes rapidly the point of which he is in search and states it ably, another, working far more slowly, has yet the sounder judgement and

so detects the weak spot in his rival's conclusions. The former, perhaps, will succeed in poetry or in the abstract sciences; the latter in real studies and practical pursuits.[23]

These distinctions he elaborates even further with the express purpose of widening the range of abilities that might be considered appropriate for receiving a liberal education.

Following his emphasis on varying qualities of mind, Vergerio puts forward the corollary that each individual needs a different arrangement of studies, invoking the generalized authority of Aristotle for support:

> Respecting the general place of liberal studies, we remember that Aristotle would not have them absorb the entire interests of life: for he kept steadily in view the nature of man as a citizen, an active member of the state. For the man who has surrendered himself absolutely to the attractions of Letters or of speculative thought follows, perhaps a self-regarding end and is useless as a citizen or as a prince.[24]

This notion of individuality, in his view, demands a much more thorough scrutiny of the occupation of schoolteaching, and in this respect Vergerio is in significant contrast to Petrarch. The latter's bitter invective in the letter of 1350 to Zanobi da Strada stands as testimony to the limitations of Petrarch's thought with respect to the cultivation of the humane studies. Vergerio, by contrast, recognizes that the cultivated society begins with the careful education of children, and his emphasis on the prime necessity of the thoughtful conduct of schooling in *De ingenuis moribus* initiates a greatly increased attention to educational theorizing that reaches its most profound expression almost a century later in the writings of the Dutch humanist, Erasmus of Rotterdam.

Almost all the advanced educational thinking of the fifteenth century, however, is a concerted attempt to recover and reapply the educational theory and practice of Greece and Rome 1500 years previously. Vergerio, in fact, uses classical examples to secure his own point that the teacher is of prime importance and must be chosen carefully, emphasizing – doubtless with some thought to his own relationships with Francesco Carrara – that 'Philip entrusted Alexander to Aristotle even for the alphabet'.[25] The teacher himself, then, is of crucial significance – it is he who mediates knowledge. Vergerio's analysis thereby achieves a special distinction: he makes the emphatic point that learning is not immediate, since knowledge is not somehow pre-existent in the mind as Neoplatonic and Augustinian theory held. The new approach to knowledge developed by Thomas Aquinas in his thirteenth-century *De magistro*, chiefly for the purpose of supporting his arguments for the rational apprehension of absolute knowledge, is now applied to the thoroughly secular and humane studies. Vergerio's insistence on the mediating role of the teacher, between student and knowledge, is one of the fundamental characteristics of the new educational theory of humanism. From this postulate Vergerio draws a number of implications for classroom procedure: the need to order material and to introduce it in small, easily assimilated amounts; the importance of mastering one point before proceeding to the next and of organizing all learning around systematically arranged bodies of content; the utility of spacing learning and instruction throughout the day. He recommends employing a number of pedagogical strategems to facilitate learning, such as regular revision, frequent classroom discussion, and setting the student to teach others what he has previously learned in order to make his knowledge more active. All of these suggestions are eminently practical and, although their origins in Quintilian are quite apparent, in the early fifteenth century they were patently in need of restatement.

Recovery of *Quintilian*'s Institutio oratoria

Vergerio's views found a response in wealthy Italian circles: the educational programme that he put forward took hold increasingly and by the time of his death in 1420 the court tutor existed in many – perhaps in all – of the aristocratic homes. Nor did Vergerio's essay remain an isolated achievement; his lead was followed by other scholars, of whom the next of importance were two Florentine citizens, both distinguished students of Chrysoloras. These were Poggio Bracciolini and Leonardo Bruni. Throughout the first half of the Quattrocento, Poggio and Bruni were major figures in the advancement of the humanist ideal: Poggio became the greatest discoverer of manuscripts of the century, Bruni became Florence's greatest historian and panegyrist.

After Vergerio's tract no single event did as much to further the humanist cause as Poggio's celebrated *coup*: the discovery in 1415 of the complete text of Quintilian's *Institutio oratoria*, the circumstances of which had a large element of the purely fortuitous. Poggio Bracciolini (1386–1459), an alumnus of the Studio Fiorentino, was a notary by profession who entered the service of the Cardinal of Bari in 1403, a year after his admission to the notarial guild. This brought him into contact with the government of the church in Rome, the papal Curia, which itself was passing through the period of profound disturbance of the Great Schism, so called because at the time there were two rival popes, one in Rome, one in Avignon. In 1377 Gregory XI (r. 1370–8) returned to Rome from Avignon; on his death there were two claimants to the succession, Clement VII at Avignon, Urban VI at Rome, and for the next thirty-six years in the period of the Great Schism this rivalry continued. By 1414, while Poggio was employed in the Curia, the situation had become impossible. Moreover, the authority of the church was challenged by a resurgence of alleged heresy, this time by the rector of the University of Prague, Jan Hus. In 1413 the Holy Roman Emperor Sigismund forced Pope John XXIII to convoke a church council to meet at Constance in southern Germany to elect a single, universally acceptable pope – the number meanwhile having grown to three: John XXIII, Gregory XII, Benedict XIII – and to deal with the heresy of Hus. So clerics, diplomats, lawyers and scholars began to converge on Constance in readiness for the first session scheduled for November 1414. It was, incidentally, to this council that Chrysoloras set off on his last mission.

Poggio, who attended in a secretarial capacity, made no direct contribution to the ecclesiastical proceedings; instead he became excited by the possibilities of finding hitherto undiscovered manuscripts. The Benedictine monastery at nearby St Gall, founded at the beginning of the eighth century, had maintained a reputation for the high quality of its library; Poggio set out from Constance across extremely difficult roads. There his enthusiasm was justified and his searches rewarded – among other valuable works of Latin scholarship he found a complete version of the *Institutio oratoria*. In ecstatic letters he announced his find to two friends, Leonardo Bruni and Niccolò Niccoli:

> In the middle of a well-stocked library, too large to catalogue at present, we discovered Quintilian, safe as yet and sound, though covered with dust and filthy with neglect and age.[26]

Poggio's discovery, coming out of his boredom with the council – 'wasting our time in idleness at Constance' is his phrase[27] – was to provide a great stimulus to the educational hopes of the humanists. For, it is worth recalling, the *Institutio oratorio* still remained the best practical treatise on education ever written and down through the centuries it had developed special attraction for scholars and schoolmasters, in part because the complete text was tantalizingly elusive. Indeed, knowledge of the work fluctuated considerably from century to century. Dante, for example, betrays no knowledge of Quintilian although Petrarch made many references, Boccaccio reveals a passing acquaintance, and the scholar Gasparino da Barzizza even attempted to restore the lacunae of one of the mutilated manuscripts. With the full text, which supplied the missing parts from Books I, V, VI, VII, VIII, IX, X, XI and XII,[28] the humanists believed, in a sense, that they had found the long lost grail in which the educational wisdom of the ancients had been placed.

Early reactions to humanism

Opposition to humanism, meanwhile, had been evident as early as the beginning of the fifteenth century when a vigorous criticism was made by the mendicant priest, Giovanni Dominici, vicar of the Dominican convent of Santa Maria Novella in Florence. Dominici's protests[29] followed the line of orthodox religious conservatism, arguing that the new humanism extolled pagan ways and neglected the teaching mission of the church. Salutati provided an answer, putting the counter-argument that classical learning contains allegorical and secret truths. The patristic writers themselves had recognized this fact, and Basil particularly, in Chapter II of his *Address to Young Men on Reading Greek Literature*, had used the metaphor of the bee to make his point: 'all flowers could be visited, and the nectar of each variety gathered to make honey'. That fourth-century homily was invoked on several occasions to support the humanist position. Bruni translated it early in the period as *De legendis gentilium libris* and, like Vergerio, he made conciliatory references to religious studies in *De studiis et literis*.

Other attacks on humanism appeared from various writers, of whom two were particularly prominent, although their lives remain obscure. These were Cino Rinuccini and Domenico da Prato, both apparently contemporaneous with Bruni.[30] Their invectives, appearing before 1407 and in 1420, respectively, expressed an opposition that was of some considerable size. Unlike the attack by Giovanni Domenici which stressed the conservative religious position, those of Rinuccini and da Prato attempted to conserve the humanism of the Trecento, especially the emergence of a vigorous vernacular proposed by Petrarch. These two polemicists stood for the efforts of Dante, Petrarch and Boccaccio in making the vernacular (*volgare*) a worthy literary vehicle. Domenico, in particular, argued that emphasis on a revived classicism, with its concentration on Latin and

Greek language and literature, would paralyse creative energy.[31] The innovating humanists, the *scuola erudita*, were opposed then by the *scuola volgare* who sought to develop the vigorous literary vernacular that had been incipient in the period of Trecento creativity. In large part these invectives were based on ignorance of the humanist intentions, and, in fact, in 1436 Bruni defended the Florentine *volgare* as having its own perfection. None the less, these writers spoke for an opposition that did not see humanism as an acceptable educational programme.

Leonardo Bruni and the study of literature

Humanism continued to gain acceptance despite opposition, and in the second quarter of the Quattrocento its most vigorous proponent was Leonardo Bruni d'Arezzo (*c.* 1370–1444). Arriving in Florence in 1390, or soon after, to study law, he was attracted subsequently to the circle around Chrysoloras and thereafter he remained a vigorous champion of his adopted city. Bruni became one of the most eloquent of the new generation of civic humanists that grew up in Florence, himself composing a large number of influential works on the theme of civic humanism, of which the greatest was his massive six-volume opus, *Historiae florentini populi*. This history of the Florentine peoples was a monument to the humanist concern with maintaining a consciousness of the past, of its continuity with the present, and its examples for the future. This work occupied him for his mature life, being commenced in 1415, about his forty-fifth year, and completed fifteen years later.

While working on his great historical study, Bruni found time to consider problems of education. Some time in the middle of this period, probably between 1423 and 1426, he composed a short letter *De studiis et literis (On Study and Literature)*[32] which continued Vergerio's scholarly concern with relatively simple educational matters. This epistle was addressed to a woman of noble family, Baptista di Montrefelto (1383–1450), who, having been joined in an incompatible marriage to Galeazzo Malatesta, sought diversion and happiness in intellectual pursuits. Although composed with those particular circumstances in mind, *De studiis et literis* bears no excessive consolatory bias; on the contrary, it is largely a positive, uncompromising statement on the educational values of the humanist programme. The modifications that exist result solely from the fact that it was addressed to a woman, for whom some different prescriptions would obviously be necessary, chiefly the elimination of rhetoric, because it is a preparation for direct civic activity, and of physical education as a preliminary to military duties. Even then Bruni takes the opportunity to make oblique references to strategy through a discussion of Homer and Aeschylus, ostensibly as examples of poetry. The emphasis of the letter, however – as the title implies – is on the study of literature, that central concern of the humanist.

Literature, for Bruni, is a generic term including within it the separate studies of history and classical Latin literature in oratorical compositions and in poetry. Although the discussion of these studies in his letter is preceded by a reference to the necessary value of Christian studies, particularly in respect of morals, and perhaps as a concession to female sensitivities, there is no doubt where Bruni's emphasis lies:

> We must not forget that true distinction is to be gained by a wide and varied range of such studies as conduce to the profitable enjoyment of life, in which, however, we must observe due proportion in the attention and time we devote to them. First among such studies I place History: a subject which must not on any account be neglected by one who aspires to true cultivation. For it is our duty to understand the origins of our own history and its development, and the achievements of peoples and kings.[33]

To this primary study, Bruni adds injunctions to read the historians Livy, Sallust, Curtius, and perhaps even Caesar, as well as the great orators, although these are not named. Poetry completes the range, this study being important because it had shaped the great minds of the past. In this respect Bruni saw in poetry merely an instrumental value; if it so influenced the mental development of the ancients – he refers specifically to Aristotle, Plato, Cicero, Jerome, Augustine, Lactantius and Boethius – it should be equally useful for the modern age. Poetry, in his view, means ancient poetry; he cites the works of Homer, Hesiod, Pindar and Euripides among the Greeks, and Ennius, Accius and Virgil among the Romans. Literature, in this general sense, should constitute the content of a liberal education; as Bruni argues, 'a high standard of education is only to be reached by one who has seen many things and read much. Poet, orator, historian, and the rest, all must be studied, each must contribute a share.'[34]

Along with this content, however, Bruni gives equal importance to expression and the method of study itself, insisting that content and method are interdependent:

> These two sides of learning should not be separated: they afford mutual aid and distinction. Proficiency in literary form, not accompanied by broad acquaint-

ance with facts and truths, is a barren attainment; while information, however vast, which lacks all grace of expression, would seem to be put under a bushel or partly thrown away. Indeed, one may fairly ask what advantage it is to possess profound and varied learning if one cannot convey it in language worthy of the subject.[35]

To this end, like Vergerio, Bruni urges close attention to the methods of instruction, although he deals only with the specific problems of making literary study as efficient as possible. Consequently his letter points out that the attainment of literary elegance comes partly through such practices as reading aloud and by attending even to the care with which notebook exercises are performed as well as through the careful choice of authors. In making these observations, Bruni was apparently the first European scholar to deal with a new schoolroom procedure: the keeping of individual exercise books. He recommends that students make notes on vocabulary, inflections, tropes, metaphors and other literary devices, as well as apt quotations on as many topics as possible so that these can be incorporated into the student's own writing and speaking.[36] Bruni apparently learned this use of notebooks from Chrysoloras, it being already the practice in Constantinople. The employment of notebooks in Europe, however, depended on the availability of sufficient cheap paper, and that commodity, despite its manufacture in Spain around 1150, France around 1189 and Italy in 1276, was still in limited use. Bruni's comments were obviously directed towards the wealthy; paper was to remain relatively expensive and this prevented its widespread use in popular education for several centuries to come.

Bruni's letter on education covers much the same ground as Vergerio's, and in many respects simply repeats the same principles, notably the preeminence of history. Perhaps the most interesting aspect of Bruni's statement, however, is his emphasis on Latin scholarship, and his lack of concern with philosophy – which, in a restricted sense, had been Vergerio's second study. Bruni had been educated by Chrysoloras, and his proficiency in Greek was sufficiently advanced for him to translate several Greek works; in addition to the tract on the education of children by the pseudo-Plutarch, he also translated a considerable amount of other Greek writing: eight of Plutarch's Lives, six of Plato's dialogues, and the pseudepigraphic letters, along with major works of Xenophon, Aeschines, Demosthenes and Homer. Yet Bruni retained his stress on the instrumentality of these studies in cultivating civic responsibility, and nowhere does he suggest that literature might be read for its aesthetic values or for other reasons:

for example, social criticism, historical insight, political acuity. Despite the seeming liberality of his letter, it placed a restriction on studies as narrow as the surviving scholasticism it sought to displace.

The *studia humanitatis*

By the time of Bruni's *De studiis et literis* humanism as an intellectual movement was extremely influential in Italy; the new learning was well established among the wealthier classes and the efforts of the previous thirty years in promoting a programme of studies were proving successful. The term *studia humanitatis*, in regular use by 1430, designated a sequence of learning following that proposed by Vergerio and Bruni, covering the entire period of formal learning from the child's early years until early adulthood. It encompassed even the idea of mature scholarly research as pursued by the humanists themselves. In that period, however, such learning was not ordered in terms of content, nor were there any generally agreed institutional sequences. Parents sent their children to a number of places which offered separately the various elements of instruction, or else tutors were hired. Gradually a sequence of instruction took shape, and the new institution of the *gymnasium* had its origins in Italy at that time. The name itself suggested a revival of the classical Greek school, and presumably its increasing use came from an attempt by the humanists to indicate the wider scope of its activities and its classical orientation, in contrast to the grammar school which was the alternative institution north of the Alps. After the *gymnasium* the student could then move on to the university, *studium generale* (*studio pubblico* in Italian), although the sequence of progression was not clearly defined. The universities, moreover, were not yet humanist in outlook and their curricula were either strictly vocational or else based on Aristotelian studies. In that period possession of an academic degree was not as important as having studied with an eminent scholar, particularly since the intellectual world was sufficiently small for personal reputation and distinction to become widely known. Growing independently of both the *gymnasium* and the *studium* was another institution, the academy, its title also a classical revival. The academies were extremely diverse in their functions, their common link, apart from their title, being the fact that they were free associations of scholars, and frequently dilettantes, who met to discuss intellectual and cultural affairs.

Some of these were quite significant in the advancement of the *studia humanitatis*, the academy of Luigi Marsili being the forerunner.

In this new growth of the *studia humanitatis* the figure of the schoolmaster becomes most important. His contemptuous dismissal by Petrarch in 1350 is no longer a feature of humanist writing. On the contrary, the schoolmaster is essential to the success of the humanist project, and it is in this period that the prototype of a new kind of teacher appears, exemplified in the persons of Vittorino da Feltre and Guarino da Verona, both court tutors, at Mantua and Ferrara respectively.

Vittorino da Feltre and the Casa Giocosa

Vittorino da Feltre (1378–1446)[37] set a large number of educational precedents which, although they were not accepted universally throughout Europe, were to influence considerably the conduct of schools, particularly those of the courts and those organized by tutors. Little is known of his early life,[38] and since his writings were few and none of them survives, present knowledge is consequently quite limited. He first appears in the record in 1396 when he arrived at Padua, its *studio* then being a leading centre of the liberal arts. There Vittorino was influenced by two outstanding scholars: Vergerio who taught at Padua until he left for the position of court tutor in the same city, and Gasparino da Barzizza, then the leading Latinist of the day. Gasparino – who attempted to restore the *Institutio oratoria* – introduced Vittorino to both Cicero and Quintilian, thereby interesting him in the two leading classical writers on education. Following graduation, some time before 1411, Vittorino remained in Padua where he conducted a school until 1415. After this, until 1423, his movements are somewhat obscure, although he is known to have been in Venice (*c.* 1415–16) with Guarino, who was also a student of Gasparino, and to have taught in a school conducted by Guarino in Venice about 1415. Around 1420 Vittorino returned to Padua, teaching in the university where he evidently secured increasing recognition as a teacher, sufficient for him to be offered the position of court tutor to the Gonzaga family, lords of Mantua, in 1423. From then until his death in 1446, Vittorino built that court's *gymnasium palatinum* into the finest school in Europe, a school distinguished by its patronage, its *alumnae*, and its example to the rest of the continent.

From the start Vittorino's relations with both Gianfrancesco Gonzaga and his wife, Paola di Malatesta, were cordial. In contrast to many courts, that at Mantua was reasonably well conducted, certainly enough for the somewhat ascetic and religiously zealous Vittorino to accept appointment there. Gianfrancesco employed Vittorino in the first instance as tutor to his three sons, all in their childhood; the enrolment increased with the birth of further Gonzaga children and the admission of some boys from other important Mantuan families. In time some leading humanists, including Guarino da Verona, Poggio Bracciolini and Francesco Filelfo, sent their sons there. These boys were housed in a building that stood separately in the palace grounds, designed originally as a house of pleasure, La Gioiosa. With a clever neologism, Vittorino converted its title to La Giocosa, the 'pleasant house',[39] whose pleasures were decidedly more intellectual.

Vittorino's teaching followed closely the educational ideals and pre-scriptions set out by Vergerio and Bruni. The emphasis of instruction was on Latin letters – *volgare* was discouraged – and though the curriculum was extended beyond letters to include some study of the quadrivium, this aspect was not stressed. Physical activities, chiefly exercises and games, were conducted in all seasons, apparently regardless of prevailing weather. Vittorino himself was always inclined towards asceticism and is reported to have dressed lightly and used no other footwear than sandals throughout the year.[40] This attitude of physical hardihood, along with other abstemious attitudes such as moderation and plainness in food and drink, he impressed upon his charges. The school's programme, in fact, was designed to cultivate moral, ethical and religious uprightness as essential elements of a proper education.

Despite Vittorino's emphasis on physical and moral welfare, and his concern to make the school building itself physically attractive and hygienic, he had no doubt that the *studia humanitatis* were the fixed point of his educational enterprise. In the first years, he himself taught Latin letters, beginning by having the children read aloud in order to secure proper enunciation and good diction. Such exercises were practised from the beginning on simple passages from leading classical writers, chiefly Ovid, Virgil, Cicero, Livy, Sallust, Homer and Demosthenes. One document indicates that the study of Plato was also intended since the Florentine book dealer Johannes Aurispa reported in 1425: 'I have received an offer from a correspondent named Vittorino who is attached to the Mantuan court . . . and proposes to pay fifty florins for two volumes of Plato and Plutarch.'[41] Since Aurispa had imported only two complete sets of Plato the year before – the first copies in Italy – it testifies both to the intellectual acumen of Vittorino and to the cultural and fiscal liberality of the Gonzagas that such costly works were sought for the school. Indeed, under Vittorino the library of La Giocosa grew into a particularly fine feature whose reputation, like the school's, spread throughout the learned world.

Whether Vittorino gained the volumes of Plato is not certain although Ambrogio Traversari records having seen a Platonic manuscript in Vittorino's library; none the less, the fact that Vittorino had a number of Greek manuscripts by various authors suggests the study of Greek which, following Quintilian, he may have sought to teach simultaneously with Latin in his school. Vittorino himself was unequal to the task since his Greek did not match his Latin, and a master of Greek had to be brought in. At the same time, however, the enrolment of his school continued to grow and Vittorino himself in time became director of studies, the teaching being performed by other scholars. Information is difficult to find on this point: the first major scholar to join the school was the Byzantine Greek, George of Trebizond, around 1430;[42] the second was Theodore of Gaza, around 1440, who had come to Italy from Constantinople two years earlier in a diplomatic mission to secure help against the ever-encroaching Turks.

In addition to the two classical languages and their literatures, the Casa Giocosa gave some attention to logic and rhetoric, but only for their possible instrumental value. Logic's place was seen to lie in offering assistance in analysing and resolving arguments or difficulties; Vittorino refused to be drawn into scholastic disputes. Similarly, a limited role was given to mathematical and nature studies; there is evidence that masters were engaged to teach arithmetic, geometry, the new study of algebra, natural philosophy and music.[43] Little is known of these, however, and it seems likely that they were taught either as simple skills or as additional polite accomplishments; certainly they were not integral with Vittorino's educational theory.

Vittorino's school became highly regarded for the quality of its instruction, particularly the teaching methods themselves. Again it appears that the reputation of the Casa Giocosa depended on the successful implementation of the recommendations of Vergerio and Bruni. Vittorino seems to have used their prescriptions in ordering and presenting his lessons, although a premium remained on memory and frequent oral drill, in part necessitated by the relative scarcity of books. One of Theodore of Gaza's attractions to Vittorino was his ability to transcribe manuscripts accurately and beautifully and to provide scholarly editing as well –

absolutely mandatory requirements if classical studies from hand-produced manuscripts were to be pursued successfully. During Vittorino's own incumbency two further innovations were under way that were to change the character of the schoolroom: the use of notebooks, as recommended by Bruni, and the development of printing from movable type. Their influence, however, was not significant until a century later.

Within ten years of Vittorino's appointment the Casa Giocosa developed a reputation that rivalled many of the *studia* of Italy. In 1433, in fact, it received a university charter from the Emperor Sigismund which was renewed by his two immediate successors, Albert II (r. 1438–9) and Frederick III (r. 1440–93).[44] Its designation as a *studium generale*, however, did not progress beyond this first formal recognition; none the less, it stands as evidence of the high regard in which the school was held. Judging from the curriculum, moreover, it appears that the instruction and content must have surpassed that given in many *studia* of the time. One of Vittorino's students, Lorenzo Valla (1405–57), was to become a leading intellectual, distinguishing himself, among other things, for his new attitude to historical criticism. Vittorino apparently did not press his claims for public recognition, and continued to conduct the school according to his two standards: the primacy of Christian faith and the necessary validity of the humanist way. By the time of his peaceful death in 1446, Vittorino, more than any other single figure, had become the personification of the new conception of the schoolmaster.

Guarino da Verona: changing emphasis in the humanist programme

The renewed emphasis on teaching and on humanist education was not sustained by Vittorino alone: among the others who were working simultaneously, Guarino da Verona was equally well regarded and was seen perhaps as a more colourful figure. Throughout his life Guarino Guarini (1370–1460) was in frequent contact with Vittorino, although his personality was in marked contrast. Guarino had studied Greek under Chrysoloras at Florence and later followed him to Constantinople, living in his house as *contubernalis*[45] in the years 1403–8, even though Chrysoloras was absent. In 1415 Guarino established a humanist school in Venice, the first in that city, and was joined for a time by Vittorino. Guarino's prominence as a schoolmaster, however, dates from his acceptance of the court tutorship at Ferrara, offered in 1429 by the lord of Ferrara, Niccolò d'Este. Guarino directed this school until 1436, when it became the basis on which a *studium generale* was founded, thereby achieving the transition that had not eventuated three years earlier at Mantua. For the rest of his life, the years 1436–60, Guarino held the chair of rhetoric in Ferrara's *studium*.

Guarino, like Vittorino, wrote nothing on the theory of education; unlike Vittorino, however, he was active in other branches of humanist letters. He was a particularly competent Greek scholar and by 1435 had translated two of Isocrates' political works, *Evagoras* and *Nicocles*, and the *Geographia* of Strabo (*c.* 1440). In addition, he translated pseudo-Plutarch's *On the Education of Children* (*Peri paidon agoges*) in 1411 under the title *De liberorum educatione* and produced a Latin translation and abridgement of Chrysolaras' *Erotemata sive quaestiones* (or *Erotemata Chrysolorae*) which became known alternatively as the *Erotemata Guarini* and was used very widely. Despite the absence of his personal writings on education, there is one relevant document, *De ordine docendi et studendi* (*On the Order and Method of Teaching and Reading Classical Authors*), written in 1459 by his twenty-five-year-old son, Battista.[46] This youngest son of Guarino was born in 1434 at the court of Ferrara and after a precocious childhood, during which he attended the court school, he became professor of rhetoric at Bologna at the age of twenty-one and then, two years later, professor at Ferrara. The treatise itself was probably instigated by the elder Guarino; in its introduction Battista states that the tract is 'a summary of the theory and practice of several scholars, and especially does it represent the doctrine of my father Guarino Veronese'.[47]

De ordine docendi et studendi in itself offers nothing new in educational thought beyond the earlier treatises of Vergerio and Bruni. Indeed, it contains virtually the same prescriptions with regard to the value of a humanist education, the care to be exercised in the choice of a schoolmaster, and the importance of kindly, persuasive methods of teaching rather than brutal coercion. Its prescriptions on content stress letters and history; another large portion of the tract, Sections 2 and 3, give very explicit instructions on grammatical points; while Section 5 deals with methods of individual study in some detail. Those three sections, in fact, mark a significant development in humanist education. They reveal a growing preoccupation with technical matters, the emphasis being less on broad questions of liberal education as asserted by Vergerio, more on such minutiae of classroom procedure as how to ensure that children learn by heart, how to grade the teaching of grammar, how to secure the best exposition of authors in reading aloud, how to grade the pupils' progress and the systematic preparation and presentation of lessons. Battista Guarino amplified Bruni's thoughts on notebooks considerably:

> In reading an author it is not enough to be content with the exposition of a single scholar. Every commentary of importance must be consulted to enable us to form our own judgement as to the precise meaning of the text and the force of each individual word. Our notes should be regularly written up, as carefully and as fully as though we destined them to publication. This practice quickens our intelligence and concentrates our attention: it tends to careful construing, to ready composition, to more exact recall of details. A volume of notes duly ordered serves the purpose of a common-place book . . . The practice of making extracts, where the interest of the subject matter suggests it, and of collecting parallel passages from different authors, is an important help to the student.[48]

This passage illustrates the entire spirit of Battista's tract, and emphasizes the growing schoolmasterly concern with specific procedural tasks of the classroom and the assertion of the centrality of Latin and Greek in education, thereby marking a distinct break with the growing vernacular. The elder Guarino himself was opposed to the use of *volgare*; his follower Angelo Decembrio recalled that Guarino considered 'writers in the Volgare were best fit to be read to women and children on a long winter evening, but deserved no admittance to the library of a *literatus*'.[49]

The final section indicates even more specifically the changing emphasis in humanist educational theory; letters are defined as an 'adornment of leisure'[50] and in this recapitulation learning is urged as much for its recreational value as for anything else. Despite a metaphorical genuflection to the spirit of civic humanism – Battista ends by equating *studia humanitatis* with the Greek *paideia* – there remains the sense of a much narrower attitude towards the *studia humanitatis* than developed by Vergerio nearly half a century earlier.

At the same time, however, it must be emphasized that Vittorino and Guarino were exceptional teachers and that most children of the time were certainly not taught by comparable masters, nor were they exposed to such a vigorous sequence of studies. On the contrary, there is much surviving evidence, particularly in contemporary writings and woodcuts of classrooms, to indicate that Petrarch's polemic against schoolmasters continued to have some basis in fact. In his day, as indeed in all previous periods, many were particularly unenlightened, and the contemporary testimony indicates that, in general, perhaps the majority were ill prepared with respect to their own learning as well as in pedagogical technique. This is, of course, one explanation of the humanist tracts: these were intended in part as simple prescriptions to help schoolmasters, thereby continuing the tradition of Quintilian's writing. The direct evidence comes from other writers, of whom Giovanni Conversino da Ravenna is the most descriptive. His autobiography, *Rationarium vitae*, gives harrowing accounts of punishments meted out to boys between the ages of six and ten: imprisonment on frosty nights, naked in an unheated cellar; daily floggings until the blood flowed; trussing of children, including a case where a child was suspended for hours in a well.[51] Giovanni Conversino himself was the most eminent humanist in Padua between 1390 and 1405, and the teacher of a number of notable scholars including Vergerio, Vittorino and Guarino. Conversino, for his part, secured some notable improvement in the vocation of teaching, although his influence was expressed chiefly through his equally celebrated students.

The prevailing practices, however, were certainly different from those of Conversino, Vittorino and Guarino. Indeed, we must ask ourselves why such brutality and coercion were necessary, and tolerated, and the answer seems to lie in the fact that the curricula of most schools were very narrow. It would be quite exceptional for schoolboys to have books of manuscripts in that period and the stress in learning remained on mnemonics and other forms of rote memorization. Most schools consisted still of a single classroom, furnished solely with forms and bare of desks, in which the children learned everything that was offered, usually the elements of literacy and some Latin grammar. Since masters in many towns continued to teach only the subject of their speciality, this forced many children to move around from one building to another to secure instruction in different subjects. If we add to this the fact that schooling was generally a winter activity, with poor illumination on account of the short days and restricted window space, we can get some appreciation of the difficulties under which many schools had to operate. Humanism as an educational programme made considerable demands for materials, and highly educated teachers. For that reason alone it was not capable of being implemented on any wide scale.

CHAPTER 8

Italy: Higher Learning in the Quattrocento

Universities and academies

Early Italian universities

It was not until the later years of the fifteenth century that the doctrines of the humanists began to influence the universities which, hitherto, had developed independently along the lines of their original traditions: in the early centuries of their development, the twelfth and thirteenth, no Italian university taught theology; this was generally a fifteenth-century development. Philosophy was offered, but in contrast to Paris, where it was an instrument of theological speculation and controversy, the Italian universities used it as a basis for medicine and as a guide to the study of the natural sciences.

Data on the development of the Italian universities are not easy to find,[1] being in no way as abundant as those for Paris. It is clear, however, that Bologna stimulated the establishment of the first wave of universities, chiefly through secessions: the first definite case is that of Padua in 1222, although Vicenza may have been settled by a secession of 1202 – the facts are uncertain. A secession from Padua in turn led to the establishment of Vercelli in 1228. An exception to this pattern was the university at Naples, founded specifically by Emperor Frederick II in 1224 as a centre for the training of administrators for his empire. Like Paris, however, most other early Italian *studia* were not founded formally; they appeared, generally, as extensions of previously existing schools of various sorts. The conferring of formal charters which gave the universities authority to grant the *jus ubique docendi* was the second step in securing their legitimacy. The universities, by autonomous right, could award only their degrees; the *jus* was granted by either pope or emperor who alone could guarantee its legality, and the universities therefore conferred the *jus* by delegated authority. The assumption by pope and emperors of the right to confer the *jus ubique docendi*, and so effect a Europe-wide recognition of university degrees, was a legal recognition of an earlier and less certain practice. Bologna itself, it must be remembered, did not gain official papal approval until the bull of Pope Honorius III in 1220, eleven years before Paris received similar authorization from Pope Gregory IX in the famous *Parens scientiarum* by which that *studium* was re-established after the great secession of 1229–1231. The motivation behind the original royal approval of Paris by Philip Augustus in 1200 was a challenge to the growing papal tendency to assume authority over the universities, and as part of the general church answer, Gregory IX stimulated the foundation of Toulouse, in southern France, in 1229. There were some cases of official intervention in the universities of northern Italy: Treviso was founded in 1318 and lapsed immediately; Siena in 1357, Pavia in 1361 and Florence in 1364 were strengthened by royal decrees of the Emperor Charles IV.[2]

Throughout the thirteenth and fourteenth centuries universities became established in many North Italian cities, including Reggio, Perugia, Vicenza, Piacenza, Verona, Pisa, Florence, Siena, Pavia and Padua. In general they were municipal institutions and were little affected by outside intervention, yet their growth, like that of their counterparts north of the Alps, remained unsteady and uncertain: traditions of institutional life were not yet secure. Florence had a particularly difficult parturition. It was established as a civic *studium* in 1321, chiefly to teach civil and canon law, along with notarial studies and their prerequisites of grammar and rhetoric. In 1348 it had to be refounded; three years later in 1351 Petrarch refused an appointment there, and in 1357 and again in 1364 further attempts were made to revive it. Not till the incumbency of Salutati as the city's chancellor, and the appearance of Chrysoloras, did that university become secure. Pisa, itself a city in the Florentine orbit, also found difficulty maintaining its *studium* which did not really begin to prosper until the 1470s when the Florentine ruler, Lorenzo, moved the faculties of law, medicine and theology there in an attempt to strengthen it. In the Quat-trocento in the time of Vittorino and Guarino, Mantua failed to sustain its *studium generale* despite the royal charter of 1433. Ferrara, under the influ-ence of Guarino, fared better, and Guarino's school made the transition successfully to a *studium generale*. This *studium* however was a revival of one that had appeared in the mid-thirteenth century and had lapsed in 1391. It is interesting to note that in 1442 a petition was addressed to Leonello, Marquis of Este, urging him to recognize by a charter the university which had been operating from 1436, since such improved status would be an adornment to the city and bring increased wealth from students and travellers.[3] This suggestion was probably made because both Bologna and Padua were seen to have benefited in exactly these ways.

The slow growth of the Italian universities is explained in part by their adherence to professional training, which was not in great demand, since it could also be met through direct practice and apprenticeship. In addition the non-religious character of the early universities meant that their students were drawn chiefly from the laity. Paris and the ultramontane universities continued to attract clerics for whom theological, or at least a theologically oriented arts curriculum, would be more suitable for voca-tional advancement. In Italy, then, the humanist movement developed largely outside the universities, although at times the stimulators, such as Petrarch, Marsilius and Poggio, were clerics of various kinds. By the middle of the Quattrocento the *studium* at Florence had become a centre of humanist studies, but this was largely an exception. For the rest of the century, in fact, the further development of the *studia humanitatis* and the elaboration of higher learning generally took place outside the univer-sities. The institution that met this need was the academy.

Emergence of the academies

In many ways description of the academies as institutions is unsatisfactory since it might be assumed that they were organized according to certain formal considerations as were the universities. On the contrary, the term academy was used by, and is applied to, the large number of loosely organ-ized associations of *literati* and *dilettanti* that appeared in fifteenth- and more particularly sixteenth-century Italy. None of these academies was more than a group of persons with some common intellectual interest. The origins of the institution can be discerned in the exchanges of Lovato and Mussato late in the thirteenth century, the first historically significant

Ficino, Landino, Poliziano, de' Becchi, detail of fresco by Ghirlandaio in S. Maria Novella, Florence, 1490.

University lecture, tomb design by Bellini for a scholar, probably a professor at the University Padua, fifteenth century.

10 University lecture in college of Henricus de Allemania, German miniature of fourteenth century.

academy being the group that met in the monastery of Marsilius in late Trecento Florence. Not until the middle of the Quattrocento, however, was there an academy of great significance when Cosimo de' Medici (r. 1434–64) became effective if *de facto* ruler of Florence. Cosimo brought with him the desire to establish a scholarly academy devoted to the study of Plato.

Cosimo, born in 1389, himself had received an education in Latin and logic that included little of the new humanist studies. None the less he was attracted to the new learning and had his enthusiasm whetted more sharply in 1438, four years after his rise to authority. In that year an ecumenical council gathered in Florence to discuss reunion, in an effort to repair the schism of 1054 between Catholics and the Orthodox Church. A secondary, but integral aspect of the council was the Greek need for assistance against the Turks; ecumenism was the price the Byzantines had to pay for security. Their mission, like that of the 1390s, included a distinguished Greek scholar, Gemistus Plethon (*c.* 1355– *c.* 1450), who was accompanied by two other scholars, John Bessarion of Nicaea (*c.* 1400–72) and Theodore of Gaza. Yet it was not by diplomacy that Plethon won the Florentines, it was with philosophy. Plethon was an ardent Platonist, and in Florence, where scholars were eager to hear the exposition of Platonic teachings, Plethon lectured to deeply appreciative audiences. Cosimo resolved to revive the study of Plato on a truly comprehensive scale, and urged Plethon to remain for that purpose. Events went otherwise; Plethon returned to Constantinople and the revival of Platonic studies lapsed temporarily. Undeterred, Cosimo continued to maintain the patronage of learning.

In the year 1437 Cosimo had already acquired the 800-volume personal library of the recently deceased Florentine humanist Niccolò Niccoli, which was probably the largest personal collection in existence. Thereupon he commissioned the architect Michelozzo to design a library building in the monastery of San Marco; it was finished in 1444 and was opened as the first public library in Europe, perhaps in the world. Libraries were in existence prior to this, but only as private or restricted access collections, allowing entry only to persons personally acquainted with, or recommended to, the owners. Of this kind, the papal library and those of the ducal houses, including Mantua, are conspicuous examples. The library at San Marco was a departure since it could be used by all citizens. Equally significant to the future of humanist scholarship was Cosimo's detection of great promise in the son of his court physician. This boy was Marsilio Ficino (1433–99).

When Marsilio reached his late adolescence Cosimo provided him with patronage so that he could study Greek and, in particular, Plato. This Marsilio did with great energy and the insight of genius. By establishing the library of San Marco, even, according to rumour, hiring forty-five scribes initially to meet the need for the expansion of holdings,[4] and by encouraging the talents of Ficino, Cosimo de' Medici laid the basis of the further elaboration of humanist studies, and certainly provided for the continued pre-eminence of Florence as the centre of European intellectual development. Cosimo did even more: on a lavish scale he promoted the arts in Florence, attracting the greatest single group of artists and scholars the West had seen since the Periclean age of fifth-century-B.C. Athens. The names are now some of the greatest in the history of art: Brunelleschi, Donatello, Lippi, Botticelli, del Sarto, Cellini, Ghiberti, Fra Angelico, Masaccio, Uccello, del Castagno. However, Cosimo could only stimulate the intellectual movement, it was his grandson Lorenzo who brought it to fruition.

Cosimo – known as 'father' of his homeland, *pater patriae* – died in 1464 and was succeeded by his son Piero (r. 1464–9), under whom the dominance of the Medici in Florentine politics was maintained. The Medici of the Quattrocento never actually held princely title to Florence, on the contrary they preserved all of the offices of the republic and preferred to exercise their authority through this sort of machinery. Their influence came by patronage; in return for financial assistance, they expected, and received, support. In general, the *literati* they assisted were inhibited from taking part in political activity. Piero himself was sickly and his short tenure did not produce many new developments in learning. It was the accession of his son Lorenzo that brought a period of great vigour to Florentine humanism.

Lorenzo de' Medici (r. 1469–92) was a great bibliophile, and encouraged the pursuit of arts and letters; in addition to consolidating the Medicean dominance of Florence, he continued to promote the fine arts and humanities. Although he was unable to finance the fine arts to the same extent as his grandfather, he did patronize Michelangelo Buonarroti (1475–1564). In this respect it is interesting to observe the contrast with his equally brilliant contemporary Leonardo da Vinci (1452–1519), who through apprenticeship in a workshop (*bottega*) had been trained as a painter. Leonardo's career was less acclaimed, in part because of the contempt of the early humanists for painting in their educational programme – Vergerio actually spoke against it – and because the stress was on literary accomplishment to the exclusion of technological studies which had been identified, since Greek antiquity, with the mechanical crafts. Lorenzo's patronage of the arts was directed towards the humanities, of which a leading practitioner now was the maturing Ficino.

Marsilio Ficino and the Platonic Academy of Florence

Marsilio Ficino brought the philosophical development of Quattrocento Italy to its apogee. He justified the promise Cosimo saw in him and fulfilled Cosimo's ambition to make Platonism a living intellectual force in Italy. Ficino's early years in Florence are obscure.[5] In 1462 Cosimo installed him in the Villa de' Careggi, and there, in the years following, Ficino set himself to the task of translating the entire *corpus Platonicum*. By 1482, that great project was complete: all thirty-six dialogues were now in Latin, although it was to take more than the whole of the following century for them to be further translated into the Italian and French vernaculars. English and German translations, in quantity, were much later still in appearing. As well as translating Plato, Ficino completed a translation of Plotinus' *Enneads* with a commentary, by 1491, just a year before his death. In addition to these signal achievements, which made him the greatest translator of the century, Ficino wrote a number of commentaries and translations of the important Neoplatonists – Porphyry, Proclus, Dionysus the Areopagite – and two major original works, *Theologica platonica de immortalitate animae* and *De christiana religione*.

During Ficino's tenure the Villa de' Careggi became the centre of a revived Platonism; round him gathered disciples, of whom the youthful and short-lived Pico della Mirandola (1463–94) was the most promising, all concerned with the study of Plato. It must be remembered, in this connection, that in Europe most of Plato's works had not been available in Greek before 1424 and that a renewed appraisal of Platonic theories had been made possible only by the gifted exposition of the two Byzantines, Chrysoloras and Plethon. Ficino's group of Platonists probably saw themselves as the spiritual heirs of the original Academy in Athens: Ficino in a letter referred to his new circle in just such terms,[6] and it has been known since as the Platonic Academy of Florence. The term itself is most imprecise since it suggests a formal institution – the closest this Academy came to a schedule was its annual convivium every November the seventh. 'Platonic Academy' was a metaphorical allusion, symbolizing the spirit of the new studies.[7]

Not every member of the Platonic Academy, of course, was a scholar; the majority of participants were more interested in the literary and visual arts, poets and painters forming the two largest single interest groups. As the leading intellectual, Ficino directed the Academy's philosophical pursuits towards the reconciliation of Platonism with Christianity. Ficino himself had undergone a grave intellectual crisis at an early age, probably between the years 1458 and 1473, because of his inability to harmonize faith with reason. This in part explains Ficino's interest in the Neoplatonists, especially Plotinus, since those early scholars had begun the task that Augustine completed – the 'baptism' of Plato. In company with others, chiefly Pico della Mirandola, Francesco Cattani di Diacceto and Peregrino Aglio, Ficino sought again to make secure the relationship between philosophy and faith. From the outset he accepted Plato's philosophy as an absolute doctrine, akin to divine law, and saw his own task as explicating Christianity in terms of the Platonic assumptions.[8] In this respect he diverged from the Neoplatonism of Augustine which accepted only those aspects of Plato that harmonized with the revealed faith. This marked a profound change in the history of the encounter between faith and reason: it was now Christianity that had to be accommodated to philosophy.

Central to Ficino's philosophy is his insistence on the primacy of man and particularly of man's intellect. For Ficino this provides a fixed point in his inquiry. Mind itself, demonstrably self-evident, is imbued with motion which impels it to seek its object, a state of contemplative rest within the harmony of the cosmos. 'What, then,' he asked, 'does the intellect seek if not to transform all things into itself by depicting all things in the intellect according to the nature of the intellect?'[9] To this rhetorical question he added the further assertion that 'by a natural instinct every soul strives in a continuous effort both to know all truths by the intellect and to enjoy all things by the will'.[10] The terminus of this effort to know rests 'in boundless truth and goodness, . . . in the infinite'.[11] This belief in an infinite, the original Platonic realm of being, provides him with a concept of god which combines a number of separate ideas. The idea of the motion of the mind is linked with that of universal design by 'one certain orderer who is most full of reason';[12] the idea of universal design indicates the existence of an 'infinite' which 'must alone be its [universal design's] especial origin'.[13] Man, then, strives to know god, and this is his proper, naturally derived vocation. With his unique possession of intellect, man, in distinction from the rest of the created universe, should seek god through knowledge: '. . . where intellect is present, intellect which is, as it were, a kind of eye turned towards the intelligible light, there also the intelligible light which is God shines and is honoured and loved and worshipped'.[14] And in the notion of love Ficino finds the ultimate meaning of existence: god created and sustains the world out of love.

This kind of philosophy enjoyed a considerable vogue, part of its appeal deriving from the warmth of its doctrines. The earlier accommodation of religion and Aristotle via the Thomist synthesis was much more austere and, in many ways, less satisfying. Man's need for security, especially in that other world of eternity beyond the frail boundaries of present physical existence, is met most satisfyingly in the belief that there is indeed a fixed, eternal order in which all things have their ultimate rest:

> In the body the soul is truly far more miserable, both because of the weakness and infirmity of the body itself and its want of all things and because of the continual anxiety of the mind. [True freedom comes only when the soul] is either free from the body or in a temperate immortal celestial body. . . . In this condition alone, the highest blessedness of man is indeed perfected.[15]

In many ways Ficino's explication provided a security as well for the humanist programme; the emphasis on man through the cultivation of personality (*virtù* and *fama*) and of intellect was given an intellectually satisfying focus in a permanent after-life.

Application of Platonism to the arts

The immediate appeal of these doctrines, however, was not as evident in philosophy as it was in the arts. In the Platonic Academy poets and artists followed Ficino's lead and sought to apply his conceptions to poetry, painting and sculpture. In doing so, they set to the task of constructing a formal theory of aesthetics, the first attempt since classical times. Within the Academy there was a group interested particularly in poetry, known as the Medici Circle; only two of the members had a real stature as poets, Lorenzo de' Medici himself and the tutor of his children, Angelo Poliziano, who is generally believed to have been the better poet. In their poetry they sought to give expression to the rehabilitated Platonism, in particular the theme of divine love.[16] Despite the fashion for visionary poems, and the cult of Dante, whose *Divine Comedy* was the prototype of this genre, none of this literature reached the status of the work of Dante or Petrarch, since that was not its purpose; none the less it did spread throughout the courts of Italy and Europe generally, becoming the basis of a style of courtly literature in the following sixteenth century. This poetry became stylized particularly in the *trattato d'amore* (love poem) of which the originator and examplar was Pietro Bembo (1470–1547) whose works began appearing in the new medium of print after 1505.[17] The poems of the Medici Circle, and those of Bembo, were written as serious metaphysical speculations on Platonic themes akin to those elaborated in Ficino's formal philosophy, seeking particularly to give meaning to man's striving after the absolute. As this style developed in the courts, however, it became less lofty and speculative, the *trattato d'amore* being written primarily to entertain. In the sixteenth century, it became purely manneristic with no serious intellectual quality whatever.

The visual arts too were subjected to philosophical speculation. Not until the Quattrocento, however, did sculpture or painting begin to exist in complete independence. By that time the artist, although still dominated by craft conceptions, and subject to the discipline of his guild, was beginning to paint and sculpt individual pieces. It was this development that the Medici recognized and encouraged. Indeed, encouragement and patronage depended upon the existence of the concept of 'art' itself.[18] When that movement reached its peak in the second half of the Quattrocento, it became the subject of speculation in the Platonic Academy, and this in itself was a highly significant development. At the beginning of the century Vergerio had dismissed drawing, and so all visual art, as irrelevant to humanist studies, regarding it as an individual predilection of the ancient Greeks, not as an activity worthy of any universal consideration. The discussions on art in the Academy of Ficino were directed specifically towards setting out an acceptable theory. Since the agreed basis was Platonism, the approach was to find in art its universal qualities. The artists frequenting the Villa de' Careggi were all highly self-conscious of their work; in attempting free pieces which no longer had to conform to the demands of architecture or book production they had of necessity to determine criteria of form, and these they found readily in Platonism. Just as the philosopher sought to explain the laws of existence in terms of the immortality of the soul and its longing for a final and eternal transcendental encounter with god, and just as the poet sought to express this desire in visionary writing, so the artists of the Academy attempted the same task in visual terms. They sought to express symbolically the idea of love and beauty.[19]

This is one of the central problems of Platonism: how indeed can beauty be adequately apprehended? The Florentine artists attempted to make just such a visual solution, to express in concrete terms the essential elements of beauty. This involved them in the search for ideal form which, since man was the focus of their interest, they found in the human body. In the painting of Alessandro Botticelli (1446–1510) and the sculpture of Michelangelo Buonarroti (1475–1564), for example, this new approach received expression. Both of these artists conceived nudity as beautiful, and believed that in the human nude rests perfect form. For the principles of beauty, following Plato, are ideas – often with a mathematical basis – and the nude is eminently suitable for revealing them. In this they broke with the assumptions underlying much of Western art up to that point in time. Medieval man saw in the unclothed figure mere *nakedness*, man, that is, symbolized in his fall. This notion was employed as a motif in countless medieval works, perhaps most notably in the *Fall* on the bronze doors of Hildesheim cathedral; it was the symbol of a *natura inferiora*. Botticelli, in his *Birth of Venus* for example, and Michelangelo in all of his great free-standing nudes symbolized instead man's *natura superiora*. Nudity became equated with beauty,[20] and the artist could attempt, in his work, to overcome the corruptive processes of matter. In establishing this tradition they were supported firmly by the philosophers, not only Ficino, but others. Pico della Mirandola, in his twenty-fourth year, published in 1486 the celebrated *Oration on the Dignity of Man*, itself an assertion of the inherent capability of man to order his own affairs and his vision of the cosmos, after the fashion of his own intellect. At the creation itself, Pico wrote allegorically, god said:

> We have set thee at the world's centre that thou mayest from thence more easily observe whatever is in the world. We have made thee neither of heaven nor of earth, neither mortal nor immortal, so that with freedom of choice and with honour, as though the maker and moulder of thyself, thou mayest fashion thyself in whatever shape thou shalt prefer.[21]

That was precisely what the Platonists of the Academy were seeking to do, and with every intention of giving man the best possible shape.

Further developments in higher learning

Decline of civic activity in Florence

Yet, it is very important to observe, the progress of philosophical studies was accompanied by a growing concern with the private, intellectual life.

Marsilio Ficino and his entourage, of course, considered themselves at the centre of important action because of their very involvement with the Platonic doctrines of the reality of existence, although in their own writings the replacement of the ideal of *vita activa* by that of *vita contemplativa* is documented clearly in the growing emphasis on mind. Cristoforo Landino, a member of the Academy and one of Lorenzo's tutors, argues through one of his characters in a dialogue:

> The mind, however, which alone makes us men, attains its perfection in immortal knowledge, not in earthly action. It is there that the final good exists, the good desired for its own sake; that which is the cause of all and to which everything refers. Hence who does not see that contemplation is far superior?[22]

Pico della Mirandola's *Oration on the Dignity of Man* published about eleven years later, around 1486, echoes the same theme of Platonic idealism: '[Man] if intellectual, will be an angel and the son of God';[23] 'let us disdain earthly things, despise heavenly things, esteeming less whatever is of the world, [and] hasten to that court which is beyond the world and nearest to the Godhead'.[24] In another sustained passage, Pico stressed beyond all doubt his surrender to the life of contemplation:

> I have never studied philosophy for any other reason than that I might be a philosopher; I have neither hoped for any pay from my studies, from my labours by lamplight, nor sought any other reward than the cultivation of my mind and the knowledge of the truth I have ever longed for above all things. I have always been so desirous, so enamoured of this that I have relinquished all interest in affairs private and public and given myself over entirely to leisure for contemplation, from which no disparagements of those who hate me, no curse of the enemies of wisdom, have been able in the past or will be able in the future to discourage me.[25]

This avowal of Pico symbolizes a new attitude to learning, one clearly dominated by the persuasiveness of Platonic thought and characterized at its best by an appreciation of the profundity of Plato's poetic vision. At the same time it is an outlook far removed from those ideals of the civic humanist which had been developed with such thoroughness from the thought of Aristotle and Cicero and which had consequently provided such stimulating educational inspiration and direction earlier in the century. The assurance that the Florentine humanists of the first half of the century derived from the ideals of the *vita activa et civilis*, which rested so certainly on the educational programme of studies drawn from history, poetry eloquence and philosophy, in both Latin and Greek, had led Poggio in

1438 to assert that Florence's pre-eminence was due to 'our ability for the cultivation of *virtus*'.[26] Yet, in the second half of the Quattrocento, we find few Florentine scholars indeed possessed of any political vigour; on the contrary, the relatively large educated class in that city became increasingly bookish and its learning, exemplified in the cult of love in the Platonic Academy with its major interests in philosophical investigation of the literary and fine arts, was remote from the affairs of practical politics.

Here, then, is a seeming paradox. How is it that the great patronage of learning initiated and maintained by the Medici did not lead, in the later decades of the Quattrocento, to any further development of civic human-ism? What, we can ask further, caused the profound difference between the cultural styles of the two halves of the century? It is necessary to ask these questions, and to seek their answers, for the example of Florence is particu-larly conspicuous since that city had been at greatest pains to promote the ideal of the civic humanist and since, moreover, it claimed a superiority over all Italy – indeed, over all Europe.

A starting-point for an explanation can be found in that assertion of Poggio. In claiming that Florence's pre-eminence was due to its citizens' ability to cultivate *virtus*, he depended on the prior assertion that this culti-vation had been made possible 'by the effects of liberty alone'[27] and *libertà*, of course, was a key concern of Florence in the early Quattrocento. The ideas of Dante and Petrarch, which had helped to develop a theory of humanist education, were basically aristocratic; indeed, a secular approach to educa-tion – in distinction to the claustral style which dominated ultramontane Europe – could not, in the first instance, be otherwise. In seeking an explanation for the ready acceptance of classical ideals by the Florentines, and their zealous cultivation of the *studia humanitatis*, it is obvious that this historical revival provided a satisfactory rationale for the seizure of power by the citizenry who were, in a sense, an oligarchy, even if one of relatively larger numbers. And the threat to their rule posed in the crisis years of the first decade of the Quattrocento forced this citizenry to cultivate a heightened sense of civic identity, which the revived ideals of antiquity assisted handsomely. So the concepts of *libertà* and *fortunà*, respectively liberty and the vagaries of external circumstance, set as it were in opposi-tion to each other, guided civic action. And the human characteristics of *virtù* and *fama*, virtue and renown, were simply new varieties of the Greek *areté* and the Latin *virtus*, both thoroughgoing aristocratic traits. It is significant that Vergerio, in extending his educational rationale for this class of society, drew upon pseudo-Plutarch's educational writings, and made the point specifically that education prepares youths for high offices in the state. It was to assist this process that history and poetry – the latter in its classic sense of epic – were regarded as prime studies, history because, in Lorenzo Valla's words, it teaches by example ('per exempla docet');[28] poetry because it enlarges the imagination and heightens sensitivities. History, it was believed, should be a central study because it assists in the solution of contemporary problems.[29] These kinds of ideas were readily seized upon by the aristocracy and it was because of the compatibility of humanist teachings with oligarchic ambitions that the *studia humanitatis* were favoured at the courts and so consequently prospered. Moreover, regardless of the specific course of political events the Medici of Florence, and the aristocracy of the other Italian courts generally, saw that their children received a humanist education and this applied to the important families as well as to the ruling groups.

Throughout the first half of the Quattrocento there is no doubt that the Florentine concern with liberty produced a heightened need for vigilance and civic activity, and that this was successful in maintaining the city's independence. But the intellectual comfort drawn from humanism was in no way responsible, in a directly causative sense, for this. In fact, in the period when Poggio was eulogizing Florence's capacity for cultivating *virtù*, the Medici family was insinuating itself into city politics, beginning with Cosimo's securing of control in 1434. For the ensuing sixty years the Medici were virtually absolute rulers of Florence, and their skilful manipulation of affairs to maintain a pretence of republicanism demonstrates that the *studia humanitatis* were not, in themselves, capable of securing genuinely republican government; they may – although it is by no means certain – have been a necessary precondition, but they certainly were not sufficient alone. The Medici were superbly capable politicians and they demonstrated this through the way in which they stimulated intellectual concern with aesthetics and art instead of politics. Platonism, as it developed under Medicean influence, seems to have provided a satisfying theory of life to those who otherwise would have felt frustrated and helpless. Because of the autocratic nature of Medici *realpolitik*, much of the activity of the Platonic Academy appears to have been directed towards rationalizing the interior life, which was increasingly becoming the only possible way for most intellectuals. Not that the process was obscure or hidden from everyone. It led Niccolò Machiavelli, who himself had been provided with a superb humanist education,[30] to ask 'whether in a corrupt state it is possible to maintain a free government'.[31]

From civic humanist to courtier : Baldesar Castiglione

Towards the end of the Quattrocento the ideals so earnestly desired by Salutati, Bruni, Poggio and Valla, and exemplified in their own lives, had become formalized and correspondingly devitalized. In Leonardo Bruni's thought, for example, the *studia humanitatis* had been regarded as a necessary and integral part of the civic humanist's training; only through a thoroughly rigorous education in the philosophy, history and literature of classical antiquity, he believed, could the new humanist gain those insights and experiences that would fit him to participate actively and meaningfully in the life of city-state politics. But this belief had not been borne out by the development of Florentine affairs and in the late Quattrocento the ideal of the civic humanist was in eclipse. Elsewhere in Italy, the lack of vigour by scholars was less marked because it had been much less developed; everywhere the absence of intellectuals and scholars from the direction of political affairs became apparent. Having been systematically discussed by two generations of schoolmasters, the humanist programme was now an affair of the classroom. No further literature was written anywhere. Meanwhile, throughout Italy, a new ideal was appearing, that of the courtier[32] who displayed a far more dependent style of personality. The growth towards courtly studies, like the courtier's code of behaviour, had been slow and barely perceptible and did not gather force until the sixteenth century. When this new style of educational writing became fashionable, it was all based upon a single archetype, *The Book of the Courtier* (*Il Libro del Cortegiano*) by Castiglione, which was written in the Lombard vernacular between about 1513 and 1519, although not published until twenty years later.

Baldesar Castiglione (1478–1529) was born in Cassanatico and worked in the service, in turn, of the dukes of Milan, Mantua and Urbino. Castiglione had a talent for diplomacy, which he exercised in his various appointments, and in 1519 he became Mantuan ambassador to Rome. He was subsequently appointed Nuncio to Spain by Pope Clement VII and arrived there in 1529, although just previously, in January of the same year, he had accepted the bishopric of Avila. Castiglione was well equipped to write of the life of the court, and *The Book of the Courtier* draws from his intimate knowledge of Italian courtly and diplomatic life.

Castiglione set out the purpose of his treatise in the first chapter

... to describe what, in my view, is the form of courtiership most appropriate for a gentleman living at the Courts of Princes, by which he will have the knowledge and ability [*sappia perfettamente*] to serve them in every reasonable thing, winning their favour and the praise of others. . . . [Let me then], if it is possible, create a courtier so perfect that the prince who is worthy of his service, even though his dominion is small, can count himself a truly great ruler.[33]

The lengthy treatise that follows develops this theme, using the literary device of a courtly dialogue among a number of appropriate persons. The contributions of the various speakers, all living members of the Italian aristocracy at the court of Urbino, add up to a composite portrait, and, like all synthesized productions, the final picture lacks integrity. In a sense it reflects faithfully an emerging educational ideal of eclectic design. Castiglione's own statement of the intentions of the treatise, however, is not fully accurate; only the first two of its books deal with the courtier; the third treats of the desirable qualities of the gentlewoman (courtesan being an infelicitous parallel), while the fourth and final book is a disquisition, in more general terms, on the practice of statecraft. This composition by Castiglione is, however, a valuable document in educational history, since it gives a comprehensive picture of a highly popular educational ideal in the years around 1500.

In developing his ideal courtier, Castiglione deals with specific skills and attainments in Book One, with qualities of temperament and character in Book Two. The primary qualification is to be 'of noble birth and good family',[34] and to have received 'from Nature not only talent and beauty of countenance and person but also that certain air and grace [*una certa grazia*] that makes him immediately pleasing and attractive to all who meet him'.[35] The next qualification 'must be that of arms; and this above everything else I wish him to pursue vigorously'.[36] This particular accomplishment is extended to include proficiency in all of the current military skills, including horsemanship: 'to ride well with the rein, to handle spirited horses very skilfully, and to tilt and joust'.[37] To these attainments he added such gymnastic skills as vaulting, running and jumping, as well as that 'noble sport' of tennis.[38]

Formal education is passed over rather lightly. The courtier should 'know both how to write and how to speak well',[39] and his good vernacular speech must be free of rustic provincialisms; he must be able to write well in that vernacular, 'and not in Latin. . . . so those writings by learned men which you mention are not to our purpose'.[40] Castiglione's attitude to the *studia humanitatis* appears somewhat undecided: there is clearly some considerable merit in them, for Count Ludovico later expounds at length on 'the necessity of letters', instancing the lessons to be learned from the study of the Greek and Roman classics, and stating that the courtier should be more than an average scholar ('più che mediocremente erudito'), at least in those studies we call the humanities ('che chiamano d'umanite'); and he should have a knowledge of Greek as well as Latin, because of the many different things that are so beautifully written in that language. He should be very well acquainted with the poets, and no less with the orators and historians, and also skilled at writing both verse and prose ('versi e prosa'), especially in our own language ('massimamente in questa nostra lingua vulgare').[41] The concluding phrase really gives the clue to the educational conditions of the times. Count Ludovico's classical authors are cited at second hand from Dante, Petrarch and Boccaccio; his list refers to the examples offered by Scipio Africanus, Alcibiades, Alexander, Xenophon, Hannibal and Cyrus. The *studia humanitatis* had become equated with the study of Trecento and Quattrocento Italians rather than direct acquaintance with ancient Greek and Latin works, and the *volgare* itself, chiefly Tuscan, had become the dominant language, both for speech and writing. The courtier's vernacular, in fact, should contain 'clear and beautiful words from the speech current in all parts of Italy'.[42]

Letters, however, are considered by Castiglione to be only part of the courtier's formal preparation; an equal place is to be accorded to an understanding and appreciation of the arts, particularly poetry, music and painting. This prescription indicates a marked change in educational values from Vergerio's time, due in large part to the influence of the Platonic Academy. Music must be understood and appreciated, and some performing skill attained, the lute being singled out especially. Castiglione argued that music in itself is educative and stands alongside the visual and graphic arts generally, because they all train aesthetic discrimination, which is of everyday relevance; painting in particular is valuable because 'it reveals the beauty of living bodies, with regard to both the delicacy of the countenance and the proportion of the other parts, in man as in all other creatures'.[43] Here we find a direct application of Platonic theory.

Castiglione devotes an entire book to consideration of the character of a courtier. Basically, he should be a reserved person free of curiosity, always careful of his good reputation, of great discretion, readily adaptable to other people, well mannered whether in conversation, at the table or in any other social situation. The courtier should not be a busybody; rather, he should respect the privacy of others. Concerning his own career, he should 'enjoy favours, but not value them so highly as to appear unable to exist without them. And when they are granted to him, he should not let himself appear unaccustomed or alien to the experience, or amazed that such things should happen . . .'[44] In his clothing, the courtier should dress soberly, for as Castiglione remarks, 'it seems to me that the most agreeable colour is black, and if not black, then at least something dark',[45] and in his pastimes, such as dancing, singing and sporting, he should conduct himself decorously and in his conversation be convivial, perhaps lightly jesting, but never rancorous.[46] In all his attainments he must remain a gentleman of grace and moderation.

Castiglione: on the education of women

The Book of the Courtier belongs to the genre of the *trattato d'amore*; indeed Bembo himself appears as a character. However, it represents the maximum departure from that syle, for though it is in *trattato* form and so is designed for courtly entertainment, it maintains as its primary feature a didactic and moralizing intent. In developing his treatment of the ideal life at court, Castiglione goes beyond the literary conventions of the times and argues that the responsibility of the courtier is to guide his prince towards righteous ways, pointing to the danger of vanity in courtiers unless their accomplishments are directed to a good end. With Books Three and Four his *trattato* introduces the multiple theme to didactic literature as he considers the two further topics of the ideal gentlewoman and the guidance of the prince.

The third book is concerned with the ideal of the gentlewoman, with an emphasis on tales of thwarted love, departing from a conventional mode only in the length of its exposition. It is significant that in the history of Western education there is no body of literature on the education of women. Plato dealt with women in *The Republic* chiefly by implication; Jerome's letter *To Laeta, Concerning the Education of Her Daughter* (A.D. 403) is comparatively brief and restricted. Even the tract of Bruni, addressed around 1423–6 to the Lady Baptista, is relatively short and concerned pre-eminently with the study of literature. The middle classes of northern Italy in this period certainly educated their daughters in intellectual, literary and artistic pursuits, probably equally with their sons, and in many conspicuous cases women of the courts became highly respected for their achievements, not only in the polite accomplishments but also in the more difficult and at times dangerous affairs of commerce and politics.[47] None the less, Castiglione is concerned only with the qualities desirable in a 'court lady' ('donna di palazzo'), and his recommendations are highly conservative. With respect to her character, she should be trained to complement the courtier; with respect to formal educational attainments Castiglione is rather vague:

> I want this lady to be knowledgeable about literature and painting, to know how to dance and play games adding a discreet modesty and the ability to give a good impression [*bona opinion*] of herself to the other principles that have been taught the courtier.[48]

The cultivation of such modesty is an essential ingredient in the education of women. Since their major purpose in life is motherhood, they should never show any wantonness, and in large part Castiglione's concern with the upbringing of gentle girls centres on the preservation of sexual innocence and its accompanying traits of modesty and propriety. In this period the courtesan was a familiar figure in the social scene, immortalized in Carpaccio's painting, now in the Museo Correr, Venice. These true courtesans were distinguished by their superior manners and style, some were quite wealthy and in many respects they paralleled the *hetairae* of classical Greece. Since there is an implicit recognition throughout this section of a greater latitude allowable to the courtier in sexual morality, it is to be assumed that the courtesan provides such additional companionship. In politer court circles, the gentlewoman is expected to be a moderating and restraining influence.

Castiglione and the education of princes

Perhaps the most interesting part of *The Book of the Courtier* is the fourth, centring on the education of the prince. Castiglione here reflects the general political trend towards absolute rule which then was exemplified in the emergence of the three major national states of Europe: Spain, France and England. Republican government in Florence throughout the fourteenth and fifteenth centuries had not been successful, and the situation was similar in other Italian city-states. In the majority of cases, centralized control was exercised by a single family: Visconti in Milan, Medici in Florence, Este in Ferrara, Gonzage in Mantua, Malatesta in Rimini. In other cities successful mercenary generals, *condottieri*, consolidated themselves as Francesco Sforza did in Milan after the fall of the Visconti in 1450. Rome was held by the papacy. All of the Quattrocento had been a period of intrigue and political complexity from which various forms of tyranny and despotism had emerged. *The Book of the Courtier* comments on this process with a discussion of the three good forms of government, themselves of classical Greek origin – monarchy, rule by the good, and civic democracy – and their three corresponding perversions – tyranny, oligarchy, mob rule. For his part, Castiglione preferred 'rule of a good prince'.[49]

Recognizing the inevitability of princely rule, Castiglione sought to moderate its tenor through his discussion of the relationships of the prince and his courtiers. The justification for princely authority stems from god, for 'men have been entrusted by God to the protection of their rulers',[50] but, on the other hand, the obligation rests unavoidably on the prince to discharge that responsibility adequately, to keep his subjects 'properly governed and well ordered'.[51] Sedition, it is argued, is the consequence of bad rule. For these reasons, the prince himself stands in need of firm guidance, and this, Castiglione maintains, is the proper office of the highly trained courtier. He is a tutor to his prince, and the relationships between the two, in their respective public offices, become subtly changed: 'I would believe you deserved the name of a good schoolmaster [*di bon maestro di schola*] rather than a good courtier, and he would be a good governor rather than a great ruler.'[52] Castiglione provides the evidence of classic examples, referring to the experience of Plato at the court of Dion and the relationship of Aristotle to Alexander. So he suggests, 'we can perhaps say that the courtier's final aim is to become his prince's instructor'.[53] This sentiment reflects the realities of Castiglione's day; with the decline of civic humanism, the educated gentleman is seen as being relegated to a position behind the lines of political power, using his erudition and cultivation indirectly by persuasion and example, not by authority.

The most vivid example of the decline of the educational ideal of civic humanism and its replacement with that of the courtier occurred in Florence itself. Lorenzo de' Medici died in 1492 and was succeeded by his twenty-two-year-old son, Piero. Meanwhile the growing strength of France led its king, Charles VIII (r. 1483–98), to invade Italy with the intention of annexing Naples, to which he laid claim. Naples, which was the most backward kingdom in Italy, was formerly part of Alfonso's kingdom of Aragon and since his death in 1458 had been ruled by his son Ferrante as a separate Italian kingdom. Florence stood in Charles's path on his way south; the inept Piero bungled diplomatic exchanges with Charles who had actually entered Florence, and Piero consequently was expelled from the city. Charles occupied Florence temporarily, and then withdrew. Effective rule in the city passed to an excessively zealous Dominican priest, Girolamo Savonarola (1452–98), in 1494. The government of Savonarola was marked by mounting tension and hostility all round: this passionate friar attacked the Florentines and the office of the papacy, and reviled the person of the pope. In 1498 the citizenry revolted against his rule, hanged him and burned his body in the city square. The invasion of Charles VIII had even more disastrous consequences for the Italian city-states as a whole. Spain fought to retain the kingdom of Naples and for more than half a century the peninsula was devastated periodically by the military encounters of the two most powerful monarchies of Europe. When the Treaty of Câteau-Cambrésis of 1559 finally confirmed Spanish suzerainty over Sicily, Italy was a ravaged land, and had ceased to be the intellectual and cultural centre of Europe.

Throughout the period of conflict, however, especially in earlier decades, Italy remained the source of virtually all educational innovation, and in fact, when it had lost its ascendancy by the mid-sixteenth century, almost all educational effort in Europe was directed towards acquiring the Italian achievement. This educational achievement was considerable: it included not only the now extensive literature on the *studia humanitatis*, the schoolmaster, the courtier and the prince, but also the accurate recension and translation of Greek classics and the consequent revival of Platonic studies. Two further developments in Italy were to become increasingly influential: the application of the craft of printing to scholarly matters, and the growth of a vigorous opposition to Platonism in the form of a more rigorously naturalistic Aristotelianism.

Defence of Aristotle: Pietro Pomponazzi

Platonism, largely owing to the stimulus provided by Ficino, gained a wide following and influenced effectively many aspects of the theory and practice of the arts – poetic, literary and visual. It set ideas on education in the direction of emphasizing the quest of the individual mind for perfection of form, which could be found chiefly in the arts. At the same time, the study of Aristotle gained a new impetus from the work of Pietro Pomponazzi (1462–1525) who reacted vigorously against the wave of Platonism. Pomponazzi's influence came later than Ficino's by several decades, not becoming well developed until the last decade of the fifteenth century and the first of the sixteenth century when he was active as a professor of philosophy successively in three Italian *studia*. He secured appointment to Padua in 1488, remaining there until 1509. In 1510 he moved to the *studium* at Ferrara, and in 1512 moved again to Bologna where he lectured for the remaining thirteen years of his life.

Pomponazzi spent his entire professional career in the defence of Aristotle, and in doing so he had to contend not only with the Platonists, but also with the scholastics who were still maintaining various other versions of Aristotle. Thomism and Averroism were the chief doctrines to which he was opposed mainly because they had become *mélanges* of competing philosophical views, resolved into uncomfortable compromises. Averroism, to his mind, surrendered itself to a hopelessly pessimistic determinism; Thomism, in an effort to avoid this position, made innumerable compromises with Neoplatonism. Neither of these positions, in his view, was a satisfactory explication of the fundamental Aristotelian philosophy. The problem of course had been complicated by textual difficulties. The Moslem commentators had worked from corrupted versions; the scholastics, in many cases, had been compelled to use texts at one remove further, working from Latin translations of Arabic versions. Aquinas' own great commentary, although based on Latin translations made direct from the Greek by William of Moerbeke, still suffered from the lack of critical Greek texts. The humanist period improved philological and critical techniques, made possible by a closer acquaintance with the sources. Throughout the fifteenth century Aristotle's works were scrutinized, criticized, emended and translated continually. By the time of Pomponazzi the *corpus Aristotelicum* existed in definitive, critical editions.

In Pomponazzi's view, Thomism and Averroism suffered from a fundamental defect, and one that was crucial for the development of the humanist programme: they were unable to give an adequate account of the human apprehension of knowledge. Both Averroes and Aquinas stressed the reality of the external world and the capacity of the mind to apprehend it directly in the passive intellect, and both experienced difficulty in explaining how the knowledge apprehended by this passive intellect could be universally real. Averroes fell back on the doctrine of the external active intelligence which informs all men; Aquinas suggested the existence of a permanent, divine intellect which maintains ultimate truth. Both of these doctrines differed little, if at all, from Platonism and Plato's doctrine of the One. Pomponazzi, seeking to promote the humanist cause, but by means of the Aristotelian philosophy, pointed out that in this important respect both Averroism and Thomism made concessions to

Platonism and incorporated it in their doctrines. Two significant consequences resulted from this: firstly, man was seen only collectively, the
individual mattering not at all; secondly, truth itself remains remote
from human understanding for it is maintained by the divine intellect.
These two consequences hindered the attainment of the full dignity of
man; they retarded equally the construction of a body of knowledge by
active investigation, that is, through the development of the sciences.

Pomponazzi's chief concern was to maintain the emphasis on the centrality of man in the universe – which had become a prominent feature of
humanism during the immediately preceding period, particularly due to
the Platonic Academy – and also to emphasize man's dignity, which he
wished to do without resorting to the Platonic viewpoint, for this, in his
view, strained reason excessively. The explanation of man and the universe
could be found in an analysis of the natural world which itself alone, he
felt, contained sufficient reason for existence. Pomponazzi saw man as
part of a natural universe and in 1516 he completed his highly contentious
and stimulating treatise *De immortalitate animae* (*On The Immortality of the
Soul*). For several years after its publication it provoked strong criticism:
it was burned in Venice, and examined in Rome for heresy. No heresy was
found but the controversy provoked rejoinders from both sides. Although
Pomponazzi made some concessions in his replies to the critics, he did not
retreat from his basic thesis that the human soul is not immortal; rather, it
is definitely and necessarily mortal.

De immortalitate animae is really a lengthy essay in fifteen chapters,
developed according to the techniques of scholastic argument, and as
such it stands in contrast to much of the humanist literature of the period.
Its continued return to the same theme, its constant appeals to authority,
chiefly Aristotle and the Bible with numerous references to others –
Averroes, Aquinas, Porphyry – and its employment of all the techniques
of medieval dialectic, mark it as a scholastic work. Yet there is a profound
difference since, unlike the scholastics, *De immortalitate animae* seeks to
prove the mortality of the soul. In Pomponazzi's view, this is a vital need
for the Christian since only the concept of a mortal soul can make the
doctrine of grace meaningful. This was precisely the difficulty of Averroes
and Aquinas. In seeking to make the soul immortal they found it difficult
to escape from cosmic determinism, since man is unable to know whether
his actions have merited grace and hence salvation and so is tempted
simply to surrender himself to the play of events. Averroes surrendered to
it entirely, Aquinas invoked the two principles of free will and divine

love, but neither of these was satisfactory in Pomponazzi's view. There remains no really decisive, positive role for man. Good humanist that he was, Pomponazzi sought to make man his own moral agent, to place on him responsibility for his own actions. He did this through a consideration of man's intellect.

The human intellect, he argued, is located in a middle range in the universe; the lowest kind of intellect is that of the beasts who know the world only through themselves, 'they need the body for their operations both as subject and object'.[54] The highest kind is that of the intelligences, such as angels, which need no body; they are 'totally separated from matter and hence in their knowing neither need a body as subject nor as object'.[55] Man, possessing body, shares with the beasts the sensory origin of knowledge and so uses his body as subject. Yet man, by being able to observe his own processes of knowing, can extract himself from pure subjectivity and transcend the limitations of the finite and the particular. Pomponazzi wrote, on this point:

> . . . there is a mean which is neither totally abstracted nor totally immersed . . . This is the human intellect, . . . which is in none of its operations wholly freed from the body or wholly immersed in it, whence it will not need the body as subject but as object . . . The human intellect in all its operations is the act of an organic body, since it always depends on the body as object.[56]

From this he developed the notion of reflective thinking:

> Wherefore the intellect can reflect upon itself, think discursively, and comprehend universals, which organic and extended powers cannot do at all. But all this comes from the essence of intellect, since as intellect it is not dependent on matter or on quantity. . . . But although the human intellect does not use quantity in knowing, nevertheless, since it is joined to sense, it cannot be released entirely from matter and quantity, since it never knows without a phantasm, as Aristotle says in *De anima* III: 'The soul does not know at all without a phantasm.'[57]

Having established the dependence of the human intellect on images abstracted from external reality, and its dependence on the human body, Pomponazzi then examines the relationship between the soul and the body. The intellect, in his view, following Aristotle, is the form of the body, or its soul.[58] Since the intellect is dependent on the body, it is finite in the sense that it cannot operate without the body. Pomponazzi thereby disposes of the Averroist and Thomist conceptions of an external intellect – active intelligence or possible intellect – and emphasizes the total dependence of the human intellect on physical existence. 'We also say', he argues, 'that the human soul is produced, not by creation but by generation. . . . We do not assert, however, that man remains after death so far as his soul is concerned, since its existence has a beginning. [As] Plato says, in the *Laws* [X.893E–894A] "Whatever in any way at all begins to be, ceases to be".'[59] This finiteness of the soul in fact, allows god to operate. Only if the soul is mortal does the doctrine of individual merit, leading to the conferring of grace, have any real meaning for Pomponazzi. He concludes his essay, therefore, with the deliberately ambiguous statement that 'It seems to me that no natural reasons can be brought forth proving that the soul is immortal, and still less any proving that the soul is mortal, as very many scholars who hold it immortal declare.'[60]

Despite this concession to rational impartiality and the considerable body of contrary opinion, there is no doubt in this essay of Pomponazzi's own beliefs. Nor was there any doubt in the minds of his critics. In the ensuing controversy, which continued from the tract's publication in 1516 until around 1519, Pomponazzi answered his detractors, acquitting himself quite competently. The University of Bologna made its own support of Pomponazzi abundantly clear: in 1518 his salary was doubled and he was reappointed for an eight-year term under conditions better than those enjoyed by any other professor in Italy at that time.[61] Pomponazzi continued in his chair and died a year before his tenure expired. His teaching, however, was not lost; on the contrary it attracted students from all Europe, and increasingly throughout the sixteenth century his revived and purified Aristotelianism influenced Western thought, especially in the new technologies and sciences that were to grow with considerable vigour out of the craft traditions and the restricted studies of the quadrivium of preceding centuries. In particular, Pomponazzi's earlier university, the Studio Patavino, was to become a great centre for foreign students to whom was transmitted the new spirit of rational thinking. Pomponazzi's contribution to the new developments of the sixteenth century was part of a much wider development in the style and content of learning at that time. The emerging technologies and empirical sciences themselves were instrumental in effecting change, although their effects were not felt immediately. The two most striking immediate outcomes of this trend were the invention of printing and the great voyages of discovery. In both of these cases, traditions of investigation and activity were brought into a synthesis that in turn had the most profound effects.

Development of printing and the Italian contribution

Printing was never really invented; its origins are lost in prehistory, and the first appearance of literacy is in terms of pressed seals found in Mesopotamia, estimated to date from at least 3000 B.C. Sumerian cylinder seals are early instances of printing. The Chinese made rubbings on to paper from carved inscriptions in the ninth century A.D.; between 836 and 846 there was an especially vigorous period when the classical literature of the T'ang Dynasty was cut in stone. The technique of duplication through rubbings from carvings and the subsequent step of cutting blocks for printing spread to the West during later centuries. Early in the fourteenth century woodcuts were used in Europe for printing – playing cards being a popular application – and some time in this period blockbooks became established. These were books printed on paper from woodblocks, with text and illustration for each page cut in a single block of wood; the earliest in fact were of northern European manufacture and were collections of pictures with small portions of text, written on banners and streamers, placed within the illustration. They were generally on religious topics, three being particularly popular, the *Apocalypse* (*c.* 1440), *Biblia pauperum* and *Ars moriendi* (*c.* 1450). The blockbooks were all in a popular strain, being designed for the use of a wide and relatively unsophisticated public. At the same time books intended for serious scholarly use depended on a different development, that of printing from movable type. By the end of the fifteenth century encyclopedic compendia were exemplified in such notable productions as Bartholemaeus' *All the Proprytees of Thinges* (1495) and Gregor Reisch's *Margarita philosophica* (1496).

The several elements of the printing process were already in existence by the fifteenth century. The winepress had been used by the ancient Romans; paper had been introduced into Europe, first in Spain in 1150, probably from Morocco, and had spread to France before 1200, Italy before 1300 and to Germany by 1390; punches for hallmarking metalware were used by gold- and silver-smiths; and, after 1410, oil-based paints, which would adhere to metal surfaces, were being used by painters, this discovery being credited to Jan van Eyck. And, moreover, the principle of printing an entire page of a book in one operation, in contrast to the prevailing practice of scribal copying, letter by letter, was already established in the blockbook tradition. All that was needed was someone to recognize the possibilities of combining these various elements. In the early decades of the fifteenth century that step was taken. While the records are not sufficiently comprehensive for the precise developments to be known, the credit is given, generally, to Johann Gänsefleisch, or Gutenberg (1394/9–1468), who was experimenting in Mainz, Germany, with printing from movable type around 1439.[62] The technique of printing from movable type became firmly established within the following twenty years and by 1468 printing presses employing movable type were in existence in every major European state.

Early printed works resembled manuscript books, since it was the inexpensive multiplication of such books that was the primary objective. Through the preceding centuries scribal writing had become very heavy, particularly in the Germanic regions, and this variety, known as 'black letter', was difficult to read. In Italy, where the first press was established in 1465, early typographers turned instead to the style of handwriting used in the papal court for its documents which was known as chancery cursive (*cancellaresca corsiva*).[63] This style had evolved successively through various Northumbrian and Hibernian bookhands into Carolingian minuscule – possibly due to the work of Alcuin – and thence into chancery cursive. This development of the writing of antiquity, named appropriately by the humanists as *antiqua*, became the basis of Italian type design. In the first century of printing, roughly 1450–1550, northern Europe employed black letter, Italy used *antiqua*. After 1550, the use of black letter remained only in Germany, where it survived to the twentieth century; elsewhere it was replaced by *antiqua*, except for works of a religious character and for special display purposes, particularly in single-page documents, printed charters and calendars for example. The Italian form of *antiqua*, or 'roman' as it is now called, became the standard European bookface.

Meanwhile, as presses were set up, it is significant that, with the sole exception of Wittenberg, they were established in commercial and not university towns. The universities, however, exercised some control over book production; many of them had ordinances governing the production and sale of required texts, and doubtless their conservatism tended to the preservation of black letter which must have given to such texts the appearance of scholarly authority. In this early period, in fact, there was some considerable reluctance to use printed books. Duke Federigo of Urbino, formerly a student of Vittorino, would have none in his splendid library. It was the commercial towns, used to the lighter and more 'secular' look of chancery cursive, that took to this typeface and employed it for printing works of literature. The first book printed in Italy, coming off a press in Rome in 1470, was a complete copy of Quintilian. Indeed, printers recognized from the beginning that schoolbooks would be a staple of their trade. As early as 1458 three separate editions of Donatus' *Ars minor* had been printed in Paris, in black letter, and this short catechetical Latin grammar continued to be printed for two centuries to come; Gutenberg himself issued twenty-four separate editions of it. Another German printer, Wynkyn de Worde, who settled in England as William Caxton's assistant and then became his successor, issued many *Donats*, as they came to be known, and about two-fifths of his output were school textbooks.[64] So enthusiastic were the printers and the public that all of the major Latin classics were printed between 1465 and 1473, and the printing of Latin translations of Greek classics soon followed. The great labours of Ficino in translating Plato into Latin between 1463 and 1482 were consummated with their appearance in print in 1491, just a year before their patron, Lorenzo de' Medici, died.

Late in the fifteenth century there was a second great printing movement to publish Greek classics in a Greek typeface or fount. This was the achievement of one of the greatest scholar-printers of all time, the Venetian, Aldo Manuzio (*c.* 1450–1515), under whom the Aldine press in the city of Venice became the leading centre of scholarly book production in the early sixteenth century. He has remained famous for the beauty and clarity of his roman founts, particularly those developed by his master designer, Francesco Griffo, and was responsible also for another typographical innovation, the imitation of sloping handwriting which is known to this day as italic. Aldo, known also by his latinized name, Aldus Manutius, was influenced towards Greek studies by his acquaintance with Pico della Mirandola, and upon founding his press in Venice in 1490 he turned almost immediately to the printing of Greek works. The immediate problem was the lack of a fount. The first book ever published in Greek had appeared in 1476 in Milan – a grammar, the *Erotemata* by Constantine Lascaris. It was printed, however, in roman upper-case, or capitals, with the addition of specially cut letters for which there were no roman equivalents. In 1495 Aldus reissued it in his new, all Greek face, developed from the Greek manuscript style then circulating in Europe. Greek script of the Hellenistic and early Christian period had been particularly simple and legible, but over the centuries it had lost much of that early calligraphic grace, becoming cramped and heavily accented, with many of the letters tied together in ligatures as a result of scribal efforts at speed. Aldus, unfortunately, attempted to reproduce the appearance of this handwriting and his Greek founts were cut with that intention. So influential was Aldus' example that his Greek type styles, incorporating the relatively meaning-less convention of accents, were transmitted to Greece itself and adopted as the model for all subsequent printing in Greek.

Aldus was enthusiastic in publishing classical literature and the printing of *Erotemata* marked the launching of his projected series of Greek texts. Thereafter works of scholarly import appeared, Aristotle's complete works between 1495 and 1498, Plato's by 1513. In this period were produced many of the first printed editions, *editiones principes*, of the Greek classics. In accomplishing this, Aldus collaborated with numerous scholars, his most famous editor being the leading humanist of the day, Erasmus of Rotterdam, who did editorial work for Aldus, and in 1507-8 visited Venice for just that purpose.

One further achievement of Aldus is of importance: the invention of the small pocket-sized book. Before his time, books were generally large, and often used on tables or lecterns. The production of books small enough to be carried by hand (the *vade mecum*) was a powerful force in the spread of learning. Early in the sixteenth century the humanist achievement was in process of becoming extended to all of Europe, and in the saddlebags of countless humanist scholars and secretaries seeking employment away from the oversupplied cities of Italy, the pocket editions of Aldus, along with the productions of other Italian presses, were carried into Germany, Spain, France and beyond – to England, Bohemia, Poland and Sweden. Foreign scholars, for their part, travelled from as far afield as England to study in Padua – the chief centre of expatriate learning in sixteenth-century Italy, despite the continued Franco-Spanish war – and the humanist learning and its spirit of scholarship became the basis of a new period of educational endeavour.

CHAPTER 9

Expansion of Education and Humanism: I. France and Germany to 1500

The north on the eve of educational change

The sixteenth century was a period of considerable change in Western education, both in thought and practice, of which the expanding influence of Italian humanism was the major, although not the only, element. In this period the political structure of Europe altered radically with the extension of Spanish suzerainty under the house of Habsburg throughout most of southern Europe; the fragmentation of the Holy Roman Empire continued, and stronger central governments appeared in France and in England. Furthermore the north of Europe was emerging from the long period of economic depression associated with the Hundred Years War (1337–1453) and the Black Death of 1348–9, and subsequent plagues in the later fourteenth century, which had been reflected in England by the Peasants' Revolt of 1381. Conditions were ameliorated gradually by improvement in trade and commerce, particularly in the region of Flanders which became an *entrepôt* and manufacturing centre. These changes towards greater secular authority and increased economic activity, along with their correlative stimulation of the commercial outlook, were accompanied by even further decline in the church's fortunes. The ending of the Great Schism (1377–1417) by the Council of Constance (1414–17) restored the papacy to Rome but it in no way repaired the damage to papal authority and its claims to temporal and spiritual sovereignty. The church remained rent with discord, and by the end of the fifteenth century it was becoming attacked for its alleged corruption. Lorenzo de' Medici, for example, was made a cardinal on his fourteenth birthday and such examples provided ready cause for the blistering denunciations by Savonarola in Florence. Abuses within the church continued throughout the early decades of the sixteenth century and led directly to the various reforming campaigns of Luther, Calvin and Loyola. Royal, and to some extent papal, intransigence precipitated conflict in England with Henry VIII, resulting in the disestablishment of the pope's authority in Henry's realm in 1534.

These various movements influenced intellectual life markedly and produced significant changes in education. The difficulties of the church resulted in less direct ecclesiastical control of education in Germany and England where the papacy was thwarted, and in a greater and more stringent religious conservatism in France and the Habsburg domains of southern Europe where Catholicism became secure. Economic and commercial developments also contributed to the growing secularism of educational thought and practice in Germany and England, although the chief impetus to educational change came from the expansion of Italian humanism in these areas. Spain, and particularly Aragon, remained largely outside humanist influence; intellectual life centred on the court and the university at Salamanca where learning was always subservient to theology. The one real influence came from the powerful and influential Cardinal Francisco Ximénez (1436–1517) who, as a patron of learning, founded in 1508 – out of his own private fortune – the University of Alcalá, to which he attracted some notable scholars, although this was a relatively isolated achievement. Humanism made some little headway in Flanders, chiefly through the *Devotio moderna*, and also in France as a result of the efforts of Guillaume Budé and Robert Gaguin, but the major centres of humanist impact were in England and Germany. The efforts of a large number of English scholars, from Duke Humphrey of Gloucester in the mid-fifteenth century to John Colet, Thomas More and William Lily fifty years later, and of an equally enthusiastic group of Germans, notably Rudolphus Agricola, Johannes Reuchlin and Beatus Rhenanus, ensured that these two countries in the sixteenth century dominated educational thought in Europe, and provided the models in practice that other countries were to follow. And, as a citizen of Europe, contributing internationally, was the intellectually commanding figure of Erasmus whose writings were to provide the most systematic and comprehensive expression of the new movement.

Education in France to 1500

Maintenance of educational tradition

Educational leadership in Europe from the ninth century onwards had been exercised very largely by France, and it maintained this position until the end of the thirteenth century. Yet, when the new learning of Italy expanded north of the Alps in the sixteenth century, France played a relatively minor part; in fact, when the initiative in that movement was taken by England and Germany, French education was in a period of marked decline and did not recover until more than a century later. The history of education in France up to 1500 is a record of conservatism, internal conflict and intellectual exhaustion that resulted in considerable loss of opportunity and the absence of any significant French contribution to Western education until the seventeenth century.

The source of France's difficulties can be found as early as Carolingian times when the conflict between the authority of church and crown was already an incipient issue. Education in the eighth and ninth centuries, however, was not an extensive enterprise and so the issuance of capitularies by Charlemagne and decretals by the church led to little overt conflict, especially since Charlemagne's educational officials were clerics in any case. None the less the basis of conflict had been laid then, and the determination of the relative rights of both church and king in educational matters, as heirs to Rome, was to become an acute issue in later times; the fight for independence of the University of Paris in the thirteenth century was the most conspicuous instance. The two Lateran decrees of 1179 and 1215 which required bishops to maintain schools free of charge[1] gave a stimulus to cathedral schools and assisted the development of some of them, in turn, into *studia generalia*; these decrees also gave effective control of schools to the universities, since the cathedral chapter was charged with the schools' maintenance, and this authority was maintained while ever the universities had the strength to do so.

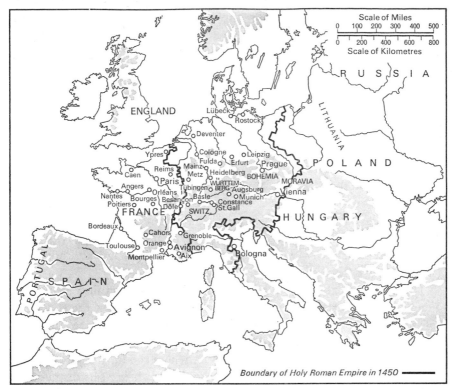

RENAISSANCE EUROPE IN 1450

By 1300 it seems that most cathedral chapters included in their number an *écolâtre* – for the French term now appears along with the traditional Latin equivalent of *scholasticus* – whose duty it was to supervise the school, appoint teachers and look after the chapter's library. Around this time, moreover, it seems that the position of *écolâtre* was filled usually by a theologian.[2] Almost simultaneously towns in France also began to establish schools, under municipal control,[3] and although these foundations are documented very sparsely,[4] the surviving evidence makes it clear that this encroachment was resisted strongly by the church. As early as the pontificate of Adrian IV (r. 1154–9) a conflict of this nature erupted in Reims occasioned by the complaints of the abbot of St Rémi,[5] and the ensuing decision of the pope established a precedent for church authority. None the less the towns as they expanded, particularly in the twelfth and thirteenth centuries, sought the establishment of secular schools in which the skills of reading, writing and reckoning could be taught. The clerics invoked the ruling of Adrian IV as their authority for control; the towns-men, since they paid part of the cost, demanded the right at least to share in the appointing of masters.[6]

This kind of conflict had a rather different course when it erupted in Flanders. In the middle of the twelfth century the cathedral school of Ghent was destroyed by fire and the monks of nearby St Peter's thereby hoped to have the school incorporated into their own. However, the citizens of Ghent took the initiative in establishing a municipal school for the now homeless scholars and this led the monks of St Peter's to appeal to Rome. Pope Alexander III (r. 1159–81) gave a verdict against the burghers which incensed the count of Flanders who sided with the townsmen. As a result, the count established a secular school in 1179 with a notary in charge. This was followed in 1195 with a similar foundation in nearby Ypres and throughout the following century municipal schools of three levels, elementary (*scholae parvae*), middle (*scholae minores*) and advanced (*scholae majores*) became common in Flanders.[7]

There is, unfortunately, a paucity of evidence concerning schools in France in the fourteenth century, but the general tenor of the surviving information gives the clear impression that struggles for control between church and secular interests continued. There is a record of such a conflict erupting in 1412 in the diocese of Évreux where the inhabitants of Saint Martin de Villers, having founded a school, had their right disputed by the bishop who claimed that such a school injured his own institution. The dispute was settled by both parties agreeing to share supervision and by the townsmen conceding to the bishop the right to appoint the master.[8] These conflicts continued throughout the fifteenth century and not until 1476 was any significant change effected. In that year Louis XI gave control of charitable institutions – almonries, hospices, orphanages – to local authorities, although the church still asserted its rights and continued to retain control of many of these schools.

Growth of French universities

By the fifteenth century, however, higher education in France was not particularly vigorous, as is reflected in the continued popularity north of the Alps of such mediocre treatises as *De disciplina scholarium* and *Commendation of the Clerk*. The universities, Paris in particular, were strongly challenged by the *studia* of Italy, and this situation obtained for several centuries to come, in spite of the founding of new *studia*, and some efforts at reform. Only two other universities had been founded in the same period as Paris, those at Montpellier and Toulouse, their first documentation dating from 1170 and 1229 respectively,[9] although neither of these developed enough institutional strength to sustain a vigorous intellectual life. Montpellier had developed chiefly as a school of medicine, stimulated in all likelihood by the exodus of Jewish physicians from Spain during the period of Christian attacks on the Moslems in the twelfth century, and these Jews brought with them the Arabic treatises on medicine. During the first fifty years there was a lack of both professional discipline and supervising authority which led the Holy See to introduce some regulation. By a statute of 1220 the *studium* at Montpellier was put under the superintendence of the Bishop of Maguelonne who 'shall elect one of the masters, with the help of some other masters . . . to dispense justice to masters and scholars alike, to such others who act against them, after complaint has been lodged with him'.[10] The statute had the usual provisions for controlling university affairs, including those for licensing. It is interesting to note that the superior role of physicians was preserved: they alone were required to be examined.

> Since it often happens that on account of ignorance of the causes and lack of training physicians cause the death of the patient when there was hope for his life; we order and command [therefore] by the present edict that nobody dare practice unless previously examined by two masters chosen by the venerable Bishop of Maguelonne from the college of masters and after he had been examined and passed he shall receive a certificate by the Bishop and the doctors who examined him.[11]

This examination, it must be stressed, was entirely scholastic; there was no attempt at practical testing. The same clause of the statute makes it clear that these regulations provide an 'exception [for] surgeons who are not required to pass an examination'.

The foundation of Toulouse appears to have resulted from very different circumstances. One of the terms of the peace settlement imposed by the Treaty of Paris in 1229 which ended the Albigensian wars was an agreement by Count Raymond VII of Toulouse to provide funds, to the extent of 400 marks annually for ten years, to support a new *studium*. Now as events happened this treaty came in the very year that the secular masters had left Paris in the Great Dispersion. The pope recognized a chance to establish orthodoxy in these heretical territories and so Toulouse came into existence. The religious intentions are revealed very clearly in one of its earliest documents in which the foundation masters sought to increase their membership:

> To all Christs' faithful and especially to masters and scholars studying in any land who may see this letter, the university of masters and scholars of Toulouse, about to plant a new *studium*, wish continued good life with a blessed end. No undertaking has a stable foundation which is not firmly placed in Christ, the foundation of holy mother church. We therefore with this in mind are trying in Christ with all our might to lay the permanent foundation of a philosophic school at Toulouse, on which others may build with us whose good will is lighted to this by luminous rays of the Holy Spirit.[12]

In order to entice the dispersed Paris scholars, and others, to Toulouse, the same document points out that many imagined difficulties no longer existed, for the foundation masters had already 'sustained the first hardships' and the French cardinal legate had, by papal authority, 'decreed that all studying at Toulouse, both masters and disciples, should obtain plenary indulgence of all their sins'. The same passage continues, 'Therefore, for this cause and because of the continuity of lecturing and disputing which the masters exercise more diligently and frequently than they did at Paris, many scholars are flocking to Toulouse.' This, however, has a suspicious sound as indeed much of the latter part of the document has, particularly when it states that all should know that 'Toulouse and the university . . . is the second land of milk and honey, green with lush pastures'. To this it adds a further claim, which must have appealed to the *clerici vagantes* at least, that 'Bacchus reigns in the vineyards'. Perhaps the most telling part of the document is the express disclaimer of any difficulty in studying Aristotle, which, of course, had been the cause of the Paris dispersion. Employing much the same language as an earlier papal decree prohibiting such activities, this letter makes it clear that 'those who wish to scrutinize the bosom of nature to the inmost can hear [at Toulouse] the books of Aristotle [*libri naturales*] which were forbidden at Paris'. Despite the allurements of the letter, however, the new *studium* did not prosper at first. In 1233 Pope Gregory IX issued a bull providing for the *jus ubique docendi* to be granted to its graduates and this was repeated in 1245. But Toulouse was too artificial a foundation and scholasticism which flourished so readily at Paris was not so easily transplanted. Only later, when Toulouse began teaching civil law, did it begin to develop strongly.

The lack of this subject in French universities was, in fact, a stimulus to the development of other *studia* in France. Pope Honorius III had expressly prohibited the teaching of civil law in the city of Paris and its environs in 1219, chiefly in order to protect and encourage theology. Two results followed: Bologna and then other Italian *studia* were able to exploit the situation and to consolidate their pre-eminence; in France, scholars interested in law simply turned to canon law as a substitute. But France's need for civil lawyers stimulated the foundation of universities of legal studies at Orléans, Angers, Nantes and Avignon. At the end of the thirteenth century France had three *studia*: Paris, Montpellier and Toulouse. In the fourteenth century six more *studia generalia* were founded – Avignon, Orléans, Cahors, Grenoble, Angers, Orange – and eight followed in the fifteenth – Aix, Dole, Poitiers, Caen, Nantes, Besançon, Bourges, Bordeaux – but none displayed any particular vigour and they were, moreover, of most uneven quality.[13] Some in fact, were little more than grammar schools or else were specialized schools, generally of theology. The obvious youth of some of their students is emphasized by a later decree of Henri IV, who in 1601 issued revised statutes for Paris, to correct a problem of long standing, which required that no child under the age of nine years could be admitted to the university.[14]

Introduction of humanism into France

While the universities of France remained preoccupied with scholasticism there was some movement into Italy of French scholars, for example Jacques Lefevre d'Étaples (1450–1536), and a resulting effort to take the new humanism back across the Alps. Later in the same century some Italian scholars moved to Paris and attempted to support themselves by teaching the new humanism; prominent among this group were Janus Lascaris, Georgius Hermonymus and Gregoria Tifernas. Yet neither movement was very successful. Apart from the general hostility of French scholars to Italian humanism – after all, the classical movement revived the antiquity of Italian and not French civilization – there was no institutional support for humanist scholars. Nor were the courts of Charles VII (r. 1422–61) or Louis XI (r. 1461–83) at all supportive at a time when France was drained of resources by the Hundred Years War with England. No royal or princely patronage was given and both Hermonymus and Tifernas found difficulty in attracting students; Hermonymus, in fact, was imprisoned for debt on one occasion and for part of his stay was reduced to the task of scribal copying.[15] Tifernas fared better at times, finding a few mildly interested students, and one exceptionally good one, Robert Gaguin, who established himself as a historian. The first real stimulus to French acceptance of humanism came when Charles VIII (r. 1483–98) invaded Italy in 1494 in his so-called Promenade. Despite initial victories this expediton turned into a political fiasco. Charles was stalemated at Florence, and despite his occupation of the peninsula as far south as Naples he was forced to withdraw, encountering resistance as he did so from an Italian army sponsored by Venice. By mid-1495 he had retreated across the Alps and in Italy his campaign was only a memory. The real effects were on France: the civic and cultural achievements of Italy overwhelmed the French, as they did all other travellers to Italy, and the resulting captivation of the French imagination promoted an interest in humanism in France.

Foremost among French humanists at the end of the fifteenth century was Guillaume Budé (1468–1540), a lawyer trained at the University of Orléans. Budé (Budaeus in the usual Latin form of the period) became interested in humanism around 1491, but not until 1508 did he become a significant figure when, in humanist style, he issued his well-received commentary on Roman law, *Annotationes ad pandectas* (*Notes on the Laws of Justinian*). The significance of his commentary was its close relationship to the original text: this was a humanist method and marked a departure from the usual medieval approach of commenting on other commentaries. Budé's interest in Greek and Latin studies was stimulated during his employment in Italy as an envoy of Louis XII between 1501 and 1508; that period of Italian residence gave him an opportunity to study those languages, and the other facets of Italian humanism, at first hand. In 1515 Budé published another humanist-type treatise, this one on Roman coinage: *De asse et partibus ejus* (*On the As and its Divisions*).[16] Other scholars dabbled with humanism but none achieved the distinction of Budé, who was, in effect, more European than French. This was to be the position in France throughout the sixteenth century – its most important scholars, like Montaigne and Cordier, were international with the significant exception of François Rabelais. Among fifteenth-century French scholars Budé, like Robert Gaguin, was conspicuous in his isolation; humanism in France tended to be derivative and manneristic. There simply was no adequate foundation for any rapid development.

Education in Germany to 1500

Medieval practices

Germany was very late in developing an indigenous education. The Benedictine monastery of St Gall in Switzerland claims continuity back to A.D. 612 when St Gall (*c.* 550–645) crossed from Italy and founded a monastery there. Parts of the present building date from the eighth century. This establishment accumulated a great supply of classical manuscripts – it provided Poggio with a treasure trove in 1416, including the complete *Institutio oratoria* – and served as an example to other institutions. Missionaries pushed north into Germany and some of their monasteries became citadels of an abbreviated learning in an otherwise unlettered environment. Chrodegang, bishop of Metz (r. 742–66), made a nearby abbey of Gorze famous; at Fulda the Benedictine foundation dating from 744 became distinguished under the direction of Hrabanus Maurus, himself one of Alcuin's most celebrated students. Despite these pioneering efforts Germany remained largely illiterate; it was far from the established centres of Western civilization, its economy almost totally agricultural. By the twelfth and thirteenth centuries when trade developed around the Baltic, organized by the Hanseatic league, the merchants remained preoccupied with affairs of business and their interest in learning was utilitarian. Even the twelfth- and thirteenth-century educational movements in France, Italy, England and Spain produced little echo in Germany.

By 1300 there were about fifty bishoprics in the country and hundreds of monasteries, but only a few of these were important centres of learning. Pre-eminent was Cologne, whose Dominican monastery school in some respects rivalled the *studium* at Paris. Also of importance in the thirteenth century was Erfurt where most of the major orders – Benedictines, Dominicans, Franciscans and Augustinian Canons for certain – had established monasteries and schools.[17] One of the earliest of these schools seems to have been St Mary's which was in existence in the early twelfth century.[18] The growth of Erfurt as an education centre of some size and importance is attested by the promulgation of the Ordinance for Schools of 1282 which contains detailed regulations for the remedy of numerous shortcomings, chief of which were delinquencies by students, both boys and youths, of the kind commonly committed in the period. At this very time, in fact, Nicholas of Bibera published his poetic satire on Erfurt academic life, *Carmen satiricum*, which mentions that the city accommodated, in his estimation, a thousand scholars ('. . . ibi sunt puto mille scolares').[19] His text makes it clear that this is a guess, and although modern scholarship discounts this as poetic hyperbole, it shows none the less that Nicholas was concerned to stress the relative size of the school population there. Generally, however, the monasteries of Germany were intellectually insignificant and the cathedral schools too were of no great consequence and made little development; certainly none of them ever achieved the transition to a *studium generale*. We find one aspect of the languor of much German schooling preserved for us in the famous late thirteenth-century composition, *Carmina Burana*, which is a collection of songs and other pieces from the Benedictine monastery of Benediktbeuern some sixty kilometres south of Munich. One piece informs us:

> Learning that flowered in days of yore,
> In these times is thought a bore.
> Once knowledge was a well to drink of,
> Now having fun is all men think of.[20]

Admittedly this is pure Goliard writing, but it has the ring of authenticity, as does this fragment also, the 'Philosophers' Holiday' (*Omittamus studia*):

> Lay aside our studies
> It's well to be unwise
> Father all the sweetness
> Of youth as it flies;
> Leave it to old men
> To ponder and advise . . .
> Swift age it overtakes us
> While study holds us down;
> It's young blood that makes us
> Frolic through the town.[21]

University of Prague: foundation by the Emperor Charles

Yet, considering the number of important German scholars and the high quality of their contribution to Europe's intellectual life up to the thirteenth century, it is rather curious that Germany was so lacking in educational institutions. Certainly there were some provisions at elementary and grammar school level for a minority, but why is it that the monasteries and cathedrals never produced any *studia generalia*? For it is a simple fact that when Germany gained its first university, at Prague in 1346, there were thirty altogether in Italy, France, Iberia, England and the papal territories, but none in Germany, Switzerland, the Low Countries, Poland, Bohemia, Hungary, Scandinavia, the Balkans and Russia.[22] And the *studium* at Prague itself was a highly conscious, politically motivated foundation, totally lacking in those features of slower academic growth which had characterized many of the earlier *studia* in Western Europe. There were, it seems, many contributing causes: certainly the German territories were racked with dynastic conflict which was exacerbated by the lack of central government during the Great Interregnum, and the more eastern regions, particularly the Slavic, had been depredated by Mongol invasions. Moreover, the cities of the existing *studia generalia* were attractive, civilized centres and Paris and Bologna certainly could have drawn students from Germany because of the more exciting life those cosmopolitan places offered. And, it has been suggested, much of eastern Europe had always been outside the reach of Roman law. The landed nobility had no interest in promoting the foundation of universities, which brought with them the study of Roman law with its doctrines of monarchic supremacy.[23] The foundation of the first university in Prague by Charles IV, king of Bohemia and Holy Roman Emperor, consequently, is of considerable interest. And, as events developed, this *studium* was to become responsible, within the first sixty years of its existence, for very significant changes in European life.

The establishment of the university at Prague reflects the vigorous political policy of the king of Bohemia, Charles IV (r. 1346–78). Bohemia had developed as one of the feudal kingdoms which constituted the Holy Roman Empire, its population being composed predominantly of German nobles and urban burghers and a Czech rural population of minor nobility and gentry and agricultural peasants, a mixture that was always rather unstable. Charles himself was born in 1316 to a Luxemburger father and a Czech mother. His father, King John of Bohemia, was frequently away and the kingdom languished until Charles, in addition to being margrave of Moravia, became regent. Charles demonstrated very early a flair for administration and diplomacy; Bohemia flourished under his regency and with his accession in 1346, following the death of his father, Charles was enabled to consolidate the strong rule he had begun to impose. In the same year, Charles IV also became Holy Roman Emperor, and this was the situation in which the University of Prague was conceived. Charles was determined to make his Bohemian capital of Prague the metropolis of the Holy Roman Empire itself, a rival to all of the great cities of Europe. Charles had therefore to establish religious independence for his new imperial capital, first by having it removed from the jurisdiction of the archiepiscopal see of Mainz. This step, in fact, had been taken during his regency, two years before his accession; Benes of Weitmil, the court chronicler, recorded that in 1344 the 'pope with the consent of the whole Curia, at the instance of Charles, released the church of Prague from all obedience to the metropolitan church of Mainz, and raised it to an archiepiscopal see'.[24] It is of more than passing interest that this pope, Clement VI, had been tutor to Charles, when the former was Pierre de Rosiers. It was this Benedictine abbot who was also responsible for cultivating Charles's intellectual interests, and this is reflected in the foundation of Bohemia's first university. Behind these events, moreover, there are some curious circumstances. The archbishop of Prague, who had been one of Charles's boyhood tutors, had had the presumption to discipline the young prince. The contemporary *Limburg Chronicle* by the clerk and notary Tilman von Wolfhagen (d. 1402) records the circumstances that Charles 'once had a master who led him to school; to whom he smote an eye out, for the master chastised him'. But this, the *Chronicle* continues, Charles 'well amended by creating him Archbishop of Prague, and later cardinal'.[25] As a further testimonial to Charles's character, the *Chronicle* tells us that 'this Charles ruled and governed as a lion for more than thirty years', and this we can readily believe.

When the *studium generale* was established at Prague in the years 1347–8 there had already been several unsuccessful attempts at its foundation. In 1294 King Václav (Wenceslaus) had proposed a university for Bohemia but was opposed by the Czech nobility, and further action was inhibited because of the regicide of Václav III in 1306 and the ensuing period of political turmoil. Charles, however, was an extremely strong ruler and he recognized that a university at Prague would strengthen his kingdom by bringing an influx of outside scholars and by providing a centre to draw together Bohemia's intellectuals, instead of having them dispersed throughout the other *studia* of Europe. In this way the distinctive identity of Bohemia could be built, and it is for this reason that humanism, particularly the study of history, was promoted at both the court and in the new *studium*. And, moreover, Charles's administration could now depend upon an assured supply of trained personnel. So in January 1347 Charles's former mentor Pope Clement VI issued a papal bull stating:

> . . . it would be advantageous to [Charles's] hereditary kingdom of Bohemia and to the other neighbouring regions and lands, where there was no *studium*

generale, to have one, and that the metropolitan city of Prague, situated in the middle and in the healthiest part of the kingdom, visited by people from divers lands, and abounding in food and other necessities of life, was most suited for such a *studium generale* . . .[26]

In April of the following year (1348) Charles promulgated his famous 'Golden Bull' by which he gave a royal charter to the university at Prague, and, in the process, asserted an equal share of royal authority over the institution. The bull asserted the specifically national character of the new *studium* in its statement that this institution was intended for 'the faithful inhabitants of this Bohemian kingdom, that they may not have to go to distant parts of the world to beg from others the desire of their hearts'; in addition, the document expressed the hope that scholars from elsewhere might be drawn there.[27] And, indeed, as part of his plan to encourage such visiting, Charles received Cola di Rienzo at his court in 1350, and Petrarch six years later.

The institutional model for Prague was drawn from both Paris and Bologna, that is, it was a *universitas magistrorum et studentium*. The chancellor was, *ex officio*, the archbishop of Prague and the vice-chancellor his nominee. Administrative authority was vested in a rector elected by the university as a whole. All four traditional faculties – arts, theology, law, medicine – were established, and in general the programme of studies and awards of degrees followed the general European pattern. The students organized themselves into nations reflecting their origins, as was now customary: there were two 'German' nations, Bavarian and Saxon, one of mixed Polish and German membership designated nominally as 'Polish' and one Czech. Again, as in other European universities, students lived in rented accommodation such as lodgings, in hospices and a few in endowed colleges of which Charles's own foundation of the Carolinum in 1366 for twelve masters in arts was the first.

University of Prague: Jan Hus and religious conflict

In the early decades of its existence the *studium* flourished and fulfilled the high expectations that Charles had held for it. This, however, was not sustained, chiefly because of the political and religious instability of Europe in the later fourteenth century. Bohemia's mixed population reacted variously to the Great Schism; the Germans generally supported the Roman pope, for Avignon, although nominally papal territory, was under French domination, while the Czechs became influenced by the reforming ideas that were becoming current. Moreover the Czechs, unlike the Germans, had always been less romanized by the church. Prague's reputation as a university was well deserved; it became as vigorous as Paris in the study of theology and it was in this area that conflict grew. At the same time, the Czechs were generally chafing under the domination exerted by the Germans who, through the nations, had three-quarters of the voting power. By the end of the century, then, the university was seriously divided, and it had become one of the major places of religious conflict in Europe.

Theology was, of course, the central intellectual study of the universities from the time of their emergence, and the issues and problems that were engendered from religious inquiry were taken up at Prague. A number of Czech scholars in theology had been urging the reform of church abuses throughout the second part of the fourteenth century. One of the first was Jan Milíč (d. 1374) who, although not a member of the university, none the less influenced the early development of its theological studies. Milíč, who worked in the imperial chancery up to around 1363, argued for a return to a simple, primitive apostolic Christianity. This type of doctrine, similar in many ways to the one being voiced at the same time in England by Wycliffe, was taken up by Milíč's student, Matěj of Janov (d. 1394). Matěj (Matthias in English) had spent some ten years studying at Paris. Both of these men produced a large body of vernacular writing on theology, thereby encouraging the autonomous development of that language. Matthias, in particular, suggested the notion, extremely similar to Wycliffe's, that the church is the 'invisible communion of the elect'.[28] These doctrines were taken up by the Czech scholar Jan Hus (c. 1369/71–1415), who had graduated as a master of arts at Prague in 1396 and was elected dean of its faculty in 1401. In 1409 he became rector of the university, a position he held till he was deposed by the king in 1412.

The period of Hus' incumbency in those first years of the fifteenth century encompassed some of the most turbulent years of the university's history. By this time, particularly after 1406, Wycliffe's ideas had reached Prague. Just how they did so is not entirely clear. England, at the time, was linked to Bohemia by royal marriage, King Richard II (r. 1377–99) having married Anne, sister to Václav IV (r. 1378–1419), the reigning king of Bohemia. Although conjectured at times, the court and diplomatic links hardly seem the means by which Wycliffitism could have been transmitted. More likely, although the situation is still not clear, both Oxford and Paris were the intermediaries. One of the Czech critics of the church, Jerome of

Prague, was at Oxford between 1399 and 1401.[29] None the less, in the first decade of the fifteenth century it is clear that Wycliffe's works and ideas were being actively studied at Prague, giving support and confirmation to the independent tradition already developing among the Czechs. The course of the conflict was very complex, involving the problems of national rivalries in Europe and the support of the various contenders for the papal throne, the issues of church corruption and the increasing resentment among Czech scholars of German domination. This last problem, in fact, had become particularly acute because, in the meantime, during the latter years of the preceding fourteenth century, several German universities had been founded and had drawn off many German scholars – which led to a Czech majority still represented by only one nation.

Generally, the Czechs, in a manifestation of emerging identity, supported the religious position of Hus and his predecessors and eagerly accepted and adopted the teachings of Wycliffe. The Germans held to an orthodox Catholic position, generally that of scholastic nominalism. So ensued a decade of mounting tension and hostility: Pope Boniface IX, in Rome, withdrew his recognition of Václav IV's position as Holy Roman Emperor in 1403 and in the same year the German scholars condemned alleged Wycliffite heresies among the Czechs. In 1408 the Germans formally charged Matthias of Knín with heresy; the Czechs countered by electing him to a post of honour (*Quodlibetarius*) for the following year. Václav, meanwhile, strove desperately to steer a middle course until the papal issues were settled. But the university was in ferment and in 1409 the king promulgated the very influential decree of Kutná Hora. In that document the king asserted the principle that one's fellow countrymen are deserving of preference, and

Since, then, reliable information has reached the king that the German nation, which has no right of citizenship in the Bohemian kingdom, has in all the business of the university arrogated to itself the use of three votes, while the Bohemian nation, the true inheritor of this land, has and uses only one; and whereas the king considers it wrong and most unfitting that foreigners and strangers should enjoy in abundance the favours that belong to the natives of the country, who feel themselves oppressed by so hurtful a deprivation, he commands the rector and the university that hereafter the Bohemian nation, in all the councils, courts, examinations, elections and all other activities and proceedings of the university, shall . . . enjoy the right to three votes, and in virtue of this privilege shall preserve that right for ever in peace and without hindrance.[30]

The immediate consequence was the secession of many German masters to the other newly emerging German universities; before long, this weakened the *studium* at Prague and kept it basically a local, national institution.

Peace, of course, did not ensue after the decree and the German secession. Hus, now a vigorous spokesman for the Czechs, maintained his pressure against the Germans, the church and the Roman claimant to the papacy, who had German support, Gregory XII (r. 1406–15). In a bid to restore peace, Václav IV removed Hus from the rectorship. No peace ensued; in that same year Hus, with support from some of the patriotic Czech nobility, denounced Rome further, particularly the practice of selling, for cash payments, indulgences remitting punishment for sin. In this period Hus wrote his major work *De ecclesia*, based largely on Wycliffe, and, in Czech, his *Postilla*. Hus was summoned in 1414 for examination at the Council of Constance, on a promise of safe conduct. One of the conditions was that he would say no Mass; Hus did not observe that condition, and, using his transgression as a pretext, his accusers seized and tried him. Intercession by the emperor was unsuccessful and in 1415 he was burned at the stake. So the incipient Czech nation, struggling under German domination, found its first national hero in the martyred Hus, who provided, by his example, a stimulus to educational development.

In large part Hus had been motivated by nationalistic feelings: the Czechs were an ethnically homogeneous people who had been evangelized from Byzantium, not Rome, and who had been brought under German hegemony into the kingdom of Bohemia when Rudolf of Habsburg defeated their king Ottakar II in 1278. The Bohemians, or Czechs, never accepted this situation, and in Hus they found a spokesman for their cause. After the execution of Hus the mood of the Czechs led them to open rebellion. The Bohemian Diet met to consider the insult to their nation by the affront at Constance and a document was prepared, receiving 452 signatures, which defended the freedom of preaching in Bohemia, the primacy of scriptural authority, and the final right of the university of Prague to determine matters of faith at issue.[31] Hussitism, meanwhile, had spread throughout the nation; everywhere there was open preaching of defiance and demands for religious independence. In Prague the famous Four Articles were drafted as a Hussite platform and in 1420 were presented to the world. They prescribed freedom of preaching, communion of the laity in both bread and wine, the primacy of Christ and punishment for sins of all social classes. The Articles were unacceptable to Rome. The political atmosphere of the towns was tense; across the countryside popular preachers found large audiences, stimulated by a heightened emotionalism, much of it interpenetrated by Chiliasm – belief in the imminent return of Christ. Pope Martin V (r. 1417–31) and Sigismund, king of Germany and Hungary, began preparations for a crusade against Bohemia. The peoples of Bohemia were divided in their beliefs and expectations, however. In the towns, where the bulk of the German population lived, the burghers wanted only the basic demands of Hus, embodied in the 1415 resolution of the Diet and the Four Articles of 1420; they sought no final separation from Rome. The rural population, almost entirely Czech, differed. As peasants with long traditions of closely integrated communal life, they resisted the growing pressures of the wealthy classes, whether Czech or German, and sought greater – even absolute – independence. Anticipating the return of Christ, they began to organize their own churches and services and to appoint clergy as a counter to the unattractive and even frightening aspects of a religion mediated by a priestly class who reserved the sacrament of wine for themselves and who conducted services in a language they could not understand.[32]

In late 1419 sporadic revolts broke out across the countryside: in 1420 the urban poor of Prague and other towns, along with the peasants, began gathering some fifty miles south of the capital on a mountain to which they gave the biblical name Tábor. And to guide their activities their leaders drew up a revolutionary manifesto abolishing all privilege and private property, known as the Taborite Articles of 1420.[33] These Taborites became the radical core of the impending revolution. After the rejection of the Four Articles of Prague in 1420 by Rome, all Bohemia united against the outside attack. The townspeople or Utraquists, along with the Taborites, came together under the leadership of Jan Žižka (1358/60–1424),[34] who proved to be the military genius of the century. Žižka led them to victory. Altogether five crusades were mounted against Bohemia between 1420 and 1431 and all failed. Negotiations were mandatory. In the Compactas of Basle in 1432 and Prague of 1433 a compromise was reached, at least with the Utraquists. To avoid further schism, Rome allowed the operation of a new church, Utraquist or Calixtine, with its own particular privileges within the broader fold of Latin Catholicism. The central doctrinal issue was conceded; henceforth the laity also had the right to receive communion in both kinds, wine and bread. That is, the people had access to the chalice (Greek *kylix*, Latin *calix*, a wine-cup), hence the name of the church.[35] In addition some autonomy of church government was granted

along with freedom from Roman fiscal dues. Of equal emotional significance to the granting of the chalice, however, was the fact that church
services henceforth were to be allowed in the Czech language.

Although the Hussite movement was not to end with the Compacta of
Prague, a temporary stability ensued during which Bohemia made great
progress in education. Already a popular vernacular educational movement
had appeared, stimulated by the enthusiasm of the people for personal
access to the scriptures. This need was met, in the first instance, through the
work of Tomáš Štítný. A widowed member of the minor gentry living
near Tábor, in the late fourteenth century, just before the time of Hus,
Štítný had written for his children, to replace the instruction of their lost
mother, the famous *Books of Christian Education* (*Knihy naučení křesťanského*),
whose ideas foreshadowed the reforming views of Hus and Wycliffe.
These readily found a wider market and became extremely popular books
by which children learned to read in the Czech vernacular.[36] In addition to
this movement, burgher schools appeared in the towns offering instruction
in both Latin and the vernacular. In 1442 the Italian humanist, Aeneas
Sylvius, entered the service of the Holy Roman Emperor, Frederick III.
One of the tasks entrusted to Sylvius, hostile to the Czech cause, was the
education of the young king of Bohemia, Ladislaus, and it was under these
circumstances that Sylvius composed his famous treatise on a liberal
education, *De liberorum educatione*, in which he counselled young Ladislaus
to 'beware of wasting time over such a subject as the history of Bohemia or
Hungary'.[37] Yet even that opponent of the Czechs remarked in 1452 that
the common people knew their Bibles better than many Italian bishops
and that in Tábor he found 'pupils and many burghers who knew Latin.
As it is, this perfidious human breed have one good quality: they love
education more than anything.'[38] The University of Prague became a
centre of a new Utraquist orthodoxy, and in this compromise situation the
future educational development of Bohemia occurred, paralleling generally
that of the rest of Europe.

The Bohemian Brethren

The position was different in the rural areas where developments reflected
the totally different consequences of the Hussite revolution among the
peasantry. While Utraquism was basically Catholicism, the Taborites and
Adamites, the latter being a minority group of extremely Chiliastic persuasion, were radicals of a different bent. The Compacta of Prague res-

tored Sigismund to the Bohemian crown but this acceptance came only from the cities and until the end of the century the countryside remained obdurate. Throughout this period the common peoples were disunited and remained in continued conflict with each other and with the government. Basically, the difficulties stemmed from the lack of an integrated alternative doctrine to Catholicism; each individual community had attempted to explicate its own from as early as the time of Žižka who himself led the first schism among the common peoples and opposed the Taborites.[39] After Žižka's death in 1424 his followers, calling themselves Orphans, competed with Adamites and Taborites until a secession from the latter created a fourth group. These were led by an obscure figure, Peter Chelčický (c. 1390–1460), who could have been, quite possibly, a Waldensian migrant who brought those doctrines into Bohemia.[40] By 1467 his group had organized themselves as the Unity of the Brethren (*Unitas Fratrum*) and they began to practise a form of communal living that apparently had ancient traditions in eastern Europe, although its history is largely unknown.[41] This brotherhood, living in obscurity in the adjoining Margravate of Moravia, came to assume an importance in the history of education, not through its doctrines, but because from among its members it produced the most internationally respected educational reformer of the seventeenth century, Comenius.

A powerful stimulus to the maintenance of independent communities was the fear of social and hence religious domination. In Utraquist lands, the peasants fared badly, they lost most privileges and were reduced to serfdom, *ascripti glebae*, progressively throughout the century. To avoid this, various Chiliast groups retreated to the remoter areas of Bohemia, finding refuge where they could on the estates of sympathetic or at least tolerant landholders. In this situation, during a period of political quiet in Moravia, the Unity of Brethren organized their social life. Their central feature was an attempt to secure the most simple and Christian form of life possible and to this end they tried to minimize social differences, the lead to be taken, so a decree ran, by 'Priests and those who teach [who] should give an example to others in word and deed'.[42] The Brethren, like the early Taborites, put emphasis on elementary literacy, chiefly because of its instrumentality in giving access to the scriptures. Revolutionary Tábor, in 1420, had set up a school to give such instruction to all children, girls as well as boys, in Czech, although little is known about it. The Brethren began by providing reading schools in the home, and in 1482 their first regular school was organized by Havel of Zatek at Brandýs and

Orlici.[43] Within twenty years a large number of such elementary reading schools was in operation; they were highly regarded in Catholic quarters for their efficiency and depreciated equally for their obvious satanic support.[44] Initially the Brethren were concerned only with skill in reading the Bible and they made no provision for higher learning. The inherent limitations in that position soon became manifest. Those Brethren who found their way into the cities needed more than literacy and their schools expanded to include the skills of commerce and the traditional Latin grammar. As the Brethren identified with burgher life, indeed, as they became socially accepted and prosperous, their original discipline improved, their children were given the regular grammar school education and their priests began to form an intellectual class, although they were not necessarily instructed in Latin, Greek or Hebrew for their vocation.[45]

This middle-class identification of some Brethren precipitated yet another schism between a major party – predominantly burgher and educated – and a minor, who were rural and apparently minimally literate. In the early sixteenth century the major party, led by the well-educated Lucáš of Prague (c. 1460–1528), became dominant and by the mid-sixteenth century the minor party had disappeared. The hostility to higher learning, particularly at the universities, was no longer sustained as it was in the first decades of the Unity's existence when one of its founding fathers, Řehoř, warned the Brethren from his death-bed in 1474 'to beware of educated and learned persons who might corrupt the faith'.[46] This suspicion of university men, despite the fact that many of them were prominent in founding the Unity, came from the belief that Christendom itself had been perverted by excessive learning. Řehoř wanted to return to that putatively felicitous condition of the early church in the time of Christ, without realizing the agonies even then of such reformers as Tatian. By the year 1567 one of the Brethren, Jan Blahoslav (1523–71), in his *Philippic Against the Enemies of Higher Education in the Brotherhood*, insisted that 'Youth should learn! They should learn when and wherever they find anything good. For example, a precious stone or pearl, artistically and skilfully cut and polished – how it differs from one which is neither cut nor polished!'[47] In this same period the Brethren were able to maintain some centres of peaceful existence in Bohemia and Moravia and, although they sought privacy, their educational activities, or rather the reform of them, made one of their pastors, Comenius, the greatest educational figure of the seventeenth century.

Foundation of further German universities

The University of Prague was well received by the Bohemians in the first years of its existence, but to other German rulers it was a challenge. In 1365, in an effort to surpass Charles IV, his rival for the imperial crown of the Holy Roman Empire, the Habsburg duke, Rudolf IV of Austria, founded a university at Vienna. Charles, for his part, did his best to suppress it although he was unsuccessful. He did, however, succeed in preventing any further universities being founded in his lifetime. Vienna did not begin to function properly, however, until 1383 when the Great Schism led many German scholars to return from Paris rather than accept the Avignonese pope, Clement VII. For, in effect, this pope had no real authority in Germany and could not appoint German graduates to benefices in their own country. This, it seems, was a widely felt problem that vexed many students. Just as the Germans had difficulty in gaining desirable clerical offices in Germany, so the Czechs experienced similar difficulties, *vis-à-vis* the Germans, in Bohemia. So Jerome of Prague, at his controversial heresy trial in Constance in 1416 declared, *inter alia*, that in the university of Prague

> ... many Germans secured prebends and fellowships, so that the Czechs had nothing ... The Germans were in complete control of the university and of all its benefices; they held the seal of the foundation and all the insignia. ... Whatever the Germans wanted in the university was as good as done. The [Czech] Bohemians could do nothing.[48]

And, in this complaint, we get a fascinating glimpse of the low esteem in which university students held schoolteaching as an occupation:

> ... [for] when a Czech had graduated in arts, if he had no other means of livelihood [that is, in default of an ecclesiastical prebend] he had to go to the towns and villages and earn his living by teaching in some private school.[49]

Three years after this virtual refounding of Vienna, a second purely German university was established at Heidelberg as the result of the desire by Rupert, count palatine of the Rhine, duke of Bavaria and elector of the Holy Roman Empire, for such an institution of prestige. Rupert's move was also part of the political manœuvring during the Schism. He secured Heidelberg's charter from Urban IV in Rome, the latter so acting to strengthen his influence among the German princes. Like Vienna, Heidelberg profited from the continued exodus of Germans from Paris and other

French universities. Yet both German foundations modelled themselves on Paris, this being recorded expressly in the foundation charter of Heidelberg issued by Rupert in 1386:

> [We, Rupert] do decree that the University of Heidelberg shall be ruled, disposed, and regulated according to the modes and manners accustomed to be observed in the University of Paris. Also that, as a handmaid of Paris – a worthy one let us hope – the latter's steps shall be imitated in every way possible.[50]

He invited to be rector the distinguished German scholar Marsilius of Inghen, who had already spent a term as rector of the university at Paris. Marsilius got the *studium* off to a good start. In his own record of the foundation he tells us that Rupert's original submission was dispatched to Urban in October 1385 and that the papal authority, *litterae bullatae*, was received in June of the ensuing year. Within three months the senior faculty members, whom he names specifically, had been appointed, and by October in the same year (1386) the university was a going concern. So he recorded that 'on the next day, on the feast of St Remigius [8 October] at the request of Master Marsilius the . . . Duke granted many and substantial privileges to the *studium*, its masters, scholars and their attendants'.[51] Instruction began almost immediately, for

> . . . on the day [of 19 October] the said master Marsilius started lectures for the faculty of arts very early in the morning – for this year he was to lecture on logic – and . . . master Reginald representing the faculty of theology took up lectures on the Epistle to Titus in the eighth hour and finally in the first hour after noon master Heylmann, also of the faculty of arts, lectured on the Book of Physics [of Aristotle]. Thus they inaugurated the *studium* in honour of God, the most blessed Virgin, all saints and the whole celestial court; and thus the *studium* was begun.[52]

The foundation of the university at Cologne followed in 1388, prompting the German theologian Henry of Hesse, rector of the new *studium* at Vienna, to comment in a letter to Duke Robert of Bavaria on the contrast between the promising developments in German universities and the decline among those of France:

> For why is it that the universities of France are breaking up, that the sun of wisdom is eclipsed there? Learning withdraws to light another people. Are there not now four lamps of learning lighted among the Germans, that is four *studia generalia* [Prague, Vienna, Heidelberg, Cologne] shining in concert with rays of glorious truth?[53]

Further foundations of German universities occurred during the Great Schism: Erfurt, 1392; Leipzig, 1409; Rostock, 1419.

In the latter half of the fifteenth century a second wave of university foundation took place, and inside just fifty years a further nine universities were established,[54] the dates of their charters coinciding with the period of the outward expansion of Italian humanism and with the development of printing, this latter being in large part Germany's contribution to civilization. Henry of Hess's observations were as true of the late fifteenth century as of the fourteenth, although his optimism concerning the new world of learning had been a little premature when he stated in the same letter that German rulers should 'employ learned men and through them stabilize a changing world'.

Humanist scholarship in Germany

Change in Germany was actually occurring quite rapidly in relation to the times. German scholars took Italian humanism into their own country throughout the fifteenth century and by 1500 the intellectual condition of the country was vastly changed from that of a century before. One of the first Germans to become significant was Peter Luder (c. 1415–c.1474) who, after an education in Italy, chiefly at Padua and also at Rome, returned in 1444 as professor of classics at Heidelberg. Despite Luder's enthusiasm for Latin humanism he did not attract a following and in 1460 he returned to Padua. Although Luder remained an academic for the final years of his life, he abandoned classics and devoted himself to medicine. Of more lasting importance in the movement to spread humanism was Rudolph Agricola (1442/4–1485) who, in the words of an almost contemporary document, 'was the first person to import into Germany a knowledge of Greek'.[55] Agricola gained his master's degree at the new university at Louvain at the age of seventeen and after finding the scholasticism of Cologne unrewarding, spent ten years in Italy, where at Ferrara he studied Greek with Battista Guarino and Theodoros Gaza. In 1480 he returned to Germany determined to promote classical studies, and in 1482 he was invited to join the faculty of arts at Heidelberg, although he did not do so, entering instead into the employment of the elector until September 1484.

In the meantime, Alexander Hegius (1433–98), a master of outstanding ability, had been given charge of the Deventer school, of the Brethren of the Common Life, in 1475. Hegius was not an original thinker, but was impressed by the influence of Agricola who visited Deventer and, from the testimony of Rhenanus, taught Hegius some Greek.[56] This apparently led Hegius to modify the rigid pedagogy of the school, and in the recollections of Erasmus, at that time a young student at Deventer,

> That school was still barbarous [1475]. The *Pater Meus* was read over, and the boys had to say their tenses; *Ebrardus* and *Joannes de Garlandia* were read aloud. But Alexander Hegius and Zinthius were beginning to introduce some better literature.[57]

Hegius remained a conservative and his school was not known for its innovations or its liberalism; it was, nevertheless, popular and during his incumbency its enrolment is reported to have reached the exceptionally large number of 2,200, although this declined after his death.[58] Hegius, however, was not a brother of the *Devotio moderna* and his school was, in all likelihood, less rigid as a result. Erasmus speaks more mildly of Deventer under Hegius than he does of schools run by the Brethren themselves, recalling in one instance that 'I know particularly well a certain Churchman of great distinction who selected the masters of his school from amongst the more accomplished wielders of the birch. Flogging, in his educational doctrine, was the prime instrument for "softening and purifying" boys' natures.'[59]

The great figure of early German humanism, however, overshadowing all others before 1500 is Johannes Reuchlin (1455–1522). After a grammar school and university education in his native Germany, the latter at Heidelberg, Reuchlin travelled abroad, studying in turn at Paris and Basle and at Orléans where he read law. His interest in Greek was growing even in this period: in a letter of 1478 Georgius Hermonymus wrote that he was sending Reuchlin the Greek introductory grammar of Theodoros of Gaza, but the lexicon (apparently also requested) was unavailable, since it belonged to a friend who considered it too valuable to lend – an interesting comment on the scarcity of Greek texts before the advent of printing.[60] In 1481 Reuchlin became teacher of Greek at the newly founded University of Tübingen for a short period before returning to Italy in the train of the count of Württemberg who had become his patron. In Italy this time Reuchlin met Pico della Mirandola and became even more strongly converted to humanist teachings. At the same time Reuchlin sought to move beyond Latin and Greek to the study of the sources of European culture and scriptural authority in the original Hebrew. In Germany, humanism made much of its headway because it supported religion in the search for absolute scriptural authority, in contrast to Italy where its motivation was decidedly secular, and Hebrew for Reuchlin was the ultimate goal of the humanist search. Reuchlin became skilled in the language and by 1500 had made progress on a Hebrew grammar. In 1502 Aldus Manutius of Venice wrote that the grammar had not been printed yet;[61] it appeared in 1505 under the title *Rudimenta hebraica* (*Elements of Hebrew*). In 1506, following its publication, Reuchlin wrote that Latin was of only limited value in allowing access to scriptural truth – an allusion to the authorized Vulgate, in all possibility – and that only through Hebrew could a return to sources be made and Christian faith be supported fully.[62]

Unfortunately for Reuchlin his Hebrew studies led him to an interest in the Jewish book of religious mysteries, the *Cabbala* (Heb. *qabbālāh*, tradition). The *Cabbala* is of ancient origin reaching back to Gnostic times (first to third centuries A.D.) and consists of attempts to interpret the scriptures by unusual means, since the Hebrew alphabet is used also for numerals so that numbers can be words and words can be seen as numbers. In this way the *Cabbala* offers a system of scriptural interpretation. This fascinated Reuchlin who became an exponent of the possible values of the system, leading him to publish in 1517 *De arte cabbalistica*. This brought him into violent conflict with the Dominicans of Cologne, through the original accusations of Johann Pfefferkorn, a converted Jew who was concerned to extirpate the study of Hebrew works. Eventually, in 1530, after lengthy suits and counter-suits, Reuchlin was convicted in Rome of heresy. Yet the issue was never really settled; in the course of the controversy educated interest was aroused and a group of anonymous scholars joined the dispute on Reuchlin's side by publishing satirical attacks on the orthodoxy of the Dominicans. These satires, the so-called *Letters of Obscure Men* (*Epistolae obscurorum virorum*),[63] mocked the current ecclesiastical teachings and represented the growing support in Germany for greater independence from Roman authority.

Contemporaneous with Reuchlin was Conrad Celtes (1459–1508)[64] whose activities helped create the great enthusiasm for humanism in the country around 1500. Celtes was in spirit, and often in practice, a *clericus vagans*, roving through Germany and Italy studying and collecting manuscripts. His introduction to learning came at the universities of Cologne and Heidelberg, and, after a time in Italy where he became attracted to Platonism and also met with Manutius, he returned to Germany in 1487 to be made poet laureate by Frederick III. Then in 1492 came his first significant pronouncement on education. He had moved that year to a position at the University of Ingolstadt and there delivered an inaugural lecture, *Oratio in gymnasio in Ingolstadio publice recitata*. It turned out to be far more than a public lecture on his subject; it was a manifesto urging the intellectual reform of all Germany, on humanist lines. Celtes, along with other Germans who had studied abroad, was sensitive to the reputation his country had for intellectual and cultural barbarity: gluttony, drunkenness, indolence, violence, ignorance were all synonymous with the word 'German' in the foreign – and Celtes meant Italian – mind. The German people, he exhorted, must

> . . . do away with that old disrepute of the Germans in Greek, Latin and Hebrew writers who ascribe to us drunkenness, cruelty, savagery and every other vice bordering on bestiality and excess.[65]

The image, he complained, was painted in the days of classical antiquity, 1500 years before. Germany had developed considerably since then and its achievements should be not only a source of just pride for Germans, they should also be actively propagandized abroad.

So Celtes stimulated a new period of German intellectual endeavour: the assimilation of humanist learning on the one hand, the propagation of a national literature on the other. To implement the former he founded a society modelled on the informal Italian academies which he called a sodality (L. *sodalis*, comrade). His own, the Danubian Sodality, was concerned primarily with Latin versification and questions of poetry; its example was followed in other German localities. He was even more successful in stimulating patriotic writing, making a beginning himself with his monumental conception of a vast historico-geographical account of the country to be called *Germania illustrata*. To achieve this he enlisted the support of other humanists and his Danubian Sodality, and contributions of articles and chapters came from enthusiastic scholars throughout the country. Although the project never came to fruition – it waned after Celtes' death – none the less the idea had promoted a new humanist activity in Germany, in a new literary genre: the national topography.[66] A full generation later, in the period between 1530 and 1550, Celtes' topographical approach became a popular German scholarly activity, coming to influence both intellectual life and the process of education.

Topographical writing was concerned fundamentally with complete literary description of a country: its physical and surface features, natural and human landscape, and its relationships with other countries. Two studies associated with topography were revived: the intensive study of a single region, called chorography; and, at the other extreme, the comprehensive study of the total world of man, known as cosmography. So three studies appeared, each with an increased range: chorography, topography, cosmology.[67] With the growing interest in cosmography the ancient tradition of encyclopedism started to revive, but this time with a much wider emphasis. Classical encyclopedias were basically catalogues, however expanded, of the content of the seven liberal arts; the new cosmographies looked anew at man and his works, using categories that hitherto had not been exploited fully, of which the most prominent was the emerging study of geography. Celtes' concern, in part, was to give a greater definition of German identity, and this new topographical movement was the first concerted effort to provide a clearer understanding of the country. Its success was assured by the intense receptivity of the Germans to anything that would provide identity and in this regard topography and cosmography were seized upon readily by some visionary schoolmasters who saw a study of potential educational vigour. Cosmography particularly became a German interest and it rapidly became assimilated into the school curriculum.

Grammar schools in Germany

When the vanguard of topographical studies began to enter the German schools early in the sixteenth century there were in existence enough schools of appropriate inclination to provide a favourable reception. For in Germany, in contrast to France, the grammar schools had managed to shake off much clerical control. Information is lacking on the German grammar schools throughout the Middle Ages but it is clear that, in general, they were established in cathedrals and some parishes according to various church injunctions, particularly the two Lateran decrees of 1179 and 1215 which applied to all dioceses under Rome's authority. Throughout the same period burgher schools (*Ratsschulen*) appeared, perhaps as extensions of parish schools and certainly in some cases as developments of guild schools.[68] These were under the administration of municipal authorities who hired and discharged teachers, and their curriculum was the traditional Latin grammar, presumably because even the strictly utilitarian needs of the burghers demanded knowledge of the language of law and of international communication. In Germany in particular it seems that the number of *clerici vagantes* was very great and these often settled, even if temporarily, in various towns as schoolmasters.[69] Friction with the church ensued, as in France, although in Germany the burghers were more successful in retaining control of their municipal schools.

It was probably in the Duchy of Brabant and the neighbouring regions of the Low Countries that education and grammar schools first became securely established. We know of grammar schools in the cities of Flanders, Ghent and Ypres, for example, and we are informed about those conducted by the Brethren of the Common Life. In Brabant the existence of what can be inferred as reasonably good grammar schools is documented with the foundation of a university in the capital of Louvain in 1426. This university chose to establish only two faculties, those of law and medicine. The teaching of the arts it entrusted to the grammar schools of the city which became known as pedagogies. These schools were regarded as part of the university itself (*partes integrantes*) and concerned themselves with teaching the trivium and the quadrivium of the traditional liberal arts. They seem to have taught boys from a variety of backgrounds, many of whom apparently had no regular elementary instruction. The pedagogies, therefore, made up this lack in their courses. By 1446 only four such schools retained accredited status as *partes integrantes*, both because of the need to maintain standards and to avoid fragmentation of the faculty of arts. Despite the intention of teaching the whole of the liberal arts, these pedagogies, like all schools of the period, directed most of their interests to Latin grammar. Towards the end of the fifteenth century they were taken over by the Brethren of the Common Life and conducted according to the methods the brothers had been developing in their schools.[70]

The teachers in virtually all German schools in the Middle Ages were, of necessity, clerics, although in the late fifteenth century secular schoolmasters began to appear, probably in response to the demand for elementary schools that could teach reading, writing and reckoning. The manner in which these were established in the towns is suggested by a Holbein painting of 1516 (Plate 11).[71] This is a sign-board (*Firmenschild*) intended to be hung outside such a school, its lengthy caption indicating that instruction in reading and writing German is offered to anyone seeking it, boys and girls being welcomed specifically. On one side of the board a master, birch in hand, is shown standing at a lectern teaching a boy of about ten to write, while a dame seated on the opposite side of the room is similarly instructing a young girl; in the centre of the room two older boys are sitting on a wooden form, reading. The other side of the board, however, shows the same master seated at a table between two men of mature age, commenting on a page of written work. Pen, ink, pen-knife and blank paper lie on the table: this too is a writing class, for adults; the small enrolment is most likely an advertising stratagem, and the sign seems to refer to a practice already well established. The action of a schoolmaster in commissioning Holbein, one of the most promising German artists of the period, suggests that the occupation was becoming competitive and warranted the best advertising possible. The teaching of German on a large scale inevitably accompanied the growth of the vernacular, a trend discernible throughout the fifteenth century. Reuchlin's letters, for example, along with those of his contemporaries are mixtures of German and Latin; the former usually for simple, everyday comments, the latter for scholarly and intellectual matters. Indeed, it has been argued on the basis of the size of the book trade that by 1500 all townspeople except the lowest classes were literate.[72]

Parallel with the growth of vernacular literacy and of greater instrumental significance in the extension of humanist learning was the increasing appearance of the grammar schools. Complete figures are not available, those that do exist indicating that the enrolment of 2,200 at Deventer during the incumbency of Hegius was exceptional. In 1485, at that very time, Nuremberg had four schools with a total of four masters and twelve ushers (assistant masters), 245 fee-paying students and a large but unspecified number of free scholars. By 1532, in fact, the free places had to be restricted to 110. Augsburg, in 1503, had five schools and a total of 523 students.[73] In the same period, around 1500, the total enrolment of all German universities has been estimated to have been between 3,000 and 4,000 students; including Vienna, Prague and German students abroad the number is estimated to have approximated 6,000.[74] Despite the paucity of evidence it is clear that Germany was quite educationally advanced regarding provision of either vernacular or Latin grammar instruction for the burgher classes by the beginning of the sixteenth century, and that the rudiments of an educational system existed. Yet the people of the countryside lacked any comparable facilities, in contrast to even the modest provisions of the Czech dissenting communities. In rural Germany, schooling of any kind for the common people was not yet entertained although intimations of a growing social conscience and concern for the plight of the common people is reflected in the account of a sixteenth-century humanist Willibald Pirckheimer who travelled through the great pass between Germany and Italy, the Val Tellina, after it had been ravaged in the war between the Swiss and the Habsburgs in 1499. He wrote:

I passed through a large village which had been burned to the ground. Two old women, herding about forty boys and girls before them, met me on the road. All were emaciated and deathly pale of face, a gruesome sight to behold. I inquired of the crones where they were leading their pitiful charges. 'You shall see presently,' was the reply. The children had by now reached the meadow. There they squatted and began to graze among the grasses and herbs, like cattle, except that they tore them not with their mouths but with their hands. . . . I stood stunned and speechless. 'Now do you see', one of the women spoke, 'where I have led these wretches, who would be better off had they never been born? Their fathers fell before the sword, their mothers succumbed to hunger, their belongings became the booty of the enemy, their houses the victim of flames.' Having seen and heard this, I could not suppress tears while I bewailed the piteous fate of man and cursed the fury of war.[75]

The echo of this cry was heard in Germany later in the century by many Germans, foremost of whom was Martin Luther. A humanitarian concern for children and their education was to develop in Germany as one of that country's outstanding contributions to the development of Western education.

CHAPTER 10

Expansion of Education and Humanism: II. England to 1500

The medieval background

Although humanism gained a following in France and Germany during the course of the fifteenth century, neither of those countries displayed an enthusiasm for the new movement comparable with England where we find its most vigorous acceptance. In England humanism was welcomed initially as a support to religion, with the grammar schools embracing it more for its possibilities of affirming faith than for any liberalizing qualities. Later, however, the religious aspect was progressively discarded and the English became the most avid followers of Italian secular humanism, and the first people outside Italy to introduce it into their schools. It is in England, itself a model for many other nations, that we find the first clearly distinguishable practical results in education of the humanist programme.

Elementary and grammar schools: before the Conquest

Yet the educational history of England before the sixteenth century gives no clear indication of potential vigour or of a future role in exercising considerable leadership in education. On the contrary, education and learning in England before 1500 were inferior to practices in continental Europe in many ways, and the great cathedral schools of France had no eleventh- and twelfth-century counterparts of comparable reputation in England. In part this can be traced to the breakdown in English educational life which occurred at the time when Alcuin joined the service of Charlemagne late in the eighth century during the Norse invasions.

England, by the time of Alcuin, had developed an educational tradition that was entirely religious. There certainly had been a minimal secular system in operation during the centuries of Roman occupation but that had disappeared entirely with the departure of the imperial legions and the ensuing barbarization of the Romano-Britons by the Anglo-Saxon invaders. Christianity, meanwhile, had reached Britain and Hibernia, and since this was generally sustained by Benedictine monasteries, education in those regions became almost entirely claustral and intended solely for oblates. The evidence is very sparse and only fleeting references to schools have come down to us. Apart from a vague mention by the monk Gildas of some schools in Wales around the period 517–40, the first firm documentation occurs in Bede's *History of the English Church and People (Historia ecclesiastica gentis Anglorum)* where we read that when Sigibert returned from exile in Gaul to the kingship of East Anglia, he established a school around 631, or earlier, on the model of those in Gaul, where boys could learn grammar, and that he was assisted by Bishop Felix of Kent who brought with him teachers and masters trained in the techniques in use at Canterbury.[1] Bede records further that, partly through the efforts of two missionaries from Italy, Archbishop Theodore and Abbot Hadrian, such schools multiplied, with the result that anyone wishing to study the scriptures could secure a master for instruction.[2]

Of course, Britain in this period was a totally agricultural region, and this claim of Bede's must be understood as enthusiastic hyperbole. Perhaps, relatively speaking, he was right, in so far as the advantages of education would have been recognized by only a few, and for that tiny minority the monasteries may indeed have been able to provide places. Benedictinism in the seventh and eighth centuries expanded rapidly throughout Europe and extended into Britain where Benedict Biscop – that is, Bishop Benedict – founded the twin cloisters of Wearmouth in 674 and nearby Jarrow in 682, close by the already flourishing monastery of Lindisfarne, on Holy Island, and to these child oblates were drawn. Bede himself was taken in his seventh year, around 680, by his parents and offered to the community at Wearmouth. After four years he was transferred to Jarrow where he remained till his death some fifty-five years later in 735. Bede was out-standing as both teacher and scholar and his achievements are evidence of the distinction of the monastic schools in this period. His own teachers, Benedict Biscop and Abbot Ceolfrid, were themselves notable scholars, and Bede's writings give testimony to the high quality of his learning, which included acquaintance with the Latin grammatical tradition. Lindisfarne, Wearmouth and Jarrow, in fact, were among the best centres of learning in the West in the seventh and eighth centuries, but they were still capable of making only a limited contribution.

The English church in the mid-eighth century was not well organized. Pope Zacharius (r. 741–52), who ruled energetically, censured the English church for its laxity, stimulating it to convene a council in 747. This, the Council of Clovesho, was the second of at least eight held at that place, although, curiously, its location is now unknown. It was mainly concerned with amending laxity of discipline among English churches and with enforcing them to follow the Latin Rite; Zacharius had threatened ex-communication for these shortcomings. In addition, this council decreed the establishment of a school in every parish in which 'boys be compelled and exercised in the love of learning, so that they may be found well learned for all the needs of God's church, and not become rectors so greedy for earthly business that the house of God is depraved for want of spiritual adornment'.[3] But what resulted we do not know.

The monasteries appear to have remained virtually the sole centres of scholarship, which itself continued to be restricted to internal needs. Some literacy had to be acquired by the parish clergy but of this there is no record whatsoever. So it was in this environment that England's greatest scholar of the period, Alcuin of York (c. 730/5–804), received his education. Alcuin's appointment to take charge of the cathedral school at York in 778 lasted only a few years before he moved in 782 to the court of Charlemagne to continue his highly distinguished career. At the time of Alcuin's emigration, the Norse invasions prevented the extension of Northumbrian learning and checked the development of education for several centuries. The evidence indicates that the invaders destroyed much of the country's scholarship – monasteries were pillaged, schools disrupted, books destroyed – and not until the time of Alfred the Great (r. 870–99) did learning become re-established.

Alfred's concern for the restoration of learning is brought out clearly in his biography *De rebus gestis Aelfredi* (*Life of King Alfred*) written by his contemporary, Bishop Asser.[4] This record tells us that Alfred, during his

RENAISSANCE ENGLAND

kingship, learned to read and translate from Latin and to communicate this to others; at the same time he required also that the officials of the court should be able to read.[5] To promote these ends he set a personal example by translating Boethius' *Consolation of Philosophy* for his subjects to read – with Asser's help, according to William of Malmesbury[6] – and with a third portion of his revenues, established a palace school for the children of nobles and others (*gentis nobilibus et etiam pueris ignobilibus*).[7] But we know very little more than we can draw out of these few references, and thereafter, for the next three centuries, English education is just as precariously and sparsely documented.[8]

Elementary and grammar schools: twelfth and thirteenth centuries

The Norman invasions of 1066 depressed English learning even more since a French-speaking landed aristocracy now became superimposed on the people. After Latin, French became the most widely used written language, indicated by the fact that legal and political documents of the period are generally either in Latin or French, and only rarely in Anglo-Saxon. England was reduced to virtual cultural vassalage of France, and the French, for their part, had no doubts about their superiority. The *Ecclesiastical History* of Oderic Vitalis gives due credit to the achievements of the Northumbrian scholars, referring specifically to Alcuin, Aldhelm and Bede, but it observes, quite trenchantly, that English society had so languished under poor leadership that at the time of the conquest 'the Normans found the English a rustic and nearly illiterate people',[9] and the Englishman William of Malmesbury expressed a similar opinion.[10] Schools for oblates continued to exist in monasteries, and others were attached to cathedrals. The most elementary of these taught only reading from the Latin as the one skill necessary for chanting the offices of the church services, and were known as song or chantry schools (*scolas cantuales*). Others added some Latin grammar and perhaps reading and writing and were known as grammar schools (*scolas grammaticales*). There was also a third kind of school which taught writing, apparently as a scribal skill, but very little is known about it.[11] In the monasteries the writing school was possibly an adjunct to the *scriptorium*, in the cathedrals it was probably connected with the grammar school.

Throughout the twelfth and thirteenth centuries the cathedrals of England, as on the continent, enjoyed a period of accelerated growth. Some of the cathedrals of England operated differently from those of Europe, however, and this had some effect on the development of education. Because England was not organized on the diocesan system in the early years of Christianity there, the custom developed, as dioceses were established later, of bishops' choosing important monastic churches for their seats, and in this way nine English cathedrals came to have monastic chapters, Benedictine in every case: Canterbury, Winchester, Worcester, Rochester, Durham, Ely, Norwich, Coventry and Bath. In 1133 a tenth was founded at Carlisle, under the care of Augustinian monks. All of these retained their monastic character. A separate parallel development was the growth of the so-called secular cathedrals which were located in the larger towns and discharged similar functions to their counterparts in Europe. There were nine of these: York, Salisbury, Lincoln, Chichester, Lichfield, Wells, Hereford, Exeter and London. In the post-conquest period some of these were moved from small villages to the large towns; the see of Lincoln was previously at Dorchester, and Chichester at Selsey. Very little is known of education in the monastic cathedrals, probably because they remained inward-looking; it was chiefly in the secular cathedrals that educational developments occurred, and, even so, information exists only for some as late as the twelfth and thirteenth centuries.[12]

Generally, however, the cathedrals, whether monastic or secular, had a song school. The performance of the liturgy was of the highest order of importance and the office of precentor – or cantor – was one of the four senior positions within the chapter, the others being those of dean, chancellor and treasurer. The precentor, assisted at times by a deputy, the succentor, had responsibility for organizing and conducting the music for all of the cathedral's services, and in this capacity he supervised and taught the boy choristers. This office is recorded as existing by the late eleventh century in the cathedrals of York, Lincoln and Salisbury.[13] It does not seem to have been widespread in the monastic cloisters and could have been restricted to the larger communities; there are mentions of song schools at Durham and Westminster Abbey.[14] Yet, despite their importance to the liturgy, these schools were not very large; between ten and fourteen choristers was the number enrolled.[15]

The cathedral schools of England seem to have had even more modest beginnings. In earlier times, during the sixth and seventh centuries, evidence shows that the bishop himself often taught the few boys that came to the cathedral for instruction. By the eleventh century, when the numbers had grown larger, and the activities of the cathedral greater and more complex, the bishop became fully engaged with administration, and the teaching function was delegated to a subordinate. In France, during the eleventh and twelfth centuries, the cathedral school became a significant institution and its head, the *scholasticus*, an important – often renowned – official, some being later translated to episcopal chairs. In England, however, the process was much slower. With the growth of the schools and the need for a full-time master, the position of chancellor seems to have been created,[16] and gradually this office grew in responsibility and prestige, having responsibility for the school and the cathedral library, including its archives. With further increase in the size of the school and the appointment of assistant masters (ushers), the chancellor gained the further specific title of *magister scholarum* or *scholasticus* (literally, master of the school). But there was nothing about these schools to distinguish them from similar ones in Europe, except perhaps that those of England were smaller and more restricted in their curriculum than those of France.

When it comes to precise numbers of schools, and their enrolments, however, the evidence completely fails us. Apart from the generalized information contained in passing references which implies that all or certainly most cathedrals had schools of varying size and quality, there is very little of a statistical nature. Probably the closest approximation here is the record that London in the twelfth century, the most populous city, had three schools: St Paul's (in the cathedral), along with St Mary-le-Bow (of the Arches) and St Martin-le-Grand, and this information has been preserved in the contemporary account (*c.* 1190) of William Fitzstephen. This is a life of Thomas Becket in which he reports yet another of those conflicts arising from rivalry between schoolmasters; his reference is to a decree of about 1138 issued by the acting bishop of London, Henry of Blois, which enjoined the chapter of St Paul's to excommunicate any master attempting to teach in the city except those in charge of the three schools specifically mentioned.[17] Apart from these allusions, nothing more definite in the way of statistical records is available for the twelfth and thirteenth centuries.

The major concern of the schools in this period – apart from the song schools – was the liberal arts which in this period were restricted almost entirely to the trivium with a major emphasis on grammar. One very interesting account of this is contained in the *Description of London* which Fitzstephen used as a preliminary to his biography of Becket. Fitzstephen, himself a cleric and member of Becket's staff, has left a memorable description. On special school festival days, he writes, the masters assemble their students at the church whose feast day it is. There,

. . . the scholars dispute, some in demonstrative rhetoric, others in dialectic. Some 'hurtle enthymemes' [syllogisms with missing premises], others with greater skill employ perfect syllogisms.

The passage continues with references to verbal wrestling, sophistic disputations and oratorical harangues. Competition is a major element and

. . . boys of different schools [St Paul's, St Mary-le-Bow, St Martin-le-Grand] strike against one another in verse, or contend concerning the principles of the art of grammar or the rules governing the use of past or future, and all this with a certain deliberate, trenchant aggression – 'they lacerate their comrades outspokenly . . ., they hurl abuse and jibes'. In the evenings, they apparently engaged in sport and on certain occasions,

> . . . older men and fathers and rich citizens come on horseback to watch the contest of the juniors and after their fashion are young again and with the young.[18]

The whole passage has a distinct flavour of fourth-century Athens about it: rhetoric and dialectic employed in oratory and debate, the latter of marked eristic quality. At one point Fitzstephen refers to scoring points with 'Socratic wit' and there is the possibility that his account reflects the new awareness in medieval England of the uses of the classical trivium.

Yet there is nothing in this account that conflicts with the general educational practice. European education in this period was all of one piece and England followed, in fact was largely dependent upon, developments across the channel. This does not deny the ability of England to produce an occasional front-rank scholar, John of Salisbury being a conspicuous example. Yet John's distinction was a rare achievement and even points up the superiority of France in this period. Moreover, John's writings are in the mainstream of the European intellectual tradition.

Like their French counterparts, the English secular cathedral schools of the twelfth century also attempted to develop their studies beyond the trivium so as to provide the professional training in theology and law that was becoming necessary. Again there is a serious shortage of reliable data and only fragments exist. It is, however, reasonably certain that York and Exeter taught law (probably civil) and that Exeter and Lincoln taught theology.[19] Indeed, all secular cathedrals seem to have offered some instruction in theology and had a resident *theologus* on their staff. The most reliable information in this regard concerns the minor figure of William de Montibus who was in charge of the theological school at Lincoln cathedral, and his activities there provide some insight into the nature of educational experiment in that century.

William de Montibus (*c.* 1140–1213)[20] was born in Lincoln where he apparently received his early schooling in the cathedral. He studied in Paris some time between 1160 and 1170 when theology was undergoing significant development there, and he brought this experience back with him to Lincoln where in 1186 he became chancellor of the cathedral, a position he held for the remainder of his life, some twenty-seven years. As part of his duties he had the task of giving theological instruction to

11 Schoolmaster's signboard by Hans Holbein, 1516 (both sides).

12 Student's notes at William Sellyng's lecture, late thirteenth century.

intending secular priests, and his attempts at introducing some innovation in this respect are preserved in his major work, the *Numerale*. This was a manual of the new speculative theology being developed in Paris and already made so exciting by the activities of Abelard and Gilbert de la Porrée, among others, earlier in the century. In addition, Hugh of St Victor had become well known for his pedagogically innovative *Didascalicon* which by William's time, half a century later, was receiving wide circulation. Hugh's efforts, like those of William, were directed towards providing systematic instruction for the less academically gifted secular clergy. William's *Numerale*, following in the tradition of Hugh of St Victor, attempted a formal scheme based upon the cultivation of certain arts and techniques of memorization.

Remembering had always presented serious problems. In the absence of ready supplies of books and paper, educated persons in antiquity were compelled to rely very heavily upon their memories, and if this reliance were to be justified, then memory had to be accurate. Plato and Aristotle, along with many other Greeks, had given much attention to the way in which the mind operates and the associated role of memory.

In antiquity, both Greek and Roman, the cultivation of memory was of signal importance. The ancients went so far as to distinguish two aspects, the 'natural' memory, that is the inherent mental powers of reception and recall, and the 'artificial' memory. The latter was a body of precepts which assisted a person to 'fix' ideas, facts, thoughts or whatever in his mind and to recall them at will. The usual method was to devise some mnemotechnical scheme of organization, of which the most favoured was the image of classical architecture. As facts were learned the individual 'arranged' them as if upon the various parts of a building: beside columns, on the porch, in niches, above doorways, for example. Then, as recall was necessary, the learner visited each of these locations in his mind, retrieving the necessary pieces of information. This technique found a special application in rhetoric, for it enabled the speaker to maintain a ready flow of prepared material. So throughout antiquity memory became a necessary aspect of the orator's art, and every writer on the subject, especially Cicero and Quintilian, stressed the value of memory. Unfortunately, however, the actual manuals of mnemotechnical instruction have been lost and we have only references to them. Cicero and Quintilian did not traverse the same ground, for they assumed their readers had a prior acquaintance with these handbooks. Throughout the Middle Ages this tradition of imprinting the mind with a visual storehouse in which to arrange facts continued to survive although, in common with the rest of the classical tradition before the Quattrocento, in attenuated and poorly understood form. This tradition goes a long way to explain Hugh of St Victor's attempt to structure both his *Didascalicon* and *De tribus* in the *ars memorativa* tradition.

William de Montibus is one of the first recorded representatives in England of the attempt to apply this approach to education. The *Numerale* does not go so far as to employ visual images; its approach is through a numerical system of organization, hence its title. Under heading one are listed: one god, one faith, one church; under two come two testaments, faith and works; under three is listed the holy trinity; twelve includes the articles of faith and the hours in a day. This work was very successful and survives in a large number of copies.[21] Equally well received, it would appear, was his other pedagogical text of sermons, the *Similitudinarius*, which brought together, in an alphabetical listing, a large number of religious statements from various sources, and these, within entries, were arranged so as to provide preachers with a variety of exegetical interpretations for key biblical concepts, in order to widen the scope of sermonizing. 'Christ', it claims, for example, can be conceived of in several ways: he is metaphorically the instrument, or staff, of god (Lat. *vitis*, the centurion's rod); he was believed to have been descended directly from David and his son Solomon; he was sacrificed as a paschal lamb – originally a Jewish Passover sacrifice that early Christians regarded as becoming symbolized in Christ (I Cor. 5:7); and he was believed in reality to be the god of mankind. So William set out, in his *Similitudinarius*, along with his written examples, some diagrammatic ones on the lines of his analysis. In this example of Christ, the centre column contains the level of interpretation, the right hand one the key scriptural terms being explained.[22]

	per similitudinem	vitis
Christus est	per nominis interpretationem	David, Salomon
	per significationem	agnus paschalis
	per rei veritatem	deus homo

The two universities: Oxford and Cambridge

Throughout the twelfth century, then, there was a great deal of activity and development occurring in the secular cathedral schools in England, but none came to have any lasting significance. When the clerks of England organized their first *studia* they chose not cathedral cities but minor towns of which one was certainly Oxford and another could have been Northampton. Oxford, some sixty miles north-west of London, was within the jurisdiction of the bishop of Lincoln whose seat lay 100 miles to the north. Why the clerks chose it is uncertain, although several advantages can be suggested: it was quite centrally situated, with relatively good communications; it was a place of resort and, perhaps, rather import-antly, it was conveniently distant from episcopal supervision. As early as 1133 Oxford appears to have been a gathering place for students; two documents of the period refer to a master named Robert Pullein lecturing there on the scriptures in 1133,[23] and to students congregating there in 1135.[24] References to teaching at Oxford appear for the years 1135 and 1149, in the respective phrases 'Magister Oxinfordie', 'Hic in Oxone-fordia legem docuit' ('he taught law in Oxford'),[25] but these do not mention a school explicitly, although one must have been in existence. The strengthening of this school may have come from the injunction of Henry II of England who in his dispute with France at the time of Becket ordered English scholars to leave Paris in 1167. Whether any scholars did so, and whether they in fact descended on the incipient *studium* at Oxford, is one of the major historical controversies on the foundation of that university.[26]

A distinct gathering of scholars at Oxford had certainly taken place by 1184–5, for which we have the evidence of Gerald of Wales who tells us that he resolved to read his *Topographica Hibernica* there because in Oxford 'the clergy of England flourished and excelled in clerkship'. He records, moreover, that 'on the first day he received at his lodgings all the poor scholars of the whole town; on the second all the doctors of different faculties and such of their pupils as were of greater fame, on the third the rest of the scholars with many knights, townsfolk and burghers'.[27] By the end of the twelfth century it is certain that the university was organized – approximately at the same time as Paris, perhaps twenty years later – on the evidence of a document of about 1200 from the scholars who style themselves *universitas magistrorum et scolarium Oxonie* (the society of masters and scholars at Oxford).[28] The theologian Alexander Nequam was teach-ing there late in the twelfth century and he had among his distinctions the record of being the first person in the West to know Aristotle in trans-lations from both Greek and Arabic.[29] Moreover, he demonstrated a wider command of Moslem learning by introducing the doctrines of Avicenna.[30] Theology, in fact, seems to have been an important study at Oxford quite early, for there is a reference to the masters John Grim and Simon of

Gloucester teaching theology around 1201–3, and in a document of 1201 Grim is referred to as a master of the school at Oxford (*magister scolarum Oxonie*).[31]

At Oxford, as in Paris, the students organized themselves into nations, but they found it more convenient to divide simply into two: Southerners (*Australes*) composed of those coming from places south of the river Trent,[32] along with the Welsh and Irish, and Northerners (*Boreales*) who were those from north of the Trent, along with the Scots. The office of chancellor, too, was a local innovation, arising out of disturbances which led also to the foundation of England's second university, at Cambridge.

This conflict took place in the year 1209 after an incident in which a student apparently killed an Oxford townswoman by accident and then fled. When the sheriff hanged his three room-mates for reprisal, the entire *studium* declared a cessation of activity, the famous *suspendium clericorum*. The university's future wavered and not until 1214 was stability regained. The conflict was chiefly one of authority over students who, for their part, claimed clerical privilege. Eventually, by the Legantine Ordinance, the students were put under the authority of their bishop – at far-off Lincoln. He, of course, was unable to exercise effective supervision so he appointed a deputy who, from the beginning, was elected by the Oxford masters. This deputy, styled 'chancellor', in time came to side with the university rather than with the bishop and hence the pope. Moreover, since the Legatine Ordinance also marked a victory over the townspeople, who were supported by royal authority, this development of the office of chancellor meant that the *studium* became virtually independent. In the meantime, however, some scholars had moved to the village of Cambridge where they established a new university. The first specific mention of Cambridge as a centre of studies is a document of 1231 which refers to a 'collection of disorderly and incorrigible clerks in our town of Cambridge'.[33] This document is a royal injunction to the sheriff of Cambridge to arrest and imprison or expel those delinquent students who refused to submit to the authority of the chancellor and masters there. The existence of a *studium generale* at Cambridge is obvious.

As the thirteenth century progressed both universities, but especially Oxford, became involved in the intellectual controversies that occupied those on the continent, although neither Oxford nor Cambridge played dominant roles; Oxford for its part was engaged in continued internal conflict that absorbed much of its energies. Much of this centred on the activities of the mendicant friars, both Dominican and Franciscan, who arrived in Oxford barely a few days after landing in England, in 1221 and 1224, respectively. Both orders wished to secure the same privileges that they already had at Paris, chief of which was the right to proceed directly to degrees in theology in their own schools, without taking a first degree in arts. The Franciscan Rule, in fact, forbade secular learning, and hence studies in arts, although it was necessary for them to study at least some theology. The Dominicans, of course, were positively enthusiastic about theology and, to an extent, canon law. Yet their demands to study independently in their own schools struck at the fundamental concept of a university and so provoked a bitter conflict with the seculars who upheld the faculty of arts as the heart of the *studium*. We find these early struggles reflected in one of the earliest and most famous statutes of Oxford, that of March 1253 which stated that 'no one could incept in theology without having first taken a university degree in arts'.[34] This was moderated two years later, owing to the precedent created by the Franciscan, Thomas of York, to allow certain friars, under special circumstances, to petition for a dispensation or 'grace' by which they could proceed directly to a bachelor's degree in theology and subsequently to a doctor's in the same subject.[35] This conflict between the mendicants, along with some of the other great monastic orders too, and the university continued intermittently throughout the thirteenth and fourteenth centuries, although at Oxford the university generally retained its ascendancy and the orders never gained the same status and privileges that they held at Paris.

Yet the mendicant schools were not as negative in their contribution as this conflict might suggest; on the contrary, they were hosts to a number of great scholars and they helped to provide many stimuli to fresh and innovatory thought, and two of Oxford's greatest thinkers taught in Franciscan schools. In the early years of Oxford's foundation the most notable among its scholars was Robert Grosseteste (*c.* 1175–1253) who had probably been at Paris as well. Between 1224 and 1235 he taught at the Franciscan house of studies in Oxford although he was not of their order. In 1235 he became bishop of Lincoln and thereby titular head of the university. Grosseteste's interests covered a wide range of topics, tending towards mathematical studies, and his influence was considerable. His tenure as bishop, however, was marked by continued disputes with the university, the canons of Lincoln, and the pope. None the less, his interest in mathematical studies and their immediate derivatives, optics for example, early gave a special character to Oxford studies, and these were pursued in turn by the Franciscan, Roger Bacon (*c.* 1214–92), who had been active at Paris during the Scholastic Controversy and may have played a part in stimulating it. Certainly his own writings were themselves the subject of considerable dispute. Bacon followed another of Grosseteste's interests, that of Greek studies.[36] Grosseteste was one of the first English scholars after the Norse invasions to attempt a revival of Greek, and his efforts at learning that language and subsequently translating some of Aristotle and a few patristic writers were remarkable achievements. Bacon went further: he wrote both Greek and Hebrew grammars, although nothing is known of any major translations by him from these two languages.

Interest in foreign languages was growing in this period; a decretal of Innocent IV in 1248 urged the training in theology at Paris of ten clerks already skilled in Arabic and other languages as preparation for missionary work on the frontiers of Christendom. In 1256 Humbert of Romans, a master-general of the Dominican order, repeated this idea in a plea for the study of oriental languages for precisely that purpose, mentioning Maronite (Syrian), Arabic and Prussian specifically; while in 1276 Raymond Lull successfully petitioned the king of Aragon for the establishment of Arabic language studies at Majorca.[37] These studies were, of course, thoroughly utilitarian, having no connection with the Oxford concern with Greek and Hebrew for the purposes of scholarship, and in this respect both Grosseteste and Bacon were ahead of their time, anticipating by a century the pioneer work of Petrarch.

The list of Oxford's important scholars in this period, moreover, is incomplete without mention of its most distinguished theologian, Johannes Duns Scotus (1264–1308). Duns' name, unfortunately, has received a wide popular currency in the word 'dunce', due to the vindictive attacks on him much later, in the early sixteenth century, by another Oxford scholar, William Tyndale (c. 1494–1536), whose reforming zeal, manifested chiefly in his English translation of the Bible, led him to attack Duns and his followers: 'Dunce's disciples,' he called them, and in this term he attempted to stigmatize the Scotists as dull and stupid. The attack came from Tyndale's impatience with Duns' very unusual and subtle style of thinking.

As his cognomen indicates, Duns came from Scotland, just north of the English border, in Roxburgh. Nothing is known of him till he appeared at Oxford, as a Franciscan, late in the thirteenth century; in 1302 he moved to the University of Paris and in 1307 went to Cologne where he died the following year. Duns was active in the period following the condemnations of Thomism – before Aquinas was canonized and his teachings given papal sanction – and he was responsible for developing what for many was a superior version of scholasticism. Duns put a premium on man's need to study the nature of god's being; he insisted that man cannot know god solely by rational means as Thomism argues. God's ultimate quality is not his reason but his will, and man can never come to know this by rational inquiry. For this reason Duns objected to the Thomist assertion that man's end is one of an intellectual vision of god; on the contrary, it must be one of man joined to the divine will by love. In his day Duns was known as the subtle doctor, 'Doctor Subtilis', and the later pejorative use of his name is as perverted a testimony as can be imagined.

Yet discussion of the famous scholars of early Oxford must not obscure the fact that, like their counterparts on the continent, the *studia* of Oxford and Cambridge were fundamentally educational institutions concerned with the more mundane tasks of preparing clerks to enter the service of church and crown. In doing this, these English *studia* followed closely the practice of Paris; there was indeed a very considerable movement of English scholars across the channel throughout the medieval centuries, particularly the thirteenth and fourteenth. The most obvious feature of the studies of both universities in England is that medicine was not taught; they concentrated on arts, theology and law, and of these three Oxford quickly became a leading centre for the study of theology, which received special distinction because of the concern shown there for the Greek scriptural and patristic sources and for their systematic collection.[38] Of major importance in this respect is the contribution of the Dominican, Robert Kilwardby (d. 1279). In his time at Oxford, after graduating master of arts at Paris and before his appointments in turn as archbishop of Canterbury in 1273 and cardinal bishop at Porto in Italy in 1278, Kilwardby advanced the study of theology and particularly the thought of Augustine. Using his considerable grammatical and logical knowledge, developed in the years at Paris, Kilwardby sought to provide students with means of theological study (*instrumenta studiorum*) and to do this he too resorted to some innovative pedagogical writing, producing his three-part guide to theology consisting of the *Intentio*, *Tabula* and *Concordantia*.[39] All three are concerned solely with the patristic *corpus*, the *intentiones* being a summary of the main topics and ideas, the *tabulae* being alphabetical indices of the content, and the last mentioned an alphabetical concordance of key words.[40] Kilwardby's work became a major textbook for the teaching of theology, not only at Oxford, but also at Paris.

We are much less well informed on the study of arts at Oxford and Cambridge, although in general there is no evidence of any departure from the Paris procedures. Students were admitted some time in adolescence – perhaps their fourteenth or fifteenth year – and followed the usual studies in grammar and logic through to the baccalaureate. Many of course failed to reach this level, and only a select few would have reached inception as a master of arts. In this respect, there is some hint of evidence that Oxford may have followed Italian practice and offered less demanding courses in *ars dictaminis* to provide the necessary training of clerks for the numerous secretarial positions that were being created in that period. Certainly some *ars dictaminis* was taught there in the first years of the fourteenth century: Richard de Bury promoted it at Oxford between 1302 and 1312 and in the same years a compilation of *dictamen* was circulating, the *Tractatus de litterarum composicione*.[41] Moreover, by the end of the fourteenth century there were two important such teachers there, John de Briggis and Thomas Sampson.[42] Yet the evidence is by no means conclusive and just how early the rhetorical tradition arrived at Oxford and how institutionally entrenched it became is still a matter for speculation – and controversy.[43]

One of the more interesting aspects of the basic concern to prepare educated clerks for the expanding society is the vexed status of the Oxford degree. Now Oxford claimed its right as a *studium generale* through tradition, *ex consuetudine*, and on the strength of this its degrees were accorded proper respect. But, in point of fact, Oxford had no papal charter, and therefore it had no legal right to confer the *jus ubique docendi*. Now, of course, when the early cathedral schools were in process of forming themselves into *studia*, formal chartering and licensing did not exist: these were subsequent regulatory procedures, but, when they were instituted, the ancient universities were motivated to secure these new legal sanctions. For Paris, recognition had come, in a sense, with the bull of 1231, *Parens scientiarum*, although a formal charter was not given till 1291, and all of the other European *studia* held either papal or royal charters – with the exception of Oxford. It seems, moreover, that throughout the thirteenth century the university made no effort to secure official recognition until 1296 when the bishops of Lincoln and Carlisle jointly approached Pope Boniface VIII, using in their request the precedent of Paris and the dubious claim that Oxford itself was a prior foundation, being in fact *fons et origo* of Paris.[44] The request was denied; twenty-one years later, in 1317, it was renewed, this time by King Edward II to Pope John XXII, and again it was turned down, although, rather astonishingly, the following year (1318) Cambridge received a charter.[45] Regrettably the circumstances are unknown; the puzzling fact remains that Oxford never was accorded any legal right to confer on any of its graduates the licence to teach.

The most distinctive feature of academic organization at both Oxford and Cambridge has always been their system of colleges, for these, as virtually independent foundations, are unique to the two universities. Again, early details are wanting, but one of the first to be founded was that endowed by Walter Merton some time before 1264.[46] Merton's intention was to bequeath his two manors for the support of scholars at Oxford,[47] chiefly for the provision of residences and perhaps for tutorial assistance although this latter provision is not explicit. Similar colleges were founded – University and Balliol in the thirteenth century; Exeter, Oriel and Queen's in the fourteenth – but none at Oxford in the years from 1340 to 1379. The position was similar at Cambridge where colleges were founded from the late thirteenth century into the first half of the fourteenth.

Suddenly, right at mid-century, academic acitivity at Oxford and Cambridge became markedly restricted and for a period of 150 years, a span corresponding almost exactly with that when Italy was the centre of great humanist activity – Petrarch to Pomponazzi – nothing of significance happened in either *studium*. The original decline around 1350 is generally attributed to the great plague of the previous year, and Cambridge appears to have been hit much harder than Oxford. In 1352 Corpus Christi was founded at Cambridge to train new scholars after the loss caused by the plague, but none thereafter until God's House (later retitled Christ's College) was founded in 1439 on the petition of William Byngham which argued that the realm of all England 'is like to be empeired and febled, by the defaute and lack of Scholemaistres of Gramer' and permission was thereby requested to found 'a mansion ycalled Goddishous the which he hath made and edified in your towne of Cambrigge for the free herbiage of poure Scolars of Gramer'.[48] God's House is, therefore, the first establishment in England, perhaps one of the first in Europe, intended specifically for the training of teachers.

Other English studia: *Northampton and Salisbury*

Oxford and Cambridge were not, however, the only places where *studia* were founded in England; there were at least two others, Northampton and Salisbury. Northampton is the more interesting for it is possible that it was in existence in the twelfth century and, through an emigration of its scholars, stimulated and strengthened the growth of Oxford. The evidence for Northampton as the site of a *studium* in the twelfth century, however, is even more slight than that for Oxford; the first significant reference comes from a citation for criminal action recorded in a document of about 1192 which concerns 'scolares de Norhamtone'.[49]

In documents from the later decades of the twelfth century there are several references to schools in the town, one of them concerning a dispute between two masters in the period around 1175–81. This particular record, apparently a rhetorical self-justification, was made by one of the contestants, Geoffrey de Vinsauf. In this document, *Causa magistri Gaufredi (The Plea of Master Geoffrey)*, we read that he has been deceived in his expectations of earning a living through teaching in the school of Northampton. This suit, nominally addressed to a high-ranking prelate – either the pope or the archbishop of Canterbury is implied – tells us that 'the undivided office I held was split up, lest I should be the only teacher and teach poorly, solely for my own profit'. The second master, formerly one of Geoffrey's colleagues in Paris, is now denigrated for being 'a low fellow from the North who could teach quarrelling better than anything else. He vexed me with insults; he terrorized my pupils; he upset the town with his errors; he was much given to making protests.' The suit continues in this tone, Geoffrey making it clear that he was mightily wronged: 'I was mild; he was fierce; I was guileless; he was violent: I was hurt; he inflicted the wound.'[50] What action was taken on his plea – 'who will avenge me?' – is unknown but it is interesting that the contretemps bears a striking similarity to one which erupted in Winchester some time between 1154 and 1159, involving the schoolmasters Jordan Fantosme and John Joichel. The letter of Archbishop Theobald to the pope concerning this latter case states that 'they both appeared before us, bringing a number of charges against each other'.[51] Such conflicts, and appeals to the ecclesiastical authorities, are symptomatic of the times. Clerks were jealous of the living to be obtained from school teaching, despite its low social status and poor pay, and frequently brought their suits to the licensing authority, who was generally the relevant bishop.

Geoffrey's evidence is reinforced by another contemporary reference, that of Daniel of Morley, who reports that the liberal arts, including the quadrivium, were flourishing at Northampton[52] and this, if we consider the criminal citation of *c.* 1192 issued on behalf of the 'scholars of

Northampton' gives some weight to the inference that Northampton had a developing *studium*. Again, its location has the same features as Oxford: on another main road north-west of London, in this case some seventy miles away, and beyond immediate episcopal supervision. The document of *c.* 1192, moreover, implies one of the ever-present 'town–gown' conflicts and it has been suggested that as a result the students of Northampton migrated to Oxford, thereby strengthening the latter in the very years when it suddenly emerged into prominence. But did this struggling *studium* of Northampton entirely disappear? There is the possibility that it did not, for some forty-six years later, in 1238, when there was a second *cessatio* at Oxford, owing to a dispute in which some students had been excommunicated, part of the student body repaired to Northampton,[53] where they remained firmly established for some decades. This, it can be argued, would only have been possible if a *studium* were already in existence there. In 1261 the *studium* at Northampton was given formal approval by Henry III,[54] but troubles continued to erupt. In 1264, after yet another town riot, when clerks from Oxford, which meanwhile was again operating, came to the assistance of their fellows at Northampton, the king threatened to hang them all, but his anger was mollified and the threat revoked. Northampton, however, was suppressed the following year (1265); acting on the advice of his academic advisers, the king ordered the university to dissolve.[55]

When the Oxford scholars dispersed in 1238, not all went to Northampton; others went south to Salisbury[56] where already there were some distinguished scholars among the cathedral chapter, and for the ensuing thirty – perhaps forty – years Salisbury seems to have been, in effect, a *studium generale*, whose chief interest was in theology.[57] This school struggled for existence, however, after the migrant scholars returned to Oxford some time between 1264 and 1279. Salisbury was unable thereafter to sustain itself as a *studium* – the precise reasons are unknown – and it soon fell into abeyance. Oxford and Cambridge remained, although they too were weakened. In the early decades of the fourteenth century there were some scholars of wide repute, chiefly William of Occam (*c.* 1300–*c.* 1349) and Thomas Bradwardine (*c.* 1290–1349). Occam was a Franciscan teacher at Oxford; Bradwardine, celebrated for his theological and mathematical scholarship, was educated at Oxford, but moved later into church administration, ending his career as archbishop of Canterbury. In the year he was consecrated he died of the plague. So too, in all likelihood, did Occam. With the sole exception of the highly controversial John

Wycliffe (*c.* 1330–84) no scholar of international significance is known in England until the late fifteenth century when humanism began to reach there from Italy.

The fourteenth century

Almonry and grammar schools

The initiative of the English universities in setting up grammar schools is well attested, and this stands in contrast to France where schools gave rise to universities. The early statutes of Merton College, for example, make provision for a teacher of grammar to be among the number of scholars,[58] clearly for conducting a grammar school. Walter Merton's generosity stands in considerable contrast to the widespread reluctance on the part of those responsible for providing schooling that is suggested by surviving documents for the fourteenth century. Other grammar schools were founded in the various university colleges, but after the plague their numbers show no significant increase until the early fifteenth century.

Schools undoubtedly suffered as a result of that great pestilence and the general economic decline it created, as well as from the social and political dislocation accompanying the Hundred Years War with France. Just how numerous the schools were, and how available any kind of learning was, is difficult to determine. Despite the fact that, from the twelfth century on, popes and bishops continually deprecated the charging of school fees, and local priests (and even bishops) were frequently ordered to provide free education, fee-charging evidently continued and it is equally certain that only a very small minority – much less than one per cent of the total population – attended school, being chiefly drawn from the growing, but still very small, class of townspeople. While it is tempting to believe that churches and monasteries gave schooling free of charge, this does not appear to have been the case. The only instances of charitable institutions are the almonry schools for which there are some thirteenth-century references,[59] but which belong more to the fourteenth century when they were established generally in Benedictine monasteries. The stimulus seems to have been the cessation of child oblation in the previous century which apparently encouraged the monastic houses to recruit some of their number from poorer people by opening free schools. There were, however, very few of these; one of the first recorded was set up at Ely in

1314, the second perhaps at St Albans around 1330.[60] Their enrolments, too, seem to have been small – less than a dozen in any one place, and as few as three or four.[61] A passing reference survives from Durham where a chronicler reports: 'Ther weare certaine poor children . . . which weare called children of the Aumery going daily to the Fermery schole.'[62] These schools taught chanting and perhaps provided an avenue for a grammar education for those boys sufficiently capable.

In addition to almonry schools the Benedictine houses also conducted regular claustral schools – which may have been merged together – this having been required of them by Pope Benedict XII when he issued revised Constitutions for the order in 1336. These, which he called schools of 'Primitive Sciences', because the designated studies, grammar, logic and philosophy, were propaedeutic to theology, apparently offered elementary instruction, grammar schooling and, for the advanced students, logic and philosophy up to bachelor of arts level at the universities, so as to enable the Benedictines, like the mendicant friars, to enter the university faculties of theology directly.

All of this raises a pertinent question concerning the social origins of such students. From whence did they come? It would be interesting to know how many came from the land since, by law, serfs were expressly forbidden to allow their daughters to be married away or their sons tonsured as this deprived the lord of his rightful property: the children of serfs had the legal status not of *familia* (family) but of *sequela*, that is, progeny or issue, the same as the animals born on the estate. So, by law, such children belonged to the lord.[63] None the less some agricultural workers did so assign their children and the manorial court rolls of England in the thirteenth and fourteenth centuries contain injunctions against the practice and records of their breach; in 1365, in just one of many examples,[64] a certain Richard was fined the considerable sum of forty pence for failing to recall his son from school where the boy was apparently preparing for some form of clerkship.[65] Fines such as these indicate that evasion of the laws occurred but the practice could not have been too widespread, simply because the closed nature of English society before 1350 would have made easy the detection and recovery of fugitives, and because, moreover, it would have been impossible for the religious orders and churches to have acted too widely or consistently against the law of the land. In 1349, none the less, the Statute of Labourers and Apprentices was specifically enacted to forbid serfs from attempting to raise the social status of their sons by sending them to school or allowing them to be apprenticed, for these forms of training opened the way to church positions and membership of guilds; both of these possibilities were considered by the ruling class to be undesirable. After the plague of 1349 and the Peasants' Revolt of 1381 the flight of servile children was easier, and this may have partly motivated a second royal statute of 1388 which again emphasized:

> It is ordained and assented. That he or she which used to labour at the plough and cart, or other Labour or Service of Husbandry till they be of Age of Twelve Years, that from thenceforth they shall abide at the same labour, without being put to any Mystery or Handicraft; and if any Covenant or Bond of Apprentice be from henceforth made to the Contrary, the same shall be holden for none.[66]

Education and learning: the literary evidence

England of the fourteenth century was very much a stratified society: the upper classes and most educated persons spoke French; the clerics and *literati* used Latin for intellectual and educational purposes; the peasants and townspeople spoke English dialects. Court records and other public documents were in either Latin or French; schoolboys translated from Latin into French, and English was considered an uncouth tongue. It was only in the late fourteenth century that English began to emerge as an acceptable language; in 1327 the monk Ralph Higden (d. 1364) complained in his *Polychronicon* that schoolboys had to construe – translate and analyse grammatically – their Latin into French. Not until 'the year of Our Lord 1385, in all the grammar schools [did] children leave French and construe and learn in English' according to Higden's younger contemporary and translator, John Trevisa.[67] But the English vernacular was by no means a universal vehicle of education; indeed, the evidence indicated that it was ill-regarded as a medium in comparison to Latin, and seems to have been used only because it had become entrenched as the mother tongue of so many children.

Middle English was not yet a literary language although it was beginning to gain this status through the activities of a number of writers, one of the most significant being Geoffrey Chaucer (*c.* 1343/4–1400). Employed as a royal official, Chaucer was appointed in 1374 Controller of Customs and Subsidy of Wools, Skins and Hides for the port of London, a minor position, but still with some degree of social standing, indicated by the fact that he was sent frequently on diplomatic missions for the crown both before and after the accession of Richard II in 1377. Although remembered chiefly for his *Canterbury Tales*, he wrote a large number of other poems in Middle English which, apart from their stature as some of the first significant examples of English vernacular writing, give a vivid picture of social customs in England in the late fourteenth century. As important as Chaucer is his contemporary, William Langland (*c.* 1362–*c.* 1399), but, while a lot is known about Chaucer the man, absolutely nothing is known of Langland except what can be inferred from his great poetic allegory, *The Vision of William Concerning Piers the Plowman*. In a rough parallel, Chaucer can be considered the Boccaccio of Middle English literature, Langland the Dante. Throughout their writings there are continued references to the state of learning in fourteenth-century England and from these we can gain a great deal of valuable insight into the educational thought and practices of the period.

In the first instance, though, it is essential to keep in mind the fact that education in England was totally in the hands of the church. Very few literate men in the fourteenth century would not have been in some form of holy orders, of which there were seven. The major three orders of bishop, priest and deacon were relatively few compared to the four minor orders, collectively called 'acolytes' and subdivided in descending order of rank, into acolyte proper, exorcist, lector and porter; and it was within this lower division that most clerics were to be found. So virtually all writings of this period come from the pens of clerics and England can be considered as consisting of two groups: the literate few and the illiterate masses. The clergy, considered as a whole, had every possible level of competence, from Roger Bacon and Robert Grosseteste down to complete ignoramuses like the priest who, upon reading in his missal the phrase 'Te igitur clementissime Pater' (literally, 'Of thee, therefore, most merciful Father . . . '), preached a sermon in which he explained that Te Igitur was the name of St Clement's father.[68] In making a distinction between the literate and the illiterate it is important to put probably the great majority of those in minor orders in the latter group. Most people in England in this period, therefore, as for all ancient and medieval times, were in literary terms necessarily mute; they had no voice and we learn nothing from them directly. Our knowledge comes solely from writings by the literate and from court and manorial records.

Both Chaucer and Langland reflect this educated bias in writing of the intellectual climate of their day. Chaucer was from a middle-class family of wine merchants and had received a courtly education from clerics;

Langland, clearly a man of literary genius, was in minor orders and earned a meagre existence in London saying prayers – for a pittance paid by relatives – for departed souls. Each was deeply concerned about the abuse of learning by clerics who were in a privileged position, but their approaches were different: Chaucer chose a ribald, robust satire – with its elegant and subtle touches – as the style for his *Canterbury Tales*; Langland wrote intensely and urgently, finding no space for lightness or humour. However, the major theme of *Piers Plowman*, and a constant refrain in the *Canterbury Tales*, is this concern for the condition of the church and the state of the clergy.

Langland makes it quite clear in many places that the common people suffer a great deprivation. They cannot even read their scriptures; indeed the Latin text humiliates them, and is a constant reminder of their ignorance:

> Thanne Scripture scorned me . . .
> And lakked me in Latyne.[69]

In another place, a simple cloth dealer's assistant excuses his ignorance by stating that he never learned to read and cannot understand the educated tongue of French because he comes from far-off rural Norfolk:

> I lerned never rede on boke
> And I can no Frenche in feith · but of the ferthest ende of Norfolke.[70]

Against this can be contrasted the avarice of friars who go to school to learn logic and law so as to prove that all earthly property should be shared in common,[71] and we are left in no doubt that this is an abuse of learning. The general disorder of the clergy, in fact, is a major theme in the allegory; early in the *Prologue* Langland writes of a 'heap' of hermits, with hooked staves, en route to Walsingham, accompanied by their concubines:

> Hermites on an heep · with hoked staves,
> Wenten to Walsyngham · and here wenches after . . .[72]

and this theme recurs throughout.

Langland's criticisms, of course, were not isolated; already Lollardy was a growing intellectual, although not yet popular, force, and there are numerous contemporary criticisms of clerical laxity, usually written by other religious. It was standard exhortatory procedure for the church leaders to constantly reprove the clergy and the common people and this can be found as easily in the writings of Aquinas and Bacon as in those of local priests. The highly educated clergy were, of course, more elegant in their turn of phrase; Aquinas wrote of 'the inexperience of many priests, who in some parts are found to be so ignorant that they cannot speak Latin, and among whom very few are found who have learnt Holy Scripture'.[73] Roger Bacon was not so restrained. At least, however, we can admire the tremendous vigour of his torrent of denunciation in the *Compendium studii philosophiae*, where he fulminates against a 'whole clergy intent upon pride, lechery and avarice' as well as against 'certain men [who] have arisen in the universities who have created themselves masters and doctors in theology and philosophy, though they themselves have never learned anything of account'.[74]

At the other end of the scale there were simpler exhortations such as that by Mirk, prior of Lilleshall in Shropshire around the year 1400, who urged his priests to be chaste and well spoken, to give up drunkenness, gluttony and lechery; to keep out of taverns, wrestling and archery contests; to be soberly and fully clothed, shaved and tonsured: the catalogue is quite lengthy. He ends with the injunction

> And of the Day of Dome have drede;
> And evere do gode agheynes [in return for] evele,
> Or elles thow myghte not lyve wele.[75]

Another writer – unknown to us – wrote more bluntly, around 1382, about the corruption and worldliness of friars:

> I have lyved now fourty yers
> And fatter men about the neres [paunch]
> Yit sawe I never than these frers
> In contreys ther thai rayke [wander].[76]

And this is borne out by the indolent clergy's own productions in the Goliard literature where appetite, both visceral and libidinal, is one of their major preoccupations. As one monk put his erotic fancies:

> Much too hard, it is, I find
> So to change my essence
> As to keep a virgin mind
> In a virgin's presence.[77]

Another, how vicariously we cannot tell, but ascribed to Abelard, describes his amatory encounter:

> The wiles of Venus
> Grow slyer and slyer –
> She cloaks her fierceness,
> Her hand creeps nigher –
> Before we know it
> The fat's in the fire.[78]

And in harmony with this is the poem of a young nun – so anyway is the alleged authorship according to the source, Orderic Vitalis – who wrote:

> All Abbesses deserve to die
> Who order subject nuns to lie
> In dire distress on lonely bed
> Only for giving love its head.
> I speak who know, for I've been fed
> For loving, long on stony bread.[79]

It was this worldliness that Chaucer satirized so exquisitely in the *Canterbury Tales*. His monk, for example, while competent to have been an abbot, was more concerned with his stable of fine horses, his greyhounds and the hunt, which he preferred to follow rather than 'upon a book in cloystre alwey to poure'.[80] The monk, moreover, wore robes trimmed – expressly against the rules – with costly grey squirrel fur, 'and that the fyneste of a lond', while his hood was fastened 'under his chyn [with] gold wroght ful curious pyn: A love knotte in the gretter ende ther was'.[81] Likewise is the prioress, Madame Eglentyne, depicted. She is indeed an elegant character; modest of speech, dainty of deportment. Yet in dress, 'Ful semely hir wympel pynched was, [and] she hadde fair forheed – It was almoost a spanne brood I trowe.'[82] To understand the significance of this observation it is necessary to read the Rule of her order which existed at the time, in a Middle English version which the prioress most certainly would have known well:

> Thay sal be clede ful wele, . . .
> Efter ther place es cald or hate . . .
> And al it sal be purvayed playne.[83]

The express intention is for nuns to be fully clothed, whether their cloister is cold or hot, and the habit must be plain. The prioress however, exposed her forehead – a very erotic piece of anatomy to the medieval mind – a full hand's span, having pleated her wimple, that medieval headress, in coquettish fashion so as to reveal her face as fully as possible rather than to conceal it, which was the express purpose of that veil-like covering. Moreover, like the monk, she too affected costume jewellery: to the end of her rosary beads was attached 'a brooch of gold ful sheene, on which ther was first writen a crowned A, and after it *Amor vincit omnia*'.[84] The significance of the gold brooch and its motto 'Love conquers everything' lies in the fact that the Latin *amor* meant profane as well as spiritual love.

Such a clergy was an affront to church and society; not only were they worldly, they lacked even the saving grace of some educational achieve-ment. Surviving statistics from early fourteenth-century Exeter, which was one of the best administered (and recorded) dioceses in England, show that during the incumbency of Bishop Stapledon, there were only twenty-five university graduates in the whole of the diocese; men, that is, with at least the minimum of the master's degree in arts.[85] Langland again illustrates this laxity when he writes in *Piers Plowman* of a priest, presented as a generic type, who has been ordained for thirty years yet can neither read the solfa musical notation nor chant the offices, nor can he read the saint's lives, or even a line of canon law:

> I have be prest and parsoun · passynge thretti wynter,
> Yet can I neither solfe ne synge · ne seyntes lyves rede,
> ... in canoun ne in the decretales · I can noughte rede a lyne,[86]

and this is repeated elsewhere:

> Ne nought on[e] amonge an hundreth · that an auctor can construe,
> Ne rede a lettre in any language.[87]

Against this prevailing image Langland, and Chaucer to a lesser extent, put up a normative vision of the good clerk, one who pursues the religious life with dedication. In Chaucer he appears as the scholar of Oxford, a man of abstemious – even ascetic – demeanour who is chiefly engrossed with learning:

> A Clerk ther was of Oxenford also
> That unto logyk hadde longe ygo.
> As leene was his hors as is a rake
> And he nas nat right fat I undertake.

This lean appearance, we read, was due to his lack of concern with worldly advancement and his preference, instead, for books:

> For hym was levere have at his beddes heed
> Twenty bookes clad in blak or reed
> Of Aristotle and his philosophye.

This clerk was totally reserved, studious, and careful of utterance:

> Sowynge in moral vertu was his speche
> And gladly wolde he lerne and gladly teche.[88]

In Langland, the true cleric is the character Piers Plowman himself, in the successive roles of farmer, priest and bishop as he progresses from the kingdom of England to the kindom of Heaven; it is the education of both Piers and William – a composite picture – that illustrates the worthy clerical life, and in the process the author describes the educational practices of the day. Langland's account begins with the fact that his father and friends provided the fees for his schooling: 'Whanne ich yong was, my fader and my frendes founden me to schole,'[89] and at this point, perhaps in his seventh year, he would have been tonsured as an acolyte.

Chaucer's Prioress's Tale provides additional evidence here, in which the activities of a 'litel scole of cristen folk'[90] are discussed. Located ostensibly in Asia, the model is clearly that of a contemporary English school where a widow's son 'a litel clergeon, seven yeer of age'[91] daily is taught his first prayers and hymns, learning,

> . . . to syngen and to rede,
> As smale children doon in hir childhede.[92]

For reading he uses a primer and an antiphonary – an elementary prayer book and type of hymnal respectively – these books, both in Latin, being learned by rote, without understanding, in preparation for church services. Seeking the meaning of the Latin, the young 'clergeon' – that is, cleric – asks an older student who gives a brief explanation of the meaning of the hymn *Alma redemptoris*, excusing himself with the statement

> I kan [can] nomoore expounde in this matere;
> I lerne song, I kan [know] but smal grammere.[93]

This evidence suggests that in the song school children at first learned to read Latin by rote, only later having the meaning of the Latin words explained in the vernacular – 'I' expounden hym this song in his langage'. The next stage, that of studying the Latin text itself – 'to construe and declare' – was not pursued in the song school; that was the task of the grammar school. In teaching the absolute beginner to read, the standard methods of antiquity were used, commencing with the separate letters of the alphabet. In this respect, some very interesting evidence has survived in the form of alphabet wall tiles. These, of some three or four inches square, were embossed and coloured individually with letters of the alphabet and set into the surfaces of the walls in medieval churches in the manner of a dado or frieze, and from them the child often gained his first acquaintance with letters.[94] At this time the so-called 'horn-book' may have made its appearance. This was a wooden bat, with a handle and thong, that could be hung up when not in use. On the surface of the bat was pasted some copy, usually the alphabet, the ten numerals and a few maxims or prayers. Its name came from the practice of covering the copy with a fine layer of transparent animal horn to retard excessive wear.

The grammar school, though, was always the focus of activities: without Latin, no progress could be made. 'Gramer [is] the grounde of al'[95] wrote Langland, and this is underscored in the stricture of Holy Church herself to him, for in adult life William regretted his lack of application:

> To litel latyn thou lernedest · led, in thi youthe;
> *Heu michi, quod sterilem duxi vitam iuuenilem!*[96]

– 'Oh what a barren life I led as a child.' The whole vision of *Piers Plowman* is supported by the belief that man's purpose in life should be one of devout religiosity, and this is secured for many by application to study. Both Chaucer and Langland held scholarship in the highest regard and their criticisms of the religious, who held a monopoly, are strongly felt and vigorously presented expressions of concern for what they considered a flagrant misuse of a precious stewardship. The clerical laxity, by now in popular opinion being equated with corruption, and fanned by the trenchant criticisms of such men as Wycliffe, makes a heightened contrast with the inability of many to gain any access to learning whatsoever.

It would be a mistake, however, to assert either that a majority of persons actually sought learning, or, on the other hand, that literacy was rarely attained at all in fourteenth-century England. Probably the majority of labourers had neither need of, nor appreciation for, any book learning. Moreover, a likely explanation of the clerical disregard was the inability of the predominantly agricultural economy to carry as many educated persons as it did. Indeed, some further evidence from Chaucer may be useful here: his use of the terms 'learning', 'schools', 'books' and 'writing' is revealing: in his total published work, and not only the *Canterbury Tales*, the word 'scholar(s)' appears only five times, of which three instances are qualified as 'poure scoler'; the term 'school(s)' is used twenty-three times. On the other hand, 'book(s)' and 'read' in their various forms occur much more frequently – of the order of one or two hundred – giving the impression that books were available rather freely and that reading was a more widespread attainment than the heightened protests of William Langland – who after all was pleading an impassioned case – might indicate, and that this facility was gained, in all probability, outside schools, or at least in institutions that did not rate as such. This interpretation is supported by his use of the words 'write', 'writing' and 'written' – these, when they occur, are generally synonyms for books. When Chaucer does refer to the skill of writing he always links it to a person of explicitly learned status, such as a clerk.[97]

The fifteenth century

Development of grammar schools

In the fifteenth century England entered a phase of commercial expansion and the demands for an increase in educational attainment by a larger number of persons could not be met by the song or almonry schools. Their continued existence into this century is documented to a limited extent, and a change in their specific function seems evident. Some song schools added the study of grammar, and there are suggestions that some grammar schools may have added the song school function, that of giving elementary instruction in reading but not specifically for church purposes, to their basic activities of teaching grammar.[98] Likewise, the almonry schools appear to have operated on a very restricted basis; while Norwich had fourteen scholars at the end of the century, the numbers elsewhere were much smaller: Leicester had six in 1440, and other monasteries had as few as two or three.[99] What did expand rather rapidly, in distinct contrast, was the Latin grammar school.

In 1387 the actual English vernacular phrase 'grammar scole' appears to have been used for the first time in John of Trevisa's translation of Higden's *Polychronicon*,[100] and with it is expressed also the concept: by the early fifteenth century the idea of the grammar school in England was quite widely developed. Some curious early testimony to this is the Cambridge degree, first heard of in 1399, of master of grammar. The requirements for this degree were less stringent than those for the master of arts: the rhetoric and philosophy elements were shortened or eliminated altogether, the content consisting chiefly in knowledge of grammar sufficient to teach in the developing grammar schools.[101] In October of that year, 1399, the archbishop of London appointed Thomas Barym 'master in grammar' to the charge of the school of St Mary-le-Bow.[102] At the same time guild schools, and transactions associated with them, appear in the records, one of the earliest of these being a record of a church guild, the Guild of the Holy Cross, in 1401–2, showing a payment by John Scholemayster for rent of a chamber in Stratford-upon-Avon.[103]

In 1405–6 existing barriers to the education of peasants were removed by a statute of Henry IV which effectively nullified the provisions of the Statute of Labourers and Apprentices of 1349. By this new act, written not in Latin but in French, parents of any social standing whatever ('de quele estate ou condicion qil soit') were enabled to apprentice their children, if they held lands with an annual rental value of at least twenty shillings, although the statute included the liberal provision that,

> Provided always, that every man or woman, of any social status at all, shall be free to set their son or daughter to study in whatever school they care to choose within the kingdom.[104]

Serfdom was now no legal barrier to education in England; moreover it is significant that this statute made no restrictions on the type of school. All schools up to this time were church controlled and staffed, but the way was clear for attendance at secular schools. In 1432 such a school was supported near London by the action of William Sevenoaks who bequeathed a legacy as an act of charity for the needy and poor to

> . . . find and maintain for every one a Master; an honest man, sufficiently advanced and expert in the science of grammar and a Bachelor in Arts, by no means in holy orders [*infra sacros ordines minime constitutum*] to keep a Grammar School in some convenient house within the said town of Sevenoaks with my goods . . . to teach and instruct all poor boys whatsoever coming there for the sake of learning, taking nothing of them or their parents or friends for the teaching and instructing them.[105]

Throughout the fifteenth century the foundations of schools continued, seeking to provide for all social classes, in a number of studies. After 1428 the boy-king Henry VI was educated in a palace school, to which other sons of the nobility were invited, which may have been modelled on Vittorino's Casa Giocosa, established in 1423.[106] If this were the case, it indicates the growing influence of Italy on England. Henry VI, in turn, founded Eton college in 1440, to have 'four clerks and six chorister boys whose duty it shall be to serve divine worship there daily, and twenty-five poor and needy scholars whose duty it shall be to learn grammar',[107] although Henry's provisions were subverted later by Edward IV who withdrew its endowment and allowed it to become an aristocratic preserve. In London the expansion is clearly evident. For 300 years, since the mid-twelfth century, only the three schools of St Paul's, St Martin's and St Mary's were authorized. However, in 1446, because there were by then a number of clandestine schools operating, conducted by 'many and divers persons not sufficiently instruct in gramer, presumynge to hold commune [public] grammer scoles, in great deceipte',[108] the king's chancellor was empowered to issue authority for two more schools, St Dunstan's and St Anthony's. The following year, four more petitions to open schools were received from London parsons and at least one was allowed; the success of three of them is not known. Within the claustral schools further improvements were sought and a Benedictine chapter of 1444 required in their schools a master who could teach the 'primitive sciences' (*sciencias primitivas*) of grammar, logic and philosophy as set out in Benedict XII's revised Constitutions of 1336, more than a century before. If such a master could not be obtained, the schools were to be put in charge of a master who could at least teach grammar.[109] This movement towards founding and improving schools continued and met with some success so that by the end of the fifteenth century schools had increased in number throughout England. About 1502 a Sir John Percyvall left money in his will to establish a free grammar school at Macclesfield in Cheshire since 'right fewe Techers and scolemaisters ben in that contre, wherebye many children for lake of such techyng an draught in conyng fall to Idlenes, and so consequently live disolutely all their dayes'.[110]

The foundation of schools in England during the fifteenth century, however vigorous it may appear from the surviving records – and in this respect it must be remembered that England is better documented for this period than any other European country – was not an operation of any great magnitude. The bulk of children, tied to the land (*ascriptae glebae*) and to serfdom, received no instruction at all, and the song and grammar schools were few in number and generally minuscule in enrolment. What learning was given must have been minimal and achieved at great cost. The most widely used schoolbooks were those perennial survivors, the *Ars minor* of Donatus and the more recent (1199) *Doctrinale* of Alexander de Villa Dei. When printing from movable type took hold after the mid-fifteenth century these books were given a much wider circulation. Classroom procedures were generally standardized: the rules and paradigms of Latin words were memorized by chanting, and throughout the long school day, lasting ten hours as a rule – the boys seated on forms with no bench or table – these rote achievements were expanded. They were applied in various syntactical constructions in the morning, and studied in various passages of classical poetry that were set for afternoon work.

The use of physical punishment

The pedagogical futility of this kind of procedure was somewhat obscured, and the system prevented from collapse, by a brutal and frequent resort to punishment with the birch. Indeed the bundle of birch rods was a necessary element of all teaching, and medieval school seals and woodcuts from printed books often depict the master or his usher holding or applying the birch rod as a symbol of authority. Physical coercion was not considered abnormal and it was, moreover, quite consonant with the general religious acceptance of bodily mortification, including flagellation. Church practice approved it under certain circumstances and canon lawyers gave favourable rulings. There was, however, a fine line of distinction to be drawn. Striking of clerics by others generally was forbidden, under pain of excommunication, and this was in part due to the need to preserve the safety of the unarmed religious. They could be corporally chastised under specific circumstances, but the blows had to be administered with just cause and under proper authority. John of Salisbury gives an interesting account of the promulgation of relevant decretals in his memoirs of the papal court, *Historia pontificalis*, for the year 1148. He relates that in the Curia

> . . . there was also some doubt about the precise application of the canon that anyone who had laid violent hands on clerks, monks, lay-brethren or nuns must go to the pope for absolution. But the pope made his intention clear by saying that this canon was not to be applied to those who committed such violence in the performance of their just duty.[111]

John gives several examples of legal propriety and points out:

> . . . the canon would not apply if a master in the schools [*doctor in scolis*] struck his pupil, or one pupil another, or one monk another monk, or one lay-brother another, or the head of a household his son or servant. For it is more desirable to settle such matters in the schools or cloisters [*in scolis uel claustris*] than to provide an excuse for the idle and dissolute to roam about under pretext of going to the pope.[112]

This became the general position and in the early fourteenth century we read in a theological dictionary which drew from these canons and subsequent affirmations, that 'a master in the schools may chastise or beat his disciple, even though this latter be a clerk, provided only that he exceed not due measure'. The same passage makes it explicit that clerics

may be beaten with rods and that the master runs no risk of excommunication, 'if the chastisement be for discipline's sake'.[113] The acceptance of
the practice of corporal punishment into academic life is symbolized by the
mime of 'palming' which constituted part of the ceremony of inception as
master of grammar at Cambridge in the early fifteenth century. The
incepting master was required to strike – with what force we do not know –
a boy across the palm with a broad bat provided by the bedell for the
purpose, an act reminiscent of the dubbing of a knight with sword taps
on the shoulders. In return for his services, the boy was paid the then
large sum of four pence.[114]

There is abundant evidence for these practices in the schools, but none
is more directly informative than *Piers Plowman* where we read that, while
the better the child the more benefit there is to be gained from teaching
him, it is important to beware of maudlin sentiment of childhood indulgence. So, in one of its many Latin quotes, the poem warns:

> *Qui parcit virge, odit filium*
> The Englich of this latyn is · who-so wil it knowe,
> Who-so spareth the sprynge · spilleth his children.[115]

'Discipline', of course, was interpreted to mean enforcing followership
and so the use of the rod, birch bundle or 'palming-bat' was quite consonant
with the legal position. Again in *Piers Plowman*, it is stated very clearly that
the master birched ('baleised') his class for failure to learn:

> And bette hem with a baleis · but if thei wolde learne,[116]

the birch, he points out, being applied not only to the palms of the
hands, but also to the bare buttocks:

> And baleised on the bare ers · and no breche bitwene.[117]

Given these circumstances, then, we should not be at all surprised to read
in the Oxford Coroners' Roll for 1301 the account of an inquest into
'John de Neushom, clerk and schoolmaster, found dead by Cherwell bank,
hard by Petty Pont', the tragedy, it seems, having happened when John

> went after dinner seek rods for the chastisement of the boys whom he taught,
> and climbed upon a certain willow to cut such rods . . . where by mis-
> adventure he fell into the water and was drowned.[118]

It would be very informative to know what the pupil's responses were
to John's demise, and perhaps some indication might be gained from this
very eloquent – and anonymous – lament from a later fifteenth-century

writer, although he could hardly have penned it in his youth; perhaps it is
a retrospect:

> Hay, hay, by this day,
> What vayleth it me thowgh I say nay?
>
> I wold fayn be a clarke,
> But yet hit is a strange werke;
> The byrchyn twygges be so sharpe
> Hit makith me have a faynt harte;
>   What vayleth it me thowgh I say nay?
>
> On Monday in the mornyng whan I shall rise,
> At vi of the clok, hyt is the gise,
> To go to skole without avise,
> I had lever go twenti myle twyse;
>   What vayleth it me thowgh I say nay?
>
> My master lokith as he were madde:
> 'Wher hast thou be, thou sory ladde?'
> 'Milked dukkes, my moder badde.'
> Hit was no mervayle thow I were sadde;
>   What vayleth it me thowgh I say nay?
>
> My master pepered my ars with well good spede;
> Hit was worse than fynkyll sede;
> He wold not leve till it did blede;
> Mych sorow have he for his dede!
>   What vayleth it me thowgh I say nay?
>
> I wold my master were a watt,
> And my boke a wyld catt,
> And a brase of grehowndes in his toppe;
> I wolde be glade for to se that.
>   What vayleth it me thowgh I say nay?
>
> I wold my master were an hare,
> And all his bokes houndes were,
> And I myself a joly hontere;
> To blow my horn I wold not spare,
> For if he were dede I wold not care.
>   What vayleth it me thowgh I say nay?[119]

Yet even this experience of learning, repugnant as it must have been even
in an age much more accustomed to brutality, was restricted to a minority.
As late as 1500 a Venetian travelling in England made an interesting

commentary in a letter home, on the more likely lot of the middle-class child, when he observed:

> The want of affection in the English is strongly manifested towards their children: for after having kept them at home till they arrive at the age of 7 or 9 years at the utmost, they put them out, both males and females, to hard service in the houses of others . . . and few are born who are exempted from this fate, for everyone however rich he may be, sends away his children into the houses of others, while he, in return, receives those of strangers into his own.[120]

Introduction of humanism: the new scholarship

Stimulus to change, that is to humanist learning, came from the two universities of Oxford and Cambridge. Following their long period of torpor the universities, particularly Oxford, began to revive in the first decades of the fifteenth century, probably as a consequence in the first instance of the influence of the Council of Constance. That gathering had been attended by many of the great scholars of Italy, including Chrysoloras, Poggio and Bruni; in one sense it could be called a council of humanists. By 1400 Greek studies, in terms of the record, appear to have died out in England; contact with humanists at Constance led to renewed interest. The first conspicuous figure in this movement was the profligate, dissolute Humphrey, duke of Gloucester (1390–1447), one of the major peers of the realm and for a time regent during Henry VI's infancy.[121] In his political career Humphrey was outmanœuvred and finally discredited and perhaps assassinated; his memory is now sustained for his services to education. Always a keen intellectual, he began collecting books and manuscripts early in life; later when his political career began to falter, Humphrey turned to this interest with greater vigour. In 1434 he inquired after books by Guarino and Bruni for his library and later commissioned Pier Candido Decembrio to prepare for him a Latin translation of Plato's *Republic*. These instances are but two of many contacts with Italian humanism made by Humphrey. In 1439 he commenced his great benefactions; having already donated some books to Oxford, he now presented the university with 120 volumes and in 1444 sent a further 135 volumes.[122] These works covered a number of subjects then commonly taught in universities: theology, philosophy, history, medicine, astrology; they included as well works by leading humanists – Dante, Petrarch, Boccaccio. In addition to these activities Humphrey was instrumental in bringing to

England, for visits, Lapo da Castiglionchio and Antonio Beccaria. To this day, Duke Humphrey's benefaction remains in use at Oxford in the original building, now a wing of the Bodleian.

Meanwhile other Italian humanists were travelling in England, Poggio Bracciolini for example, and many English scholars were studying in Italy, particularly at Padua, Vercelli, Vicenza and at Bologna, where there was an English 'nation'. During the fifteenth century numerous Englishmen travelled and studied throughout Italy, of whom the most prominent were the Oxford scholars John Tiptoft, William Grey, John Free, Robert Flemmyng and John Gunthorpe. All of these studied with Guarino of Verona, and his son Battista Guarino approved the scholarly migrations, recording that students were coming even from far-off Britain.[123] The most conspicuous of these men was John Tiptoft, earl of Worcester, who had the financial means to become both a great collector of manuscripts – an interest stimulated by his first experiences in Italy at Padua – and a patron of other Englishmen in acquiring humanist learning. This first wave of scholars was followed by the next generation, later in the fifteenth century, among them William Selling who studied at Padua and Bologna, and translated into Latin a work by John Chrysostom, in turn influencing his student Thomas Linacre. The latter was one of a group of Oxford friends which included William Grocin and William Latimer, a trio responsible for the re-establishment of Greek studies in England and for the firm transplanting of humanism in the years around 1500.

Thomas Linacre (c. 1460–1524), after a period as student and fellow of All Souls College, Oxford, went in 1485 to Rome, accompanying Selling who at the time was ambassador to the papal court. Linacre busied himself with humanist studies, including philological work with Greek manuscripts, and studied for a time with Politian, a leading teacher of the day, as did Grocin and Latimer. In Venice, Linacre met Aldus Manutius who stimulated further his interest in Greek studies; Aldus interested Linacre in preparing translations from the Greek for the Aldine press. Linacre's interests were in scriptural criticism and medicine, and some twenty years later he translated three works of Galen from Greek into Latin for Aldus.[124] When Linacre returned from Italy in 1494, he began teaching Greek at Oxford, later becoming a royal tutor, and while furthering his interests in medicine helped found the Royal College of Physicians in London.

William Grocin (c. 1446–1519) was equally influential in reviving Greek studies at Oxford although much of his life is obscure; the total of his surviving works seems to be his will and a letter to Aldus. His library books were taken by Thomas Linacre, the executor of his estate, to Oxford where many of them found their way into college libraries.[125] The list of Grocin's books that were lodged in Merton is itself a record of the changed condition of learning at Oxford – if Merton can be considered at all representative. A Merton catalogue of *c.* 1320 records 25 titles, all Latin versions of Aristotle or expositions of his works; a catalogue of philosophy books in 1375 gives 91 titles, again of Aristotle and commentaries, but including one work each by Euclid, Ptolemy and Grosseteste; yet another list for 1437 of 38 titles is only of Latin texts and these of wide variety – Aquinas, Isidore, Scotus and Augustine are mentioned along with a large number of other kinds of expositions and commentaries.[126] The list of Grocin's books, 54 in all, although 23 are duplicate copies, provides a strong contrast: they are all Greek manuscripts, their content ranging from introductory grammars to Platonic dialogues; it includes works by Chrysostum, Aristotle, Basil, Boethius, Porphyry, Thucydides and Euclid.[127] Grocin's books, of course, represent a personal interest and are therefore only a sample of a much wider range of available literature. By the end of the fifteenth century, partly because of the readier availability of printed editions, books on a wide variety of topics, both in Latin and Greek, were in use.[128]

The new learning in England was far less secular than in Italy; indeed the entire spirit of English humanism was concerned to ameliorate many of the austerities of scholasticism and to replace its aridities with what the period considered to be more meaningful doctrines; the temper of the English movement remained decidedly linked to Christianity and the church.[129] Throughout the whole period of Italian, and now European, humanism, one of the most distinctive characteristics of the humanist movement had been a constant and deep concern for education; the greatest scholars had considered it entirely proper and indeed necessary for them to write not only on lofty themes but also on the problems of school organization, order of studies, methods of teaching, and the behaviour of children. Many of these scholars even bent their efforts to furthering educational reforms by themselves teaching and by writing textbooks which they considered to be improvements. And, in all Europe, this movement received its most vigorous implementation in England, particularly after Grocin and Linacre had prepared the way. In the efforts of their three most distinguished students – Colet, Erasmus, More – the application of humanism to the support of Christianity and improvement of education reaches its highest level.

CHAPTER II

Christian Humanism: I. Desiderius Erasmus and the Ideal of Piety

By the late fifteenth century humanism had become quite widely disseminated across western Europe as the dominant intellectual style. Yet, despite enthusiastic acceptance by many of the educated persons of Europe, it had not penetrated into the schools to any significant extent. Then, early in the sixteenth century, educational thought and practice were to receive a tremendous fillip from two of the greatest personalities in the history of Western civilization: Desiderius Erasmus and Martin Luther. Between them – although they worked apart and even, in some respects, in opposition – they were responsible for making education, at the levels of both ideology and practice, into a major preoccupation of rulers and influential citizens. Each was motivated primarily by religious issues and saw education, particularly the humanist programme, as a ready instrument by which faith could be promoted, strengthened and maintained. As a consequence of their efforts, humanism, in its Christian version with an emphasis on piety, swept the last vestiges of scholasticism aside and became established, unchallenged, in virtually all of the schools and universities of Europe.

Erasmus of Rotterdam

Life and education to 1500

In this new promotion of humanism as an instrument for the advancement of faith, Desiderius Erasmus (*c.* 1466–1536) was the prior figure. In his lifetime he became one of the most influential persons in Europe, being in every sense a universal citizen, travelling continually across the continent and devoting his energies to the *studia humanitatis*, particularly to the study of Latin, the international language of scholars. Some of his closest links were with England where he obtained much of the support his style of life needed, particularly in the early years of his career, and it was there that the most direct results of his efforts at educational reform were achieved.

Details of his early life are wanting, perhaps because Erasmus was always particularly sensitive to his illegitimate birth, and his concern to mitigate this distasteful fact led to a certain vagueness in his own accounts. Born around 1466 to the priest Gerard of Gouda and a widow, Margaret, he was baptized Erasmus (from the Greek *erasmios*, 'beloved' or 'desired') and in adult life latinized this to Desiderius, acquiring the tautological name by which he remained known.[1] His addition of the city of his birth produced the full version by which he frequently styled himself: Desiderius Erasmus Roterodamus. As a child he was instructed first at Gouda and then at Deventer, where he was enrolled in St Lebuin's school conducted by Alexander Hegius, and where he was influenced by the Brethren of the Common Life, although it is not clear whether he attended one of their schools.[2] Certainly Erasmus thought well of Hegius and St Lebuin's, while the influence on him of the Brethren seems mainly to have been his acquisition of a violent antipathy towards their scholastic methods, the sterilities of their lesson content and the brutality of their coercive discipline.[3] By 1486 Erasmus became a member of the Augustinian Canons, a quasi-monastic order given church approval in 1059, and organized according to the ancient Rule of Augustine of Hippo; in 1492 he was ordained priest, but he seems to have accepted his entry into the priesthood with little enthusiasm. Considering the circumstances of his life, however, there was little alternative open, particularly since he demonstrated an intellectual precocity that only a career in letters could satisfy. Unlike his later friends, Colet and More, Erasmus had no wealthy family connections to provide an alternative way.

14 Boy being birched, initial from English manuscript, mid-fourteenth century.

13 A drinking monk, initial from late thirteenth-century manuscript.

15 Erasmus, charcoal drawing by Dürer, 1520.

16 John Colet, drawing by Hans Holbein, 1530s.

Erasmus was introduced to the world of humanism in Paris where he went in 1494 to study theology. Although disappointed with both the city and university, where he cut short his studies, he made the acquaintance there of the young English nobleman William Blount, Lord Mountjoy. This encounter developed into a firm friendship, and in 1499 Erasmus visited Blount in England, as his guest. In London, as a consequence, Erasmus made the further acquaintance of two like-minded persons, Thomas More (1478–1535) and John Colet (1466–1519), and this period marked the beginning for Erasmus of strong interests in education and humanist scholarship. More was young – twelve years junior to Erasmus – and still unknown, but already he was becoming attracted to both religion and humanism. The son of a judge, More had been a brilliant under-graduate, and after leaving Oxford in 1494 at the age of sixteen, studied law in London at Lincoln's Inn. The Inns of Court at this time were becoming concerned with the liberal arts, providing a metropolitan centre for studies to balance the relative isolation of Oxford and Cambridge.[4] Colet was the same age as Erasmus, and like More he came from a highly respected London family, had excelled at Oxford and, after graduating in 1490, also travelled in Europe, particularly in Italy where he studied Greek with Politian. In 1496 Colet was ordained and commenced ten years at Oxford where he composed and delivered his most important lectures.[5]

Early concern with education

Erasmus expressed his concern with humanism as the basis of education as early as 1947 when he wrote, in a letter to Thomas Grey, that good authors form the mind well, while lascivious and indecent ones have an opposite effect. To secure the worthiest purposes of learning 'of these good authors you [should] read among the first Virgil, Lucan, Cicero, Lactantius, Jerome, Sallust and Livy'.[6] In 1500 Erasmus returned to Paris and began the implementation of that idea – the first of his important pedagogical labours – with the compilation of a book of proverbs drawn from ancient authors. In March of that year he wrote to his friend James Batt, formerly schoolmaster and now town clerk of Bergen-op-Zoom, with whom Erasmus maintained a continued correspondence, that 'I am deep in Letters, bent on compiling a collection of ancient Adages. It will be a hasty work. I see some thousands may be collected, but I propose to publish only two or three hundred.'[7] A month later he wrote further: 'I am devoting all my strength to the preparation of my Adages, which I hope will be made public soon after Easter, a work of some length and demanding an infinity of pains. We have collected some eight hundred proverbs, part Greek and part Latin.'[8] In order to do this successfully, Erasmus recognized his need of Greek and so began studies in that language which he continued throughout his life, achieving in time a complete scholarly mastery. About June of 1500 the *Adages* appeared, dedicated to Lord Mountjoy.[9] The work was an instant success, as Erasmus had anticipated, since he had used a prototype of the idea with students whom he tutored while studying in Paris some years previously. The first edition of 144 pages and 818 adages, all in Latin, was enormously successful and quickly made Erasmus one of the best-known pedagogical writers in Europe. Reprinted in 1505, the *Adages* were republished in 1508 by Aldus Manutius, and further reprinted at Basle in 1513 and at Tübingen in 1514.[10] Their subsequent use, emendation and example to others not only sustained the name of Erasmus, they indicated the need for a wider variety of school texts than existed hitherto, and testified to the growing expansion of schools in Europe. And, moreover, they signify Erasmus' recognition and use of the print ing press as a major instrument in the achievement of educational ideals.

On the Christian life

Preparation of school texts, however, was not the consuming interest for Erasmus in the early years of the sixteenth century. Like so many others, he was deeply concerned with the continued decline of the church, particularly regarding its moral example, and with the frequent wars that were destroying peace and preventing the cumulative development of all that was best in civilization. In 1501, the year after the publication of the *Adages*, Erasmus composed in Latin his first systematic treatise on the moral problems of Europe, his *Enchiridion militis Christiani* (*Handbook of the Militant Christian*) which appeared in print two years later.[11] The title itself is a *double entendre*, a literary device Erasmus enjoyed using. *Enchiridion*, a Greek word, means either a dagger or a handbook,[12] and this metaphor is used to sustain his argument for a new kind of armour and weaponry for the Christian: prayer and knowledge, thereby continuing to express the concept of Christian piety. 'These two', he wrote, 'are inseparable, the former imploring but the latter suggesting what should be prayed for.'[13] This led him to a discussion of preparation for this holy war:

> If you but dedicate yourself entirely to the study of the Scriptures, if you meditate day and night on the divine law, nothing will ever terrorize you and you will be prepared against any attack of the enemy.
>
> I might also add that a sensible reading of the pagan poets and philosophers is a good preparation for the Christian life. We have the example of St Basil, who recommends the ancient poets for their natural goodness. Both St Augustine and St Jerome followed this method. St Cyprian has worked wonders in adorning the Scriptures with the literary beauty of the ancient. Of course it is not my intention that you imbibe the bad morals of the pagans along with their literary excellence. I am sure that you will nonetheless find many examples in the classics that are conducive to right living. Many of these writers were, of course, very good teachers of ethics.[14]

The rest of this section expands the humanist argument for return to the classics, although Erasmus stresses their value in serving Christian ends, in contrast to the Italian humanists who saw the classics as means to the *vita activa*, independently of Christian goals.

Although *Enchiridion* is a guide to the Christian life and not a treatise on education, it none the less deals explicitly with education, since, following the traditions of Western Christendom, Erasmus conceived Christianity as a way to both spiritual and intellectual understanding. It is necessary for the good Christian to recognize within himself the warring of factious passions and, following the classical dictum of moderation in all things, he must attempt to subject the body to the spirit.

> This then, is the only road to happiness: first, know yourself; do not allow yourself to be led by the passions, but submit all things to the judgement of the reason.[15]

Nor, he suggested, should the Christian put too much faith in the efficacy of attending divine services – mass, vespers, novenas. Without an inner assent of the soul – that which 'really constitutes us as human beings'[16] – these are useless activities.

To show how this might be pursued, Erasmus then gives twenty-two rules for guiding man through 'the labyrinth of this world'[17] towards the goal of Christ; in addition, he suggests remedies for seven particular vices, five of these belonging to the traditional seven deadly sins. In adopting this form, Erasmus followed an established convention in such devotional works of which the most popular predecessors were Thomas à

Kempis' *Imitation of Christ* of 1418 and the *Ladder of Perfection* written some time in the same period by the obscure Englishman, Walter Hilton, a member, like Erasmus, of the order of Augustinian Canons. The way advocated by Erasmus – and it is a thoroughly and consciously Platonic approach – is one of physical abnegation and spiritual search. 'The things that we see with our physical eyes are mere shadows of reality,'[18] he argued, in an image taken from Plato's *Republic*, and just as the visible world is transformed in the mind of god, so also is the human soul transformed. To help the Christian effect this transformation of vision Erasmus recommended study of the church fathers, particularly Augustine who, in his use of the language and ideas of Platonism, will 'lead you to an inner penetration of the word of God, to an understanding of the spiritual worth it contains'.[19] This particular point was made expressly to disavow the contemporary northern strain of Aristotelianism which Erasmus found so distasteful at Paris – he had as yet no contact with the revived Aristotelianism of Pomponazzi – and because, like Colet, Erasmus was influenced profoundly by the Platonist revival in Italy which had been accepted eagerly at Oxford. Most modern scholastics, he commented, are 'content with Aristotle, treat the mysteries of revelation in the tangled fashion of the logician [and . . .] strangle the beauty of revelation.'[20] At the same time, however, Erasmus also stressed the importance of the scriptures, this being the opening dictum of his first rule: 'Be convinced there is not a single item contained in Holy Writ that does not pertain to your salvation.'[21]

Despite the intensity of his argument for the primacy of faith in the scriptures, Erasmus advanced no specific programme of the ways in which it could be applied to life – his exhortations have all of the evanescence of emotional appeals; they give no precise indications of how a Christian can order his daily affairs. On the contrary, there is an acceptance of life as it is. Consider, for example, the uneven distribution of wealth in society which had vexed so many Christian thinkers. On this issue, Erasmus' observations are both realistic and compatible with a Christian approach; in one passage he pointed out:

> It is not wrong to have money. It only becomes wrong when money is loved as an end instead of looked on as a means. If you should become rich, act like the generous steward; if you should become poor, do not feel robbed, but rather feel as though a friend had relieved you of a dangerous thing.[22]

In the course of the next years Erasmus became as much concerned with education as with theology, and he drew closer to the work of both More and Colet, particularly after he met them again in 1505 during his second visit to England. The following year Erasmus left for Italy where he travelled for three years, visiting Aldus in Venice and thence proceeding to Rome. The moral decadence of Italy disappointed him and in 1509 he departed for England where the second Tudor sovereign, Henry VIII (r. 1509–47), had recently succeeded to the throne.

Education and the Christian way

Erasmus arrived in England in June of 1509 and, while a house guest of Thomas More, composed a light-hearted satire on the foibles of society that became celebrated throughout Europe. Dedicated to More, its title too, is another *double entendre*; although written in Latin it received a Greek title, *Morias enkomion* (*Praise of Folly*) since the word *morias*, Greek for folly, provides a pun on its recipient's name, intended expressly, Erasmus stated in its dedication, to provide the maximum contrast with More's own character. Now this work, it is important to note, is one of the most amazing paradoxes in his career. Although Erasmus himself avowed that it had been written in jest, it had an instant appeal throughout Europe, its popularity continuing for more than a century, in which time it appeared in some 600 printed editions. There is no doubt that it was not read for its triviality, but because, not too deeply hidden, there lay a criticism of current society that was neither lighthearted nor inconsequential.

In the satire, folly is personified as a woman – itself a comment on the social attitudes of the times – and despite what is easily recognized as superficial and trivial writing, Erasmus is unable to conceal a deep concern for the poor condition of learning in his day and at times a sympathy for ignorance. Folly, he points out early in the piece, is a necessary ingredient of life; it mitigates excessive seriousness and provides a buffer against preoccupation with daily misfortunes. Throughout the early pages the essay deals extensively with the various ways in which people employ folly to implement and sustain simple, and necessary, deceptions: marriage, for example, can only succeed if the partners ignore each other's short-comings and uphold the relationship by flattery, joking, compromise, ignorance and duplicity. As the narrative progresses, however, its mood changes and Erasmus gradually barbs his prose, searching out the most foolish members of society. These he finds within his own particular world: they are the men of learning and, since they have abused their rank and station, they are the most culpable. So his invective proceeds to uncover the absurdities and errors of men of knowledge, worthy, he remarks pungently, not of the title 'philosophers' but rather 'fool-osophers'.[23]

The ambiguous nature of the writing in this satire can be well illustrated with respect to grammar and the occupation of schoolmastering. Erasmus commences in jesting style: society's troubles have their origin in the fall from grace. In that state of original innocence all men spoke the same language, none sought to take advantage of another, so there was need neither for rhetoric and law nor for scientific curiosity, much less for the study of grammar. Compounding the enormity of the expulsion from Eden was Jehovah's destruction of the tower of Babel (Genesis 11:1–9) and the consequent multiplicity of languages on earth. Numerous tongues, Erasmus argues, still in jest, led to the 'idle speculation of the Greeks' in the study of language and this in turn to philology and comparative grammar, an agonizing procedure 'since even one grammatical system is enough to make life one endless moment of torture',[24] and this sort of statement will evoke a wry smile from every grammarian and philologist. But then his strictures against the grammarians begin to run to extremes; among the foolish, he writes,

> . . . the grammarians hold first place. Nothing could be more disaster-stricken or more afflicted than this generation of men . . . they are famished and filthy in their schools, or even better stated, in their think-shops, or shambles, among herds of boys. There they grow old with their labours, they are deafened by the noise, and they become ill from the stench and filth.[25]

In this polemic, however, it is clear that Erasmus is condemning the *grammaticus*, the grammar-schoolmaster, and not the philologist, and doubtless he is recalling quite emotionally his own schooldays. Yet his diatribe is extended to include a much wider range of supposedly educated men: poets, 'they are fools praising fools, and dunces praising dunces'; scientists, 'they can never explain why they always disagree with each other on every subject'; priests and monks, 'they think they are upholding the universal church, which is otherwise about to crumble to ruins, by the influence of their syllogisms'; rhetoricians, 'when they close their oration it is apparent that their only reason is that they are too breathless to utter anything else'; courtiers, 'no group of men is more sordid, more obsequious, more idiotic, or more contemptible than this set of men'.[26]

The target of his attack throughout is the middle range of scholars and *literati*, those who perform the daily intellectual tasks of the world and who in a broad and pervasive way act as teachers. For teaching, as he brings out so clearly, is not only an affair of the schoolroom, it is present in every act of life when men extend the range of human understanding. Erasmus reserves a special condemnation for banal ecclesiasticism and those who make patently false interpretations of Christianity; these seem, in his words, 'to have a certain relationship with some kind of folly but [fail] to agree at all with wisdom'.[27] And, in making this claim, Erasmus chides the early church fathers for their hostility to classical learning. At this point Erasmus advances the Platonic position, and it becomes clear that his essay is, in effect, a double argument. He agrees with Socrates, although not explicitly in this work, that the unexamined life is not worth living, yet it is clear that Erasmus believes that, for the masses, the examined life is no better. The myth of Plato's cave[28] is developed seriously to explain the beliefs of the masses, and in this respect Erasmus accepts the division of mankind into two groups, the majority – the vulgar – who seek only material possessions and continued diversions, and the minority of the pious – not by any means churchmen – who seek the spirit of god. The vulgar live for their appetites, and this is a never-ending treadmill, sustained of necessity by folly and continued self-deception. For the pious, life is a quest for 'absorption of the body by the spirit', the movement to 'share in the Highest Good which draws all to Itself'.[29] Final vision is for a few.

Language and learning: the improvement of school texts

Already Erasmus reveals in these writings his perception that religion is intertwined with education. For the remainder of his life, his twenty-five years of maturity, he devoted himself to the twin goals of the reform of religion and the reform of education. In 1511 he moved to Cambridge[30] at the invitation of John Fisher, chancellor of the university, and there he lectured in Greek, from the *Erotemata Chrysolorae*. Writing to his friend Andrew Ammonius in the same year he expressed the hope that the class would grow and that he could change to the grammar of Theodore of Gaza.[31] In addition he taught some theology, studied manuscripts of Jerome and began to work on the Greek text of the New Testament. It was in this period also that he published his first major treatise on education, *De ratione studii*, at Paris in 1511, and his second school textbook, *De copia verborum*, at Basle the following year.

De ratione studii (*On the Right Method of Instruction*)[32] is a systematic statement of his own educational views, and in its day it was the only work of its kind. Not since Quintilian had anyone produced such a carefully constructed theory; indeed Erasmus admits that his study rests heavily on that predecessor, stating at one point that 'as regards the methods of the rudiments – that is, of learning to talk and knowing the alphabet – I can add nothing to what Quintilian has laid down'.[33] The express purpose of the treatise, given in the conclusion, is to 'carry forward youths of merely average intelligence to a creditable standard of scholarship, and of conversation also, in Latin and Greek, at an age when, under the common schoolmaster of today, the same youths would be just stammering through their primer'.[34] This might seem a narrow goal but in 1511 the classics still represented the entirety of school instructional material; the newly printed school texts were mostly in Latin, the remainder in Greek.[35] In any case, Erasmus himself believed that the vernacular had to be avoided since in his view the two classical languages were the only proper medium of the cultural heritage. In the opening sentence of *De ratione studii* Erasmus sets out his pedagogical argument, a concept that is basic to all of his thought, religious as well as educational. With great perception he writes:

> All knowledge falls into one of two divisions: the knowledge of 'truths' and the knowledge of 'words'; and if the former is first in importance, the latter is acquired first in order of time.[36]

The educational task, he recognized – and it is true of all times – is to get beyond words, as words, to the truth they contain: Erasmus' rapidly maturing Platonism is well illustrated in this treatise.

Of major importance to the success of the method proposed by Erasmus is the precondition that children begin life speaking Latin, and not the vernacular, in the home, and so his tract is necessarily limited to the social stratum of the well-to-do intelligentsia, although he suggests that a clever schoolmaster can stimulate such conditions in the classroom. A beginning should be made with grammar in both Latin and Greek, but the basis of linguistic ability, he argues, comes from reading extensively in good prose, not from memorizing the grammatical rules as Donatus' grammar provides. Indeed, this concern for a quick progression from the aridities of formal grammar to virtual immersion in the literature of both Latin and Greek is one of his most distinctive pedagogical attitudes.

Content of passages is the first aspect to which attention should be given. Erasmus gives his own preferences for this stage of instruction, recommending those passages he collected separately and had published the same year in *De copia verborum* (*A Plenitude of Expressions*). This was an anthology of the standard classical authors favoured by humanists, and included among others Pliny, Macrobius, Plato, Aristotle, Origen, Basil, Ovid, Homer and Hesiod. In reading a classic for appreciation he recommended that the master should begin with a biography of the author and locate him in time and place, then move directly to the piece itself, progressively narrowing the focus until the diction itself is studied, 'noting any conspicuous elegance, or such peculiarities as archaism, novel usage, Graecisms; bringing out anything that is involved or obscure in phrases or sentence-forms; marking, where necessary, derivations and orthography, metaphors and other rhetorical devices'.[37] The precepts of Bruni, almost a century before, receive firm and explicit statement here. Subsequently, and gradually, by means of encouragement and prizes, children should be taught to discriminate the rules of accidence and syntax, the teacher arranging these in order and dictating them for entry into notebooks.[38] In turn this suggests a method for proceeding to the next stage, that of exercises in composition. The same topic may be set in both Latin and Greek and the two versions compared so as to appreciate the 'peculiar genius of each language',[39] although Erasmus does modify this method by suggesting also that, as a prior exercise, topics might first be written on in the vernacular. Having given further elaboration of the method of proceeding in the study of literature, Erasmus observes, somewhat wryly, that a schoolmaster of more than 'slight learning and experience' is required. But he offers no counsel for the right method of training teachers; he simply asserts that 'given these qualities [that is, of pedagogical expertise and scholarly attainment, in the master] I have no doubt that the class will speedily absorb the kind of knowledge which I have indicated'.[40]

De copia verborum had been projected in 1499; the next year Erasmus began writing it. Throughout the following decade he worked at it intermittently, and after some vicissitudes a final version was published in 1512, dedicated to Colet and offered to him, as a reward for patronage, as 'some small literary present to assist in the furniture of your school'.[41] At this time Colet, then dean of St Paul's in London, was establishing in the grounds of the cathedral a new school which was planned on humanist lines. The statutes prescribed 'good litterature both laten and greke' and as a means of access to this for the 'chyldren [to] lerne ffirst above all the Cathechyzon in Englysh and after the accidence that I made or sum other yf eny be better to the purpose to induce chyldren more spedely to laten spech'. Once the catechism and accidence were learned, the boys were to go straight 'to the Institutum Christiani homin[i]s which that lernyd Erasmus made at my request and the boke called Copia of the same Erasmus'.[42] The boys then were to read directly in the literature of Christian humanism.

Erasmus' *De copia verborum*, which was essential to this educational scheme, is a work on literary composition with numerous examples; basically it is a grammar book intended for children. Its first part deals extensively with vocabulary and the numerous ways in which words can be substituted; the second part, *De copia rerum*, extends the use of vocabulary to whole sentences and passages. Despite the censure of Guillaume Budé, writing from Paris in 1516 that it seemed worthy neither of such a great title nor such an author,[43] it was received eagerly and in the following fifty years appeared in more than thirty editions.[44]

Ideas on education and government

In 1514 Erasmus left England for Flanders and then Basle, meanwhile continuing his steady output of editions and translations, as well as his indefatigable letter-writing. Then in 1516 appeared his first major venture into political writing, the *Institutio principis Christiani* (*Education of A Christian Prince*),[45] the same year in which his friend Thomas More published the first version of *Utopia*, also a political treatise although of markedly different temper. The *Institutio principis* is not an educational treatise in any specific sense, and its prescriptions for the formal schooling of the prince are only slightly sketched. Rather, this work belongs in part to the tradition of the *speculum principis*, or mirror for princes, a literary genre of ancient lineage.[46] The *speculum principis* as a literary form began as early as Isocrates in the fourth century B.C. and was employed by scholars throughout the ages to set forward views on political theory and the role of sovereigns. Many great thinkers attempted this genre: Plato in the *Republic*, Aristotle in *Politics* and *Ethics*, and Cicero in his *Offices* are the first writers of significance. Thereafter the list increases steadily, encompassing works from the Roman Empire up to the time of Erasmus. Even contemporaneously with his *Institutio principis* other *specula* were being written, notably More's *Utopia* and Machiavelli's *Il Principe* (*The Prince*), although this latter work stemmed equally from the *trattato d'amore* tradition and was not published until 1532, nine years after it was first drafted. In composing his own *speculum* – although the work is much more besides – Erasmus was not only conforming to a standard literary convention, he used it also as the most appropriate means to spread his views on maintaining the peace, a perennial problem in Europe but one that was becoming exacerbated at this particular time.

Erasmus' view of princely government rested on some firm principles: the prince should be a wise and sober man, morally irreproachable and temperamentally austere, concerned primarily with the good of the state and occupied with ruling constitutionally. He must be a paragon of human virtues, displaying the qualities of justice, mercy, tolerance, equity, charity and impartiality.[47] In comparison, Machiavelli's *Il Principe* is a much more penetrating study of the craft of politics, a classic essay in *realpolitik* which concentrates its message on the strategy of maintaining sovereignty, advising the prince to avoid flatterers or other court sycophants, and to be loved rather than feared since these actions are conducive to effective control. Yet, as Machiavelli pointed out, the prince should not misuse his mercy:

> . . . [he] must not mind incurring the charge of cruelty for the purpose of keeping his subjects united and faithful; for, with a very few examples, he will be more merciful than those who, from excess of tenderness, allow disorders to arise, from whence spring bloodshed and rapine; for these as a rule injure the whole community, while the executions carried out by the prince injure only individuals.[48]

Erasmus' view of the prince is in strong, at times direct, contrast. The prince should avoid flattery and dispense justice, not because they are politically effective, but because they are fundamentally good qualities. The conception of the state in Erasmus' *Institutio principis* is basically that of Plato's *Republic* – as the numerous references to the latter work indicate – with the significant addition of a Christian emphasis: 'Before all else the story of Christ must be rooted firmly in the mind of the prince.'[49] Erasmus attempted to rewrite the *Republic* for his own day.

If the prince is to be formed for such a task then he must, in himself, be proper material: inherent talent, rather than royal lineage, is suggested as the ideal qualification for princedom, although Erasmus wisely presses the point no further than the opening paragraphs since the tract was written expressly for the instruction of the sixteen-year-old Prince Charles, the future Charles I, Habsburg King of Spain and Holy Roman Emperor. Whatever the prince's native talents, Erasmus advances the Platonic argument for careful and extensive exposure to the good, since 'the chief hope for a good prince is from his education'.[50] A competent tutor is mandatory, but Erasmus, as in his other works, fails to elaborate on what these pedagogical qualities of competence in the teacher might be. In addition, from his earlier days the prince should be reared in a carefully selected environment, one resembling closely that recommended for the future guardians in Plato's *Republic*. Only in this respect does Erasmus give any detail on the content of education and again he follows Plato closely: good books, carefully selected, are the best means of forming right thoughts:

> The first matter is the selection of authors, for the sort of books the boy first reads and absorbs is of prime importance. Wicked conversations ruin the mind, and in no less a degree do wicked books. . . . To make use of my plan, as soon as the elements of language have been taught [the tutor] should set forth the *Proverbs* of Solomon, *Ecclesiasticus*, and the *Book of Wisdom* . . . that [the tutor] may fitly show in a few words whatever pertains to the functions of a good prince.[51]

The passage then lists in sequence the works that Erasmus recommends: the gospels, Plutarch's *Apothegmata* and *Moralia*, Aristotle's *Politics*, Cicero's *Offices (On Duty)*, Plato's *Laws* and *Republic*. Historians – Herodotus, Xenophon, Sallust, Livy – are useful, but they must be read critically, as, indeed, must much of the Old Testament. All this, then, to the end that 'whenever the prince picks up a book, he should do so not with the idea of gaining pleasure but of bettering himself by his reading'.[52]

In setting out this programme of princely education Erasmus captured much interest. As with his other works, this one was distributed widely: four printed editions appeared the first year, further ones in 1518, 1519, 1523 and 1525.[53] The last edition came in 1641, but translations continued for some time after. Despite the popularity of the work – and it was read by emperors and princes across Europe – the work is founded on a political idealism that was in marked contrast to the current world of diplomacy and the march of events. Europe at that very moment was on the eve of tremendous conflict.

Christian education and the way to peace

The role of scholarship in a troubled world

The following year (1517) Erasmus turned his gentle and scholarly mind to the problems of civil strife, publishing his *Querela pacis* (*The Complaint of Peace*).[54] At the time Erasmus was in Basle, where he forsaw the great tragedy about to envelop all Europe in a devastating series of wars that, having already commenced in some places as early as 1494, were to continue to rage, intermittently and in various locations, throughout the century. The Turks were consolidating their penetration of south-east Europe after their conquest of Constantinople in 1453 and were on the point of a new wave of advances. Meanwhile the French house of Valois contended with the Spanish Habsburgs for control of Italy; Castile was still in conflict with Aragon; the Holy Roman Empire remained a chaos of disorganized states and principalities. The papacy in Rome, moreover, was both worldly and corrupt, drawing considerable wealth from the Holy Roman Empire – more, in fact, than the emperor himself. Pope Julius II (r. 1503–13), known as the 'warrior pope', not only weakened the moral hegemony of his office by leading in person a papal army in an effort to reconquer the papal estates, he also allowed the governing Curia in Rome to become more corrupt by conceding many of their claims for further financial privileges, specifically, the right to collect revenues by delegating the sale of relics and indulgences. Meanwhile in 1511 the obscure Augustinian monk Martin Luther left Rome for Wittenberg where he became involved in profound theological speculation. In 1513 he even criticized Pope Julius, and gradually his thought became increasingly critical of many church abuses. Then, in the same year that Erasmus wrote his *Querela pacis*, Martin Luther produced in Wittenberg his Ninety-Five Theses, simply offering, in the custom of the time, to debate them with all comers. The debate involved much of Europe for the following two centuries.

Erasmus himself found little in the Christian society of his day to reassure him and *Querela pacis* is a record of his despair. Perhaps his greatest disappointment came from the lack of intelligent leadership by men of learning. Both *Enchiridion* and *Institutio principis* deal seriously with the theme, while *Praise of Folly* treated it in apparent jest; in this new tract the same growing despair is recorded. Why is it, he asks, that 'unanimity is of absolute necessity for man, yet neither nature, education, nor the rewards of concord and the disadvantages of disunity seem to be able to unite mankind in mutual love?'[55] Particularly culpable are man's leaders – princes and scholars – for while princes have failed to maintain equity and concord, scholars have neglected to provide knowledge and vision. Scholars, in fact, actually abuse learning. 'They fight until the heat of argument leads to slanders and to blows. Their weapons are not daggers but venomous pens. They tear one another with taunts.'[56] The way of man should be social unity as a means to spiritual unity in Christ, and to suggest the values of this way Erasmus examines and propagandizes the many advantages to be gained from peace, although he concedes, in conclusion, that nothing will come of his plan until princes rule constitutionally, according to law, and all men acknowledge Christ.

The problem, he maintained, is in large part one of education – a belief he held to all his life – and Erasmus continued his efforts in this direction. Here lay his talents; moreover, it satisfied his own impulses to act ethically according to his own stringent precepts. In 1516 there appeared his highly influential version of the New Testament, consisting of a new edition of the Greek text accompanied by a parallel rendition in classical Latin. This was his understanding of his own kind of contribution; Erasmus already had made public confession that he possessed no grand heroic courage. Continuing his scholarly efforts he published in 1518 the first version of his famous colloquies under the title *Familiarium colloquiorum formulae*.[57] These *Colloquies*, exercises for teaching Latin conversation, set the final seal on his pedagogical endeavours; few books have achieved such wide acclaim in educational circles. Like his other works, this one was reprinted seven times, in Paris, Antwerp, Leipzig, Vienna and Cracow, within eighteen months of the first printing. It was then rewritten, enlarged and reissued intermittently between 1522 and 1533 in a total of twelve editions and more than a hundred impressions.[58] The first edition was a set of schoolroom exercises in catechetical style; simple Latin questions followed by appropriate answers which were intended to teach good Latinity by actual conversational practice. Erasmus was displeased with the first version, and the emended edition of 1522 included fully expanded dialogues with sustained passages of writing, along with elementary plots and characterization. 'The Wooer and the Maiden', dealing with a youth's numerous ploys bent on seduction, and the girl's tactics of defence, is a fresh and vigorous treatment of a timeless theme. The robust character of these colloquies must have enlivened classroom Latin considerably, and indeed, in their day, some were criticized for excessive coarseness. These dialogues soon found a much wider audience outside the classroom; they were in effect a literary form that met current fashions of taste.

During this period the Lutheran controversy became steadily worse and Erasmus was dragged into it, albeit reluctantly. So far, he had avoided involvement in the dispute, but by now Rome needed support and in Basle, as a result of pressure from the pope, the Holy Roman Emperor and various secular princes, Erasmus published his position in 1524 in *De libero arbitrio*.

Despite its title, *On the Freedom of the Will* is really a diatribe against Luther; the question of the freedom of man's will is in part a pretext for examining the entire question of the search for meaning in the universe. The scriptures themselves are manifestly ambiguous, Erasmus states, as Henry VIII of England was demonstrating with regard to remarriage: Leviticus 20:21 forbids marriage with the wife of one's deceased brother, Deuteronomy 25:5 enjoins a man to take that wife into his tent. How can man decide? Discussing the general problem of scriptural conflict – although he does not refer specifically to these two passages – Erasmus claims that if scriptural authority were all that is needed, he would 'readily take refuge in it'[59] as a means of reaching solutions. But the history of theology does not show that men have been equally persuaded by scripture, as the great debates of the scholastic period made him acutely aware. Nor, in the opinion of Erasmus, is general consensus of the whole population enough, for most people, despite the popular teachings of such men as Wycliffe and Hus, are in no position to judge. Here the viewpoint of Erasmus resembles closely that of Plato which the latter summarized in the dictum that 'democracy treats all men as equal, whether they are equal or not'.[60] Indeed Erasmus points out that doctrinal disputes are better not discussed in front of all and sundry, 'before common ears'.[61] Ultimate truths, he again feels, are for the intellectual few. At times Erasmus shows a close, although unacknowledged, acquaintance with the Moslem controversies of the twelfth century that had centred on Averroes; his discussion of man's freedom of will versus cosmic determinism traverses the same arguments as the Moslem debates, and at one point Erasmus uses the very same illustration, namely the cause of fire burning.[62] Most curiously Erasmus moderated the deterministic and free-will positions: man works in concert with grace to achieve salvation. God created the universe in its entirety, good and bad, and in this sense determines its composition. At the same time, god has given man a will sufficiently free for him to recognize the conflict of good and evil and to choose the right path to salvation: 'For myself, I prefer the view of those who do attribute much to free choice, but most to grace.'[63] Yet Erasmus did not come out firmly in support of the church; he asserted that the scriptures alone give no clear account of the way to salvation, and so guidance is necessary, but this is not said to come necessarily from the church in Rome. He ended on the ambiguous note, akin to that adopted by Plato, Averroes and

Maimonides, that it is dangerous to allow the masses to question faith.

Despite the publication of *De libero arbitrio*, Erasmus was subjected to attacks from within the Catholic church. Two years earlier, in 1522, the inquisitor Egomondanus had denounced the *Colloquies* as containing heresies and in 1526 the Paris faculty of theology, by this time called the Sorbonne, condemned them; in 1538, two years after the death of Erasmus, a consistory of cardinals prohibited their use. Finally in 1564 Pius IV confirmed the decrees banning them passed earlier by the Council of Trent – a convocation that had met between 1545 and 1563 to determine a programme of church reform – and they were put on the catalogue of forbidden books, *Index librorum prohibitorum*, which itself had been first issued by Pope Paul IV in 1557 as a means of controlling the appearance of works contrary to Catholic faith and morals. Erasmus, while he lived, defended his work, and its popularity was kept well before the public by this controversy. The pedagogical method it employed, moreover, was followed readily by many others, most strikingly by Juan Luis Vives in *De tradendis disciplinis* (*On Education*) of 1531 and by Mathurinus Corderius in his *Colloquiorum scholasticorum* (*School Colloquies*) of 1556. In the final years of his life, however, Erasmus found the opportunity to write his last significant essay on schooling, *De pueris instituendis* (*On the Education of Boys*),[64] which is one of the most penetrating studies on education ever written. With its acuity of perception, soundness of judgement and humane sense of moderation it is, despite its brevity, one of Western civilization's most important documents in the history of education.

A programme of education

Everywhere, Erasmus writes in this work, first published in 1529, may be seen the results of bad teaching: ignorant masters, chiefly monks, clerics and Common Life brothers who are beggarly in their own scholarship and so ignorant of the purposes of education that their schoolroom procedures are at times orgies of cruel torture, schools themselves frequently being 'kept by some incompetent, ill-tempered, perhaps drunken creature'.[65] So bad were many schools, particularly the claustral ones, that Erasmus urges parents either to choose a 'public' school, that is, one conducted outside the cloisters, usually in a parish church, or else to keep their child at home.[66] If the boy should be so intractable that only flogging makes him conform, it would be better by far to turn him loose. The pressing need in schools, he argues, is for good schoolmasters, men approaching the temperament of Aristotle, who could teach a new generation as he taught Alexander. Indeed, it is the public duty of both church and state to provide such persons, since schoolboys are not only the sons of citizens, they are future citizens themselves. The proper education of children demands teachers of insight, for as Erasmus observes with great acuity – in marked contrast to the blurred perception of his time – children are individuals, differing considerably in capacity and interests, and developing mentally and physically according to subtle patterns of growth that are imperfectly understood. The good master can watch for learning readiness, thereby recognizing the individualities of each child's nature, and so devise appropriate studies, since not all studies favour all children equally; this will enable him to time his pedagogical efforts more carefully.

Now it is important to note that Erasmus always held the highest respect for the office of schoolmaster, in distinction to his contempt for individual worthless practitioners. In 1511, for example, he involved himself in an acrimonious debate on the intrinsic validity of schoolteaching that had arisen from the pejorative challenge, 'who would submit to pass his life in [that] school among boys, who could live in any fashion whatever, elsewhere?'[67] Erasmus' defence survives in his account contained in a letter to Colet, where he writes that his reply to the taunt was that 'I thought it a highly honourable office to bring up youth in virtue and learning; that Christ had not despised that age, upon which kindness was best bestowed, and for which the richest harvest might be expected, . . . there was no duty by which [one] could serve God better than by drawing children to Christ.' And to the further taunt of his unknown antagonist that if one really wanted to serve Christ then it were better to enter a convent or monastery, Erasmus countered by asserting the pervasive nature of Christian piety: 'Paul places all religion in offices of charity, and charity consists in doing all the good we can to our neighbours.'[68] Some two years later, Erasmus again extolled the office of teacher in a letter to the schoolmaster Robert Caesar, urging him to 'proceed, my Robert, in your noble work of preparing the youth of Ghent for the reception of the best learning and [not to] let your mind be moved by the clatter of the envious'. And, as a further reinforcement, Erasmus added, 'I showed your pupils' writings to our friends, and could scarcely persuade any one that they came from boys'.[69]

So, in the essay On the Education of Boys, having again emphasized his long-standing belief in the intrinsic validity of the office of schoolmaster,

Erasmus then proceeds to show how the teacher should be concerned with the development of the mental powers of his students. The distinguishing quality of man is his reason, Erasmus asserts, and in its cultivation lies man's earthly way. Following Aristotle in this belief, Erasmus argues that man has a capacity for training; this indeed is 'the chief aptitude which has been bestowed upon humanity'.[70] Reason, he continues, is the mark of man and as such it is superior to appetite; it must control the natural passions, else humanity cannot be realized. The existence of reason carries its own implicit educational directives: reason impels man to seek intellectual cultivation. Again his educational arguments, particularly the teleological assumption of man's end being to cultivate intellectual virtue, follow Aristotle, despite his own preference for Platonic philosophy. The need for man to realize his latent reason and to cultivate it through capacity for training, is, in fact, a duty we owe both to god and to the state. At the same time, Erasmus makes clear his perception that the cultivation of reason needs time and a proper sequence of activities. The education of the child should begin in his earliest years, in the first three, and not after the seventh as was customary from early classical times. Virtue, that necessary correlative of rationality, must be nurtured at the first possible opportunity; if education is delayed until after the seventh year, bad habits and attitudes could already have taken firm hold of the child. Nature, method and practice are the three cardinal concepts the educator must appreciate and employ to the best tactical advantage. Nature means the physical and mental endowment of the child, including his latent capacity for realizing humanity; method is the skilled application of instruction and guidance; practice comprehends the continued and varied interplay between personality and method.

Erasmus was aware that current pedagogy objected to any instruction before the eighth year chiefly because most if not all of it would be lost – and he answers this objection by suggesting that although maturity can make up for earlier lack of instruction, the patent difficulty has to be faced of teaching boys already indifferent to learning. The earliest beginning, then, is best. Another objection he dismisses is that of injury to the child's health – indeed the extent of popular concern for the bad effects of excessive early memorizing on children must be weighed against the common stories of frequent brutality towards them. Erasmus himself makes this point rather shrewdly when he recalls a child whom he knew personally – perhaps in his own school days – who was hung up by the arms and flogged till the master was too tired to continue, and that 'was the least disgusting part of the punishment'.[71] The most educationally advantageous procedure is to mediate the two positions: to begin early but to respect immaturity, to go with the nature of the young child. This means, in practice, the recognition of childish delight in games, competition, prizes, stratagems, rewards, puzzles, emulation – all these, in that period, being largely foreign to the classroom.

The basis of all learning, Erasmus maintains, is verbal; it cannot be otherwise. So the classroom should have, in the first instance, a verbally stimulating atmosphere. Stories delight the young, and which, he asks, are better than Aesop's? Comic stories too have a particular appeal; they teach many deep truths of life in lighter vein. Music, arithmetic and geography also have some educational value and can be introduced to leaven the curriculum. None the less, language remains the centre of classroom endeavour and the one really significant means whereby man realizes his potential. Already Erasmus had made clear in the *Adages* and *Colloquies* his belief in the graded sequence of language instruction. In *De pueris instituendis* he reaffirms this, pointing out continually that children delight in games and the pleasantly challenging, and these are the best procedures for the schoolmaster. Even that bugbear, memorization, necessary in much learning and particularly in Greek and Latin, can be alleviated, often indeed made into fun, by the use of appropriate mnemonic devices. Education, Erasmus insists, is a positive process, it cultivates reason, affirms humanity, leads to god; its methods, therefore, if they are to achieve these ends, must be consonant with them.

The programme implemented: Colet and St Paul's school

Erasmus himself never attempted any practical implementation of his ideas on education, but in his lifetime he stimulated many others, of whom the most outstanding was John Colet; and for one example of how the theory of Christian humanism became translated into educational practice we can turn to Colet's foundation of a new school in St Paul's cathedral in London.

Colet himself, of course, was also a significant figure in English Reformation life. In the ten years of his lectureship at Oxford (1496–1505) he turned away, according to Erasmus, from 'the race for professorships and fees [which he believed] spoilt everything and adulterated the purity of all branches of learning',[72] and devoted himself vigorously to attacking the corruption of the church as manifested, for example, in granting bishoprics to ignorant men by secular princes.[73] Indeed, in the work that contains this criticism, *Super opera Dionysii* (later edited as *Two Treatises on the Hierarchies of Dionysius*), he reached a high point of rhetorical invective against the venality of the church, declaiming:

> Out upon this wicked generation! these abandoned principles! this madness of princes! this blindness and folly of ecclesiastics! a blindness whether more to be had in derision or wept over, I know not. All order is being overthrown; the flesh waxes wanton; the spirit is quenched; all things are distorted and foul. Unless Christ have pity on His Church, death, which is already at the door, will seize on all. For how shall that endure, which is being administered with destructive counsels and murderous hands?[74]

This attack was sustained in his other writings, and chiefly in his lectures on St Paul's epistles in which, like other reformers of the times, he advanced the argument for a return to simple, primitive, apostolic Christianity. In following Paul, Colet also followed Platonism and so his ideas were markedly similar to those of Erasmus. It was this similarity of thought and temperament – although Colet was much more radical, being accused even of Lollardy – that first brought the two humanists together in 1498 when Colet wrote to Erasmus expressing interest in meeting him, and the latter replied, offering friendship.

In April 1505 Colet was appointed dean of St Paul's cathedral in London and almost immediately began the reform of its chapter. The staff was considerable, more than fifty – including thirty canons – and all, in Colet's view, leading indolent lives on large and undeserved revenues. The cathedral activities were minimal and the school, like everything else there, was degenerate. Yet London was short of schools and, since they were the subject of clerical monopolies in that city, there was little that could be done to effect improvement. Colet seized the chance to reform education on Christian humanist lines about 1509 when he received a large bequest from his deceased father's estate. Ignoring the decadent cathedral school, by now apparently an insignificant song school, he established a new foundation, as we read in the Statutes of St Paul's:

> Prologus
> John Colett, the sonne of henry Colett, Dean of paules desyring nothing more thanne Education and bringing vpp chyldren in good Maners and litterature in the yere of our lorde a mli fyve hundreth and twelff [1512] bylded a Scole in the Estende of paulis Church for cliij [153] to be taught free in the same.[75]

To supervise this school the statutes provide for a 'Maister and a Surmaister and a Chapelyn'; that is, a master, an assistant and a chaplain. To the senior position, later termed – as in places it still is – 'high master', he appointed the Oxford grammarian of Magdalen College, William Lily (*c.* 1468/9–1522).

In large part the Statutes deal with necessary legal matters: the income from properties that are to provide the endowment, the vesting of the governance of the school in the 'honourable Compeny of Mercers of london' – in whose archives the Statutes still remain – and the requisites for office of the three incumbents, along with their emoluments, privileges and conditions of tenure. The master, it is specifically provided in the section 'Capitulum primum de magistro primario', shall be 'a man hoole in body honest and vertuouse and lerned in the [?] good and clere laten litterature and also in greke yf suche may be gotten'. From an educational viewpoint, however, the most important sections are those two entitled 'The Children' and 'What Shalbe Taught'.

Both of these sections are very brief – less than a thousand words together – but they do give a clear indication of the way in which Colet desired to improve schooling and to promote Christian piety. So the first clause provides that 'There shalbe taught in the scole Children of all nacions and countres indifferently to the Noumber of cliij [153] acordyng to the noumber of the Setys in the scole', although this is followed by the proviso that they shall already be prepared in catechism and able to 'rede and wryte competently'.[76] An initial registration fee – the only one charged – was four pence and this money was to provide a scholarship for 'the pore Scoler . . . that swepith the scole, and kepith the scole clene'. The school was to be divided into 'forms', the term coming from the backless benches on which the boys sat, and for each form 'one principall chylde shalbe plasid in the chere president of that fforme'. Apart from religious holy days, the boys were to attend throughout the year 'boith wynter and somer' from seven till eleven in the morning and one till five in the afternoon, with three daily prayer sessions. The students were enjoined not to bring into or consume within the school any food or liquor, as was their common practice. Nor were they to indulge in the customary diversions: cock-fighting, riding about or disputing, but instead, at all times, to go about 'soberly and not sing out'.[77]

The curriculum followed standard Christian humanist theory: students were to be

> . . . taught all way in good litterature both laten and greke, and good auctors [authors] suych as have the veray Romayne eliquence joyned withe wisdome specially Cristyn auctors that wrote theyre wisdom with clene and chast laten.

This, Colet stated, was for the specific purpose of increasing

> . . . knowledge and worshipping of god and oure lorde Crist Jesu and good Cristen lyff and maners in the Children.[78]

To achieve this end, it was advocated that the boys commence with the catechism and Latin grammar ('accidence') written by Colet himself,[79] proceeding next to the *Institutem Christiani hominis* and *De copia verborum* of Erasmus and thence to the 'good Latin authors'. Here the statutes are rather surprising: we would expect at this point to read the names at least of Cicero, Virgil, and perhaps Sallust, Ovid and Horace, along with some expressly Christian authors, but instead we find Lactantius, Prudentius, Probus, Sedulius and Juvencus and, astonishingly, the recent Quattrocento writer, Baptista Mantuanus. Every one of these is a marginal figure; how can their prescription be explained? Certainly they meet the criterion of being Christian authors for, with the exception of Probus, who is probably Valerius Probus, an obscure but frequently quoted grammarian of the first century A.D., and Baptista Mantuanus (1448–1516), a minor but voluminous poet, best remembered for his *Eclogues* and possibly included because Erasmus considered him close in stature to Virgil, the other four – Lactantius (A.D. *c.* 250–*c.* 317), Prudentius, (A.D. 348–after 405), Sedulius (*fl. c.* A.D. 435) and Juvencus (early fourth century A.D.) – were all Christian apologists of the patristic age. It is quite conceivable that Colet, being fervently reformist, was sceptical of the major authors and preferred minor writers whose works would be free of any taint of pagan contamination. The prescription of these authors probably came from Colet's need to provide an education in Latin and that these authors were the best available to him, at least for classroom purposes. Yet their value in serving as a corrective to 'all corrupcion [and] laten adulterate which ignorant blynde folis brought into this worlde' must have been severely limited, especially since the Latin which had been adulterated and 'poisoned' and which Colet sought to improve was, paradoxically, 'the veray Romayne tong which in the tyme of Tully [Marcus Tullius Cicero] and Salust and Virgill and Terence was vsid, whiche also seint Jerome and seint ambrose and seint Austen [Augustine] and many hooly doctors lerned in theyr tymes'.[80] The interpretation that Colet sought to promote an excessively pietistic, Christian character – which made the great pagans still suspect – is strengthened by his rhetorical, pulpit-style outburst in the final sentence of this section of the Statutes:

> I say that ffylthynesse and all such abusyon which the later blynde worlde

brought in which more ratheyr may be called blotterature thenne litterature I vtterly abbanysh and Exclude oute of this scole and charge the Maisters that they teche all way that is the best and instruct the chyldren in greke and Redyng laten in Redyng vnto them suych auctors that hathe with wisdome joyned the pure chaste eloquence.[81]

Certainly Colet shows none of the humane breadth of vision so manifest in Erasmus, and his interpretation of Christian humanism is markedly narrow. However, under the capable management of William Lily the school became established successfully, and it continued in operation down through the following centuries.

Erasmus and the Reformation in Germany

Throughout his life Erasmus himself had striven to affirm the Christian vocation of man and to demonstrate the centrality of education in achieving that end. Yet he never really felt secure in his attitudes towards the institutional church and this is illustrated in his relationships with his order, the Augustinian Canons. After leaving the monastery, he ceased to wear an ecclesiastical habit and was, throughout the early years of the sixteenth century, intermittently at odds with them, this reaching a climax in 1514 when his superior, Servatus Rogerius, instructed him to return to the cloister at Steyn. Erasmus refused and in 1517, after some diplomatic manœuvring, was released from his vows.

In much of his writing, of course, he was vigorously critical of religious behaviour and covertly condemnatory of the church itself. Yet it was very much against his inclinations that he became drawn into the religious disputes in Germany, and the writing of De libero arbitrio was a reluctant action which, in some effort to withdraw from further involvement in the conflict, he included the statement that 'I have never sworn allegiance to the words of Luther'.[82] This disavowal gave some support to Rome's policy at the time (1524) when the movement of dissent was clearly getting out of hand, but apart from this, Erasmus resisted any further involvement and attempted to maintain his scholarly – if ambiguous – detachment till his death at Basle in 1536. Even in his last moments of physical agony, reflecting in a sense the great conflict raging in Europe, Erasmus maintained the Christian way he had striven for all his life and as he expired uttered his last words in Dutch, 'Lieuer Got' ('Dear God').[83]

Erasmus was, however, unable to influence the course of political events and he certainly did not reach Luther; on the contrary, Luther's doctrines, supported by his brilliant, intellectual colleague Philip Melanch-thon, were not easily dismissed and in fact they took firm hold, and were to result, not only in the religious separation of much of Germany from Rome, but also, as a consequence of this independence, in new attitudes to education. This, in effect, was to lead to the first foundation of a specific-ally nationalistic education since the time of imperial Rome.

CHAPTER 12

Christian Humanism:
II. Martin Luther and
the Reformation in Germany

Humanism and the Reformation

Luther and the Ninety-Five Theses

Martin Luther (1483–1546) was born in the Saxon village of Mansfeld, son of a miner. Although intending to become a lawyer, he entered an Augustinian monastery in 1505, after a traumatic encounter with lightning in a storm had precipitated his religious conviction. The order that Luther joined, known as the Hermits or Friars, had been founded in 1256 by a group of Italians modelling themselves on the Dominicans while taking the rule of Augustine of Hippo as their constitution; like the Augustinian Canons who received approval two centuries earlier in 1059, the Friars looked back to the founder of Latin monasticism.

After his ordination in 1507 Luther taught at Wittenberg until 1510 when he went to Rome on business for his order. While there he was disturbed by the obvious corruption of the church, and after he returned to the chair of theology at Wittenberg in 1513 his concern grew, so that increasingly he came to diverge from orthodox doctrine. By this time the fund-raising activities of the church in Rome had reached the point of open scandal, aggravated by the excessive crudity of many schemes. The new craft of printing allowed the rapid multiplication of indulgences –

papal documents remitting punishment for sins.[1] Simultaneously vast numbers of relics were appearing – fragments of the true cross, milk from Mary's breasts, thorns that had pierced Jesus' brow, and a dozen others, equally ludicrous. Indulgences had a well-defined market price: twenty-five guilders for kings, queens and princes; ten for abbots and the higher nobility; six for the lesser nobility; three guilders for merchants of high station, one for those of low; proportionately less for those of poorer means.[2] In Germany, these sales were carried out by a braggart Dominican, John Tetzel, whose behaviour led to the first stirrings of unrest. Luther saw the sale of indulgences and relics not simply as gross crudities, but, more seriously, as symbols of papal arrogation of the means to salvation. The thought was disturbing; the scriptures and man's faith were put at one remove from god, interposed by the church claiming a mediating role. The teachings of Wycliffe and Hus had already found a response in Germany, and Luther began to fear that continued papal claims to mediation would weaken this direct evangelical faith. In 1517 Luther composed his Ninety-Five Theses and is believed to have nailed them to the cathedral door at Wittenberg,[3] thereby signalling, according to the academic convention of the period, his willingness to debate the issues.

The Ninety-Five Theses are a list of statements in Latin repudiating many of the abuses and church claims of the day, as these two examples show:

> The Pope neither wishes nor can remit any punishment except that which he imposed by his or by canonical authority.

> Christians are to be taught that it is not the desire of the Pope that the buying [of indulgences] should in any way be compared with works of mercy.[4]

The posting of the theses created immediate response; they were almost immediately put into print, and became circulated widely and quickly throughout Europe, the craft of printing proving to be an impartial instrument since theses multiplied as rapidly as indulgences. Luther was no longer obscure although, at this point, neither was he famous. Rome, for its part, had no need to feel any particular urgency – heresies had arisen before and had been handled. At first Pope Leo X attempted to persuade Duke George of Saxony to restrain Luther; then, in 1518, Cardinal Cajetan was dispatched to interview the fledgling heretic. In Luther's own account of that meeting, the mature form of his theological thinking can be discerned: the belief that man is saved by faith. Luther asserted to Cajetan his conviction that the theses were not contrary to church teachings. 'All that I have said today seems to me to have been sensible, true, and catholic.'[5] The following year Luther debated the theses publicly with John Eck at Leipzig, and although Eck claimed victory neither side was really satisfied. Luther, in fact, stepped up his activities and the next year wrote three of his famous tracts urging church reform: *An den christlichen Adel deutscher Nation* (*To the Nobility of the German Nation*); *De captivitate Babylonica ecclesiae* (*On the Babylonian Captivity of the Church*); and *Von der Freiheit eines Christenmenschen* (*On the Freedom of a Christian*). 'Thus we owe', he wrote in *De captivitate*, 'whatever of good there may be in our penance, not to our scrupulous enumeration of sins but to the truth of God and our faith.'[6]

The position worsened. In 1520 Luther was judged in error on forty-one points of belief in the bull *Exsurge domine*, which offered him sixty days in which to recant.[7] Luther responded by publicly burning the bull and other papal books, thereby making the rift even wider. The pope now moved to silence Luther; yet one more chance to recant was offered him at the Diet of Worms where Luther appeared, under promise of safe conduct, in 1521. Again Luther refused to recant, and he requested permission to withdraw from the city, doubtless aware that the promise of safe conduct to Constance had failed to save Hus. Barely out of the city, Luther was pseudo-kidnapped by his protector Elector John Frederick of Saxony and hurried to safety in Wartburg Castle where he remained in seclusion for the ensuing ten months. Lutheranism began to spread, much as Hussitism had done; Rome had again miscalculated the steadily increasing nationalism north of the Alps. The activities of humanists and the correlative growth of patriotic literature brought to a focus the Germanic urge to independence. In religion as in other matters, support of Luther came from a widespread popular sentiment. While in hiding in the Wartburg, Luther wrote vigorously, his major production being his translation of the New Testament in German, this 'September Bible' of 1522 becoming the basis of public scriptural literacy.

Thought of Luther and Melanchthon

Luther came out of hiding in 1522 and returned to Wittenberg where he devoted himself even more energetically to the cause of reform, securing at the same time the support of his fellow academics. Of these the most scholarly, and constant, was a youthful prodigy who had arrived at the university some years before and whose very youth, at his first appearance, had made him the object of much suspicion, in which Luther had initially joined. This was Philip Melanchthon (1497–1560). Born in the obscure Rhenish village of Bretten as Philipp Schwarzerd, he demonstrated his intellectual precocity early in childhood, receiving his schooling chiefly from his grandfather. In his twelfth year, when both father and grand-father died, the young Philip was sent to school in Pforzheim near Stuttgart, where he became a ward of his great-uncle, the renowned humanist Johann Reuchlin (1455–1522). Noting the child's ready skill in the classics, Reuchlin translated the peasant name of Schwarzerd (literally, 'black earth') into its Greek equivalent, Melanchthon, thereby foreshadow-ing the classical career that was to make Melanchthon as renowned in the middle decades of the sixteenth century in Germany as his great-uncle had been in the first two. Melanchthon studied at Heidelberg and Tübingen, tutoring children meanwhile, and at the age of twenty was appointed, as a result of Reuchlin's influence, and on the evidence of a promising thesis presented in 1517, *De artibus*, to the faculty of Wittenberg. Here he met Luther and the friendship of the two became fixed when Melanchthon demonstrated the quality of his intellect in a brilliant inaugural address of 1518: *De corrigendis adolescentiae studiis (On Improving the Studies of Youth)*.[8] In that lecture Melanchthon surveyed the direction that learning was taking in Germany, arguing forcefully that the goals of humanism should be pursued more vigorously and that this would assist the pietist aim of getting to the truth of the scriptures. The early Latin fathers had excelled in Greek, he declared, because they recognized its values for reading the scriptures, which exist only in Greek and Hebrew, the pure stream from which the Latin-speaking theologian must drink if he is to be at all knowledgeable. Without Greek and Hebrew, he asserted, the theological scholar must be silent.[9] Melanchthon continued to point out that it was neglect of the sources of scriptural truth that contributed to the decay of the church;[10] only through a return to the sources, to evangelical truth ('quam quod Evangelicae Veritati'), can man find his way.

Melanchthon was accepted enthusiastically; the suspicion surrounding his appointment vanished and Reuchlin's effort[11] in securing the young man's appointment was seen, not as naked nepotism, but as the proper support of a promising scholar. For his part, Melanchthon plunged with vigour into his task of leading men back to the font of evangelical truth. Very shortly after Melanchthon commenced teaching, Luther wrote of him to Johann Lang, vicar of the Augustinian monastery at Erfurt, that

> The most learned and perfect Grecian Philipp Melanchthon is teaching Greek here. He is a mere boy in years, but one of us in various knowledge, including that of almost all books. He is not only master of Greek and Latin, but of all the learning to which they are the keys, and he also knows some Hebrew.[12]

The following week Melanchthon wrote to Christopher Scheurl in Nuremburg that he had introduced classes in Greek and Hebrew[13] which turned out to be extremely popular. Students came to him in increasing numbers, the enrolment doubling each year for the first two years: in 1520 it was reported that 600 attended one of his lectures.[14]

In addition, Melanchthon became very active in the encouragement of grammar schools, even establishing one in his own home, in 1520, which offered Latin, Greek, perhaps Hebrew, mathematics, ethics and Aristotelian physics. His advice was sought from elsewhere, and in 1525 Melanchthon was requested by the council of Nuremburg to become rector of a school they were planning. He declined but the following year accepted an invitation by the count of Mansfeld to establish a school at Eisleben. From that venture Melanchthon gained much practical experience which was expressed a year later, in 1526, when he gave the foundation speech of the new school set up at Nuremberg. In that humanist panegyric, in praise of new schools, *In laudem novae scholae*, Melanchthon described the function of the school as promoting learned piety through a sound classical education, properly applied.[15] In addition to these two schools, he also assisted in the foundation of one at Magdeburg, and he was largely responsible for selecting the masters of all three institutions. Simultaneously Melanchthon was just as busy stimulating university reform, beginning with Wittenberg in 1523. Melanchthon quickly became known as much for his administrative and organizing skill as for his academic brilliance, and his advice was sought for upgrading the universities of Tübingen, Leipzig and Heidelberg, as well as for the planning of new ones at Marburg and Königsberg.[16]

In the same period Melanchthon played an indispensable although unobtrusive role in the debates of Luther, first against Cardinal Cajetan and later against Johann Eck, in which his task was to prepare Luther's arguments. At times Eck himself was moved to criticize and inveigh against this silent advocate whose eloquence was beginning to tell. By 1519 the close bonds between Luther and Melanchthon disturbed Reuchlin, who was himself embroiled with the Dominicans of Cologne;

Reuchlin wrote to Melanchthon counselling him to break with Luther and to join him at the University of Ingolstadt. Melanchthon refused and Reuchlin broke off all further contact with his great-nephew, never seeing him again. Reuchlin, for his part, while being strongly and openly critical of the scholastics and also adopting a humanist position, was none the less as far removed from secular humanism as possible. He was a pious conservative, a Catholic and a competent Hebraist, interested chiefly in understanding the Bible.

Melanchthon and Luther too were chiefly concerned with the inculcation of piety but saw that the humanist literature was a vital element; it was, in fact, only through classical studies that an approach could be made to biblical truth. Indeed, Melanchthon became strongly influenced by Luther in this respect and before long became the moderator of Luther's educational doctrines. The problem, however, was extremely complex, since the implementation of Protestant teachings needed a systematic, institutional basis. The vernacular September Bible provided a start, but it would remain a closed book for many unless reading were extended through a programme of popular schooling. Yet an adequate system of schools did not exist, and could not be established anyway for such a purpose. Luther himself recognized this impossibility as early as 1524 when he composed his famous address to the councilmen of all German cities urging them to establish and maintain schools for the Christian education of youth.[17] In this document is contained one of Luther's most comprehensive statements on education.

Opposition to Luther from Erasmus

Meanwhile Rome had begun to realize that Luther was a much more serious threat to the Catholic faith than had been imagined in the first years of the controversy. Criticism of the church was spreading throughout Europe, particularly in Switzerland where another schismatic priest, Huldreich Zwingli, was leading a movement of reform. By 1524 the course of the Lutheran conflict was most complex; in Zürich, for example, many of the church sacraments and liturgical practices had been discarded, including belief in transubstantiation, although in Wittenberg and much of Germany that particular doctrine was retained – Luther was a firm believer in it; generally, however, the seven sacraments were reduced to two, Eucharist and Baptism. And it was in that same year that Erasmus produced, under pressure from the church, his tract against Luther *On the Freedom of the Will.* Not that Luther and his supporters were deterred; the very next year Luther himself wrote a spirited reply, *De servo arbitrio* (*On the Bondage of the Will*), in which he argued that man's will is incapable of following the good, and that guidance is therefore necessary, to be provided by good pastors and good teachers. By this time Luther had a considerable following, including adequate princely and civic support; he had, moreover, already taken the first steps to put his educational theories into practice.

Towards the establishment of schools

Luther's Letter to the Councilmen of Germany

The earliest specific comment by Luther on education is preserved in a letter of 1523 to a humanist friend at Erfurt, Eobanus Hessus (1488–1540), in which Luther counselled him not to give way to the fear, expressed earlier by Hessus, that the increasing emphasis on theology would lead to a decline in humanist studies in Germany, thereby making the German people more barbarous than ever. Indeed, Luther reassured him, literary studies must be encouraged, for they were vital to the success of the Reformation theology. 'I am persuaded', Luther declared, 'that without an expert training in literary studies no true theology can establish and maintain itself.'[18] Moreover, the only way to a 'revelation of divine truth . . . is through a revival and practice of the study of languages and literature. Surely there is nothing I should less desire to happen than that our young men should neglect poetry and rhetoric.'[19] Some thirteen months later, in April 1524, he underscored these beliefs in a similar letter to Jacob Strauss in Eisenach, writing:

> I beseech you, do your utmost in the cause of the training of young people, for I am convinced that the neglect of education will bring the greatest ruin to the gospel.[20]

In this same year (1524) Luther also published his famous letter, *To the Councilmen of All the Cities in Germany that They Establish and Maintain Christian Schools*,[21] provoked in large part by a widespread public sentiment that the promotion of humanist studies, of the kind suggested in the letters to Hessus and Strauss, would benefit only a few and create an 'aristocracy of letters' having little value for the common people. There was, in fact, a widespread and deep-rooted distrust of book learning, pithily summarized in the popular rhyming apophthegm of the time, *Gelehrte sind verkehrte*: 'the learned are daft'. So, to gain the support of the burghers, Luther argues from a largely utilitarian position. Schools, he writes, are an asset to any city: they provide learned and law-abiding citizens, and promote peace and foster good government. In fact, the existence of an educated citizenry would save money, for it would release people from paying for the numerous exactions and imposts that priests currently obtain from the ignorant and credulous. The savings made by eliminating these ecclesiastical parasites could be used for the maintenance of schools, thereby furthering the cause of religious enlightenment. And, Luther adds with evangelistic vigour, such an action would be in accord with god's purposes, since young people, boys and girls, would be allowed access to the scriptures.

The conjunction between useful and scriptural learning is effected in this essay without any rational link. Luther provides no explanation of why schools should give instruction in both secular learning and the Testaments; on the contrary he asserts that the study of scriptures is required of us by god, and for that reason it is sufficient. Clearly he anticipated widespread opposition to the study of Latin, Greek and Hebrew in schools intended for the education of youth in civic duty and useful knowledge. While acknowledging that Greek and Hebrew belong to the higher levels of culture,[22] they are none the less necessary because god, in his inscrutable way, has made these two languages the vehicle of his truth; the study of Latin is required also because god chose Rome as the agency by which his truths are to be disseminated. Against the mysterious workings of the divine will of god there can be no appeal; reason cannot penetrate into that realm. Man can only recognize that these languages are 'the sheath in which this sword of the Spirit is encased; . . . the casket in which this jewel is enshrined; . . . the vessel in which this wine is held; . . . the larder in which this food is stored; . . . the baskets in which are kept these loaves and fishes and fragments'.[23] The study of these languages, then, is a means of reaching gospel truth, yet already, Luther claims, such learning is declining because of the primacy given by clerics and the church to commentaries and scholastic interpretations based on Aristotle. The evidence for the rapid disappearance of knowledge, he continues in the same passage, can be seen in the

> . . . deplorable example of the universities and monasteries in which men have not only unlearned the gospel, but have, in addition, so corrupted the

17   Luther preaching,
painting by Lukas Cranach.

18   Melanchthon, miniature by Hans Holbein, *c.* 1530.

rerum humanarum fortunatrix, mecũ
adeo consentiat, ut sapiẽtibus istis sem/
per fuerit inimicissima . Contra stultis
etiam dormientibus, omnia commo/
da adduxerit? Agnoscitis Timotheum
illum, cui hinc etiam cognomen, & pro/
uerbium ἠ εὔδοντῶ κύρῖῶ αἴρει . Rursum
aliud γλαὺξ ἴπῖαῖη. Contra insapientes q̃/
drant illa, ἐν πῖρᾳδί γεννηδέντες, & equũ ha/
bet Seianum, & aurum Tolosanũ. Sed
desino παρoιμιάζεϑ, ne uidear Erasmi
mei cõmentaria, suppilasse. Ergo ut ad
rem

nes, triste i fere habu/
isse exitũ, idignatus
scripsit, Σωκράτηυ ὁ
κόσμῷ πεποίηκε σο
φὸμ εἶναι κᾳὶ κακῶς
ἀνἕλε τῷρ σοκρατιώ ὁ
κόσμῷ Ἐρ τῇ φυλαῖ
κῇ, κώνσιορ ὅῖι πιῶρ τέ
θνηκερ πχλύποδα φα
γὼρ ὁ διογὲνῆς ὠμὸρ
τέθνηκερ Ἀἰχύλω γρά
φοντί ἐπιπεέπῶκε χε
λὤνη Σοφοκλῆς ῥᾶσα
φαγὼρ σαφυλῆς πνι/
γείς τέθνηκε κωνές οἱ
καῖα θράκιω, εὑριπι/
δῆυ ἐξωγορ τὸρ θεῖορ

Dum ad hunc locum p/
nichat Erasmus, sepi/
sir uidens exclamaut,
ohé, si Erasmus althu/
tis esset, ducerat profe/
uxorem.

ὅμηρορ, λιμὸς καπεδαπάνκσερ .i. Socratem mundus fecit sapientem esse . Et
male sustulit Socratem mundus. In carcere cicutã, quoniã bibens mortuus
est. Polypedẽ comedens Diogenes crudum mortuus est. Aeschylo scriben/
ti incidit testudo. Sophocles acinũ comedens uuæ, suffocatus perijt . Canes
Thracij Euripidem uorauerunt. Diuinum Homerũ fames confecit. Timo/
theum.) Hic dux erat Atheniensiũ, longe omniũ fortunatissimus, de q̃ Sui/
das sic scripsit, Ἐποίουμ πε αὐτὸμ ἐν εἰκόσιμ oἱ ζωγάφοι κοιμώμονορ, κᾳὶ πὰς τύ
χας φορόσας αὐπῷ εἰς δίκτυα πόλις, ἢ πορθῦν τα αυῖας, αἰνιῖόμμυοι πὺν εὐδαι
μονίαμ αὐῖ, ἀλαζονευό μονος ἐπὶ εὐπυχίᾳ ὁ τίμοθεος, ἔφη αὐῖ εἶναι μᾶλλορ, ἢ
τῆ πύχης, τὰ καῖορθάμαῖα. δ᾽ ὁ ἢ ἠτύχνσερ ὕσρορ, νεμεσησάσης αὐῖῷ τ πύχηρ .i.
Finxerũt ipsum in imaginibus pictores dormientẽ, & fortunas ferentes ipsi
in retia ciuitates, & populantẽ eas inuentes felicitatẽ ipsius, supbiens aũt p̃/
pter bonã fortunã Timotheus, dixit ipsius magis q̃ fortunæ esse, egregie fa/
cta. Quocirca infelicior euasit postea, indignãte ipsi fortuna. ἠ εὔδ ούτος κύρ/
ῖος αἴρει) .i. dormiẽtes rete capit. Hoc puerbiũ q̃drat in eos, qbus citra labo/
rẽ & conatũ, oia q̃ cupiũt, eueniũt. Natũ ab ipsoTimotheo, q uulgo εὐτυχὴς
.i. felix cognominat' est, q̃ fortunatior q̃ prudẽtior haberet. γλαὺξ ἴπῖαῖη)
.i. noctua uolat. Noctua sacra est Mineruæ. Ea dicta est Atheniẽsiũ male cõ
sulta, in bonũ uertere exitũ, unde puerbiũ, Noctua uolat. Ἐρ πῖρᾳδί γεννηθέν
τες) .i. q̃rta luna nati, puerbiũ est in eos, q ex durissimis laboribus, qb' alijs
prosunt, ipsi nihil fructus capiunt. Quod Hercules hac luna natus ferat.

Equũ habet Seianũ) Vtruq̃ puerbiũ dicebat de extremo infortunio, uñ
de natũ sit, explicat Au. Gellius. παρoιμιάζεϑ) .i. puerbiari, siue puer/
bijs uti. Suppilasse) .i. furtim usurpasse. Neminẽ nominatim taxauit, præ/
ter seipsum

---

19   Page from Erasmus' *Encomium moriae,* showing Greek and Latin texts, with marginal
drawing by Hans Holbein, from Basle edition of 1515.

Latin and German languages that the miserable folk [inhabiting them] have been fairly turned into beasts, unable to speak or write a correct German or Latin, and have well-nigh lost their natural reason to boot.[24]

Behind the polemic there was the substance of truth.

Luther continues to temper this appeal with the utilitarian argument: children need also the useful arts, which he suggests are the three scriptural languages along with German, history, singing, instrumental music and mathematics. Children, of course, cannot teach themselves these subjects and neither can most parents. Even if parents can, he suggests, it is an uneconomical use of their time. Intelligent and educated adults recognize that schools should be provided – 'for what purpose do we old folks exist, other than to care for, instruct, and bring up the young?'[25] – but clearly this task is best performed by well-trained teachers, and, significantly, he includes women ('gelerte und züchtige menster und mensterynn');[26] in this respect he foreshadows the development of an independent vocation. His view of teaching maintained throughout his life is extremely generous; next to preaching, he considers the occupation of schoolmaster to be 'the best, greatest and most useful office there is' ('nützlichst, grössest und beste ist').[27]

The schools themselves should be kept in suitable buildings and supported by good libraries with systematically organized holdings. Luther suggests, provisionally, four classifications: Holy Scriptures in Latin, Greek, Hebrew, German and other languages; literary works, pagan and Christian, that support grammar teaching and thereby give access to the scriptures; the corpus of the arts and sciences; books on jurisprudence and medicine. Again, keeping the practicalities of his plan in mind, Luther suggests that boys and, significantly, girls, need spend only an hour or two a day at school and then go home to their household tasks and so gain the rudiments in time that otherwise would have been wasted. In this respect Luther implies instruction for these children in the vernacular only, and in immediately practical subjects, since he states:

... it is not my intention either to have such schools established as we have had heretofore, where a boy slaved away at his Donatus or Alexander for twenty or thirty years and still learned nothing. My idea is to have the boys [the girls are not specified] attend such a school for one or two hours during the day, and spend the remainder of the time working at home, learning a trade, or doing whatever is expected of them. In this way, study and work will go hand in hand while the boys are young and able to do both.'[28]

And, perhaps in a bid to reassure the children as well as parents, he speaks out firmly against excessive punishment and meaningless learning. 'Today', he asserts – with what evidence we cannot tell – 'schools are not what they once were, a hell and purgatory in which we were tormented with *casualibus* and *temporalibus* [cases and tenses].'[29] The library that he suggests for these schools is for the brightest students, those who give promise of becoming preachers, teachers and other such educated persons able to render future service to the community. These students should be in full-time attendance.

Improving the schools in Saxony: the Visitation Articles

Luther's *Letter to the Councilmen* appeared at the same time that Germany was undergoing even greater social disorder with a peasants' uprising in the spring of 1524, which developed into a virtual war the following year. Basically, this was a widespread popular movement concerned with gaining greater personal freedom and relief from taxes. The peasants' indiscipline, however, and numerous excesses, led Luther to denounce them and to side with the Protestant princes who, through their collective army, the Schwabischer Bund, stamped out the insurrection by 1526. Although it secured his position with the princes, it cost Luther much grass-roots support. The next year (1527) the Protestant Elector, Duke John Frederick of Saxony, sought Luther's guidance in organizing religion in his territories, and in accepting the invitation Luther found the chance to implement his educational theories.

The first step was to make a survey of the condition of religion throughout Saxony, and for this purpose it was divided into five territories, in each of which a group of Wittenbergers was charged with preparing a report on the condition of the new religion and the schools. Melanchthon accompanied one group and in their allotted region they found conditions deplorable; many of the clergy were immoral and unenlightened in the new faith, and schools, where they existed at all, were extremely poor. Immediate reform was indicated, and as a first step Melanchthon suggested that a set of criteria of good religious and educational practice be determined. Accordingly, he drew up a short list of Articles of Visitation, the famous *Unterricht der Visitation an die Pfarhern ym Kurfurstenthum zu Sachssen*.[30] This document, originally in Latin, was then subjected to scrutiny, and owing to objections from Agricola, who felt that too many concessions were made to Rome, Luther mediated and drafted in German the final version of 1528 which contains two parts: detailed instructions in the Lutheran faith and a programme for the visitation, or inspection, of schools. The first part consists of eighteen articles of faith – a basis for the twenty-eight articles of the Augsburg Confession two years later. The second part of the document outlines the proper method of conducting schools so as to inculcate what Melanchthon termed eloquent piety (*pietas litterata*) or, as it is expressed in the German, *Beredsamkeit*, literally eloquence, not in the popular sense of glibness but as a term expressing the thoroughgoing articulation of man's intellectual and spiritual powers. At the same time, Melanchthon recognized the manifold dangers of eloquence, and expressed the sentiments of many classical scholars centuries before him in seeking to avoid mere demonstrative artifice and persuasive superficiality.[31]

In the *Visitation Articles*, Luther and Melanchthon placed responsibility for the establishment and maintenance of schools on the civil authorities, with the recommendation that teachers worthy of appointment should be learned in both Latin and Greek so that they would be able to draw upon a wide background of scholarship and not teach merely at the limits of their own knowledge. At this time there was no firm expression of the ideas that the schools could be used as the particular agents of specific faiths, and in both Catholic and Protestant schools either the scholastic or humanist programmes, or blends of the two, were in operation. This situation changed by the middle of the century, and in the later decades divergencies began to appear which, in the seventeenth century, were to harden into lines of virtually complete separation between the two confessions. In the plan of 1528, still relatively unconcerned with these issues, the school was to be organized into three divisions, one for beginners, the second for those learning grammar, the third for those who were able to complete the second-division programme successfully. The plan not only set out subjects of instruction in detail, it also specified the hours at which they were to be taught.

The first-division children were to begin with a manual containing the alphabet, the creed and the Lord's Prayer. After they had memorized these they were read Cato and Donatus as an introduction to Latin and then to proceed to regular instruction in reading and writing Latin, along with singing. The study of Latin was to be, in fact, the overwhelming concern of the school. The opening paragraphs on 'Schools', *Von Schulen*, state explicitly that 'schoolmasters are to be concerned about teaching the children Latin only, [and] not German or Greek or Hebrew', and this sentiment is repeated at the end:

> ... pupils shall also be required to speak Latin. The schoolmaster himself, as far as possible, should speak only Latin with the pupils so that they become accustomed to and are encouraged in this practice.[32]

The second division (*der ander hausse*) had a much more extensive curriculum. The day was to begin with explanation by the pupils of their understanding of one of Aesop's *Fables* set, the previous day, for home study. This was to be followed in turn by lessons in declining Latin nouns and conjugating verbs, the memorization of passages from the two Latin comic playwrights Plautus and Terence, and exercises in Latin grammar, etymology, syntax and prosody, all taught by the method of constant repetition. The afternoon programme began with singing; next the teacher was to set one of Aesop's fables for homework and then a passage from Petrus Mosellanus' *Paedologia*, a set of Latin colloquies, followed by a colloquy from Erasmus. Then, before the school closed, when the children were to be sent home for the night, they were to be given a short maxim, preferably from a classical source, to memorize and repeat the next morning, such as *Fortuna quem nimium fovet, stultum facit* (Fortune makes a fool of him on whom it smiles too much) or from Ovid, *Vulgas amicitias utilitae probat* (the crowd praises friendship for its usefulness).[33] The second and third divisions were to spend the morning in common; in the afternoon the third group, composed of the very best students (*geschicktisten*), were to be given instruction in music and then were to proceed to the study of Virgil, Ovid's *Metamorphoses* and Cicero's *Officia* or *Epistolas familiares* (*Familiar Letters*). Once grammar was sufficiently mastered, the students should be instructed in dialectic and rhetoric. To round out their work, they were to be set a weekly exercise in prose composition, and one day a week was to be given over completely to religious instruction.

These *Visitation Articles* received the assent of the Elector and henceforth became the basis of Saxon educational endeavour, being issued in a revised version in 1539. In the previous year a Latin translation had been adopted in Denmark and in 1545 they were used to organize education in the Diocese of Naumberg.

Luther's sermon On Keeping Children in School

Despite the success of the visitation programme, it is not the case that Germany was rapidly won over to the cause of a wider education; on the contrary, Luther had to fight longer to achieve this goal. In fact, by 1530, despite the examples of individual cities, the burghers were conspicuously tardy in establishing and maintaining schools, and this prompted Luther to issue a second tract on education in 1530, of comparable length and importance to his *Letter to the Councilmen*, this being his equally famous Sermon *On Keeping Children in School* (*Eine Predigt, dass man Kinder zur Schulen halten solle*).[34]

Although nominally called a sermon (*Predigt*), this tract *On Keeping Children in School* was never preached; it was written specifically for wide distribution and reading, being sent first to Melanchthon before release to the public. Luther spent some time in composing it, during a year of enforced inactivity in Coburg Castle. Dedicated to Lazarus Spengler, Syndic (magistrate) of Nuremberg, in recognition of his efforts to make his a leading city in educational matters, it was prompted by the lack of sufficient response to the *Letter to the Councilmen* of 1524, and, like that earlier letter, it traverses the same ground, although even more forcefully. Indeed, this new homily has all the rhetorical hallmarks of the sermonical style, and as such it does not, on first reading, appear to develop a consistent theme. Rather, as a sermon might be expected to do, it moves from arguments of utility to those of intrinsic validity rather freely, it has its elements of hyperbole and emotionally heightened appeals to parental vanity on the one hand, and sense of shame on the other. But within, it has a consistent and carefully constructed argument: everything depends primarily on a precondition of civil equity and continuity maintained by the rule of law; and this, in turn, can only prevail if the people are educated to a sufficient level of understanding. This will require a higher standard of public education than that currently existing, not simply to provide the necessary proportion of skilled persons, but in order to create a wider public consciousness of, and appreciation for, the desirability of a well-ordered and well-governed society. The whole argument has a particular urgency in view of the chaotic times that stimulated it.

Luther knew that he had to overcome burgher mistrust of formal booklearning, so readily identified in Protestant Germany with its Catholic history and, certainly to an extent, irrationally linked therefore with that corrupt church. Moreover, the merchant classes, his chief target, generally – despite obvious exceptions of the great families who patronized arts and culture – had a disdain for the apparently leisured and easy life of scholars, compared to the hard work of daily commerce in which a knowledge of the basic elements of literacy – reading, writing, reckoning – sufficed. So we find Luther attacking this directly, acknowledging that, 'as they say, the learned are daft' ('denn die gelerten heisst man die verkereten').[35] Yet, as he picks up the same argument further on, 'although the pen is light, certainly, and needs only the physical effort of three fingers, yet it requires the whole body and soul to work at it too' ('aber gantz leib und seel erbeiten dran').[36] And the argument for minimal accomplishments is just as vigorously dismissed in answer to the common burgher assertion that 'if my son can read and write German and do arithmetic, that is enough [because] I am going to make a businessman of him'. Luther counters with the argument that 'if preaching and law should fail, the businessman will not be [one] for long'.[37]

What, then, is Luther's chief positive argument for education, and just why do citizens have a duty to keep their children at school? Fundamentally, because the law was given to man by god, via Rome as agent, and cannot be maintained by fists and weapons, but only by heads and books.[38] From this premiss all of his sermon is derived. The law is maintained by all of the learned professions: professors and scholars, schoolmasters, community pastors right down to 'medicine and other liberal arts' ('ertzney und andern freyen künsten').[39] As a society sees to the maximum realization of the talents of all of its citizens so it will move towards greater stability and rule of law and, therefore, to a more godly condition. At the same time, Luther knew his audience: even if assent were given to the general principles of his arguments, how could individual parents be persuaded to educate their own particular children and not simply leave it to others? It was Luther's awareness of this reluctance of individuals to act that caused him to assert that compulsion really is the only effective means: just as taxes are levied for bridges, roads and works necessary for the public good, so education should be included, and therefore 'it is the duty of temporal authority to compel its subjects to keep their children in school, especially the promising ones'.[40] But compulsion at that time was not possible and so he resorted to exhortation, and this explains the continued rhetorical style and the constant appeals of all kinds, in specific terms.

So, at the outset, the sermon does not postulate the basic premiss of the maintenance of the rule of (god's) law; that comes later. Instead, Luther begins by stating his concern with the 'common people' (*gemeinen leuten*)[41] whose children are given to them, not for their own, but for god's service. Having denied parents any property rights in their children, the sermon then elaborates the reasons for keeping children at school: there are many good jobs going for the educated, it helps discharge one's duty to god, society will benefit. For ambitious and vain parents he holds out the promise that their sons can become 'highly learned doctors and masters of Holy Scripture' and so participate in performing great works – 'You can have a share in all this.' For those who have some idea of the intrinsic validity of learning, he adds, tantalizingly, that 'I shall say nothing about the pure pleasure a man gets from having studied.'[42] At the same time, to allay the fears of those whose children are more modestly endowed, the sermon stresses that not everyone has to reach the highest flights, for there are still many occupations requiring simpler attainments, and every boy 'ought at least to read, write and understand Latin'. His argument also anticipates financial opposition in stressing that great periods of time at school are no longer needed. The techniques of schooling are now so advanced that 'one can learn more now in three years than was formerly possible in twenty'.[43] Furthermore, he praises the benefit of literacy in the vernacular for all; 'even women and children', he continues, in an effort to make his argument more compelling, 'can learn from German books and sermons more about God and Christ – I am telling the truth! – than all the universities, foundations, monasteries, the whole papacy, and all the world used to know'.[44] He even adduces statistics to bolster his points: without much greater provision of schooling the reformed church will be in great danger, for in Saxony alone there are 1,800 parishes which require therefore 3,600 clerics at the usual ratio of two clerics per parish. Since in all of Germany there are only presently 4,000 boys in school – perhaps a figure gained from the school visitation programme – a severe shortage of pastors is predictable, especially since, on account of the disorders of the times, schools and universities, 'here and there . . . are so deserted that it is distressing to behold'.[45] So the sermon moves, in the form of traditional rhetorical persuasion, from point to point, even employing direct abuse, emphasizing that 'if you keep your intelligent son from school you are serving the devil' and that if a parent does not prepare his son for a glorious career, he is a 'gross, ungrateful clod'.[46] The sermon concludes, grandiloquently, 'Well then, my beloved Germans, I have told you enough. You have heard your prophet.' (' . . . ihr habt erwn Propheten gehort.')[47]

Knowledge and the limits of reason

Throughout his writings on education, and in his specific plans for its implementation, Luther gave explicit approval to secular knowledge, and thereby to the development of human intellect. Yet, since his evangelical theology was based on a rejection of any rational understanding of god, that is, on the assertion that man cannot, by reason, acquire any knowledge of god because he cannot know who, or what, god is (*quid sit Deus*),[48] it is important to explore Luther's views on secular learning and the legitimacy to be accorded to human reason. For Luther, there are two realms: *regnum mundi* and *regnum Christi*, and it is the latter, the realm of Christ, that is beyond any rational access. Luther's metaphysics were derived in large part from William of Occam; like that fourteenth-century scholastic, Luther rejected universals and accepted only the reality of particular, individual experiences. In denying the reality of universals Luther limited the scope of reason to experience of this-worldly phenomena, to the *regnum mundi*, and so came close to holding a theory of double truth.[49] Reason, he affirmed, is limited completely to the *regnum mundi*; within this realm of earthly events, reason is autonomous and yields demonstrable knowledge. He called it natural reason, *ratio naturalis*, and regarded its legitimacy beyond question or doubt. Luther's well-known hostility to reason, expressed dramatically in his last Wittenberg sermon of 1546,[50] but manifested throughout much of his writing, was directed towards what he considered a presumptuous reason, one which has arrogated to itself claims to know the realm of faith. *Ratio naturalis* is nothing more than the method of logical discussion and inquiry and is necessary to man; arrogant reason, through the work of the scholastics and Thomas Aquinas in particular, has become no longer a method but a body of established doctrines. This, for Luther, is the prostitution of reason in the service of man's unwarranted presumption to know god definitively; such reason could be only in the service of the devil and Luther castigated it as Frau Hulda, the Devil's Whore.

Repeatedly, Luther argued from the primacy of the scriptures:

For whatever worldly order and reason disclose is very far below divine law. Indeed, Scripture forbids one to follow reason (Deut. 12:18; Gen. 6:5) ... Therefore, the attempt to guard or to base God's order upon reason, unless previously it has been grounded in and illumined by faith, is the same as if I wanted to illumine the sun with a dark lantern or use a reed as the foundation for a rock.[51]

While condemning such use of arrogant reason, Luther accepted the limited role of natural reason:

> Philosophy understands naught of divine matters. I don't say that man may not teach and learn philosophy; I approve thereof, so that it be within reason and moderation. Let philosophy remain within her bounds as God has appointed.[52]

Indeed, if man uses his reason for its own temporal ends, his way to salvation is facilitated. Opposing the method of Thomas Aquinas which employed reason as a way of guaranteeing faith, Luther asserted instead that natural wisdom and understanding must be set aside in matters of faith.[53] So Luther charted the course of Christian scholarship and learning: it was one of biblical study, with close attention to grammar and exegetical method, designed to provide access to the scriptures under the guidance of approved teachers already committed to the faith. Like Augustine, more than a millennium earlier, Luther emphasized the primacy and mystery of faith, and of god's correlative, grace. Man's faith and god's grace rest in ineffable mystery, and no amount of rational doctrine can elucidate or secure them.

The educational problem lay in reconciling the classical and the philosophical traditions with the stringencies of the evangelistic position, and in large part this task fell to Melanchthon. Like Luther, he accepted Christian Rome as the vehicle by which god chose to disseminate his message; behind Rome lay the cultures of the Greeks and Hebrews, the founts of god's wisdom. Melanchthon recognized the need to study the classical writers, and particularly to purify Aristotle from the commentators; without him, he stated in 1544, we cannot make any intellectual progress.[54] Melanchthon's only objection to Aristotle was his conception of the eternity of the world,[55] and in this respect Melanchthon examined the most ambiguous of Aristotle's teachings and the aspect that had been most emphasized by the Averroist commentaries: this was the uncertainty whether the world had existed from eternity, or had a finite creation by god. The whole Christian eschatology, and hence much of the legitimacy of the Protestant position, as part of the divine plan of continuing revelation, rested in the acceptance of a finite creation: the need to know certainly that god had created the world was crucial to the success of the evangelistic educational programme, although it admitted of no final demonstration. The best that could be done was, proceeding from a deeply held conviction of faith, to organize school studies around a study of the scriptures and to attempt the cultivation of learned piety (*pietas litterata*). It was this task that Melanchthon had begun quite early in his association with Luther, and it was from Melanchthon's efforts, in large part successful, that the pietistic character of German education in the sixteenth century, and thereafter, was derived.

Owing in no inconsiderable part to Melanchthon's efforts, the implementation of Christian pietistic education and the expansion of schools became accelerated and, in contrast to Luther's letter of 1524, the sermon of 1530 stimulated a greater response; in a sense it was an affirmation of a new spirit which had begun to take hold of the country. In the decades that followed schools were founded increasingly on this Lutheran model. Even the universities were influenced by the new educational ideal of *Beredsamkeit*. Under Luther's influence Wittenberg dropped much of the traditional study of Aristotle and substituted humanist studies: languages, mathematics and classical authors in the quadrivium, while in the trivium emphasis moved from dialectic to grammar. Wittenberg, and subsequently other German universities, dropped the scholastic and philosophical outlook of medieval provenance and henceforth took on a scriptural-exegetical cast in their approach to knowledge.

The role of the schoolmaster

For his part, Luther never ceased to expound the virtues of education and to extol the office of schoolmaster. As schools spread and enrolments increased he found less need to speak out as strongly as before, but, none the less, education remained an active idea in his writings. In his *Lectures on Galatians*, delivered in 1535, five years after the sermon *On Keeping Children in School*, he reaffirmed the concept of law. Indeed, since 'the devil reigns in the whole world and drives men to all sorts of shameful deeds, . . . God has ordained magistrates, parents, teachers, laws, shackles and all civic ordinances so that, if they cannot do any more, they will at least bind the hands of the devil and keep him raging at will'.[56] Again, the chief burden of one of his short Table Talks of 1540 is a summary of the sermon of 1530 to the effect that all civilized society depends upon education, mediated by the schoolmaster. Here, it is rather interesting to read Luther chiding young preachers for being too ready with their tongues and suggesting, with no apparent sense of contradiction, that he wished 'nobody would be chosen preacher unless he had first kept school',[57] for among other benefits it would induce humility 'for it involves much work and is held in low esteem'.[58] But, it is important to note, neither here nor elsewhere does Luther ever grant any autonomy to the process of education; it is always tied to an instrumental role in preserving religion, and the reformed church. Two years later, in a Table Talk for 1542, *Scholae*, he wrote that 'when schools flourish things go well and the church is secure . . . God has preserved the church through the schools'.[59] And, in a sense, this imposes definite limits on his conception of education in so far as it never escapes a totally instrumental role. Indeed, in his final, and sixty-seventh, year, in his last sermon from Wittenberg, he expressed a profoundly Augustinian conviction that reads like a passage either from Augustine's *City of God* or Clement's *Paidagogos*:

> If we were altogether pure, we should have no need to be admonished, and would be like the angels in heaven with no need for a schoolmaster, and do everything willingly of ourselves.[60]

Religious schism and church response

In respect of religious matters the church in Rome had not remained indifferent to developments in Germany; on the contrary it had been intensifying its diplomatic activities to achieve some conciliation and possible accommodation of the Lutherans, although there were numerous difficulties in the way, resulting from the ferment throughout much of Europe. In 1525, not only were the peasants of Germany in revolt; in addition, Charles V, the Holy Roman Emperor, was at war with France and the Turkish spectre loomed ever closer. The following year (1526) the Imperial Diet convened at Speyer to attempt mediation, but nothing was settled and Germany drifted even further away from Rome. A second Diet of Speyer met in 1529 and the conservative majority, in full control, voted to revoke all toleration of Lutherans in Catholic regions; in response, the petition, or *Protestatio*, of the Lutherans to the Archduke Ferdinand urged freedom of individual conscience and respect for the rights of minorities. Apart from introducing the term Protestant into religious discussion in Europe, that second Diet did no more than prepare for yet another meeting to be held at Augsburg in 1530. For this conference Melanchthon was charged with supervising the writing of a conciliatory statement representing the position of the Protestants, as they were known thereafter; the document that he produced, known as the Augsburg Confession, contains twenty-eight articles of faith and a conclusion. It was rejected by Charles V and, after a period of charge and counter-charge, both sides reached the brink of war. By 1532 war was averted only because of the presence of the Turks outside Vienna and the protective confederation formed by the Lutherans in the League of Schmalkald, named after the town in which they drew up their convenant. Charles V, moreover, was still at war with France. When the conflict with France was concluded in 1544 Charles turned to Germany, meeting the Protestant army and defeating it in 1547. No real victory ensued for him. The German states fell apart into their separate elements and Charles, who, as the Protestants knew, coveted his sovereignty, had no one to treat with.

Meanwhile Luther, growing old and irascible, committed diplomatic blunders, particularly when he approved the bigamy of Philip of Hesse in 1540. He died in 1546, ten years after the death of Erasmus. Melanchthon lived on to see the success of the Protestant cause; in 1552 the Peace of Passau prepared the way for an agreement – by no means permanent as it happened – at Augsburg in 1555. In that settlement Lutheranism was recognized as a legitimate faith, although other Protestant movements such as Calvinism which had been growing, particularly in Switzerland, with its headquarters in Geneva, were not given recognition. This recognition of Lutheranism was, in a very real sense, Melanchthon's triumph, and when he died five years later in 1560 his students gave him the accolade *praeceptor noster communis, praeceptor Germaniae*: our teacher, indeed, teacher of all Germany. Augsburg, for which he had fought so valiantly, was still a compromise, a settlement *cuius regio, eius religio*: as the prince chooses his faith, so must the people follow him.[61] Individual conscience was not yet tolerated. Yet by the mid-century the efforts of these three – Erasmus, Luther, Melanchthon – had prepared the way for a new approach to learning and piety, although their influences came from different motivations, and were felt in various ways. The work of Erasmus was reflected on the continent, but most particularly in England where the philosophic approach to religious understanding and education was culti- vated; in Germany both theology and education continued to reflect the philological and scriptural approaches urged by Luther and Melanchthon.

Further schism from Rome: Switzerland

Many of the developments in Switzerland which gave an added com- plexity to the disputes of the period occurred independently of those in

Germany, although of course there was much intercommunication of ideas. The first movements to reform came as a result of the teaching of Huldreich Zwingli (1484–1531) who had been preaching doctrines of religious simplicity since 1506 at Glarus where he commenced his priesthood in his twenty-third year. Zwingli went to Zürich in 1518, after an interval at Einsiedeln, and became an outspoken supporter of the primacy of scriptural authority – signalled in his first major tract of 1522 *Von Erkeisen und Freiheit der Speisen* (*On Choice and Freedom of Food*) – although his stimulus and inspiration, rather ironically, came from Erasmus rather than from Luther. By 1530 Zürich and its surrounding canton was overwhelmingly Protestant and in that year the emissaries of Zürich presented their confession at Augsburg, along with the Lutherans, and had it rejected out of hand. The following year, 1531, the Catholic cantons marched on Zürich and, in the Battle of Cappel that followed, Zwingli was killed, his troops defeated. Zwingli was succeeded as chief pastor of Zürich by Johann Bullinger (1504–75), while his place as leader of the reformed churches of South German and Swiss Protestantism was taken by Martin Bucer (1491–1551), who had been a Dominican priest until his excommunication in 1523, resulting from his support for Luther and the latter's marriage to Katherine von Bora in 1522.

The battle of Cappel checked the expansion of Zwingli's form of Protestantism, although it was not eradicated. Geneva, another city in the Swiss Confederation, by 1538 had turned to the reforming cause under the leadership of the Frenchman, Jean Calvin (or Cauvin). The son of a secretary to the bishop of Noyon in France, Calvin (1509–64) was sent to study at the University of Paris where he graduated master of arts in 1528. In this period he became influenced by the new Protestant doctrines and in 1534, as a result of active proscriptions of the new faith in France by Francis I, he left for Basle in Switzerland, where in 1536 he published the first version of his widely studied Latin theological treatise *Christianae religionis institutio* (*Institutes of the Christian Religion*) which was reissued in an enlarged edition of 1539; a French translation by Calvin himself followed in 1541, and two final editions some years later, the Latin version in 1559, the French in 1560. These *Institutes* became the fundamental doctrines of the reformed faith in Geneva and were adopted by Protestants in France, Germany, the Netherlands, England and Scotland, in a movement that spread north from Geneva through the valleys of the Rhine and Meuse to the North Sea and across to Britain. Calvin left Basle in 1536 at the time of the first publication of the *Institutes* and soon after settled for a time in Geneva until disputes there led him to leave for Strasbourg in 1538. Three years later he returned to Geneva to lead its religious and civic life. Although his return was not universally welcomed he gradually assumed full control and by 1555 was the acknowledged director of all of that city's life, remaining so until his death in 1564. Calvin maintained an autocratic rule and imposed austere standards of behaviour on its people, imbuing them with his particular additions to Lutheranism: denial of the doctrine of grace, assertion of the certainty of salvation, and absolute predestination. The incompatibility of the last-mentioned two was reconciled through the argument that those who recognize these doctrines – that is, Calvinists – are among those whom god has preordained for eternal salvation. Calvin established the Geneva Academy in 1559 to train ministers in his new faith and Geneva remained the centre of the reformed church.

The establishment of the Geneva Academy – the first avowedly Protestant religious seminary although similar teachings had been going on for years in various universities – in the same year as the Peace of Augsburg marked a new stage in the development of Western culture: religious pluralism was now a *fait accompli* and Rome ceased to have a monopoly on the means to salvation. This pluralism, moreover, was not confined to continental Europe but spread in the same period to England and Scotland where it assumed other forms. Since the achievement of this religious pluralism was almost totally the result of intellectual developments, education was involved too and the way was prepared for finding new relationships between the dictates of faith and the inquiries of man's restless mind. Not that conceptions of education were altered dramatically; tradition remained the mainstay of practice, but, by this time, the way was opened, irreversibly, to an ever-increasing acceleration of the rate of educational change.

CHAPTER 13

Extension of Educational Thought and Practice in the Sixteenth Century

The sixteenth century was in general a period of heightened awareness of education indicated by the fact that the greatest scholar of the period, Erasmus, and the most charismatic, Luther, gave it their close scrutiny and support. At the same time they were not isolated in their endeavours; on the contrary, they expressed, perhaps more articulately and to a wider audience, what was being said and written by numerous others. Evidence of this more general concern with education comes from a multiplicity of sources, and this in itself gives the century a particular identity and complexity. Many thinkers concerned themselves with the process of education and sought to expand its range of concepts: scholars everywhere, whether connected directly with educational activities and institutions, or linked indirectly through a public-spirited concern, wrote about schools, colleges and universities. The early sixteenth-century scholar, moreover, as exemplified by Erasmus, was a European rather than a national figure. Specific developments of course were regional, notably in Germany where Luther and Melanchthon initiated the principles and procedures of making the schools into instruments of a particular religious persuasion, but generally the efforts of most educational reformers were directed towards the improvement of schools and their curricula free of any doctrinal issues. Formal school education was still considered a single process with the one ultimate aim of leading man to god, and for many of the scholars of Erasmus' day it would have appeared contradictory to qualify the word with such adjectives as national or vocational. Yet, at the same time, movement towards educational diversification and extension was also characteristic of the sixteenth century.

There was, however, no unanimity of viewpoints concerning education: both Erasmus and Luther express considerable idealism in many of their statements, and even a certain impracticality, although, of course, they cannot be blamed for this. Their thought simply reflected the circumstances of the times which were dominated not only by the cataclysmic events of the various Protestant schisms, but also by profound changes in social, political and economic life. Feudal society was generally obsolescent, having been replaced in western Europe by central governments, those of France and England being particularly powerful; even when feudal customs lingered they did so only at courts and then in vestigial or highly manneristic forms, the only major exception to this being the continued and necessary training of the upper classes in the techniques of military warfare. The significant social and political changes of the century came from the considerable growth of the urban bourgeoisie, and in Italy their further development into powerful princely houses. This in itself, although part of a long process already in evidence by the fourteenth century, was now associated with the rapidly widening economic base of Europe resulting from the more efficient use of the land and the expansion of trade, particularly into the new world of the Americas. The period also saw continued increases in population and greater social mobility with resulting pressures towards more extensive provisions for education. This heightened awareness of the possibilities of education was stimulated by the expansion of Italian humanism north into Transalpine Europe and the influence exerted by the humanist programme of literary studies, in which, it is important to recall, the concept of the active, civic life was decidedly utilitarian. The promotion of *vita activa* had come from the Florentine response to political and economic threats, and the humanist statesman-scholar was conceived essentially as the type of person able to secure and to maintain liberty. The economic motive remained very strong. Interludes of aesthetic diversions such as were pursued by the circle of poetasters who clustered around Ficino's Academy cultivating the romantic style of *trattato* writing sometimes obscure the fundamental belief of the period that education in nearly if not all of its senses was conceived to be eminently practical, although this concept of practical must not be confused with the immediately instrumental. The ultimate embodiment of the *trattato* in courtesy books intended to train the courtier or, as he was sometimes called in England, the Italianate gentleman, is consistent with the utilitarian view. The education of the courtier, like the training of the priest or protestant pastor, was recognized as a need to be met, and only gradually, it might seem, did it become evident that this and other emerging developments had to be reconciled within a wider concept of education.

The writers of the period, however, did not themselves always appreciate the fact that they were responding to new developments in European culture, and in many cases they assumed that they were merely regularizing existing practices or intensifying current theories of education. Yet in the same period as Erasmus and Luther there were a number of significant scholars who, while working within the established framework of the received intellectual tradition, in the process of seeking to improve the schools and colleges of their day, actually extended the limits of current conceptions of education. Quite a few important thinkers made effective contributions and of these More, Sadoleto, Vives, Sturm and Elyot, whose writings influenced many of the schoolmasters and less conspicuous educational writers and administrators throughout Europe, deserve special mention. And, indeed, a consideration of their nationalities and the places where they worked shows very clearly how widespread was the belief that education should remain within the established tradition of the *studia humanitatis*, using Latin and thereby transcending national boundaries. Erasmus, it will be recalled, was a Netherlander; More and Elyot were Englishmen, Vives a Spaniard who lived in England and Flanders, Sadoleto an Italian, Sturm a German.

Knowledge as the way to peace: More, Sadoleto, Vives

Thomas More and English independence of Rome

Thomas More (1478–1535) was the son of a judge, Sir John More. From grammar school he was sent to Oxford where he studied under two of the scholars who were introducing humanism into England, Grocin and Linacre. After graduating at Oxford in 1494 More began further studies for the law at Lincoln's Inn – then becoming a popular London centre of

REFORMATION EUROPE

higher learning – and after some interlude he remained in legal practice for the rest of his life. His vocation was marked by exceptional success; he was promoted from one public position to another quite swiftly and in 1529 succeeded Cardinal Wolsey as lord chancellor of England, a post from which he resigned in 1532. Five years later in 1534, by the Statute of Supremacy, King Henry VIII repudiated the authority of Rome over the church in England, thereby climaxing a long-developing process; this involved More profoundly.

The immediate stimulus to the break with Rome was Henry's excommunication in 1533 by Pope Clement VII for illegally divorcing Catherine of Aragon and marrying Anne Boleyn, but Henry's arrogation to himself of all ecclesiastical authority in England was no act of mere caprice. England always had a strong religious hierarchy, who in the fourteenth century referred to themselves in their various documents as *ecclesia Anglicana*, meaning both the church *in* England and the church *of* England. Almost two centuries before Henry's action, the Statue of Provisors in 1351 had guaranteed that clerics should be elected to their benefices by the king and his lords, not by the pope; specifically the statute decreed 'the King and other lords shall present unto benefices of their own, and not the Bishop of Rome'. The power of the king of England was strengthened throughout the later decades of the century while the papacy was stricken in the Great Schism, and the king retained this ascendancy throughout the fifteenth century. In the person of Henry VIII this authority was held tenaciously, particularly since Henry was a strong monarch and himself the embodiment of current princely ideals – a scholar of religious matters and thoroughly schooled in humanist learning. Henry had no intention of abandoning the Catholic faith; on the contrary he had been given the title *Fidei defensor* (Defender of the Faith) in 1521 by Pope Leo X for his arguments against Luther. Henry's action of 1534 was in part – although it was also much more – a regularization of the *de facto* independence the *ecclesia Anglicana* had enjoyed. To secure his authority, one of his first acts was the dissolution of the monasteries over a three-year period between 1536 and 1539 and the transfer of their wealth to the crown for redistribution, for which the recipients generally had to pay in hard cash. This had little immediate effect on education, however, since the monasteries had generally ceased by this time to be important centres of learning.

Changes in the Catholic faith necessary to sustain the new situation soon came, although in Henry's reign, until his death in 1547, these were relatively minor. What was of major significance, however, was the translation of the New Testament into English by the evangelistic Protestant William Tyndale (*c.* 1494–1536). Although opposed by the English hierarchy when it appeared in 1526 – and Tyndale in fact published it in Worms where he had fled earlier – this became established in English religious life. Henry's successor, Edward VI (r. 1547–53), allowed the first steps towards Protestantism by authorizing Thomas Cranmer, archbishop of

Canterbury, to issue the Book of Common Prayer in 1549, followed by a second in 1552, and in 1553 the specific doctrines of Anglican faith known as the Forty-Two Articles. Mary Tudor, daughter of Henry VIII and Catherine of Aragon, succeeded Edward VI in 1553 for five years and attempted, unsuccessfully, a Catholic revival and the persecution of Protestants. By this time, the reformed faith had taken hold and despite her proscriptions England remained Protestant, a proclivity given vigorous affirmation with the accession in 1558 of Elizabeth I.

More did not live to see these developments. When Henry VIII proclaimed independence of Rome he required all English subjects to swear allegiance to the crown as head of the Church of England. More remained a steadfast Catholic and his intransigence regarding Henry's demand resulted in his execution for treason in 1535. By this time, however, More had already demonstrated his great talents for serious writing which established him in the ranks of Europe's leading scholars.

Incipient social conscience: Utopia

The first indications of More's concern with social problems and their connection with educational reform came from his continuing friendship with Erasmus ever since the two met in 1499 through their mutual acquaintance, Lord Mountjoy. It was in More's household in 1509 that Erasmus wrote *Praise of Folly* (*Morias enkomion*), and dedicated it to his host. In the following years when Erasmus was occupied with writing some of his most influential works on education – *De ratione studii* (1511), *Institutum hominis Christiani* (1514), *Querela pacis* and *Institutio principis Christiani* (both 1516) – More too was composing his major work. Completing it in 1516 he entrusted it to Erasmus for publication, writing 'I send you our *Nowhere* [*Nusquamam*], nowhere well written; and have prefixed to it a letter to my Peter. For the rest I have learned by experience, there is no need of my exhorting you to give it your best attention.'[1] This Latin work was published in Louvain the same year under the equivalent Greek title *Utopia*, literally, 'no place'.[2] It was an immediate success and More spent the following two years improving it, bringing out a Paris edition in 1517, and two editions in Basle, both of 1518. It was reprinted regularly thereafter and remains to the present day a popular literary work as well as a significant contribution to Western thought.

Utopia, which was written as a lighthearted exercise, is perhaps too deceptively simple, being a fanciful account of an ideal community isolated from the corrupting influences of the day on a remote island, the recent discoveries of Amerigo Vespucci in the new world described in his account of four voyages, his *Quatuor nauigationes*, providing an exotic setting. Yet the lightness of the prose, and the improbability of such an ideal society, should not obscure the fact that this work was a significant departure from the thought of the times, including that of Erasmus. More was a highly cultivated scholar, deeply versed in the humanist tradition, and in *Utopia* his erudition enabled him to examine the pressing social problems of the day, chiefly those of sustaining peace and securing justice. The theme, of course, has its *locus classicus* in Plato's *Republic*, and in many ways *Utopia* depends on the ideas of that classical formulation of an ideal society. More adds to it, however, ideas gathered from many subsequent writers[3] of Greek, Roman, medieval and humanist times. It is not, in the first instance, a study of education; rather it is unique in its style, and its educational discussions arise incidentally to the theme, chiefly because More seeks to give an account of an ideal society and so finds it necessary to include education as one important aspect. Most probably he had no intention of making it an educational treatise, and certainly the book makes no mention whatsoever of pedagogical or other classroom practices; none the less it becomes clear that his vision of the ideal state rests upon an informed society, itself organized as an enlightened democracy, electing an assembly, a senate and a governor.

The peoples of *Utopia* are organized into an appropriate number of balanced occupations, divided between rural and urban activities, sharing their production in common. In many respects their lives are abstemious, even ascetic, and they avoid many of the vices that afflict society: gambling, idleness, usury, vanity and cosmetics, for example. All citizens contribute actively to production, even at times engaging in agricultural labouring, and every citizen is required to learn a craft to which he is naturally suited.[4] The educational activities of the society immediately become apparent when leisure is considered. Since the communal life provides a just distribution of wealth, easily secured in a six-hour working day, time for recreation is amply available, and as idleness is absent citizens are free to devote this time to some occupation according to taste, 'these periods [being] commonly devoted to intellectual pursuits'.[5] This is a particularly popular activity and

> ... it is their custom that public lectures are daily delivered in the hours before daybreak. Attendance is compulsory only for those who have been specially chosen to devote themselves to learning. A great number of all

classes, however, both males and females, flock to hear the lectures, some to one and some to another, according to their natural inclination. But if anyone should prefer to devote this time to his trade, as is the case with many minds which do not reach the level for any of the higher intellectual disciplines, he is not hindered; in fact, he is even praised as useful to the commonwealth.[6]

There is a realistic acceptance in *Utopia*, revealed in this passage, of the limitations of many with regard to intellectual ability, and formal schooling is not demanded beyond reasonable levels of attainment requisite for the various crafts. Utopians in fact are extremely teachable. All children are introduced to good literature, and all schooling is given in their native tongue (*ipsorum lingua*).[7] Their remoteness means that they are totally unacquainted with European learning,

> . . . yet in music, dialectic, arithmetic, and geometry they have made almost the same discoveries as those predecessors of ours in the classical world . . .

although, More adds satirically,

> . . . while they measure up to the ancients in almost all other subjects, still they are far from being a match for the inventions of our modern logicians. In fact, they have discovered not even a single one of those very ingeniously devised rules about restrictions, amplifications, and suppositions which our own children everywhere learn in the *Small Logicals*.[8]

During More's visit with them, the Utopians were introduced to Greek and

> . . . they began so easily to imitate the shapes of the letters, so readily to pronounce the words, so quickly to learn by heart, and so faithfully to reproduce what they had learned that it was a perfect wonder to us. The explanation was that most of them were scholars picked for their ability and mature in years, who undertook to learn their tasks not only fired by their own free will but acting under orders of the senate. In less than three years they were perfect in the language and able to peruse good authors without any difficulty unless the text had faulty readings.[9]

It is from scholars such as these that 'they choose ambassadors, priests, tranibors [chief officials] and finally the governor himself'.[10] and this in itself is not a closed class; indeed, if a craftsman makes good use of his leisure hours in study and becomes accomplished, 'he is relieved of his manual labour and [is] advanced into the class of men of learning'.[11]

Towards an enlightened citizenry

Utopia is concerned with all the activities requisite for a balanced, equitable society, and it is abundantly clear that success depends on an enlightened citizenry. In a number of ways *Utopia* is more realistic than the *Republic*, and in this respect More shows himself influenced rather by the educational theories advanced in Plato's *Laws*. Despite much of its fanciful innocence, *Utopia* is decidedly allegorical and certainly it makes some sharp breaks from contemporary educational practices in Europe. The contrast is most evident in his concern for personal merit and his frequent appeals to individual nature as the basis for schooling and for social advancement, reflecting no doubt More's awareness of his own progress from a relatively obscure background, and that of Erasmus, among many others. More's aversion to scholasticism is revealed while his decided preference for vernacular instruction in the childhood years receives explicit assent, and during adolescence at least by implication; he is searching for the concept of vernacular maturity as the best basis for learning the classical languages, and this represents a pronounced contrast with his own times when boys were usually set to learning Latin in their seventh year or even earlier. More himself gave his own daughters a classical education at home by means of tutors, and his attitudes towards the instruction of girls, given some brief affirmation in *Utopia*, are also untypical of his times. The very notion, in fact, that all children should receive enough vernacular instruction to fit them for their craft, if not revolutionary, was certainly not commonly accepted. *Utopia* is significant not so much for its allegorical intimations as for its clear demonstration in the early sixteenth century of an expanding social conscience.

Utopia appeared at a time of intense religious feeling and increasing conflict – Erasmus, Luther and Pomponazzi were publishing simultaneously – and the whole of European intellectual life and its social bases were being subjected to new standards of evaluation. When the *De pueris instituendis* of Erasmus appeared some years later in 1529 it was the next realistic indictment of the barbarous school practices of the time and the relative insensitivity of society to the need for good schools and a well-articulated programme of education. Other voices were added to that of Erasmus, and in the next two years his work was followed by two similar treatises, which continued to express a new social conscience, although neither was as intense as More's. These were Jacopo Sadoleto's *De liberis recte instituendis* (*The Proper Way to a Liberal Education*) of 1532 and Juan Luis

Vives' *De tradendis disciplinis* (*On Education* or, literally, *On the Transmission of Knowledge*) of 1531, both of which sustained the arguments of Erasmus. Sadoleto's treatise[12] is important because it is the considered statement of one of the most learned and influential clerics of the day.

Sadoleto and universal harmony

Born at Modena, Jacopo Sadoleto (1477–1547) came from an intellectual background, his father having been a colleague of Battista Guarino and a professor of civil law at Ferrara. He rose rapidly through the church hierarchy, becoming papal secretary in 1513 to Leo X, who was formerly Giovanni de' Medici and second son of Lorenzo. In 1517 Sadoleto became bishop of Carpentras, and in 1536 cardinal. Like Erasmus, Sadoleto was deeply sensitive to the continued wars of the period, waged often in the name of Christian brotherhood, and his experience of conflicts in Italy motivated him to write on education. In 1520 the twenty-year-old Habsburg Charles of Spain had been elected Holy Roman Emperor, defeating his opponent, the young French king, Francis I. Tensions towards war increased, exacerbated by the growing Lutheran schism in Germany and the support given it by many German princes, by the continental ambitions of Henry VIII in England, and by the demands of the Turks, now occupying Hungary, for arrears in tribute moneys. By 1525 Charles V was at war with Francis I, the latter being assisted by forces from the papal and Italian republican states and from Henry VIII of England. Northern Italy was the locale of conflict, and from the siege of Pavia in 1525 until 1529 when hostilities ceased, that region was ravaged; Rome itself was sacked, and Sadoleto, in the city for part of the period on papal business, sought the pope's permission, granted reluctantly, to leave for the scholarly quietude of Carpentras, near Avignon, a place which he described, quite correctly, as being free from the terror and tumult of Rome.[13] Sadoleto lived through the period and in 1538, after his appointment as cardinal, he became papal mediator between the houses of Valois and Habsburg in one of the periods of truce.

The sack of Rome had precipitated his educational writing since it led him, as it did Erasmus, to see war as a contingent evil, resulting from ignorance and indiscipline, the alleviation of which he felt would come in part from a more widespread and effective programme of education in which the public support of schools was a necessary element. Sadoleto, in fact, had become much more involved with education following his appointment to the see of Carpentras, since he became charged with the supervision of the schools of the cathedral and the diocese. In this he was most assiduous, taking care to appoint good masters. As a direct consequence of his episcopal concerns he was moved to compose his major educational work, *De pueris recte instituendis*, which was first published in Venice in 1533, followed by editions in Paris in 1534 and Lyons in 1535. This treatise, written in the form of a dialogue between Sadoleto and his eighteen-year-old adopted nephew Paullus, was composed ostensibly as marital advice to William du Bellay – 'the best of all my friends' – who is complimented, in the opening pages, for having married a woman of superior physical and intellectual qualities and so maintaining the principle of good breeding. Indeed, the interpretation of marriage as a largely procreative and parental role is dominant. And it is not surprising to find the essay, having taken this theme, expounding what is basically a Platonic position with many ideas taken from the *Republic*. The dialogue form even strengthens the resemblance to Plato.

De pueris, then, sets out a twofold division of education into moral and intellectual, and deals with each in turn. The family must be the basic foundation of a sound moral education; the parents are necessarily responsible for their children's moral growth and this they achieve in the first instance by ensuring that their children are brought up in a disciplined environment. Discipline is used in its classical Greek sense of the cultivation of virtue – the Greek *areté*, the Roman *virtus* – and Sadoleto sees this as requiring two stages of development; a first in which the child is habituated 'to the authority of another's virtue',[14] this in turn leading to the emergence of personal virtue in which the child comes to act 'in obedience to its own authority'.[15] Sadoleto is careful not to confuse coercion and beating with discipline, and strictly forbids the father to flog his son, for this is fit only for slaves.[16] Indeed, the father must exemplify good moral character himself and so must display those cardinal traits of self-respect and its correlative, reverence for others, expressed by the classical Greeks as *aidos*, as well as exhibiting a sense of moderation in all things, which had received expression in the classical doctrine of the mean, *to meson*.[17] So we read that the child is to be raised first in a good home with his circle of acquaintance progressively enlarged to include carefully chosen companions,[18] all this to the end of reaching towards truth, which in a strikingly Platonic metaphor he gives as 'the luminary by which all forms of knowledge and learning are revealed'.[19] In this attainment of individual moral growth, Sadoleto asserts, the communal good is also secured.[20]

Truth, however, does not lie in the moral realm, but in the intellectual, and so the child, or rather young man – for Sadoleto envisages a twenty-four-year period of education [21] – must follow the Platonic path of seeking to cultivate intellectual virtue (*dianoetikos*). So the curriculum recommended includes the full range of humanist studies, Latin and Greek grammar and literature, rhetoric, ethics, arithmetic, geometry, music and gymnastics – virtually the seven liberal arts. In keeping with his times, Sadoleto saw the *studia humanitatis* as pre-eminent, this being reflected in his appointing in 1535 as master of the cathedral school, a Scot, Volusenus, whose competence was in teaching Cicero, Virgil and the elements of Greek.[22] Philosophy is considered to be the highest study since it is the integrator of experience; it provides an understanding of the interrelationships of knowledge and offers the widest possible vision, an awareness of the unity of all existence, although, as we would certainly expect, Sadoleto makes it clear that philosophy should be guided at all times by the Christian religion.[23] So he exhibits in his essay, despite its many traditional features, a profound interest in the social good, developed very clearly from the belief that a philosophic vision of the unity of all things will lead to peace and harmony.

Knowledge for the common good: Juan Luis Vives

An even more systematic and influential expression of the same ideal came the following year from the expatriate Spaniard, Juan Luis Vives (1492–1540),[24] who was born in Valencia. After attending the university there in 1508 he left the following year for the University of Paris where he remained until 1514, becoming acquainted with Erasmus who was variously in Paris and Flanders at that time. Subsequently Vives became a teacher, both in the position of tutor to William de Croy and then at the Collegium Trilingue which was founded in the University of Louvain in 1517 to teach Latin, Greek and Hebrew. Then in 1523, at the request of the lord chancellor of England, Cardinal Thomas Wolsey (c. 1474–1530), Vives went to England to occupy a chair at Oxford in the new Corpus Christi college, founded seven years earlier, where he came to establish a friendship with Thomas More. In 1528 Vives became involved in a dispute over Henry VIII's divorce of Catherine of Aragon, herself a Spaniard, and found it prudent to move across the channel to Bruges where he lived the remaining twelve years of his life. In Bruges, at the centre of the intellectual life of Europe, he remained in contact with Erasmus and More, and there in 1531 he issued his mature and systematic educational treatise, *De tradendis disciplinis* (*On the Transmission of Knowledge*).[25]

Vives had distinguished himself as an intellectual before this treatise appeared;[26] as early as 1519 at Paris he had written a vigorous attack on the arid scholasticism of the day entitled *In pseudo-dialecticos* (*Against False Dialectic*); in 1523, at the invitation of Queen Catherine, when he was newly established in Oxford, he wrote a very short tract on the education of the Christian women, *De institutione feminae Christianae*. His criticisms of scholasticism, begun in his essay against the false use of dialectic, were amplified in a new attack of 1531 entitled *De causis corruptarum artium* (*On the Causes of Corruption of the Arts*), a treatise in seven books. This corruption, he argues, issues from many sources having generally a common origin in human ignorance and lack of personal and social discipline. It is from these causes he observes, with Sadoleto, that the evils of war and political instability spring. Scholars are exceptionally culpable, for they are ignorant of their disciplines, lack any deep understanding of the classical languages or any thoroughgoing acquaintance with their literatures. The debt to Erasmus, and particularly to the 1509 treatise *Praise of Folly*, is clear; equally observable is Vives' dependence on the thought of other humanist scholars and the classical writers whose educational theories they sought to revive – Aristotle, Plutarch and Quintilian. To this invective Vives added two additional sections, one in five books dealing with the transmission of knowledge, and one in eight books on its content, the three sections being gathered together to form a twenty-book treatise on education that appeared as *De tradendis disciplinis* in 1531. The middle part, dealing with the transmission of knowledge, in five books, became the most popular and was singled out in the sixteenth century for special study.

In many respects its contents and arguments present no further advance on the humanist position; rather they represent in intensified and more systematic form the concepts already becoming current. Yet throughout this section Vives does present some ideas that are new and these, along with the clarity of his statement, help give his treatise some fresh force. The opening chapter, in fact, offers a quasi-anthropological account of the beginnings of society,[27] a marked departure from the conventional account of the Book of Genesis. God, he argues, is necessary in order to light man's way, and in this Vives casts him almost in an instrumental role. Further, god is the highest good, and from his love man has issued.[28] Beyond this, Vives has little to say on ultimate matters, although these two concepts reveal clearly his affinities with the theology of Aquinas and the teachings of Aristotle. He locates the centre of man's concern in the observable physical world; man makes his way by intellection, which is, in his view, a way of great importance. In selecting books, for example, it is important to choose wisely from the plethora available, otherwise 'life will fleet away before it has come to the bearing of fruit'.[29] Man's urgent task is one of achieving intellectual clarity, since from an awareness of the structure of the world comes vision of god's cosmic design and so awareness of ultimate truth, which itself is the terminus of all human intellectual endeavour. To meet this need man must utilize his own reason and become correspondingly preoccupied with the search for knowledge. Reason itself – the Latin *ratio* – is identified in the Aristotelian notion of intellectual clarification, it is the instrument by which man can discriminate and classify the data of the external world, it is reason alone which can yield knowledge. Vives is clear on the function of reason in directing observation through the senses:

> But I only call that knowledge which we receive when the senses are properly brought to observe things and in a methodical way to which clear reason leads us on, reason so closely connected with the nature of our mind that there is no one who does not accept its lead.[30]

The operation of reason in educing demonstrative knowledge acts as a natural theology or, as he says, 'advances piety',[31] this attitude being reinforced in his argument that knowledge permits man's scrutiny of the world. Knowledge itself consists in a number of divisions, and he instances history, natural history, dietetics, medicine, ethics, economics, politics, grammar, rhetoric, philology, practical wisdom or polyhistoria, geometry, arithmetic, poetry and theology.[32] There are two innovations to be observed in this respect: firstly, Vives has expanded the concept of knowledge considerably, the traditional liberal arts being augmented by studies that hitherto would have been considered practical, and therefore illiberal; secondly, his argument that knowledge both pre-exists in divisions and yet can be elicited by the inquiring mind, which is actually an attempt to set out the concept of scientific inquiry. Indeed, Vives was quite explicit on this point, writing that

> ... knowledge founded on experience is necessary to determine in what manner these means [of inquiry] should be secured and preserved ... we must partly learn to accept what has been handed down to us, and partly think it out for ourselves and learn it by practising it.[33]

Vives: the way to knowledge

In his argument, the school has a major role since it is by definition the institution committed to the pursuit of knowledge. Vives, like Erasmus and Luther, shared the current interest in the founding of schools: 'Let a public academy be established in each province of a country,'[34] he writes, referring to the local units of autonomous government throughout Europe as provinces. He conceives academies on the model of Oxford colleges as communities of scholars 'equally good as learned, met together to confer the same blessings on all who come there for the sake of learning'.[35] The academy so conceived could include lower schools – elementary and grammar – in addition to the advanced college.[36] Vives does make some specific recommendations for a lower school, separate from the academy, which he designates rather ambiguously: 'Let a school [*ludus literarius*] be established in every township and let there be received into it as teachers men who are of ascertained learning, uprightness and prudence. Let their salary be paid to them from the public treasury.'[37] This institution, called here simply a school of letters, evidently comprehends an elementary function although the bulk of his recommendations refer clearly to the Latin grammar school's activities. The children chosen for admission must have demonstrated an aptitude for learning, although the teacher should be a person of sufficient acumen to discern variability among the pupils, to respect their individual emerging capabilities and provide the proper stimulation for each type of personality. Reliance on Quintilian is evident here, as indeed it is from allusions throughout *De tradendis* where Quintilian is referred to at times by name but often is quoted directly without reference.[38] Like the *Institutio oratoria* of Quintilian, Vives' book is a manual of teaching method and its points are set out in full detail since it is addressed, at least in part, to an audience unfamiliar with the conduct of schools. It stands, consequently, as evidence of a growing interest in the expansion of provisions for education.

Vives deals explicitly with the vexed question of the use of the vernacular in the school. Usual practice was either to avoid it, or else denigrate it, and it was considered desirable to accept into schools children who had already learned enough Latin, probably from a tutor, so as to begin school instruction directly in that language. Certainly in this period there was no general acceptance among schoolmasters of the vernacular as a means of beginning instruction, and *De tradendis disciplinis* is significant in this respect since it attempted to accommodate the vernacular into the first stages of school instruction. The problem was a serious one, and Vives was sensitive to the role of language in mediating knowledge, seeing language in fact as 'the shrine of erudition'.[39] Although Vives makes no claim for Latin as an absolute language, he does argue that, in every practical respect, it is the most adequate and fully developed available and on that count alone should be the basis of instruction. Following his belief in the origin of human conflict in ignorance, he adds, wistfully, perhaps referring to the Ottoman advance through south-eastern Europe, 'I would that the Arabs and we had some language in common; I believe that within a short time many of them would cast in their lot with us.'[40] A teacher should know the children's mother tongue exactly so 'that by means of their vernacular he may make his instruction easier and more pleasant for them',[41] since, Vives argues, a clear exposition in the vernacular will lead to exactitude in Latin expression. There is here at least implicit recognition that the vernaculars of Europe were capable of permitting this precision of expression. With regard to classroom procedures, Vives gives rather well-established prescriptions: foundations of writing should be laid while pupils are being taught to read, details should be recorded in paper notebooks since writing fixes ideas in the mind, although this is not so necessary with Greek, since 'we only want to know the literature',[42] and the teacher should be moderate and restrained in his expectations, judicious in his use of rewards and punishments. The vernacular, however, is to be used only as a bridge to Latin, and the entire curriculum should consist in Roman writers, with the desirable addition of Greek authors.

To explain his ideas on the teaching of the classical languages, Vives gives some details. Latin studies should be graded, the child beginning preferably with Donatus as a guide to the rudiments of the language and thence proceeding either to Linacre's *De emendata structura* (*On Right Syntax*) or the *Rules* of Melanchthon or that grammar sketched out originally by Erasmus and subsequently emended by Colet and William Lily and known as *Lily's Grammar*,[43] which was just then gaining wide support. From there, the child could progress to properly censored selections from Terence, Virgil, Horace, Ovid, Martial, Livy, Valerius Maximus and Cicero. If possible Greek should be studied simultaneously with Latin so that both languages proceed together and give mutual reinforcement. The first book could be the grammar of Theodore of Gaza, and the second Aesop's *Fables*, followed by selections from authors including Isocrates, Lucian, Chrysostom, Euripides, Homer and Aristophanes. Along with this should proceed study of Greek grammarians, while all the time the child should be keeping notes in his paper book and attempting the construction of personal dictionaries in Latin and the vernacular, Greek and the vernacular, and vice-versa.

Vives deals also with higher learning and again his prescriptions follow the humanist position: Greek and Latin are the way to wisdom since through their literatures 'the works of great minds are handed down to us'.[44] Yet again his thought contains some distinct departures; Vives gives a much greater emphasis to the study of nature since man needs knowledge directly,[45] although he adds with some perception that nature of itself cannot give rise to certainty. The beginnings of knowledge are to be found in nature since 'the senses open up the way to all knowledge',[46] but this is merely the primary stage: to become true knowledge the data of the senses must be subjected to the discipline of philosophy. Here Vives shows his aversion to dialectical skirmishing and warns his reader to avoid mere nominalism since 'names in themselves of natural objects are not adequate for giving knowledge'.[47] Dialectic, rhetoric and logic are indeed valuable, but only, he cautions, as instruments for ascertaining the truth. Vives gives no clear statement on how truth is secured, although his writing exhibits an unresolved awareness of the need to use logic as a genuine tool. In a sense, he is feeling for a scientific method and for a logical process of induction.

The underlying restlessness of Vives' thought with respect to higher studies, however, is revealed most strikingly in his discussion of their values. History, moral philosophy, ethics, economics, politics, jurisprudence and law are all examined and recommended for their value in promoting 'right living', and it is this concept, closely akin to the classical ideal of the good life, that provokes some original thinking in Vives. At base, the intellectual activities of life are directed towards achieving the 'skill of accommodating all things, of which we make use in life, to their proper places, times, persons, and functions'.[48] Vives is here attempting to explicate the notion of an ordered logical design of the universe which, if extracted and apprehended by the human mind, will yield ultimate knowledge, or what he terms 'the connections of events' which 'lead to God'.[49] Throughout Book Five, subtitled 'Studies and Life', Vives attempts to expand the conventional limits of higher learning to include the experiences of practical affairs which might bear, conceivably, on understanding the cosmic design. In promoting his view of the interconnected structure of society and the cosmos, Vives has a rather different view of scholarship and the scholar.

Unlike Erasmus whose Platonic notions reserved final vision for a few, Vives argues that knowledge is a public possession, the common property of all men which should be shared freely: if, 'therefore, each man, for his part, to the utmost of his strength, will himself contribute, and will freely help others to contribute'[50] then the common good will be best promoted. All men, he insists, stand in need of ultimate vision: the poor to alleviate their condition, the rich to temper theirs; the happy to put energy into the right channels, the unhappy to bear misfortunes. Sustaining the intellectual search is the scholar who has the special task of striving towards moral rectitude and, emulating the example of Christ, passing on the same learning to others.[51]

Although similar in many respects to the thought of Erasmus, that displayed by Vives in *De tradendis disciplinis* reveals a more affirmative approach to the problems of the times. Vives attempted to incorporate the vernacular in the educational process and to extend education to a wider public, including a limited amount to women, who should study chiefly the Bible and patristic writers, following the advice of Jerome in his letter *To Laetia*. In seeking to expand the traditional and socially acceptable studies into the realm of useful and practical knowledge Vives was sensitive to the increasing preoccupation of the times with these matters. His perceptions on the abuse of learning, and his practical suggestions for improving schools, were in the forefront of the times, although other thinkers were dealing simultaneously with the same ideas.

Reform of the school

The ideas of More, Sadoleto and Vives illustrate the belief that civil concord and social harmony in a distressed world could be secured by the wider dissemination of knowledge and in More we find the express recognition that society itself can be an educational instrument. The thought of the times, however, generally remained preoccupied with the school as the prime agency; this is again reflected in the literature. The role of the school in disseminating knowledge and extending education received close attention, a considerable part of this being directed towards the need to ensure that the school's practices were suitably organized to fulfil its functions as adequately as possible. Yet men remained in the grip of their traditional practices, and when it came to the specific problem of seeing

20 Education in the early sixteenth century, woodcut from manual of astronomy, *Compotus manualis ad usum Oxoniensium*, 1519.

Ons escollers qui tant tendes
Aux formes des verbes scauoir
Je vous requiert que mentendez
Car par moy ce que pretendez
Pourres incontinant auoir
Il nest richesse ne bien auoir
Qui ne viengne de la pratique
Des formes qui bien la pratique

La premiere en droicte nature
Est nommee meditatiue

21 Sixteenth-century scholars and teacher, woodcut from Pierre Michault's *Doctrinal*, 1522.

that the organization of the school was as good as could be, this was interpreted, not in terms of any major change in the pattern of rote learning of
classical authors, but simply as improving the grading of traditional studies
and the correlative matching of the student's capabilities and attainment.
In this respect, Europe had an undisputed master whose example became
the most admired and widely emulated: this was Johann Sturm.

Sturm at Strasbourg: pietas litterata *and the graded school*

During the fifteenth century the Brethren of the Common Life had extended their schools from Deventer and the Low Countries throughout
the regions of Germany, and it was in one of their schools at Liège that
Joannes Sturmius (1507–89) began his Latin grammar studies, progressing from there to the university at Louvain and thence to Heidelberg
where he was influenced by the great humanist Jacob Wimpheling (1450–
1528), who was at the time a leading humanist of Germany, and who held,
long before Melanchthon, the title *Praeceptor Germaniae.* Sturm then went
to Paris where from 1530 to 1536 he lectured on rhetoric and the classics,
becoming influenced simultaneously by the Protestant teachings of Martin
Bucer.

Meanwhile, the magistrates of the free city of Strasbourg, which was
situated at one of the major crossroads of Europe, and was Protestant in
allegiance, had taken the decision in 1528 to reform their schools in order
better to promote the new evangelical faith. They appointed, accordingly,
a commission of three 'scholarchs' to recommend the best procedures,
and these in turn put forward the name of Sturm. Accepting the invitation,
Sturm left Paris at the end of 1536, taking up residence in Strasbourg in
January of the following year where he remained for most of his life.[52]
Sturm's talents were decidedly pedagogical and in 1538 he submitted an
educational plan on the model urged by Melanchthon. Accordingly, the
town's various schools, the earliest being a cathedral school founded in
1509, were disbanded and a single institution, with Sturm as principal, was
established the same year, 1538. It was given a new designation as a
Gymnasium, this being probably the earliest use of the term to describe the
Latin grammar school of sixteenth-century Germany, and reflecting, of
course, the self-consciousness of the classical revival which looked back to
ancient Greece and the emergence of higher learning in the precincts of
their *gymnasia.*[53] Sturm directed this gymnasium, to which a higher school
or academy was added in 1567, for forty-four years, until 1581 when he

was expelled from the city for his liberal political views. He was allowed subsequently to return and he died there in 1589.

The gymnasium at Strasbourg, early in its career, became the centre of European interest in educational methods. In the very first year (1538) Sturm set out his theory of method or *ratio*, which is a central term in all his writing, in his *De literarum ludis recte aperiendis* (*On the Correct Setting Out of School Studies*) which is concerned primarily with a 'ready way to the Latin tongue'. The purpose of education, he asserted, is to cultivate a wise and eloquent piety, piety, in fact, being the end of learning ('pietatem finem statuimus studiorum').[54] This central goal of piety was the outstanding characteristic of Sturm's endeavours throughout his lengthy tenure. Yet piety itself had to be cultivated, and this is the significance of the double qualification – wise and eloquent – for Sturm recognized that piety came from knowledge and the correlative ability to articulate such awareness. Accepting in general the conservative Christian humanist position, Sturm believed that the approved Latin and Greek classics – the *pietas litterata* – were the way to knowledge and hence to wisdom, and to an understanding of the divine plan of the universe. At the same time, an attempt to incorporate the rhetorical tradition raised a serious problem, one that had been a continuing concern of Christian educators since patristic times – that of the pursuit of eloquence subverting the attainment of piety. Sturm could not separate the two, however, pointing out that if speech is discordant and graceless then knowledge itself is barbarous: in consequence men fail to achieve awareness of the truth and substitute their own imperfect understandings.[55]

Developing Latin fluency, then, was the key to his method, and Sturm, like Erasmus, followed the practice of total 'immersion' of the student in classical literature. The proper method of schooling, he believed, is to get to the Latin and Greek authors quickly. For this purpose, the school, which accepted only the sons of the wealthy, amounting to around 500 altogether, was organized into fifteen grades: nine junior and six senior. Within each grade the boys were subdivided further into groups of ten, *decuriae*, so as to provide classes of optimal size for learning Latin effectively.[56] Entering around their seventh year of age, in the lowest, or ninth form, the children began in Latin using Donatus, and for the first three years they studied only this language, progressing from grammar as soon as possible to selections from Cicero – the exemplar of perfect Latinity – along with Horace, Catullus, Tibellus and Virgil. Thereafter the Latin curriculum extended progressively to the reading of longer works –

Plautus, Livy, Terence, Cicero, Caesar – with a pronounced emphasis on textual studies. To secure good Latinity, moreover, Sturm banned the use of the vernacular altogether, although he compensated for this by providing constant practice in speaking and writing Latin. Greek was introduced, as was more or less customary, in the fourth year of the junior school – the sixth form – and followed the same pattern as Latin although it was not used as the basis for speech and the demands on the students were not as great. In this way the course of studies introduced them to selections from Demosthenes, Aristotle and Plato.

In addition, Sturm's school taught some Hebrew, though with caution; it was not introduced until the final year – the ninth form – so as not to inhibit the acquirement of pure Latinity. Theology too was treated with reserve, and, although it naturally enough had its place, Sturm was conscious of the scholastic accumulations of the preceding centuries with their commentaries, *glossae* and *sententiae*. He was anxious to avoid any taint of scholasticism and strove to keep the *pietas litterata* and the reformed evangelical faith at the forefront of studies. So in the higher grades further subjects were added, the most important being the scriptures, chiefly the Greek New Testament, although this was supplemented by the addition of mathematics, consisting of arithmetic and astronomy; history, read in Livy and Tacitus; and geography, this study being concerned with the new nationalistic literature that had its beginnings in the early sixteenth century. Beyond these nine grades of studies in the gymnasium was the six-year sequence of the academy which offered liberal arts and instruction in several vocations, including law and medicine, and had authority to confer degrees. In its organization the gymnasium provided a solution for the systematic instruction of large numbers of children, and Sturm's use of a graded sequence of instruction, with corresponding classes or forms, was to become a major feature of most subsequent classroom practice.

Sturm was a prolific writer, and he corresponded, though not always punctually, with educators around Europe. In 1550, following the visit of Martin Bucer to England, he was introduced, through correspondence, to the Englishman Roger Ascham (*c.* 1515–68), then tutor to Princess Elizabeth, the future queen. Sturm and Ascham maintained contact thereafter, and thus helped to enable the methods of the Strasbourg gymnasium to reach England. Sturm's greatest direct influence, however, was in Germany where his school became the model for the large number that proliferated as a result of the proselytizing of Luther and Melanchthon. His work exerted an even greater influence on European educational practices through the activities of the new religious order known as the Society of Jesus which grew rapidly in the second half of the sixteenth century and came to exercise a virtual monopoly on Latin grammar schooling in the Catholic regions of Europe. The *ratio* of Sturm was the model for the Jesuit version which by the end of the century received its definitive form in the Jesuit *Ratio studiorum* of 1599 which was the most thoroughly systematic explication of pedagogical method ever devised for teaching the *studia humanitatis*.

Improvement of education in England: Thomas Elyot

One of the most interesting and equally progressive contemporaries of Vives and Sturm was the Englishman, Thomas Elyot (*c.* 1490–1546), whose widely read work, *The Boke Named the Governour*, published in 1531, the same year as *De tradendis*, expressed many similar observations. Elyot, who was the son of a judge, received a classical education, probably from a tutor. It is uncertain whether he went to university, but he did enter the law. Early in adult life, around 1522, he attracted the favourable attentions of Wolsey and entered public life, rising steadily in rank and eventually into diplomatic service. Following the end of his appointment as clerk of Wolsey's Council in 1530, he turned to writing and the next year published *The Governour* as it was known by its short title. In itself the title is highly significant: it is in English, and in fact this was the first book published in English on education. Moreover, it represented a continuation of the theme initiated by Castiglione's *The Courtier* which although written in 1508 was not printed until 1528. *The Courtier* did not appear in English until Thomas Hoby translated and issued it in 1561; in the meantime it was Elyot who provided the English model in this 'set-book' which became very widely used in England, especially in the households of the provincial gentry. Hitherto all reforming tracts on education had been written in Latin, and though they may have been read by the more progressive among the educated men of the day, it is doubtful whether they influenced many schoolmasters, whose continued ignorance, documented in many surviving accounts of the ghastliness of the bulk of schools, makes it far less certain that they were reading Erasmus, More, Sadoleto or Vives. Elyot's *Governour* is concerned deeply with this considerable discontinuity between the best thought and the usual practice, and possibly it was in order to reach the common schoolmaster that he wrote in the vernacular, since he realized that an ability to teach Latin grammar, aphorisms and pithy apophthegms is no guarantee of a master's skill in comprehending the polished Latin in which the reformers generally wrote. The decay of training, already attacked by Vives in his *In pseudo-dialecticos*, is discussed further by Elyot, and although the express intention of *The Governour* is to expound on the theme of advanced education for the higher ranks of public officials, he finds it necessary to survey the current lamentable condition of schools. Leaving no doubt of his own appraisal of the condition of teaching, he writes pungently: 'Lorde god, howe many good and clene wittes of children be nowe a dayes perisshed by ignorant schole maisters.' Elyot, in the same context, makes the charge that many masters can do no more than teach rules, and from these he withholds the title of grammarian, which should be given only to him, who

> ... by the autoritie of Quintilian, that speakyng Latine elegantly, can expounde good autours, expressynge the invention and disposition of the ma[s]ter, their stile or fourme of eloquence, plicating the figures as well of sentences as wordes, levying nothyng, person or place named by the autour, undeclared or hidde from his scholers.

Undoubtedly, Elyot declares, there are many such competent scholars in England but they remain unattracted to the schools because the vocation is held in contempt and salaries are so low. This cycle of decay is completed by parents who themselves fail to recognize the value of education and of employing good masters, or else out of personal avarice refuse to offer a reasonable salary.[57]

Elyot's theory of education for leadership

His central theme, however, is the training of boys for the highest civil posts, and for this Elyot gives a complete prescription. He offers the classical prerequisites of good birth and a wisely chosen nurse and, in advising on the early upbringing of the child, writes:

> I will use the policie of a wyse and counnynge gardener: who purposynge to have in his gardeine a fyne and preciouse herbe ... he will first serche throughout his gardeyne where he can finde the most melowe and fertile erth: and therein will he put the sede of the herbe to growe and be norisshed.[58]

This is a clear introduction into educational thought of the organic metaphor, presentiments of which already existed in More's notion of going along with human nature. At the age of seven the boy must be taken from the company of all women, since this is intrinsically deleterious, and put under the charge of a morally and intellectually competent tutor. Even

before this, however, Elyot recommends that the child should previously have been introduced to Latin and Greek – contrary to established
opinion which considered seven an adequate age – since neither of these
languages is the child's vernacular and therefore there is already much
lost time to be made up. If there must be a choice between these two, it
is better to concentrate on Greek since Latin is learned easily in the home
if he is a nobleman's son.[59] At the same time, Elyot is against meaningless
learning and retributive punishment: 'I wolde not have them inforced by
violence to lerne, but accordynge to the counsaile of Quintilian, to be
swetely allured therto with prasies and suche praty gyftes as children delite
in.' Without difficulty, he suggests, a start can be made with meaningful
learning so as 'little and little to trayne and exercise them in spekying of
latyne: informing them to knowe first the names in latine of all thynges
that cometh in syghte, and to name all the partes of theyr bodies'.[60] In
addition, the young child should be given activities in music, drawing
and carving before proceeding to the grammar master.

Progression to this master should be made when the boy is acquainted
thoroughly with the parts of speech in the vernacular, so that instruction
in Latin and Greek can proceed unhindered. Just as Elyot moderated the
early years of instruction with a careful consideration of young children's
interests and capabilities, so he is innovatory in respect of formal grammar
instruction. He suggests that only three years be devoted to grammar – 'I
wolde advyse [the master] nat to detayne the childe to longe in that tedious
labours, eyther in the greke or latyne grammer, for a gentyll wytte is there
with sone fatigate';[61] it is better to proceed as soon as possible to the
classical authors themselves. In Greek, a beginning can be made with
Aesop's *Fables* followed by selections from Aristophanes, Lucian and
Homer, with additional readings from Latin authors for reinforcement,
such as Virgil, Ovid and Horace, until the boy reaches the age of thirteen,
perhaps fourteen, when his 'reason waxeth rype, and deprehendeth
thinges with a more constant judgement'.[62] This is the signal to introduce
the boy to more serious works: Aristotle, Cicero and Agricola for the
study of logic; Quintilian and Cicero for Latin rhetoric; Isocrates and
Demosthenes for Greek. Yet a further innovation comes in his extension
of studies to include history – in its wider sense of 'inquiry' – and he
mentions both Ptolemy (Claudius Ptolemais), referring implicitly therefore
to the latter's *Geographia*, and Strabo, these two serving 'to prepare the
mind' for the study of Xenophon, Julius Caesar, Sallust and Tacitus. It is
most important, Elyot cautions, to sustain the boy's studies beyond the

age of eighteen since it takes all the time till then for him to grasp Latin; only at this age can true learning begin, commencing with three years of philosophy and then, in the twenty-first year, with the study of law, which itself is based on rhetoric. In addition, the young man should be exercised in wrestling, running, swimming, swordsmanship and skill with the battleaxe, archery, horsemanship and dancing, the last being given a lengthy, elaborate and highly symbolic explanation, most likely because it was not yet considered fully apposite.

The Governour stems from two sources: the first that of pseudo-Plutarch's *Education of Children (Peri paidon agoges)*, which was virtually the standard treatise on childhood education, although honoured perhaps more in the breach; the second, Castiglione's *The Courtier*, which represented the trend of current thinking on higher education outside the narrow circles of the universities which throughout Europe were still involved, in varying degrees, with scholasticism or its latter-day developments. Elyot in his opening pages avows himself a monarchist, favouring government by a single ruler, but at the same time he is aware that the expanding basis of sovereignty necessitates the delegation of more authority to officials, and this in a sense represents a widening of public responsibility. Like his friend Thomas More, whose career closely resembled his own, Elyot had emerged from the rising and increasingly articulate middle class whose aspirations and widened social and intellectual horizons were an aspect of the considerable changes then occurring. His own prescriptions for schooling, like those of Sadoleto and Vives, appear on the surface to be narrow and restrictive since Elyot addresses himself to the wealthy; yet he and his equally sensitive contemporaries reveal an awareness of increasing needs for schools and institutions of higher learning. Their concern over the lack of teachers is clearly genuine though the evidence does not suggest that teachers were in decreasing numbers so much as that the growing demands for their services created a shortage from which charlatans sought to profit.[63]

Recognition of the need to seek better-qualified teachers and to pay them adequate salaries is not limited to Elyot. In his 1524 *Letter to the Councilmen* of German cities Luther had argued that teachers should be much better educated, and to this end no expense should be spared.[64] Later, in a sermon of 1548 delivered in St Paul's church in London, one of the leading clerics of the day, Hugh Latimer, declared:

> Therefore for the love of God appoint teachers and schoolmasters, you that have charge of youth; and give the teachers stipends worthy their pains, that

they may bring them up in grammar, in logic, in rhetoric, in philosophy, in the civil law, and in that which I cannot leave unspoken of, the word of God.[65]

Beyond the school: expansion of educational activities

Although the central concern of most educational writing in the sixteenth century was with improving the grammar school and the teaching of Latin, since it was a mandatory language in many aspects of commercial life, it is clear that many reformers were searching, perhaps at times unconsciously, to extend the provisions of education, and as a first step came efforts at widening the concept. More, Vives and Elyot were all concerned with this. In Germany the introduction of nationalistic topography to the schools is an instance of this movement. Luther knew that he stood his best chance of promoting the cause of education generally through the improvement of schooling. Clearly, the needs of the times could not be met solely by upgrading grammar teaching. Expertise had become necessary for many vocations, and the customary pursuit of long-established craft practices was often inadequate: rapid improvement in techniques of ship-construction, navigation and chart-making, for instance, demanded the training of a new kind of ship's officer. Further examples exist in the relatively rapid growth of civil law, prompted both by the decline of authority and jurisdiction of canon law and by the correlative increase in commercial activities that demanded regulation; in the pressing need for improved methods of reckoning and accounting for business life; in the wide recognition of the need for acquiring the skill of writing, now absolutely necessary in virtually every aspect of middle-class life. Clearly these examples all reflect the widening interests and activities of the urban bourgeoisie. New subjects and instructional rationales had to be devised and implemented, and this concern is evident not only with respect to traditional higher learning but also in a new sphere of adult training. In both areas, attempts to extend the limits of traditional schooling were met inside, but more generally outside existing institutions. Hitherto higher learning had been virtually monopolized by the universities which had accommodated the professional studies of law, medicine and theology quite openly in their graduate faculties, and the preparation of teachers rather more covertly in the guise of the liberal arts, since the thirteenth century at least. Yet the initial developments were not sustained in later centuries at a sufficiently progressive pace and the universities, in many cases, were conservative. As a consequence, higher learning in the six-teenth century often developed new disciplines outside the university.

In England civil law had become centred near London ever since the early thirteenth century, when the Court of Common Pleas was established at Westminster in 1223. Lawyers found it necessary to rent quarters, and in nearby London several inns became virtually lawyers' dormitories, in time becoming known as the Inns of Court, of which Gray's, Lincoln's, Middle Temple and Inner Temple were dominant.[66] Students, *addiscentes apprenticii* (learners by apprenticeship), gathered there also, learning their future calling by beginning with the menial tasks of legal offices. This carried the rank of inner barrister,[67] which was followed by that of utter barrister (that is, *outer*) when the student was formally recognized as a lawyer by being called to the bar. There followed a period as a teacher of law in the Inns as well as further practice until the third rank of Serjeant at Law was reached which carried full legal qualifications. The three grades corresponded roughly to the Oxford and Cambridge equivalents of undergraduate, bachelor and doctor; indeed, the Inns initially appear to have copied their law curricula.[68] The Inns were self-disciplining and by the mid-fifteenth century students were bound to residence in, and obedi-ence to, their respective *hospitia*. By the sixteenth century the curriculum had expanded beyond law to include the liberal arts, and a contemporary writer, Sir George Buck, referred to the Inns as the third university of England.[69] The attraction in part was the cosmopolitan location of Lon-don; in addition, many students of the rural gentry enrolled, not for a legal education, but to gain a general background in the law so as to help them in administering their estates and, more importantly, so they could act as justices of the peace.[70] Since they needed also some general learning, this was supplied by the traditional liberal arts, thus broadening the curriculum and providing a type of education previously unavailable in England's capital and most populous city.

Further developments occurred on the continent and of these the Geneva Academy, founded by Calvin to train clerics of his new faith, is one of the most conspicuous. This academy is also notable since it was probably the first institution intended to provide a specifically religious training, in contrast to the traditional courses in arts, theology and canon law which were offered elsewhere.

Another significant development was the establishment in 1517 of a new college of biblical-exegetical studies in Louvain, which although organized under the aegis of the university was virtually an autonomous institution. This was the Collegium Trilingue provided through the will of Jerome de Busleyden (*c.* 1470–1517), a lawyer who became interested in promoting the study of literature and languages. Busleyden was advised by Erasmus, and others, chiefly Jean Robbyns and Jean Stercke, that this could best be achieved through founding a new institution for the study of Greek, Latin and Hebrew.[71] Soon after Busleyden's death the college was established, the chairs of Hebrew and Latin being filled immediately by Mattheus Adrianus and Johann Becker of Borselen respectively. Greek proved more difficult. An invitation to Janus Lascaris was unsuccessful – he could not be found – and eventually the youthful Rutger Rescius was appointed. Lectures in all three departments prospered from the start, although there was a period of subsequent internal conflict. This stimulated further similar foundations which appeared either as independent institutions, or as incorporations within existing universities, at Utrecht, Leipzig, Wittenberg and Heidelberg, as well as in Corpus Christi at Oxford and Fisher's college at Cambridge.

Liberal arts, theology, law and languages, being relatively formal activities, were amenable to institutional study along more or less traditional lines; at the same time the need for further education of adults outside these forms was experienced, amounting often to demands for self-improvement. To meet this, private instructors and tutors appeared offering courses in writing, computation and navigation, for example.[72] Another major contribution was that of the printing press from which came a proliferation of autodidactic books. Many of these, of which *The Courtier* and *The Governour* are the major exemplars, were intended to train the person who sought accomplishment beyond formal cognitive skills. There were numerous other kinds of these self-help manuals which seem to parallel those of classical Rome – the *ars*, *introductio* and *manuale* which served a similar purpose. In this same period the public need for knowledge is reflected in a second classical revival with the appearance on an extensive scale, entirely on account of the printing-press, of the popular encyclopedia. The term itself was used by Thomas Elyot in probably one of the first instances of the revived concept: 'Wherefore in as moche as in an oratour is required to be a heape of all maner of lernyng: whiche of some is called the worlde of science, of other the circle of doctrine, whiche is in one worde of greke *Encyclopedia*.'[73] The compendium offered the sum of knowledge, the fulfilment of the ideal sought by many reformers and expressed succinctly in the words of Vives as 'the connections of events which lead us to knowledge of god'. This promise captured not only the uncultivated minds but many a sophisticated one as well and encyclopedism was embraced eagerly as yet another means of education.

CHAPTER 14

The Search for Method: Towards a *Ratio*

Sixteenth-century concern with grammar

Reform of the grammar school: concepts of ordino *and* ratio

Despite the interest of intellectuals in the sixteenth century in extending the limits of formal education, and the numerous ways in which this extension began to be implemented, the dominant educational motif of the period was the quickening tempo of concern with the inadequacy of traditional institutions and their curricula. Many persons were attempting to improve the procedural aspects of schooling, ranging from Erasmus, whose *Adages* and *Colloquies* received a very wide acceptance, down to an uncountable number of less well-known schoolmasters. The basic educational institution was the Latin grammar school, and the most conspicuous efforts at reform centred on its curriculum since Latin was a mandatory language in many aspects of commercial and cultivated life throughout Europe.

A fundamental preoccupation was the search for the best method of instruction, itself a basic Aristotelian concept, designated in Latin by the terms *ratio* and *ordino*. *Ratio*, usually translated as reason, actually had a number of meanings including that of a theory, doctrine or systematically ordered body of knowledge. Sharing in this sense, *ordino* contains the idea of arranging things in their correct sequence. Intimations of this idea can be discerned in Quattrocento humanism, Battista Guarino's *De ordine docendi et studendi* being the first major explicit presentation of the concept, while the *De ratione studii* of Erasmus was the most systematic and stimulating contribution. Implicit in this search was the belief that learning and teaching would be facilitated if a *ratio* could be found, a belief reinforced by the further conviction that such a logical structure already existed as part of an inherent world order. Aristotle had taught that knowledge itself can be ordered into an overall pattern of relationships, and that the mind with its congenital discriminative structure can apprehend this order and so become one with its object.[1] The basic pedagogical task, then, is to seek out the structure of knowledge, in this case of the Latin tongue, reduce it to a systematic sequence and present it as a programme of classroom instruction.

Not, of course, that the task was set out as directly as this at the time; none the less such was the underlying motivating principle, and the search for a logical method of teaching Latin – and Greek, to a lesser extent – dominated much of the formal pedagogical activity of the sixteenth century, establishing a pattern for the following centuries. In terms of sixteenth-century thinking the problems faced were the immediate ones: to write grammar books in clearer language, to grade the sequence of instruction and the presentation of linguistic concepts, and, as a growing practice, to accommodate Latin more to the vernacular. Concomitantly, efforts were also made to improve the internal organization of the school itself, realized in the widespread acceptance of class grades arranged according to the pupil's progress, in the introduction of novel strategems to initiate and maintain interest and in the use of a varied pedagogy, chiefly mnemonic schemes and devices intended to facilitate learning and remembering. Both theory and practice were combined quite often in the work and writings of many scholars and schoolmasters in the first part of the sixteenth century, and since the vernaculars had not yet become established sufficiently to promote regional insularity and to isolate scholars, reform of the grammar school can still be discerned throughout Europe as virtually a single process.

Grammar texts: tradition and innovation

The universal feature of all educational prescriptions up to the year 1500, and in many treatises even for several decades into the sixteenth century, was the recommendation to commence instruction with the *Ars minor* of Donatus or the *Doctrinale* of Alexander villa Dei, and then to proceed to a simple reader, usually a collection of short pieces and known by the Latin title as a *florilegium*, itself a translation of the Greek *anthology*, meaning literally a gathering of flowers. Erasmus' *Adages* of 1500 was just such a work. Both Donatus' grammar, composed in the fourth century A.D., and Alexander's of 1199 were designed for the minimum classroom, that is, one consisting of the barest elements: a master reading or expounding to pupils seated on forms, with no further necessary equipment such as a blackboard or writing equipment – desks, pens, ink and paper. The *Ars minor* was arranged catechetically to secure responses by the pupils, the *Doctrinale* consisted of hexameter verses – another kind of mnemonic device.

The introduction of paper and its use in notebooks helped children to become involved more actively in learning; the development of printing from movable type made it possible to put a grammar into the hands of each individual pupil, in the ideal situation at least. So the pedagogical organization of the fifteenth- and sixteenth-century classroom underwent a minor revolution, and the new possibilities of the textbook and notebook used in combination were realized very quickly. Grammars and florilegia proliferated, of which one of the earliest was written in England in 1483 by Joannes Anwykll under the title *Compendium totius grammatice* (*A Complete Grammar*). This work is an early example of a departure from Donatus and Alexander since it includes explanations of grammatical and syntactical usage.

Some years later – just after 1490 is the estimated date – an even greater departure from tradition occurred when John Holt published in English his *Mylke for Children* which was accompanied by the parallel Latin title, *Lac puerorum*. Not only did Holt describe Latin grammatical rules in English, although his examples were given in Latin verse, but he also included a simple woodcut illustration of an outstretched hand to show the declensions of nouns, in which the cases were written on the fingertips. None the less, Holt's work was a primitive production even by contemporary standards. The pages of *Lac puerorum* were closely set in a poorly cut, black-letter face on very small pages, generally in the style of Caxton's school books, and the quality of explanation was limited, as these two examples illustrate:

I ¶ The subiunctyf mode
The present. quū amer. whan I be loued

The preterin. quū amarer. whan I was loued
The preterper. quū amatus sim vel fuerim. whan
I haue be loued
The preterplu. quū amatus essem vel fuissem
The future. quum amatus ero vel fuero

II Consulo is āglice to aske counsell is a verbe actyf and may gouerne an
accusatyf of the persone that I ask of/a genityf or els an ablatyf a preposicyo
of the thynge that I counseyll for as te remedij vel de remedio[2]

Yet we must appreciate the positive intention in these examples to render
the material more meaningful and to bridge the considerable gap that
existed between the bare descriptions of Donatus or Alexander and the
first Latin reader.

Other books based on the principle of describing Latin grammar and
syntax much more fully and giving verbal illustration soon followed. In
France three volumes by Despauterius (1460–1520) were remarkably
successful: the *Orthographiae isogoge* of 1510, the *Rudimenta* of 1512 and the
Syntaxis of 1515. These three, consisting respectively of an introduction to
spelling, the elements of grammar and a syntax, were gathered together
in 1536 and issued under the title *Commentarii grammatice*. In Germany,
Melanchthon's Greek grammar of 1508 was followed by one in Latin in
1525 and both of these were edited by later authors and issued with various
emendations.

Meanwhile in England several grammars became popular, the first
being John Stanbridge's *Accidence* of 1520, the title indicating that it was
concerned chiefly with the inflections or 'accompanying changes' of the
endings in the four parts of speech – nouns (including adjectives), pro-
nouns, participles and verbs – the term 'accidence' itself being a literal
translation of the Greek word *parepomena* ('accompanying things') which
was employed to describe the phenomenon of inflection. More famous
was one first sketched out by Erasmus but actually written by John Colet,
and by William Lily, for use in the school Colet established some time after
1508 in St Paul's. Lily became headmaster in 1512 and their joint publication was in fact the first version of the longest-lived Latin grammar in
England, its first definitive edition appearing in 1527. Its popularity was
partly due to the fact that it became a required text: in order to strengthen
the Church of England after the break with Rome in 1536 Henry VIII
decided to issue a standard schoolbook, and Lily's was chosen. Between
1540 and 1542 it was emended and expanded and in the latter year appeared
with an introductory treatment of the eight parts of speech, followed by

an intensive grammatical section, along with the catechism and prayers of the new Anglican church, and a foreword written by the king himself.

Parallel with the grammars or 'accidences' as they were usually called were extended treatments of syntax illustrated with short selections from classical writers. These, called *vulgariae*, were in effect florilegia with syntactical glosses, and although their immediate parent was the *Adages* of Erasmus, the vulgariae soon took on a character of their own. In England the first notable ones in the new style were Stanbridge's *Vulgaria Stanbrigiana* of 1519, William Horman's *Vulgaria* of the same year, and Robert Whittinton's of 1520.[3] These books all dealt with grammatical rules as did the accidences, but they went beyond by giving explanations and illustrations. Lily's grammar, in contrast, is quite spare in its content, as this example shows:

THE CASE OF THE RELATIVE

When there cometh no nominative case between the relative and the verb, then the relative shall be the nominative case to the verb.

When there cometh a nominative case between the relative and the verb, then the relative shall be such case as the verb will have after him of whom he is governed, as:

It is a man whom I love.	*Est vir quem diligo.*
Whom I desire to see.	*Quem cupio videre.*
Whom I pity.	*Cuius misereor.*
Whom I favour.	*Cui faveo.*
Whom I use familiarly.	*Quo utor familiariter.*
Whose wit I commend.	*Cuius ingenium laudo. . . .*[4]

The precept is lengthy and conceptually involved, the illustrations do not clarify immediately, unless, of course, the child is able to recall the paradigm of the relative pronoun *qui* meaning *who* or *which* and to recognize its cases in the examples, in descending order, as an accusative (direct object), another accusative, a genitive (possessive), a dative (indirect object), an ablative (instrumental case), and finally another genitive.

To avoid the artificiality of this, and to supplement such desiccated instruction, the vulgariae were used, Stanbridge's being a noted example. His phrases begin with simple greetings and become more complex as the following selections, not sequential in the original, illustrate:

Good morning.	*Bonum tibi hujus diei sit primordium?*
How fare you?	*Qua valitudine praeditus es, ut vales?*

I fare well, thanked be God.	*Bene me habeo alithrono sit gratia.*
Whither goest thou?	*Quo tendis?*
It is a great help for scholars to speak Latin.	*Non nihil conducit discipulis loqui Latine.*
I was set to school when I was seven years old.	*Datus sum scholis cum septennis eram.*
From that day hidewards, I was never kept from school.	*Ab eo tempore huiusque nunquam a studio detentus sum.*[5]

Horman and Whittinton both used this style of presentation, the latter incorporating grammatical rules as well, but in comparison to Lily's grammar the precept is shortened considerably and the number of examples is increased, although only a few are reproduced here:

PRAECEPTUM

Cum pretij nomen, etc. [Monetary value expressed by the genitive.]

EXEMPLA:

Beef and mutton be so dear that a pennyworth of meat will scant suffice a boy at a meal.
Bovine et ovine carnes adeo sunt care | ut denarij obsonium vix puerum saturet | vel unica refectione.

When I was a scholar at Oxford, I lived competently with seven pence commons weekly.
Cum Oxonie studui: septenorum denariorum convictu singulis ebdomadis (sic satis) reficiebar.

PRAECEPTUM

Artificem signans, etc. [Genitive used in signifying a craftsman.]

EXEMPLA:

We have in our ward bell founders, pewterers, plumbers, braziers.
Sunt in nostra vicinia fusores companarij | stannarii | plumbarij | erarij.
And a little beneath, there dwell tailors, shoemakers, hosiers, upholsterers, glovers, sewsters, cobblers.
Et paulo inferius habitant sutores vestiarij | calcearij | caligarij | lectarij | chirotecarij | sutrices linterie | et sarctores calcearij.[6]

William Horman's *Vulgaria* also attempted to improve the presentation of material for reading by marking off phrases and presenting them in parallel translation, shown in these few examples:

> There is no near way to come to cunning than to read good authors and draw to learned men and be present when they be gathered in communication.
> *Nihil efficacius reddit eruditum | quam: ut quis probatos legat authores: et in celebri doctorum hominum coitu versetus | et in circulis frequentioribus inseratur.*

> Eloquence is most allowed and made of among all other science of the people.
> *Studia humanitatis | sunt alijs disciplinis magis popularia.*

> I am very glad that thou goest so lustily to thy book.
> *Voluptati | vel volupe est | quod tam aventer studeas.*

> By reading of substantial authors, thou shalt bring about or attain to speak elegant and substantial Latin.
> *Legendis clarissimis authoribus adipisceris gravitatem | candoremque sermonis. . . .*

> Paper first was made of a certain stuff like the pith of a bulrush in Egypt; and since, it is made of linen cloth soaked in water, stamped or ground, pressed and smoothed.
> *Chartae | seu papyri usus | olim ex Aegypto petebatur | fierique coepit ex papiro frutice; aevo autem nostro ex macerato lino | vel cannabo e tritis et pertusis panniculis.*

> The principal commendation of paper is that it be thin, hard, white and smooth.
> *In chartis spectantur tenuitas | densitas | candor | et lever.*

> There is other fine and thin paper, serving for missive letters, but it will not bear ink on both sides.
> *Est papyri genus | quod dicunt sugustum | caeteris tenuius | et epistolis dicatum | quod tolerandis non sufficiat calamis | adhoc tramittens literas.*[7]

These examples from English texts illustrate some of the developments in schoolbook writing that were occurring in western Europe generally, the most evident features being the parallel use of the vernacular with Latin, the explanation of Latin rules in the vernacular, and an attempt, modest as it is, to use the format of typesetting to stimulate visual learning. Stanbridge's *Accidence* of *c.* 1520 had already offered tabular presentations of verbs of the kind that are still used in grammar books.

Latin readers: colloquies by Erasmus, Vives, Corderius

Further innovations were also proceeding in extending the range of reading materials beyond the grammars and vulgariae to a third level, that of the conversations or dialogues, known as colloquies. Again Erasmus had initiated this development in 1516 with his first version of the *Colloquia*, which appeared in its finest edition in 1523. Soon many colloquies were being written which also extended the Latin version of Erasmus by adding parallel vernacular readings. One of the first of these was written by Seybaldus Heyden and published in 1530 as *Formulae puerilium colloquiorum*, and it begins with this dialogue:

SALUTATIO MATUTINA

DIALOGUS I

Andreas	*Balthasar*
A Bonus dies.	B Talem et tibi precor.
Ain güter tag.	*Ich bit dir auch so vil.*
B Deo gratia.	A Bene sit tibi hoc die.
Gott sey danck.	*Dir sol an dem tab wol sein.*
A Opto tibi bonum diem.	B Nec tibi male sit.
Ich wünsch dir ainen güten tag.	*Es sol dir auch nit übel sein.*[8]

Then follows a dialogue on midday greetings and a further twenty-five short exchanges dealing generally with the various aspects of schooling including going to school, reading activities, making pens, and writing exercises. This German work was followed by the more widely used colloquies of the Spanish educator Vives who published his *Linguae latinae exercitatio* in 1539, and the Frenchman Corderius, whose imitative *Colloquia selecta* appeared in 1564. Vives, however, who worked in several countries, made no attempt to use a vernacular gloss.

The colloquies of Vives, along with those of Erasmus, were by far the best constructed in the period, although their contents differ considerably. Whereas the *Colloquia* of Erasmus consisted of lengthy stories on a wide variety of topics, the *Linguae latinae exercitatio* are similar to the dialogues of Heyden and Horman in that each one is shorter and the content deals with everyday affairs likely to be encountered by the schoolboy. Vives wrote twenty-five dialogues in this work, each with three or four speakers, beginning with one on getting up in the morning, followed by a second on morning greetings similar to that of Heyden. The third colloquy, *Deductio ad ludum*, concerns going to school and in this the child's father as one of the speakers, observes that the school is a 'laboratory for the formation of men' while the teacher named Philoponus (literally, lover of labour) is referred to as 'artist-educator', although the fourth dialogue mentions him as justly thrashing miscreants with a rod (*ferula*). The first fifteen of the colloquies deal with activities relevant to the school, chiefly reading, writing, returning home and playing games, school meals, students' chatter, equestrian advice, getting dressed and taking a morning walk, the school itself, and studies by night. The last ten cover a variety of topics, but their central aim is to provide appropriate forms of gentlemanly decorum, since they include discussions of the kitchen, dining rooms, banquets, drunkenness, the king's palace, the young prince, card playing and paper games and the rules for them. The final three dialogues deal, respectively, with the exterior of a man's body, the general practice of education, and precepts of education.[9]

Two basic groupings of topics occur in Vives' book as they do in so many other colloquies, namely, descriptions of the school and its activities, and didactic, moralistic situations. The former grouping contains such straightforward discussions as how to read, beginning with the five vowels and proceeding in turn to consonants, syllables and words, although even in this there is a didactic intrusion in introducing the etymology of the word for school:

> It is indeed called *ludus*, but it is *ludus literarius* because here we must play with letters as elsewhere with a ball, hoop and dice. And I have heard that in Greek it is called *schola*, as it were a place of leisure, because it is true ease and quiet of mind, when we spend our life in studies.[10]

Both etymologies are reasonably correct; *ludus*, meaning originally a child's game, became extended some time during the third century B.C. to include children's activities generally, so coming to encompass the work of the school. In this sixteenth-century discussion Vives demonstrates his awareness of the classical use of the term and attempts to restore its association with pleasant activity.

The tenth chapter, *Scriptio*, considers the ultimate value of writing in its transcendence of time and space and then goes on to discuss quills and ink and how to prepare them, and to the uses and grades of paper. The school itself and its activities are the subject of much didactic moralizing; Chapter 10 points out that 'true nobility' comes from possession of the symbolic skills of reading and writing; Chapter 13, *Schola*, discusses the division of the school into three stages, elementary and advanced grammar, rhetoric and dialectic, and the 'liberal or noble arts', so called, Vives says, 'because every noble-minded person must be instructed in them. The liberal arts are contrasted strongly with the illiberal subjects of the market-place which are practised by the labours of the body or hands, and pertain to slaves and men who have but little wit.' Continuing to promote the advantages of schooling, Vives in Chapter 20 on the young prince, entitled *Princeps puer*, drops the aside that persons 'so far as they have not learned, will regret that they did not take the pains to acquire knowledge'.

The most direct exhortation to learning, however, comes in Chapter 24, *Educatio*, a discussion between the two masters, Flexibulus and Gorgopas, and the boy-prince Grympherantes – which is, in effect, a miniature *speculum principis*. The case is put at the beginning with the boy's recognition that princely behaviour comes from proper education; it is this that distinguishes him from the masses. Flexibulus then leads him to a deeper understanding by arguing that mind and reason constitute man's essence and failure to cultivate these return him to the brute condition. The prince needs to cultivate himself, to aim at the 'good', and this is defined by its qualities, calling for the personal attainment of a keen intellect, wise and mature judgement, wide and varied knowledge, wisdom, piety, temperance, justice, liberality, magnanimity, equability and bravery. All these are necessary, the prince is advised and

> If thou doest these things then wilt thou get the real solid, noble education itself, and true urbanity; and if, as we are supposing now, thou followest after a courtly life, thou wilt be pleasing to all and dear to all. But even this thou wilt not set at high value, but what will then be the sole care to thee will be, to be acceptable to the Eternal God.[11]

Vives here gives a practical application of his ideas on education written eight years previously in his 1531 treatise, *De tradendis disciplinis*, with the sustained argument for the primacy of reason and the cultivation of the intellectual virtues. Although in that earlier theoretical work Vives had expanded the concept of the liberal arts to include a number of relatively practical studies – dietetics, medicine, economics, natural history, philology, history – and had argued for the use of observation and personal experience as necessary additions to the operation of pure reason, this later book of exercises shows him still well within the tradition of accepting as truly educational studies only those activities considered amenable to intellection. The market-place remains beyond scholarly consideration.

Closely modelled on the colloquies of Vives, and significant chiefly because they were so widely adopted for such a long period, were those written by Mathurinus Corderius (1480–1564) and published in 1564 as *Colloquia selecta*. These colloquies are derived directly from the *Linguae latinae exercitatio* to the extent at times of using even the same phrases.[12] Most of the same topics, although not all, are used, along with some of Vives' practical suggestions such as the employment of paper notebooks.[13] Corderius' work was even more successful than that of Vives – the twentieth English edition being issued in 1824 – and for this reason it deserves consideration. Corderius was pre-eminently a practical schoolmaster who is known to have been a priest at Rouen in 1514.[14] Later he was at the University of Paris and then held a chair of rhetoric at the Collège de la Marche, from which he resigned in 1527 to become a grammar master. Between 1530 and 1534 he was principal of a school at Nevers. Meanwhile the city of Bordeaux was attempting the reorganization of its grammar school, and for this purpose appointed the widely respected master André Gouves, whom the leading French writer of the century, Michel de Montaigne, called 'the greatest teacher of France'. He began by attracting a large body of scholars as masters to form the new Collège de Guyenne, and the scholarship of Corderius was recognized in an invitation to join its faculty in 1534. Remaining there only two years, Corderius then left in 1536 for Switzerland to join with John Calvin, chiefly to help him reorganize the schools. Corderius lived out the rest of his life in Geneva reforming schools, in the Protestant cause, and not until the year of his death were his colloquies published.

In his Latin text, Corderius, like Vives, had no intention of using vernacular parallel glosses; on the contrary he was a stern opponent of the vernacular – in this case French – and it was to counter the lack of suitable speaking experience in Latin for schoolboys that he wrote his colloquies. The conversational topics are much the same as those used by Vives: going to school, meeting the master, the values of learning, meals, play, ethics, Christian morality, making pens, journeys, although not in the same order. However in later editions it was not considered possible for the work to be kept purely in Latin; other schoolmasters added glosses and as late as the nineteenth century these remained in use. One of the common methods of presentation was to put the Latin text by itself on the upper half of each page and in the lower part a double column of Latin and vernacular with the phrases in exact correspondence as in this example:

Sed quis docebit me ista verba?	*But who shall teach me those words?*
Scribam ea tibi in tuo commentariolo.	*I will write them for thee in thy note book.*[15]

The complete text was then followed by a list of all the words construed, in order of their use. Already word-lists had become necessary, and these were to form yet another kind of schoolbook, which was to develop into the dictionary.

Introduction of dictionaries

Primitive dictionaries were in use in the fifteenth century such as the Latin–English list of verbs and nouns known as the *Promptorium parvulorum* (*The Small Handbook*) and the 1500 publication, *Ortus vocabulorum* (*Beginners' Vocabulary*). At Paris, in 1531, the royal printer Robert Estienne published his prototypical dictionary *Thesaurus linguae latinae*, and in 1550 he brought out a small dictionary for schoolboys. In England there was no adequate dictionary for the grammar school, a lack referred to by Vives in *De tradendis disciplinis*, and Thomas Elyot himself attempted to correct this, publishing in 1538 *The Dictionary of Sir T. Elyot* from which these two examples are taken:

Abactores. Thieves that steal cattle.
Abacus. A counting-table or cupboard.
Abaculus. Of pliny is taken for 'accompt'.
Abalienatus. He whom a man putteth from him.
Abaliena, avi, are. To put or turn away.
Abana. A river in the country of Damascus under the hill called Libanus.
Abanec. A girdle that the priests of the Jews did wear.

Medica. An herb which I suppose to be clover-grass with purple, round flowers.
Melandria. The lean parts of the fish called tuna.
Melanurus. A kind of perches called ruffes.
Melita. An isle lying between Sicily and Africa, which is now called Malta, where at this time the company of the Knights Hospitallers do inhabit as they did at the Rhodes.
Merula. A fish called merling or whiting.
Minutum, Idem quod [λεπτά same as *lepta*, that is, fine or thin].
Mygala. A field mouse with a long snout called a shrew.[16]

The interesting feature of this dictionary is that where possible it defines the Latin word in terms of the English equivalent, as well as with a description. This was a highly successful work and received a wide circulation in the version amplified and emended by Thomas Cooper as *Bibliotheca Elyotae*.

The question of Greek and Hebrew studies

Greek and Hebrew studies did not progress anywhere near as favourably as Latin, even though all scholars recognized their value; Hebrew, in fact, seems to have made little headway in schools and was generally restricted to theological faculties of universities and to the new seminaries that were appearing such as the Calvinist Academy at Geneva. Greek was recommended highly by More, Sadoleto, Vives and Elyot, and of these four it was Thomas More who considered it more appropriate for mature scholars able to approach it with a high degree of motivation, no doubt reflecting his own experiences since he learned Greek at university and rapidly reached a high level of proficiency. He collaborated, for example, with William Lily in translating a Greek florilegium into Latin under the title *Progymnasmata*. The recommendations of both Vives and Elyot regarding Greek probably reflect the current situation, that is, that the boy begin with a grammar – Vives referred specifically to Theodore of Gaza, Elyot specified none – and then proceed to reading Aesop followed by selections from classical writers. Both mentioned particularly Lucian, Homer and Aristophanes. Elyot then suggested Isocrates and Demosthenes for higher studies in rhetoric.

None the less Greek was in a considerably different position from Latin since the latter was a spoken tongue whereas Greek was the language of the classics, for which a reading knowledge was generally sufficient. For this reason it always took a second place in the school and so discussion of Greek does not dominate the pedagogical theory and practice of the period to the extent that Latin does. In England it did not begin to take on until the later years of the sixteenth century. Records exist of Greek being introduced into the more prominent grammar schools – Eton in 1560, Harrow in 1591 – and to meet these needs Edward Grant wrote *Tis 'Elleniken glosses stachyologia*, which was later emended by William Camden and received a wide distribution. One sixteenth-century German schoolmaster, Thomas Platter (*c.* 1500–*c.* 1580), writing of his own country, recorded that in the early decades

> The Greek language was not yet anywhere in the land. No one had printed books, the preceptor [Philip Melanchthon] alone had a printed Terence. What one read must first be dictated, then defined, then construed, and then only could he explain it; so that the bacchantes [students] had to carry home great miserable books when they went away.[17]

Melanchthon was the driving force in promoting Greek studies in Germany and his own grammar was the one usually employed for beginners, both in the municipal schools that he and Luther helped establish and in those of the Brethren of the Common Life which also introduced Greek and Hebrew into their curricula. Nor was the position any better in France since it was not even as amenable to humanism as England and Germany in the same period. Some Greek was taught at the University of Paris but generally not until the fifth year of instruction in its grammar school, that is, between the boy's eleventh and twelfth year, since entry was made usually at the age of seven. Greek studies became much more widespread in France and Germany in the late sixteenth century, and much of this interest was due to the growth of Protestant schools where the language was useful for the study of the New Testament.

The ratio *in the organization of the school*

The attempt to embody a *ratio* in the textbooks of the grammar school and so to effect a graded sequence – grammar and dictionary, vulgaria, colloquies – was made also in relation to the school itself. Philip Melanchthon had made the use of very general grades one of the features of the Visitation Articles, and in that regulation three divisions were specified. Previously, grading was rather indeterminate and the principles of sequential instruction were not at all well described or understood. The new sequences of textbooks allowed a more precise grading to be implemented in schools in various parts of Europe, of which the first and most celebrated was that conducted at Strasbourg by Johann Sturm, itself the chief model for grammar schools throughout both Protestant and Catholic Europe. Within the school a further step was the development and application of the principle of the child's regular progression through grades at intervals of about a year. The initiative in this respect was seized by a new Catholic religious order, the Society of Jesus, which became so successful in its conducting of grammar schools that its members came to enjoy the title of the 'schoolmasters of Europe', and to have for a time a virtual monopoly of schooling in Catholic lands, including those of the New World.

The Society of Jesus

Foundation: Ignatius Loyola and the Constitutions

This new society, which received papal approval in 1540, was founded as a result of the spiritual growth of a minor Spanish nobleman Ignatius of Loyola (1491–1556). The son of Don Beltran Yanez de Oñaz Loyola, the young Inigo (his vernacular name) was given a minimal formal schooling before receiving the customary training in military skills appropriate to his aristocratic station. In 1521 he was severely wounded in the legs in a battle at Pampeluna and his military career was apparently ended. In his ensuing convalescence, however, having taken to reading a life of Christ – Ludolf of Saxony's *Vita Christi* – and other religious literature, he resolved to pursue his calling as a soldier of Christ. The first step was a vigil in 1522 when he divested himself of all worldly goods; the second was a spiritual retreat in Manresa where he wrote the initial version of his manual of *Spiritual Exercises*, a regimen planned for a four-week period of personal self-examination. Subsequently he made a pilgrimage to Jerusalem, and on his return in 1524, recognizing his need of formal learning, he enrolled in a school, an adult among small children, in Barcelona. Two years later he went to the University of Alcalá but, making little progress, he left the following year (1527) for Paris where his studies prospered and he became licentiate in 1533 and master of arts twelve months later, in the process having made a profound impression on some of his fellows. At Paris he established a firm friendship with Peter Faber and Francis Xavier, the nucleus from which the society was to grow. In the next few years they were joined by others and in 1539 this band of ten zealots formed themselves into the Society of Jesus. Their asssumption of the name of Christ was resisted by many, since the tradition was that orders generally took the names of their founder; despite this, they received verbal approval from Pope Paul III in 1539 and his formal assent the following year in the bull *Regimini militantis ecclesiae*.

The primary purpose of the new order was missionary, originally for Turkish lands, although this became diffused to cover all territories, particularly the New World which Spanish and Portuguese explorers and settlers had been opening up to European domination. Papal approval in 1540 was only the beginning; the following year Ignatius was elected General of the order and he commenced the task of organizing this still inchoate group. All members were to be priests – Ignatius had been ordained in 1538 – and they were to renounce all worldly titles, including church preferments and promotions, so as to avoid being diverted from their purposes. The most pressing task was the clear definition of these purposes, amounting, in effect, to the formulation of a Rule, the first draft of which Ignatius began in 1547 and completed in 1550. This was reviewed by a convocation of Jesuits in 1551–2, and further revised in a final and definitive version of 1556, the year of Ignatius' death. It was entitled formally *The Constitutions of the Society of Jesus*.[18]

The *Constitutions* consist of ten parts, covering admission and acceptance into the order, the spiritual and educational care of novices, and the government of the order. Half of the length of the *Constitutions* is in the fourth part, with the title, *Concerning the Instruction in Letters of Those Who are to be Kept in the Society and in Other Things Which Pertain to the Helping of the Neighbour*, which itself consists of a Preamble and seventeen chapters. The Preamble contains a clear definition of the purposes of the society:

> . . . the direct objective at which the society aims is to help the souls of its members and of the neighbour to attain the final end for which they were created.[19]

and this entails, consequently, an obligation on the society to set

> . . . a good moral example, [and, since] learning and methods of presenting it are necessary for the attaining of this end, therefore, after it seems that a fitting foundation for self-denial and for the necessary progress in virtue has been laid for those who have been admitted to probation, the education in letters and of the manner of utilizing them, so that they can aid to a better knowledge and service of God, our Creator and Lord, will be treated.[20]

It had become abundantly clear to the early Jesuits that education was the only proper means to achieving their purposes in a world in which the proliferation of knowledge and the rapid expansion of competing and conflicting systems of education were already altering conceptions of faith and influencing the attainment of man's ultimate end. And, since schools were not freely available, it was necessary for the Jesuits to establish their own.

Definition of Jesuit educational policy

The Fourth Part of the *Constitutions* in large measure provides essentially a programme of Christian education. Despite his own leanings towards mysticism and his concern with the primacy of the interior spiritual life already recorded in the *Spiritual Exercises*, Ignatius readily adopted the general attitudes to learning of his day, accepting without reservation the programme of the *studia humanitatis* and the philosophy of Aristotle as interpreted by Thomas Aquinas. So the foundations of studies for the Jesuit novitiate were in grammar, rhetoric and logic, followed by natural and moral philosophy and metaphysics. Progression could then be made to both scholastic and positive theology, although care had to be exercised that students should not be strained beyond their intellectual means and those unfit for the rigours of the full programme should be put to other tasks.[21] The order of studies is outlined, beginning with a solid foundation in Latin language, which must always be spoken,[22] proceeding then to the trivium – grammar, rhetoric, logic – of the liberal arts, along with poetry, history and some mathematics,[23] in so far as the last study is relevant to preparing the mind for theology. The philosophical studies of logic, natural philosophy and metaphysics are to be taken from Aristotle, these being a preparation for theology, both scholastic and positive, the former being a study of Aquinas. Positive theology is concerned with church dogma and doctrine and for this all of the foregoing studies, along with scriptural study, are prerequisites. The three languages of Latin, Greek and Hebrew are necessary, and, if possible, those of Chaldaic, Arabic and Indian are to be studied too, simply because of their instrumental value for missionary work in eastern lands.[24] In addition, positive theology is to encompass the reading of both Old and New Testaments and the master of sentences, Peter Lombard.[25]

Other chapters in the Fourth Part of the *Constitutions* are concerned with the general affairs and management of the Jesuit schools, called colleges, along with admissions policy, spiritual and apologetics training, church attendance, and decorum of novices, all of this reflecting the growth of the society in its first fifteen years and its patent need to regularize all its procedures. The seventh chapter of this part has the most direct bearing on the condition of schools in the period, and indicates the extent to which the missionary activity of the order was becoming directed towards public education:

> Taking into account with due reason not only the progress in letters of our Scholastics but also the progress in letters and morals of externs whom we take to be instructed in our colleges, let public schools be opened where it can be done conveniently, at least in the liberal arts. In regard to the more advanced disciplines, schools may be opened according to the needs of the locality in which our colleges are situated.[26]

This provision confirmed a practice already in operation: the Jesuits had been admitting externs (those not seeking membership of the society) into their schools since 1546 when students were allowed into classes of philosophy held at their first foundation in Gandia in Spain and to grammar classes two years later.[27] In 1548, as a result of a petition from the citizens of Messina in Sicily, a fully constituted classical college was opened there offering instruction to externs in the rudiments of Latin through to the study of Cicero and Quintilian. Greek and Hebrew were also offered, on similar lines. Eight years later, when the final version of the *Constitutions* was issued, thirty-five colleges were operating in Sicily, Italy, Spain, Portugal, Austria, France, Bohemia and Germany, most of them already admitting externs.[28] It was this practice that the Jesuits expanded into the most comprehensive single school system in Europe, and to regulate this they devised the most precisely detailed and thoroughgoing programme of school instruction ever seen.

The Jesuit *Ratio studiorum*

Search for a ratio

The development of such a *ratio* was emphasized in the *Constitutions* where the need for a comprehensive programme is set out:

> Concerning the stated hours for lectures and the order and mode, and concerning the exercises both of compositions (which ought to be corrected by teachers) and of disputations in all the faculties and of giving public orations and odes, all this will be treated separately in a certain treatise approved by the General, to which this Constitution refers us, giving however this admonition that these matters ought to be accommodated to the times, places, and persons although as far as possible it would be advisable to follow this order.[29]

In the years following the death of Ignatius the number of Jesuit schools for externs multiplied, as did their own seminaries, and by 1586 they had 162 colleges of which about 147 were open to externs.[30] It was towards the end of that period of expansion that deliberate steps were taken to formulate a *ratio*. Earlier the rector of Messina, Jerome Nadal (1507–74), had produced an *Ordo studiorum* in 1551, three years after the college had been founded, and this was copied by other schools of the order. In the same year that Nadal produced his *ratio* a free school of grammar, humanities and Christian doctrine was opened in Rome by fourteen Jesuits, with the advertisement tablet about the entry inscribed, significantly, in the Italian vernacular: *Scuola di grammatica, d'humanità e di dottrina Christiana, gratis.*[31] This was the Roman College, as it became known. It was subjected to Ignatius' influence for its first five years, and for a method its masters turned to Nadal's *Ordo studiorum.*[32] The next major effort came from James Ledesma (1519–75) who taught at the Roman College for most of his Jesuit career which began in 1557, two years after the Peace of Augsburg. Ledesma was sensitive to that partition of Europe between the Catholic and Lutheran faiths, and his attempt to construct a thoroughgoing system of school instruction reflected the growing efforts of the Jesuits to counter the spread of Protestant teachings. From 1560 until his death he worked at a *ratio*, projected as *De ratione et ordine studiorum Collegii Romani*: the method and order of studies of the College of Rome. Although he made an outline of its five parts, it remained largely incomplete at his death.[33]

Ratio *of 1599*

The need for a *ratio* was imperative since the proliferation of colleges required co-ordination if the society, spread throughout Europe and its overseas colonies, were to survive in a corporate form. In 1581 Claudius Aquaviva became fifth General of the society; three years later he convened a committee of six senior members to prepare a final *ratio*. They completed one by 1586, using the *Constitutions* as their reference point – 'We read the Constitutions again and again, especially the fourth part, with the steady purpose of building everything on this norm'[34] – and this was distributed throughout the society for comment. From the criticisms that followed a second draft was issued in 1591, *Ratio atque institutio studiorum*, which was further criticized; eventually, in 1599 General Aquaviva promulgated a much shorter version as the definitive and binding form, the *Ratio atque institutio studiorum Societatis Jesu*, a document of thirty chapters expanding in detail the broad prescriptions of Part 4 of the *Constitutions* of forty-three years earlier. The bulk of the chapters are rules, arranged in order of descending authority: for the provincial (head of the basic division of the society's operations, corresponding approximately to a diocese), rector, prefect of studies, and professors of all grades, from theology down to introductory grammar. A large number of the rules are procedural, providing specific guides for decision-making in the numerous matters requiring attention – enrolment, progress, discipline, examinations, prayers, school decorum – these being frequently common-sense prescriptions. The educationally significant aspect of the *Ratio* is its attitude to learning itself and the concept of the school.

There is an absolute acceptance of the content of education in the same terms as conceived and practised by contemporaries, Catholic or Protestant: this is the pursuit of *pietas litterata*. The basic institution is designated the college, throughout which there is to be a single method of teaching, this injunction being given to the Prefect of Lower Studies who is to

> . . . take great care that new teachers carefully retain the method of teaching of their predecessors, and other customs not foreign to our plan, thereby giving outsiders less justification for condemning our frequent change of teachers.[35]

The college is to be divided into five lower grades, although there can be multiple classes within each grade if numbers are too large for single classes, consisting in ascending order of lower grammar, middle grammar, higher grammar, humanities and rhetoric. This is not necessarily a five-year sequence; it is likely to be much longer for some since 'it is impossible to prescribe exactly the time to be devoted to the study of humanities and rhetoric'.[36] A minimum of two years rhetoric, and a further three years philosophy is specified, additional time requirements being left to the judgement of the rector. In addition, for interns seeking admission to the society itself a further four years of theology are required, this being the first instance of a formal theological training for the priesthood, in distinction to the treatment of theological topics in the courses in philosophy or the graduate work in the university faculties of theology which was not taken by ordinary priests. The shortest possible period of instruction then for interns was thirteen years, although the grammar studies of the three lowest grades and the work in humanities and rhetoric probably required at least eight years, possibly ten, making the more likely length of at least fifteen years. For externs, eleven or twelve years of studies culminating in rhetoric, philosophy and humanities could be obtained.

Rules and methods of studies: praelectio *and* concertatio

Rules prescribing studies and progression for all of the various grades are quite explicit, and follow a uniform plan. For every level there are prescriptions on the division of time – a daily schedule, in effect – and the procedures for both master and pupils to follow in respect of classroom behaviour, both for decorum and intellectual activity. The basis of pedagogical method rests on the use of prelection, a medieval technique that the Jesuits made into the distinctive feature of instruction in all of their schools. The *Ratio studiorum* gives a very explicit definition of the method as presented by the master:

The form of the prelection shall be about as follows:

1. Let him [the master] read the whole passage without interruption, unless in rhetoric and the humanities it would have to be too long.

2. Let him explain the topic and, if necessary, its connection with what has preceded.

3. After reading a single sentence, if he is interpreting Latin, let him explain the more obscure parts; let him connect one to another; let him explain the thought, not in inept metaphrase by giving for each Latin word another Latin word, but by expressing the same thought in some intelligible phrases. But if he does it in the vernacular, let him preserve the order of words, as much as possible; for so he will accustom their ears to the rhythm. But if the vernacular does not lend itself to this; let him explain everything first word for word, and then in the vernacular. But if the vernacular idiom will not allow this, let him first explain all things word for word, and afterwards according to the vernacular idiom.

4. Starting from the beginning, unless he prefers to insert them in the explanation itself, let him give observations suited to each class; but they should not be many, for he shall order them to be taken down, either by interrupting the explanation or by dictating them separately when the prelection is finished; but it is usually considered better that grammar pupils write nothing, unless ordered.[37]

This method of prelection was applied to all of the *studia humanitatis*: grammar, literature, poetry, history; a modification was used also for mathematics, rhetoric, philosophy and theology.

Paralleling the use of prelection was a second technique known as *concertatio*, the Latin etymology coming from Cicero who extended the usual meaning of physical contest to that of a contest in words or dispute, and this also was intended to be used for all studies. The nature of this contest is also defined explicitly:

The concertatio, which is usually conducted by the questions of the master or the corrections of rivals, or by the rivals questioning each other in turn, must be held in high esteem and used whenever time permits, so that honourable rivalry, which is a great incentive to studies, may be fostered. Some may be sent individually or in groups from each side especially from the officers; or one may attack several; let a private seek a private, an officer seek an officer;

or even let a private attack an officer, and, if he conquers, let him secure his honour or some other award or sign of victory, as the dignity of the class and the custom of the place demand.[38]

Reinforcement of both prelection and concertation was secured by the setting of written exercises, to be corrected carefully by the master, and by oral repetitions intended to cultivate and strengthen memory, to be given as frequently as possible. Prelection, concertation, exercises and repetition were the pedagogical techniques by which Jesuit schools proceeded, and around which the curriculum was constructed.

The problem of a Jesuit grammar

Instruction began with Latin grammar, and for this study the *Ratio studiorum* prescribed the text published in 1572 by the Portuguese Jesuit, Emmanuel Alvarez, under the title *De institutione grammatica libri tres.* This prescription itself resulted from several decades of conflict over the use of grammar texts. In France the early Jesuit schools used the widely adopted 1536 text of Despauterius, the three-volume *Commentarii grammatice*, and its use spread. Soon, however, in Sicily and Italy first, objections to this grammar became more frequent,[39] chiefly because of its prolixity and difficulty, although there are suspicions that it was also identified with France at a time of emerging nationalism. By 1554 Ignatius himself urged the adoption of a better text, and several Jesuits produced efforts: Coudret produced a text between 1548 and 1553, followed by Frusius' *Summa latinae syntaxeos* of 1556 and Ledesma's two-volume set, *Grammatica brevi* and *Syntax plenior* of 1569. Meanwhile in Lisbon, Emmanuel Alvarez, who had taught in the first Jesuit college there since its foundation in 1553, had been writing a grammar which was published nineteen years later in 1572 in a three-part format: Etymology, Syntax, Prosody. This gained a ready acceptance and soon appeared in a number of versions and emendations, followed by a revised edition of 1583 by Alvarez himself. The following year a committee of Jesuits in Rome issued a further revision which was the basis of the prescriptions of the early *Ratio studiorum* of 1586. The 1584 edition was not accepted unanimously; the French Jesuits in particular resisted it, preferring Despauterius. Eventually, after much dispute, Emmanuel Alvarez's grammar was accepted, with the reservation that another grammar could be used if it proved unsuitable to a particular locality. This it did in France, so that the French schools continued to use Despauterius; in most other places Emmanuel was used.

Grammar instruction, whether from Emmanuel or Despauterius, began with an introduction to syntax, moving on to the construction of the eight parts of speech, and to the use of figures of speech and the measuring of syllables, all studied from the prescribed text by the methods of prelection and concertation. In the first grade of the three-stage grammar sequence, that is the Lower Grammar class, the student should have a 'perfect knowledge of the rudiments and a beginning knowledge of syntax',[40] including declensions of common nouns and the conjugations of common verbs, except for preterites and supines,[41] both for Latin and Greek. At this stage only the grammatically simple works of Cicero are specified, and it is suggested also that Greek need not be taught as intensively as Latin. In the next grade, the Middle Grammar class, the aim is to achieve 'the knowledge, indeed, of the whole of grammar',[42] although not exhaustively, and with less demands in Greek. Cicero and Ovid are set for prelection, and some simple works in Greek, if the latter is taught. In the third stage, the Higher Grammar class, the requirement is 'a complete knowledge of grammar; for he [the student] shall so repeat syntax from the beginning as to add all the appendices, and then explain figured construction and the art of versification; but in Greek [only] the eight parts of speech.'[43] Readings in Latin are to be made from Cicero, Ovid, Catullus, Ribullus, Propertius, Virgil, and in Greek from Chrysostom, Aesop, Agapetus and similar, but unspecified, writers.

The pietas litterata

After this three-stage sequence progression should be made to the humanities, in which the student is to make daily prelections of Cicero, and of studies from Caesar, Sallust, Livy, Curtius and Virgil. The fact that Greek did not parallel Latin is revealed in the prescription that 'Of the Greek language, that part belongs to this class which is properly called syntax, taking care in the meantime that they understand the Greek writers fairly well and know how to write Greek somewhat.'[44] Greek authors set include Isocrates, Plato, Chrysostom, Basil, Synesius, Nazianzus, Theognis and Phocyllis, all but the first two being writers of the Christian era, most of them patristic. In addition students of humanities should be encouraged to write poems on classical models with the intention that students' writing 'be directed to the imitation of Cicero as much as possible, to his standard of narration, persuasion, congratulation, admonition and other forms of that nature'.[45] Overlapping these studies are those of the rhetoric class, to which the student moved next since 'the grade of this class cannot be easily assigned to certain definite ends: for it instructs to perfect eloquence, which embraces the two highest faculties, oratory and poetry (of these two, however, the preference is always given to oratory); nor does it serve only for usefulness, but also nourishes culture'.[46] Quintilian and Aristotle are to be added to Cicero – although only Cicero is to be a model of style – and Demosthenes, Plato, Thucydides, Homer, Hesiod and Pindar are to be studied. Significantly, the classical Greek writers are now admitted in force. At the same time, however, Aristotle's works on rhetoric were read only in Latin translations and, since it was recognized by the Jesuits that a thorough study of rhetoric demands the reading of the Greek authorities in the original language, it was decreed that to achieve this purpose, 'Greek syntax and prosody, if necessary, are to be explained on alternate days', although no text is specified.[47]

Generally this completed the instruction offered to externs. Beyond the class of rhetoric there were the classes of mathematics, philosophy and theology, although these were intended mainly for interns. Mathematics is not specified in any detail, it is mentioned simply as providing explanation of the elements of Euclid and 'something of geography or of the sphere or other matters which students are glad to listen to'.[48] Philosophy is divided into moral philosophy, consisting in 'the principal heads of moral science which are had in the ten books of ethics of Aristotle',[49] and the remaining philosophic studies, chiefly logic and metaphysics. Philosophy should take three years, the first being devoted to the logic of Aristotle given in *Perihermenias*; the second year covering the eight books of the *Physics* along with *De caelo* and the first book of *De generatione*; the third year encompassing the rest of *De generatione*, and *De anima* and all of Aristotle's *Metaphysics*. Although Aristotle is to be followed carefully the professor at the same time should avoid treating authors hostile to Christianity, Averroes being mentioned specifically.[50] Aquinas is to be taken always as a guide; let the professor 'never speak except with respect of St Thomas, following him readily as often as it is proper, or reverently and gravely differing from him if at any time he does not approve of him'.[51] Indeed, only those professors 'well disposed towards St Thomas' are to hold chairs of theology, the final study, and those 'who are averse to him or not much devoted to him should be removed from the office of teaching',[52] since 'All members of our Order shall follow St Thomas in scholastic theology and consider him as their special teacher'.[53] Theology required four years of study, encompassing dogma, doctrine, sacraments and some aspects of canon law and church administration. In addition, students were required to take courses in Hebrew and Sacred Scripture, either concurrently or subsequently, to complete their formal training for admission to the order.

This completes the content of the *Ratio studiorum* respecting the programme of studies. However, the document makes a few other pedagogical comments, including a brief mention that an academy for training teachers should be set up as a separate institution,[54] although no further detail is supplied. At the same time, the *Ratio studiorum* is itself a carefully composed and thoroughly well-set-out manual of teacher instruction, standing far in advance of any other work hitherto written. The definitive version of 1599 is an impressive document and remains a monument to the care and industry with which the Jesuits sought to translate their religious zeal into a viable programme of education. By the time of its publication the Jesuits had become well established throughout the Catholic south of Europe – Spain, Portugal, France, Italy, Austria and southern Germany – and had begun to expand further afield, into Russia, formerly a largely illiterate country, although evangelized from Byzantium in the ninth century, and abroad into the Spanish and Portuguese colonies in the New World – the Americas, Africa, India and the East Indies. Wherever they went they established schools, organizing them according to the prescriptions of their *Constitutions* and the *Ratio studiorum*. Indeed, the 1599 version of the *Ratio*, with slight emendations in 1616, remained their official school programme until 1773 when Clement XIV (r. 1769–74) suppressed the order by the bull *Dominus ac Redempter noster*, as a result of tremendous political pressures brought by France, Spain and Portugal. Jesuit zeal had not been contained within the limits of spiritual and educational activity; the order became involved in the political intrigues of the day, and, consequently, they were the losers.

A major factor in the decline of Jesuit fortunes was the inherent discontinuities built into their system, these being discernible in the *Ratio* itself. Ignatius responded to the difficulties of his times, which were manifested in continued religious schisms and social upheavals, themselves the symptoms of an expanding universe of knowledge and social conscience, by accepting many of the reforming programmes and attempting to make them compatible with Catholic doctrine. So the *pietas litterata* were accepted, in addition to the Thomist synthesis with its assertion of the validity of man's reason, but Ignatius himself never developed his own thinking beyond what he learned from scholars before him: his genius was systematization. It was in this field that he failed to provide an adequate basis for the continued validity and effectiveness of his programme. The initial success of his system was due to the acceptance of current styles of thought, although the Jesuits remained a safely conservative distance from the most innovatory of contemporary thinking. Prelection and concertation were little more than regularized applications of the medieval *lectio* and *disputatio*, the acceptance of *pietas litterata* did not embrace modern authors – 'in prelections only the ancient authors are to be explained, by no means the recent writers'[55] – and the Jesuits' attitude towards studies beyond the trivium was not enthusiastic. The *Ratio* mentions mathematics and geography only minimally, the *Constitutions* allow the study of 'logic, physics, metaphysics, moral science, and even mathematics in so far as it helps toward the attaining of our proposed end'; that is, in so far as 'the arts and natural sciences dispose the mind for theology, and serve to perfect its knowledge and application and of themselves help toward the same end . . . seeking in all things the honour and glory of God'.[56]

In accepting contemporary intellectual fashions, and translating them into the best educational programme of the day the Jesuits took much of the pedagogical initiative in Europe; yet, they failed to recognize the fact that the very times that had created them and allowed their success would move on relentlessly, leaving the intellectual fashions of the sixteenth century outdated even as early as the seventeenth. The Jesuits built two cardinal limitations into their educational system: the first was to accept the thought of their day as permanently viable, the second was to regularize this into a conservative, rigid system. Even as they wrote the *Ratio* these difficulties must have occurred to them, for this document contains so manifest a discontinuity as the prescription of Latin speech for all possible occasions, and the allowance of the vernacular in prelections.[57] Even though the universe of knowledge was expanding, it was still held to be a closed system, that is, it was believed that all knowledge could be discovered and causally interrelated, and the Jesuits are no more culpable in failing to question this than any other educational thinkers of the period. In fact, they were conspicuously ahead of much alternative thought by the year 1600, although many significant changes were already in process. Apart from their intrinsic interests in developing a *ratio* of education, the Jesuits were responsible for helping to create another dimension to the character of education, namely the development of the school as the agent of a particular system of belief.

The end of an era

By the time of the Jesuits, however, the civilization of Europe was approaching the end of an era, one that had begun some eight centuries earlier with Charlemagne's attempt to effect a *renovatio* of the Roman Empire through military conquest and an ambitious educational programme. In the Holy Roman Empire, as he envisaged it, the classical traditions of Greece and Rome – such as they were understood – were to be restored and revivified through the divine agency of Christian revelation, leading, he hoped, to the rebirth of ancient civilization in Europe as an *imperium christianum*. The recovery of the classical tradition that this required was undertaken eagerly, although it proved to be an extremely long and complicated enterprise. In this process which continued during the following centuries, a considerable educational apparatus was assembled and maintained, and this, as so often happens, came to assume a life and character of its own. Education became increasingly formalized and its institutions acquired considerable independence, a position illustrated vividly by the universities which, although originally made up of little more than groups of pious scholars, developed into autonomous centres sustaining and advancing much of the intellectual and cultural life of Europe. The universities came to dominate all educational thought and most of its practices, so that for centuries higher learning was conducted almost entirely under the aegis of this corporate body.

Sustained throughout this era, however, was the dominant motif of Europe as a Christian society, of which the visible symbol was the Holy Catholic Church. For centuries the bishop of Rome maintained an effective and almost complete authority over Christian Europe, and the schools were an integral part of the structure by which this was secured. In its fullest and most widely accepted sense, education was conceived as the means whereby man achieves his vocation of union with god and this, by definition, is an activity integral with the church's mission to care for souls. So, as the universities and other institutions of education developed, the church could claim that it was bound in conscience to exercise supervision. While in one sense the hierarchical structure of the church imposed faith and morals from above – from the bishop of Rome speaking *ex cathedra* – yet, in another, his office came to be very dependent upon the scholars of Christendom, so that European educational thought became shaped by the interplay in intellectual life between universities and the papal court.

By the sixteenth century the Holy Roman Empire had become – at least in theory – coterminous with Europe, and throughout this region educational ideals and procedures exhibited a pervasive unity which is reflected in the literature of education. Certainly there was a total consensus that the highest aim of education is the inculcation of the religious life, and that an educational programme based on a blending of classical and Christian culture, expressed in the concept of the *pietas litterata*, is the best means of effecting this. At the same time, however, the path was not easy; there were many difficulties in the way of securing and maintaining a Christian society. The forces of evil – whether personified in the devil or projected into the surrounding environment – were believed to be ever-present, and many churchmen saw their task to be not only educational but also defensive; it is therefore not surprising to find the concepts of warfare applied to the procedures of promoting and maintaining faith. Since ancient times Christians had considered theirs to be a Church Militant, and this was reflected in the organization and terminology of the Franciscans and Dominicans in the early thirteenth century. Two centuries later, Erasmus acted in a way quite consonant with this tradition when he chose to call one of his inspirational works a *Handbook of the Militant Christian*, this being given added force in Latin by the double meaning of 'handbook' (*enchiridion*) as 'sword'. Luther, also, in his *Letter to the Councilmen of Germany*, used the same metaphor in calling classical education the 'sword of the spirit'. The military character of the Jesuits was nothing unusual.

Yet, despite this zealous vigilance by a militant church, the Christian civilization of Europe remained far from secure. The very processes whereby the church sought to promote itself proved to act against it: the universities insisted on the pursuit of the autonomous life of the intellect; the Dominicans, in an effort to buttress faith, accepted the Thomist synthesis and so prepared the way for rationalism; Luther in his reforming zeal split Catholic Christendom and provided the stimulus and example for a continuing fragmentation. At the same time the unity of European civilization was challenged by the growth of trade and commerce, the consequent increasing urbanization, and the development of crafts and technologies, all of which depended upon a practice of education and a supportive theory that necessarily remained outside the traditional system. The classical concept of education as the pursuit of virtue, which had lent itself so easily to Christianization, gave no useful support to the simpler workaday processes on which society basically depends. Even the apparently progressive acceptance of Thomism proved to be a limiting intellectual framework and came to pose enormous obstacles in the way of construct-ing an adequate theory of science and technology. During the sixteenth century this conflict became particularly evident in the study of astronomy. By virtually canonizing Aristotelian thought, authority was given equally to all of Aristotle's works so that, along with his theory of knowledge, the church also accepted his theory of what he called the 'heavenly spheres'. In his cosmology Aristotle held that the universe is geocentric and finite, being limited by an outer sphere whose motion is 'continuous, regular and eternal'.[58] The earth, which 'must be at the centre and immovable',[59] occupies an inner sphere of change and decay, while the heavens, in accordance with his doctrine of contraries, are considered not subject to change, nor to the same laws that govern earth, 'for order and definiteness are much more plainly manifest in the celestial bodies than in our own frame; while change and chance are characteristic of the perishable things of earth'.[60] The papal acceptance of this patently limited viewpoint in-hibited the epoch-making work of Copernicus (1473–1543) in the six-teenth century and even led to church opposition to aspects of inquiry in the natural sciences, with the further consequence that seventeenth-century investigators attempted to develop their scientific studies independently of all considerations of religion and morality.

By this time, the secular and empirical activities by which society was sustained were unable to be held back, and, because they were excluded from traditional education through their 'illiberality', they developed separately, largely within the vernacular tradition. Indeed, the growth of Jesuit education stemmed in part from a reaction to the increasing domin-ance of the vernacular languages in everyday life. For as the civilization of Europe developed, so too did its many vernaculars, and by the sixteenth century these had generally displaced Latin for most purposes: not only was Latin proving unable to accommodate to new terms and concepts from the trades and sciences; in educational matters as well it is important to recall that Colet wrote his statutes for St Paul's in English, Luther's exhortations on the value of a classical education were published in German, and even the Jesuits had painted the signboard in Italian for their school in Rome. At the same time, however, the vernaculars of Europe were highly developed: Italian had reached a high point in the Trecento with the work of Dante and Petrarch; by the sixteenth century the Spanish of Vives, the German of Luther, the French of Montaigne and the English of Shakespeare were more than capable of sustaining an advanced intel-lectual and cultural life. But their vigour struck at the unity of the *imperium christianum* which had depended on the use of a common tongue. So the Jesuits appeared as heirs to a movement to sustain the cultural unity of Europe at a time when it was most threatened. By concentrating their energies on the teaching of Latin and the transmission of the classical tradition, however, the Jesuits, like the other reformers of the grammar school, exerted a stultifying and retrograde influence on education: fundamentally, they were teaching what was largely a dead language in a dead manner.

Already criticisms of education were being voiced throughout Europe, quite strongly, for example, in Italy by Giambattista Gelli and in France by Michel de Montaigne, both of whom advanced the cause of a vernacular basis, and their statements were echoed in the works of many educational writers in the same century. It was not only the medium of instruction that was being questioned, but the entire conception of education itself. Yet the schools remained dominated by highly conservative theories and methods, and their traditions were not to be discarded with any haste. On the contrary, the development of education to serve the wider needs of an increasingly secular and pluralist Europe was a discontinuous, saltatory process. Many uncoordinated movements in this direction are evident in the complex period that marks the Western age of expansion: the printing presses, for instance, were producing a wider range of contemporary books reflecting current interests, including the study of the natural world, its plants, animals, rocks, lands and peoples. Meanwhile, the teaching of the skills needed for development in cartography, navigation and the trades was carried on outside the existing educational institutions, although there were some relatively unspectacular efforts to broaden the traditional curriculum of these.

In general, however, the reformers of grammar schools in the sixteenth century, like the leaders of the Protestant reformation in the fifteenth, were traditionally oriented in their educational aims and programmes. Newer theories and proposals that challenged the conservative view were given expression at this time, but generally these were to find their application and acceptance much later, and their discussion is not pursued here. Indeed, the steps by which conscious efforts were made to transcend the limitations of the established process of education as it had been formulated in Europe during the preceding millennium is the main theme of the history of Western education from the sixteenth century to the twentieth. In this latter period, however, the history is no longer confined to Europe itself, it becomes extended to a modern West: Europe and the New World.

Notes

Chapter 1

1 Cf. W. Ullmann, *The Carolingian Renaissance and the Idea of Kingship* (1969), Ch. 1, *passim*.

2 Cf. *Oxford Dictionary of the Christian Church* (1958), s.v. 'The Pope'.

3 This is the general theme of Ullmann, op. cit.

4 *Vita Karoli imperatoris ab Einhardo dictata* (Oxford text, 1915). XXIX. 2: 'Post susceptum imperiale nomen, cum adverteret multa legibus populi sui deese – nam Franci duas habent leges, in plurimus locis valde diversas – cogitavit quae deerant addere et discrepantia unire, prava quoque ac perperam prolata corrigere . . .'

5 Notker, *De Carolo magno*, Section I, in Einhard and Notker the Stammerer, *Two Lives of Charlemagne*, trans. L. Thorpe (1969), p. 93.

6 *Vita Karoli*, Walahfridi prologus ll. 10–16, in Thorpe (ed. and trans.), op. cit. p. 23.

7 Ullmann, op. cit. *passim* and esp. Ch. 1.

8 There has been a long controversy on the authorship of the *Libri Carolini*. The attribution to Alcuin of York now seems discredited and Theodulph of Orléans the most likely major author. Cf. Ann Freeman, 'Further Studies in the *Libri Carolini*', *Speculum*, XL (1965), pp. 203–89.

9 *Vita Karoli*, XIX, 1, 1–7; trans. Thorpe, op. cit. p. 59: 'Liberos suos ita censuit instituendos ut tam filii quam filiae primo liberalibus studiis, quibus et ipse operam dabat, erudirentur.'

10 Ibid. XXV. 1: '. . . ui quibus Latinam ita didicit ut aequa illa ac paeria lingua orare sit solitus . . . graecam vero melius intellegere quam pronuntiare poterat.'

11 Ibid. XXV. 2.

12 Ibid.: '. . . sed parum successit labor praeposterus ac sero inchoatus.'

13 Ibid: '. . . artes liberales studiosissime coluit, earumque doctores plurimum veneratus magnis adficiebat honoribus.'

14 For a biography see E. S. Duckett, *Alcuin, Friend of Charlemagne* (1959).

15 Cf. Pierre Courcelle, 'Les Sources antiques du prologue d'Alcuin sur les disciplines', *Philologus: Zeitschrift für das klassische Altertum*, Band 110, Heft 3/4 (1966), pp. 293–305.

16 Ullmann, op. cit. pp. 31, 36 ff.

17 Text and translation in W. S. Howell, *The Rhetoric of Alcuin and Charlemagne* (1941).

18 Cf. L. Wallach, *Alcuin and Charlemagne* (1959), pp. 48 ff.

19 Howell, op. cit. III. 53–8; pp. 68–9.

20 Ep. 145, D.231.17.

21 J. P. Migne, *Patr. Lat.* CI, col. 975C–D; collected and trans. in M. W. L. Laistner, *Thought and Letters in Western Europe, A.D. 500–900* (1931), p. 156.

22 Cf. Wallach, op. cit. pp. 210–11.

23 Cf. Howell, op. cit. pp. 44 ff.

24 On the extent of Greek scholarship – or really the lack of it – in Carolingian times, see Laistner, op. cit. Ch. X, 'The Study of Greek', pp. 191 ff.

25 Howell, op. cit. pp. 58–61.

26 *Monumenta Germaniae historica; Capitularia regum francorum*, XXII; cited in C. J. B. Gaskoin, *Alcuin: His Life and Work* (1904, reprinted 1966), p. 181 n. 3.

27 *Patr. Lat.* XCVIII. col. 895, 'De litterarum studiis'.

28 'Admonitio Generalis', Capitularia, XXII, cap. 72, trans. H. Bettenson, *Documents of the Christian Church* (1963), p. 135.

29 Cf. C. W. Jones, 'An Early Medieval Licensing Examination', *History of Education Quarterly*, III, 1 (Mar. 1963), pp. 19–30, for a discussion of *computus* and an early Latin text (with an English translation) of an examination in *computus*. The text is from the Sirmond MS, Bodleian MS. 309, fol. 141.

30 Cf. M. L. W. Laistner, op. cit. pp. 173–4.

31 C. W. Jones, op. cit. pp. 22–3.

32 *Admonitio generalis*, XXII, cap. 72.

33 On this see Donald Bullough, *The Age of Charlemagne* (1965), pp. 99–100.

34 *Mon. Ger. hist.* Epistolae IV, 172.

35 Cf. L. Wallach, *Alcuin and Charlemagne*, p. 47.

36 For the various interpretations see R. Sullivan, *The Coronation of Charlemagne* (1959).

37 Text in F. V. N. Painter, *Great Pedagogical Essays: Plato to Spencer* (1905).
38 *De clericorum institutione*, III. 2.
39 Ibid. III. 1.
40 Ibid. III. 18.
41 Ibid. III. 20.
42 Ibid.
43 On this see Bernard Bischoff, 'The Study of Foreign Languages in the Middle Ages', *Speculum*, XXXVI, 2 (April, 1961), p. 215.
44 Iohannis Scoti Eriugenae, *Periphyseon* (*De divisione naturae*), Liber primus, ed. and trans. I. P. Sheldon-Williams (1968), I. 448A. 10–13; pp. 50–1.
45 Ibid.
46 Ibid. I. 493C. 17 – 494A.30.
47 Ibid. I. 475 B.16.
48 Ibid. I. 475 A.32 – 475 B.14.
49 Einhard, *Life of Charlemagne*, trans. Thorpe, op. cit. XIX. 1. 1–3, p. 59.: '. . . more Francorum equitare, armis ac venatibus exerceri fecit.'
50 *Policraticus*, VI. 8 (trans. J. Dickinson, 1927).
51 Einhard, op. cit. XIX. 1. 3–5; p. 59.
52 C. J. Hefele, *Histoire des conciles d' après les documents originaux* (1907 f.). French trans. H. Leclerq, II, Part 2 (1908), pp. 1110–15: 'tous les prêtres chargés de paroisses de recevoir chez eux en qualité de lecteurs des jeunes gens, afin de les élever chrétiennement, de leur apprendre les psaumes et les leçons de l'Écriture, et toute la loi du Seigneur, de façon à pouvoir se préparer parmi eux de dignes successeurs.'
53 Council of Eugenius, A.D. 826, 'Bishops should Establish Masters and Teachers in Fit Places', in A. Leach, *Educational Charters and Documents* (1911), p. 21.
54 Cf. L. Wallach, 'Education and Culture in the Tenth Century', *Medievalia et Humanistica*, IX (1955), pp. 18–22.
55 Collected in J. H. Robinson, *Readings in European History* (1904), Vol. I, pp. 259–60.
56 Ibid.
57 Ekkehard IV, *Casus S. Galli;* in *Mon. Ger. Hist.* Scriptt. II. 122; quoted and trans. in G. G. Coulton, *Life in the Middle Ages* (1954), Vol. IV, pp. 57–8.
58 *Liber legum ecclesiasticum*, Articles XIX, XX; in Leach, op. cit. p. 37. 'Presbyteri: semper debent in domibus suis ludimagistrorum scholas habere . . .'
59 Cf. R. W. Southern, *Medieval Humanism and Other Studies* (1970), pp. 61 f.; and, below, Ch. 2, n. 25.
60 Cf. D. J. Geanakoplos, *Byzantine East and Latin West* (1966), Ch. 4, *passim* and p. 113, n. 2.

Chapter 2

1 There is very little information on this topic. Some discussion, bearing chiefly on the later medieval period, will be found in L. R. Shelby, 'The Education of Medieval English Master Masons', *Mediaeval Studies*, XXXII (1970), pp. 1–26.

2 Richer, *Histoire de France (888–995)*, [*Historiarum libri IV*], 2 vols, edited by Robert Latouche (Paris: Librarie Ancienne Honoré Champion, 1930–7), II, pp. 54–6.

3 Ibid.

4 See Richard McKeon, 'Rhetoric in the Middle Ages', *Speculum*, XVII, 1 (Jan. 1942), *passim*.

5 Richer, op. cit. pp. 58–60.

6 C. H. Haskins, *Studies in the History of Medieval Science* (1927; reprinted 1960), p. 8.

7 Ibid., p. 9.

8 Cf. J. R. Williams, 'The Cathedral School of Rheims in the Eleventh Century', *Speculum*, XXIX, 4 (Oct. 1954), pp. 661–77.

9 Ibid. pp. 663 f.

10 *Gesta abbatum Gemblacensium*, in L. MacKinney, *Bishop Fulbert and Education at the School of Chartres* (1957), Appendix 3, p. 52.

11 *Historia ecclesiastica* [*The Ecclesiastical History of Orderic Vitalis*], ed. and trans. M. Chibnall (1969), II. iv (ii.209), pp. 248–9.

12 Ibid. II. iii (ii.126), pp. 146–7.

13 Ibid. II. iv (ii.210), pp. 250–1.

14 Ibid.

15 Ibid. II. iv (ii.211), pp. 250–1.

16 Ibid.

17 *Proslogion*, III. Translated by H. Bettenson, *Documents of the Christian Church* (1963), p. 191.

18 'Neque enim quaero intelligere ut credam, sed credo ut intelligam.' The most accessible of Anselm's writings is probably *Dialogue on Truth* (*Dialogus de veritate*), trans. and ed. Richard McKeon, *Selections from Medieval Philosophers*, Vol. 1 (1929), pp. 150–84.

19 Peter Abelard, *Historia calamitatum*, Ch. 2.

20 Abelard's writings on the topic are relatively inaccessible. They have been edited by B. Geyer, *Die Philosophischen Schriften Peter Abaelards*. A translation of the *Glosses on Porphyry* collected by Geyer has been made in R. McKeon, op. cit. Vol. 1 (1929), pp. 208–58. The most accessible source is Victor Cousin, *Ouvrages inédits d'Abélard* (Paris: Imprimerie Royale, 1836). This volume contains *Dialectica, Sic et non* and a few minor works.

21 Cf. R. McKeon, 'Rhetoric in the Middle Ages', *Speculum*, XVII, 3 (Jan. 1942), *passim*.

22 *The Letters of St Bernard of Clairvaux*, trans. B. S. James (Chicago: Henry Regnery, 1953), pp. 325-17.

23 *Glosses on Porphyry*, in R. McKeon, op. cit. pp. 219-20.

24 Ibid. p. 221.

25 Ibid. pp. 250-1.

26 A moderating interpretation of the importance of Chartres is L. C. Mac-Kinney, *Bishop Fulbert and Education at the School of Chartres* (1957); since then the view has been put more forcefully by R. W. Southern, *Medieval Humanism and Other Studies* (1970), pp. 61 f.

27 John of Salisbury, *Metalogicon*, ed. C. C. I. Webb (Oxford University Press, 1929), I. 24, pp. 55-7. Coll. and trans. H. Wieruszowski, *The Medieval University*, p. 126; cf. also, D. D. McGarry, *The Metalogicon of John of Salisbury* (1962), pp. 67-9.

28 Ibid.

29 Ibid.

30 *Historia pontificalis*, ed. and trans. M. Chibnall (1956), VIII. 17-18, p. 16.

31 Ibid.

32 C. H. Haskins, *Studies in the History of Medieval Science* (1927; repr. 1960), p. 225, and Ch. XI, *passim*.

33 *Life* of Bernard, J. P. Migne, *Patr. Lat.* Vol. 185, col. 479.

34 For a detailed account of the career of the *Institutio oratoria* up to its final recovery in 1416 see the introduction to F. H. Colson, *M. Fabii Quintiliani: Institutionis oratoriae*, Liber I (Cambridge University Press, 1924).

35 The Latin text is edited by C. H. Buttimer, *Didascalion de studio legendi* (1939); the translation is J. Taylor, *The Didascalicon of Hugh of St Victor* (1961).

36 *Didascalicon* I. 1; in Taylor, op. cit. p. 46.

37 Ibid. I. 18; p. 73.

38 Ibid. III. 3; pp. 86-7.

39 Ibid. II. 20; p. 75.

40 Ibid. II. 28; pp. 78 f.

41 Ibid.

42 Ibid.

43 Ibid.

44 Ibid. V. 10; pp. 90 f.

45 Ibid. III. 3; p. 87.

46 Cf. *Nich. Ethics*, I. xiii. 9 (1103a).

47 *Didascalicon*, ed. Taylor, I, p. 54.

48 Ibid. III. 6, p. 90.

49 Cf. *Posterior Analytics*, II. xix (996).

50 The Latin text is W. M. Green, 'Hugo of St Victor *De tribus maximis*

circumstantiis gestorum', *Speculum*, XVIII (1943), pp. 484–93. An English translation is in C. P. McMahon, 'Pedagogical Techniques: Augustine and Hugo of St Victor', *History of Education Quarterly*, III, 1 (March 1963), pp. 33–7, and a summary of the contents of *De tribus* is in C. P. McMahon, 'The Teaching of History in the Twelfth Century', *History of Education Quarterly*, II, 1 (March 1962), p. 50.

51 *De tribus* . . . Prologus; McMahon, *Hist. Ed. Q.* III. 1 (1963), p. 36.
52 Ibid.
53 Ibid.
54 Ibid. p. 33.
55 Ibid. pp. 33–4.
56 Ibid. p. 35.
57 Ibid.
58 Ibid.
59 On this topic generally see F. A. Yates, *The Art of Memory* (1966).
60 Cf. J. Taylor, *The Didascalicon of Hugh of St Victor* (1961), p. 4.
61 C. P. McMahon, *Hist. Ed. Q.* II, 1 (1962), p. 49 and p. 51, n. 15, referring to W. M. Green, 'Augustine on the Teaching of History', *University of California Publications in Classical Philology*, XII (1944), pp. 315–32, 331.
62 Quoted and translated in C. P. McMahon, *Hist. Ed. Q.* III, 1 (1963), p. 32.

Chapter 3

1 A translation of the text, with full documentation, is in H. Bettenson, *Documents of the Christian Church*, 2nd ed. (1963), pp. 135–9. The authenticity of this document was finally discredited in the fifteenth century by Lorenzo Valla, although its spuriousness was known to church officials as early as the tenth century. Cf. W. Ullmann, *A History of Political Thought in the Middle Ages* (1965), p. 98 n.
2 Kingdom is a more appropriate translation of the Latin *civitas* than the word city. Augustine's great treatise is better rendered as the *Kingdom of God*.
3 See particularly G. L. Burr, 'Anent the Middle Ages', *American Historica Review*, XVIII (Oct. 1912–July 1913), pp. 715–18.
4 'Ut non solum Romanum imperium nostro modermine disponatur, verum etiam regnum Graeciae ad nutum nostrum regi et sub nostro imperio gubernari debeat.' Quoted and discussed in W. Ullmann, 'Reflections on the Medieval Empire', *Transactions of the Royal Historical Society*, 5th series, Vol. 14, p. 101.
5 Cf. Ullmann, op. cit. p. 98.
6 See C. H. Haskins, *Studies in the History of Medieval Science* (1927), Ch. IX, and particularly Ch. XII, 'Science at The Court of the Emperor Frederick II'.

7 The only complete modern translation is Daniel D. McGarry, *The Metalogicon of John of Salisbury: A Twelfth-Century Defense of the Verbal and Logical Arts of the Trivium* (1962).

8 *City of God*, V. 24.

9 Hans Liebeschütz, *Mediaeval Humanism in the Life and Writings of John of Salisbury* (1950), p. 93.

10 D. D. McGarry, *Metalogicon;* Introduction, xxi.

11 Ibid. I. 5, 7.

12 *Policraticus*, in J. B. Pike (ed.), *Frivolities of Courtiers and Footprints of Philosophers* (1938). (Trans. of Books I, II, III and parts of VII and VIII.) This quote, VII. 12, p. 137.

13 Ibid.

14 Ibid. VII. 9, p. 123. Proteus: cf. Homer, *Odyssey*, IV. 385 ff.

15 Ibid. VII. 9, p. 122.

16 *Metalogicon* (McGarry, op. cit.), I. 7.

17 Ibid.

18 Ibid. I. 10.

19 Ibid. I. 13.

20 Ibid. II. 4.

21 Ibid. II. 9.

22 Ibid. II. 12.

23 *Policraticus* (Pike, op. cit.), VII. 9, p. 126.

24 Ibid. II. 18, p. 106.

25 Ibid.

26 *Metalogicon* (McGarry, op. cit.), IV. 13.

27 Ibid.

28 *Policraticus* (Pike, op. cit.), VII. 7, p. 114.

29 *Policraticus, passim.*

30 The standard account remains C. H. Haskins, *Studies in the History of Medieval Science*, p. 225, Ch. XII, *passim*. See also S. M. Afnan, *Avicenna: His Life and Works* (1958), Ch. IX, 'Avicenna and the West'.

31 Discussed in Fernand van Steenberghen, *The Philosophical Movement of the Thirteenth Century* (1955), pp. 29–31; see also S. M. Afnan, *Avicenna: His Life and Works* (1958), p. 260.

32 Haskins, op. cit. p. 10.

33 Ibid. Ch. I, *passim.*

34 Ibid. pp. 131 f.

35 Ibid. Ch. XI, *passim.*

36 *Bayt* and *Dar* both mean 'house', although the former carries the emotive meaning of 'home', the latter refers more to physical structure or location. The two meanings, however, blend into each other. Cf. *Encyc. Islam*, Vol. II, pp. 126–7.

37 A recent monograph is S. M. Afnan, op. cit. Avicenna's views are embedded in his numerous writings, and discussed by Afnan, Ch. 2. A selection of Avicenna's works have been collected in Ralph Lerner and Muhsin Mahdi, *Medieval Political Philosophy: A Sourcebook* (1963).

38 S. M. Afnan, op. cit. Ch. IV, *passim*.

39 Ibid. p. 130. Cf. Henry Corbin, *Avicenna and the Visionary Recital* (1960), Ch. 11, Part 10 and *passim*.

40 See Simon van den Bergh, *Averroes' Tahafut al-Tahafut* (1954), p. xiii.

41 On this topic see Majid Fakry, *Islamic Occasionalism* (1958).

42 Quoted from al-Ghazali by Averroes in *Tahafut al-Tahafut* (Bouyges' notation, 518:5–9); given in van den Bergh's translation, pp. 316–17. This is probably the most accessible source of al-Ghazali's writings since the arguments, at least, are cited in detail by Averroes in his critical refutation. See *below*, n. 56.

43 Fakry, op. cit. p. 61. The Latin phrase is from discussion of the Arabic works in the West in the twelfth and thirteen centuries.

44 A short biography will be found in the Introduction to George Hourani, *On the Harmony of Religion and Philosophy (Kitab fasl al-maqal)* (1961).

45 The commentary survives in a Hebrew text by Samuel ben Yehuda of Marseilles, written *c.* 1320 and published in a critical edition with an English translation by E. I. J. Rosenthal, *Averroes' Commentary on Plato's Republic* (1956).

46 Hourani, op. cit. Introduction, p. 17.

47 *Fasl al-maqal*, 1. 15.

48 Ibid. 2. 10.

49 Ibid. 21. 4–8.

50 Ibid. 2. 9.

51 *Commentary on Plato's Republic* (trans. Rosenthal), I. xii, 6; p. 129.

52 *Fasl al-maqal*, 15. 10.

53 Ibid. 5. 20 to 6. 9; also 18. 5–15.

54 This interpretation is clearly warranted by the text of *Fasl al-maqal* and is emphasized by Hourani in his *Introduction*; it is also stressed by van Steenberghen *The Philosophical Movement in the Thirteenth Century* (1955), p. 89. This view therefore conflicts with the often stated belief that Averroes presented a theory of a 'double-truth', that is, that there are two realms of truth, one for phenomenal experience, one for spiritual, and that they are mutually separate.

55 Hourani, *Fasl al-maqal*, Introduction, p. 41.

56 The critical edition is Maurice Bouyges, Volume III of his *Bibliotheca Arabica Scholasticorum* (1930); the standard English translation is Simon van den Bergh, *Averroes' Tahafut al-Tahafut* (1954).

57 Bouyges, op. cit. Preface, p. xi.

58 *Tahafut al-Tahafut*, 'About the Natural Sciences: First Discussion', (Bouyges notation, 520: 10–521:2). In van den Bergh's translation, p. 318.

59 *Fasl al-maqal*, 11. 17–18.

60 *Tahafut al-Tahafut*, 521. 11–12. Cf. Aristotle, *Physics*, II. iii (194b) ff.

61 *Tahafut al-Tahafut*, 522. 7–14.

62 Ibid. Introduction, pp. xv–xix.

63 Aristotle, *De anima*, III: 4–5.

64 Ibid. III: [430:1]

65 See S. M. Afnan, *Avicenna: His Life and Works*, Ch. IV, 'Problems of Metaphysics'.

66 *Maimonides' Treatise on Logic*, trans. Israel Efros (New York: American Academy for Jewish Research, 1938).

67 Maimonides wrote the text in Arabic under the title *Dalalat al-hairin*. The *editio princeps* is *Le Guide des égarés*, edited and with a translation by S. Munk (Paris, 1850–66). There are two important English translations: M. Friedländer (1904) and Shlomo Pines (1963).

68 *Talmudic Commentaries* (before 1160), Essay on the *Jewish Calendar* (1158), *Letter on Apostasy* (1160), *Mishnah Commentary* (1168), *Book of Precepts* (1170), *Letter to the Yemen* (1172), *Mishneh Torah* (1170/80).

69 *Guide* (trans. Pines), Introduction, p. 4.

70 Ibid. I. 33.

71 Ibid. I. 46.

72 Ibid. I. 69. (This section begins Maimonides' arguments on the sequence of cause and effect.)

73 The conflicting opinions are given in Majid Fakry, *Islamic Occasionalism* (1958), pp. 83, 126 n.; and Shlomo Pines, *The Guide of the Perplexed* (1963), pp. cvii f.

74 Maimonides wrote the *Guide* in the Arabic language but using the Hebrew alphabet. He later regretted using Hebrew characters and would have liked to have made the translation himself. Pressure of events prevented him, although he collaborated with Tibbon by offering him advice.

75 See Leon Roth, *The Guide for the Perplexed* (1948), Ch. 8, 'Maimonides in the Synagogue', *passim*.

76 The story, with background information, is told in S. Runciman, *The Medieval Manichee* (1947), esp. Ch. VI, 'The Cathars'.

Chapter 4

1 Orderic Vitalis, *Historia ecclesiastica II* (ed. and trans. M. Chibnall, 1969), III (ii. 20–1); pp. 20–1; 'ad bene legendum, ad canendum, ad scribendum, et ad alia bona studia . . .'

2 Migne, *Patr. Lat.* CLVI, col. 843; coll. and trans. in G. G. Coulton, *Life in the Middle Ages* (1954), Vol. 4, p. 138.

3 W. J. Millor *et al.*, *The Letters of John of Salisbury*, Vol. 1, 'The Early Letters (1153–1161)'. Ep. 56, 'Archbishop Theobald to the Pope', c. 1154–9, pp. 94–5.

4 *Chartularium universitatis Parisiensis*, I. xii, p. 10; cf. footnote 11 below.

5 Innocent III, Decretal V, tit. 5; in Leach, *Educational Charters* (1911), pp. 142–3.

6 The population of France in the thirteenth century has been estimated at 22 million. The standard work is R. Mols, *Introduction à la démographie historique des villes d'Europe du 14e au 18e siècle*, 3 vols (Gembloux, Belgium, 1954–6). Extracts of relevant tables appear in R. R. Palmer, *Atlas of World History* (Chicago: Rand-McNally, 1957), pp. 193–5.

7 *Hist. eccl.* II, iii (ii. 70), pp. 76–7: ' . . . nam in grammatica et dialectica in astronomia quoque scientiam tam copiose habuit . . . physicae quoque scientiam tam copiose habuit, ut in urbe Psalernitana ubi maxime medicorum scolae ab antiquo tempore habentur . . .'

8 The standard work on the medieval university in English remains the 1895 two-volume edition by Hastings Rashdall, *The Universities of Europe in the Middle Ages*, revised in a three-volume edition by F. M. Powicke and A. B. Emden. For Salerno, see Rashdall, pp. 75–86.

9 Rashdall suggests 1158 for the masters' *collegium* (p. 146) and c. 1178 for the students' *universitas* (p. 162). Recent research, however, has advanced these dates considerably forward.

10 C. H. Haskins, *The Rise of Universities* (1923), p. 292.

11 The standard source of records for Paris is the *Chartularium universitatis Parisiensis*, 4 vols, ed. H. Denifle and E. Chatelain (1889–). A useful selection is printed in Lynn Thorndike, *University Records and Life in the Middle Ages* (1944). For Collège de Dix-Huit, *Chartularium* I: 49, see Thorndike, Document 10, p. 21.

12 Rashdall, op. cit. p. 6; Ch. 1, *passim*.

13 Ibid. pp. 15–17.

14 *Chart. univ. Par.* I: 516–18, in Thorndike, op. cit. Doc. 39, p. 81.

15 Text of the charter is collected in University of Pennsylvania, *Translations and Reprints from the Original Sources of European History*, II: 3, pp. 5–7.

16 *Chart. univ. Par.* I: 5–6, Thorndike, op. cit. Doc. 8, p. 19.

17 *Chart. univ. Par.* I: 78–9, Thorndike, op. cit. Doc. 15, p. 27.

18 *Letter (Parens scientiarum)* of Gregory IX, 23 April 1231, in *Chartularium*, I: 136–9, Thorndike, op. cit. Doc. 19, p. 36. The title of this bull, as with all papal documents, comes from the words with which it opens: 'Mother of sciences . . .'

19 These kinds of wandering scholars had existed, as early as the fifth century in

Egypt, and known in the Greek as *bakantiboi*, from the testimony of Synesius, bishop of Ptolemais (*c*. 410–*c*. 414). Synesius' complaints of their irregular behaviour were part of a general feeling against them that led to fifth-century regulations forbidding the ordination of priests without parishes. The etymology of both *bakantiboi* and *vagantes* is unknown, but later medieval belief connected both terms to Bacchus (Dionysos in Greek), who was considered to be the god of wine. The word *vagantes*, in fact, was believed to come from a double consonant shift, the 'b' and hard 'ch' being replaced by 'v' and 'g'; although its derivation from the latin *vagus* (wandering) is equally plausible. The former etymology was strongly reinforced by the vagantes' reputations for carousing and bibulous living. *Goliardi* has a more fixed origin. It derived from the scholars' acceptance of a certain now obscure Golias Episcopus as their patron. At the same time, however, the word goliard is Old French for glutton. There seems no escape from the general contemporary feelings about them. See Helen Waddell, *The Wandering Scholars* (1927); cf. Paul Monroe, *Thomas Platter and the Educational Renaissance of the Sixteenth Century* (1904), p. 19.

20 Pearl Kibre, *The Nations in the Medieval Universities* (1940), p. 10.

21 *Chart. univ. Par.* I: 103; cited in Pearl Kibre, op. cit. pp. 14–28.

22 A detailed account is given in Kibre, op. cit. pp. 10 f.

23 Apparently so named from the custom of students using the straw as a floor covering on which to sit during lectures. In Latin it was called *Vicus stramineus*. See Kibre, op. cit. pp. 90 f.

24 Friedrich Paulsen, *German Education: Past and Present*, trans. T. Lorenz (1908), p. 26. In ancient Rome the *paedagogium* was a place where boys of servile birth were trained as pages; in Greece the παιδᾰγωγεῖον was the room in which the παιδαγωγοί waited for their charges.

25 *Chart. univ. Par.* I: 136–9, Thorndike, op. cit. Doc. 19, p. 38.

26 In Richard McKeon, *Selections from Medieval Philosophers* (1930), Vol. II, pp. 240, 268.

27 *Chart. univ. Par.* I: 227–230, Thorndike, op. cit. Doc. 26, p. 53.

28 Rashdall, op. cit. pp. 450–4; p. 207, n. 2.

29 *Chart. univ. Par.* I: 78–9, Thorndike, op. cit. Doc. 15, pp. 27 f.

30 Rashdall, op. cit. p. 461.

31 Cf. F. M. Powicke, *Ways of Medieval Life and Thought* (1949), Ch. 8, 'Bologna, Paris, Oxford: Three *Studia Generalia*', Ch. 9, 'Some Problems in the History of the Medieval University', *passim*.

32 Ibid. pp. 158–9.

33 Paulsen, op. cit. pp. 26–7; Wieruszowski, *The Medieval University*, p. 31.

34 Petri Lombardi, *Liber quattuor sententiarum*, selection translated in R. McKeon, *Selections from the Medieval Philosophers*, Vol. 1, pp. 189–201.

35 Bk I. Distinction III, Ch. 1, ibid. p. 189.

36 The etymology is dubious; perhaps because they 'came after' they were considered *post illa verba* and so received their name this way. Cf. Beryl Smalley, *The Study of The Bible in the Middle Ages* (1952), p. 270.

37 Smalley, op. cit. p. 366.

38 Ibid. p. 271.

39 *Chart univ. Par.* I: 65, in Thorndike, op. cit. Doc. 13, pp. 25–6.

40 *Chart. univ. Par.* I: 8, p. 67; cf. Wieruszowski, op. cit. p. 137.

41 *Chart univ. Par.* I: 78–9; cf. Wieruszowski, op. cit. pp. 138–9, Thorndike, op. cit. Doc. 15, p. 29.

42 *Chart. univ. Par.* I: 32, pp. 91–2; cf. Wieruszowski, op. cit. pp. 144–5.

43 *Chart. univ. Par.* I: 136–9; cf. Thorndike, op. cit. Doc. 19, p. 38.

44 These four studies are mentioned specifically in a Paris statute of 1288, *Chart univ. Par.* I: 112–13; cf. Thorndike, op. cit. Doc. 16, p. 31.

45 *Chart. univ. Par.* I: 419, p. 473; cf. Wieruszowski, op. cit. pp. 146–7.

46 Which can be inferred from *Chart. univ. Par.* I: 385–6; cf. Thorndike, op. cit. Doc. 32, pp. 79–82.

47 Augustinus Triumphus of Ancona, *On Ecclesiastical Power*, in Thorndike, op. cit. pp. 161–2.

48 Ibid.

49 *Chart. univ. Par.* I: 516–18; cf. Thorndike, op. cit. Doc. 39, pp. 81–2.

50 *Chart. univ. Par.* I: 488–90; cf. Thorndike, op. cit. Doc. 40, pp. 83–5.

51 Cf. Helene Wireuszowski, 'Arezzo as a Center of Learning and Letters in the Thirteenth Century', *Traditio*, IX (1953), p. 328, n. 28, for discussion and documentation.

52 C. H. Haskins, *The Rise of Universities* (1923), p. 7.

53 Latin text in O. Holder-Egger and B. von Simson (eds.), *Die Chronik des Propstes: Burchard von Ursberg* [Scriptores rerum Germanicum, ex Monumentis Germaniae Historicis] (Hannover and Leipzig: Hahnsche Buchhandlung, 1916); English trans. in Wieruszowski, *The Medieval University*, p. 164.

54 Ibid. However, Wieruszowski's date of 1125 is doubtful. The MGH gloss gives 1132/3 as the probable date of the reference to Gratian and the f.n. p. 15, n. 2, suggests soon after 1140: '... wahrscheinlich bald nach 1140 enstanden'. For confirmation of the latter see *Oxford Dictionary of the Christian Church*, s.v. 'Gratian'.

55 Ibid.

56 Herman Kantorowicz, 'Note on the Development of the Gloss to the Justinian and the Canon Law', in Beryl Smalley, *The Study of the Bible in the Middle Ages* (1952), pp. 52 f.

57 Ibid.

58 Ibid. p. 54.

59 Pearl Kibre, *Scholarly Privileges in the Middle Ages* (1961), pp. 10–11.

60 Ibid. n. 28.

61 Ibid. p. 12.

62 Pearl Kibre, *The Nations in the Medieval Universities* (1948), p. 3.

63 Kibre, *Scholarly Privileges* . . ., pp. 20–1.

64 Ibid. Ch. 1, *passim*.

65 Ibid. p. 21, n. 15: 'Decretum consilii Bononiensis quo urgente bello doctores et scholares a militia esse caretur.'

66 Wieruszowski, 'Arezzo as a Center of Learning . . .', op. cit. p. 326, nn. 21, 22.

67 Wieruszowski, *The Medieval University*, p. 167.

68 Kibre, *Scholarly Privileges* . . ., p. 32: 'Scholaribus, qui ab archiadiacono Bononiensi utriusque iuris laureas adept; fuerint, civiles, ac canonicas leges ubique gentium docere posse decernit.'

69 Ibid.

70 A bibliography for the examination of this is in the footnotes to Helen Wieruszowski, '*Ars Dictaminis* in the Time of Dante', *Medievalia et Humanistica*, I (1943), pp. 95–108.

71 Ibid. p. 96, n. 9 and Rashdall, op. cit. I. 108 ff.

72 Wieruszowski, 'Arezzo as a Center of Learning . . .' p. 329.

73 'Buoncompagni da Signa on the New Rhetoric, 1235', in Thorndike, *University Records and Life in the Middle Ages*.

74 Ibid.

75 A full exposition, with further references, is in Wieruszowski, '*Ars Dictaminis* in the Time of Dante'.

76 Ibid. p. 98, and n. 24.

77 Ibid. p. 103: 'Tullio disse che la più nobile parte di tutte le scienze di governare la città si è la retorica, cioè la scienza del parlare.'

78 Ibid. p. 107

79 Wieruszowski, 'Arezzo as a Center of Learning . . .', pp. 336–7.

80 Wieruszowski, '*Ars Dictaminis* . . .', p. 103.

81 Trans. in C. H. Haskins, *The Renaissance of the Twelfth Century* (1927); coll. in Wieruszowski, *The Medieval University*, p. 165.

82 Ibid.

83 Heinrich Denifle, 'Die Statuten der Juristen-Universität Bologna', *Archiv für Literatur- und Kirchengeschichte des Mittelalters*, III (1887), p. 284, coll. and trans. in Wieruszowski, op. cit. p. 170.

84 Ibid. p. 171.

85 Rashdall, op. cit. I. pp. 588–9; coll. in Wieruszowski, op. cit. p. 172.

Chapter 5

1 The standard biography is from his contemporary, Thomas of Celano. See A. G. F. Howell (ed.), *The Lives of St Francis of Assisi by Brother Thomas of Celano* (1908).

2 *Regula Francisci*, Sections 2, 3. The rule is collected in E. F. Henderson, *Select Documents of the Middle Ages* (1896), and P. Robinson (ed.), *The Writings of St Francis of Assisi* (1906).

3 *Regula Francisci*, Sect. 5.

4 There are numerous biographies of Dominic; one of the most recent is B. Jarrett, *The Life of Saint Dominic* (Westminster, Maryland: Newman Press, 1955).

5 This term, from the Greek σχολαστικός and the Latin *scholasticus*, meaning studious or learned, came into use in the sixteenth century to refer to the philosophical activities of the thirteenth-century *studia generalia* or 'schools'.

6 *Chartularium universitatis Parisiensis*, I. 47-8; cf. L. Thorndike, *University Records and Life in the Middle Ages* (1944), Document 11, pp. 22-4.

7 *Chart. univ. Par.* I. 70; Thorndike, op. cit. Doc. 14, pp. 26-7.

8 Ibid. 78-9; Doc. 15, pp. 27-8.

9 Ibid. I. 154; Doc. 20, pp. 39-40.

10 Ibid. I. 173-4; Doc. 23, pp. 47-8.

11 Fernand van Steenberghen, *The Philosophical Movement in the Thirteenth Century* (1955), p. 47.

12 *Chart. univ. Par.* I. 227-30; Thorndike, op. cit. Doc. 26, pp. 53-4.

13 Ibid. I. 277-9; Doc. 28, pp. 64-5.

14 *Munimenta academia Oxon.* I. 34 (Rolls Series), in A. F. Leach, *Educational Charters and Documents* (1911), pp. 192-3.

15 Letters of the University of Paris to prelates of the church and scholars generally in which religious orders, especially the Friars Preachers, are attacked; *Chart. univ. Par.* I. 252-8; cf. Thorndike, Doc. 27, pp. 56-64.

16 *Commentaria in quattuor libros sententiarum magistri Petri Lombardi* (*Commentary on the Four Books of Sentences of Peter Lombard*). A selection will be found in Richard McKeon, *Selections from Medieval Philosophers* (1930), Vol. II, pp. 111-48.

17 A term applied by van Steenberghen, op. cit. Chapter IV: 'Saint Bonaventure or Augustinian Aristotelianism'.

18 Thomas's life is documented in three major sources: (1) three biographies all written between 1318 and 1330 by Dominicans, William Tocco, Bernard Gui, Peter Calo; (2) minutes of the first canonization inquiry; (3) fifteen chapters from Tolomeo Lucca's *Historia ecclesiastica* (1317). The relevant materials from all of these sources are collected in Kenelm Foster, *The Life of Saint Thomas Aquinas: Biographical Documents* (1959).

19 *Summa de veritate fidei catholicae contra gentiles.* There are several English translations.

20 *Summa theologica*, I. 79, 1–2. (Thomas echoes Aristotle's idea of a discriminative capacity, cf. Aristotle, *De anima*, IV. 430a.)

21 Ibid. I. 85, 1, c.

22 *Quaestiones disputatae de veritate*, I. 11, c (R. W. Mulligan *et. al.*, *Truth*, 3 vols (Chicago: Regnery, 1952–4)); *Summa theologica*, I. 17, 3, c.

23 *Quaestiones disputatae de veritate*, I. 12, c.

24 Ibid. I. 4, c.

25 Ibid.

26 *Super librum de causis expositio*, Lecture 1.

27 *Summa theologica*, I. 76, 1.

28 *Super librum de causis expositio*, Lecture 1.

29 *De unitate intellectus contra Avveroystas* (incl. French trans.), *Opuscules*, XVI (Paris, 1857).

30 *Summa contra gentiles*, I. 29; II. 28–29; see also Majid Fakry, *Islamic Occasionalism*, Ch. 4, Pt 3, 'Causality as an Instance of Divine Love and Generosity', pp. 148–65.

31 *Quaestiones disputatae, De veritate XI, De magistro*, West Baden trans. (Chicago: Regnery, 1953).

32 Ibid.

33 Ibid. *Reply.*

34 Ibid.

35 Ibid.

36 Ibid. *Answers to Difficulties*, No. 4.

37 Ibid. No. 11.

38 Ibid. No. 17.

39 *Chart. univ. Par.* I. 486–7; Thorndike, op. cit. Doc. 38, pp. 80–1.

40 These have only recently been recovered and are not readily available. All editions are European; for a definitive bibliography cf. *Oxford Dictionary of the Christian Church*, s.v. 'Siger of Brabant'.

41 Detailed in van Steenberghen, op. cit. Ch. v, 'Siger of Brabant or Radical Aristotelianism'.

42 The condemnation is developed at length in Etienne Gilson, *History of Christian Philosophy in the Middle Ages*, 'The Condemnation of 1277'. The text of all propositions will be found in R. Lerner and M. Mahdi, *Medieval Political Philosophy* (1963), pp. 335–54.

43 For example, the important treatise on Being and Truth, *Commentaria Oxoniensia ad IV Libros magistri sententiarum* (*Oxford Commentary on the Four Books of the Master of the Sentences*), collected in McKeon, op. cit. pp. 313–50.

44 *Quodlibeta septem . . .*, in McKeon, op. cit. Vol. II, pp. 360–421.

45 Ibid. I. xiii.

46 Quoted in Kenelm Foster, *The Life of Saint Thomas Aquinas: Bibliographical Documents* (1959), p. 4.

47 Texts from all of these writers are collected in Lerner and Mahdi, op. cit.

48 Translation of the text of *Clericos laicos* and *Unam sanctam* is given in Norton Downs, *Basic Documents in Medieval History* (1959); E. F. Henderson, *Historical Documents of the Middle Ages* (1896).

49 *Unam sanctum*, Downs, op. cit. p. 165.

50 Cf. J. A. Robson, *Wyclif and the Oxford Schools* (1961), pp. 97 f.

51 Augustinus, *De correptione et gratia*, 39.

52 Wycliffe, *De ecclesia* 107 f.; cf. G. Leff, *Heresy in the Later Middle Ages* (1967), Vol. II, p. 517, n 4.

53 Two important works by A. F. Leach are relevant to the period: *Educational Charters and Documents* (1911) gives a selection of materials for English education, and has formed the basis for his later extensive monograph, *The Schools of Medieval England*. No comparable works exist in English for continental Europe although the position in England in general paralleled that in Europe until the end of the fourteenth century. Thereafter there were some marked divergencies.

54 There is no English translation of this document. Latin text appears in J. P. Migne, *Patr. lat.* LXIV, Cols. 1223–38; and an explanatory essay by J. W. Adamson in *The Illiterate Anglo-Saxon* (1946), Ch. VI, 'De disciplina scholarium: A Medieval Student's Handbook'.

55 Ibid. pp. 111–16.

56 Thirteenth-century date has been put forward by A. L. Gabriel, 'Source of the Anecdote of the Constant Scholar', in his *Garlandia: Studies in the History of the Medieval University* (1969).

57 The Latin text, an English translation, and a short bibliographic description is given in Thorndike, *University Records and Life in the Middle Ages* (1944), pp. 409–33; 201–35.

58 Ibid. p. 211.

59 J. W. Adamson, op. cit. Ch. IV: 'Medieval Education', p. 73.

60 *Commendation of the Clerk*, Thorndike, pp. 223–34.

61 *De disciplina scholarium.*

62 See especially Ch. VII, 'Concerning the Principal of a Boys' School', Thorndike, op. cit. pp. 223–5.

63 *De commendatione cleri*, I. i: '... penne columbe deargentate et posteriora dorsi eius in pallore auri.'

64 Described comprehensively in G. G. Coulton, *Europe's Apprenticeship* (1940), and given in numerous items in his four-volume collection of documentary sources, *Life in the Middle Ages* (1944).

65 Robert de Graystanes, *Chronicle*; quoted and trans. in G. C. Coulton, *Life in the Middle Ages*, Vol. II, pp. 86–7.

66 Ibid.

67 Ibid.

68 Ibid.

69 Coulton, op. cit. II, p. 39.

70 Ibid.

71 *Register of St Osmund*, Rolls Series, Vol. I, p. 304; in Coulton, op. cit. II, p. 39.

72 Ibid.

73 Ibid. p. 40.

74 Coll. and trans. in Coulton, op. cit. Vol. I, p. 104.

75 Odo Rigaldi, *Regestrum visitationum*; Coulton, op. cit. Vol. II, p. 42.

76 Ibid.

77 Ibid.

78 Ibid. II, p. 46.

79 A full account of the revised constitutions will be found in David Knowles, *The Religious Orders in England*, Vol. II, *The End of the Middle Ages* (1955), *passim*.

80 *Constitutiones Benedicti Pape ejus nomine XII super monachos negros*, Cap. 7, 'De studiis', in Leach, *Educational Charters and Documents*, pp. 288–9.

81 *Register*; in Coulton, op. cit. II. pp. 113–14; also in Leach, op. cit. 'Episcopal Attack on the Classics in the Diocese of Exeter, 1357', pp. 314–17.

82 Ibid.

83 The standard monograph is Albert Hyma, *The Brethren of the Common Life* (1950). The name Groote in Dutch means 'the great'. See also E. F. Jacob, 'Gerard Groote and the beginnings of the "New Devotion" in the Low Countries', *Journal of Ecclesiastical History*, III, 1 (Jan. 1952), pp. 40–57.

84 Jacob, op. cit. p. 46.

85 Ibid. p. 50.

86 Ibid. p. 49.

87 Cited by Jacob, ibid. p. 50.

88 Gerard Groote, Ep. 4, p. 8; cited by Jacob, ibid. p. 48.

89 Jacob, ibid. p. 55.

90 Cf. ibid. p. 46 for an account of Gerard's bibliomania.

Chapter 6

1 *Trecento* is used to describe the cultural developments in Italy in the fourteenth century. It is a shortened form of the Italian way of naming a century; in full it is *milletrecento*, literally, 'one thousand, three hundred' which is contracted to simply 'three hundred'. Likewise the thirteenth century is the 'twelve hundreds', *duecento* [or, colloquially, *dugento*], the fifteenth is the

quattrocento; less frequently used are *cinquecento* and *seicento* for the sixteenth and seventeenth centuries respectively.

2 Cf. C. T. Davis, 'Education in Dante's Florence', *Speculum*, XL (1965), pp. 415–35; p. 417.

3 Ibid.

4 Ibid. p. 415.

5 *Paradiso*, X. 98–9.

6 Ibid. X. 136–9.

7 *Inferno*, XV. 58.

8 Ibid. XV. 84–5.

9 *Paradiso*, XVII. 68: 'Di sua bestialitate il suo processo / Farà la prova sì che a te fia bello / Averti fatta parte per te stesso.'

10 The standard English collection of the original works is E. Moore and Paget Toynbee, *Le Opere de Dante Alighieri*. The edition used here is the fourth (1924), from which citations from the original texts have been taken.

11 See especially R. H. Robins, *Ancient and Medieval Grammatical Theory* (1951), pp. 75 f.

12 See J. Cremona, 'Dante's Views on Language', in U. Limentani (ed.), *The Mind of Dante* (1965).

13 *De vulgari eloquentia*, I. i. 4.

14 *Convivio*, I. v. 7–15.

15 Ibid. I. v. 45–109.

16 Ibid. I. v. 66–9: 'Di questo si parlerà altrove piu compiutamente in un libello ch'io intendo di fare, Dio concedente, di *Volgare Eloquenza*.'

17 *De monarchia*, I. xv: 'quod omne quod est bonum, per hoc est bonum, quod in uno consistit.'

18 The complete text in English, with notes, has been translated by Donald Nicholl, *Monarchy* (1954); an abridgement, translated by Philip Wicksteed, consisting of all of Book I and Section XVI of Book III is included in Ralph Lerner and Muhsin Mahdi, *Medieval Political Philosophy: A Sourcebook* (1963), pp. 418–38.

19 Dante's knowledge of Aristotle's *Politics* may have come from Aquinas' commentaries, cf. Nicholl, op. cit. p. 8n. None the less, A. P. D'Entreves, *Dante as a Political Thinker* (1952), righly points out that the source of his observation is irrelevant; pp. 16, 35–6.

20 *De monarchia*, I. iii. 76–8.

21 Ibid. I. xv. 57–64.

22 The issues are treated by D'Entreves, op. cit. pp. 18–19 and Ch. 1, *passim*.

23 *De monarchia*, II. i. 1 f.

24 Ibid. III. xvi. 43–70.

25 The work that comes closest to telling us that Dante was primarily an educator is Étienne Gilson, *Dante as a Philosopher*.

26 *Inferno*, XV. 106–7.

27 Ibid. XIX. 70.

28 Ibid. XXIII. 92.

29 *Paradiso*, IX. 132–8:

> . . . Perocchè fatto ha lupo del pastore.
> Per questo l'Evangelio e i Dottor magni
> Son derelitti, e solo ai Decretali
> Si studia sì che pare ai lor vivagni.
> A questio intende il papa e i cardinali:
> Non vanno i lor pensieri a Nazzarette,
> Là dove Gabriello aperse l'ali.

30 *De monarchia*, III. xvi. 75–82: 'Propter quod opus fuit homini duplici directivo, secundum duplicem finem: scilicet summo Pontifice, qui secundum revelata humanum genus perduceret ad vitam aeternam; et Imperatore, qui secundum philosophica documenta genus humanem ad temporalem felicitatem dirigeret.'

31 R. Weiss, *The Spread of Italian Humanism* (1964), remarks that *De monarchia* and *De vulgari eloquentia* were 'medieval to the core' and that 'Dante marks the end of the middle ages', p. 19.

32 *De monarchia*, III, x.

33 Cf. Weiss, op. cit. pp. 14 f.

34 The movement is examined in detail in Weiss, op. cit. Ch. 1.

35 There was no fixed form of the family name; Petrarch is the Anglicized form. There are several reliable biographies of Petrarch, including E. H. Wilkins, *Life of Petrarch* (1961), and Morris Bishop, *Petrarch and His World* (1964).

36 *Epistolae seniles*, XVI. 1. Translated and quoted by Bishop, op. cit. p. 21. Petrarch himself collected and edited his letters, late in life. These are the standard source for his biography and his thought. There are five major collections of *epistolae*: *metricae* (in metre), *seniles* (from old age), *sine nomine* (without titles), *variae* (miscellaneous topics), *familiares* (personal records). The *Epistolae familiares* are a huge collection of twenty-four books in 1,300 pages of Latin prose. There is no comprehensive English translation; for critical details, see Bishop, op. cit. pp. 376 f. A selection is translated by E. H. Wilkins, *Petrarch at Vaucluse: Letters in Prose and Verse* (1958).

37 Bishop, op. cit. p. 91.

38 *Rerum memorandum libri*, I. 2; trans. Bishop, op. cit. p. 99.

39 *Epistolae familiares*, III. 12; trans. Wilkins, *Petrarch at Vaucluse*.

40 Details of editions in Bishop, op. cit. pp. 376 f.; Wilkins, op. cit. pp. 261–2. An English translation made by Hans Nachod of *De sui ipsius et multoram ignorantia* is collected in E. Cassirer, P. O. Kristeller and J. H. Randall, *The Renaissance Philosophy of Man* (1948), pp. 47–133.

41 Cf. Bishop, op. cit. p. 185; Weiss, op. cit. p. 27.

42 See J. H. Whitfield, *Petrarch and the Renascence* (1943), pp. 104 f.

43 *Epistolae familiares*, III. 18 (trans. Wilkins, op. cit.).

44 *Ep. fam.* VII. 4 (trans. Wilkins).

45 *Ep. fam.* XV. 2 (trans. Wilkins).

46 *Ep. fam.* XVI. 3 (trans. Wilkins).

47 *On His Own Ignorance*, in Cassirer *et al.*, op. cit. p. 112.

48 *Ep. fam.* VI, 2; cf. Bishop, Ch. IX, *passim*.

49 *Ep. fam.* XI. 3.

50 Cf. Dante, *De monarchia*, I. xii.

51 *Epistolae seniles*, trans. into Italian and collected by G. Martellotti *et al.*, *Prosa* (Milan and Naples: Ricciardi, 1955).

52 This objection occupies much of *De . . . ignorantia*. Cf. Cassirer, op. cit. pp. 77 f.

53 See, for example, *A Disapproval of an Unreasonable Use of the Discipline of Dialectic*; *An Averroist's Visit*; *Aversion to Arab Science*; *A Request to Take Up the Fight Against Averroes*; all collected in Cassirer, op. cit.

54 *Aversion to Arab Science*; Cassirer *et al.*, op. cit. p. 142.

55 *Epistolae variae*, XLII, XLVIII; *Epistolae sine nomine*, II; collected in Wilkins, *Petrarch at Vaucluse*.

56 *Ep. seniles*, VII. 1.

57 *Ep. fam.* XII, 3; trans. and quoted in Bishop, op. cit. p. 286.

58 *De . . . ignorantia*; Cassirer *et al.*, op. cit. p. 96.

59 *Ep. fam.* I, 7; Cassirer, op. cit. p. 138.

60 Ibid.

61 Petrarch refers twice to *Institutio oratoria*: XII. 2, 14 and IX. 2, 78, in his letter *Disapproval of an Unreasonable Use* of *Dialectic*, *Ep. fam.* I. 7.

62 *Ep. sen.* XIV. 1. Petrarch wrote also on the education of the Christian prince in *Ep. fam.* XII. 2.

63 Bishop, op. cit. p. 369. Bishop points out that the unlikeliness of this story does not discount the poetic symbolism with which the rumour invested his life in the public mind.

64 Set out in A. A. Vasiliev, *History of the Byzantine Empire* (1961), Vol. 2, pp. 717–18.

65 Ibid. p. 715.

66 *Epistolae de rebus familiaribus et variae*, XVIII. 2; XXIV. 12 (ed. Fracassetti, II, 474; III, 302); trans. and quoted by Vasiliev, op. cit. p. 714.

67 *Ep. var.* XXV; Vasiliev, loc. cit.

68 *De genealogia deorum*, XV. 6; cf. Vasiliev, op. cit. p. 715.

69 *De gen. deorum*, XV. 6; Vasiliev, loc. cit.

70 Earlier, in 1298/9, Raymond Lull had urged the university at Paris to establish chairs in Arabic, Tartar and Greek; *Chartularium univ. Parisiensis*, II. 83–4. As late as 1430, however, scholars at Paris were complaining that an

ancient ordinance in this respect had not been observed and requested the appointment of professors of Hebrew, Aramaic and Greek, *Chartularium*, IV, 505; see Thorndike, *University Records and Life in the Middle Ages*, pp. 125–7, 297–8.

71 *De gen. deorum*, XV. 6, *passim*.

72 *Ep. sen.* XV. 6; Cassirer, op. cit. p. 143.

73 The problems of chronology, and the relevant evidence, are given in Émile Legrand, *Biographie hellénique* (Paris, 1885; reprinted 1963), Vol. I, pp. xix f. Cf. W. H. Woodward, *Vittorino da Feltre* (1905), p. 16, n. 2. The most recent dates are given in Ian Thomson, 'Manuel Chrysoloras and the Early Italian Renaissance', *Greek, Roman and Byzantine Studies*, VII (Spring 1966), No. 1.

74 Details in Legrand, op. cit. xxi.

75 The date is uncertain; cf. Legrand, xxii.

76 Vittorio Rossi, *Il Quattrocento* (Milan, 1956), pp. 34–5; given in Lauro Martines, *The Social World of the Florentine Humanists 1390–1460* (1963), p. 319.

77 For notarial studies, see J. K. Hyde, *Padua in the Age of Dante* (1966); esp. Ch. VI, 'The Guildsmen', pp. 154–74.

78 Martines, op. cit. pp. xxiv–xxvi.

79 Thomson, op. cit. pp. 63, 80.

80 The evidence and dates, however, are not certain. Cf. Legrand, op. cit. xix.

81 *Laudatio*, ed. Klette, p. 104, in H. Baron, *The Crisis of the Early Italian Renaissance* (1955), pp. 362; 620 n. 11.

Chapter 7

1 The standard account of this period is Hans Baron, *The Crisis of the Early Italian Renaissance* (1955).

2 Cf. ibid. Ch. 7, *passim*.

3 Ibid. p. 92.

4 The modern revival of the term appears to have been the coining of 'humanismus' in 1808 by the German educator F. J. Niethammer to stress the Greek and Latin emphasis in the secondary school curriculum, in opposition to the growing demands for more technical content. See P. O. Kristeller, *The Classics and Renaissance Thought* (1955), pp. 9, 94 n. 4.

5 *Dialogi*, ed. Klette (1889), p. 80; ed. Garin (1952), p. 94; for full details see Baron, op. cit. Vol. 2, p. 454, n. 1. Cited in Baron, op. cit., p. 232, 540 n. 37.

6 There is some doubt that Vergerio was formally in Carrara's service. Documentation in Baron, op. cit. Vol. 2, p. 487, n. 20.

7 The date is given variously; the *terminus a quo* is 1392, the *terminus ad quem* is 1405. Cf. Woodward, *Vittorino da Feltre and other Humanist Educators*, pp. 14 n. 5, 93 n. 5. Woodward himself is uncertain. Cf. R. R. Bolgar, *The Classical Heritage and its Beneficiaries* (1958), pp. 258, 429; Hans Baron, op. cit.

Vol. 2, p. 487 n. 20. *De ingenuis moribus* means literally 'concerning gentlemanly ways'.

8 Woodward, op. cit. p. 14 n. 6.

9 Documentation in Bolgar, op. cit. Cf. Woodward, *Desiderius Erasmus* (1904), p. 86 n. 2, where evidence is presented to confirm the *terminus ad quem* of 1405 as a more likely date for the writing of *De ingenuis moribus*.

10 *De ingenuis moribus*, Section 3; Woodward, op. cit. p. 96.

11 Ibid. Sect. 2; p. 100.

12 Ibid. Sect. 3; p. 102.

13 Ibid. Sect. 3; pp. 106–7.

14 Ibid.

15 Ibid. Sect. 5, *passim*; p. 116.

16 Ibid. Sect. 3; p. 107.

17 Ibid.

18 Ibid. Sect. 3; p. 108.

19 An exhaustive and accurate catalogue of Greek manuscript sources, with the dates of their introduction into Italy, is given in a lengthy Appendix I to R. R. Bolgar, op. cit. pp. 455–505. Appendix II catalogues the translations of these manuscripts and Latin authors as well into the major vernaculars – English, French, German, Italian, Spanish – before 1600.

20 *De ingenuis moribus*, Sect. 3; p. 108.

21 Ibid.

22 Ibid. Sect. 4; p. 109.

23 Ibid.

24 Ibid. p. 110.

25 Ibid.

26 Letter collected in J. A. Symonds, *The Revival of Learning* (1888), pp. 135–6.

27 Ibid.

28 A full account of the history of the *Institutio oratoria* will be found in F. H. Colson, *M. Fabii Quintiliani: Institutionis oratoriae*, Bk 1 (1924), Introduction, *passim*. For list of lacunae, cf. p. lxi.

29 Documentation discussed in Baron, op. cit. Vol. 2, p. 561. Partial translation in Emerton, *Humanism and Tyranny* (1925), pp. 309–41, 346–77; ideas discussed in J. Cinquino, 'Coluccio Salutati, Defender of Poetry', *Italica*, XXVI (1949), pp. 131–5.

30 Details in Baron, op. cit. pp. 254 f.

31 Ibid. p. 257.

32 Text located in Baron, op. cit.: 'Leonardus Aretinus: De studiis et literis', in *Leonardo Aretinos: Humanische and Philosophische Schriften* (Leipzig, 1928), Vol. 1, pp. 7–10. English translation in W. H. Woodward *Vittorino da Feltre and Other Humanist Educators*. Woodward's dating of 1405 (p. 120), however, has been revised by Baron, pp. 356, 613 n. 23.

33 *De studiis et literis*; Woodward, op. cit., pp. 127–8.

34 Ibid. p. 132.

35 Ibid.

36 Woodward doesn't bring out the emphasis in his version when he translates 'we must note attentively vocabulary . . .' The text itself warrants 'note *down*': 'Diligenter curabitque ut quotiens ei loquendam sit aliqua vel scriben-dum.' The point is also discussed by Bolgar, *The Classical Heritage*, pp. 296 f., and the corresponding note on p. 431.

37 Vittorino styled himself Vittore dai Ramboldi, preferring to be considered a Mantuan rather than a Feltrese. Cf. Jacob Burckhardt, *The Civilization of the Renaissance in Italy* (1860), Part III, Ch. 5.

38 The standard account in English is W. H. Woodward, *Vittorino da Feltre and other Humanist Educators* (1897).

39 Ibid. p. 32.

40 Burckhardt, op. cit. (Harper Torchbook Edition, 1958), Vol. I, p. 221.

41 Letter to Ambrogio Traversari, cited in Woodward, op. cit. p. 68 n. 3; Traversari *Epp.* VIII, 50, cited in Bolgar, op. cit.

42 Ibid. p. 52.

43 Ibid. pp. 42–3.

44 Ibid. p. 61.

45 A young man living closely to an elder, with the intention of learning a particular vocation. It seems to have begun in Republican Rome when youths accompanied generals to war to learn the military arts (Latin, *Contubernium*, a military tent). This practice was revived in Italy; both Guarino and Chrysoloras, for example, were *contubernales* of Barzizza.

46 Translated in Woodward, op. cit. pp. 159–78.

47 *De ordine docendi et studendi*; in Woodward, op. cit. p. 161.

48 Ibid. p. 173.

49 Given in Baron, op. cit. p. 423.

50 *De ordine* . . . : Woodward, op. cit. p. 176.

51 Given in Bolgar, op. cit. pp. 257, p. 429 n. 3. Similar stories are told by Erasmus, *De pueris instituendis*, Sect. 24, 504D et. seq.

Chapter 8

1 L. Thorndike, *University Records and Life in the Middle Ages* (1944), p. xiii and Introduction, *passim*.

2 F. M. Powicke, *Ways of Medieval Life and Thought* (1949), Ch. VIII, 'Bologna, Paris, Oxford: Three *Studia Generalia*', *passim*.

3 Petition collected in Thorndike, op. cit. Doc. 142, pp. 333–4. Cf. Doc. 143, 'Decree Against Ignorant Schoolteachers, Ferrara, 1443', pp. 335–7.

4 Ferdinand Schevill, *The Medici* (1950), p. 88.

5 See Nesca A. Robb, *Neoplatonism of the Italian Renaissance* (1935), pp. 58 f.

6 The origin and use of the word 'academy' by Ficino's circle is given in Robb, op. cit. p. 57 n. 1.

7 There is no adequate account of this Platonic Academy in English; Robb, op. cit., gives a brief treatment in Ch. III, 'Marsilio Ficino and the Platonic Academy of Florence' basing it on the definitive work, Arnaldo della Torre, *Storia dell' Academia Platonica di Firenze* (Florence, 1902).

8 This theme is developed in Josephine Burrough's Introduction to the translation of Ficino's *Five Questions Concerning the Mind*, in E. Cassirer *et al.*, *Renaissance Philosophy of Man* (1948), pp. 186 f.; q.v.

9 *Five Questions Concerning the Mind*, op. cit. p. 200.

10 Ibid. p. 201.

11 Ibid.

12 Ibid. p. 195.

13 Ibid. p. 202.

14 Ibid. p. 207.

15 Ibid. pp. 211–12.

16 Robb, op. cit. pp. 90 f.

17 See Robb, pp. 179 f.; 184 n. 1.

18 Cf. E. H. Gombrich, 'The Early Medici as Patrons of Art: A Survey of Primary Sources', in *Italian Renaissance Studies*, ed. E. F. Jacob (1960), pp. 279–311.

19 The theme is elaborated in Erwin Panofsky, *Studies in Iconology: Humanistic Themes in the Art of the Renaissance* (1939), cf. Ch. V, VI.

20 Cf. Panofsky, op. cit. pp. 156–9, Ch. V, *passim*; also Schevill, *The Medici* (1950), pp. 158–9; Robb, op. cit. Ch. VII, 'Neoplatonism and the Arts', *passim*.

21 *On the Dignity of Man*, trans. E. L. Forbes, in Cassirer *et al.*, op. cit. p. 225.

22 *Disputationes Camaldulenses* (1475), in E. Garin, *Prosatori latini de Quattrocento*, p. 742; cited in Martines, op. cit. p. 297.

23 *On the Dignity of Man*, in Cassirer *et al.*, op. cit. p. 225.

24 Ibid. p. 227.

25 Ibid. p. 238.

26 *Opera* (Basle, 1538), p. 337; cited in H. Baron, *The Crisis of the Early Italian Renaissance* (1955), p. 362.

27 Ibid.

28 Cited in F. Gilbert, *Machiavelli and Guiccardini: Politics and History in Sixteenth Century Florence* (1965), p. 216, n. 28.

29 Cf. Gilbert, op. cit., for a close study of these issues.

30 Ibid. p. 321.

31 *Discorsi sopra la prima deca di Tito Livio*, I. xviii; cited in Gilbert, op. cit. p. 7, n. 1: 'Se in una città corrotta si può mantenere lo stato libero.'

32 Cf. Lauro Martines, *The Social World of the Florentine Humanists: 1390–1460* (1963), esp. pp. 271–302 for an analysis of the genesis and decline of civic humanism.

33 *The Book of the Courtier*, trans. G. Bull (1967), pp. 39–40. English citations are all taken from this rendition and the Italian interpolations from Bruno Maier (ed.), *Il Libro del Cortegiano*, 2nd ed. (Turin, 1964), which is based on the best manuscript authorities including M. L. Dolce and V. Cian; cf. *Nota ai testi*, pp. 60 f.

34 *The Book of the Courtier* (trans. Bull), p. 54.

35 Ibid. p. 55.

36 Ibid. p. 57.

37 Ibid. p. 63.

38 Ibid. p. 73.

39 Maier, p. 134: 'Anzi a cortegian tanto eccellente e così perfetto non è dubbio che l'uno e l'altro è necessario a sapere.'

40 Bull, p. 74.

41 Ibid. p. 90; Maier, p. 162.

42 Bull, p. 78.

43 Ibid. p. 101.

44 Ibid. p. 127.

45 Ibid. p. 135.

46 Ibid. pp. 186–7.

47 Cf. J. Burckhardt, *The Civilization of the Renaissance in Italy*, Ch. VI, 'The Position of Women', *passim*. Castiglione discusses this too; Bull, pp. 237 f.; Maier, pp. 383 f.

48 Bull, p. 216.

49 Ibid. p. 296.

50 Ibid. p. 299.

51 Ibid. p. 309.

52 Ibid. p. 310.

53 Ibid. p. 320; Maier, p. 507: '. . . onde forse si poria dir che 'l divenir institutor del principe fosse il fin del cortegiano'.

54 *De immortalitate animae*, trans. W. H. Hay, in Cassirer *et al.*, op. cit. p. 314; cf. p. 328.

55 Ibid.

56 Ibid. pp. 315–16.

57 Ibid. p. 319. The quotation from Aristotle is *De anima* III. vii (431a): διὸ οὐδέποτε νοεῖ ἄνευ φαντάσματος 'η ψυχή. 'Phantasm', φάντασμα, is the object of mental consideration presented by the imagination, φαντασία, which is the power of the mind to construct images.

58 *De immortalitate animae*, ibid. p. 331. Pomponazzi writes that 'the soul itself has no being save in matter'. This appears to be a reference to *De anima*, III.

viii. 43lb: 'mind, when actively thinking, is identical with its objects', ὅλως δὲ ὁ νοῦς ἐστὶν ὁ κατ' ἐνέργειαν τα πράγματα νοῶν.

59 Ibid. p. 325. This is a paraphrase of the principle enunciated in *Laws*, X. 893 E-894 A.

60 Ibid. p. 377.

61 Quoted by J. H. Randall in his Introduction to *De immortalitate animae*, in Cassirer *et al.*, op. cit. p. 275. Randall's Introduction is a valuable treatment of this obscure period of Italian scholastic thought.

62 Gutenberg's claims, and rival counter-claims, are discussed in D. C. Mc-Murtrie, *The Book: The Story of Printing and Bookmaking* (1943), Chs. X, XI, and bibliography, pp. 613-18. Cf. McMurtrie's *The Gutenberg Documents*, (New York, 1941).

63 A facsimile reprint of the three most famous examples of chancery cursive, produced by the celebrated writing masters, Arrighi, Palatino and Tagliente, has been issued by Dover, *Three Classics of Italian Calligraphy*, (1953).

64 S. H. Steinberg, *Five Hundred Years of Printing* (1955), pp. 100, 72.

Chapter 9

1 The Decree of the Third Lateran Council of 1179 is *Chart. univ. Par.* I: 10 collected in Lyn Thorndike, *University Records and Life in the Middle Ages*, Doc. 9, p. 21: Decretal of Innocent III in Leach, *Educational Charters and Documents*, pp. 142-3.

2 J.-F. Lemarignier, 'Les Institutions ecclésiastiques en France, de la fin du Xe au milieu du XIIe siècle', in F. Lot et R. Fawtier, *Histoire des institutions françaises au moyen âge* (1962), Vol. 3, p. 189.

3 ' . . . des écoles publiques rattachées aux paroisses', in Lot et Fawtier, op. cit. p. 219.

4 The depredations of the Hundred Years War was a major contributing factor. The standard account of the losses due to this is H. Denifle, *La Désolation des églises, monastères et hôpitaux en France pendant la guerre de cent ans*, 2 vols (first published Paris, 1897-9; reprinted Brussels: Culture et Civilisation, 1965).

5 The issue is in Varin, *Arch. adm. de la ville de Reims*, I.1.117; documented and discussed in Lot et Fawtier, op. cit. p. 301, n. 1.

6 Ibid.

7 Given in J. W. Thompson, *Economic and Social History of Europe in the Middle Ages* (1931), p. 501.

8 Cited in Matthew Arnold, *The Popular Education of France* (1861), p. 12.

9 Helen Wieruszowski, *The Medieval University*, pp. 78-80, 84-5; Letter from the masters of Toulouse inviting scholars from Paris to secede after 1229,

Chart. univ. Par. I: 106, pp. 156–7; in Wieruszowski, p. 178; also in Thorndike, *University Records and Life in the Middle Ages*, Doc. 18, p. 32.

10 Marcel Fournier, *Les Statuts et privilèges des universités françaises*, Vol. II (Paris, 1892). Nos 882 and 884 (pp. 4–7); cited in Wieruszowski, op. cit. p. 176.

11 Ibid.

12 Trans. Thorndike, op. cit. pp. 33–5. Another trans., Wieruszowski, op. cit. pp. 178–9.

13 Details are given in *Encyclopédie pratique de l'éducation en France* (Paris: Ministère de l'Éducation Nationale, 1960), p. 12.

14 Article X, collected in C. M. G. Bréchillet-Jourdain, *Histoire de l'Université de Paris au XVIIe et au XVIIIe siècles*, (Paris, 1862–6).

15 H. Omont, 'Georges Hermonyme de Sparte', *Mémoires de la Société de l'Histoire de la France XII* (1885); cited in R. R. Bolgar, *Classical Heritage and its Beneficiaries* (1954), pp. 306, 442 n. Bolgar gives an account in Chapter 8, 'The End of the Renaissance and the Appearance of New Patterns in Education and Scholarship', pp. 302–79.

16 The *as* was a basic unit of Roman bronze currency (as distinct from the co-existent silver used in cities) introduced in 269 B.C. for rural people. Its value was manipulated constantly and its history helps give an understanding of the course of Rome's economic fortunes.

17 Cf. G. C. Boyce, 'Erfurt Schools and Scholars in the Thirteenth Century', *Speculum*, XXIV, 1 (1949), pp. 1–18.

18 Ibid. p. 7.

19 Quoted ibid. p. 13, n. 47.

20 Coll. and trans. in G. F. Whicker, *The Goliard Poets: Medieval Latin Songs and Satires* (1949), pp. 141 f.

21 Ibid.

22 R. R. Betts, *Essays in Czech History* (1969), p. 3.

23 Ibid. p. 5. These *Essays* are a posthumous collection of journal articles, of which two are especially relevant here: 'The University of Prague: 1348', *Slavonic and East European Review*, XXVII, 68, pp. 57–66; and 'The University of Prague: The First Sixty Years', *Prague Essays*, ed. R. W Seton-Watson (Oxford, 1949), pp. 53–68. The former occupies pp. 1–12, the latter pp. 13–28, in the *Essays in Czech History*.

24 Quoted in S. H. Thomson, 'Learning at the Court of Charles IV', *Speculum*, XXV, 1 (1950), p. 4.

25 *Limberg Chronicle*, in *Monumentis Germaniae Historicis*, ed. A. Wyss, *Deutsche Chroniken*, Vol. 1. Coll. and trans. G. G. Coulton, *Life in the Middle Ages* (1954), Vol. 2, p. 80, Document 33.

26 Betts, *Essays in Czech History*, p. 6.

27 Quoted and trans. in Betts, op. cit. p. 14.

28 Cf. R. R. Betts, 'English and Czech Influences on the Hussite Movement',

Transactions of the Royal Historical Society (London), 4th series, XXI, pp. 71–102; reprinted in Betts, *Essays in Czech History*, pp. 132–59; this reference, p. 154.

29 Cf. ibid. p. 141.

30 Betts, 'The University of Prague: The First Sixty Years', in *Essays*, p. 27.

31 F. G. Heymann, *John Žižka and the Hussite Revolution* (1955), pp. 57–8.

32 Ibid. Ch. 10, 'The Four Articles of Prague' gives an account of the movement. Text of the articles is in Josef Maček, *The Hussite Movement in Bohemia* 2nd ed. (Prague: Orbis, 1958). The appendix includes most of the major Hussite documents; the text itself, however, is unreliable.

33 In the appendix, pp. 130–3 of Maček, op. cit.

34 The standard account is F. G. Heymann, op. cit.

35 'Utraquist' is derived from the words *sub utraque specie* meaning in both kinds, referring to the act of celebrating the Eucharist (or Mass) by consecrating bread (usually in the form of a wafer) and wine. The celebrant priest consumed both, but others present, whether clergy or laity, did not normally receive communion except at Easter. Then they were given bread only, not wine. Basically, Utraquism was concerned with the administration of communion. Calixtine comes from the Greek *kylix* (κύλιξ), a wine-cup, and was taken to symbolize the access of the laity to the wine in the communion chalice.

36 Betts, *Essays*, p. 153.

37 Collected in W. H. Woodward, *Vittorino da Feltre and other Humanist Educators* (1897), pp. 134 f.

38 Ibid. p. 152.

39 Probably the most accessible amount of this period in English is Peter Brock, *The Political and Social Doctrines of the Unity of Czech Brethren in the Fifteenth and Early Sixteenth Centuries* (1957).

40 Ibid. p. 28.

41 The entire social history of Bohemia in this period is poorly written up; the basic cause rests in the lack of adequate documentation resulting from the wars which depredated the regions throughout much of the sixteenth and seventeenth centuries. See Heymann, op. cit. p. 37, n. 3.

42 Complete decree in Brock, op. cit. pp. 80–1.

43 Ibid. p. 100.

44 Ibid.

45 On account of this ignorance they were chided by Luther. Cf. Brock, p. 237, n. 64.

46 Quoted in Brock, pp. 100–1.

47 Quoted from the Brotherhood Archives (*Archiv der Bruderunitat*) by Jan Herborn, *Hus and His Followers* (London: Geoffrey Bles, 1926), p. 151.

48 Quoted in Betts, *Essays in Czech History*, p. 26.

49 Ibid.

50 Collected in E. F. Henderson, *Select Historical Documents of the Middle Ages* (1896), p. 262; also in L. L. Snyder, *Documents of German History* (1958), p. 51.

51 Coll. and trans. in Wieruszowski, *The Medieval University*, pp. 186–7.

52 Ibid.

53 Collected in Thorndike, op. cit. Doc. 96, p. 257; also in Wieroszowski, op. cit. 8 B, pp. 187–8.

54 Griefswald, 1456; Freiburg, 1457; Basle, 1459; Ingolstadt, 1472; Trier, 1473; Mainz, 1477; Tübingen, 1477; Wittenberg, 1504; Frankfurt-an-der-Oder, 1506.

55 Beatus Rhenanus to Herman of Wied, archbishop of Cologne, *Origenis Opera*, Basle, 1536; collected in F. M. Nichols, *The Epistles of Erasmus* (1901; reprinted 1962), p. 23.

56 Ibid.

57 *Erasmus to Goclen*, 2 April 1524; Nichols, op. cit. p. 5.

58 Nichol's commentary, ibid. p. 17.

59 *De pueris instituendis*, Sect. 24, 504 F (1529).

60 'Mitto ad te introductionem grammatices Theodori De autem meum non est, sed amici cujusdam, precium erit scuta sex.' *Georgius Hermonymus an Reuchlin*, 8 Feb. 1478, in L. Geiger (ed.), *Johann Reuchlins Briefwechsel* (Hildesheim: Georg Olms Verlagsbuchhandlung, 1962), II, p. 5.

61 *Aldus Manutius to Reuchlin*, 18 August 1502; LXXXIII, p. 77.

62 *Johannes Reuchlin ad Dionysium*, 7 March 1506; LXXXXV, pp. 88 f.

63 An example of these letters dealing with the problem of whether eating an egg, containing a newly hatching chicken, on Friday is a mortal sin (since Catholics were forbidden to eat meat on Fridays) is collected in L. L. Snyder, *Documents of German History*, pp. 58–9.

64 There is only one biography in English: Lewis Spitz, *Conrad Celtes, The German Arch-Humanist* (1957).

65 Leonard Forster, *Selections from Conrad Celtes* (1948), p. 36.

66 The only account in English is Gerald Strauss, *Sixteenth-Century Germany: Its Topography and Topographers* (Madison: University of Wisconsin Press, 1959).

67 See Strauss, pp. 57, 116.

68 See Friedrich Paulsen, *Das deutsche Bildungswesen in seiner geschichtlichen Entwicklung* (Leipzig: Teubner, 1906), trans. T. Lorenz as *German Education: Past and Present* (1908), cf. Ch. 2, *passim*; also, Paul Monroe, *Thomas Platter and the Educational Renaissance of the Sixteenth Century* (1904), pp. 13 f.

69 Monroe, op. cit. pp. 14, 33 f.; Ch. 3 'The Schoolboy', *passim*.

70 Cf. H. de Vocht, *History of the Foundation and Rise of the Collegium Trilingue Lovaniense, 1517–1550* (1951), Ch. II, 'The Study of Languages in

Louvain before 1517', Pt 1: 'The Teaching of Latin in the Pedagogies', pp. 63 f.

71 *Firmenschild eines Schulmeisters (Schoolmaster's Sign Board)*, 1516, now in the Public Art Gallery of Basle (Öffentliche Kunstsammlung, Basle).

72 Paulsen, op. cit. p. 30. No figures are available. Thomas More made an estimate of 50 per cent literacy for southern England in the same period.

73 Paulsen, p. 32.

74 Ibid., quoting from F. Eulenberg, *Die Frequenz der deutschen Universitäten von ihrer Grundung bis zur Gegenwart* (Leipzig, 1904; no page reference given). One of the big difficulties in securing adequate documentation for German schools in this period is the great archive losses caused by the Wars of Religion in the sixteenth century, and the Thirty Years War in the seventeenth.

75 Karl Ruck (ed.), *Willibald Pirckheimers Schweizerkreig* (Munich, 1895), p. 98; trans. and quoted by Strauss, op. cit. p. 179, n. 4.

Chapter 10

1 *Hist. eccl.* III. 18.

2 Ibid. IV. 2: ' . . . et quicumque lectionibus sacris cuperent erudiri, haberent in promptu magistros qui docerent.'

3 Quoted in A. F. Leach, *The Schools of Medieval England* (1915), p. 55. Cited hereafter as *Schools*. Note that Leach errs in ascribing this to the seventh Council of Clovesho, which took place in 825. The error, though, might simply be one of transcription in his manuscript because all of the other facts are correct, including the major one that the council was held during Egbert's episcopate, which spanned the period *c.* 732–66.

4 W. H. Stevenson (ed.), *Asser's Life of King Alfred* (1904). There is a translation by L. C. Jane (1926). The genuineness of this text has been recently defended by Dorothy Whitelock, *The Genuine Asser*, The Stenton Lecture 1967 (1968).

5 *De rebus gestis Aelfredi*, Coll. 87–9.

6 William of Malmesbury, *Gesta regum Anglorum*, Col. 122; Stevenson, op. cit. p. lxviii, n. 2.

7 ' . . . tertiam scholae, quam ex multis suae propriae gentis nobilibus et etiam pueris ignobilibus studiosissime congregaverat'; Asserius, *De rebus gestis Alfredi*, Col. 102.

8 The relevant documents have been collected in text and translation by A. F. Leach, *Educational Charters and Documents: 598 to 1909* (1911), pp. 22–140. Cited hereafter as *Charters*.

9 *Ecclesiastical History*, IV. ii. 207: M. Chibnall, op. cit. pp. 246–7: ' . . . cur Anglos agrestes et pene illitteratos inuenerint Normanni'.

10 William of Malmesbury; Stevenson, op. cit. p. 246, n. 1.

11 Where there were few students the one master taught all three skills if the situation demanded it; when numbers increased these three activities were separated according to the evidence of Alcuin who recommended different masters and a separation (*separatim*) of students into the three categories of reading, writing and chanting. There is also a reference in Alcuin for the year 796 to 'those who are assigned to the writing school' ('qui scribendi studio deputentur'). Cf. Leach, *Charters*, p. 18.

12 Cf. D. Knowles, *The Religious Orders in England*, Vol. II, *The End of the Middle Ages* (1955), p. 294; and R. W. Hunt, 'English Learning in the Late Twelfth Century', *Trans. Royal Hist. Soc.* (May 1936); collected in R. W. Southern (ed.), *Essays in Medieval History* (1968).

13 K. Edwards, *The English Secular Cathedrals in the Middle Ages* (1967), p. 160.

14 Knowles, op. cit. p. 296.

15 Edwards, op. cit. p. 308.

16 Ibid. pp. 176 f.

17 Ibid. p. 188.

18 Ibid. pp. 188–9.

19 Ibid. p. 187.

20 Cf. T. A. Sandquist and M. R. Powicke, *Essays in Medieval History* (1969), Chapter II. 'William de Montibus: A Medieval Teacher', by H. Mackinnon, pp. 32–45.

21 Ibid. pp. 35 f.

22 This example occurs in the MS of *Similtudinarius* at f.102^v and has been taken from Mackinnon in Sandquist and Powicke, op. cit.

23 'Magister Robert Pullein scripturas divinas, quae in Anglia obsoluerant, apud Oxoniam legere coepit . . .': Oxford Historical Society, Collection II, 159; in Leach, *Charters*, p. 100.

24 Robertson, ed. Rolls Series, II. 97; in Leach, *Charters*, pp. 102–3.

25 Oxf. Hist. Soc., Coll. II. 153; II. 168; in Leach *Charters*, pp. 102, 108.

26 Hastings Rashdall, *Universities of Europe in the Middle Ages*, advances this theory; it is contested emphatically by Leach, *Schools*, pp. 129–30. Helen Wieruszowski, *The Medieval University*, presents Rashdall's theory (pp. 53–4) although the evidence she cites, the *Topographica Hibernica* (1184–5) of Giraldus Cambrensis, is not new. She appears simply to follow Rashdall.

27 Wieruszowski, op. cit. p. 156.

28 Oxf. Hist. Soc., Coll. II. 188; in Leach, *Charters*, p. 136.

29 R. W. Hunt, op. cit. p. 111.

30 Ibid.

31 Ibid. p. 107.

32 The river Trent, rising from several sources, including Lichfield, flows in a crescent easterly through Nottingham and thence north-easterly where it

reaches the North Sea at Hull. Generally speaking, it is the southern boundary of what is known in the present day as the Midlands of England.

33 'Scias quod cum in villa nostra Kantebrigie, ubi convenit multitudo studencium, plures sunt clerici rebelles et incorigibiles.' Cal. Close Rolls, 15 Hen III; in Leach, *Charters*, p. 148–9.

34 *Munimenta academica*, 25: ' . . . quod nullus in eadem Universitate incipiat in theologia nisi prius rexerit in artibus in aliqua Universitate'; quoted in C. E. Mallet, *A History of the University of Oxford*, Vol. I, *The Mediaeval University and the Colleges Founded in the Middle Ages* (1924), p. 49, n. 4.

35 Ibid. p. 73.

36 On the general question of Greek and other language studies, see B. Bischoff, 'The Study of Foreign Languages in the Middle Ages', *Speculum*, XXXVI, 2 (April 1961), pp. 209–24.

37 Texts and comments in Thorndike, *University Records and Life in the Middle Ages*: for Humbert, *Chart. univ. Par.* I, 317–18; for Lull, *Chart. univ. Par.* II, 83–4; both in Thorndike, Doc. 31, pp. 68–70, 125–7.

38 Cf. D. A. Callus, 'The Contribution to the Study of The Fathers Made by the Thirteenth-Century Oxford Schools', *Journal of Ecclesiastical History*, V. 2 (Oct. 1964), pp. 139–48. For studies in arts, see J. A. Weisheipl, 'Curriculum of the Faculty of Arts at Oxford in the Early Fourteenth Century', *Mediaeval Studies*, XXXVI (1964), pp. 143–85; and, 'Developments in the Arts Curriculum at Oxford in the Early Fourteenth Century', *Mediaeval Studies*, XXVIII (1966), pp. 151–75.

39 Ibid. p. 146.

40 Ibid.

41 R. J. Schoeck, 'On Rhetoric in Fourteenth-Century Oxford', *Mediaeval Studies*, XXX (1968), pp. 217 f.

42 Ibid.

43 Cf. Schoeck, op. cit., and J. J. Murphy, 'Rhetoric in Fourteenth Century Oxford', *Medium Aevum*, XXXIV, 1 (1965) pp. 1–20.

44 G. L. Haskins, 'The University of Oxford and the *Ius Ubique Docendi*', *English Historical Review*, LVI (1941), pp. 281–8.

45 Ibid. p. 287.

46 P. S. Allen and H. W. Garrod (eds.), *Merton Muniments* (1928), pp. 7, 9–10. The statutes in which this is first recorded (1264) appear to be a revision of earlier ones.

47 ' . . . ad sustentationem clericorum in scolis degentium'; Document of 7 May 1262 in *Merton Muniments*, p. 8.

48 *Munimenta*, King's College, Cambridge; Leach pp. 402–3.

49 H. G. Richardson, 'The Schools of Northampton in the Twelfth Century', *English Historical Review*, LVI (1941), pp. 595–605; p. 596 and nn. 1, 2.

50 Ibid. pp. 597–8.

51 *The Letters of John of Salisbury*, Vol. I, ed. W. J. Millor and H. E. Butler (1955); Ep. 56, 'Archbishop Theobald to the Pope', pp. 95–6.

52 H. G. Richardson, op. cit. pp. 601–2.

53 'Unde factum est ut quidam villam Northamptonie, quidam novam citatem Sarum ad studium elegerunt.' Walsingham, *Ypodigma Neustriae* (Rolls Series), 141; in Leach, *Charters*, pp. 154.

54 Pat. 45 Hen. III; Leach, *Charters*, p. 158.

55 'Vobis de consilio magnatum nosterum firmiter inhibemus ne in villa nostra de cetero aliquam Universitatem esse . . .' Close Roll, 49 Hen. III; Leach, *Charters*, p. 162.

56 Cf. n. 51 above.

57 Edwards, op. cit. p. 191.

58 'Sit etiam in ipsa congregacione gramaticus unus qui studio gramatice totaliter vacet'; . . . Founder's Statutes, August 1274, *Merton Muniments*, p. 21.

59 Leach, *Schools*, p. 214.

60 Knowles, op. cit. p. 295.

61 Ibid. and Leach, *Schools*, pp. 213–16.

62 Knowles, loc. cit.

63 Cf. G. G. Coulton, *Medieval Panorama* (1938; reissued 1961), Vol. I, p. 93.

64 A number are cited in Leach, *Schools*, pp. 206–7.

65 Memorial Court Rolls, Halmote, 1365, in *Univ. Penn. Translations and Reprints*, III: 5, p. 26.

66 Coulton, op. cit. I. p. 98.

67 Ibid. p. 15.

68 Ibid. p. 187.

69 With one exception below, n. 87, all citations from *Piers Plowman* come from the B text: W. W. Skeat, *The Vision of William Concerning Piers the Plowman* (1886). This quote, B. *Passus* XI. 1–2.

70 B. *Passus* V. 238–9.

71 B. *Passus* XX. 271–4.

72 B. *Prologus* 51–2.

73 Trans. and quoted Coulton, *Medieval Panorama*, Vol. I, p. 186.

74 Trans. and coll. in G. G. Coulton, *Life in the Middle Ages* (1954), Vol. 2, Doc. 25, pp. 55 f.

75 Mirk, *The Character of a Priest*. Coll. in A. S. Cook, *A Literary Middle English Reader* (1915), pp. 287–8.

76 *Song Against the Friars* (anon.); in Cook, op. cit., pp. 361–4.

77 'Confessions of Golias', by the unknown, self-styled 'Archpoet of Cologne', *c.* 1161–5. Coll. and trans. by G. F. Whicher, *The Goliard Poets: Medieval Latin Songs and Satires* (1949), p. 109.

78 'Time's in Prison', [*Clausas chronos*], anon., but attributed to Abelard; Whicher, op. cit. p. 49.

79 Orderic Vitalis, *Historia ecclesiastica*; quoted and trans. R. W. Southern, *The Making of the Middle Ages* (1953), p. 24.

80 *Canterbury Tales*, ed. J. M. Manly and E. Rickert, *The Text of the Canterbury Tales* (1940); Prologue 185.

81 *Prologue* 194–6.

82 *Prologue* 151–5.

83 *Rule of St Benedict*, 'The Nun's Clothing', coll. in Cook, op. cit. pp. 298–9.

84 *Canterbury Tales*, Prologue 160–2.

85 Coulton, *Medieval Panorama*, Vol. I, p. 167.

86 *Piers Plowman*, B. Passus V. 422–8, *passim*.

87 Ibid. B. *Passus*. XV. 368–9.

88 *Canterbury Tales*, Prologue 287–310, *passim*.

89 C. *Passus* VI. 35–6.

90 *Canterbury Tales*: Prioress's Tale, 61.

91 Ibid. 69.

92 Ibid. 67.

93 Ibid. 101–2.

94 Cf. Lloyd Haberly, *Medieval English Paving Tiles* (n.d., c. 19); also, 'Medieval Patterned Tiles of Warwickshire', *Trans. Brit. Arch. Soc.* LX (1940), p. 33, fig. 32. A number of these tiles are kept in the Ashmolean Museum at Oxford.

95 *Piers Plowman*, B. Passus XV. 365.

96 Ibid. B. *Passus* 139–40.

97 The words 'educate' and 'education' never appear since these were used first in the fifteenth and sixteenth centuries, respectively. Chaucer's terms are much simpler: school, scholar, learn, learning, etc. 'Book(s)' occurs 219 times; 'read', 'reader', 'readest', 'readeth' a total of 158; 'write', 'writing', 'written', a total of 120. Cf. J. S. P. Tatlock and A. G. Kennedy, *A Concordance to the Works of Geoffrey Chaucer* (1963).

98 As argued by J. W. Adamson, *The Illiterate Anglo-Saxon*, in Ch. 3, 'Literacy in England in the Fifteenth and Sixteenth Centuries'. Cf. p. 48.

99 Knowles, op. cit. p. 296.

100 S. J. Curtis, *History of Education in Great Britain*, 5th ed. (1963), p. 13.

101 Coulton, *Medieval Panorama*, Vol. II, p. 20.

102 Leach, *Schools*, p. 143.

103 Ibid. pp. 241–2.

104 7 Hen. IV. *c.* 17; in Leach, *Charters*, pp. 386–7; 'Purveux toutesfoitz que chacun homme ou femme de quele estate ou condicion qil soit, soit fraunc de mettre so fitz ou file dapprendre lettereure, a quelconq escole que leur

plest deinz le Roialme.' This statute itself indicates the continued use of French as the literary vernacular of the period.

105 *William Sevenoaks' Will* in Leach, op. cit. pp. 398 f.

106 Leach, *Schools*, says that the direct copying was made 'almost certainly' (p. 252). Against this must be weighed the consideration that five years is a very short period for such an influence to be felt in England which was much less educationally advanced than Italy in this period. R. Weiss, *Humanism in England*, 2nd ed. (1957), is much more cautious; he suggests the Casa Giocosa as a possible model for the English public schools, p. 84. The immediate link with England was the Council of Constance, which was a virtual 'council' of humanists, at which England was represented.

107 Foundation Charter, 11 Oct. 1440; Leach, *Charters*, pp. 404 f.

108 Leach, *Schools*, p. 265.

109 Knowles, op. cit. 295. Knowles quotes the text from W. A. Pantin (ed.), *Chapters of the Black Monks*, II. 205, which reads in full: 'Habeatur unus ydoneus et scientificus, sive secularis, sive religiosus, qui monachis in claustris ipsorum sciencias primitivas horis debitis legat et doceat, grammaticam videlicet ad minus.'

110 Macclesfield is the medieval Maxfield. Document in School's archives, Roll 14; coll. in Leach, *Charters*, p. 436.

111 *Memoirs of the Papal Court (Historia pontificalis)*, ed. and trans. M. Chibnall (1956); pp. 9-10.

112 Ibid.

113 Cited in Coulton, *Life in the Middle Ages*, Vol. III, Doc. 53, p. 119.

114 Coulton, *Medieval Panorama*, Vol. II, p. 20.

115 *Piers Plowman*, B. *Passus* V. 39-41.

116 Ibid. B. *Passus* X. 176.

117 Ibid. B. *Passus* V. 174.

118 J. E. T. Rogers, *Oxford City Documents*, pp. 150 ff.; in Coulton, *Life in the Middle Ages*, Vol. II, Doc. 31, pp. 74-5.

119 Anonymous, fifteenth century. Collected in H. S. Bennett, *Six Medieval Men and Women* (1955), pp. 74-5. *Avise*: argument; *fynkyll*: fennel; *watt*: hare; *top*: forelock.

120 Quoted in H. S. Bennett, op. cit. pp. 106-7. Several of Bennett's essays in this volume give interesting further accounts of early Tudor education. Ch. 1, 'Humphrey, Duke of Gloucester'; Ch. 3, 'Thomas Hoccleve'; Ch. 4, 'Margaret Paston'.

121 An account of Humphrey's exploits, both political and educational, is given in Bennett, op. cit. Ch. 1, *passim*.

122 Bennett, op. cit. p. 25.

123 'Ex Britanniae ipsa, quae extra orbem terrarum posita est', collected in Voigt, G., *Die Wiederbelebung des classischen Alterthums* (Berlin, 1893), Vol. 2,

p. 261 n.; quoted in L. Epstein, *The Italian Renaissance in England* (1902), p. 19.

124 *De sanitate tuenda* (1517); *Methodus medendi* (1519); *De temperamentis* (1521).

125 Grocin's letter and will are collected in E. M. Nugent, *The Thought and Literature of the English Renaissance: An Anthology of Tudor Prose* (1956), pp. 13–15; a photograph of his book-list with transcription is in *Merton Muniments*, pp. 46–7.

126 *Merton Muniments*, Plates XXIII, XXIV, XXV, pp. 44–7.

127 Ibid. Pl. XXVI, pp. 46–7.

128 An extensive discussion of these titles and their use will be found in R. Weiss, *Humanism in England* (1957); Ch. 12, *passim*.

129 This thesis is developed at length in Weiss, op. cit.

Chapter 11

1 Lat. *desiderium*, desired. The Greek ἐράσμιος has the same meaning.

2 Most lives of Erasmus refer simply to influence. In his introduction to the *Epistles of Erasmus* (1901, repr. 1962), F. M. Nichols gives the evidence for believing that St Lebuin was a parish church school and that Erasmus was not taught in a Brethren school.

3 *Opera* (Leyden Edn. 1704), I. 514 f.

4 There is a large literature on the Inns of Court. A short account is given in W. S. Holdsworth, *History of English Law*, 3rd ed. (1945), II. 494–512.

5 Minor works survive including *Grammatices rudimenta* (1527) and *Statutes of St Paul's School* (1518). The latter are collected in the appendices to J. H. Lupton, *A Life of John Colet, D.D.*, 2nd ed. (1909; reissued Hamden, Conn.: The Shoe String Press, 1961).

6 The standard collection of Erasmus' letters is P. S. Allen (ed.), *Opus epistolarum Des. Erasmi Roterdami*, 11 vols (1906–47); hereafter cited as Allen. The standard English translation is by F. M. Nichols, op. cit. 3 vols; hereafter cited as Nichols. This quote, Nichols, Ep. 58, *To Thomas Grey*, Vol. I, p. 140.

7 Nichols, Ep. 112, I. p. 232; Allen, Ep. 123, I. pp. 282–5.

8 Nichols, Ep. 113, I. p. 236; Allen, Ep. 124, I. pp. 285–8: 'Collegimus enim fere prouerbia octingenta, partim Graeca, partim Latina.'

9 Nichols, Ep. 121, I. pp. 243–4; Allen, Ep. 126, I. pp. 289–97. The full title of the *Adages* is *Desyderii Herasmi Roterdami maximeque insignium proemiarum id est adagiorum collecteana*.

10 The most recent edition is M. M. Phillips, *The Adages of Erasmus: A Study with Translations* (1964). Phillips gives an account of the *Adages*, *editio princeps* and the subsequent history of the work.

11 The standard edition of Erasmus' collected works is *Erasmi opera omnia*, ed.

Jean Leclerc (1704). The *Enchiridion* has been issued in English translation in J. P. Dolan, *The Essential Erasmus* (1964), from which following translations have been taken.

12 Gk. ἐγχειρίδιος, literally, in the hand.

13 *Ench. mil. chr.* Ch. 2; Dolan, op. cit. p. 35.

14 Ibid. p. 37.

15 Ibid. p. 46.

16 Ibid. pp. 51, 50. Throughout the essay Erasmus stresses the need to avoid reliance on merely external forms of worship.

17 Ibid. p. 51. This phrase has a particular significance: it recurs more than a century later as the title of Comenius' first work of Christian piety, written in Czech: *Labyrint sveta à ráj srdce* (1623) (*The Labyrinth of the World and the Paradise of the Heart*).

18 *Ench. mil. chr.* Ch. 10, p. 62.

19 Ibid. p. 64.

20 Ibid. p. 63.

21 Ibid. p. 53.

22 Ibid. p. 87.

23 Gk. μωρόσοφος, 'foolishly wise': a pun on *moria*, folly.

24 Dolan, op. cit. p. 123.

25 Ibid. p. 138.

26 Ibid. pp. 141, 142, 146, 153, 155, respectively.

27 Ibid. p. 169.

28 *Republic* VII, 514–21.

29 Dolan, op. cit. p. 172.

30 An account with a selection of relevant documents is D. F. S. Thomson and H. C. Porter, *Erasmus and Cambridge* (1963).

31 Erasmus to Ammonio, 16 Oct. 1511: Nichols, Ep. 227, II. pp. 28–9; Allen, Ep. 233, I. pp. 472–3: '... fortassis frequentiori auditorio Theodori Grammaticam auspicabimur ...'

32 First translated into English by W. H. Woodward, *Desiderius Erasmus Concerning the Aim of Education* (1904).

33 *De ratione studii*, Ch. 6, 523 F; Woodward, op. cit. p. 168.

34 Ibid. 13, 530 A–B; Woodward, op. cit. p. 178.

35 As early as 1484 Caxton published an English translation of *Aesop's Fables* which was illustrated with woodcuts and found ready acceptance among middle-class children, but neither this nor any other vernacular books – Caxton himself published seventy-four in English – were used in the classroom.

36 *De ratione studii*, 1. 521 A; Woodward, op. cit. p. 162.

37 Ibid. 10. 526F–528C; Woodward, op. cit. p. 174.

38 Ibid. 6. 524A–C; Woodward, op. cit. p. 162.

39 Ibid. 8. 525C–F; Woodward, op. cit. p. 171.

40 Ibid. 12. 529B; Woodward, op. cit. p. 177.

41 *Erasmus to Colet*, Ep. 248; Nichols, II. pp. 66–7; Allen, Ep. 260, I. pp. 510–12: '. . . officii mei sum arbitratus litterarium aliquod munusculum in ornamentum scholae tuae conferre'.

42 *Statuta Paulinae Scholae; Statutes of St Paul's School*, 'What Shalbe Taught'; in Appendix A, J. H. Lupton, *A Life of John Colet, D.D.* (1909), p. 279.

43 *Budé to Erasmus*, Ep. 422; Nichols. II. p. 301; Allen, Ep. 435, II. pp. 272–6.

44 F. Buisson, *Répertoire des ouvrages pédagogiques du XVIe siècle* (Paris, 1886), pp. 232–4; cited in R. R. Bolgar, *The Classical Heritage*, p. 448, n. 338.

45 Trans. Lester K. Born, *The Education of a Christian Prince* (1936, repr. 1965).

46 A history of the *speculum principis* is given in Born, op. cit. Introduction, III, IV.

47 The catalogue is long and occurs, not in any single place, but throughout the treatise.

48 Machiavelli, *The Prince*, trans. L. Ricci, rev. E. R. P. Vincent (1935), Ch. XVII, p. 73.

49 *Ed. Chr. Pr.* Born, op. cit. p. 148. The dictum occurs throughout.

50 Ibid. p. 140.

51 Ibid. p. 200.

52 Ibid. p. 203.

53 Details in Born, op. cit. pp. 27–9.

54 Coll. and trans. J. P. Dolan, op. cit. pp. 177–208.

55 *Querela pacis*, Dolan, op. cit. p. 179.

56 Ibid.

57 The complete version in translation, with an introduction, is C. R. Thompson, *The Colloquies of Erasmus* (1965). The same author has issued a selection, *Ten Colloquies of Erasmus* (1957).

58 Details in Thompson, *Ten Colloquies*, pp. xix–xxi.

59 *On the Freedom of the Will*, in E. G. Rupp (trans.), *Luther and Erasmus: Free Will and Salvation*, Vol. XVII, Library of Christian Classics (1969); p. 37.

60 *Republic*, VIII. 558C.

61 *On the Freedom of the Will*, in Rupp, op. cit. p. 40.

62 Ibid. p. 47: 'as fire comes from striking flint'. Cf. the comment by Averroes on al-Ghazali in *The Incoherence of the Incoherence (Tahafut al-Tahafut)*, 518:5–9 in van den Bergh's edition (1954), pp. 316–17.

63 Rupp, op. cit. p. 96.

64 Trans. in W. H. Woodward, *Desiderius Erasmus Concerning the Aim and Method of Education*, pp. 180–222.

65 Ibid. Sect. 23, 504A–D and Sect. 24, *passim*, pp. 204 f.

66 Ibid. Sect. 23, 504D, p. 204.

67 *Erasmus to Colet*, 29 Oct. 1511, 'The Schoolmaster's an Honorable Office', Allen, Ep. 237, I. p. 479; Nichols, Ep. 231, II. pp. 34 f.

68 Ibid.

69 *Erasmus to Robert Caesar, Schoolmaster*, after 1513, Nichols, Ep. 175, I. p. 360.

70 *On the Education of Boys*, Woodward, op. cit. Sect. 4, 491D, p. 184.

71 Ibid. Sect. 24, 506G–F, p. 207.

72 Erasmus, *Lives of Vitrier and Colet*, quoted in J. H. Lupton, *A Life of John Colet, D.D.* (1909), p. 37.

73 *Super opera Dionysii*, cf. Lupton, op. cit. p. 72.

74 Ibid.

75 *Statuta Paulinae Scholae* (Statutes of St Paul's School), 1512; given in Appendix A to Lupton, op. cit. pp. 271–84. The original statutes are preserved at Mercer's Hall, London, and a variant MS is in the British Museum, *Additional and Egerton* 6274. Cf. Lupton, op. cit. p. 271, n. 1.

76 Lupton, op. cit. p. 277.

77 Ibid. pp. 277–9.

78 Ibid. p. 279.

79 These are given as Appendix B in Lupton, op. cit.

80 Ibid. pp. 279–80.

81 Ibid.

82 *On the Freedom of the Will*, in Rupp, op. cit. p. 36.

83 A very useful biography of Erasmus is R. H. Bainton, *Erasmus of Christendom* (1969). This monograph brings out the conflicts and ambiguities in Erasmus' life.

Chapter 12

1 For a short account with technical details of indulgences, from the Catholic point of view, see Erwin Iserloh, *The Theses Were Not Posted* (1968), Ch. 1, *passim*.

2 Cf. H. J. Hillerbrand, *The Reformation in its Own Words* (1964), p. 39. This collection of documents contains much useful source material including contemporary woodcuts and a facsimile of the Ninety-Five Theses. See also, L. L. Snyder, *Documents of German History* (1958).

3 For the revisionist argument (which has had a very sceptical reception) that the theses were never actually nailed up, but quietly sent in a despatch to Luther's bishop and subsequently distributed through the new medium of print, see E. Iserloh, op. cit.

4 Hillerbrand, op. cit. pp. 51–2; Snyder, op. cit. pp. 63–6. The critical edition of Luther's works is *D. Martin Luthers Werke*, Kritische Gesamtausgabe (Weimarer Ausgabe) (Weimar: Herman Böhlaus Nachfolger, 1883–);

customarily abbreviated, as hereafter, WA. The standard English translation, although not in the same order as WA, is *Luther's Works*, ed. J. Pelikan and H. T. Lehmann, 55 vols (St Louis: Concordia Publishing House, 1915–58); customarily abbreviated, as hereafter, LW. The Ninety-Five Theses, in Latin are in WA I, pp. 233–8; in English, LW. XXXI, pp. 25–33.

5 LW. XXXI, pp. 261–4.

6 *De captivitate Babylonica ecclesiae*, WA. VI, pp. 497–573; trans. in H. T. Kerr, *A Compend of Luther's Theology* (1943), p. 99.

7 Text of *Exsurge domine* ('Arise, O Lord!') in Hillerbrand, op. cit. pp. 80–4.

8 Latin text in Robert Stupperich (gen. ed.), *Melanchthons Werke;* Band III, *Humanistische Schriften*, ed. Richard Nürnberger (1961). Abridged trans. in Hillerbrand, op. cit. pp. 58–60, under title, 'The Reform of the Education of Youth'.

9 'Itaque cum theologia partim Hebraica, partim Graeca sit, nam Latini rivos illorum bibimus, linguae externae discendae sunt, ne velati χωρὰ πρόσωπα, cum Theologis agumus': *Corpus Reformatorum* XI. 24, 11 f.; in Nürnberger, *Melanchthons Werke* (hereafter MW), p. 40.

10 'Hoc sanc in causa erat cur decerim usu litterarum destitutam ecclesiam; veram ac germanam pietatem traditionibus humanis alicubi mutasse.' Nürnberger, MW. III, p. 41; also in *Corpus Reformatorum* (hereafter CR) XI. 25, pp. 4 f.

11 Reuchlin, *Briefwechsel*, ed. L. Geiger (1962), CCLXIV, 21 July 1518; CCLXV, 25 July 1518.

12 WA, *Briefwechsel* I, No. 93, p. 203.

13 'An Christoph Scheurl in Nürnberg', 24 Sept. 1518. MW. VII. 1, pp. 44–6. Also CR. I. 48.

14 CR. X. 301.

15 *In laudem novae scholae*, 1526; Nürnberger, MW. III, pp. 63 f.

16 Cf. Robert Stupperich, *Melanchthon* (1966), p. 70. This translation of the German edition of 1960 by the world's leading authority on Melanchthon has a useful chapter, 'Labors for Church and School', pp. 61–75, s.v.

17 'An die Ratherren alle Städte deutsches Lands, dass sie christliche Schulen aufrichten und erhalten sollen', 1524; WA. XV, pp. 9–53. Translated as 'To the Councilmen of All Cities in Germany that they Establish and Maintain Christian Schools', LW. XLV, pp. 342 f.

18 'Luther an Eobanus Hessus', 29 Mar. 1523; WA. *Briefwechsel* III, No. 596, pp. 48–51. This trans., E. G. Dickens, *Martin Luther and the Reformation* (1967), p. 79.

19 Ibid.

20 'An Jakob Strauss in Eisenach', 25 Apr. 1524; WA. *Briefwechsel* III, No. 733, pp. 275–8: '... video enim euanglio maximam impendere ruinam neglectu educandae pueritae.'

21 Cf. n. 17 above.

22 WA. XV, pp. 36 f.; LW. XLV, p. 357.

23 WA. XV, p. 38; LW. XLV, p. 360.

24 Ibid.

25 WA. XV, p. 32; LW. XLV, p. 353: '. . . und warumb leben wir allten anders, denn das wir des jungen volcks warten, leren und auffzihen?'

26 WA. XV, p. 45; LW. XLV, p. 368.

27 WA. XXX. 2, p. 58; LW. XLVI, p. 253: 'Denn ich weis, das dis werck, nehest dem Predig ampt das aller nützlichst, grossest und beste ist.'

28 WA. XV, p. 47; LW. XLV, p. 370.

29 WA. XV, p. 46; LW. XLV, p. 369: 'Und ist itzt nich mehr die helle und das fegefewr unser schulen, da wir ynnen gemartert sind uber den casualibus und temporalibus . . .'

30 Collected in MW. I, *Reformatorische Schriften*, pp. 215–71. Also, because although actually drafted by Melanchthon they contain Luther's ideas, they are collected in WA. XXVI, pp. 195–240.

31 But, cf. Melanchthon's *Reply* of 1558, CR. IX, pp. 687–703, to Giovanni Pico della Mirandola's *Reply* of June 1485 to Ermolao Barbaro's concern to keep rhetoric and wisdom integral. See also, Quirinius Breen 'Melanchthon's Reply to Giovanni Pico della Mirandola', *Journal of the History of Ideas*, XIII, 3 (1952), pp. 384–426.

32 WA. XXVI, p. 236; LW. XL, p. 315.

33 WA. XXVI, p. 237; LW. XL, p. 317.

34 'Eine Predigt, dass man Kinder zur Schulen halten solle', 1530; W.A. XXX.2, pp. 508–88; LW. XLVI, pp. 213–58.

35 WA. XXX.2, p. 546; LW. XLVI, p. 232.

36 WA. XXX.2, p. 573; LW. XLVI, p. 249.

37 WA. XXX.2, pp. 577–8; LW. XLVI, p. 251.

38 WA. XXX.2, p. 558; LW. XLVI, p. 239: 'faust und harnsch thuns nicht, es mussen die köpffe und bucher thun.'

39 WA. XXX.2, p. 579; LW. XLVI, p. 252.

40 WA. XXX.2, p. 568; LW. XLVI, p. 256: 'Ich halt aber, das auch die oberkeit hie schuldig sey die unterhanen zu zwingen, ihre kinder zur schulen zu halten, sonderlich die, da von droben gesagt ist.'

41 WA. XXX.2, p. 545; LW. XLVI, p. 218.

42 WA. XXX.2, p. 565; LW. XLVI, p. 243.

43 WA. XXX.2, p. 547; LW. XLVI, p. 232.

44 Ibid.

45 WA. XXX.2, p. 550; LW. XLVI, p. 234.

46 WA. XXX.2, p. 560; LW. XLVI, p. 241.

47 WA. XXX.2, p. 588; LW. XLVI, p. 257–8.

48 Quoted and discussed with documentation to Luther in B. A. Gerrish, *Grace*

and Reason: A Study in the Theology of Luther (1962), pp. 15 f.; Part 1, pp. 10 f.; *passim.*

49 Ibid. pp. 53 f.

50 'The Last Sermon in Wittenberg', 17 Jan 1546; WA. LI, pp. 123–34; LW. LI, pp. 371–80. Gerrish, op. cit. opening argument, pp. 1 f.

51 'On the Papacy in Rome', 1520; WA. VI, pp. 285–324; LW. XXXIX, pp. 55–104; this quote, p. 63.

52 *Table Talk*, No. 48; coll. and trans., H. T. Kerr, op. cit.

53 *Table Talk*, No. 294; coll. and trans., H. T. Kerr, op. cit.

54 Melanchthon, *Corpus Reformatorum*, XI, p. 655, *Oratio de Aristotle*, 1544: 'carere igitur Aristotelis monumentis non possumus'. Text in MW. I, pp. 122 f. Cf. *De vita Aristotelis*, 1537, in MW. I, pp. 96 f., for further evidence of this attitude to the work of Aristotle.

55 Melanchthon, CR. XIII, pp. 222 f., 376 f. Discussed in Franz Hildebrandt, *Melanchthon: Alien or Ally?* (1946), pp. 6 f.

56 'Lectures on Galatians', 1535; WA. XL. 1, III. 19, p. 480; LW. XXVI, III. 19, pp. 308–9.

57 WA. *Tischreden*, Band 5, No. 5252, *c.* 2–17 Sept. 1540, p. 27. Also in LW. LIV, *Table Talk*, p. 403. Note that LW gives the number 5252 incorrectly as 5247. This text reads: 'Ich wolte, das keiner zu keim prediger erwelt wurde, er hett denn vor schul gehalten.'

58 Loc. cit.: 'den die arbeit is gross, und man helt sie ein wenig gering.'

59 WA. Tr. 5, No. 5557, pp. 239–40; LW. LIV, p. 452: ' . . . Deus servavit ecclesiam per scholas.'

60 WA. LI, p. 125; LW. LI, p. 373.

61 'Cuius regio, eius religio'; literally, 'whose region, [also] his religion'. Trans. of Peace of Augsburg in Hillerbrand, op. cit. pp. 412–13.

Chapter 13

1 *More to Erasmus*, 3 Sep. 1516, *Ep.* 450 in F. M. Nichols, *Epistles of Erasmus* (1901), p. 381.

2 From the Greek *ou* + *tópos*, no + place.

3 A discussion of the complexity of the sources drawn upon is given in the definitive edition, Edward Surtz and J. H. Hexter, *The Complete Works of St Thomas More*, Vol. 4 (1965); 'Sources, Parallels and Influences', pp. cliii f.

4 'Nam eo plerique natura feruntur', *Utopia*, Bk II. k4; Surtz and Hexter, op. cit. p. 126.

5 Ibid. p. 129.

6 Ibid.

7 Ibid. p. 159.

8 Ibid. The *Small Logicals* (*Parva logicalia*) by Alexander de Villa Dei was a

medieval textbook. References to it can be found in P. Boehner, *Medieval Logic* (1952), pp. 32–6, 77, 79. Cf. P. S. Allen, *Age of Erasmus*, pp. 33–65.

9 *Utopia*, Surtz and Hexter, op. cit. p. 180.

10 Ibid. p. 133.

11 Ibid.

12 The treatise has been translated by E. T. Campagnac and K. Forbes, *Sadoleto on Education: A Translation of the De pueris recte instituendis* (1916). An exposition of Sadoleto's views is given in W. H. Woodward, *Studies in Education During the Age of the Renaissance, 1400–1600* (1906, repr. 1969), Ch. IX, pp. 167 f.

13 'Sadoleto to Pietro Bembo', 1527, Ep. I.3, Vol. I, *Iacopi Sadoleti Opera Omnia*, ed. J. A. Tumerman (Verona, 1737–8); cited Campagnac and Forbes, op. cit. xvij.

14 *De pueris*; Campagnac and Forbes, op. cit. pp. 16–17.

15 Ibid.

16 Ibid. p. 63.

17 Respectively, αἰδώς, τὸ μέσον. Cf. Woodward, op. cit. p. 170.

18 *De pueris*; Campagnac and Forbes, op. cit. p. 63.

19 Ibid. p. 69.

20 Ibid. p. 66.

21 Ibid. p. 47.

22 'Ep. ad Paull', Sadoleto, *Opera omnia*, 3, Vol. II; cited Campagnac and Forbes, op. cit. Introduction, xxi: ' . . . nescio quae Ciceronis, Vergilii, Graecaquae praeterea linguae rudimenta enarraturus.'

23 *De pueris*; Campagnac and Forbes, op. cit. p. 69.

24 For Vives the definitive work is D. Adolfo Bonilla y San Martin, *Luis Vives y la Filosofia del Renacimento* (Madrid: Memoria premiada por la Real Academia de Cientias Morales y Politicas, 1903). In English, see Foster Watson, *Tudor School Boy Life* (1908); Foster Watson (trans.), *De tradendis disciplinis* (1913).

25 The literal translation of the title is *The Transmission of the Arts*.

26 For a brief and informative biography, see W. H. Woodward, *Studies in Education During the Age of the Renaissance, 1400–1600*, Ch. X: 'Juan Luis Vives', pp. 180–210.

27 *De tradendis*, I.1.

28 Ibid. 1.4.

29 Ibid. I.6. Quotations from *De tradendis* are from the translation by Foster Watson (1913).

30 Ibid. I.2; p. 22.

31 Ibid. I.4.

32 Ibid. I.5.

33 Ibid. I.4; p. 36.

34 Ibid. II. 1; p. 55.

35 *Epistolae* (ed. 1642; Col. 1505 f.); quoted and discussed in Watson, *De tradendis disciplinis*, pp. cxlviii–cliii.

36 *De tradendis*, II.3.

37 Ibid. II.3; p. 72.

38 Vives states that 'If anyone should consider the matter with close attention he will see that my view of teaching and that of Quintilian are alike'; III. 1; p. 98.

39 *De tradendis*, III. 1; p. 91.

40 Ibid.

41 Ibid. II.2; p. 103.

42 Ibid. III.2; p. 112.

43 The full title is *J. Coleti aeditio una cum quibusdam G. Lilii grammatices rudimentis* (1527).

44 *De tradendis*, IV.1; p. 163.

45 Ibid.

46 Ibid. IV.1; p. 168.

47 Ibid. IV.2; p. 175.

48 Ibid. V.1; p. 228.

49 Ibid. IV.2; p. 175.

50 Appendix to *De tradendis disciplinis*, 'The Scholar's Life and Character', in Watson, op. cit. p. 289.

51 Ibid.

52 On Sturm generally, see Pierre Mesnard, 'The Pedagogy of Johann Sturm (1507–1589) and its Evangelical Inspiration', *Studies in the Renaissance*, XIII (1966), pp. 200–19.

53 The Greek *gymnasia* themselves were concerned with exercises alone. The sixteenth-century use of *gymnasium* to refer to a school is not the first, however; the *Commendation of the Clerk* of the mid-fourteenth century complains that 'Nor is a place properly called a school house [*domus scolastica*] where they are occupied with other matters than the knowledge of letters, for example training in military agility, whose proper place is a gymnasium [*cuius receptaculum proprie gympnasium dicitur*] although because of a certain resemblance between these occupations one term is interchanged for the other.' Text and trans. in Lynn Thorndike, *University Records and Life in the Middle Ages* (1944), pp. 213, 416–17.

54 *De literarum ludis.* . . . Fol 15ʳ. There is no English translation of this, nor of any of Sturm's works.

55 Ibid. Fol 4ʳ.

56 Cf. Mesnard, op. cit. p. 211.

57 *The Boke Named the Governour*, citations from 1531 text, reprinted in the Everyman edition (1937), p. 69.

58 Ibid. p. 18.
59 Ibid. p. 35.
60 Ibid. p. 46.
61 Ibid. p. 35.
62 Ibid. p. 40.
63 The case is argued very exhaustively for England in Joan Simon, *Education and Society in Tudor England* (1966).
64 *Works*, IV, pp. 106–24.
65 *Sermons of Hugh Latimer*, ed. G. E. Corrie (1844); The Sermon on the Plough, 18 Jan. 1548; p. 69.
66 Cf. W. Holdsworth, *A History of English Law*, 3rd ed. (1945), II, pp. 494–512; IV, pp. 229–30; 263–70; and for a full account, K. Charlton, *Education in Renaissance England* (1965), Ch. VI. 'The Inns of Court', pp. 169 f.
67 The term barrister derives apparently from the bar which separated the student from the court proper, *Oxford Dictionary of English Etymology*, s.v. 'barrister'.
68 Holdsworth, op. cit. IV. pp. 229–30.
69 *The Thirde Vniuersitie of England, Or, a Treatise of the foundations of all the Colledges, ancient schools of priviledge, and houses of learning, and liberall arts, within and about the cittie of London* (1612).
70 Holdsworth, op. cit. IV. p. 267.
71 The Latin text of the will is given in H. de Vocht, *History of the Foundation and the Rise of the Collegium Trilingue Lovaniense, 1517–1550* (Louvain, 1951); pp. 24–46 in ninety-three numbered paragraphs.
72 Cf. Charlton, op. cit. Pt. III, Informal Education, *passim*.
73 *The Governour*, I. xiii. p. 56. The term appears also in Joachimus Fortinus, *Lucubrationes vel portius, absolutissima κυκλοπαιδεία* (Basle, 1541); and, Paulus Scalichius de Lika, *Encyclopedia seu Orbis Disciplinarum tum sacrum tum profanarum* (Basle, 1559).

Chapter 14

1 *De anima*, III.5.
2 John Holt, *Lac puerorum* (Antwerp: Adriaen van [Berghen], *c.* 1508); Bodleian MS Auct VII. Q VII. 45 (fragments), Fol. ii^r.
3 A good selection of excerpts from English grammars of the period is given in E. M. Nugent, *The Thought and Culture of the English Renaissance: An Anthology of Tudor Prose 1481–1555* (1956), pp. 107–55.
4 This and other examples can be found in Nugent, op. cit. pp. 120–2.
5 Ibid. pp. 114–15.
6 Ibid. pp. 127–31 for an extensive selection. Sewsters = seamstresses.

7 Ibid. pp. 123–6.
8 A selection of 8 of the 27 dialogues is given in an appendix to W. H. Wood-ward, *Studies in Education during the Age of the Renaissance, 1400–1600* (first published 1906; reprinted, New York: Teachers College Press, Columbia University, 1967), pp. 327–30.
9 Vives' colloquy remains readily accessible in a translation by Foster Watson under the title *Tudor School Boy Life* (1908).
10 Cap. 5, *Lectio.*
11 Cap. 24, *Educatio,* XIV. iii.
12 Cf. *Ling. lat. exerc.* Coll. IV, and *Coll. sel.* I. i; *Ling. lat. exerc.* X. 4 and *Coll. sel.* II. 14. Cf. also Erasmus' colloquy *Off to School* for the predecessor of both.
13 *Colloquia selecta,* IV.
14 A short biography is given in Woodward, op. cit. pp. 139–66.
15 From the *Select Colloquies of Mathurin Cordier,* ed. and with an added English translation by Samuel Loggon, 20th ed. rev. and corr. (London: C. & I. Rivington, 1824), Coll. IV.
16 Cf. Nugent, op. cit. p. 155.
17 Autobiography, trans. in Paul Monroe (ed. and trans.), *Thomas Platter and the Educational Renaissance of the Sixteenth Century* (1904), pp. 104–5.
18 Text in *Institutum societatis Iesu,* new ed. 3 vols (Rome, 1869), Vol. I., pp. 47–74; translation in E. A. Fitzpatrick (ed.), *St Ignatius and the Ratio Studiorum* (New York: McGraw-Hill, 1933).
19 *Constitutions,* Pt 4, XX, Preamble. Trans. M. H. Mayer, in Fitzpatrick, op. cit. p. 49.
20 Ibid.
21 Ibid VI. 15; IX *in toto.*
22 Ibid. VI. 13.
23 Ibid. V. 1; VI. 4; XII. 2; XII. 3.
24 Ibid. XII. 2(B).
25 Ibid. XIV. 1.
26 Ibid. VII. 1.
27 A. P. Farrell, *The Jesuit Code of Liberal Education: Development and Scope of the Ratio Studiorum* (1938), p. 25 and Appendix A, pp. 431 f.
28 Ibid. pp. 25–9.
29 *Constitutions,* Pt 4, XIII. 2 (A).
30 Farrell, op. cit. p. 25, n. 2.
31 Documentation given in Farrell, op. cit. p. 65, n. 4.
32 Description and outline of the *Ordo studiorum* in Farrell, op. cit. pp. 76 f.
33 Cf. Farrell, op. cit. pp. 168 f.
34 Cited from G. M. Pachtler, *Ratio studiorum et institutiones scholasticae societatis Jesu II; Monumenta Germaniae paedagogica,* Vol. V, p. 29; in Fitzpatrick, op. cit. p. 29.

35 *Ratio studiorum*, XII. 5. (Trans. A. R. Ball in Fitzpatrick, op. cit. p. 176.)

36 *Ratio studiorum*, I. 10.

37 Ibid. XV. 27.

38 Ibid. XV. 31.

39 An account of the movement to adopt a standard grammar is given in Appendix C, pp. 441 f., of Farrell, op. cit.

40 Ratio studiorum, XX. 1.

41 The preterite is the past tense (*preteritum tempus*); the supine (*supinus*) is used instead of an infinitive, after verbs of motion, to indicate an intention.

42 Ibid. XIX. 1.

43 Ibid. XVIII. 1.

44 Ibid. XVII. 1.

45 Ibid. XV. 30.

46 Ibid. XVI. 1.

47 Ibid. XVI. 14

48 Ibid. XI. 1.

49 Ibid. X. 1.

50 Ibid. IX. 4.

51 Ibid. IX. 6.

52 Ibid. I. 9 (1).

53 Ibid. VII. 2.

54 Ibid. I. 30.

55 Ibid. XX. 27.

56 Ibid. XII. 3.

57 Cf. ibid. II. 8 and XV. 27 are antagonistic; XV. 18 offers some concessions.

58 *De caelo*, 287a. Trans. J. L. Stocks, Vol. II, *Works of Aristotle* (Oxford, 1947).

59 Ibid. 296b.

60 *De partibus animalium*, I. 1 (641b. 20). Trans. W. Ogle *Works of Aristotle*, op. cit. Vol. V.

Bibliography

1 Medieval

ABELARD. *Ouvrages inédits d'Abélard*. Edited by V. Cousin. Paris: Imprimerie Royale, 1836.

ADAMSON, J. W. *The Illiterate Anglo-Saxon and other Essays on Education*. Cambridge: The University Press, 1946.

ADELSON, H. L. *Medieval Commerce*. Princeton, New Jersey: Van Nostrand, Anvil Books, 1962.

ALCUIN. *The Rhetoric of Alcuin and Charlemagne*. Edited and translated by W. S. Howell. Princeton, New Jersey: Princeton University Press, 1941.

ALLEN, P. S., and GARROD, H. W. (eds.). *Merton Muniments*. Oxford: Oxford University Press for the Oxford Historical Society, 1928.

ASSER. *Asserius de Rebus Gestis Aelfredi* [*Asser's Life of King Alfred*]. Edited by W. H. Stevenson. Oxford: Clarendon Press, 1904.

—— *Asser's Life of King Alfred*. Translated by L. C. Jane. London: Chatto and Windus, 1908.

BENNETT, H. S. *Six Medieval Men and Women*. Cambridge: The University Press, 1955.

BERNARD. *Some Letters of Saint Bernard, Abbot of Clairvaux*. Edited by F. A. Gasquet. Translated by S. J. Eales. London: John Hodges, 1904.

—— *Letters of St Bernard of Clairvaux*. Translated by B. S. James. Chicago: Henry Regnery, 1953.

BETTENSON, H. *Documents of the Christian Church*. 2nd edition. London: Oxford University Press, 1963.

BISCHOFF, B. 'The Study of Foreign Languages in the Middle Ages'. *Speculum*, XXXVI, 2 (1961), pp. 209–24.

BOEHNER, P. *Medieval Logic: An Outline of its Development from 1250 to c. 1.400* Manchester: The University Press, 1952.

BOLGAR, R. R. *The Classical Heritage and its Beneficiaries*. Cambridge: The University Press, 1954.

BOYCE, G. C. 'Erfurt Schools and Scholars in the Thirteenth Century'. *Speculum*, XXIV, 1 (1949), pp. 1–18.

BOYLE, L. E. 'The Constitution "Cum ex eo" of Boniface VIII'. *Mediaeval Studies*, XXIV (1962), pp. 263–302.

BULLOUGH, D. *The Age of Charlemagne*. London: Elek Books, 1965.

BURCHARD VON URSBERG. *Chronicon*. [Scriptores Rerum Germanicum, ex Monumentis Germaniae historicus, Separatim editi.] Hannoverae et Lipsiae: Impensis bibliopolii Hahniani, 1916.

BURR, G. L. 'Anent the Middle Ages'. *American Historical Review*, XVIII (Oct. 1912–July 1913), pp. 715–18.

CALLUS, D. A. 'The Contribution to the Study of the Fathers Made by the Thirteenth-Century Oxford Schools'. *Journal of Ecclesiastical History*, V. 2 (1964), pp. 139–48.

CHAUCER, G. *The Canterbury Tales*. Edited by J. M. Manly and E. Rickert. 8 vols. Chicago: The University Press, 1940.

—— *The Works of Geoffrey Chaucer*. 2nd edition. Edited by F. N. Robinson. London: Oxford University Press, 1957.

—— *A Concordance to the Complete Works of Geoffrey Chaucer and the Romaunt of the Rose*. Compiled by J. S. P. Tatlock and A. G. Kennedy. Gloucester, Massachusetts: Peter Smith, 1963.

CHRODEGANG. *Rule of Chrodegang* [*Regula Chrodegangi*]. Edited by A. S. Napier. London: Early English Text Society. Original Series, CL, 1916.

COOK, A. S. *A Literary Middle English Reader*. Boston: Ginn, 1915.

COULTON, G. G. *Life in the Middle Ages*. 2nd edition, 4 vols in 1. Cambridge: The University Press, 1930.

—— *Medieval Panorama*. 2 vols. Cambridge: The University Press, 1938.

—— *Europe's Apprenticeship: A Survey of Medieval Latin with Examples*. London: Nelson, 1943.

COURCELLE, P. 'Les Sources antiques du prologue d'Alcuin sur les disciplines'. *Philologus: Zeitschrift für das klassische Altertum*, CX, 3/4 (1966), pp. 293–305.

CURTIS, S. J. *A History of Education in Great Britain*. 5th edition. London: University Tutorial Press, 1963.

DENIFLE, H. *La Désolation des églises, monastères et hôpitaux en France pendant la guerre de cent ans*. [First published, Paris, 1897–9.] 2 vols. Reissued, Bruxelles: Culture et civilisation, 1965.

DOWNS, N. *Basic Documents in Medieval History*. Princeton, New Jersey: Van Nostrand, Anvil Books, 1959.

DUCKETT, E. S. *Alcuin, Friend of Charlemagne*. New York: Macmillan, 1951.

EDWARDS, K. *The English Secular Cathedrals in the Middle Ages*. 2nd edition. Manchester: The University Press, 1967.

EINHARD. *Vita Karoli imperatoris ab Einhardo dictata*. Edited by H. W. Garrod and R. B. Mowatt. Oxford: Clarendon Press, 1915.

—— *Two Lives of Charlemagne*. [By Einhard and Notker the Stammerer.] Translated by L. Thorpe. Harmondsworth: Penguin, 1969.

FOSTER, K. *The Life of Saint Thomas Aquinas: Biographical Documents*. London: Longmans, Green, 1959.

FOURIER, C. *L'Enseignement français de l'antiquité à la révolution*. Paris: Institut Pédagogique Nationale, 1964.

FREEMAN, A. 'Further Studies in the *Libri Carolini*'. *Speculum*, XL (1965), pp. 203–89.

GABRIEL, A. L. *The Educational Ideas of Vincent of Beauvais*. Notre Dame, Indiana: Mediaeval Institute, 1956.

GASKOIN, C. J. *Alcuin, His Life and Work*. [First published 1904.] Reissued, New York: Russell and Russell, 1966.

GREEN, W. M. 'De tribus maximis circumstantiis gestorum'. *Speculum*, XVIII (1943), pp. 484–93.

HABERLY, L. *Medieval English Paving Tiles*. Oxford: Blackwell, 1937.

HASKINS, C. H. *The Rise of Universities*. New York: Henry Holt, 1923; reissued, Ithaca: Cornell University Press, 1957.

—— *Studies in the History of Medieval Science*. [First published 1927.] 2nd edition. London: Constable, 1960.

—— *The Renaissance of the Twelfth Century*. Cambridge, Massachusetts: Harvard University Press, 1927; reprinted New York: Meridian Books, 1957.

HASKINS, G. L. 'The University of Oxford and the *Ius Ubique Docendi*'. *English Historical Review*, LVI (1941), pp. 281–8.

HOWELL, A. G. F. *The Lives of St Francis of Assisi by Brother Thomas of Celano*. New York: E. P. Dutton, 1908.

HUGH OF ST VICTOR. *Didascalion de studio legendi* [*On the Study of Teaching*]. Edited by C. H. Buttimer. Washington, D. C.: 1939.

—— *The* Didascalicon *of Hugh of St Victor*. Translated by J. Taylor. New York: Columbia University Press, 1961.

HUNT, R. W. 'English Learning in the Late Twelfth Century' from the *Transactions of the Royal Historical Society* (May 1936). Collected in R. W. Southern (ed.), *Essays in Medieval History*. London: Macmillan, 1968.

HUTCHINSON, B. 'Robert Grosseteste: The Role of Education in the Reform of Thirteenth Century English Society'. *History of Education Quarterly*, V, 1 (1965), pp. 26–39.

HYMA, A. *The Christian Renaissance: A History of the Devotio Moderna*. Grand Rapids, Michigan: W. B. Eerdmans, 1924.

—— *The Brethren of the Common Life*. Grand Rapids, Michigan: W. B. Eerdmans, 1950.

JACOB, E. F. 'Gerard Groote and the Beginnings of the "New Devotion" in the Low Countries'. *Journal of Ecclesiastical History*, III, 1 (1952), pp. 40–57.

JARRETT, B. *The Life of Saint Dominic*. Westminster, Maryland: Newman Press, 1955.

JOHN OF SALISBURY. *The Letters of John of Salisbury*. Vol. 1: *The Early Letters (1153–1161)*. Edited by W. J. Millor and H. E. Butler. Revised by C. N. L. Brooke. London: Nelson, 1955.

—— *Historia pontificalis* [*Memoirs of the Papal Court*]. Edited text, with English translation, by M. Chibnall. London: Nelson, 1956.

—— *Metalogicon*. Latin text edited by C. C. I. Webb. London: Oxford University Press, 1929.

—— *Metalogicon*. Translated by D. D. McGarry. Berkeley and Los Angeles: University of California Press, 1962.

—— *Frivolities of Courtiers and Footprints of Philosophers*. [Translation of Books I, II, III and parts of VII and VIII of *Policraticus*.] Translated by J. B. Pike. Minneapolis: University of Minnesota Press, 1938.

JOHN THE SCOT [IOHANNIS SCOTI ERIUGENAE]. *Periphyseon* [*De divisione naturae*]. Liber primus. Edited and translated by I. P. Sheldon-Williams. Dublin: Dublin Institute for Advanced Studies, 1968.

JONES, C. W. 'An Early Medieval Licensing Examination'. *History of Education Quarterly*, III, 1 (1963), pp. 19–29.

KIBRE, P. *The Nations in the Medieval Universities*. Cambridge, Massachusetts: Mediaeval Academy of America, 1948.

—— *Scholarly Privileges in the Middle Ages*. London: Mediaeval Academy of America, 1961.

KNOWLES, D. *The Religious Orders in England*. Vol. 2: *The End of the Middle Ages*. Cambridge: The University Press, 1955.

LAISTNER, M. L. W. *Thought and Letters in Western Europe, A.D. 500 to 900*. London: Methuen, 1931.

—— *The Intellectual Heritage of the Early Middle Ages*. Edited by C. G. Starr. New York: Octagon Books, 1966.

LANGLAND, WILLIAM. *The Vision of William Concerning Piers the Plowman*. Edited by W. W. Skeat. [First published 1886.] London: Humphrey Milford, Oxford University Press, 1924.

—— *The Vision of William Concerning Piers the Plowman*. The 'B' Text. London:

Oxford University Press for the Early English Text Society, 1869; reprinted, 1964.

—— *Will's Visions of Piers Plowman and Do-Well*. The 'A' Text. Edited by G. Kane. London: University of London, The Athlone Press, 1960.

—— *Visions from Piers Plowman*. Edited, abridged and translated by N. Coghill. London: Phoenix House, 1949.

LATOUCHE, R. *Textes d'histoire médiévale, Ve – XIe siècle*. Paris: Presses Universitaires de France, 1951.

LEACH, A. F. *Educational Charters and Documents*. Cambridge: The University Press, 1911.

—— *The Schools of Medieval England*. London: Methuen, 1915; reprinted 1969.

LEFF, G. *Heresy in the Later Middle Ages*. 2 vols. Manchester: The University Press, 1967.

LERNER, R., and MAHDI, M. *Medieval Political Philosophy: A Sourcebook*. New York: Free Press of Glencoe (Macmillan), 1963.

LIEBESCHÜTZ, H. *Mediaeval Humanism in the Life and Writings of John of Salisbury*. London: Warburg Institute, University of London, 1950.

LOT, F., and FAWTIER, R. *Histoire des institutions françaises au moyen âge*. Vol. 3: *Institutions ecclésiastiques*. J.-F. Lemarignier, *et al*. Paris: Presses Universitaires de France, 1962.

LUSCOMBE, D. E. *The School of Peter Abelard*. Cambridge: The University Press, 1969.

MCFARLANE, K. B. *John Wycliffe and the Beginnings of English Nonconformity*. London: English Universities Press, 1952.

MCKEON, R. *Selections from Medieval Philosophers*. 2 vols. New York: Scribner's, 1929.

—— 'Rhetoric in the Middle Ages'. *Speculum*, XVII, 1 (1942), pp. 1–32.

MACKINNEY, L. *Bishop Fulbert and the School of Chartres*. Notre Dame, Indiana: Medieval Institute of the University of Notre Dame, 1957.

MCMAHON, C. P. 'The Teaching of History in the Twelfth Century'. *History of Education Quarterly*, II, 1 (1962), pp. 47–51.

—— 'Pedagogical Techniques: Augustine and Hugo of St Victor'. *History of Education Quarterly*, III, 1 (1963), pp. 30–7.

MALLET, C. E. *A History of the University of Oxford*. 3 vols. Vol. 1: *The Mediaeval University and the Colleges Founded in the Middle Ages*. First published 1924. Reprinted New York: Barnes and Noble; London: Methuen, 1968.

ORDERIC VITALIS. *The Ecclesiastical History of Orderic Vitalis*. Edited and translated by M. Chibnall. Oxford: Clarendon Press, 1969.

PAINTER, F. V. N. *Great Pedagogical Essays: Plato to Spencer*. New York: American Book Co., 1905.

PARÉ, G., *et al*. *La Renaissance du XIIe siècle: les écoles et l'enseignement*. Ottawa: Institut d'études médiévales; Paris: Librairie Philosophique J. Vrin, 1933.

PICKFORD, C. E. 'A Fifteenth-Century Copyist and His Patron'. In *Medieval Miscellany Presented to Eugène Vinaver*. Edited by F. Whitehead *et al*. Manchester: The University Press, 1965.

POWICKE, F. M. *Ways of Medieval Life and Thought (Essays and Addresses)*. London: Odhams Press, 1949.

RAJNA, P. 'Le denominazioni Trivium e Quadrivium'. *Studi Medievali*, N.S. I (1928), pp. 4–36.

RASHDALL, H. *The Universities of Europe in the Middle Ages*. Revised by F. M. Powicke and A. B. Emden. 3 vols. Oxford: Clarendon Press, 1936.

REUCHLIN. *Johann Reuchlins Briefwechsel*. Edited by L. Geiger. Hildesheim: Georg Olms Verlagsbuchhandlung, 1962.

RICHARDSON, H. G. 'The Schools of Northampton in the Twelfth Century'. *English Historical Review*, LVI (1941), pp. 595–605.

RICHER. *Historiarum libri IV [Histoire de France, 888–995]*. Latin text and French translation edited by R. Latouche. 2 vols. Paris: Librairie Ancienne Honoré Champion, 1930–7.

ROBINSON, J. H. *Readings in European History*. Boston: Ginn, 1904.

ROBSON, J. A. *Wyclif and the Oxford Schools*. Cambridge: The University Press, 1961.

ROSS, J. B., and MCLAUGHLIN, M. M. *The Portable Medieval Reader*. New York: Viking Press, 1949.

RUNCIMAN, S. *The Medieval Manichee*. Cambridge: The University Press, 1947; reprinted with addenda, 1954.

SANDQUIST, T. A., and POWICKE, M. R. *Essays in Medieval History*. Toronto: University of Toronto Press, 1969.

SCHOECK, R. J. 'Rhetoric and Law in Sixteenth-Century England'. *Studies in Philology*, L (1953), pp. 110–27.

—— 'On Rhetoric in Fourteenth-Century Oxford'. *Mediaeval Studies*, XXX (1968), pp. 217–25.

SHELBY, L. R. 'The Education of Medieval English Master Masons'. *Mediaeval Studies*, XXXII (1970), pp. 1–26.

SHELDON-WILLIAMS, I. P. 'J. Scotus Eriugena'. *Journal of Ecclesiastical History*, X, 2 (1959), pp. 198–224.

SMAIL, R. C. *Crusading Warfare (1097–1193)*. Cambridge: The University Press, 1956.

SMALLEY, B. *The Study of the Bible in the Middle Ages*. Oxford: Blackwell, 1952.

SOUTHERN, R. W. *The Making of the Middle Ages*. London: Hutchinson, 1953.

—— (ed.) *Essays in Medieval History*. [Selected from the *Transactions of the Royal Historical Society* on the occasion of its centenary.] London: Macmillan; New York: St Martin's Press, 1968.

—— *Medieval Humanism and Other Studies*. Oxford: Blackwell, 1970.

STEENBERGHEN, F. VAN. *The Philosophic Movement in the Thirteenth Century.* Edinburgh and London: Nelson, 1955.

STUBBS, W. *Select Charters.* [First published 1870.] 9th edition, revised by H. W. C. Davis. Oxford: Clarendon Press, 1929.

—— (Co-editor with A. W. Haddon) *Councils and Ecclesiastical Documents Relating to Great Britain and Ireland.* 3 vols. Oxford: Clarendon Press, 1964.

SULLIVAN, R. E. *The Coronation of Charlemagne: What Did it Signify?* Boston: D. C. Heath, 1959.

TAYLOR, J. *The Origin and Early life of Hugh of St Victor: An Evaluation of the Tradition.* Notre Dame, Indiana: Medieval Institute of the University of Notre Dame, 1957.

THOMAS AQUINAS. *Summa Theologica.* Translated by the Fathers of the English Dominican Province. 22 vols. London: Burns, Oates and Washbourne, 1911–42.

THOMPSON, J. W. *Economic and Social History of Europe in the Later Middle Ages.* [First published 1931.] New York: Ungar, 1960.

THOMSON, S. H. 'Learning at the Court of Charles IV'. *Speculum*, XXV, 1 (1950), pp. 1–20.

THORNDIKE, L. *University Records and Life in the Middle Ages.* New York: Columbia University Press, 1944.

ULLMANN, B. L. *The Origin and Development of Humanistic Script.* Rome: Edizioni di Storia e Letteratura, 1960.

ULLMANN, W. *The Growth of Papal Government in the Middle Ages.* London: Methuen, 1955.

—— 'Reflections on the Medieval Empire'. *Transactions of The Royal Historical Society*, 5th series, XIV (1964), pp. 89–108.

—— *A History of Political Thought in the Middle Ages.* Harmondsworth: Penguin, 1965.

—— *The Carolingian Renaissance and the Idea of Kingship.* London: Methuen, 1969.

WADDELL, H. *The Wandering Scholars.* London: Constable, 1927; reprinted New York: Doubleday Anchor Books, 1955.

WALLACH, L. 'Education and Culture in the Tenth Century'. *Medievalia et Humanistica*, IX (1955), pp. 18–22.

—— *Alcuin and Charlemagne: Studies in Carolingian History and Literature.* Ithaca, New York: Cornell University Press, 1959.

WEISHEIPL, J. A. 'Curriculum of the Faculty of Arts at Oxford in the Early Fourteenth Century'. *Mediaeval Studies*, XXVI (1964), pp. 143–85.

—— 'Developments in the Arts Curriculum at Oxford in the Early Fourteenth Century'. *Mediaeval Studies*, XXVIII (1966), pp. 151–75.

WEST, A. F. *Alcuin and the Rise of the Christian Schools.* London: Heinemann, 1893.

WHICHER, G. F. *The Goliard Poets: Medieval Latin Songs and Satires.* New York: New Directions, 1949.

WHITELOCK, D. *The Genuine Asser*. [The Stenton Lecture for 1967.] Reading: The University of Reading, 1968.

WIERUSZOWSKI, H. 'Arezzo as a Center of Learning and Letters in the Thirteenth Century'. *Traditio*, IX (1953), pp. 321–91.

—— '*Ars dictaminis* in the Time of Dante'. *Medievalia et Humanistica*, I (1943), pp. 95–108.

—— *The Medieval University: Masters, Students, Learning*. Princeton, New Jersey: Van Nostrand, Anvil Books, 1966.

WILLIAMS, J. R. 'The Cathedral School of Rheims in the Eleventh Century'. *Speculum*, XXIX, 4 (1954), pp. 661–77.

YATES, F. A. *The Art of Memory*. London: Routledge and Kegan Paul, 1966.

2 Moslem and Hebrew

AFNAN, S. M. *Avicenna: His Life and Works*. London: Allen and Unwin, 1958.

AVERROES. *Averroes' Tahafut al-Tahafut* [*The Incoherence of the Incoherence*]. Translated from the Arabic with an introduction and notes by S. van den Bergh. 2 vols. London: Luzac, for the Gibb Memorial Trust, 1954.

—— *Averroes' Commentary on Plato's Republic*. Edited and translated by E. I. J. Rosenthal. Cambridge: The University Press, 1956.

—— *On the Harmony of Religion and Philosophy* [*Kitab fasl al-maqal*]. Translated by G. F. Hourani. London: Luzac, for the Gibb Memorial Trust, 1961.

AVICENNA. *The Visionary Recital*. Translated by H. Corbin. [Translated from the French by W. R. Trask.] London: Routledge and Kegan Paul, 1960.

FAKRY, M. *Islamic Occasionalism, and its Critique by Averroes and Aquinas*. London: George Allen and Unwin, 1958.

HITTI, P. *History of the Arabs*. London: Macmillan, 1960.

JAMIL-UR-REHMAN, M. *The Philosophy and Theology of Averroes*. Baroda: A. G. Widgery, 1921.

KHALDUN, IBN. *An Arab Philosophy of History*. Selections from the Prolegomena of Ibn Khaldun of Tunis translated and arranged by C. Issawi. London: John Murray, 1950.

MAHDI, M., and LERNER, R. *Medieval Political Philosophy: A Sourcebook*. New York: Free Press of Glencoe (Macmillan), 1963.

MAIMONIDES, MOSES. *Maimonides' Treatise on Logic*. Translated by I. Efros. New York: American Academy for Jewish Research, 1938.

—— *The Guide for the Perplexed*. Translated by M. Friedländer. 2nd revised edition. London: Kegan Paul, 1904.

—— *The Guide of the Perplexed*. Translated by S. Pines. Chicago: The University Press, 1963.

RAHMAN, F. *Islam*. London: Weidenfeld and Nicolson, 1966.

SHALABY, A. *History of Muslim Education*. Beirut: Dar Alkashaf, 1954.

TRITTON, A. S. *Materials on Muslim Education in the Middle Ages*. London: Luzac, 1954.

WALZER, R. *Greek into Arabic: Essays on Islamic Philosophy*. Oxford: Bruno Cassirer, 1962.

3 Italian Renaissance

BARON, H. *The Crisis of the Early Italian Renaissance*. 2 vols. Princeton, New Jersey: Princeton University Press, 1955.

BISHOP, M. *Petrarch and His World*. London: Chatto and Windus, 1964.

BOLGAR, R. R. *The Classical Heritage and Its Beneficiaries*. Cambridge: The University Press, 1954.

BURCKHARDT, J. *The Civilization of the Renaissance in Italy*. [First published 1860.] 2 vols. New York: Harper Torchbooks, 1958.

CASTIGLIONE, BALDESAR. *Il Libro del Cortegiano (con una scelta delle Opere minori)*. Edited by Bruno Maier. 2nd edition. Turin: Unione Tipografico-Editrice Torinese, 1964.

—— *The Book of the Courtier*. Translated by G. Bull. Harmondsworth: Penguin, 1967.

—— *The Book of the Courtier*. Translated by Thomas Hoby, 1561. Reprinted, London: Dent, Everyman's Library, 1928.

CASSIRER, E., *et al*. *Renaissance Philosophy of Man*. Chicago: University of Chicago Press, 1948.

CHRYSOLORAS, M. *Biographie Hellénique*. Vol. 1. Edited by E. Legrand. [First published 1885.] Reissued, Paris: Culture et civilization, 1963.

CINQUINO, J. 'Coluccio Salutati, Defender of Poetry'. *Italica*, XXVI (1949), pp. 131–5.

COLSON, F. H. (ed.) *M. Fabii Quintiliani: Institutiones Oratoriae, Liber I*. Cambridge: The University Press, 1924.

DANTE ALIGHIERI. *The Letters of Dante* [*Dantis Aligherii Epistolae*]. Edited and translated by P. Toynbee and C. G. Hardie. 2nd edition. Oxford: Clarendon Press, 1966.

—— *Le opere de Dante Alighieri*. Edited by E. Moore and P. Toynbee. 4th edition. London: Oxford University Press, 1924.

—— *Monarchy* [*De monarchia*]. Translated by D. Nicholl. London: Weidenfeld and Nicolson, 1954.

DAVIS, C. T. 'Education in Dante's Florence'. *Speculum*, XL (1965), pp. 415–35.

D'ENTREVES, A. P. *Dante as a Political Thinker*. Oxford: Clarendon Press, 1952.

GEANAKOPLOS, D. J. *Greek Scholars in Venice: Studies in the Dissemination of Greek Learning from Byzantium to Western Europe*. Cambridge, Massachusetts: Harvard University Press, 1962.

—— *Byzantine East and Latin West*. Oxford: Blackwell, 1966.

GILBERT, F. *Machiavelli and Guicciardini: Politics and History in Sixteenth Century Florence*. Princeton, New Jersey: Princeton University Press, 1965.

GILMORE, M. P. *Humanists and Jurists: Six Studies in the Renaissance*. Cambridge, Massachusetts: The Belknap Press of Harvard University Press, 1963.

GILSON, E. *Dante the Philosopher*. New edition. Translated by D. Moore. London: Sheed and Ward, 1952.

GRENDLER, P. F. *Critics of the Italian World 1530–1560*. Madison, Wisconsin: University of Wisconsin Press, 1969.

HYDE, J. K. *Padua in the Age of Dante*. Manchester: The University Press, 1966.

JACOB, E. F. (ed.) *Italian Renaissance Studies*. London: Faber and Faber, 1960.

KRISTELLER, P. O. *The Classics and Renaissance Thought*. [Martin Classical Lectures, Volume XV.] Cambridge, Massachusetts: Harvard University Press for Oberlin College, 1955.

LIMENTANI, U. (ed.) *The Mind of Dante*. Cambridge: The University Press, 1965.

MACHIAVELLI, NICCOLÒ. *The Prince [Il Principe]*. Translated by Luigi Ricci, revised by E. R. P. Vincent. London: Oxford University Press, The World's Classics, 1935.

MCMURTRIE, D. C. *The Book: The Story of Printing and Bookmaking*. New York: Oxford University Press, 1943.

MARTINES, L. *The Social World of the Florentine Humanists 1390–1460*. London: Routledge and Kegan Paul, 1963.

PANOFSKY, E. *Studies in Iconology: Humanistic Themes in the Art of the Renaissance*. New York: Oxford University Press, 1939.

PETRARCH. *Petrarch at Vaucluse: Letters in Verse and Prose*. Translated by E. H. Wilkins. Chicago: The University Press, 1958.

ROBB, N. A. *Neoplatonism of the Italian Renaissance*. London: Allen and Unwin, 1935.

SCHEVILL, F. *History of Florence: From the Founding of the City Through to the Renaissance*. New York: Harcourt, Brace, 1936; reprinted, New York: Ungar, 1961.

—— *The Medici*. London: Gollancz, 1950.

STEINBERG, S. *Five Hundred Years of Printing*. Harmondsworth: Penguin, 1955.

THOMSON, I. 'Manuel Chrysoloras and the Early Italian Renaissance'. *Greek, Roman and Byzantine Studies*, VII, 1 (1966), pp. 63–82.

VASILIEV, A. A. *History of the Byzantine Empire*. [First published 1928.] Reissued, 2 vols. Madison, Wisconsin: University of Wisconsin Press, 1952.

WEISS, R. *The Spread of Italian Humanism*. London: Hutchinson's University Library, 1964.

—— *The Renaissance Discovery of Classical Antiquity*. Oxford: Blackwell, 1969.

WHITFIELD, J. H. *Petrarch and the Renaissance*. Oxford: Blackwell, 1943; reprinted, New York: Russell and Russell, 1965.

WILKINS, E. H. *Life of Petrarch*. Chicago: The University Press, 1958.

WOODWARD, A. M. 'Greek History at the Renaissance'. *Journal of Hellenic Studies*, LXIII (1943), pp. 1–14.

WOODWARD, W. H. *Vittorino da Feltre and other Humanist Educators*. Cambridge: The University Press, 1905.

4 European Humanism and the Reformation

ARNOLD, M. *The Popular Education of France (with notices of that of Holland and Switzerland)*. London: Longman, Green, Longman and Roberts, 1861.

BAINTON, R. *Here I Stand: A Life of Martin Luther*. New York and Nashville: Abingdon-Cokesbury Press, 1950.

—— *Erasmus of Christendom*. New York: Scribner's; London: Collins, 1969.

BARNARD, H. 'Life and Educational Services of Philipp Melanchthon'. *American Journal of Education*, IV (1859), pp. 749–55.

BARNARD, H. C. *The French Tradition in Education: Ramus to Mme Necker de Saussure*. Cambridge: The University Press, 1922.

BEALES, A. C. F. *Education under Penalty*. London: University of London, The Athlone Press, 1963.

BENNETT, H. S. *Six Medieval Men and Women*. Cambridge: The University Press, 1955.

BETTS, R. R. *Essays in Czech History*. London: University of London, The Athlone Press, 1969.

BREEN, Q. 'Giovanni Pico della Mirandola on the Conflict of Philosophy and Rhetoric', and 'Melanchthon's Reply to Giovanni Pico della Mirandola'. *Journal of the History of Ideas*, XIII, 3 (1952), pp. 384–412, 413–26.

BRETSCHNEIDER, C. G., and BINDSEIL, H. E. *Corpus Reformatorum*. Halle: C. A. Schwetschke, 1834–60.

BROCK, P. *The Political and Social Doctrines of the Unity of Czech Brethren in the Fifteenth and Early Sixteenth Centuries*. 'S-Gravenhage, Netherlands: Mouton, 1957.

CAMPANA, A. 'Origin of the Word Humanist'. *Journal of the Warburg and Courtauld Institutes*, IX (1946), pp. 60–73.

CELTES. *Selections from Conrad Celtes*. Translated by Leonard Forster. Cambridge: The University Press, 1948.

CHADWICK, H. 'The Scots College at Douai, 1580–1613'. *English Historical Review*, LVI (1941), pp. 571–85.

CHARLTON, K. *Education in Renaissance England*. London: Routledge and Kegan Paul, 1965.

CLARKE, M. L. *Classical Education in Great Britain, 1500–1900*. Cambridge: The University Press, 1959.

CORDIER, M. *Select Colloquies*. Edited and translated by Samuel Loggon. 2nd edition, revised and corrected. London: C. and I. Rivington, 1824.

DICKENS, A. G. *Martin Luther and the Reformation*. London: English Universities Press, 1967.

EINSTEIN, L. *The Italian Renaissance in England: Studies*. New York: Columbia University Press, 1902.

ELTON, G. R. *Star Chamber Stories*. London: Methuen, 1958.

ELYOT, T. *The Boke Named the Governour*. London: Dent, Everyman's Library, 1937.

ERASMUS. *Opus epistolarum Des. Erasmi Roterodami*. Edited by P. S. Allen. 11 vols. Oxford: Clarendon Press, 1906–47. Continued by H. M. Allen and H. W. Garrod, Vol. 12 (Indices), 1958.

—— *Epistles of Erasmus, from his earliest letters to his fifty-first year, arranged in order of time*. Edited and translated by F. M. Nichols. [First published 1901.] Reissued, New York: Russell and Russell, 1962.

—— *Desiderius Erasmus Concerning the Aim of Education*. [Translations of *De ratione studii* and *De pueris instituendis* by Foster Watson.] Cambridge: The University Press, 1904.

—— *Ten Colloquies of Erasmus*. Translated by C. R. Thompson. New York: Liberal Arts Press, 1957.

—— *Erasmus and Cambridge: The Cambridge Letters*. Edited by H. C. Porter and translated by D. F. S. Thomson. Toronto: University of Toronto Press, 1963.

—— *The Essential Erasmus*. Edited and translated by J. P. Dolan. New York: New American Library, Mentor-Omega Books, 1964.

—— *The Adages of Erasmus: A Study with Translations*. Edited and translated by M. M. Phillips. Cambridge: The University Press, 1964.

—— *The Education of a Christian Prince*. Translated by L. K. Born. New York: Columbia University Press, 1936; reprinted, New York: Octagon Books, 1965.

—— *De Libero Arbitrio* [*On the Freedom of the Will*]. Translated in E. G. Rupp (ed.), *Luther and Erasmus: Free Will and Salvation*. Vol. XVII, Library of Christian Classics. London: SCM Press, 1969.

FARRELL, A. P. *The Jesuit Code of Liberal Education: Development and Scope of the Ratio Studiorum*. Milwaukee: Bruce Publishing Co., 1938.

FITZPATRICK, A. (ed.) *St Ignatius and the Ratio Studiorum*. New York: McGraw-Hill, 1933.

FORELL, G. W., *et al. Luther and Culture*. Martin Luther Lectures, Volume IV. Decorah, Iowa: Luther College Press, 1960.

GERRISH, B. A. *Grace and Reason: A Study in the Theology of Luther*. Oxford: Clarendon Press, 1962.

GRIMM, H. J. 'Luther and Education'. In G. W. Forell *et al.*, *Luther and Culture*. Decorah, Iowa: Luther College Press, 1960.

HEYMANN, F. G. *John Žižka and the Hussite Revolution*. Princeton, New Jersey: Princeton University Press, 1955.

HILDEBRANDT, F. *Melanchthon: Alien or Ally?* Cambridge: The University Press, 1946.

HILLERBRAND, H. J. *The Reformation in Its Own Words*. London: SCM Press, 1964.

HOLDSWORTH, W. *A History of English Law*. 3rd edition. London: Methuen, Sweet and Maxwell, 1945.

HOLT, JOHN. *Lac puerorum*. Antwerp: Adriaen van [Berghen], *c.* 1508.

ISERLOH, E. *The Theses Were Not Posted: Luther Between Reform and Reformation*. [Translation of the second edition of *Luther zwischen Reform und Reformation*. Munster: Verlag Aschendorff, 1967.] London: Chapman, 1968.

LEACH, A. F. *English Schools at the Reformation, 1546–48*. Westminster: Constable, 1896.

LUPTON, J. H. *A Life of John Colet, D.D.* 2nd edition. London: Bell, 1909. Reprinted, Hamden, Connecticut: The Shoestring Press, 1961.

LUTHER. *D. Martin Luthers Werke*. [Kritische Gesamtausgabe, Weimarer Ausgabe.] Weimar: Herman Böhlaus Nachfolger, 1883–.

—— *Luther's Works*. Edited by J. Pelikan and H. T. Lehman. 55 vols. St Louis: Concordia Publishing House; Philadelphia: Muhlenberg Press, 1915–58.

—— *Dr Martin Luthers Pädagogische Schriften und Äusserungen*. Langensalza: Herman Beyer, 1888.

—— *A Compend of Luther's Theology*. Edited and translated by H. T. Kerr. Philadelphia: The Westminster Press, 1943.

—— *De servo arbitrio* [*On the Bondage of the Will*]. Translated by J. I. Packer and O. R. Johnston. London: J. Clark, 1957.

MCCONICA, J. K. *English Humanists and Reformation Politics under Henry VIII and Edward VI*. Oxford: Clarendon Press, 1965.

MAČEK, J. *The Hussite Movement in Bohemia*. Translated by Vilém Fried and Ian Miller. 2nd, enlarged edition. Prague: Orbis, 1958.

MANSCHRECK, C. L. *Melanchthon: The Quiet Reformer*. New York and Nashville: Abingdon Press, 1958.

MASON, H. A. *Humanism and Poetry in the Early Tudor Period*. London: Routledge and Kegan Paul, 1959.

MELANCHTHON. *Melanchthons Werke in Auswahl*. General editor R. Stupperich. Gütersloh: Gütersloher Verlaghaus Gerd Mohn, 1961.

—— *Melanchthon: Selected Writings*. Edited by E. E. Flack and L. Sabre. Translated by C. L. Hill. Minneapolis: Augsburg Publishing House, 1962.

MESNARD, P. 'The Pedagogy of Johann Sturm and its Evangelical Inspiration'. *Studies in the Renaissance*, XIII (1966), pp. 200–19.

MONROE, P. *Thomas Platter and the Educational Renaissance of the Sixteenth Century*. New York: Appleton, 1904.

MORE. *The Complete Works of St Thomas More.* Volume 4: *Utopia.* Edited and translated by E. Surtz and J. H. Hexter. New Haven: Yale University Press, 1965.

MURPHY, J. J. 'Rhetoric in Fourteenth-Century Oxford'. *Medium Aevum.* XXXIV, 1 (1965), pp. 1–20.

NUGENT, E. M. (ed.) *The Thought and Culture of the English Renaissance: An Anthology of Tudor Prose, 1481–1555.* Cambridge: The University Press, 1956.

PAULSEN, F. *German Education: Past and Present.* Translated by T. Lorenz, London: T. Fisher and Unwin, 1908.

SADOLETO. *Sadoleto on Education: A Translation of 'De pueris recte instituendis'.* Translated by E. T. Campagnac and K. Forbes. London: Oxford University Press, 1916.

SIMON, J. *Education and Society in Tudor England.* Cambridge: The University Press, 1966.

SNYDER, L. L. (ed.) *Documents of German History.* New Brunswick, New Jersey: Rutgers University Press, 1958.

SPITZ, L. W. *Conrad Celtis, The German Arch-Humanist.* Cambridge, Massachusetts: Harvard University Press, 1957.

—— *The Religious Renaissance of the German Humanists.* Cambridge, Massachusetts: Harvard University Press, 1963.

—— *The Protestant Reformation.* Englewood Cliffs, New Jersey: Prentice-Hall, 1966.

STUPPERICH. R. *Melanchthon.* Translated by R. H. Fisher. London: Lutterworth Press, 1966.

VIVES. *Tudor School-Boy Life: The Dialogues of Juan Luis Vives.* Translated, with an introduction, by Foster Watson. London: Dent, 1908.

—— *De tradendis disciplinis* [*The Transmission of the Arts*]. Translated by Foster Watson. Cambridge: The University Press, 1913.

VOCHT, H. DE. *History of the Foundation and Rise of the Collegium Trilingue Lovaniense, 1517–1550.* Louvain: Publications Universitaires, 1951.

WATSON, F. *The English Grammar Schools to 1660: Their Curriculum and Practice.* Cambridge: The University Press, 1908.

WEISS, R. *Humanism in England During the Fifteenth Century.* 2nd edition. Oxford: Blackwell, 1957.

WOODWARD, W. H. *Studies in Education During the Age of the Renaissance.* Cambridge: The University Press, 1906; reissued, New York: Russell and Russell, 1965.

—— *Desiderius Erasmus Concerning the Aim of Education.* Cambridge: The University Press, 1904.

WRIGHT, L. B., and LA MAR, V. A. (eds.) *Life and Letters in Tudor and Stuart England.* Folger Shakespeare Library, first Folger series. Ithaca: Cornell University Press, 1962.

Index